POPE JOHN THE TWENTY-THIRD
AND MASTER JOHN HUS OF BOHEMIA

AMS PRESS
NEW YORK

Upper Part of the tomb of Pope John XXIII in the Baptistery at Florence. erected in 1427. the figure of the pontiff being the work of Donatello.

POPE JOHN
THE TWENTY-THIRD

AND MASTER JOHN HUS OF BOHEMIA

BY

EUSTACE J. KITTS

AUTHOR OF 'IN THE DAYS OF THE COUNCILS'

ILLUSTRATED

LONDON
CONSTABLE AND COMPANY LIMITED
10 ORANGE STREET LEICESTER SQUARE
1910

Library of Congress Cataloging in Publication Data

Kitts, Eustace John.
  Pope John the Twenty-third and Master John Hus of Bohemia.

  Reprint of the 1910 ed. published by Constable, London.
  Bibliography: p.
  1. Joannes XXIII, antipope, d. 1419. 2. Hus, Jan, 1369?-1415. 3. Sigismund, Emperor of Germany, 1368-1437. 4. Constance, Council of, 1414-1418. I. Title.
  BX1290.K55 1978   282'.09'024   77-84726
  ISBN 0-404-16127-8

Reprinted from the edition of 1910, London
First AMS edition published in 1978

Manufactured in the United States of America

AMS PRESS, INC.
NEW YORK, N.Y.

INTRODUCTION

In this book I have endeavoured to narrate the five years' history of three men and a movement; the men are Pope John the Twenty-third, John Hus, the patriot reformer of Bohemia, and Sigismund, King of the Romans; and the movement is the conciliar movement up to the middle of the year 1415.

I have already, in my book entitled *In the Days of the Councils*, given the history of Baldassare Cossa, who became Pope John the Twenty-third, up to the death of Pope Alexander the Fifth. Baldassare Cossa was in no sense a hero; there were indeed very few heroes in those days. One thing which makes history so much more interesting than fiction is that the characters have their human frailties as well as their human virtues. 'Il n'y a pas,' says M. Boissier, 'de gens parfaits que dans les romans.' Baldassare Cossa was simply a strong man placed in a position for which he had striven but for which he was eminently unfit, struggling with adversity. It is in the struggle that the interest of his story lies. Up till the battle of Rocca Secca all went well with him; after that, Fate was consistently against him. He had the misfortune to have for an enemy one of the foremost literary men of his time; and literary men then said all that they knew was true, all that they thought was true, and much that they hoped was true. They took rumour and scandal without investigation, and gave it currency as fact. Unhappily our own greatest historian accepted all that Dietrich von Niem wrote, and the glamour of Gibbon's great name has worked evil to the repute of Pope John the Twenty-third until in these last days the patient labour of German historians has succeeded in disentangling fact from fiction and in painting his character in the colours of verisimilitude.

John Hus, it is necessary to remember, was a patriot as well as a reformer. Bohemia for the Bohemians was his leading thought when he got the Teutons expelled from the University of Prague, and when he went to clear his country of the imputation of heresy at the Council of Constance. It was his hatred of the German race that made him so popular with the nobles of Hungary; it was his influence, no less as patriot than as reformer, that inspired the Hussite Wars. Personally he was a gentle and lovable man, a follower of Wyclif in philosophy and deeply imbued with the religious views of the English reformer. As to religion it is at first sight difficult to place him. He was not a Catholic, seeing that he was burned by the Council of Constance for heresy; nor was he, in the ordinary modern acceptation of the term, a Protestant, seeing that he venerated the Virgin Mary, believed in transubstantiation, and knew nothing of justification by faith. But if we leave isolated doctrines and come to fundamental principles, then John Hus must be adjudged the equivalent of a Protestant, for it is clear that he took the Bible as being alone the true standard and rule of faith, that he practically rejected Tradition, and disowned Church authority. In his unconscious appeal to the liberty of the individual conscience, a conscience duly enlightened by the study of the Scripture and meditation on the Fathers, and to the letter of the written Word as an authority superior to Pope or Council, John Hus was a precursor of the Reformation.

The character of King Sigismund is a riddle to which different answers have been given. To some he has appeared sensual, impulsive, and wanting in perseverance, while others regard him as the embodiment of all that is grandest in the German monarchy. In the five years with which I deal he had undoubtedly sobered down from the light-hearted excesses of his youth, and the influence of three fixed ideas can be clearly traced in his policy; he believed in the majesty of the Holy Roman Empire, the unity of the Holy Roman Church, and the expulsion of the Turks from Europe; and to these ideas he held true throughout.

In my previous book and in the present I have sketched the

rise of that conciliar spirit which arrogated to the councils the superiority over the papacy; and I have told the story of the Councils of Pisa, of Cividale, of Perpignan, and of Rome. With the Council of Constance I am only concerned during the first eight months of its existence, during which time its proceedings were practically unanimous and amicable, whereas later on they became conflicting and at times turbulent. I have only attempted to give the history of the Council in detail so far as the burning of John Hus. This will account for, and I hope excuse, the sketchy characters of the last two chapters of this volume.

LIST OF CARDINALS

A. LIST OF CARDINALS IN THE CONCLAVE AT THE ELECTION OF POPE JOHN XXIII.

(1) HENRICUS MINULTULUS, Neapolitan; created cardinal 18th December 1389 by Boniface IX.; at first Cardinal Bishop of Tusculum, then of Sabina; was made Papal Legate of Bologna in 1411; died at Bologna on 18th May 1412.

(2) NICOLAUS BRANCACIUS, Neapolitan; Cardinal Bishop of Albano; created cardinal by Clement VII. in January 1378; died 1412.

(3) JEAN DE BROGNY, Frenchman; born 1342; Cardinal Bishop of Ostia: also called Cardinal de Viviers; created cardinal by Benedict XIII. in 1394; was at Constance; died 1426.

(4) PIERRE GERARD, Bishop du Puy; Cardinal Bishop of Tusculum; created cardinal by Clement VII. in October 1390; died 1415.

(5) ANGELUS DE ANNA, Neapolitan; Cardinal Priest of S. Pudenziana; known as the Cardinal of Lodi; created cardinal by Urban VI.; was at Constance; died 1428.

(6) PETRUS FERNANDI FRIAS, Spaniard; Cardinal Priest of S. Prassede; created cardinal by Clement VII. in 1394; was at Constance; died at Florence in September 1420.

(7) CONRAD CARACCIOLO, Neapolitan; Cardinal Priest of S. Crisogono; created cardinal by Innocent VII. in 1405; died 1411.

(8) FRANCESCO UGOCCIONE of Urbino, Italian; Archbishop of Bordeaux; Cardinal Priest of SS. Quattro Coronati; created cardinal by Innocent VII. in 1405; died 1412.

(9) GIORDANO ORSINI, Roman; Cardinal Priest of S. Lorenzo in Damaso; created cardinal by Innocent VII. in 1405; was at Constance; died 1439.

(10) GIOVANNI DE' MEGLIORATI; Cardinal Priest of S. Croce in Gerusalemme; known as the Cardinal of Ravenna; created cardinal by his uncle, Innocent VII., in 1405; died 1410.

(11) ANTONIUS CALVUS, Roman; Cardinal Priest of S. Prassede; created cardinal by Innocent VII. in 1405; known as the Cardinal of Mileto; died 1411.

x POPE JOHN THE TWENTY-THIRD

(12) RAYNALDUS BRANCACIUS, Neapolitan : Cardinal Deacon of SS. Vito e Modesto ; created cardinal by Urban VI. in 1385 ; was at Constance ; died 1427.

(13) LANDULFUS MARAMAUR, Neapolitan ; Cardinal Deacon of S. Nicola in Carcere Tulliano ; Legate in Spain ; created cardinal by Urban VI. in 1381 ; died at Constance in 1415.

(14) BALDASSARE COSSA, Neapolitan ; Pope John XXIII.

(15) ODDO COLONNA, Roman ; Cardinal Deacon of S. Giorgio in Velabro ; created cardinal by Innocent VII. in 1405 ; Pope Martin V.

(16) PETRUS STEFANESCUS HANNIBALDUS, Roman ; Cardinal Deacon of S. Angelo in Pescheria ; created cardinal by Innocent VII. in 1405 ; was at Constance and died there in 1417.

(17) ANTOINE DE CHALANT, Savoyard ; Cardinal Deacon of S. Maria in Via Lata ; created cardinal by Benedict XIII. on 9th May 1404 ; was at Constance ; died 4th September 1418.

B. LIST OF CARDINALS OF THE SAME OBEDIENCE WHO WERE NOT IN THE CONCLAVE

(18) GUY DE MAILLESEC (or Malesset); known as the Cardinal of Poitiers ; died 1411.

(19) ANTONIO CAETANI, Roman ; Cardinal Bishop of Palestrina ; created cardinal by Boniface IX. in 1402 ; died January 1412.

(20) PIERRE DE THURY, Frenchman ; Cardinal Priest of S. Susanna ; Legate in France ; created cardinal by Clement VII. in 1385 ; died September 1412.

(21) JEAN FLANDRIN, Frenchman ; Cardinal D'Auch ; Cardinal Priest of SS. Giovanni e Paolo ; created cardinal by Clement VII. in 1390 ; was not at Constance.

22) LOUIS DE BAR, Frenchman ; Cardinal Priest of XII. Apostoli ; created cardinal by Benedict XIII. in 1397 ; not at Constance ; died 1430.

(23) LOUIS FIESCHI of Geneva ; Cardinal Deacon of S. Adriano in Foro Romano ; created cardinal by Urban VI. in 1384 ; was at Constance ; died 1423.

(24) AMADEUS DE SALUZZO, Italian ; Cardinal Deacon of S. Maria Nova ; created cardinal by Clement VII. in 1382 ; was at Constance ; died at Florence in July 1419.

LIST OF CARDINALS

C. LIST OF CARDINALS NOMINATED BY POPE JOHN XXIII.
ON 6TH JUNE 1411

(1) FRANCESCUS LANDUS, Venetian; Cardinal Priest of S. Croce in Gerusalemme; known as the Cardinal of Venice; was at Constance; died 1427.

(2) ANTONIUS PANCERA DE PORTOGRUARIO, Patriarch of Aquileia, nephew of Cardinal Caetani; Cardinal Priest of S. Susanna; was at Constance; died 1431.

(3) JOHN OF PORTUGAL; Cardinal Priest of S. Pietro in Vincoli; died on 23rd January 1415.

(4) ALAMAN ADIMAR, Florentine, Archbishop of Pisa; Cardinal Priest of S. Eusebio; was at Constance; died 27th September 1422.

(5) PIERRE D'AILLY, Frenchman; born 1350; Cardinal Priest of S. Crisogono; was at Constance; died 8th August 1425.

6) GEORGE VON LICHTENSTEIN, Bishop of Trient; never came to Rome.

(7) BRANDA DE CASTELLIO, Milanese; Cardinal Priest of S. Clemente; was at Constance; died 5th February 1443.

(8) THOMAS BRANCACIUS, nephew of John XXIII.; Cardinal Priest of SS. Giovanni e Paolo; was at Constance; died 8th September 1427.

(9) THOMAS LANGLEY, Bishop of Durham; never came to Rome.

(10) ROBERT HALLAM, Bishop of Salisbury, never came to Rome.

(11) GILLES DES CHAMPS, Frenchman; never came to Rome.

(12) FRANCESCO ZABARELLA of Padua, known as the Cardinal of Florence; born 1339; Cardinal Deacon of SS. Cosma e Damiano; died at Constance on 26th September 1417.

(13) LUCIUS ALDEBRANDINUS, also called Lucio de Comitibus, Roman; Cardinal Deacon of S. Maria in Cosmedin; was at Constance; died 1437.

(14) GUILLAUME FILLASTRE, Frenchman; Cardinal Priest of S. Marco; was at Constance; died November 1428.

D. SECOND CREATION ON 13TH APRIL 1413

(15) SIMON DE CRAMAUD, Patriarch of Alexandria, Frenchman; Cardinal Priest of S. Lorenzo in Lucina; was at Constance; died 1429.

THIRD CREATION IN OCTOBER 1413

(16) GIACOMO ISOLANO OF BOLOGNA; Cardinal Deacon of S. Eustachio; Papal Legate and Governor of Genoa; died 9th February 1431.

E. LIST OF CARDINALS CREATED BY POPE GREGORY XII.

ON 12TH JUNE 1408

(1) GIOVANNI DOMENICI; born at Florence 1340; was Legate of Gregory at Constance; known as the Cardinal of Ragusa; died 10th June 1419.

(2) ANTONIO CORRARIO, nephew of Gregory XII.; was at Constance; died 1445.

(3) GABRIEL GONDULMER, nephew of Gregory XII.; was at Constance; became Pope Eugenius IV.; died 1447.

(4) JACOBUS UTINENSIS; died 1412.

F. SECOND CREATION ON 19TH SEPTEMBER 1408

(5) ANGELUS OF RECATE; died 21st June 1412.

(6) LOUIS THE SICILIAN; died 13th September 1413.

(7) ANGELO BARBARDICO, Venetian; was at Constance; died 1418.

(8) BANDELLUS DE BANDELLIS, Etrurian; was at Constance; died August 1417.

(9) PHILIP OF RIPON, Bishop Lincoln; was at Constance; died 1417.

(10) MATTHEW OF CRACOW; died 1410.

(11) LUCAS MANZOLIUS OF FLORENCE; died 14th September 1411.

(12) PETRUS MAUROCENUS, Venetian; was at Constance; died 1424.

(13) VINCENTIUS, Spaniard; died 1410.

G. LIST OF CARDINALS IN THE CONCLAVE AT THE ELECTION OF POPE MARTIN V.

CARDINAL BISHOPS—

(1) Jean de Brogny.
(2) Angelus de Anna.
(3) Petrus Fernandi Frias.
(4) Giordano Orsini.
(5) Antonio Corrario

LIST OF CARDINALS

CARDINAL PRIESTS—

(6) Francescus Landus.
(7) Giovanni Domenici.
(8) Antonio Pancerinus.
(9) Alaman Adimar.
(10) Gabriel Gondulmer.
(11) Pierre d'Ailly.
(12) Thomas Brancacius.

(13) Branda de Castellio.
(14) Angelo Barbardico.
(15) Guillaume Fillastre.
(16) Simon de Cramaud.
(17) Antoine de Chalant.
(18) Pierre de Foix.

CARDINAL DEACONS—

(19) Louis Fieschi.
(20) Amadeus de Saluzzo.
(21) Raynaldus Brancacius.

(22) Oddo Colonna, Pope Martin v.
(23) Lucio de Comitibus.

MEMORANDUM OF ABBREVIATIONS

N.B.—The following abbreviations have been used for authorities cited in the Notes and References.

A.D.B.	*Allgemeine Deutsche Biographie.* 1875-99.
A.F.	Marmor: *Alter Fuehrer durch die Stadt Konstanz.* 1864.
A.S.I.	*Archivio Storico Italiano.* 1843.
Aen. Sylv.	*Aeneae Sylvii Opera.* Basileae.
ALTMANN.	*Eberhart Windeckes Denkwuerdigkeiten*; ed. Altmann. 1893.
ANTON.	Divi Antonini Archiepiscopi Florentini *chronicorum tertia pars.*
AMMIRATO.	Ammirato, Scipione: *Istorie Fiorentine.* 7 vols., 1853.
ASCHBACH.	Aschbach, Joseph: *Geschichte Kaiser Sigmunds.* 4 vols., 1838.
B.W.	Beda Weber: *Oswald von Wolkenstein und Friedrich mit der leeren Tasche.* 1850.
BADER.	Bader, J.: *Freiburg.*
BARANTE.	Barante, M. de: *Histoire des Ducs de Bourgogne de la Maison de Valois.* 14 vols., 1826.
BERGER.	Berger, Dr. Wilhelm: *Johannes Hus und Koenig Sigmund.* 1871.
BESS.	Bess, Bernhard: *Frankreichs Kirchenpolitik.* 1891.
BLUMENTHAL.	Blumenthal, Hermann: *Die Vorgeschichte des Constanzer Concils.* 1897.
BRANDENBURG.	Brandenburg, Erich: *Koenig Sigmund und Kurfuerst Friedrich I. von Brandenburg.* 1891.
BRANDIS.	Brandis, Clemens Grafen und Herrn zu Brandis: *Tirol unter Friedrich von Oesterreich.* 1823.
BRIEGER.	Brieger: *Zeitschrift fuer Kirchengeschichte.*
BROWN.	Brown, Horatio F.: *Venice.* 1895.
BURKE.	Burke, Ulick Ralph: *History of Spain.* 2 vols., 1895.
C.E.	The Catholic Encyclopedia: vols. I.-VI.
CAPPER.	Capper, Samuel James: *The Shores and Cities of the Boden See.* 1881.
CAPPONI.	Capponi, Gino: *Storia della Repubblica di Firenze.* 1875.

CHASTENET.	Chastenet, Bourgeois de: *Nouvelle Histoire du Concile de Constance.* 1718.
CHRISTOPHE.	Christophe, L'Abbé J. B.: *Histoire de la Papauté pendant le XIVe siècle.* 3 vols., 1853.
CIACONIUS.	Ciaconius, Alphonsus: *Vitae et res gestae Pontificum.* 4 vols., 1677.
Coeln.	*Die Chroniken der niederrheinischen Staedte.* Coeln. 1876.
COVILLE.	Coville, Alfred: *Les Cabochiens et l'Ordonnance de 1413.* 1888.
CREIGHTON.	Creighton, Mandel: *History of the Papacy.* 6 vols., 1897.
CRIVELLI.	Crivelli, Domenico: *Della prima e della seconda Giovanna, regine di Napoli.* Padova, 1832.
D.N.B.	*Dictionary of National Biography.* 66 vols.
D.R.	*Deutsche Reichstagsakten*; siebenter Band. 1878.
DARU.	Daru, P.: *Histoire de la République de Venise.* 8 vols., 1827.
DROYSEN.	Droysen, Joh. Gust.: *Geschichte der preussischen Politik; Die Gruendung.* 1868.
DUCHESNE.	Duchesne: *Liber Pontificalis.* 2 vols., 1886-92.
EGGER.	Egger, Josef: *Geschichte Tirols.* 3 vols., 1872.
EISELEIN.	Eiselein, Josua: *Geschichte und Beschreibung der Stadt Konstanz.* 1851.
ERDMANN.	Erdmann, Johann Eduard; tr. Hough: *History of Philosophy.* 3 vols., 1890.
ERLER.	Erler, Georg: *Dietrich von Nieheim.* 1887.
FINKE (*Acta*).	Finke, Heinrich: *Acta Concilii Constantiensis.* 1896.
FINKE (*B.*).	Finke, Heinrich: *Bilder von Konstanzer Konzil.* 1903.
FINKE (*F.*).	Finke, Heinrich: *Forschungen und Quellen zur Geschichte des Konstanzer Konzils.* 1889.
FINLAY.	Finlay, George: *History of Greece.* 7 vols., 1877.
GASCOIGNE.	Gascoigne (Rogers): *Loci e Libro Veritatum.* 1871.
GERSON.	Gerson, J. Charlier de: *Opera.* 1706.
GHIRAR.	*Della Historia di Bologna* del R.P.M. Cherubino Ghirardacci Bolognese. 2 vols., 1657.
GIERKE.	Gierke, Dr. Otto (tr. Maitland): *Political Theories of the Middle Age.* 1900.
GOELLER.	Goeller, Emil: *Koenig Sigismunds Kirchenpolitik.* 1902.
GOZZADINI.	Gozzadini, Giovanni: *Nanne Gozzadini e Baldassare Cossa.* 1880.
GRATIUS.	Gratius, Ortwinus: *Fasciculus rerum expetendarum et fugiendarum.* 1690.

ABBREVIATIONS

HARDT.	Hardt, Hermann von der: *Rerum Concilii Oecumenici Constantiensis.* 6 vols., 1697.
HAURÉAU.	Hauréau, B.: *Histoire de la Philosophie Scolastique.* 1872.
HAZLITT.	Hazlitt, W. Carew: *The Venetian Republic.* 2 vols., 1900.
HEFELE.	Hefele, Dr. Carl Joseph: *Conciliengeschichte.* 1869. 7ter Band: 1rste Abt.
HELFERT.	Helfert, Josef Alexander: *Hus und Hieronymus.* 1853.
Hist. Gén.	*Histoire Générale du ive siècle à nos jours*; Lavisse et Rambaud. 12 vols., 1893.
HOEFLER.	Hoefler, Carl Adolf Constantin: *Magister Johannes Hus und der Abzug.* 1864.
HUBER.	Huber, Alfons: *Geschichte Oesterreichs.* 5 vols., 1885.
HUEBLER.	Huebler, Bernhard: *Die Constanzer Reformation.* 1867.
HUNGER.	Hunger, Carl: *Zur Geschichte Papst Johanns XXIII.* 1876.
JUVENAL.	Juvenal des Ursins, Jean: *Histoire de Charles VI.* 1653.
KAGELMACHER.	Kagelmacher, Ernst: *Filippo Maria Visconti und Koenig Sigismund.* 1885.
LAVISSE.	Lavisse, Ernest: *Histoire de France.* 1905.
LECHLER.	Lechler, Gotthard Viktor: *Johannes Hus.* 1889.
LECHLER (*Lorimer*).	Lechler, Professor (tr. Lorimer): *John Wycliffe and his English Precursors.* 1 vol.
LENFANT (*C.*).	Lenfant, Jaques: *Histoire du Concile de Constance.* 2 vols., 1727.
LENFANT (*P.*).	Lenfant Jaques: *Histoire du Concile de Pise.* 1724.
LENZ.	Lenz, Max: *Koenig Sigismund und Heinrich der Fuenfte.* 1874.
LICHNOWSKY.	Lichnowsky, C. M.: *Geschichte des Hauses Habsburg.* 1839.
LINDNER (*H.*).	Lindner, Theodor: *Deutsche Geschichte unter den Habsburgen und Luxemburgen.* 2 vols., 1890.
LINDNER (*W.*).	Lindner, Theodor: *Geschichte des deutschen Reiches unter Koenig Wenzel.* 2 vols., 1875.
LOSERTH.	Loserth, Dr. Johann (tr. Evans): *Wiclif and Hus.*
LUETZOW.	Luetzow, The Count: *The Life and Times of Master John Hus.* 1909.
MANSI.	Mansi, Joannes Dominicus: *Sacrorum Conciliorum nova et amplissima collectio.*
MARMOR.	Marmor, J.: *Das Konzil zu Konstanz.* 1898.
MARTENE (*A. C.*).	Martene and Durand: *Veterum scriptorum et monumentorum amplissima collectio.* 1724-33.

MARTENE (T.).	Martene and Durand: *Thesaurus novus anecdotorum.* 1717.
MAURICE.	Maurice, Frederic Denison: *Moral and Metaphysical Philosophy.* 1873.
MAYHEW.	Mayhew, Henry: *The Upper Rhine.* 1860.
MAZELLA.	Scipio Mazella Napolitano: *Le Vite dei re di Napoli.*
MENZEL.	Menzel, Wolfgang: *History of Germany*; tr. Horrocks.
MICHAEL.	Michael, Emil: *Geschichte des deutschen Volkes.* 4 vols.
MICHELET.	Michelet, Jules: *Histoire de France.*
MILMAN.	Milman, Henry Hart: *History of Latin Christianity.* 1883.
MOLMENTI.	Molmenti, Pompeo; tr. Brown: *Venice in the Middle Ages.* 2 vols., 1906.
MONSTRELET.	Monstrelet: *Chronique de 1400 à 1444.* 1848.
MUELLER.	Mueller, Jean de; tr. Monnard: *Histoire de la Confédération Suisse.* 1837.
MUR.	Muratorius, Ludovicus Antonius: *Rerum Italicarum Scriptores.*
MUR (A.).	Muratorius, Ludovicus Antonius: *Annali d'Italia.*
OMAN.	Oman, C.: *The History of England* (from the accession of Richard II. to the death of Richard III.) 1906.
PALACKY.	Palacky, Franz: *Geschichte von Boehmen.* 7 vols. 1836.
PALACKY (Doc.).	Palacky, Franz: *Documenta Mag. Johannis Hus.* 1869.
PASTOR.	Pastor, Ludwig: *History of the Popes.* 8 vols., English translation, 1899 *et seq.*
PLATINA.	Platina, Baptista: *Lives of the Popes*; tr. Rycaut. 1688.
POOLE.	Poole, Reginald Lane: *Illustrations of the History of Mediæval Thought.* 1884.
PULKA.	Petrus de Pulka, Abgesandter der Wiener Universitaet am Concilium zu Constanz: von Friedrich Firnhaber: Archiv fuer Kunde oesterreichischer Geschichtsquellen. Band XV. Wien, 1856.
QUIDDE.	Quidde, L.: *Koenig Sigmund (Die Wahl Sigmunds).*
RADFORD.	Radford, Lewis Bostock: *Henry Beaufort.* 1908.
RAMSAY.	Sir James H.: *Lancaster and York.* 2 vols., 1892.
RASHDALL.	Rashdall, Hastings: *The Universities of Europe in the Middle Ages.* 2 vols., 1895.
RAUMER.	*Historisches Taschenbuch,* 1869; containing Erler, Dr. Georg: *Florenz, Neapel und das paepstliche Schisma.*

ABBREVIATIONS

RAYNALDUS.	Raynaldus, Ordericus : *Annales Ecclesiastici.*
REINKE.	Reinke, Georg: *Frankreich und Papst Johann XXIII.* 1900.
RELIGIEUX.	Documents Inédits sur l'Histoire de France : *Chronique du Religieux de Saint-Denys,* ed. Bellaguet. 6 vols., 1842.
RICHENTAL.	Richental, Ulrich von: *Chronik des Constanzer Concils,* ed. Buck. 1882.
ROBERTSON.	Robertson, James Craigie : *History of the Christian Church.* 4 vols., 1871.
ROSSMANN.	Rossmann : *De externo Concilii Constantiensis apparatu.* 1856.
SAUERBREI.	Sauerbrei, Moritz : *Die italienische Politik Koenig Sigmunds.* 1893.
SCHMID.	Schmid, Georg : *Itinerarium Johanns XXIII. zum Concil von Konstanz* 1414. Published in the Festschrift zum elfhundertjaehrigen Jubilaeum des deutschen Campo Santo in Rom. 1897.
SCHWAB.	Schwab, Johann Baptist : *Johannes Gerson.* 1858.
SISMONDI.	Sismondi Simonde de : *Histoire des Républiques Italiennes du Moyen Age.* 10 vols., 1840.
TSCHACKERT.	Tschackert, Paul : *Peter von Ailli.* 1877.
TUETEY.	Tuetey, Alexandre : *Journal d'un Bourgeois de Paris.* 1881.
VALOIS.	Valois, Noël : *La France et le Grand Schisme d'Occident.* 4 vols., 1884.
WESSENBERG.	J. H. von Wessenberg : *Die grossen Kirchenversammlungen des 15ten und 16ten Jahrhunderts.* Constanz, 1840.
WOLKENSTEIN.	Wolkenstein, Oswald von : *Gedichte.* 1866.
WYLIE.	Wylie, James Hamilton : *History of England under Henry the Fourth.* 4 vols.
WYLIE (C.).	Wylie, James Hamilton : *The Council of Constance to the Death of John Hus.* 1900.

TABLE OF CONTENTS

	PAGE
THE INTRODUCTION,	v
LIST OF CARDINALS,	ix
MEMORANDUM OF ABBREVIATIONS,	xv
LIST OF ILLUSTRATIONS,	xxxi

CHAPTER I

THE NEW POPE

Death of Pope Alexander the Fifth. Political outlook. Merits and demerits of Baldassare Cossa. Proceedings in the conclave. Coronation of Pope John the Twenty-third. Felicitations. Pippo Span of Ozora. His mission. Attitude of Sigismund of Hungary. Preliminary measures of Pope John. Destruction of the French fleet off Meloria. Duke of Anjou's march to Rome. King Ladislas and the Florentines. Use of the Bull in favour of the mendicant orders prohibited. Pope Gregory the Twelfth. Carlo Malatesta of Rimini. His correspondence with Pope John. With Venice and Pope Benedict. With King Sigismund. Pope John and France: his first false move. Pope John and England. Bologna, . 1

CHAPTER II

JOHN HUS

Pope John the Twenty-third and Wyclifism. Bohemia and the Czechs. King John. Charles the Fourth. King Wenzel. Sigismund in Bohemia. The introduction of Wyclifism. The *Dialogus* and *Trialogus* brought to Bohemia. The early career of John Hus. The Bethlehem Chapel. Archbishop Zbynek and Hus. Wyclifism at the University of Prague.

xxii POPE JOHN THE TWENTY-THIRD

The doctrine of the Sacrament. First breach between the Archbishop and Hus. Letter from the University of Oxford brought to Prague. Hus's doctrine on the Eucharist. His endeavours to improve the Czech language. The question of neutrality. Alteration of the constitution of the University of Prague. Feud between the Archbishop and Hus. The papal Bull. Appeal to the new Pope. Burning of Wyclif's works. Hus appeals to his congregation for support. Tumult. Decision of Cardinal Colonna. Sympathy from England. Decision of the Bologna doctors. Excommunication of John Hus for contumacy, ... 24

CHAPTER III

THREE POPES AND THREE EMPERORS

Death of King Rupert. The new election. The candidates, Wenzel, Jost, and Sigismund. Pope John resolves to support Sigismund. The Electors. Opposition to Wenzel. The Archbishops of Mainz and Cologne. The Count Palatine and the Archbishop of Trier. The other three lay electors. The imperial capitulation of the 5th August. Delay. Proposals of the Archbishop of Mainz. The Burggraf Friedrich of Nuernberg. The Count Palatine and Archbishop of Trier pronounce for Sigismund. They elect him on the 20th September. Jost elected on the 1st October. Negotiations between Sigismund and Jost. Death of Jost on 8th January. Agreement between Sigismund and Wenzel. Settlement of the religious troubles in Hungary. Archbishop of Mainz conciliated. Second election of Sigismund on 21st July. The need for a strong ruler. Communications between Pope John and Sigismund. His more immediate work, . . . 52

CHAPTER IV

SIGISMUND

Sigismund. His birth. His childhood. Betrothal to Marie of Hungary. Loses Poland. Hedwig. Sigismund married to Marie. King of Hungary. The capture of Marie and her mother. Death of Marie. Invasion of Ladislas. Nature of Sigismund's training in warfare. Character of Sigismund.

TABLE OF CONTENTS

His relations toward his cousins and his brother Johann. His ingratitude to Wenzel. Breach with Pope Boniface the Ninth. The Kumanian troops. Sigismund's fits of passion. His levity with women. His imprisonment. His release. The turning-point in his career. His good legislation. The lighter side of his character. His attitude to the clergy. His impecuniosity. His peacemaking. His three 'fixed ideas.' The majesty of the Empire. The unity of the Church. The expulsion of the Turk. The Order of the Dragon. Queen Barbara. Sigismund's attitude to Pope John. The Pope's second false move, ... 70

CHAPTER V

ROCCA SECCA

Spring of 1411. Unpropitious weather. The Pope marches from Bologna to Rome. The revolt of Bologna. Its suppression. The war with Naples. The Pope the only supporter of the Duke of Anjou. Louis of Anjou. Paolo Orsini. Sforza Attendolo. King Ladislas of Naples. The battle of Rocca Secca. Announcement of the victory at Rome. Failure to follow up the victory. The Duke of Anjou compelled to leave Italy. Fiscal measures of Pope John. Sforza leaves him, ... 95

CHAPTER VI

A CREATION OF CARDINALS

Diminution of numbers in the College of Cardinals. The new cardinals; the Pope's nephew. The Italian cardinals; Francesco Zabarella. The English nominations. The French nominations. Guillaume Fillastre. Gilles des Champs. Pierre d'Ailly. The fourteen nominations. The crusade against King Ladislas. Its failure. Peace between Archbishop Zbynek and John Hus. Death of the Archbishop. Clux and Stokes at Prague. Denunciation of the crusade in Prague. The three martyrs. Attitude of John Hus, ... 110

CHAPTER VII

THE COUNCIL AT ROME

The outlook for the Pope. Peace with King Ladislas. Pope Gregory the Twelfth. The advantage of the Peace to the Pope. Rome appointed for the Council. The Pope and France. Opening of the Council at Rome. Arrival of Representatives. The Holy Ghost in the form of an Owl. The tone of France to the Pope. Concessions to France and the University of Paris. Vacillating nature of the French policy. The only general session. John Wyclif; Nominalism and Realism. The realist theory. Ockham's philosophy as regards species and universals. Reason and Faith in watertight compartments. Wyclif's philosophy. John Hus. Wyclif on transubstantiation. Decree of the Council against Wyclifism. Adjournment of the Council, .   . 126

CHAPTER VIII

THE WAR WITH VENICE

Success of the Venetian Republic. Her aggrandisement. Her dealings with Hungary. Situation of Hungary. Relations with Poland. Sigismund resolves on war. Prosperity of Venice. Unsuccessful mediation of the Pope. Rumour as to the coronation. Hungarian successes. Retreat of Pippo Span. The first battle of Motta. Renewed intervention of the Pope. Second battle of Motta. Pippo Span unsuccessful in northern Italy. Sigismund appears in person: third battle of Motta. Hermann of Cilly negotiates a truce. Articles of agreement. Sigismund at Belluno. End of the fratricidal war among the sons of Bajazet. Sigismund now comparatively free to deal with the Great Schism, 146

CHAPTER IX

THE FLIGHT FROM ROME

The peace with Ladislas and the rupture with Sforza. The rupture with Ladislas. Simon de Cramaud made Cardinal. Pope John and the Romans. The taking of Rome. The flight of the Pope. Pope John reaches Florence. King

TABLE OF CONTENTS

Ladislas in Rome. Todi and Rocca Contrada. Sigismund and Friedrich of the Tirol. The King and the Duke at Salzburg. The affair of the burgher's daughter at Innsbruck. The Tirol. Friedrich and Wintler. Friedrich and Rottenburg. Friedrich and Georg of Trient. The enmity between Sigismund and Friedrich. Attempt to poison Sigismund at Brixen. Sigismund at Meran. The Swiss and Milan. Sigismund's appeal to the Swiss. His inadequate forces. Filippo Maria at Milan. Colloquy between Sigismund and Filippo Maria. Pope John and Leonardo of Arezzo. Negotiations with Sigismund. The papal embassy to the King. Ladislas of Naples and Pope Benedict the Thirteenth, 161

CHAPTER X

THE CONVOCATION OF THE GREAT COUNCIL

Negotiations between the King and the Pope. The Pope's ambassadors. Action of the Venetians. Constance agreed upon. The King's proclamation announcing the Council. His position. Meeting of the Pope and the King. Oswald von Wolkenstein. The Pope and the King at Lodi. Their conference. Events at Lodi. Gregory the Twelfth. Benedict the Thirteenth. Cremona. The brilliant idea of Gabrino Fondulo. The Pope and the King as church reformers. The consultation with regard to John Hus. Prague placed under an interdict. John Hus in retirement. His writings at that time. Albert retires and Conrad becomes Archbishop of Prague. Sigismund communicates with John Hus, who resolves to go to Constance. Negotiations with Pope Gregory. Sigismund at Genoa: at Asti: at Pavia: at Turin. Pope John again at Bologna. King Ladislas marches from Rome and besieges Todi. Ladislas poisoned at Perugia and returns to Naples, where he dies. The Pope's hesitation on hearing the news, . . . 182

CHAPTER XI

PRELIMINARY NEGOTIATIONS

Preliminary negotiations necessary. Negotiation with France. Sigismund abandons the Duke of Burgundy. Burgundians and Armagnacs. Projected visit to Avignon. Treaty signed at Trino. Peace between the Burgundians and Armagnacs.

xxvi POPE JOHN THE TWENTY-THIRD

French arrangements for the Council. Burgundian arrangements. Negotiations with England. Negotiations with the kingdoms of Spain and Pope Benedict the Thirteenth. King Ferdinand and Pope Benedict at Morella. Embassies to King Sigismund. Project for reconciliation of the Greek and Latin Churches. Sigismund at Bern: at Cologne: at Strassburg, Speier, and Mainz. Uncertainty about the coronation. Sigismund at Heilbronn. The coronation at Aachen, ... 205

CHAPTER XII

THE JOURNEY TO CONSTANCE

The Pope's plan. Treaty with the magistrates of Constance. Three Cardinals sent on ahead. Richental the chronicler. Pope John leaves Bologna, passes through Trient. St. Michael on the Adige. The league with Duke Friedrich at Meran. Bozen. Brixen. Innsbruck. The accident in the pass. The Pope reaches Kreuzlingen. He enters Constance. The misconceptions of John Hus. The papal inquisitor declares that Hus is not a heretic. Hus leaves Prague. His reception in Germany. Hus at Nuernberg. He decides not to join King Sigismund. Hus reaches Constance. The safe-conduct. King Sigismund's journey from Aachen to Constance, ... 223

CHAPTER XIII

CONSTANCE

Constance practically unaltered. Disappearance of the walls, towers, and gateways. Changes in some of the buildings. The streets the same. The foundation of the city. Extension of the town. Later enlargements. The clergy. The laymen. Numbers present during the Council. The Board and the College of Auditors. Police arrangements. Prices of provisions. Official visitors. Traders, workmen, and players. Amusements. A motley scene. Literary activity in Constance. Poets. Oswald von Wolkenstein, . . 237

TABLE OF CONTENTS

CHAPTER XIV

THE COUNCIL BEFORE CHRISTMAS, 1414

The nature of the Council. Celebration of Mass on 1st November 1414. The opening of the Council. Constance in winter. Early arrivals. John Hus at the house of the widow Fida. Division into nations. First general session. The arms of Pope Gregory the Twelfth. Arrival of Pierre d'Ailly. John Hus summoned by the Cardinals. Friar Didachus. Hus imprisoned. The weakening of the Pope. Hus taken to the Dominican Cloister. Commission appointed. Increasing influence of Pierre d'Ailly. Postponement of the second general session. Arrival of King Sigismund and Queen Barbara, ... 252

CHAPTER XV

REX SUPER GRAMMATICAM

The Mass on Christmas Day. Pierre d'Ailly's sermon. Question of the safe-conduct settled. The trial of John Hus. Gerson and Hus. The Legates of Pope Gregory: received in congregation. Canonisation of Saint Brigitta. The King throws over the Pope. Cardinal Fillastre proposes that the Pope do resign. Arrivals in Constance. Question as to who shall vote. Question as to how the vote shall be counted. Anonymous attack on Pope John. *Rex super grammaticam*, . 269

CHAPTER XVI

THE QUESTION OF RESIGNATION

Pope John promises to resign. Formulas of cession. Arrival of the French embassy. The embassy from the University of Paris. New formula of cession prepared: accepted by the Pope. Second general session. Difficulties as to proctors. Presentation of the Golden Rose. Breach between the Pope and the King. The parties in the Council. Cardinal Hannibaldus not allowed to leave Constance. The King's explanation and the Pope's promise. Dissension amid the nations. The King and the French nation. The King visits the Pope. The King and Duke Friedrich. The Duke's tournament. John Hus in prison, ... 285

CHAPTER XVII

THE FLIGHT

The tournament in the lists at Paradise. The flight of Pope John. The action of Duke Friedrich. Schaffhausen; the Pope's letters. The relation of Friedrich to the Pope. The Pope's mistake. Constance after the flight. The attitude of the Cardinals. The King and the Duke. John Hus. The Pope at Schaffhausen. The sermon of Jean Gerson. The deputation of the three cardinals. The Pope's motives. The cardinals in opposition. Return of the deputation. Rejection of the Pope's proposal. Fourth general session. Measures against Friedrich. Pope John leaves Schaffhausen. His stay there, ... 299

CHAPTER XVIII

THROUGH THE BLACK FOREST

The Pope's Bull from Laufenburg. Fifth general session. Its proceedings. Commission of belief. Superiority of the Council over the Pope. War against Duke Friedrich. Affairs in France. The Pope flies to Freiburg. Freiburg. The Pope's hopes and professions. Pope and the Council at hopeless variance. Death of Chrysoloras. The Members of the University of Paris at Constance. Sixth general session. Jerome of Prague. Supervision of the commission of belief. The cardinals and the nations at variance. The embassy to Pope John. The attitude of the Duke of Burgundy. The Pope goes to Breisach. The embassy with the Pope. The day at Neuenburg. Pope John betrayed by Duke Friedrich. Appearance of Louis of Bavaria: his interview with the Duke. Pope John a prisoner at Freiburg, . . . 316

CHAPTER XIX

THE DEPOSITION OF POPE JOHN

Return of Duke Friedrich. Seventh general session. Eighth general session. Condemnation of the forty-five articles. Its importance to John Hus. Submission of Duke Friedrich. Possession taken of his lands. Pope John in captivity at Freiburg. Ninth general session. Tenth general session. Petitions on behalf of Hus from Bohemia and Moravia.

TABLE OF CONTENTS   xxix

Pope Gregory the Twelfth. The Duke of Burgundy. The matter of the Bohemian heresy. The indictment of Pope John. The Pope at Radolfzell. Eleventh general session. Deposition of the Pope. The end of his reign, . . 331

CHAPTER XX

THE TRIAL OF JOHN HUS

News of the Pope's deposition received in France. Friedrich with the empty pockets. Baldassare Cossa at Gottlieben. Hus's physical condition. Hus removed to the Franciscan Cloister. First day of the trial. Hus's determination. Second day of the trial. Hus and d'Ailly. Hus and the Wyclifian heresies. Hus's appeal to Christ. Hus and the disturbances at Prague. Sigismund's warning. Hus refuses to take the advice. Last day of the trial. Hus's doctrine on the Church and church government. Hus and ecclesiastical censures. Hus explains why he did not condemn Wyclif. A Pope in mortal sin. John Stokes, . . 361

CHAPTER XXI

THE CONCLUSION OF THE TRIAL

Supposed submission of John Hus to the Council. Hus's argument with King Sigismund. The matter of the students at Prague. The letter from the University of Oxford. Hus condemned by King Sigismund. Hus's heresy. His regard for the Scriptures as the supreme rule of faith. The interpretation of Scripture. The appeal to the individual conscience. The catholic doctrine on the Scripture. The punishment of heresy. After the final audience. Communion in both kinds. Attempt to induce Hus to recant. John of Chlum's exhortation. Hus's consistency, . . 381

CHAPTER XXII

MARTYRDOM

The doctrine of political assassination. Hus's Protestantism. The cathedral square on the 6th July 1415. Condemnation. Sentence. Degradation. Hus taken to the stake. Hus is burned. The ashes thrown into the Rhine, . . . 395

xxx POPE JOHN THE TWENTY-THIRD

CHAPTER XXIII

THE BEADLE OF THE EMPIRE

PAGE

Baldassare Cossa at Mannheim and Heidelberg. The resignation of Pope Gregory the Twelfth. The firmness of Pope Benedict the Thirteenth. Preparations for the departure of King Sigismund. The King goes to Narbonne. The hopes of Pope Benedict. Sigismund reaches Perpignan. Failure of the negotiations. The Pope retires to Peniscola. The capitulation of Narbonne. The news received at Constance. The King at Avignon. The King at Chambery and at Paris. His failure in France. He goes to England. The Peace of Canterbury. Sigismund returns to Constance. Jean Gerson at Constance. The dispute regarding the doctrine of Jean Petit. Decision postponed. Disputes among the nations. The case of Jerome of Prague. The letter of Poggio Bracciolini. The burning of Jerome. Friedrich of the Tirol, ... 402

CHAPTER XXIV

THE LAST DAYS OF BALDASSARE COSSA

The Spanish nation at the Council. The deposition of Pope Benedict. The question of church reform. Discussions and recriminations. Compromise effected by the Bishop of Winchester. Arrangements for the election of a new Pope. The election of Oddo Colonna. The character of the new Pope, Martin the Fifth. His measures for reform. The reconciliation of King Sigismund with Duke Friedrich. The end of the Council of Constance. Baldassare Cossa becomes a prisoner of the Pope. Efforts for the release of Baldassare Cossa. His release. He enters Florence. He submits to Pope Martin the Fifth. His death and character. His tomb, ... 421

Popes now as there had been three hundred and sixty-five years before; and as the Emperor then had stifled the Schism by deposing all three, might not a similar solution be possible in the present difficulty?

In some respects the elevation to the papacy of Baldassare Cossa must have seemed to many to be of good omen. He was a man of action and resolution, who hitherto had succeeded in all that he had attempted. He was prompt and determined, and ready-witted as ever. An instance of this occurred in the wordy war between him and his friend, the Lord of Rimini, during the nine days of mourning for Alexander. Carlo Malatesta had always been the best of friends with Baldassare Cossa,[1] but he did not wish to see him Pope, seeing that he himself was devoted to Gregory the Twelfth. Carlo wished to postpone the election, but Cossa made answer, among other points, that the cardinals wanted a head for their protection. To which the witty lord replied by asking him to consider the fowls of the air, how our Heavenly Father protecteth them, and certainly He would protect the cardinals also; surely during the vacancy all urgent and necessary acts could be done and signed by a Cardinal-Vicar. 'Cardinal-Vicar is not Pope,' answered Cossa, ' the name makes all the difference ' (nomen Papal est illud quod totum operatur). Cossa was known to be a man of political genius, though it was of the opportunist Italian type. He had seen the necessity for a general council, and had understood its possibility; he had, more than any other single man, brought about and carried through the great Council of Pisa. The man who had won back Bologna for the Church, who had beaten back King Ladislas and recovered Rome, who had defended and rendered possible the Council which had deposed two Popes, might surely be trusted to deal adequately with the existing situation. His first task would be to crush the overweening pretensions of the King of Naples, his next to make himself sole Pope in Christendom, and his third to deal with the demand for church reform. There must have been many who looked on Cossa as the ecclesiastic best qualified to deal with at least two, if not with all three, of these questions. But, besides the fact that the Popes had long been

[1] Hardt, ii. 361.

men of peace, taking no active personal part in warfare, there were other considerations also which militated against this view.

Baldassare Cossa at this time was about forty-three years of age; a tall, spare, strongly built man, with handsome, clearcut features, a prominent nose and chin, and grey eyes that gleamed out from beneath bushy eyebrows. His accession to the papacy meant to him a total change in his manner of life. He was above all things a soldier, fitter for the sword than the cassock, taking more delight in buckler and helmet than in pall or vestments, an able man in temporal matters but of no account in affairs spiritual;[1] he was a man who, as the Archbishop of Bordeaux said, would do better as king or emperor than as Pope. Hitherto much of his time had been spent in the tented field; he had himself led the troops against Milan when he first became Cardinal Legate, and he was himself engaged in the siege of Forlimpopolo when recalled to the deathbed of Alexander the Fifth. Though a churchman and a cardinal, he was still only a deacon, a layman in all but name; church routine had occupied but little of his time, church matters had necessarily entered little into his thoughts. There were those who said that he had never confessed nor taken the sacrament;[2] there were others who alleged that he believed not in the resurrection of the dead.[3] He was now to change the camp for the chapel, the council chamber of Bologna for the Consistory of cardinals, the local politics of northern Italy for those wide schemes of church reform which were agitating nearly the whole of civilised Europe. The mere transition from an outdoor existence to the wearisome seclusion of closet and chapel meant much. The change from the free life of the open air to one of ceremonial and seclusion, the passage from scenes of prompt activity to the tedium of religious service, to the hearing of lengthy reports, to the conduct of office business must itself have been irksome in the extreme to a man of Cossa's temperament. It is small wonder that he was gradually to lose his old force and determination of character, and that a fatalistic tendency was to become predominant. He was a Neapolitan; and Naples, like other places in the earthquake zone, was noted for the fatalism

---

[1] Ciaconius, ii. 790; Mur. xix. 41.   [2] Finke (*F.*), 1, note.
[3] *Ibid.* (*B.*), 10.

of its people ; the Neapolitans, from the time of Frederic the Second onward, had enjoyed the evil repute of being more Sarasin than Christian in religion. The change of life co-operated with this native tendency to encourage habits of sloth and fatalism in the new Pope.

Not on the physical side only, but on the moral side also, was the new pontiff like to prove inadequate to the great task before him. The cry for church reform had gone abroad through England, through France, through Bohemia ; but it found but little echo in Italy. Morality was at a very low ebb, was indeed practically non-existent, in the greater part of that country ; there was in Italy a great love for strength and for the beauty that waits on strength, there was keen appreciation of art, of refinement, of literature, but there was very little admiration for the mere moral virtues. The need for the moral reform of the Church,[1] so strongly felt elsewhere, was scarcely recognised by the Italian clergy ; and the new Pope had hitherto had little intercourse with members of the Holy Roman Church outside his own country. The cry for moral reform was therefore not likely to find any echo in the breast of Baldassare Cossa. His own life and manners, as Platina said, were those of the camp.[2] Again the demand for fiscal reform, the outcry against the exactions of the Curia, was strongest outside Italy ; the Popes got but little of their revenues from the poor sees of the peninsula ; they looked on England and France as their milch-kine. And John had been brought up and had served his apprenticeship in the Court of Boniface the Ninth, where papal exaction had become a fine art, where simony and corruption had reached a height hitherto unknown, where the

---

[1] 'During the latter part of the Middle Ages, the desire for reform of the Church was constant. It was strongest and most apparent among laymen, for a famous monastic writer of the fourteenth century testified that the laity led better lives than the clergy. To the bulk of ordinary Christians reform meant morality in the priesthood. It became intolerable to them to see the sacrament administered habitually by sacrilegious hands, or to let their daughters go to confession to an unclean priest. The discontent was deepest where men were best. They felt that the organisation provided for the salvation of souls was serving for their destruction, and that the more people sought the means of grace in the manner provided, the greater risk they incurred of imbibing corruption.'—Acton, *Lectures on Modern History*, 90.

[2] 'Militaris prope habebatur ejus vita, militares mores.'—Platina, i. 342.

spiritual side of the papacy had been systematically prostituted to its temporal needs. His aim would naturally be to restore the methods and régime of his patron and exemplar. He would be intent on the temporal interest of the papacy, and for her spiritual interest he would reck little. The hopes and aspirations of such orthodox churchmen as Jean Gerson, Pierre d'Ailly, and Nicolas de Clamanges found as little sympathy with him as did those of John Wyclif or John Hus; he failed to appreciate how widespread and influential their feelings were, how momentous the question they involved had become. To deal adequately with the matters then before Christendom, it needed a Pope who fully appreciated the issues at stake and the momentum of popular feeling behind them; it needed a Pope who was a profound statesman rather than an opportunist politician. In all questions of church reform John was like to be hopelessly conservative, bent on conceding as little and as grudgingly as possible. For the immediate present, however, this question did not call for solution or treatment; the new Pope was bound by the resolution of the Council of Pisa to call another Council in three years' time, and he was a man to keep his word.

The greatest disadvantage under which the new Pope laboured was that, with the exception of a few months under his immediate predecessor, he had been living apart from the papal court, and was likely to know but little of the political situation of Europe. He had indeed sent an occasional envoy to Bohemia or to France; but for seven years he had not seen Rome; he had been Papal Legate at Bologna; as a condottiere general and as Lord of Bologna he had been eminently successful; he had regained the territories of the city and had enlarged its borders; he had brought to it peace and welfare; but his attention had necessarily been concentrated on the work under his hand and had been diverted from the troubled politics of Europe outside Italy. In the affairs of the peninsula he was an astute and consummate politician; but the concentration of his interest weakened his power of grasping the situation in France and in Germany. For the existing crisis a Pope was needed of wider experience and of deeper sympathy. Baldassare Cossa's experience had been in the main that of a condottiere general and Podesta of an Italian city; even though

THE NEW POPE

he might be 'vir nobilis et expers in agendis,'[1] still he was, as the Venetian chronicler described him, an 'uomo molto dedito all' arme':[2] his sympathy was entirely with the temporal power of the Church; he failed to appreciate the standpoint of those who desired its reform. But in other respects also Baldassare Cossa was unfitted for the high office of supreme pontiff. The activity of a soldier's life had rendered him impatient of forms and ceremonies, and he did not appreciate their effect on the generality of mankind, he saw no use in long audiences which led to nothing; the tedious Masses bored him and he cut them short;[3] he was not exact in his pontifical dress; and he was apt to indulge in unseemly levity.[4] These are points which in our day may appear of minor importance, but which at the beginning of the fifteenth century were certain to cause grave scandal.

It is interesting in this connection to notice the warnings which Dietrich von Niem gave the new Pope.[5] The abbreviator knew the Pope well. He admonished him to be attentive to the offices of the Church, to be diligent at Mass and at Vespers, to read Mass at least three or four times in the week. He agreed with John as to the time wasted in unprofitable audiences, but he desired the time saved to be expended in reading the Bible and the histories of the Popes and the Kaisers. Still more remarkable is it that he exhorted the new Pope to withdraw his attention from the lands close at hand, and to direct his thoughts to foreign lands. It is clear that Niem knew the weak points in the harness of the new pontiff.

Baldassare Cossa was elected Pope on the 17th May 1410. Seventeen cardinals[6] entered into conclave at ten o'clock at night, on Wednesday, the 14th, in the Bishop's palace; their beds were arranged in cubicles, divided by curtains of the finest silk, and adorned with flowers and sweet-smelling herbs, 'so that it seemed a Paradise,' and the arms of each cardinal were posted outside his apartment. The windows were walled up, little peepholes being left for light; the entrance to the palace was secured under double lock, a small door being made

---
[1] *Religieux*, iv. 324. [2] Mur. xxii. 853.
[3] Public opinion tolerated shortening the Mass in the case of huntsmen anxious to be off to their day's sport, but not in the case of a Pope who might have important business to transact. Every one will remember the sweet little church on the south bank of the Arno at Pisa, famed for its Huntsman's Masses.
[4] Hardt, iv. 25. [5] Erler, 198. [6] For their names see the Introduction, p. ix.

to admit food and drink, and a strong guard of soldiers was posted under the command of Malatesta of Pesaro and Nicolo Roberti of Ferrara.[1] The choice of the new Pope was due to the influence of the Duke of Anjou, who was anxious that the most powerful and most friendly of the cardinals should be pontiff. But the tongue of scandal was not idle. Some alleged that Baldassare Cossa had bribed all the poorer members of the College; others said that he had threatened the cardinals with his anger if they did not elect a Pope agreeable to him, and that the Pope most agreeable to him was himself. Philip of Bergamo told a slightly different story. There was discord, according to him, among the cardinals, and they asked Cossa who ought to be elected. ' Give me the mantle of Saint Peter,' said he, ' and I will give it to him who ought to be Pope.' As soon as he had the mantle in his hands, he threw it over his own shoulders saying, ' I am Pope.' But a similar story was told of John the Twenty-Second; and no mention of any such incident was subsequently made at the Council of Constance, when all the iniquities which could be laid to the count of John were piled together in accusation against him.[2] Cossa himself desired that Conrad Caracciolo, the Cardinal of Malta, should be Pope, and advised the cardinals to elect him. When they refused to elect the man whom he suggested, hoping still to remain the powerful cardinal behind the papal throne, the cardinals could hardly do other, having regard to the political necessities of the time, than elect Baldassare Cossa himself.[3]

At midday on the 17th the cross appeared outside the palace, signifying that the election had been made, and an hour later, the new Pope, wearing a scarlet mitre, bordered with white, issued from the conclave. Accompanied by all the cardinals, by the two patriarchs, the three archbishops, by twenty-seven abbots, by a large number of the clergy and a throng of the citizens, Pope John the Twenty-third proceeded to the church of San Pietro Maggiore; and after the sacrament had been administered, he sat on a golden chair that all might kiss his feet. His dwelling was pillaged according to custom, even the doors and windows being carried off. As he was still a deacon, he was ordained priest on Saturday, the 23rd, by

[1] Ghirar, ii. 582.   [2] Robertson, iv. 250.   [3] Christophe, iii. 346-7.

Cardinal de Viviers, Bishop of Ostia, in the chapel of his predecessor, and he was consecrated Bishop in the church of San Petronio; the Cardinal Chalant acted as deacon. On Sunday the new Pope celebrated High Mass in the Cathedral, the Marquess of Ferrara and Carlo Malatesta holding the basin for him to wash his hands; the Marquess was attended by fifty-four cavaliers, dressed in crimson and azure, and by five trumpeters and eight fiddlers to discourse sweet music. A lofty platform, covered with cloth of gold, was erected on the piazza against the wall of the church; the Pope was brought out and seated on a chair; and here, in the presence of the cardinals and clergy and of a great multitude of doctors from his old University, Baldassare Cossa was crowned Pope by his fellow-countryman Cardinal Brancacius and by the Archdeacon Modesto. The guns on the piazza were fired, and all the church bells in the city were rung; and meanwhile, to remind him that he was but mortal, tufts of tow were thrice lighted and thrice extinguished before him by six cardinals, who warned him, as the fire went out, ' Holy Father, thus passeth away the glory of this world.' Then the newly crowned pontiff, clad in full canonicals, descended from the stage, mounted his horse, which was covered with scarlet trappings, and rode under a gold-embroidered canopy, held aloft by cavaliers and doctors, through the market-place to the Piazza of San Stefano; he was accompanied by the cardinals and other prelates in their mitres and long robes, mounted on horses housed in white. Thus they rode through the streets of Bologna. In the Piazza the High Priest of the Rabbis met the Pope and presented him with the Book of the Law, to whom John answered that it was a good law, but that they understood it not aright. The Jews followed him, tearing the trappings from his horse; the streets were so thronged that the Papal Treasurer had to scatter largess to the crowd in order to make way to the palace, while the two hundred men-at-arms who accompanied the Pope struck the Jews with their leather maces as they went along, ' so that it was great joy to behold.' The next day the Pope made another joyous procession, accompanied by prelates in their red cloaks and white mitres, by dukes, counts, and cavaliers of Italy, by thirty-six trumpeters, and twenty minstrels who sang motets and virelais at the top of their voices. Having returned to his palace, the Pope blessed the people, and the cardinals kissed him on the hand, the foot, and the mouth; then they dined together, and the Pope presented the cardinals, patriarchs, archbishops, and bishops with many and divers gifts. There were grand feasts, music, and dancing; for three days and three nights the rejoicings continued.[1] Bologna now had a Pope who had lived in its midst for the best part of twenty years. 'Rarely,' says the historian, ' has such magnificence been displayed. The splendour, alas ! was far from intimating to him whom it surrounded with so much glory the incomprehensible troubles which were later to accompany a dignity so ardently pursued and so sadly acquired.'[2]

Felicitations flowed in on the new pontiff. The Signory of Florence lost no time in sending an embassy of congratulation. They knew Pope John the Twenty-third to be a man of the highest capacity, 'uomo capace del sommo grade';[3] they placed their forces at his disposal, and begged him to go to Rome and to aid Louis of Anjou in his enterprise. War was inevitable, and it was in war that Baldassare Cossa had hitherto been conspicuously successful; unfortunately the Popes no longer conducted their wars in person. The city of Rome received the news of the new Pope's accession with gladness; the insignia of Gregory the Twelfth were everywhere removed; the old form of government was re-established; Nicolo and Giovanni Colonna were won over by Paolo Orsini to John's side; traitors were rigorously punished; the attempts of Ladislas of Naples were repulsed.

Of all the embassies of congratulation, probably the most welcome was the ambassador Pippo Span; Pippo, Count of Ozora, who passed through Ferrara on the 21st, and arrived at Bologna soon after, from King Sigismund of Hungary.[4] Pippo is the ordinary Italian diminutive for Filippo, and Span or Zupan is the designation which in Hungary was given to every captain of a district. Filippo Scolari was a Florentine, and belonged to the noble old family of the Buondelmonte;[5] but his father Stefano and his mother Antonia were poor people,

[1] Ghirar, ii. 583; Monstrelet, 169-70. [2] Christophe, iii. 347.
[3] Capponi, i. 440. [4] Mur. xxiv. 177. [5] *A.S.I.*, iv. 163.

THE NEW POPE

and some said that Stefano was a shoemaker. Pippo was born in 1369 in Tizzano, seven miles from Florence, and when only thirteen years of age was taken by a trader, Luca Pecchia, to Buda. Here the boy attracted the notice of Sigismund's treasurer, brother of the Bishop of Strigonia, who took him under his protection. It so happened that Pippo went one day to Strigonia to the Bishop, in whose palace King Sigismund was then staying. After dinner a discussion arose about raising twelve thousand cavalry to guard the Danube against the Turks who had just taken Servia ; and no one present was able to calculate the expense. Pippo was called in, took pen and paper, and gave at once the necessary information. This was his introduction to Sigismund. The King was struck both with the ability and with the appearance of the young man ; for Pippo, though but of middle height and of a spare well-knit frame, had dark lustrous eyes, his face wore a perpetual smile, and he was as fond of smart clothes as Sigismund himself.[1] The King took Pippo into his service and placed him in charge of the mines. His management of these secured him the royal favour ; and Pippo ingratiated himself with everybody. In his habits he was abstemious ; as an orator he became accomplished, speaking the languages of Hungary, Poland, Germany, and Bohemia as fluently as he did Italian. On the fatal 28th April 1401, when Sigismund was seized in the Hall of Audience at Buda, Pippo Span was present and drew his sword in defence of his patron ; he would have been cut down and killed had it not been for the Bishop of Strigonia, who threw his robe over him and declared that Pippo was his prisoner.[2] Pippo lost no time in raising troops to free his master ; he wrote to Sigismund in prison, and the King no sooner recovered his freedom than he gave Pippo a castle in gratitude for his services. Pippo interceded for the rebels, at first unsuccessfully ; he let drop the clasp he was wearing, a serpent with its tail in its mouth ; the King noticed the legend on the cross on the reverse, ' How art thou merciful, just and good, oh God.' He determined to imitate the divine clemency and pardoned the rebels ; he used the motto afterwards for the Order of the Dragon. Pippo's influence in Hungary was immensely increased by his successful

[1] Hazlitt, i. 777.　　　[2] *A.S.I.*, iv. 167.

mediation. He accompanied the King in his war with Bosnia, and when on one occasion Sigismund, panic-stricken, took to flight, Pippo snatched his crown, placed it on his own head, rallied the troops, and won a splendid victory. Pippo was a born general, and this timely service so endeared him to the King that Sigismund made Pippo general of twenty thousand horse, and loaded him with wealth; henceforth Pippo Span was the right-hand man of King Sigismund of Hungary.[1]

Pippo had come to announce to the Pope the allegiance of the King of Hungary, to crave pardon for the malversation of the ecclesiastical revenues, and to set forth to the Pope the King's determination to restore the Church in Hungary to its former splendour.[2] Pippo usually appeared in a long silk mantle, which he wore, like Duke Friedrich of Austria, trailing on the ground, and with a military hat with lappets falling on his shoulders. Sigismund had sent off his ambassador in the middle of May, before the death of King Rupert, though probably about the time that he heard that Pope Alexander was dead or dying, for his letter was not addressed to the Pope by name, but merely to the Pope as the Vicar of Christ.[3] Pippo went on from Bologna to Florence and spent some time there; the Florentines commended his mission to the Pope when the ambassador left their city on the 16th August 1410. They pointed out that the King of Hungary had been harshly treated by former pontiffs and they requested Pope John to confirm the appointments which the King had made and to remove prelates displeasing to him; they pointed out, moreover, that the Pope ought to assist the King and to admonish his adversaries when the King was fighting for the common weal of Christendom against the unbelievers, and that he should allow and sanction all exactions made by the King from the clergy of Hungary for this purpose.[4] Sigismund had the war with Venice at this time in view, and the Venetians had little doubt that Pippo's embassy had to do therewith.[5]

To Pope John the attitude of the King of Hungary was of immense importance. Sigismund had not acknowledged the Council of Pisa, but had stood aloof. Now he promised obedi-

[1] Mur. xxiv. 177-8.   [2] Raynaldus, viii. 325.   [3] Goeller, 71, note.
[4] Finke (*Acta*), 93 *et seq.*   [5] Goeller, 70, note.

THE NEW POPE

ence to the Pope of the Council; but he promised this obedience only as King of Hungary; he had not at this time become a candidate for the Empire, and he made no promise to Pope John in that capacity. The new Pope had already, on the 31st May, signed a letter to the Electors of the Empire, announcing his election as Pope; and this letter was afterward taken by his messengers, the knights Hugo of Hervorst and Nicolas of Altronandis, to Frankfurt. When Pippo arrived, Pope John knew of the death of Rupert and of the demise of the German crown; he appreciated the importance of the forthcoming election and of the recognition by the new head of the Holy Roman Empire of himself as the only true Pope, the only head on earth of the Holy Roman Church. Benedict the Thirteenth could still count on the support of Spain and Scotland; Gregory the Twelfth was still backed up by Ladislas of Naples and Carlo Malatesta, and was acknowledged by the German bishoprics of Trier, Speier, and Worms:[1] it was of infinite importance to Pope John that the future King of the Romans should undo the work of the late King Rupert, and should bring all Germany under the obedience of the Pope whose status depended on the Council of Pisa. This consideration determined the relation of Pope John the Twenty-third to King Sigismund of Hungary; the support of Sigismund was absolutely necessary; friendship with him was essential. The Pope accordingly was most gracious on all points of the embassy. He removed the sentence of closure on the churches of Hungary which had been passed on the 6th April 1404;[2] intercourse between the King and the Curia was renewed, the revolutionary acts of Sigismund were indirectly legalised. Bishop Branda of Piacenza was sent as Papal Legate to Hungary to arrange for the institution of a University, to correct certain abuses and abolish certain privileges which certain bishops had received from the rival Pope, and at the special desire of the King to take thought for the creation of new benefices on the borders of the kingdom. To King Sigismund Pope John was determined to be most conciliatory.

The first year of his pontificate was spent by the Pope at his beloved city, Bologna; here the negotiations with Carlo

[1] Palacky, iii. 244. [2] Goeller, 73.

14   POPE JOHN THE TWENTY-THIRD

Malatesta were carried through; hence the Legates were despatched to France and to Spain; Bologna, moreover, was more convenient than Rome for watching the proceedings in connection with the election of the new King of the Romans. The new Pope lost no time in issuing, for the information of Christendom, an encyclical [1] in which he claimed the adhesion accorded to his predecessor, and in which he renewed against his adversaries and their adherents the sentences pronounced by the Council of Pisa. He gave them until the month of April to make their allegiance, and announced that he would then take thought for the time and place of the coming council.[2] Pope Gregory was also stimulated to promulgate a Bull in which, referring to Baldassare Cossa's boyhood, he denounced all pirates and thieves.[3] Pope John sent to Spain a Legate *a latere*, Cardinal Maramaur,[4] to try to persuade Pope Benedict to resign and to win the adhesion of the kingdoms of Castile, Aragon, and Navarre; but the mission was a miserable failure. As soon as he was elected the Pope wrote to King Ladislas of Naples demanding the sixty thousand ducats which were due from him to the Church, but that red-haired libertine answered that he would not pay a single Tornese.[5] John can have expected no other answer, considering the terms he was on with Louis, Duke of Anjou, the rival of King Ladislas. On the very first day of his pontificate the Pope had issued letters of recommendation to all lords, spiritual and temporal, beseeching them to aid the army of Louis;[6] he had entrusted the Duke with a prefecture to give him facilities for the invasion of Naples,[7] and these measures were known to the King of Naples.

The Duke of Anjou had now returned from France to try to win for himself the kingdom of Naples which Queen Joanna the First had bequeathed to his father. In his haste he had sailed on ahead with half his fleet, leaving behind him the other six galleys with his horses, arms, stores, and the larger part of his troops and treasure. This detachment, so fatally weakened, fell in with the fleets of Ladislas and the Genoese, and a fierce fight ensued near the Island of Meloria. At first the day

---

[1] Raynaldus, viii. 320.   [2] *Ibid.* viii. 331.   [3] Blumenthal, 27.
[4] Raynaldus, viii. 323.   [5] Mur. xxii. 352.   [6] Raynaldus, viii. 324.
[7] Blumenthal, 13.

THE NEW POPE

went in favour of the French; one of their enemy's ships was taken and another was boarded, and the victors at once thought of securing their prize. But the allies rallied; they reconquered their ship; they renewed the fight with deadly vigour; it continued for seven long hours. At the end of that time two of the French galleys had been sent to the bottom, three were taken, and their valuable cargoes fell to the Neapolitans; one ship only, with fifteen hundred men aboard, escaped and rejoined the Duke at Piombino. This was on the 8th June 1410.[1] The Island of Elba was also taken by the fleet of Ladislas, which then sailed off to Ischia and Procida, the possessions of the Pope's family, where they did more damage; they finally made their way south to Policastro, which they took and sacked.

The unfortunate Duke was meantime at Piombino, where he received an embassy of condolence from Florence. Thence, mounted on a black horse, clad in black raiment, and accompanied by an escort arrayed in the like mournful habiliments, he sorrowfully wended his way to Siena. Here John the Twenty-third had given orders for his cordial reception, and the Duke now donned a red uniform, and betook himself to Bologna. Outside the city, on the Wednesday after the Pope's coronation, the Duke was honourably met by the cardinals and citizens. He came to solicit aid in men and money, and presently went on to Florence on the same errand. Neither Pope nor Republic helped him with money; probably they lacked confidence in him; but troops were forthcoming. The Florentine contingent was commanded by Alberigo da Barbiano, who, however, died near Perugia, when his place was taken by Braccio da Montone. The Duke himself was able to engage the services of Sforza Attendolo—a better general could not be found—but he failed to keep him contented, because he did not pay him regularly. Regular pay for his men was the first consideration with a condottiere general, and this was precisely what Louis of Anjou was unable to ensure. The papal and ducal troops, together with two thousand five hundred men supplied by Florence and Siena, marched off toward Rome. At the same time the rest of the ducal fleet, seven large galleys and one small one, sailed

[1] Ammirato, v. 14, note; Valois, iv. 133, note.

off to Ostia under command of the Pope's brother, the Italian admiral Gaspar Cossa; from Ostia they sailed toward Naples, but soon returned. Ladislas attempted to surprise Ostia, but his troops were defeated in one or two insignificant skirmishes by Paolo Orsini, and Ostia and Tivoli acknowledged the sway of the Pope. Nothing of importance occurred in the field, but the wily King was gaining his ends elsewhere.[1]

Ladislas was quite aware of the impecuniosity of the Duke, caused by the sea-fight off Meloria, and he knew of the importance to him of his wealthy ally, the Republic of Florence. He accordingly opened communications with the Signory, and the Florentines, who had no wish to see France strongly established in Italy, listened to his overtures. The result was a peace between the King of Naples on the one side and Florence and Siena on the other; it was concluded on the last day of the year.[2] The Republic sent envoys to the Duke of Anjou and to the Pope, trying to get them also to make peace with the King. 'They might at least have waited until the term of our alliance was up,' was the Duke's remark; the Pope also scouted the idea of peace. King Ladislas had promised the Florentines not to interfere in Rome; he sold Cortona to them, and he promised to return all the Florentine goods captured by his fleet. This peace left the Duke of Anjou dependent on the Pope alone for aid against Naples. His army meantime was in a pitiable state. The French soldiers, whom he had left at Rome under the Count of Tagliacozzo, had received no pay for a twelve-month; those who remained had neither horses nor arms. Louis left Rome in despair on the 31st December, and betook himself to the Pope. War was impracticable during the winter, so the Duke had to wait until the ensuing spring.

One of the first acts of John the Twenty-third related to that Bull of his predecessor regarding the mendicant orders which had caused such umbrage in France. On the 10th June 1410 he prohibited the use of this Bull. This measure, however, failed to satisfy the University of Paris,[3] which desired that the Bull should be authoritatively annulled; but the Pope, having granted the practical relief required, refused to go further and to dishonour the memory of his friend.

[1] Mur. xxiv. 1017-8.   [2] Raumer, 224.   [3] Finke (*Acta*), 162.

THE NEW POPE

Soon after the death of King Rupert, Pope Gregory the Twelfth wrote a lengthy defence of himself and criticism of the proceedings at the Council of Pisa. He sent this to the courts of Europe, and among others to King Sigismund. He could, however, hope for little result from the King of Hungary, seeing that his own principal supporter was that monarch's hated rival, Ladislas of Naples, who was still recognised by Gregory and the Republic of Venice as rightful King of Hungary. The aged Pope desisted from further communications with King Sigismund until the summer of 1412, when he had himself been abandoned by the faithless Ladislas.[1]

The most persevering opponent of Pope John the Twenty-third in the first year of his pontificate was his former friend, Carlo Malatesta who, like Pope Boniface the Ninth and many nobles of northern Italy, was a client of Baldassare Cossa's old enemies, the Gozzadini.[2] The Lord of Rimini was an indefatigable advocate of a general Council; from the very first he did more than any other man to bring it about, and to him, next to King Sigismund, the Council of Constance was due. After the papal election at the Council of Pisa, undeterred by his rebuff there, Malatesta had urged the plan of a Council on Alexander the Fifth and on Benedict the Thirteenth;[3] and after the death of Pope Alexander he urged the scheme again on the cardinals before the election of Pope John. His endeavours had hitherto been ineffectual. Pope John, who was naturally anxious to strengthen his own position, now heard with some alarm that Carlo Malatesta was preparing to make war upon him in the interest of his rival Pope Gregory the Twelfth. An interesting correspondence ensued.

Carlo Malatesta reminded the new Pope of their friendship which had subsisted since the time when Cossa was a Chamberlain to Pope Boniface. John answered that the friendship would last as long as life itself; he added that he would hold the Council promised by Pope Alexander and would do all in his power, even if he had to remain a simple clerk, to bring back peace to the Church. Carlo replied that he had served Cossa faithfully as long as he was cardinal; now that they were opposed, he still loved Pope John, for we are bidden to love our

---

[1] Finke (*Acta*), 15. [2] Gozzadini, 25. [3] Blumenthal, 6.

B

enemies, but he could no longer serve him, for no man can serve two masters, and Carlo was the servant of his Holy Mother the Church and of her rightful Lord, Pope Gregory; he could only recommend a general Council. The Pope sent a doctor to say that he was ready to convoke a Council and to propose that Carlo and his brother should be two of the protectors; but he insisted that it was absurd to call in question his own undoubted right as Pope before his two rivals who had been condemned at the Council of Pisa; he could not recognise any Council that they might call, nor would they abide by any decisions of his Council. Another person, writing from the papal court, pointed out to Malatesta that a general Council might depose Pope John (the idea of deposing all three Popes was already in the air), and dilated on the difficulty of fixing a fit and suitable place for the meeting. Carlo Malatesta wanted to go behind the Council of Pisa; whereas Pope John took his stand on that Council. The Lord of Rimini declared that he was ready to resign his lordship if John would resign the papacy; he again proposed that the rival Popes should appoint proctors to decide as to the time and place for the new Council. Pope John answered that he was ready to hold a Council at Bologna, that he would not invite his rivals, but had no objection to their attending, that he held himself to be the only legitimate Pope and would do nothing to prejudice his right, but that Malatesta was free to communicate with the two antipopes.[1] These negotiations continued until the 15th July 1410. There was no chance of the disputants coming to any agreement, for they were approaching the quarrel from different standpoints. Carlo Malatesta wanted a Council so constituted as to go behind that of Pisa, and to reconsider the conclusions there arrived at; Pope John was determined to uphold that Council at all hazards.

The Pope then wrote to the Republic of Venice to use their influence to make Malatesta desist from his endeavours, and the Venetians accordingly advised Carlo that it was not honourable to attempt to withdraw Bologna from the Pope's allegiance, but at the same time they refused to interfere between the Lord of Rimini and the King of Naples.[2] Malatesta again sent to Pope Benedict, who answered him most graciously and was

---

[1] Martene (*A. C.*), vii. 1171 *et seq.* [2] Finke (*Acta*), 24-5.

THE NEW POPE

willing to enter into communication with Pope Gregory but not with the Pope of the Council.[1] Carlo's efforts were defeated at all points; the only conclusion at which he could arrive, and it was the only sensible and practical conclusion, was that he himself was not the person to bring about a general Council, but that the King of the Romans, as the son, the advocate, the defender of the Church, was the fit and proper person to convoke it.[2] The communications between the two old friends are interesting, because they show that not only was the Council of Pisa recognised as a failure, but that a fresh general Council was in contemplation at which it was quite possible that all three rival Popes might be deposed or be required to resign. Under these circumstances it obviously was the policy of Pope John to uphold the authority of the Council of Pisa. His aim was to checkmate his two adversaries and to acquire for himself the entire obedience of Christendom. Carlo Malatesta was apparently the author of the proposal that all three Popes should abdicate or be deposed.

Carlo Malatesta did not mean to let matters rest. He was appointed by Pope Gregory to be Rector of Romandiola and defender of the true faith, and was commanded to make war on that son of iniquity, Baldassare Cossa, who now presumed to style himself Pope John the Twenty-third.[3] As soon as Sigismund was elected King of the Romans, Carlo Malatesta wrote to him, recounting all that he had done at the Council of Pisa and since, and calling upon him to convoke a general Council. The scheme for the settlement of the Great Schism by the abdication or deposition of all three Popes was now before the King of the Romans; and Pope John knew thus early in his reign that this was the chief danger which threatened him on the papal throne. To counteract this scheme, it was necessary for him to conciliate those in power and to win them to his way of thinking. If he could induce the King of the Romans and the leading Courts of Europe to uphold the authority of the Council which had elected his predecessor, then he might flout Carlo Malatesta. He accordingly spared no pains, he overlooked no opportunity save one, to ingratiate himself with

[1] Blumenthal, 18. [2] Martene (*A. C.*), vii. 1197-1202.
[3] Raynaldus, viii. 329.

King Sigismund; he was equally desirous to get the Kings of France and England on his side. The former would naturally uphold the Council of Pisa, but of the other he was not sure. Unfortunately Pope John was not a good judge of character, and was apt to choose his instruments amiss.

Like his predecessor, Pope John was anxious to get in all available arrears of taxes due to the Apostolic See. There was very little money in the papal treasury; Alexander the Fifth, as he said, had been a beggar as Pope. John wished to levy a tenth on the clergy of France. The Archbishop of Pisa and two other legates whom he sent to announce his election were charged to obtain the consent of the French Court to the proposed tax. An audience was granted them in the King's Council on the 22nd November, and the legates were indiscreet enough to maintain that the Pope had an absolute right to levy tenths on the clergy at his pleasure, and that the King's authority was only required for the form in which the imposition was to be made. The University of Paris was up in arms at once. The clergy of France, they affirmed, could not be taxed save with the consent of the King and of their own representatives; the Pope's demand was an infringement of the rights of the Gallican Church. The legates found out their mistake; they had raised a veritable hornets' nest about their ears; they tried to appease the University, but only procured a fresh protestation that the clergy of France were not subject to any apostolic tax save with their own consent. The Pope, disgusted at the want of tact of his legates, had no intention of losing the material support of France on a mere matter of form; above all else he wanted the money. He sent a diamond heart, set in a ring of gold, to the Duke of Berri; he took Jean Juvenal des Ursins, the future historian and son of the King's advocate, into his service as secretary; he addressed a Bull, full of compliments, to the all-powerful Duke of Burgundy; he sent the King a Bull allowing him to levy a tenth on the clergy of France for the war with England, and another permitting him to levy aids from them for the next three years for the same purpose. He thus won over the Court, and was allowed to levy on the clergy a gratuitous gift, equivalent to a tenth; the unfortunate clergy were not consulted, but were compelled to pay the gratuity.

Nor was the Pope blind to the influence of the powerful University of Paris; he even went so far as to incur censure in his endeavours to conciliate that body. In 1410 it is true that they were told that those who refused to pay the tenth were no true Christians, and were checkmated in their assertion of the liberties of the Gallican Church, but the Pope subsequently tried to make it up to them. By his briefs of the 10th July 1411, and the 7th January 1412, he declared that members of the University were not to be postponed in their claims to benefices even to those who held expectative briefs from the Pope, and that Masters of Philosophy, after seven years' study, were eligible for posts in cathedrals. These privileges were so much the more valuable to the hungry members of the University inasmuch as that body enjoyed no particular favour either with the French episcopacy or with other patrons of benefices. On the 1st April 1412 Pope John conferred on Jean Gerson, the Chancellor of the University, the right of absolving all scholars and masters from censure, even in cases specially reserved for the apostolic stool; and on the same date he allowed the University the privilege for three years of bringing all their disputes for decision before the Bishop of Paris instead of taking them to the Curia at Rome. All these concessions, however, failed to conciliate the more ardent spirits or to win them over to his side in the coming struggle.

To our own country the Pope was equally complaisant. His great patron and master, Pope Boniface the Ninth, had granted to the University of Oxford a Bull making it subject to the King of England in civil matters and to the Court of Rome in matters spiritual. The University therefore claimed to be exempt from all jurisdiction of the Archbishop of Canterbury, although its Chancellor had been warned that the King would refuse to recognise the validity of this Bull, seeing that he had vested all authority in the Archbishop. Archbishop Arundel was bent on suppressing Lollardy at Oxford, its headquarters, and appeared at Saint Mary's church only to find himself barred out by the Chancellor and the Proctors. The students were in the streets armed with bows and arrows, and quite ready to use them. The Archbishop put the church under an interdict, whereupon the Chancellor threatened to excom-

municate him. It was agreed to refer the matter to King
Henry; and before him at Lambeth the Archbishop, the
Chancellor, and the Proctors accordingly appeared on the
9th September 1411. The King decided in favour of the Archbishop, who had meantime also appealed to Rome. On the
20th November 1411, Pope John issued a Bull which authorised
the Archbishop of Canterbury to exercise full metropolitan
jurisdiction over the University, thus throwing over his predecessor in order to ingratiate himself with the King and the
Archbishop. The University in the same month unreservedly
submitted itself to the Archbishop. The real object of the
contest had been ' the suppression of Lollardy—in other words,
the suppression of free speech and thought—in the schools and
pulpits of Oxford.'[1] These instances of John's opportunist
policy have taken us beyond the first year of his reign, to which
we must now return.

Trouble arose in the country around Bologna itself. Cardinal
Conrad Caracciolo was sent to rase the Castello di Barbiano.
Giorgio Ordelassi had conquered Forli, Forlimpopolo, and the
castle of Oriolo. Gian Galeazzo, the son of Astor de' Manfredi,
whom the Pope had beheaded five years earlier, surprised by
night the city of Faenza, and became himself the Signor thereof
as his father had been before him. Carlo Malatesta had
instigated the enterprise, hoping that Manfredi would restore
the city to Pope Gregory; but the youth made terms with
Pope John, and consented to hold Faenza as a fief under him.
(1st August 1410.[2])

Through the whole of the year 1410 Pope John the Twenty-
third remained at Bologna, possibly because of the impending
election in Germany. The first year of his pontificate brought
him into close relationship with two men, with whom his fate
five years later became mysteriously and inextricably involved.
They were Sigismund, the stalwart King of Hungary, and John
Hus, the patriot reformer of Bohemia. Trouble was brewing
between the King of Hungary and Venice, and in the summer of
1410 Pope John sent to the Republic, offering to mediate between them. They answered that they already had an embassy
at Sigismund's Court, but suggested that the Pope should

[1] Rashdall, ii. 435.   [2] Mur. xxiv. 176; Ghirar, ii. 583.

approach Count Pippo of Ozora on the subject, and should let them know the result of his conference; they also informed their ambassadors of the possibility of the Pope's intervention. John subsequently renewed his offer through Cardinal Branda. Eventually the King and the Republic agreed to refer their differences to the Pope. The result will appear later.

Both King and Reformer, Sigismund and John Hus, merit a detailed description in order that we may appreciate aright the parts which they play in the history of Pope John the Twenty-third and his times.

CHAPTER II

JOHN HUS

IT was one of the most serious deficiencies of Pope John the Twenty-third that, being so entirely a man of action, he had very limited sympathy with the intellectual and religious movements of his time. The two movements were almost identical, for the greater part of the best intellect was in the service of religion. The Pope indeed delighted in the society and converse of learned and clever men,[1] but this was because of his Italian *virtu*, of that love of strength, physical and intellectual, of strength and the beauty which waits on strength. But the appreciation of literature and art was, as Gian Galeazzo and others had shown, compatible with tyrannical and unscrupulous use of power. The intellect provided trifles for the lighter hours, not food for the serious thought, of the ruler. In this manner would the Pope have regarded the works of John Wyclif, if they came across his notice. Yet, as an original thinker, Wyclif was the greatest genius of his day. He had made his name as a realist philosopher and as a political writer before he was known as a theologian or a heretic. Paris was nominalist, and the University there was consequently safe from the fascination of the great realist; but the Universities at Oxford and Prague were realist, and Wyclif was in high esteem at both. Political circumstances in England were adverse to the spread of his religious views, and consequently Lollardy, except in a few holes and corners, almost died out before the Reformation; but in Bohemia the political situation was propitious, and Wyclifism took deep root and flourished, and eventually produced long and fierce warfare. In order to understand how Wyclifism became so great a force in the land of its adoption, and to appreciate the part it played in the time

[1] Duchesne, ii. 555.

JOHN HUS

of Pope John the Twenty-third, it will be necessary to glance at the political life of Bohemia and at the career of the patriot reformer, a Bohemian of the Bohemians, John Hus.

Bohemia, the lozenge-shaped country between the four ranges of hills, was a land divided against itself. It was held by a Czech nobility, a branch of the great Slavonian family, but it was peopled by two antagonistic and hopelessly discordant elements, the Czech and the Teuton. The Czech peasantry were unenterprising and inactive; Teuton settlers had been invited and were granted special privileges; a Teuton invasion was favoured by the Premsylides, themselves half Germans; Teuton peasants cleared the forests and brought under cultivation the lands once held by the wolf and the bear; Teutons worked the silver mines of Kurtenberg and Deutschbrod and other mines also; Teuton artisans and merchants founded the towns and brought prosperity to the cities by their industry and intelligence. The Czech peasants sank into the condition of serfs to the nobility, against whose power the Teutons acted as a counterpoise for the Kings. The country was exploited, civilised, and enriched by the Teutons; but the two elements in the population never coalesced. The Czechs hated the Teutons worse than the Irish hated the English; the Teutons were an object of national animosity alike to the Slavonic nobility above them and to the Slavonic peasantry below. Bohemia was a country occupied by two hostile peoples, differing in language, habits, and sympathies; the two elements never fused, but remained in perpetual antagonism.[1]

The Czech dynasty of the Premsylides became extinct in 1306; four years later the crown was offered to John, son of the Emperor Henry the Seventh, and with him commenced the dynasty of the Luxemburgs, which lasted for a century and a quarter. The new King was a knight-errant, a ubiquitous man, to be found everywhere except in his own country; nothing happened anywhere, men said, without God and King John. He added Upper Lusatia, Silesia, and Moravia to Bohemia, but he neglected and plundered the country, and when his son Charles succeeded him he could not find a single royal castle for his residence, but was obliged to live like a burgess in the

[1] *Hist. Gen.*, ii. 750-65; Hoefler, Buch I. *passim.*

town. The barons had become tyrants who feared not the King, for they had divided the kingdom amongst them. Charles's reign was one long struggle against this turbulent aristocracy, who were proud of their ancient history and determined to defend their nationality. They were sunk into an evil plight through their folly and sensual indulgence, but their struggle was not without its advantage. 'Bohemia, the centre of the Empire under Charles the Fourth, became the focus from which civilisation spread over Eastern Europe; with Hus, it dealt the first blow to the religious and political system of the Middle Age; with Ziska and Procopius, it victoriously defended the principle of independence in matters of faith.'[1]

Charles the Fourth set himself to bring back peace, order, and prosperity to Bohemia. He was the father of the land; he loved the country, he loved the people, he loved their language; he could talk Czech as readily as German, French, Italian, or Latin. His aim was to concentrate the government in his own hands and to frame a strong and absolute monarchy. He succeeded, and under him both the cities and the Church in Bohemia attained a period of unexampled prosperity.[2] The infiltration of the Teutons was slackening, but they had already covered a great part of Bohemia; in the cities German was the language of administration, of justice, of the pulpit, of education. The King put himself at the head of the Slav movement; he protected the mass of the people against the nobles, to whom he allowed their existing authority, but forbade its abuse or its extension. The peasantry obtained the 'German right' and became attached to the King. Charles, who was fond of architecture, who commenced the Cathedral of Saint Vitus and constructed the Castle of Karlstein, built the new city of Prague for the Slavs, the old city being occupied by the Teutons. He was anxious to make Bohemia the corner-stone of the Empire, and to increase its importance in every way. Being regarded with a favourable eye by Pope Clement the Sixth, he persuaded that pontiff, on the ground of difference in language, to cut off the bishopric of Prague from the metropolitan see of Mainz and to raise it into an independent archbishopric. Hereby the

[1] *Hist. Gen.*, iii. 656.   [2] Lechler, 5.

LIST OF ILLUSTRATIONS

Upper Part of the Tomb of Pope John XXIII. in the Paptistery at Florence, erected in 1407, the figure of the pontiff being the work of Donatello, ... *Frontispiece*

AT PAGE

Sixteenth-century sketch of John Hus going to execution escorted by the Count Palatine's swordsman, and wearing the heretic's head-dress, as used at the Spanish autos da fé. (From the MS. in the archives of the Counts von Königsegg in Aulendorf), ... 50

Bird's-eye view of Constance and its Environs at the time of the Council. Reduced from the map published by Von der Hardt in his *Rerum Concilii Oecumenici Constantiensis*, 1697, . . 237

The Castle on the Rhine at Gottlieben, still standing, used by the Bishop of Constance for his prisoners. In this castle both Pope John the Twenty-third and John Hus were incarcerated, ... 306

Geometrical Plan showing the exact spot, now marked by a monument, where John Hus and Jerome of Prague were burned. Reduced from the plan published by Eiselein in his *Begruendeter Aufweis des Plazes bei der Stadt Constanz*, 1847, ... 400

The Kaufhaus or Merchants' Hall of Constance, still standing, built in 1388 by Master Arnold, and used on the eighth to the eleventh November 1417 for the Election of Pope Martin the Fifth toward the conclusion of the Council, . . . 424

POPE JOHN THE TWENTY-THIRD
AND MASTER JOHN HUS OF BOHEMIA

CHAPTER I
THE NEW POPE

IN the early days of May, 1410, Pope Alexander the Fifth lay dying at Bologna. ' Let not your hearts be troubled,' said the old Franciscan Candiot, ' I ascend to your Father and to my Father.' Among the cardinals who clustered round the bed was Baldassare Cossa, who was reported by his enemies to have commenced life as a pirate, who in his youth had won renown as a student and was noted for his valour in the field, who in his manhood had proved to be a successful condottiere general and an able civil administrator, who as cardinal had engineered and defended the Council of Pisa. I have told the story of his early life in my book, *In the Days of the Councils*, and now I propose to give a sketch of his pontificate and his deposition; for little more than half the rest of his life did he wear the triple crown; five years he reigned as Pope; then followed imprisonment, succeeded by a few peaceful months at Florence at the end of his varied career.

When Pope Alexander the Fifth died at Bologna on the 5th May 1410, the political outlook of the papacy was troubled and gloomy. France had hitherto taken the leading part in endeavouring to put an end to the Great Schism which troubled and divided Christendom; but this country was now settling down to civil war between the Burgundians and the Armagnacs; the former party was allying itself with the butchers of Paris, and the latter with the Gascon ' sons of the Devil '; [1] the energies and attentions of the nobles would therefore be absorbed at home, and there would be little or no material aid

[1] Michelet, v. 269.

to place at the service of the new Pope. At the same time the Gallican Church was eager in defence of its liberties, and the University of Paris was determined to preserve its privileges. Hence it followed that unless the new Pope were extremely politic and circumspect in his bearing, he might expect more trouble than help from France. In Italy the French had been ousted from Genoa; but, on the other hand, the Duke of Anjou was on his way to prosecute his claim to the throne of Naples; while Ladislas, the reigning king, whose banners bore the device *Aut Cæsar aut nihil*, aspired certainly to the overlordship of Italy, and probably to the golden crown of the Empire. War in Italy was inevitable and close at hand. In Germany, seething with civil and ecclesiastical trouble, on the 18th May 1410 died Rupert, King of the Romans, and a new election was imminent; the choice of the new King was fraught with the utmost importance to the papacy. Everywhere there were murmurings and demands for the social and moral reform of the clergy, the reform of the Church in its head and its members, a reform which every one regarded as desirable, though the movement in its favour had not yet gained sufficient momentum of popular support to render it dangerous, so that it might possibly be neglected for a time by the Head of the Church with impunity. But, on the other hand, there was very serious discontent within the Church itself on account of the papal exactions; and it remained to be seen whether the Pope of the Council, the Pope who owned the largest obedience of the three, would be able to appease the mutinous spirit, whether he would by timely concession be able to keep the greater part of Christendom true to himself and possibly to win somewhat from the obedience of his rivals, or whether his action, by not recognising grievances which undoubtedly existed, would tend to a further outbreak of revolt. It was a situation which demanded considerable political ability, which required a sympathetic appreciation of the feeling in the various churches of Europe. Most important of all was the fact that the Great Schism itself was not healed, that it was intensified rather than alleviated, seeing that the Council of Pisa had not brought unity, that there were now three Popes instead of two. The Schism called for immediate action; there were three

clergy of Bohemia, who were possessed of no independent standing in the State like those of Germany and France, fell entirely under the control of the crown, seeing that their possessions were by Bohemian custom not church lands but crown property. In 1347 Charles founded the University of Prague on the model of Paris and Bologna, intending it as a *studium generale* for Eastern Europe. It was originally composed of the faculties of arts, theology, medicine, and law, but the last faculty seceded and formed a distinct university in 1372. The Church in Bohemia was very wealthy and over officered; but it was also extremely corrupt and licentious; simony abounded; and the clergy, who were mostly Teutons, were sunk in depravity and contempt. The King desired not only a more efficient control of the priesthood, but also an improvement in their lives and influence. His friend, the first Archbishop of Prague, Ernst of Pardubitz, a man of exemplary life and conduct, seconded the King's endeavours, and did much toward the reform of the clergy, but he was unable to contend with entire success against their entanglement in worldly pursuits, against the multiplication of benefices, and the intrusion of interlopers. The King's example made piety fashionable, but failed to make it earnest; while his establishment in the Neustadt of Prague of the Emmaus convent for Benedictine monks who observed the Eastern ritual accentuated the antagonism between the Teutonic and Slavonic elements in the capital and provided a focus for agitation.[1] At the same time education spread through the land; it was the golden age of Bohemian literature, and grammar-schools abounded.[2] The consequence of the education of the people and the abasement of the clergy was that numbers of the people became alienated from the Church, and that heresy and mysticism increased among them; faulty translations of the Scriptures were made and circulated; the writings of the Fathers were unknown or neglected, but the written word of the New Testament was held in high veneration. Charles the Fourth died as the Great Schism began and was succeeded by his son Wenzel.

The animosity between the two races increased under King Wenzel, as he gradually withdrew from interference in the affairs

[1] Berger, 4 *et seq.*   [2] Rashdall, ii. 215.

of the Empire, and became more and more exclusively, until at last he became of necessity, the mere King of Bohemia. Under him the Czech language, in addition to Latin and German, was used in the royal chancery; a Bohemian element began to creep into the towns and to acquire a share in their government; some of the younger clergy copied the example of Milic of Kremsier and preached in Czech, and in this language Thomas of Stitny wrote his books, addressing them professedly to the common people.[1] At the same time the Bohemian element in the University increased; in the first twenty years of Wenzel's reign it was less than one-sixth, in the third ten years it reached a fifth of the whole number; and whereas in the former period the Bohemians held only one-seventh of the deaneries, in the latter they held one-third.[2] Wenzel had instituted a cabinet ministry of the lower nobility, of 'grooms and kitchen-boys,' as the higher nobles termed them; and being a man averse from hard work and independent resolve, he naturally soon fell entirely under their influence. These favourites of the King were clever and able men, but were hopelessly at variance with the higher nobles and with the higher clergy. They were bent on maintaining the absolute monarchy which the Emperor Charles had set up. Some of them were advocates of reform, and among the earliest and most strenuous friends of John Hus; others were simply enemies of the Church and clergy, persecuting men whose shoe-latchets they were not worthy to unloose, and consorting with those against whom the reformer directed his warmest and best-deserved censure. The murder of the General Vicar Johann von Pomuk brought on a revolution in 1393 among the higher nobility, who were joined by the King's cousin Jost; Wenzel was captured by them in the following year.

Sigismund, King of the neighbouring country of Hungary, meantime played his own game; he was convinced that his own position in Hungary was dependent on peace and a firm rule in Bohemia, and he thought this object could best be secured if he himself became ruler of Bohemia. He would not join the nobles in their revolt, but made use of their discontent to ingratiate himself with his half-brother, and in 1396 he became his repre-

[1] Helfert, 51.   [2] *Ibid.* 54.

sentative in the Empire. Then followed the campaign which ended in the disastrous defeat of Nicopolis; this drew Sigismund away from Bohemia, and the favourites regained their power; Wenzel went to Germany and to France to settle the Schism; he appointed his cousin Prokop his representative in Bohemia, and Prokop, with an army formed of the scum of Europe, soon had the nobility and clergy of Bohemia against him. Sigismund again appeared with an army. Even the deposition of Wenzel and the elevation of Rupert to be King of the Romans failed, however, to reconcile the half-brothers. In 1401 Sigismund was in his turn imprisoned by his vassals; as soon as he escaped the brothers became reconciled, and at Koenigingraetz on the 4th February Wenzel made over to Sigismund the rule of Bohemia and appointed him to be Vicar-General of the Empire. Sigismund had now attained his object, but the good understanding between the brothers was of short duration. When Wenzel became restive, Sigismund cast him into prison and ruled Bohemia with a rod of iron. Herein he over-reached himself. On the 11th November 1403 Wenzel escaped. Sigismund was checkmated. All parties were glad to get rid of him. The higher nobility, who had won something in the restriction of the royal power, were patriots enough to prefer the reign of King Log to King Stork. The favourites came back to power again.[1]

Meanwhile two movements had taken shape which contributed to accentuate and strengthen the patriotic feeling in Bohemia. One was religious and the other was rational. The religious agitation was commenced by the preaching of Conrad Waldhauser; it was continued by the mystical teaching of Milic of Kremsier and Mathias of Janow; it was fostered by Thomas of Stitny and Adalbert Ranco. All these reformers inveighed against the vice and immorality of the laity, against the superficiality and degeneracy of the clergy. They all alike claimed to be faithful sons of the Church, and were all alike ignorant of Wyclif's heresies. But their preaching had entered into the souls of thinking men and had penetrated the understanding of the masses, and so had prepared the ground for the reception of Wyclif's teaching.[2] The rational agitation in

---

[1] Berger, 33.   [2] Helfert, 40.

Bohemia was for the admission of Wyclif's teaching into the circle of theological and philosophical studies. There were many points on which Wyclif's views appealed to the patriotic party in Bohemia. The refusal by England to send money out of the country to Avignon, to the material injury of the nation and to the material advantage of a Pope who was the partisan and tool of a hostile king, was an example actually followed. The recognition by Pope Boniface the Ninth of Rupert as King of the Romans and of Ladislas as King of Hungary placed these two countries in the same relation to him as was England to Pope Clement the Seventh, and was the reason why Sigismund, following the precedent set by the English parliament in 1366, interdicted all intercourse between those countries and the Roman Curia. The right of the nobility to resume church goods, another doctrine of Wyclif, was one which might have commended itself to the Emperor Charles the Fourth, for he had threatened the Bishop and Chapter of Constance with the deprivation of their temporalities, pending reference to the Pope, if they neglected to reform the clergy in their diocese. The attack on the possessions and on the political status of the clergy was as appropriate to Bohemia as to England. Wyclif's views had not merely an intellectual but also a political and economical aspect which ensured sympathy and appreciation; and it was their practical political value which won for them acceptance in the Court of King Wenzel. They were translated into the Czech language and were widely circulated among the Bohemian nobility. His political teaching thus ensured for his doctrinal system a ready entrance into Bohemia. In this way, both for political and for social reasons, on the grounds of economy and of morality, the country was ready to listen to the new doctrines and to give them a favourable hearing. And at this time the race feeling, the animosity and jealousy between Czech and Teuton, was at its height. It was believed that the innovations in Church and State, the introduction of celibacy of the clergy, of communion in one kind, the confirmation of bishops by Rome, had been coincident with the introduction of the German element into Bohemia; the political and the religious deterioration alike were ascribed by the Bohemians to the foreign element in their country. The Germans had ousted the old nobility and had usurped the direction of affairs, they had by their commerce and industry acquired a great part of the wealth of the country, they had taken from the sons of the soil the Church livings and the good things of the new University; patriotism and religious reform were certain therefore to go hand-in-hand in Bohemia, and religious reform became bound up with the name of John Wyclif.

Wyclif, who ' was famous as a philosopher before he became a theologian at all, and famous as a theologian before he became a heresiarch,'[1] died on the last day of 1384; he was regarded in Bohemia as the fifth Evangelist.[2] Some of his works were known in the country as early as 1391; Jerome of Prague, who visited England in 1399, copied out the Dialogus and Trialogus and brought them back with him; ' it was the works of Wyclif which first called forth the deep religious feeling in Bohemia.'[3] The movement, up to the time of the Council of Constance, was known almost exclusively by his name; he was called the Arius of his time, and it was to the Wyclifites that King Sigismund referred when he said, ' Truly I was but a youth when this sect arose and spread in Bohemia, and behold to what strength it has already attained.' The foremost disciple and promulgator of Wyclifism in Bohemia was John Hus.

John Hus, John the son of Michael as he was originally called, was born at the little market-town of Husinez, near Prachtice, in the south of Bohemia, close to the Bavarian frontier, where the Czech and German languages met, and where the racial strife was consequently fiercest. The year of his birth has generally been given as 1369, but it is not exactly known.[4] He was one of several brothers, and was his mother's favourite son. His parents were peasants of but moderate means, and the boy received his early education at the parish school at

---

[1] *D.N.B.*, lxiii. 219.   [2] Loserth, xv.
[3] Loserth, 70, 75, 77; for a different view see Helfert, 39; Luetzow, 18.
[4] Berger, 38, gives 1470 as the date. Luetzow, 64, says: ' We are unable to state positively in what year Hus was born. The oldest traditions stated that he was born on July 6, 1373. More recently such great authorities as Palacky and Tomek gave July 6, 1369, as the date of the birth of Hus. According to the latest researches the exact year of his birth cannot be affirmed, but it undoubtedly took place between 1373 and 1375. The day is quite uncertain. The tradition that Hus was born on the 6th July is merely founded on a fanciful analogy with the day of his death, which occurred on July 6th.'

Husinez or at Prachtice.¹ When he was still a mere boy he went to the University of Prague and became an inmate of the College founded in 1386 by King Wenzel in the fruit market.² He was so poor that he was often obliged to beg in the streets and to sleep on the ground; he earned a little money as singing boy and as ministrant at religious services in some of the many churches in Prague. 'When I was a hungry little student,' he says, 'I made a spoon out of bread till I had eaten the pease, and then ate the spoon also.'³ He joined in the sports of his fellow-students, and was fond of chess; his ambition was to become a priest, that he might have a good house and clothes, and be looked up to by his fellow-men. In 1393 he became Bachelor of Arts, in the following year Bachelor of Divinity, and in 1396 Master of Arts; but he never became a Doctor of Divinity. As he was placed in the middle of the list of those who graduated with him, he does not appear to have been particularly distinguished at this time;⁴ but he was from the beginning fond of theological disputations, and was noted for his profound piety and religious zeal. He was always a singularly lovable man, whose absolute simplicity and blameless life won the respect of all, whose tenderness of heart extended even to his enemies, and whose indomitable faith and enthusiasm kindled the lasting devotion of his adherents. The University in his time reached the zenith of its popularity; it was there that Hus met Stanislas of Znaim and Stephen Palec, at first his firm friends but afterwards his bitterest enemies, and there too that he was a fellow-student with Jerome of Prague and with Jacob of Stribro, or Jacobel, the originator of utraquism. In 1398 Hus became a public teacher and delivered lectures at the University; in 1401 he preached at the church of St. Michael and was made Dean of the Faculty of Philosophy, and in 1402 'he became, at an unusually early age, for the first time Rector of the University.'⁵ In this same year the great fame which he had already acquired as a preacher led to another appointment which in great degree determined his future career as patriot and reformer.

On the 25th May 1391, Hans Milheim, one of the favourite

---

¹ Berger, 38; Luetzow, 65.   ² Rashdall, ii. 219.
³ Luetzow, 69, note; Lechler, 27.   ⁴ Palacky, iii. 191.   ⁵ Luetzow, 72.

courtiers of King Wenzel, connected through his wife with the
old Bohemian nobility, had founded in the present Bethlehem
Square in Prague a chapel, a somewhat extensive building,
roomy enough to contain over a thousand people, known as the
Bethlehem Chapel.[1] The foundation was an offshoot of Milic's
reform movement. Associated with the founder was a wealthy
tradesman, Kriz, ' the shopkeeper,' who gave the ground.
Their object was that whereas Germans had hitherto been able
to hear preaching in open churches, and Bohemians had been
obliged to seek it in private houses and out-of-the-way corners,
the Rector of the new foundation was to be a secular priest bound
to preach in the Bohemian tongue on the morning and afternoon
of every Sunday and Saint's Day.[2] The priest's house, the
door of which still remains, was erected close to the chapel.
Johann Protiva of Neudorf was the first preacher; Stephen of
Kolin was the second; they had both been renowned for their
eloquence. On the 14th March 1402, Hus was appointed
Rector and Preacher, being confirmed in the post by the General
Vicar of Prague.[3] His eloquence and earnestness attracted
crowds of listeners, and his fame speedily eclipsed that of his
predecessors. The chapel, ' the scene of his triumphs, became
to him in reality a home, to which he was ever fervently
attached.'[4] He had already studied Wyclif's philosophical
works, now he began to immerse himself in the theological
tractates of the Reformer. Pious Bohemian ladies, Anezka,
daughter of Thomas of Stitny, and other noble dames, made
their habitations close to the chapel. Queen Sophia, the second
wife of the King, was a frequent visitor. The Queen made Hus
her confessor, and through her influence he became Court
chaplain. Wenzel's sister Anne, through her marriage with
Richard the Second of England, and the intercourse between
the two Courts which thus sprung up, had been the means of
introducing the writings of John Wyclif into Bohemia; Wenzel's second wife, Sophia, made John Hus a Court favourite
and secured his commanding influence with the King and the
nobility. The heavy, good-natured King, when sufficiently
sober, was fond of a theological argument, and delighted to pit
Hus against a more orthodox opponent. But Hus's influence

[1] Leutzow, 73-5. [2] Helfert, 58. [3] Lechler, 33. [4] Loserth, 69.

rested not merely on the Court, but also on the people; he was not only a reformer, but also a patriot. He spoke strongly against the German soldiers whom King Rupert had sent into Bohemia, he spoke equally strongly against the German members of the University who favoured that King. ' The Germans in Bohemia should go to King Wenzel,' said he, ' and swear to be faithful to him and to Bohemia, but this will only be when a serpent warms itself on the ice.' From this time forward Hus took the lead in Bohemia both as patriot and as reformer.

The Archbishop of Prague died in 1402, and in October 1403, a month before King Wenzel escaped from his imprisonment in Vienna, a new Archbishop was elected. This was Zbynek Zajic of Hasenburg, a noble, nominally a priest, but really a distinguished soldier, with all a soldier's contempt for theological disputation, and with a good soldier's readiness to carry out all commands received from headquarters. He was a man with a clear head and of sound common-sense; he saw that the chief danger to the Church lay in the evil lives of the clergy, that drastic measures of internal reform were necessary. He saw too that John Hus was not only powerful and popular, but that he was a man of clean life and of unimpeachable morality, one, moreover, who was filled with the zeal for reform. He took Hus into his favour and confidence; he appointed him and his friend, Stanislas of Znaim, to be synodal preachers; he required him, whenever he noticed any defect in the government of the Church, to bring the same, either personally or by letter, to his notice.[1] For five years the two men worked together in unity. The Archbishop intrusted him with the supervision of the clergy. In 1405 Hus exposed the fraud of the bleeding wafer at Wilsnack. The experience which Hus during this time acquired of fraud and immorality rendered him still more bitter both in speech and in writing against the Bohemian priests, and brought upon him their hatred. They complained that he called them heretics because they took fees for confession, communion, baptism, and the like ecclesiastical functions; his sermons, they said, had ' lacerated the minds of the pious, extinguished charity, and rendered the clergy odious to the people.'[2] There

[1] Palacky (*Doc.*), 3.   [2] Luetzow, 85.

would be no more loaves and fishes for them unless Hus were stopped. But it is very doubtful whether his diatribes against the clergy, which every one knew to be well merited, would have done Hus any harm. As Andrew of Brod had said : ' Ye may speak as ye list on the grievous irregularities of the clergy; only be silent about the errors and books of Wyclif, of which ye are the protectors. I, poor child of man, say to you : If not for other things, merely because ye preach against the clergy, no one will put you under excommunication ; for even from ancient times have Conrad, Milic, Stekna, and very many others preached against the clergy without any of them being placed under an interdict.'[1]

Wyclifism, however, had struck deep root in Bohemia ; and indeed, considering the intercourse between the two countries and the number of Bohemian students who frequented the University of Oxford, there was little wonder that it should be so. For Wyclif was the greatest schoolman since William of Ockham ; he was indeed the last of the great schoolmen, and the University of Oxford and the Bohemian Nation of the University of Prague had rallied to his modified realism just as the other three nations at Prague and the University of Paris had stuck to the thoroughgoing nominalism of the Doctor Invincibilis. The University of Prague was anxious that its alumni should be taught nothing but sound doctrine, and to that end the Faculty of Philosophy on the 20th April 1367 had formulated a rule that mere bachelors should not lecture on their own account, but should use the note-books of well-known masters of Prague, Paris, or Oxford, ' dummodo sint ab aliquo famoso de universitate Pragensi, Parisiensi vel Oxoniensi magistro compilata.'[2] What more natural, therefore, than that the note-books of Wyclif's philosophy should be taught at Prague, seeing that the University was realist like Oxford, and that Wyclif, though without an atom of poetry or humour in his nature, was noted for the depth of his reading, for the acuteness of his intellect, and for the uncompromising character of his logic. Even before his death his theological views had not escaped condemnation. Of twenty-four propositions based upon the doctrines maintained in his extant

[1] Loserth, 77.   [2] Loserth, 69 ; Helfert, 56.

writings, ten were described as heretical, and the others as erroneous and contrary to the determination of the Church. But the Earthquake Council, held at the Blackfriars' Convent in May 1382, which passed this condemnation had been a packed body,[1] and Wyclif had not been condemned by the Pope. In the University of Prague in 1403 a German master of theology had brought to the notice of the chapter these twenty-four propositions and twenty-one others which he professed to have derived from the writings of Wyclif. A general meeting of the members of the University was presided over by its Rector, and a stormy debate was held in the great hall of the Carolinum College. The accuracy of the propositions was denied. Hus exclaimed that ' such falsifiers of books better deserved to be burnt than the two adulterators of saffron ' who had recently been executed. Stephen Palec threw one of Wyclif's books on the table, saying, ' Let who will stand up and speak against any word contained in this book ! I will defend it.' Stanislas of Znaim rose in his wrath and waxed furious on the same side.[2] The forty-five articles were not declared to be heretical, but the majority of the meeting, probably the three foreign nations in opposition to the Bohemians,[3] passed a resolution that no one should teach, repeat, or affirm them either publicly or privately. But the discussion after all had been merely academical, and the prohibition had no effect.

Political circumstances also favoured the reformers. Sigismund had withdrawn the obedience of Bohemia from the Pope at Rome, and Wenzel, when he escaped from his imprisonment, was not inclined to restore it to the Pope who had favoured his rival Rupert. The King's long captivity had done him good. He showed himself more energetic and discriminating. He set to work to rid the land of robbers and freebooters. The warlike Archbishop captured Nicolas Zul of Ostredek, and John Hus accompanied him to the gallows, where the robber made an edifying end. The waning influence of King Rupert induced Wenzel to hope that the Pope might again recognise him as King of the Romans, but the refusal of Gregory the Twelfth

[1] *D.N.B.*, lxiii. 213. [2] Loserth, 97 ; Luetzow, 80 ; Palacky, iii. 196.
[3] Helfert, 65.

JOHN HUS

to go back on the finding of his predecessor strengthened Wenzel's hostility to Rome.

Until 1408 the influence of Hus with the Archbishop of Prague continued unabated. In 1405 Pope Innocent the Seventh, in response to a denunciation from Prague, ordered the Archbishop to stop the spread of Wyclifism; and next year at the summer synod the clergy were ordered to publish and preach the Church's doctrine of the sacrament. This was a point in which Hus refused to follow the teaching of the English reformer; and the order to the clergy, which was renewed the following year when Gregory the Twelfth renewed his predecessor's warning, was probably drafted by John Hus, for it did not mention the name of Wyclif.[1] Hus preached the synodal sermons in 1406 and 1407, and was commended by the Archbishop. In 1407 some laymen and clerks were accused before the Archbishop of Wyclifite heresy, but they all either exculpated themselves or renounced their errors and were acquitted.

In 1408 the Cardinals of both papal obediences resolved to hold a general council the year following. In view of the coming council King Wenzel was anxious to clear his land of the imputation of heresy under which it lay. He accordingly issued orders to the end that Wyclifism and all who favoured it should be driven from the land. The Archbishop hereupon summoned the Bohemian Nation of the University, the only nation suspected of heresy, and sixty-four Doctors and Masters, a hundred Bachelors, and upwards of a thousand students appeared. They were told to condemn the forty-five articles. John Hus objected to an unqualified condemnation, and the resolution was passed that no member of the Bohemian Nation, under pain of excommunication, should teach or maintain any of those articles in an heretical, erroneous or offensive acceptation. Furthermore it was determined that no Bachelor should in the future hold any public lecture on Wyclif's *Dialogus*, *Trialogus*, or *De Eucharistia*, or any public disputation on any proposition of Wyclif.[2] This was on the 20th May, and on the 30th June several preachers were summoned to appear before the General Vicar. One of them, Nicolas of Welenowic,

[1] Berger, 43; Palacky, iii. 214.   [2] Palacky, iii. 222.

also called Abraham, was found guilty and delivered to the Inquisitor of Prague, who cast him into prison. Hus interceded for him with the Archbishop, who banished Abraham from his diocese. Hus took it ill; the Archbishop, he said, got rid of the pious and good shepherds of the flock, and kept the foul and sinful. This was the first open breach between John Hus and Archbishop Zbynek. The high ecclesiastic had, however, carried out orders; he was able, on the 17th July 1408, to assemble a synod of his clergy and to declare that after diligent search through the country he could find no unbeliever or heretic in Bohemia. In order that no heresy might arise in the future he ordered all who possessed any of Wyclif's books to bring them to him. This last order evoked more of ridicule than of compliance.

At this time [1] a curious incident happened. Two wandering students, Nicolas Faulfisch and George of Knyehnicz,[2] both of them Bohemians, brought to Prague a letter which purported to issue from the University of Oxford and to be addressed to the reformers of Bohemia. Faulfisch also brought with him a piece of the gravestone of Wyclif, which was subsequently held in reverence in Bohemia as a holy relic.[3] The letter set forth that the whole of England, with the exception of some false mendicant friars, was on the side of Wyclif.[4] Hus was naturally overjoyed at receiving this testimony to the orthodoxy of his spiritual master, and did not hesitate to read the letter and to exhibit the seal, which was perfectly genuine, from his pulpit in the Bethlehem Chapel; he used it also in his discussions at the University.[5] It has been suggested that the letter was 'passed by a snatch vote of congregation during the long vacation.'[6] But there is very little doubt that its substance was an impudent forgery, the work of one Peter Payne or Clerk, a Master of Arts at Oxford. This heretic was the son of an Englishman by a French wife; he was born at Hough-on-the-Hill about the year 1380, and he had been introduced by Peter Partridge to the writings of Wyclif,[7] which produced a great impression on him. It has been supposed that he stole the

---

[1] Berger, 48, note.   [2] Loserth, 101.   [3] Palacky (*Doc.*), 313.
[4] *D.N.B.*, xliv. 114.   [5] Berger, 48.   [6] *D.N.B.*, xliv. 114.
[7] *D.N.B.*, xliii. 431.

JOHN HUS

seal of the University and affixed it to the document which was afterwards presented to John Hus.[1] A passage in the report of the Convocation held in December 1411, however, refers to this testimonial and ' seems to make it certain that the testimonial was actually sealed with the real University seal by the University officials whether regularly or irregularly. As it was customary for the Regents to grant themselves a general leave to have what testimonials they required passed under the University seal, the testimonial was even less than most testimonials an indication of the deliberate opinion of the testimonialists.'[2] Of this Hus was naturally quite unaware. The forgery was not suspected in Bohemia; it gave a great impetus to the Wyclifite movement; Hus himself was greatly moved by it and expressed the wish that his soul might one day be where that of John Wyclif now was.[3]

There was much truth, or at any rate plausibility, in the declaration of Archbishop Zbynek that there was no heretic in Bohemia. For the head and forefront of Wyclif's offending was his doctrine on the Eucharist, his rejection of the Catholic tenet of transubstantiation. Others of the propositions derived from his works were open to explanation or to argument. The theories on which Hus and Wyclif were agreed, says Dr. Luetzow, ' were mainly common property of all mediæval opponents of the Church of Rome, while the natures and characters of Hus and Wyclif were in most respects different, even antagonistic. The somewhat pedantic and matter-of-fact nature of Wyclif, devoid of artistic instincts, contrasts absolutely with the enthusiastic and fanciful character of Hus.'[4] In his doctrine as to the Eucharist the English reformer was hopelessly at variance with the teaching of Rome. On this point, however, Hus clearly and definitely separated himself from Wyclif. Both alike were realists; but Hus clave to the doctrine which had held the field among orthodox realists since the days of Lanfranc. ' The substances of the bread and wine were changed, it was held, by the act of the priest into the substance of the body and blood of Christ, while the accidents remained the same ';[5] the sensible properties remained the same, but

[1] Gascoigne, 5-6, 20, 186-7. [2] Rashdall, ii. 433 note.
[3] Palacky (*Doc.*), 154.   [4] Luetzow, 299.   [5] Rashdall, i. 47.

the substance itself had altered. Wyclif's logical mind denied that there could be an alteration of the substance without a corresponding alteration of the accidents. Hus was an independent thinker and found no difficulty in accepting the theory held by the Church. He and his friends claimed to be, and believed themselves to be, true sons of the Church, ready to acknowledge the rightful Pope as soon as they knew who he was. No thought of revolt from the Pope or of appeal to any higher power had at this time entered the mind of the foremost churchman in Bohemia. He believed the Archbishop to be amply justified in the declaration he made.

A friend hitherto of the Archbishop and powerful in the Church, a favourite of the King and confessor to the Queen, the idol of the Bohemian populace, on whose common speech he had formed his style, while he ennobled and raised it ' to the rank of a language adapted to the expression of theological and philosophical thought,' Hus was opposed at every turn by the German element in Bohemia. He was a patriot indignant at the manner in which the Germans had monopolised the majority of the offices of state and the benefices of the Church, reducing his countrymen to a humiliating and subordinate condition. He condemned mixed marriages between Bohemians and Germans. He endeavoured to improve the Czech orthography; he introduced diacritical marks; he tried to establish a universally recognised written language; he began to revise and correct the translations of the Bible; he was indefatigable in his endeavours to improve and elevate his native tongue. Furthermore he encouraged the taste for sacred music. Before his time church song had been left almost entirely to the monks or the clerks in minor orders, who did their work in an irreverent, mechanical, and negligent manner. Sometimes they sang out of time, sometimes they roved about the church and scoffed at the congregation, they were always in an unseemly hurry. Hus believed in the importance of devotional music, and availed himself of the critical taste innate among Bohemians. He established a school for church song at the Bethlehem Chapel. Only four Bohemian hymns had hitherto been recognised by the Church of Rome. Ancient Bohemian hymns were now revived and sung; new ones were composed; translations were made from the Latin; sacred songs, the work of unknown writers, suddenly appeared in the country; singing became a marked feature in the services at the Bethlehem Chapel. But the clergy were in opposition to Hus, and the majority of them were Germans.[1] By the Germans in Bohemia Hus was regarded much as, in the first half of the nineteenth century, an ordinary Englishman would have regarded an Irish hero formed of Daniel O'Connell and Father Mathew rolled into one person.

The time for the Council of Pisa was now drawing nigh. King Wenzel desired to declare the neutrality of Bohemia between the rival Popes. He had sent an embassy to the Cardinals, and two of this embassy, Stanislas of Znaim and Stephen Palec, were, at the end of October 1408, arrested at Bologna by Baldassare Cossa on a suspicion of Wyclifism, but were subsequently released by order of the Cardinals at the King's intervention. Wenzel had already forbidden the Archbishop to recognise any appointment to a benefice made by Pope Gregory,[2] and probably thought he could carry the Archbishop with him now; he desired also to have the University on his side. A meeting of the members of the University was held late in the year; Hus and the Bohemian nation were on the side of the King and of neutrality, but the three German nations remained true to Pope Gregory. No formal vote was taken; but shortly afterwards Archbishop Zbynek declared Hus to be a disobedient son of the Church and forbade him the exercise of ecclesiastical functions. It was from this meeting that Hus dated the loss of the Archbishop's favour. As soon as the King returned from Silesia he sent for some of the more important members of the University. Hus and Jerome and two other Bohemians were among the deputation, as were the Rector and some German masters. The King turned first to the Rector, who seized the opportunity to complain of the scandal which the Wyclifite movement had brought on Prague and on Bohemia. The bait drew. The King was very gracious to the Rector, but turned in fury on Hus and Jerome; he accused them of fomenting disorder and threatened them with death. Hus was of a gentle and sensitive disposition and the

[1] Luetzow, 293-303. [2] Palacky, iii. 212.

loss of the King's favour threw him into a violent fever so that he became seriously ill and was confined to his bed. When the King cooled down, he soon recognised that it was the Bohemian nation in the University which was on his side, and the three Teuton nations which were thwarting his wishes. The Archbishop also refused to throw off his allegiance to the Pope who had granted him his pallium. Then commenced the agitation as to the constitution of the University. The story has been already told, and need not be repeated here.[1]

On the 18th January 1409 King Wenzel arbitrarily altered the constitution of the University of Prague, giving three votes henceforth to the Bohemians and one vote to the three Teuton nations. The University had been originally Bohemian; the masters had been Bohemians; there had been no German among the earliest teachers.[2] The King declared that his father had desired mainly to benefit his Bohemian subjects, and that though they had originally been inferior in learning to the Germans, they had now become stronger and superior in all arts and sciences.[3] 'Let therefore those who had formerly been advantaged at the expense of the true owners of the land give way to them, and let these true owners rule the University for all centuries.' A copy of the decree was sent to Hus, who seized it with trembling hands as he lay on his sickbed. Two of his friends came in. 'Would it be just,' he asked them, 'if we had three votes?' 'Would God but grant it,' answered they, 'we shall never have that power.' He gave them the decree to read, and they were transported with joy.[4] The German students shortly afterwards abandoned Prague; Hus and the Bohemian nation remained masters of the situation. They and the Polish students obeyed the King, and the University declared for neutrality. Hus was elected the new Rector. He was now, says his latest biographer, ' at the height of his political position. Wenzel was undoubtedly grateful to the man to whose action it was principally due that the University of Prague had discarded Pope Gregory. The Queen and the Bohemian nobles treated him with greater favour than ever. He was the recognised leader of the University, and his

---

[1] *In the Days of the Councils*, 295-7. [2] Luetzow, 67.
[3] *Ibid.* 109. [4] *Ibid.* 106.

JOHN HUS

popularity among the citizens of Prague was very great.'[1] His sympathy and his influence extended beyond the Slavs of Bohemia; he was in direct communication with the King of Poland, who later sent a special messenger to inform John Hus of his victory over the Teutonic Order at Tannenberg. He continued to preach in the Bethlehem Chapel; he could afford to disregard the archiepiscopal prohibition, for Zbynek, through his adhesion to Pope Gregory, had incurred the displeasure of the Cardinals at Pisa. Hus was on the side of the Cardinals and of the coming Pope, of that Pope who, so many then dreamed, was to restore unity to Christendom.

Archbishop Zbynek saw that his position in Bohemia, with the King and the Pope alike against him, was absolutely untenable. Some of Hus's adherents had complained of him, and Pope Alexander had cited the Archbishop to appear and answer their charges. Zbynek on the 2nd September 1409 publicly recognised Alexander the Fifth as the only legitimate Pope. The summons for his appearance was annulled. ' The Pope preferred as an ally the mighty archbishop to the humble preacher.' Fortune had hitherto smiled upon Hus in his endeavours, but now the fickle goddess turned her wheel. The Archbishop, who had been his firm friend, now became his deadly enemy; he was a good hater, and Hus found that the work of church reform was a very different matter when he had the Archbishop and the King at his back from what it became when he had the Archbishop and the Pope behind him to contend with. Zbynek summoned Hus to appear and answer certain charges. The first charge referred to Wyclif's doctrine that a priest in a state of mortal sin could not validly administer the sacraments. Hus answered that he did not so believe, seeing that the grace of God operated equally through a bad as through a good priest. It was next said that Hus did speak, and did not blush to speak, slightingly of Pope Gregory the Great; this charge also he had no difficulty in refuting. It was further charged that he had said, and had not blushed to say, that it was absurd to suppose that the city of Prague should be placed under an interdict because of the death of Johann von Pomuk, to which Hus answered that he saw no reason why all should be deprived of

[1] Luetzow, 114.

religious consolation because of the death of one man. Other similar charges were brought and met. The forefront of Hus's offence is to be found in the charge that he had stirred up strife between the Teutons and the Bohemians, and this he denied, adding that he loved a good Teuton better than a bad Bohemian even though the latter were his own brother.[1] What Hus had done, and this it was which raised such bitter enmity, was that he had preached, nor only in his synodal sermons in Latin, but in the Bethlehem Chapel in the common tongue, against the vices of the clergy, thereby setting the people in judgment over them and destroying their influence. Up to the beginning of the thirteenth century the clergy of Bohemia had been married men, but John Hus was a firm supporter of Hildebrand's reform which was then introduced. The rule of celibacy was too hard for most of the priests, and they kept concubines; and for this Hus was never weary of upbraiding them. The parochial clergy were almost universally immoral, but they naturally objected to public denunciation. After hearing Hus the Archbishop sent an embassy to Alexander the Fifth, deploring the corruption which had been brought by the spread of Wyclifism, and suggesting that preaching should be prohibited except in cathedral, collegiate, parish, and cloister churches. The Pope issued a Bull on the 20th December adopting the Archbishop's suggestion as to the prohibition of preaching, instructing him to consult a council of four doctors of theology and two of canon law, and directing him to order all those who possessed any of Wyclif's writings to deliver them up in order that they might be removed from the sight of the faithful.[2] Owing to the bad state of the roads this Bull did not reach Prague until about the 9th March 1410. On the 1st June Pope John the Twenty-third wrote to the Rector and University of Prague informing them of the death of Pope Alexander the Fifth and of his own succession.

The Papal Bull which the Archbishop had obtained was the first blow dealt by the Pope to John Hus and his followers; it staggered and astonished them; they could not believe it was genuine; it had been obtained by bribery; it was the forgery of an Olivetan monk.[3] The Archbishop proceeded to action;

[1] Palacky (*Doc.*), 164-9. [2] *Ibid.* (*Doc.*), 374-6. [3] *Ibid.* (*Doc.*), 387 *et seq.*

JOHN HUS

he appointed his six councillors, men ready to back him up in carrying out the Pope's orders. On the 16th June, at the general synod of the clergy in Saint Vitus's Cathedral, the Papal Bull and the decree of the councillors were read; seventeen of Wyclif's works were declared to be heretical; all who possessed any copies of them were required to bring them to the Archbishop's palace within six days that they might be removed from the eyes of the faithful by a whirlpool of fire (*per ignis voraginem*). The prohibition of preaching, already mentioned, was renewed, and the Archbishop announced that in case of need he was ready to appeal for secular aid to the King. Henceforth all hope of a peaceful internal reformation of the Bohemian church was at an end.

The University was on the side of John Hus. A general meeting was held on the 15th, and on the 21st June a declaration was published dissenting from the condemnation of Wyclif's writings and protesting against their being burned; they appealed to the King. Wenzel induced the Archbishop to postpone the cremation for the time, until the arrival of the Markgraf Jost, a learned man, a lover of books, to whom Hus had already presented a copy of his translation of Wyclif's *Trialogus*.[1] On the 25th June Hus and his friends appealed to the new Pope against the Archbishop's order. They pointed out that the University was not under the jurisdiction of the Archbishop, that many of Wyclif's works did not deal with theology but with logic, mathematics, and other matters, that they had the right of reading these books which they had collected at much trouble and expense; they relied particularly on the argument that the death of the late Pope annulled the powers conferred on the Archbishop. John the Twenty-third allowed the force of this last argument.

As the Markgraf Jost delayed his coming, the Archbishop proceeded to action. Hus had brought his copies of Wyclif's works, and had asked the Archbishop to examine them and to point out the errors in them; others had also obeyed the archiepiscopal order; over two hundred volumes had been delivered at the palace. On the 16th July the court of the palace was barricaded; an armed force was assembled;

[1] Palacky, iii. 250.

a stake was erected in the middle of the court; the books were burned, the Archbishop himself lighting the pile, and all the assembled prelates and ecclesiastical dignitaries singing the Te Deum. This done, the Archbishop immediately escaped to his castle at Roudnice. On the 18th July he published a ban of excommunication against John Hus and his friends, forbidding him to officiate in any church in his diocese.

The result was a popular tumult, ' a great storm and much strife.' Brute force was used on both sides. The Court—the favourites had always been Hussites—and the people were mad with rage against the parochial clergy, whose immorality was patent to all. They wanted a reform of the Church; they felt that the charges of heresy were a mere blind, a false trail meant to put the Pope off the scent. Hus himself lost his customary prudence and caution. He preached in the Bethlehem Chapel to an immense crowd. He told them how the late Pope had written to the Archbishop that the hearts of many were turned aside to heresy because of Wyclif's writings, whereas he had himself affirmed and thanked God that there was no Bohemian a heretic. The congregation burst out with a shout, ' He lies, he lies.' Hus went on : ' Now is fulfilled the prophecy of Jacob of Taramo that in the year 1409 one should arise to persecute the Gospel and the faith of Christ, for the late Pope, I know not whether he be in heaven or in hell, has written on his wretched parchments (*in suis cutibus asininis*) to the Archbishop to burn the books of Master John Wyclif, wherein are many good things.' Hus went on to say that he had appealed against the Archbishop's order, and he asked the congregation if they would stand by him; to which the whole people with one voice made answer, ' We are ready to stand by you.' Hus continued his discourse : he must preach or be banished or die in prison; popes might lie and did lie; his people must not fear excommunication, for they would be excommunicated together with him; now was the time when they must gird on the sword and be ready to defend God's law.'[1] The sermon is noteworthy; it is the first occasion on which John Hus shows a disposition to rebel against the Pope; but it was not an act of open rebellion, for he had appealed to the Pope and was

[1] Palacky (*Doc.*), 405.

JOHN HUS

awaiting his order. His party was the stronger in Prague; they prevented the publication of the Archbishop's ban in most of the churches; they sang ribald songs ridiculing Zbynek, one of which ran thus—

> 'Zbynek, Bishop A.B.C.
> Burnt the books, but ne'er knew he
> What was in them written.'[1]

On the 22nd July, as the Archbishop was about to publish his ban in the Cathedral, an uproar arose, and he and forty of the clergy were obliged to withdraw. On the same day six armed men made a murderous attack on the officiating priest in Saint Stephen's church. There were reprisals on the other side. The choir boys who lived in the Castle sallied out to capture adherents of Hus, dragged them into the common room, and whipped them unmercifully. After these tumultuary outbursts it was comparatively a small thing that at the end of the month John Hus and his friends held a public disputation in defence of Wyclif's writings. The King had been absent from Prague during these scenes; as soon as he returned, he stopped the disorder in the streets, and prohibited the singing of abusive songs. Wenzel was on the side of Hus, and ordered the Archbishop to suspend any measures on his ban and to make good to the owners the value of the books which he had burned. When the Archbishop delayed compliance, the King attached his revenues.[2] Two Doctors from Bologna meantime arrived, sent by Pope John to settle certain Church questions. The King, the Queen, and many of the nobles besought these envoys to get the Bull of Pope Alexander annulled. When the Doctors left Prague on the 16th September, they carried with them letters to the Pope and to the College of Cardinals. The King's letter of the 12th set forth that the Bull had been obtained by false representations, and complained of the prohibition of preaching and the burning of Wyclif's books. ' How should the vineyard flourish when the vines are cut down by the roots?'[3] The Queen wrote on the same day interceding for the Bethlehem Chapel, which she had found most useful ' for hearing the word.'[4] She wrote again four days later

---

[1] Luetzow, 126. [2] Berger, 69.
[3] Palacky (*Doc.*), 410. [4] *Ibid.* (*Doc.*), 411.

protesting against the stopping of preaching and the burning of Wyclif's works. The King and the Queen both wrote to the College of Cardinals asking that the obnoxious order might be rescinded. The two Barons of Krawar and the Baron of Potenstein and the Consuls and Seniors of the city of Prague likewise appealed to the new Pope.[1] There had, as a matter of fact, been no alteration in the circumstances since the day when the Archbishop had officially declared that there was not a heretic in Bohemia, so that they were technically right in affirming that the late Pope's Bull had been obtained under false pretences. The Archbishop, on his side, forwarded the appeal of John Hus before the end of June to Bologna, and denounced the appellants as the authors of all the evil that had arisen. Pope John entrusted the conduct and decision of the process to Cardinal Oddo Colonna. The Cardinal made no independent examination nor local inquiry; he proceeded hurriedly and *ex parte*;[2] and at once on the materials before him on the 25th August he upheld the action of the Archbishop and cited John Hus to appear in person at the papal court, there to answer the charges against him. The Archbishop was directed to proceed with the work intrusted to him by Alexander the Fifth, and to invoke the aid of the secular arm if necessary.[3] When the Cardinal's letter was received in Prague does not appear, but the citation to Hus was made on the 20th September.[4]

The religious struggle in Bohemia had aroused attention and sympathy in England. Richard Wiche, a Lollard, wrote to Hus, rejoicing in the fact that the Bohemians were walking in the path of truth, and exhorting him not to be cast down by reason of tribulation or suffering. The letter was joyfully received and was read by Hus in the presence of, as he says, nearly ten thousand people.[5] It was so comforting a letter, said Hus, that he would have risked his life for this message of Christ. The incident is chiefly noteworthy as a proof of the interest which Hus had excited outside Bohemia, and of the importance which the movement under him had attained. Had these facts been adequately realised by the Pope and the

[1] Palacky (*Doc.*), 412 *et seq.* [2] *Ibid.* (*Doc.*), 190. [3] *Ibid.* (*Doc.*), 407.
[4] Berger, 70. [5] Palacky (*Doc.*), 12.

JOHN HUS

Cardinals they would probably have dealt more seriously with the whole matter. It was not until King Sigismund interfered that they realised its importance.

Hus had been summoned to appear at Bologna, but he had no desire to put his head into the lion's den, and he doubted whether he might not be kidnapped or murdered on the road. Notwithstanding this he probably would have gone had he not been dissuaded. He therefore sent three proctors to Bologna, and the King and Queen also wrote, begging that, because of dangers on the road, his personal attendance might be excused.[1] They doubted whether his enemies would ever let the reformer reach Bologna alive. King Wenzel also, on the 30th September, wrote to the Cardinal, saying that he had sent a protonotary, one Johannes Nas, to him to ask that, for the King's honour and for the quietude and weal of the kingdom, John Hus might be absolved from personal appearance, that Hus was ready to appear before any tribunal in Bohemia, even before the University of Prague; finally Wenzel expressed the wish that Oddo Colonna would himself come to Prague.[2] The King believed in John Hus; he was also sincerely anxious to clear his country from the imputation of heresy which lay on it. Furthermore if Hus had started for Bologna, and had been captured by the Bishop of Passau or any other enemy on the way, there would have been such a revolution in Bohemia as it would have been difficult to quell. On the 2nd October Queen Sophia wrote a letter to the College of Cardinals asking for resumption of service in the Bethlehem Chapel and that her devout and beloved chaplain might be excused from personal appearance in Bologna, failing which the King and the barons would have to take measures to prevent further disturbances.[3] Archbishop Zbynek also sent his messengers to Bologna. Pope John laid the question of the burning of Wyclif's books before the University, but did not otherwise interfere with the Cardinal's proceedings. A meeting of the Bologna doctors, some from Paris and Oxford also being present, was held in the church of Saint Dominic. A few of the masters approved the burning, but the great majority condemned it, and finally all agreed in this opinion. It was, they said, a scandal to the University of

[1] Palacky (*Doc.*), 190, 422-3.   [2] *Ibid.* (*Doc.*), 424.   [3] *Ibid.* (*Doc.*), 425.

Oxford, where Wyclif had been professor of theology; it created greater confusion in the University of Prague and greater schism in Bohemia; and it was absurd that works on logic, philosophy, morals, and theology, containing much that was true, good, and useful should be removed from the students and scholars.[1] A copy of this judgment was sent to Prague. 'Hus and his friends probably overrated the importance of this decision.'[2]

This, however, did not settle the question whether Hus was to appear personally at Bologna. Wenzel had suggested that a papal legate should be sent to Bohemia at his expense. The Pope had committed the affair to Cardinal Colonna, who would hear of no excuse. As John Hus did not appear in person at Bologna within the time prescribed, the Cardinal, in February 1411, excommunicated him for contumacy. A copy of his order was sent to Prague, and the sentence was published in all the churches of the city, two alone excepted, on the 15th March. It was a lamentable decision, for it decided nothing and it satisfied nobody but the Archbishop, whose change of front had produced all the recent trouble in Bohemia. It has been suggested that the Cardinal was influenced by 'the rich gifts brought by the envoys of the Archbishop' to display 'that hatred of Bohemia which was to be a prominent feature in his later life';[3] but Oddo Colonna, who was afterwards Pope Martin the Fifth, was probably as good a man as there was then in the College. He, however, like Pope John, underrated the importance of the matter, and was anxious to get it off his hands before he returned to Rome. Except for the altered attitude of the Archbishop, the situation was the same as it had been when in 1408 the orthodoxy of Bohemia was certified. A very slight independent examination would have revealed this to the Cardinal. But he merely examined a few witnesses sent by the Archbishop; the accused persons were not present nor represented; the whole inquiry was hurried and *ex parte*. The judgment did not decide whether Hus was a heretic, nor whether there was any heresy in Bohemia. It merely decided that Hus was contumacious for not appearing, and it decided this apparently without evidence, though the letters of the King

---

[1] Palacky (*Doc.*), 426-7.   [2] Luetzow, 132.   [3] *Ibid.* 130-2.

SIXTEENTH-CENTURY SKETCH OF JOHN HUS going to execution escorted by the Count Palatine's swordsman, and wearing the heretic's head-dress, as used at the Spanish autos da fé. (From the MS. in the archives of the Counts von Königsegg in Aulendorf.)

and Queen and of at least three Bohemian nobles made out a strong *prima facie* case for the reformer. The whole process was almost farcical in its insufficiency, and this was felt to be so by Hus and his friends. The moral effect of the judgment was deplorable, for it confirmed Hus, who still accounted himself a faithful son of the Church, in the belief that he had no justice or right judgment to expect from the Curia of Rome.

The further development of the controversy becomes involved with the question of the choice of a new King of the Romans, and to this question it is now necessary to turn.

CHAPTER III

THREE POPES AND THREE EMPERORS

RUPERT, King of the Romans, died on the 18th May 1410, the day after Baldassare Cossa became Pope John the Twenty-third. In the well-meaning but ineffective King Pope Gregory the Twelfth lost his most considerable supporter. On the 7th July he wrote a letter of condolence to Louis, Count Palatine, saying that he could not contain himself in his grief for the loss of so distinguished and prominent a ruler who, as he had sincerely hoped, would have made an end of the unfortunate and lamentable state of Christendom. The son returned an appropriate answer. Louis was determined to follow his father's example and to remain true to Pope Gregory. There was no further correspondence between the Pope and the Count until the autumn of 1413.[1]

Now that King Rupert was dead, a fresh election to the dignity of King of the Romans became imminent, and it was practically certain that the new King would be of the House of Luxemburg. This was indeed a necessity if Bohemia, Moravia, Silesia, and Brandenburg were not to be separated from the Empire.[2] The choice of the new sovereign was to Pope John a matter of the gravest importance. Not only was it eminently desirable that the temporal head of the Holy Roman Empire should acknowledge him as the spiritual head of that Empire; there was the need also for material aid; furthermore it behoved the new King of the Romans to draw into the obedience of the Pope of the Council that portion of Germany which still adhered to his rival, Pope Gregory the Twelfth. There was a party in Germany which held that Wenzel, King of Bohemia, had never ceased to be King of the Romans and that therefore no fresh election was necessary, and Wenzel was already

[1] Finke (F.), 4. [2] Brandenburg, 11.

THREE POPES AND THREE EMPERORS 53

pledged to acknowledge the Pope of the Council; but, on the other hand, Wenzel's sloth and incapacity were so notorious that his support and countenance could be of very little practical value. Pope John needed a stronger ally than Wenzel for the troublous times which he saw ahead. He had no doubt that the candidate who would be of most value to him as friend and supporter was Sigismund, King of Hungary. It was true that Sigismund held the very meanest opinion of Italians generally; he counted them to be the scum of the earth;[1] but the Pope knew him to be a 'person very stout, and fit for all brave actions,'[2] and he determined to back up his candidature. He believed that Sigismund would support him. As early as the 10th June 1410 he told the envoys of Carlo Malatesta that he had hope of obtaining the obedience of the whole of Germany, and that the King of Hungary and the Queen of Sweden had promised him their obedience.[3] Pope John supported Sigismund throughout, because he felt that Sigismund's support was vital to himself.

There were three candidates in the field for the imperial crown. The first was Wenzel, King of Bohemia, who claimed to be still King of the Romans, never having been rightfully deposed; he had been elected in the lifetime of his father, the Emperor Charles the Fourth, and his position as King had recently been acknowledged by the Council of Pisa. But Wenzel had drowned one high dignitary of the Church, and had insulted and threatened an Archbishop; he had shot a monk in the forest, saying that monks ought to be in the cloister and not in the greenwood; he had had his own cook cooked at his kitchen fire for spoiling the dinner; he had, with his own hand, executed his own executioner for too complaisantly carrying out his orders; he had acknowledged that if he were not already a second Nero he soon would be;[4] he was cursed by such an intolerable thirst that it was popularly attributed to the effects of poison lurking in his system; he exhibited all the helplessness, the indolence, the self-indulgence of a spoiled child; he not only altogether neglected the affairs of the Empire, but he failed even to maintain obedience in his own country. On the

[1] 'Faex mundi': Mur. xix. 828.   [2] Platina, i. 343.
[3] Martene (*A. C.*), vii. 1176.   [4] Aschbach, i. 267.

54 POPE JOHN THE TWENTY-THIRD

other hand his cause had lately been gaining ground; he had been acknowledged at Liège and Rotenburg; he had been recognised as King of the Romans by the Council of Pisa. On the 8th June 1409 he and the Council had entered into an agreement together; he had promised to recognise the Council and its proceedings, to come to Italy within the year and to reconquer the States of the Church; the Council had promised that the new Pope should recognise him as King. Accordingly on the 2nd September 1409 Zbynek, the Archbishop of Prague, had recognised Alexander the Fifth as Pope,[1] and on the 10th December Alexander the Fifth had recognised Wenzel as King of the Romans. But although the Electors Rudolf of Saxony and Jost of Moravia were on his side, there was little chance that the rest of the Electors would recognise the claim of so hopelessly incompetent a ruler. John of Nassau, the Archbishop-Elector of Mainz, and the Archbishop-Elector Frederic of Cologne, had both been at the Council of Pisa, but they ignored the agreement of that Council with Wenzel.[2] The second candidate was the Markgraf Jost of Moravia himself, who aspired to the crown if Wenzel was not to wear it. He was first cousin of the King of Bohemia, being the eldest son of John Henry, brother of Charles the Fourth, the first husband of Margaret Maultasch. That lusty virago, ' pock-mouthed Meg ' of the Tirol, had, in 1339, divorced John of Bohemia's second son, saying she was sure she should get no children by him; but John Henry subsequently gave her the lie by begetting three sons, of whom Jost, the eldest, was born in 1340. Now the Markgraf, with his long, flowing, white beard, was nearly seventy years of age; he was to the knowledge of all men the meanest and most miserly, the most shifty, intriguing, and untrustworthy, in every way the most despicable scion of the House of Luxemburg; but he was learned, wealthy, and very cunning. The third candidate for Empire, belonging to the same house, was Sigismund, Wenzel's half-brother, six years his junior, of determined character and fixity of purpose, a man of war from his youth up; he was King of Hungary, and by hard fighting he had compelled Bosnia, Servia, and part of Dalmatia to acknowledge his suzerainty.

[1] Palacky, iii. 83, 245.   [2] Goeller, 66.

Pope John the Twenty-third had very little difficulty in making up his mind to support the candidature of Sigismund, a man after his own heart, an invaluable friend and supporter. If he could secure that Sigismund should be elected King of the Romans and that Sigismund should be his faithful adherent, they two would be able to face the world. He and the King of Hungary had a mortal enemy in common in the person of King Ladislas of Naples; the embassy of Pippo Span gave John hope that Sigismund would support him against the rival Popes, and Sigismund was undoubtedly the strongest of the three candidates. The Pope therefore resolved to recommend his claims to the Electors. If by his support he could ensure the election, he would thereby earn a claim to Sigismund's future gratitude and lay the foundation for their future friendship and co-operation. His two envoys left Bologna on the 31st May 1410. Their mission was to announce the election of the new Pope, to bring back to the obedience of Pope John the adherents in Germany of Pope Gregory, and to express His Holiness's desire to restore unity to the Holy Church and Empire. To these same envoys, as soon as he heard of King Rupert's death, did Pope John by further instructions, deliver the task of persuading the Electors of the Empire to choose Sigismund to be King of the Romans.[1] From Frankfurt the two knights went to Mainz, Cologne, and Trier; they visited other chiefs on the Rhine; they journeyed as far as Guelders, and thence they returned with the Archbishops of Mainz and Cologne to Frankfurt.

The number and persons of the Electors had been definitely fixed by the Golden Bull framed in 1356 by the Emperor Charles the Fourth, the father of the half-brothers Wenzel and Sigismund. The number of the Electors was seven; three were ecclesiastics and four were lay chiefs. The three spiritual Electors were the three Archbishops of the Rhine. The first of these was the Archbishop of Mainz, Chancellor of Germany, whose duty it was to summon the Electors for election when a vacancy occurred. The present Archbishop of Mainz was the energetic warrior-priest John of Nassau, who had first met Baldassare Cossa at Rome when he went there thirteen years

[1] Hunger, 37.

earlier to procure his own election to the Archbishopric; since then the two men had worked together in Germany for neutrality and the Council, and they were firm friends. The Archbishop had already summoned the Electors to meet at Frankfurt on the first day of September. The second ecclesiastical Elector was the Archbishop of Cologne, Chancellor of Italy, whose duty it was to crown the elected King at Aachen; the present Archbishop was Friedrich of Mors, who acted together with his more youthful comrade of Mainz. The third was the Archbishop of Trier, Chancellor of Burgundy and Gaul: it was an Archbishop of Trier who, a hundred years earlier (1308), had secured the imperial crown for his own elder brother, Henry the Seventh, and who had lived to see that crown worn by Henry's grandson, Charles the Fourth. The present Archbishop of Trier, Werner, had been an adherent of the late King Rupert, and was now acting in concert with that King's son, Louis, the Count Palatine, himself one of the lay electors, the sword-bearer and grand justiciar of the Empire. A second lay elector was the Duke of Saxony, hereditary Marshal of the Empire; the present Duke was Rudolf, who was acting in concert with Jost, the cousin of the half-brothers. The King of Bohemia, the imperial cupbearer, had been recognised by the Golden Bull as an elector, and Wenzel, the present King, claimed to be still King of the Romans, refusing to recognise his deposition ten years earlier. The seventh and last elector was the Markgraf of Brandenburg. The right to this vote was disputed; it was claimed by both Sigismund and Jost. Sigismund had been Markgraf of Brandenburg, but in 1385 he had borrowed money from Jost, and had executed in his favour a simple mortgage of the Mark; in 1397, as Sigismund was unable to repay the amount borrowed, the simple mortgage was changed into an usufructuary, and Jost was enfeoffed of the Mark. Jost was generally regarded as being the Markgraf, and was summoned in that capacity by the senior elector,[1] the Archbishop of Mainz, but King Sigismund still claimed to be owner of the Mark, with right of redemption; he alleged that the vote for Brandenburg belonged to him as owner.

Never had an election been more beset with difficulties. One

[1] Hunger, 32.

point was abundantly clear, that no one but a Prince of the House of Luxemburg had any chance of being chosen. The Count Palatine saw this, and did not venture to become himself a candidate for the crown which his father had worn. Wenzel, King of Bohemia, claimed that, being still King of the Romans in virtue of the election held in 1376, the usurping King Rupert being dead, no new election was necessary. His cousin Jost, the Elector, and Duke Rudolf of Saxony took the same view and therefore declined to answer the summons issued to them by the Archbishop of Mainz. Inasmuch as the Council of Pisa had expressly recognised that Wenzel was still King of the Romans, and inasmuch as two of the three Archbishops had taken part in that Council and had approved its proceedings, it might have been expected that they would also recognise the claim of Wenzel's; but they were little troubled on the score of consistency. The three Archbishops and the Count Palatine scouted the acknowledgment by the Council of Wenzel; it was they who deposed him in 1410; it was they who had elected Rupert in his place; and they declined to stultify their former action. But though they were agreed in their opposition to King Wenzel, their agreement extended no further; in their choice of a future king, they were divided, two against two.

The Archbishop of Mainz had opposed King Rupert in the matter of the Council; he had stood firmly by the Cardinals at Pisa, and now he would support no candidate who was not ready outspokenly to acknowledge his old friend Baldassare Cossa, John the Twenty-third, the Pope of the Council, and no other to be the rightful Pope. The future King must acknowledge Pope John and be confirmed by him. On two other points also John of Nassau insisted. No new tolls should be levied on the Rhine without the assent of the Electors, nor should any Vicar of the Empire be appointed without their consent and approval. Already under King Wenzel the Electors had endeavoured to assert this right, and to Sigismund who foresaw that, if elected, his occasional absence from Germany would be necessary, who indeed foresaw a war with Venice looming in the immediate future, this innovation implied a serious circumscription of power and authority. Friedrich of

Mors stood by John of Nassau; the two Archbishops of Mainz and Cologne formed the first body among the Electors.

The Count Palatine, on the other hand, stuck to his father's opinion that Gregory the Twelfth was the true and only Pope, and with him concurred the Archbishop of Trier. Count Louis was anxious in the new King to find an ally against his political enemies, and Friedrich of Nuernberg, who had left the service of King Rupert only the year before for that of King Sigismund, acted as intermediary. The King of Hungary was ready to promise to the Count Palatine confirmation of all his privileges; he had not yet himself formally abandoned the obedience of Pope Gregory, but he was not ready to promise to recognise him as Pope; he was already in communication with Pope John, and all that he would promise was, that if elected, he would proclaim toleration and would work for the suppression of the Schism. The King of Hungary became forthwith the accepted candidate of this, the second party among the Electors.[1]

The third party consisted of the three lay Electors of Bohemia, Saxony, and Brandenburg. King Wenzel himself and Duke Rudolf of Saxony were of opinion that no election was necessary, that Wenzel was, and from 1376 had been, King of the Romans. The Markgraf Jost was also of opinion that his cousin had never lost his dignity, though, if Wenzel were no longer King of the Romans, then Jost himself was a candidate for that dignity.

The proposals of the Archbishops of Mainz and Cologne reached King Sigismund at Wissegrad on the 25th July 1410;[2] he was already in communication with Pope John on the one side and with his cousin the Markgraf Jost on the other; he did not desire to buy the crown of the Empire for gold, nor to inflict an open insult on his half-brother Wenzel; furthermore he had no intention of alienating the Count Palatine and the Archbishop of Trier;[3] he therefore had no hesitation in rejecting the terms offered by the imperious Archbishop, John of Nassau. It was on the 5th August that he signed the imperial capitulation in which, though he no longer promised to support the Pope whose obedience he had hitherto acknowledged, he did

---

[1] Quidde, 7.   [2] *Ibid.* 8; Hunger, 39.   [3] *Ibid.* 39.

THREE POPES AND THREE EMPERORS 59

solemnly engage to protect the adherents of Pope Gregory the Twelfth against all adverse exercise of power. With this modified promise of support the Count Palatine and the Archbishop of Trier were content.

The day appointed by the Archbishop of Mainz for the election was drawing on, and as yet there was only one candidate in the field. The Markgraf Jost and the Elector of Saxony, in response to the Archbishop's invitation, wrote at first that there was no need for any election, seeing that Wenzel was already King of the Romans; afterwards they wrote asking that the election might be postponed. The ambassadors of the Archbishops of Mainz and Cologne, after receiving no definite answer from King Sigismund, had gone on to the Markgraf and had been favourably received by him. Having won their votes, Jost had little difficulty in bringing Wenzel and Rudolf of Saxony round to his side. But this took time, causing a certain delay, and the consequence was that the representatives of these electors did not reach Frankfurt until the 28th September. Before this date arrived an important development had occurred.

When on the 1st September, the date fixed for the election, the Markgraf Jost had not expressed his readiness to take up the thorny crown of Rupert, the Electors of the Rhine were left in a state of indecision. Friedrich, the Burggraf of Nuernberg, had appeared, and they had admitted him, not as proxy for the Elector of Brandenburg, but as representative of the King of Hungary. The King and Jost both claimed the Brandenburg vote, and the question between them was as yet undecided. Duke Stephen of Bavaria also appeared as the head of the Wittelsbach family, but the Electors, acting on the authority of the Golden Bull, refused to acknowledge him as one of their number. The Archbishops of Mainz and Cologne were anxious that the question as to who was the rightful Pope should be decided before the election took place; they wanted the Count Palatine and the Archbishop of Trier to acknowledge Pope John the Twenty-third. If this could be secured, then John of Nassau thought that a circumscription of the powers of the King of the Romans could be brought about as effectually by an agreement between the four Electors of the Rhine as by a rescript of the King himself. His great aim was to limit the kingly authority and to increase that of the Electors. He was willing to enter into an agreement with the other two Electors to this effect, but they anticipated him. The Archbishop of Mainz decided to await the arrival of the other Electors or their representatives, but the Count Palatine and his ally determined on immediate action.

With them was acting Friedrich, the Burggraf of Nuernberg, the younger son of the old Burggraf Friedrich the Fifth. He was an able, energetic, and far-seeing man, popular, though generally short of cash. He was the devoted personal adherent of King Sigismund, at whose side he had fought at Nicoplois, and with whom he had had diplomatic relations on behalf of King Rupert in 1403.[1] He had been the faithful servant of that ineffective King; but when Rupert had been flouted by the city of Rotenburg, flouted by the League of Marbach, flouted and set at nought by the Diet at Frankfurt and the Archbishop of Mainz, Friedrich had recognised that no good thing was to be hoped for from the ineffective King, and that the Empire no less than the Church needed a reformation in its head and its members. With the permission and good will of King Rupert he had gone over to King Sigismund. He saw in him a man who had brought to his own kingdom welfare and security, who had reduced Bosnia to obedience, who had won back Dalmatia, who had compelled Servia to acknowledge his suzerainty; he saw in him, moreover, the only hope of the House of Luxemburg. Hence, at the death of Rupert, he recognised in Sigismund the man fit to be King of the Romans, and he worked steadfastly and loyally to win the crown for him,[2] for he knew that he was the only man strong enough to make his authority felt.

Sigismund had openly announced that he had no desire to be King of the Romans; it was a difficult and thankless office; he wished his half-brother to retain the dignity but himself to have the power, for this was necessary to him; he still, though he was a stranger to Germany, called himself and acted as the Vicar of the Empire. He and the Burggraf of Nuernberg rejected absolutely the advances of the Archbishops of Mainz

[1] Brandenburg, 7, 9, 21.   [2] Droysen, 185.

THREE POPES AND THREE EMPERORS 61

and Cologne ; he also declined to say definitely that he acknowledged Pope John, for he would thereby have lost the votes of the other two Electors. He had, on the 25th August, as already mentioned, issued through the Burggraf an ambiguous pronouncement that, if he were elected, he would work for the unity of the Church, and would see that no harm came to Pope Gregory or his adherents. This obviously might mean that he would acknowledge any one, or more probably no one at all, of the three Popes. The influence of the Burggraf, the staunch and active supporter of Sigismund's claims, his most faithful and zealous adherent, prevailed with the honest Louis of the Palatine and the good-natured Werner of Trier, and they declared themselves satisfied with the capitulation and ready to vote for the King of Hungary. The other two Archbishops, on the contrary, declined to accept any assurance so ambiguous and unsatisfactory to them. John of Nassau declared that the defeat of the Teutonic Order at Tannenberg (15th July 1410) had caused the delay of Rudolf of Saxony and Jost of Moravia, and that it was necessary to await their arrival or that of their representatives. The two Archbishops packed their baggage on the boats and were ready to leave Frankfurt.

More than a fortnight had already passed since the day fixed for the election. Disgusted and discontented at the delay, Sigismund's supporters resolved on a *coup d'état*. One of the rules of the Golden Bull was that should any one of the Electors not appear in person or by representative on the day fixed, the other Electors then present were to proceed with the election according to rule. Acting on this authority the Archbishop of Trier and the Count Palatine, accompanied by the Burggraf of Nuernberg, appeared on the morning of the 20th September before the doors of the church of Saint Bartholomew, within which, after the Mass of the Holy Spirit had been sung, the election was by the Golden Bull appointed to be held. The church, however, lay under an interdict, and its doors were closed, so that it was impossible for the Mass to be sung or the election to be held therein. The Archbishops of Mainz and Cologne, getting wind of their opponents' scheme, had on the day previous declared that no election should take place, and the former had pronounced the interdict, and had caused the church doors to be closed accordingly. Nothing daunted, the two Electors proceeded to the churchyard, acknowledged the Burggraf Friedrich as the accredited agent of the Elector of Brandenburg, and forthwith elected Sigismund to be King of the Romans. Having done this they left Frankfurt, and Friedrich, the Burggraf of Nuernberg, went back to report progress to King Sigismund.

Eight days later the representatives from King Wenzel, Markgraf Jost and Duke Rudolf of Saxony appeared. What it was that had induced this change of front in the King and the Duke, and had caused them to support the candidature of the Markgraf, we do not know. Wenzel's representatives were fully empowered, and in the subsequent announcement of the election it was stated that Wenzel had renounced the crown, although he himself still appeared and acted as King of the Romans.[1] There is nothing to show that he and his cousin had come to any definite agreement on these points, and probably their relationship was still unsettled and undetermined. A second election was held on the 1st October, and Jost was declared to be King of the Romans. There were four votes in his favour; counting the vote for Brandenburg as his, there were five; in any case the majority of the Electors had pronounced for him. And if, as is probable, Wenzel had not as yet renounced the title which he still claimed to hold, there were now three Kings of the Romans even as there were three Popes. There were thus three heads of the temporal world, and three heads of the spiritual world, in Christendom. Those faithful souls who regarded the Pope as the sun, and the Emperor as the moon, must have been sore dismayed when they beheld three suns and three moons in the firmament at once. Once before, in 1046, there had been three Popes simultaneously; once before, in 1347, there had been three who claimed to be Kings of the Romans; but never before had there been three Popes and three Kings of the Romans at one and the same time, and the like was never to happen again.

Although Sigismund and Jost had both been elected King of the Romans, neither made any attempt to obtain actual possession of the state and dignity, nor was there any attempt

[1] Quidde, 11.

made by their partisans to prepare for a fight and to refer the decision to the God of Battles. Although on the 20th September the Burggraf Friedrich declared that Sigismund accepted the crown, the King himself made no declaration. The ostensible reason given was that the royal seal was not yet ready; the real reason was that he and his cousin were arranging a meeting together. They were to have met on the 8th January 1411, but did not. Sigismund's briefs announcing his acceptance of the crown were dated the 12th and 21st January, but were probably prepared some time earlier. It appears beyond doubt that during the last three months of 1410 and the beginning of 1411 negotiations were proceeding between Sigismund on the one side and Jost and his Electors on the other, though it is impossible to say what was their trend or object.

Nor for long was the confusion in the temporal world to prevail. On the 26th December the Markgraf had executed an imperial capitulation confirming the rights and privileges of the Archbishop of Mainz, but he had made no preparations for the customary siege of Frankfurt.[1] He was seventy years of age and of feeble health. On the 18th January 1411 the greybearded Markgraf Jost died. Some thought, as men in those days were prone to think, that he had been poisoned, but of this there was no proof whatever. His rival and cousin, Sigismund, was far off, fighting the rebels in Bosnia; the Fates had been suspiciously kind to him, as they had been at the death of his brother, Johann of Goerlitz, and at the death of his cousin Prokop, Jost's brother. It was six days before his cousin's death that Sigismund had formally announced that he was willing to accept the election made in his favour nearly four months earlier; it was three days after the death that he wrote to Frankfurt to the same effect. The death of Jost left the question of the succession to be fought out between Sigismund and his half-brother Wenzel.

Now that their own candidate was dead, John of Nassau and Friedrich of Mors had to bethink themselves of the course they should pursue. They had on the 1st October written to Sigismund's counsellors, and though they had asked that the King might be persuaded to decline the irregular election and to

[1] Hunger, 45.

acknowledge Jost, still their letter had not been uncompromising in tone. But inasmuch as Sigismund had not acknowledged Pope John, they now declined to recognise him as the only possible King, and twice approached Wenzel with the offer of the crown. He declined, on the ground that he was already, without any election, King of the Romans, but at the same time he asked them to defer proceedings until his emissaries arrived at Frankfurt. The meaning of this was that, unknown to the two Archbishops, negotiations were already pending between him and his half-brother. On the 27th January the Burggraf Friedrich had hinted at such an arrangement in announcing that Sigismund was coming to Germany to be crowned. The Archbishop of Mainz fixed the 11th June for the new election, and on the 6th Wenzel wrote to him; the definite agreement between the Kings of Bohemia and Hungary was, however, not reached until the 21st June. There was to be no truckling for Empire on the part of Sigismund. Wenzel was tenacious of the dignity, Sigismund wanted the reality, of power. Pope John sent repeated messages to the Electors urging them to elect Sigismund,[1] and it was clear that he would be the future King. The two half-brothers arranged their differences over the heads of the Archbishops through the agency of Count Stibor of Transylvania: Sigismund was not to aspire to the imperial dignity while Wenzel lived, but was to help his half-brother to become Emperor of the Holy Roman Empire; he was to leave him the regalia and to share with him the revenues and possessions of the crown; Wenzel was to give his vote for Sigismund, who in vain strove to avoid the formality of a new election; Sigismund was to be King of the Romans and to rule as such. On the 30th June news of this agreement reached Frankfurt, where the Archbishops of Mainz and Cologne received it; they would rather the half-brothers had remained at variance.[2]

These negotiations between the two royal half-brothers had the effect of bringing the religious troubles in Bohemia again before Pope John. The excommunication of John Hus for contumacy, however pleasing to the Archbishop, merely raised popular feeling in the city to fever heat. The King was on the

[1] Hardt, ii. 260.   [2] Quidde, 12-14; Brandenburg, 19.

THREE POPES AND THREE EMPERORS 65

side of the reformer; he ordered the magistrates of Prague to attach the lands and revenues of the Archbishop and other clergy; the Archbishop retaliated by excommunicating those who carried out this order, and finally laid the entire city under an interdict. The King banished certain of the clergy; others were pillaged; on the 6th May Wenzel came to the Cathedral and had the treasures removed to the Karlstein to prevent the Archbishop taking them to his own castle.[1] We have seen that logically it was the Archbishop who was in the wrong. Wenzel felt this, and what is more Sigismund felt it also. Wenzel was childless and Sigismund was his next heir, and for this reason, and also because of the propinquity of his own country, he took a deep interest in the affairs of Bohemia, and followed them closely. It was of great moment to him that Bohemia should be at peace within itself and respected without, and hence he desired that the imputation of heresy under which it lay should be cleared away, and that the country should once again be pronounced free of all taint. Pope John would do very little for a king of the kidney of Wenzel, but he would do anything for King Sigismund, whose favour and support were essential to him. Seeing that Sigismund was interested in Bohemia, Pope John removed the process against Hus from the hands of Cardinal Colonna and entrusted it to a commission of four cardinals presided over by Zarabella, the famous Florentine, noted alike for his knowledge of law, his careful judgment, and his eloquence. The commission set to work earnestly and deliberately to inquire into the matter in June 1411;[2] but it was clear that their work would be lengthy, and the Pope desired to arrange the matter speedily to the satisfaction of King Sigismund. He therefore sent a hint to Archbishop Zbynek that he had better show himself more compliant, and the Archbishop was not the man to neglect such an intimation from such a quarter.[3] It was at the end of June that the two royal half-brothers were fully reconciled; it was on the 3rd July that the Archbishop and his clergy met John Hus and the masters of the University and agreed together with them. It was settled that the whole matter in dispute should be referred to arbitration. The King himself was to preside over the committee; Duke

[1] Palacky, iii. 265.   [2] Berger, 74.   [3] Palacky, iii. 267 and note.

Rudolf of Saxony, Count Stibor of Transylvania and Baron Lacek of Krawar were to assist him; other laymen and priests were consulted. The committee met at once and published their decree on the 6th July. It was a lengthy document stipulating for the removal of excommunication and interdict, the restitution of revenues and annuities, of rights and privileges, the cessation of pending lawsuits, and a further inquiry by the King as to the existence of vice and heresy. But the most important stipulations were that the Archbishop was to be reconciled to the King and was to write to the Pope that he knew of no heresy in the kingdom of Bohemia, but merely of a private quarrel between Hus and himself which the King was endeavouring to settle. In other words, the Archbishop was to repeat his official declaration of 1408 that there was not a heretic in Bohemia. He also promised to write to the Pope interceding for Hus. Once more it seemed as if the religious strife in Bohemia was at an end. John Hus himself wrote to Pope John protesting that he was a true Catholic, who did not believe in Wyclif's doctrine of the Eucharist, and who never said that a sinful priest could not administer the sacraments validly. The letter was approved by the University and was sealed with their seal. Every one hoped that a peaceful settlement had now been reached.

To return to the question of the election of the King of the Romans. In the spring of 1411 the pugnacious John of Nassau, Archbishop of Mainz, had nearly come to open war with the Count Palatine. The Archbishop, however, recognised that if he hoped to make good any of the pretensions of the Electors against Sigismund, he must agree with his adversaries quickly. He accordingly approached the Archbishop of Trier. The King of Hungary had made a negative pronouncement; he had not promised that he would acknowledge Pope John, nor that he would seek approbation and confirmation of his election from him, if he were elected; but he had promised that he would seek such approbation and confirmation from no one but Pope John or his successor. This precluded him from seeking confirmation of his title from Pope Gregory, but it left him free to seek it or not to seek it, as he chose, from Pope John. With this negative assurance were the Archbishops of Mainz and

THREE POPES AND THREE EMPERORS 67

Cologne fain to content themselves when they approached their fellow-electors, and on this basis an understanding was reached. King Sigismund in his second imperial capitulation further promised to bring back to his obedience and to restore to the Holy Roman Empire the lands which had fallen from it, and this stipulation had special reference to Milan.[1] His most important undertaking was to end the Great Schism and to restore unity to the Church. He made the customary promises to confirm to the Electors their existing privileges. On the 3rd May the Archbishop of Mainz and the Count Palatine agreed that the clergy on land belonging to the Palatinate in the diocese of Mainz should be free to acknowledge whichever Pope they pleased; while the Archbishops of Mainz and Trier agreed together that they would not acknowledge any Vicar of the Empire, nor any Vicar for any part of the Empire, unless he were appointed with their knowledge and consent. Sigismund also agreed that he would not appoint any Vicar of the Empire without the knowledge and goodwill of the Electors (ane sinen wissen und gutten willen).[2]

The Archbishop had fixed the 11th June for the new election; Sigismund had announced that he would appear on that date, and the Archbishop of Trier sent troops to uphold him. The King of Hungary, however, did not come; the troops went home again; and on the 10th July the accredited agents of the Kings of Bohemia and Hungary and of the Duke of Saxony appeared at Frankfurt. The customary ceremonies prior to the election began on the 17th, and the election itself was held on the 21st July. The Count Palatine and the Archbishop of Trier refused to stultify their former proceedings by appearing in person; they sent their counsel, who declined to take the seats allotted for their Electors in the church, and who disappeared before the oath was administered. The remaining five Electors unanimously elected Sigismund, who was represented at the altar by the Burggraf of Nuernberg. In France the election was attributed to the influence of Pope John the Twenty-third.[3]

Thus was Sigismund, King of Hungary, elected King of the Romans on the 21st July 1411, though he himself always dated

[1] *D.R.*, vii. 108. [2] *D.R.*, vii. 108; Droysen, 198. [3] Chastenet, 138.

the year of his reign from his previous election on the 20th September 1410. He had not been in Germany for thirty-five years; the Electors knew little of him, save that he was a strong man; and in raising him to the throne, they had taken a veritable leap in the dark. But at that juncture a strong ruler was above all things necessary. Never had the power of the King of the Romans sunk so low as during the thirty years which had elapsed since the death of the Emperor Charles the Fourth. Private feuds in the Empire had been endless and unceasing; the right of private warfare had been exercised wantonly and ruthlessly; harvests, vineyards, and fruit-trees had been wasted; cattle had been driven off; the husbandmen were in despair; whole villages had been blotted from the map, never to re-appear. For the internal welfare of Germany itself a strong rule was necessary; while the rest of Christendom awaited a strong ruler of the Empire to put an end to the accursed Schism. Men felt that the Council of Pisa had been a failure, that the infamous duality had been replaced by an accursed trinity, and that the only hope lay in the interference of the head of the temporal world. ' So long as there shall not be a single lawful, strong, and universal Emperor or King of the Romans,' said Jean Gerson, ' so long will the Schism not only endure, but there is reason to fear that it will wax worse.' [1]

In his imperial capitulation Sigismund had promised the Archbishops of Mainz and Cologne to seek the ratification of his election from no other Pope than John the Twenty-third or his successor, but as to the question of the ending of the Great Schism he had kept a free hand; his promise to these two Archbishops was therefore consistent with his promise to the Count Palatine and the Archbishop of Trier. Pope John had done his utmost to ensure the election of Sigismund; the King had been elected, and had undertaken to put an end to the Schism; but Pope John had nothing beyond the King's gratitude to count on; he had no definite promise that Sigismund would recognise him as the only rightful Pope.[2] The King and the Pope had indeed been for some time in communication with each other. On the 1st August 1410 Bishop Branda of Piacenza had been nominated Papal Legate to Hungary,

[1] Droysen, 177.   [2] Hunger, 31 *et seq.*

THREE POPES AND THREE EMPERORS 69

and had been instructed to choose a site for the University, and also to reform certain abuses rife among the Hungarian clergy.[1] On the 5th of the same month Pope John had written to King Sigismund transferring to him the dues and revenues accruing to the Church, a transfer which simply legalised what the King had been taking on his own authority since the days of Boniface the Ninth. On the 16th August Pope John had commissioned the Legate Branda to take precautionary measures in Hungary against King Ladislas of Naples; and the Bishop was further ordered to restore the churches which had been laid waste by the unbelievers, to provide their congregations with worthy pastors, and to annul all privileges which had been granted by any anti-pope. The Pope professed to be ready, and clearly was ready, to do all that the King desired.[2] In his dealings alike with Wenzel and with Sigismund, Pope John the Twenty-third omitted nothing that could conciliate and win over to his side the future King of the Romans. He wanted a strong man to be King of the Romans, and he wanted that strong man to be his own active supporter and ally. With Sigismund on his side he could face the rest of Europe.

But would King Sigismund be definitely on the side of Pope John? He had no sooner become King of the Romans than Carlo Malatesta, Lord of Rimini, wrote to him detailing all his own endeavours for the unity of the Church, laying suspicion on the good faith of Pope John, and suggesting that he, as well as the other two Popes, should be required to abdicate or should be deposed by a General Council. Before, however, Sigismund could take up the question of the Church, he had his own differences with Poland and Venice, and with the Dukes Ernest and Friedrich of Austria to settle.

The new King of the Romans plays such an important part in the history of the next few years that it will be well to study his character in the light of his former history, in order to form a just appreciation of the manner of man he was, and of the part he was likely to play.

[1] Raynaldus, viii. 325; *Vid. sup.*, 18.   [2] Hunger, 40, 49.

CHAPTER IV

SIGISMUND

The new King of the Romans was from head to foot a true king of men. He was now forty-three years of age, and his curly hair was turning grey, but he was still handsome in face, lithe, strong, and well built;[1] his noble presence, his accomplishments and his knightly deportment, his love of splendour and magnificence were certain to ensure him popularity.[2] He was to be the most powerful Emperor since the days of Frederic the Second.

Sigismund was the son of the Emperor Charles the Fourth by his fourth wife, Elisabeth of Pomerania, the granddaughter of Kasimir the Great of Poland. He was the son of both his parents; for his character displayed the western blood and breeding, the astuteness and tenacity of purpose, of his father, no less than the daring and ferocity of his mother's house. He inherited also the comeliness and personal strength of his mother. Elisabeth of Pomerania-Stettin, renowned for her beauty, was a veritable daughter of Anak, who could bend a horseshoe with her fists or tear in shreds a shirt of mail. Of her was born on Saint Valentine's Day, 1368,[3] a sturdy son of remarkable beauty, to whom no trace of his father's gout and palsy descended. The boy was named Sigismund, in memory of the Burgundian martyr-prince, whose bones Charles the Fourth had enshrined at Prague a few years earlier.

As a child Sigismund had been betrothed to the daughter of Friedrich, Burggraf of Nuernberg; but the engagement was soon broken off as brighter prospects promised. Louis the Great of Hungary was then at the zenith of his power; he had united with his own kingdom the lands of Red Russia, Moldavia,

---

[1] Mur. xix. 936.   [2] Robertson, iv. 253.
[3] Aschbach, i. 5; Lindner (*W.*), i. 17; contradicting *A.D.B.*, xxiv. 267.

SIGISMUND

Wallachia, Bulgaria, Servia, Bosnia, Dalmatia, and Poland, countries which his own power alone sufficed to keep together, which fell apart as soon as that bond of union was removed. Louis ruled from the Baltic to the Black Sea and Adriatic; he was a mighty king both in war and in peace. He had no son, but three daughters; the eldest, Katharine, died when she was young, and Louis offered his second daughter, Maria, in betrothal to young Sigismund. The children were related, for the mother of Louis of Hungary was sister to Kasimir of Poland. The prospect was too alluring to be rejected, but the betrothal was not completed when Charles the Fourth died. Charles left to Sigismund, a lively, beautiful, and talented boy of ten, the Mark of Brandenburg as his portion; and the widowed Queen Elisabeth took up the marriage negotiations with Hungary. Louis not only approved, but he was anxious that Poland as well as Hungary should fall to his daughter Maria; so that when in 1380 Sigismund was formally betrothed to his future bride, and was recognised by the bishops and nobles as entitled to the investiture of the crown, he was the prospective ruler of two vast kingdoms.

The death of Louis the Great of Hungary, however, brought a change in the boy's prospects. Sigismund was now fourteen years of age; his mother-tongue was German; he talked Bohemian, Hungarian, French, and Italian; he knew Latin, though not as the grammarians and doctors; he had picked up Polish since his betrothal. But he soon had to renounce the crown of Poland. Elisabeth, the Queen-Regent of Hungary, was by no means enamoured of the Luxemburg alliance; she would have preferred to marry Maria to Louis, Duke of Orleans. The Polish nobles were as little favourable as was Elisabeth to the pretensions of Sigismund; they were willing to receive a daughter of Louis as their queen, but they made it a condition that she and her husband should live in Poland. Hungary was not a country that could be ruled from without, so that this meant that the two kingdoms were to be separate. If the Poles could not have a queen on their own conditions, they were ready to elect a king of their own. To prevent the loss of the Polish crown altogether, Elisabeth, the Queen-Mother, announced to the Polish nobles that they were not bound to do homage to the boy Sigismund provided they would take one of her daughters as their queen. They answered that they were ready to accept the younger daughter Hedwig on their own conditions; and by this decision Sigismund, before he obtained the crown of Hungary, lost all hope of that of Poland.

The Hungarians disdained the name of a queen, and consequently, when Maria was crowned on the 17th September 1382, she was crowned *King* of Hungary. The Queen-Mother thus hoped to keep the two crowns for her two daughters; and though she had been so hostile to his prospects, she still retained her hold of Sigismund, who invaded Poland two years running, 1383-84, on her behalf. The reason for this hostility was that Elisabeth was unwilling that her beautiful daughter should be banished to that wild country, and she stood out against the condition on which the Poles insisted; but eventually she had to give way, and on the 15th October 1385, Hedwig was crowned at Cracow. Hedwig's love-story was rather sad. As a child she had been brought up with Wilhelm, the eldest son of that Leopold of Austria who fell at Sempach. Wilhelm was the senior by two or three years, but the children had played together from infancy, had been in love with each other from childhood, and had been formally betrothed since 1375, when Wilhelm was but five years old. Now in 1385, three years after her father's death, Hedwig, a girl of extraordinary beauty, was to be separated from the young knight whom she loved, and was to be wedded for reasons of state to Jagello of Lithuania, whom she despised as a heathen and hated as a man. She sent to Wilhelm, who came to Cracow with a splendid retinue; the youthful lovers met, but it was only to say farewell. The Austrian Duke remained true to his first love, and never married while she lived; though after her death in 1400 he married Joanna, the sister of King Ladislas of Naples, and thus became the enemy of Sigismund of Hungary. Jagello of Lithuania was baptized in order to wed a Christian princess, and assumed the name of Ladislas. The Lithuanians, like their ruler, became Christians, and their country was annexed to Poland.

In Hungary meantime there had been a revolution, brought about by the Horwathi faction, who had invited Charles the

SIGISMUND

Small of Naples to seize the throne. It was necessary for the Queen-Mother to bind Sigismund nearer to her, for hitherto he had been allowed no voice in the government of his future kingdom. Accordingly at the end of November 1385, Sigismund was married to Maria, and was declared Protector of the kingdom; he was also called king, although to this last step the Hungarian nobles had not given their consent. His first duty now was to checkmate the Horwathi faction by bringing troops to dispose of the pretender from Naples. He went off to the court of his half-brother to raise an army, but want of means hampered him. All through life Sigismund was improvident and extravagant. Before he could come to the aid of his wife, Charles the Small had made good his pretensions, had been crowned King of Hungary, but was then foully murdered and Maria was now again King. The delay of the youthful bridegroom enraged the Queen-Mother. Impecuniosity and lightheartedness with women were already Sigismund's besetting faults; the first was indirectly the cause of his mother-in-law's anger; the second was the cause of his wife's estrangement; she was young, and could not bear to be deserted for the first pretty face which caught her husband's fancy. Sigismund might thus by his own fault have lost the crown of Hungary as well as that of Poland but for a series of tragic events. The two queens, mother and daughter, were captured in July 1386, by the Horwathi faction; their faithful Cupbearer and Palatine was murdered at their feet, and they themselves were thrown into prison. At first they were immured in the Castle of Krupa, then in the mountain fortress of Novigrad on the Adriatic. The Horwathi faction sent word of their successful *coup* to Naples. But there were the Venetians also to be reckoned with; and the Republic had no desire to see the same rulers on both sides of them, in Naples and in Hungary. Ships were fitted out; and while Sigismund still delayed his coming, the Venetians besieged Novigrad. The Horwathi faction tried to scare them off by a deed of blood. The Queen-Mother was strangled by her gaolers in her daughter's presence, and her body was thrown over the walls before the Venetian fleet. With Maria a prisoner, and Sigismund away, there was no king in Hungary. Hedwig's husband, the King of Poland, claimed

74 POPE JOHN THE TWENTY-THIRD

the government in the name of his wife. In order to preserve the independence of their country, the Hungarian nobles accepted Sigismund as their King, and crowned him at Stuhlweissenburg on Palm Sunday, the 31st March 1387. Thus did Sigismund gain the crown of Hungary. When he was crowned he knew not whether his wife were living or dead. It was the Venetians who brought about the deliverance of Maria, and who forced her captors to set her free on the 4th June; she and her husband met at Agram on the 4th July 1387.

Maria was but a girl of twelve when her father died; for the next three years she was nominally King of Hungary, but her mother actually ruled. Then had come the successful invasion of the King of Naples, when the two queens were his prisoners, kept close at hand that their movements might the better be watched; then Maria witnessed the cruel assassination of Charles the Small; five months later she and her mother were attacked, Nicolas von Gara and Balsius Forgacz were killed before her, she and her mother were imprisoned: she had seen her mother strangled, and for ten months and ten days she had lived in the hands of her deadly enemies, daily expecting a similar fate. It is small wonder that this fearful experience should have made the girl of seventeen old before her time. She was married to a man whom she neither respected nor loved, who was notoriously unfaithful. But an opportunity arose which proved her worth. A conspiracy was formed to murder Sigismund; the conspirators assembled in the Queen's bedchamber; but she told her husband, and they were seized and executed. From that day forth Sigismund loved Maria and trusted her entirely. She, however, did not live long; she died on the 17th May 1392.

Sigismund had to fight to win the kingdom of Hungary and had to fight to retain it. The Horwathi faction was strong in favour of the King of Naples and against the Luxemburger. Twartko of Bosnia asserted his independence, made an alliance with the Turks, and instigated the Woivods of Moldavia and Wallachia also to throw off the Hungarian yoke. In 1390 Sigismund conquered Moldavia, and the Woivod swore allegiance. Then the King turned his arms against Bosnia and the Horwathi faction, who held Dalmatia, Croatia, and Slavonia. Luckily King

SIGISMUND

Twartko died on the 16th February 1392, and the new prince submitted and did homage for the kingdom which was secured to him for his life. Johannes Horwathi, the chief of the rebels, fled from the Castle Dodor, where he was besieged by Nicolas and Johannes von Gara, sons of the murdered Palatine; he was captured, tied on the back of a wild horse, torn to pieces with hot irons, and finally quartered; thus was Maria revenged. Still the Horwathi faction was not subdued. It was strong for conspiracies, and strong also for rebellion. In 1396, when the King was but twenty-eight years of age, there came the bloody fight of Nicopolis, and the flight down the Danube, when the Venetian fleet alone enabled him to escape from his victorious enemies. When Sigismund got back to Dalmatia at the end of the year, Hungary was in uproar, the vassal King of Bosnia had died and the country was in revolt, the nobles of Croatia had cast in their lot with the rebels of Hungary; and the powerful city of Zara, whose loyalty Sigismund had forfeited by his adverse decision in favour of the independence of the island of Pago just before he opened his campaign against Turkey, headed the cities of Dalmatia in taking the side of Sigismund's rival, King Ladislas of Naples. The allies joined the Turks, and Ladislas thought of wedding Bajazet's daughter; fortunately he was too much engaged with Duke Louis of Anjou and too afraid of following in his father's fate, to take an active part just then in recovering Hungary. Sigismund managed to win his way back to his kingdom, and when the head of the rebels appeared at a diet accompanied by as many armed men as the King himself, Sigismund seized and executed him and hung his body from the window to encourage his followers.

Such were the scenes of fierce strife and bloody warfare which formed the education of the future King of the Romans. He was a man of war from his youth up; for five-and-twenty years after the death of Louis of Hungary, from his fifteenth year to his fortieth, Sigismund was in arms at some time of every year of his life. He was, moreover, a warrior of the East of Europe, not of the West. There was comparatively little of courtly honour or knightly chivalry in the East; it was war to the death, war by fair means or foul, wherein each party desired to kill or exterminate its rivals. Sigismund on one occasion was

76 POPE JOHN THE TWENTY-THIRD

forced to flee in a little boat and to stave off hunger with a few grains of corn; on another occasion a Turkish scimitar had cleft him to the chin had not the speedy shield of Blasius Czerei caught the stroke; on another he had to ride for his life through a hail of poisoned arrows protected by the shields of his comrades. In 1404, when he and Duke Albert of Austria were besieging Znaim, they were both poisoned by a dish of black pepper; the Duke succumbed; Sigismund, by his doctor's advice, was hung by his heels for twenty-four hours that the poison might trickle from his mouth, and his vigorous frame recovered both from the poison and the treatment.[1] The fighting in Hungary, where the Magyars had lost little of that fierce savagery which distinguished them five hundred years earlier, was of a very different kind from that of the day of Roosebeke when Charles the Sixth with his French cavaliers mowed down their thousands of the Flemish footmen, of a very different kind from that of the day before Liège, when John of Burgundy won his soubriquet and left twenty-five thousand of his enemies dead on the field, of a still more different kind from the warfare of the condottiere in Italy, where each general was anxious not to press the other too shrewdly and so to spoil the market for war. It was a training which could not fail to make Sigismund bold and masterful and unscrupulous.

In the character of Sigismund, says the historian,[2] the qualities of intrigue, cunning, dissimulation, violence, ingratitude, and avarice were harshly prominent; but openness, sincerity, loyalty, fair-mindedness and unselfishness were not seldom mixed with them. In his intrigue, his cunning, his dissimulation, he was meeting his enemies on their own terms, but he was inferior to them; he was, on the whole, a man more sinned against than sinning. He never circumvented his elder cousin Jost. The old Markgraf—he was seventy when he was elected King of the Romans—was a model of meanness; he had taken advantage of Sigismund's impecuniosity at every turn; he had betrayed the Luxemburg cause for his own advantage; he had the reputation of being the greatest liar in the Holy Roman Empire. Jost had a long white beard, by which he was in the habit of swearing; and when he swore by

[1] Altmann, 98.   [2] Aschbach, i. 48.

SIGISMUND

his beard, then was the knight most frequently forsworn. No one could get the better of Jost; he was always ready to play the traitor for his own advantage, and in his dealings with the old Markgraf, Sigismund, like others, invariably came off second best.

Jost had a younger brother Prokop, whom he hated fervently; and Prokop died in 1405. Sigismund had twice got Prokop into his own power by treachery; and such instances of treachery among near relatives were tolerably common in the East of Europe. Sigismund himself was on his guard against them. He and the King of Poland had married sisters for their first wives, and cousins for their second; moreover, in 1394, Ladislas of Poland had befriended Sigismund in the hour of need. Yet, when the war between Poland and the Teutonic Order was threatening, and Ladislas sent to Sigismund a safe-conduct to come to his Court as mediator, Sigismund dared not risk the journey for he had heard that Ladislas had posted troops in the passes to cut him off and make him prisoner.[1] When Prokop died there were some who said that his death was the result either of poison or of hunger while he was in Sigismund's custody;[2] but Aschbach, who never seeks to screen Sigismund, does not believe the story, so that it is probably untrue.

Sigismund had a younger brother, Johann of Goerlitz, an 'honourable, pious, capable, and truthful man,'[3] father of the beautiful heiress who subsequently married Antony of Brabant: and when King Wenzel, in 1394, was seized as he was dining at the Franciscan Cloister at Beraun, and was hurried by the conspirators from one fortress to another, he was eventually, after twenty-eight days' imprisonment, liberated through the agency of Johann of Goerlitz. Jost was at the head of the conspiracy, and Sigismund was supposed to be privy to it. Johann, despite his good qualities or perhaps by reason of them, was hated by his brothers and cousins, ' and therefore must he die from poison in his youth '[4] on the 1st March 1396, being then but twenty-six years of age. This was a very black stain on the character of Sigismund, if indeed he was privy to the

---

[1] Aschbach, i. 247.   [2] *Ibid.* i. 209 note.
[3] So says Eberhard Windecke: Altmann, 3.
[4] Eberhard Windecke: Altmann, 3.

crime. Neither death can be said to be proved against him; and in any case he did not, as did John of Burgundy, take the Holy Communion with his victim beforehand.

With comparative justice has Sigismund been reproached with ingratitude to his half-brother Wenzel, who had done so much to help him to the throne of Hungary. But it must be remembered that up to the year 1393 Sigismund was completely true to Wenzel; and that since 1389 Wenzel had not only given up all attempt at government of the Empire, but had become a victim to crapulous sloth, had disgraced himself indelibly by his dealings with the Archbishop and the clergy, had given way to fits of brutal violence, and had incurred the hatred and contempt of the lay and spiritual nobles of his kingdom. Of Wenzel it was already hopeless to expect any good thing when in December 1393 Sigismund and Jost entered into a general league of defence and defiance with Duke Albert of Austria and Markgraf Wilhelm of Meissen. Next year Sigismund was privy to the conspiracy for the capture and imprisonment of his half-brother; and from that time forth he played entirely for his own hand. He might, had he chosen, have marched with Wenzel against King Rupert in 1400; but he demanded first to be assured of the hypothecation of Silesia and Lusatia, of the reversion of Bohemia on the death of Wenzel, and of the present government of that country; and when his half-brother, on hearing these conditions, rode off in scornful silence, Sigismund left him to his fate. Wenzel, on the other hand, had the sense to recognise that Sigismund, rather than Jost, was the surest hope of the House of Luxemberg; and therefore when Sigismund was imprisoned by the nobles of Hungary, he sent men and money to aid in his liberation.

Even after this, when all the members of the House of Luxemberg were at peace and amity together, when Sigismund was appointed vice-regent of Bohemia (18th February 1402), he proceeded to harsh measures against Wenzel. He had determined to take him to Rome to be crowned Emperor; he himself was his next heir. King Rupert returned in April from his luckless expedition into Italy, and had little difficulty in persuading the brothers Jost and Prokop that they had been overreached by the masterful King of Hungary and that they would find their own advantage in an alliance with him. Wenzel himself began to regret having parted with the rule of Bohemia. It was necessary for Sigismund to take strong measures in self-defence. Accordingly he took Wenzel into his custody; he invited Prokop to a conference and treacherously imprisoned him; Jost he could not get into his power. But the dangers of the road through the machinations of King Rupert with the Austrian Dukes, and the unrest in Hungary and Bohemia, obliged him to abandon his project of taking Wenzel to Rome; he determined to remain in Germany; he made a league with the Austrian Dukes (16th August 1402); he made over King Wenzel to them for safe custody; he imprisoned Prokop at Pressburg and turned his own attention to Jost.

The breach with the other members of the House of Luxemburg and the alliance with the Albertine House of Austria were henceforth the cardinal features of Sigismund's policy; he and Duke Albert were recognised as each other's heirs; and this arrangement was sanctioned on the 21st September by the prelates, nobles, and cities of Hungary. When the Duke died, Sigismund took his widow and son under his special protection. In his government of Bohemia Sigismund and his troops treated the country like an enemy's territory; the soldiery committed the most outrageous excesses; the officials favourable to Wenzel were removed and were replaced by friends of the vice-regent; heavy taxes were mercilessly levied; Sigismund made himself universally hated. Troubles in Hungary prevented him from marching against Jost. On the 1st October 1403 Pope Boniface the Ninth had recognised Rupert as King of the Romans, so that the project of crowning Wenzel at Rome had to be for ever dropped. The Pope, moreover, encouraged King Ladislas of Naples to invade Hungary, and stirred up the wealthy and powerful clergy of the realm to rise and to use their influence in his favour. To crown the misfortunes of Sigismund, Duke Wilhelm of Austria, the former love of Hedwig, who had remained faithful to her during her life, married the sister of King Ladislas, and incontinently allowed Wenzel to escape from custody. By Christmas 1403 Sigismund's reign in Bohemia was at an end, and he had to hurry back to save his own kingdom from the invader.

During his wars in Eastern Europe the King of Hungary had learned rough methods; to gain his own ends there was very little which he allowed to stand in his way. His favourite troops were the Kumanians, an untameably savage and fierce tribe, who had settled in the Theiss lowlands three centuries earlier. In the war with Bohemia at the beginning of the fourteenth century, the Kumanians had strung the Czech children together, by boring holes through the palms of their hands, and had flung them across their saddle-bows as they tore through the land; these ruffian troops served Sigismund faithfully, and he rewarded them handsomely. Moreover he allowed robbers and freebooters to take refuge in Hungary, and thence to plunder the neighbouring states; the Austrian dukes did the like, and patronised such bandits even more unblushingly. Every method of injuring one's adversary was deemed permissible; there was little public morality.

In addition to dissimulation and ingratitude there were other unpleasant traits in the character of Sigismund. Like all the Luxemburgers, he was subject to fits of uncontrollable passion, of Berserker rage, and while the paroxysm was on him, he was often guilty of wild injustice or wanton cruelty. When, after three years of hard fighting, he captured Twartko Schura, the King of Bosnia, in the Castle Doboy on the Bosna River, he cut off the heads of a hundred and twenty-six of the Bosnian lords and had them flung from the ramparts into the river. When the embassy of Duke Wilhelm of Austria met him at Pressburg, Sigismund fell into a paroxysm of rage at the defiant speech of Reinprecht von Walfe and dismissed the ambassadors in anger; but he cooled and reconsidered the matter; he not only reopened the negotiations for peace, but he bestowed marks of special favour on his adversary's loyal and bold spokesman. At an earlier time when the conspiracy of the Thirty-two of the Horwathi faction was discovered, the conspirators, with Stephen Konth at their head, were surprised in their sleep and captured. The Thirty-two were brought before Sigismund, but they neither bowed their heads nor greeted him in any way; they had sooner die than acknowledge him to be their king. Sigismund fell into one of his fits of violent anger, and ordered them all to instant execution. They died fearless, still scorning the King, and refusing him reverence. As Stephen Konth stood facing Sigismund, and was cut down from behind, his swordbearer, a noble boy named Chowka, burst into bitter tears. The grief of the lad touched Sigismund's heart; he tried to console the boy, offered him presents, and promised him a better master. But Chowka answered scornfully, ' I will serve no Bohemian swine,' and he perished with the rest.

It was also a disadvantage to Sigismund that he was a foreigner in Hungary and had no sympathy with the nobles of the country. Before he became King, he got into trouble by attempting to mortgage Hungarian lands. When he was crowned, his reckless generosity in bestowing civil and spiritual dignities, forfeited by the rebels, while it increased the number of his friends at the same time exasperated the Hungarians. He made no attempt at first to govern Hungary through the nobles of the land. The Garas were indeed of an old Hungarian family; but Count Hermann of Cilly was a Styrian, Stibor of Stiborzieze was a Pole, Pippo Span was a Florentine; these were his chief adherents—these were the men whom he delighted to honour. His levity with women was also against him. His bright sparkling eyes, his ruddy cheeks, on which the flush of youth still mantled, his long tawny beard, his limber frame, his prowess in the lists, rendered him irresistible with the ladies; and where he conquered he was generous; but the husbands of the ladies did not appreciate his success with their wives and daughters. Yet it was long ere Sigismund learned to restrain himself. The discontent in Hungary went on increasing until on the 28th April 1401 he was made prisoner by the prelates and barons in the Hall of Audience at Buda. It was a surprise to the King. As they attempted to unarm him, Sigismund drew back, plucked out his sword, and faced his adversaries. ' Who of you dare lay his hand on his King,' said he fearlessly; ' what offence have I committed that you should fall on me; if any of you think himself injured, let him stand forth and meet me in honourable fight.' The King was disarmed and the imprisonment which followed for eighteen weeks in Siklos Castle gave him time for reflection.

There were four parties in Hungary when the King was thus

captured. Some were in favour of an Austrian duke, and others were for the King of Poland; but both these parties were weak and vacillating, and allowed the favourable moment to slip by. The two stronger parties were those who were in favour of King Ladislas of Naples, and those who desired the restoration of Sigismund. The King of Naples also tarried; while the party led by Nicolas von Gara and Hermann von Cilly, assisted by Wenzel and Prokop, who wanted to preserve Hungary for the House of Luxemburg, went to work quickly. Sigismund in his prison went on his knees to the mother of the Garas, the widow of the murdered Palatine; he promised to marry Barbara von Cilly, the Count's nine-year-old daughter; he obtained his liberty after eighteen weeks' confinement on the 27th October 1401; he met Wenzel and Jost at Kuttenberg in December, and was appointed vice-regent of Bohemia on the 18th February 1402. The danger from Naples was merely postponed; Ladislas invaded Dalmatia in 1403 and was crowned King of Hungary at Zara on the 5th August. The King of Naples was, however, a coward at heart; he feared his father's fate; his crowning was the turning-point of his fortune. The Bishop of Agram, the Ban of Machow, the brothers Gara assembled their troops against him; Stibor of Stiborzieze won a great victory; Ladislas was driven back to Dalmatia. Then King Sigismund appeared, promised an amnesty to the rebels who returned to their allegiance, and at the end of October 1403 King Ladislas took ship for Naples. His dream of the Hungarian throne was at an end; a stronger than he was in possession.

The imprisonment and the invasion were a turning-point in the life of Sigismund; he had learned at last the lesson that he must govern Hungary for the good of its people, that he must curb his passions, that he must rule to ensure the peace, the safety, the well-being, the improvement of his subjects.[1] The magnates of the country came gradually to see that their interest lay with the King rather than against him; the Garas, the Maroths, the Perenys were on his side. The need of recompensing them for their aid in his frequent wars, and his own reckless generosity, impoverished

[1] Aschbach, i. 253.

the King and made these barons and his foreign favourites extremely powerful; and Sigismund was wont to say that if Pippo Span turned against him, he could give the King a little white staff and could force him, naked and forlorn, to abandon his kingdom. At the same time, Sigismund had, through the suppression of the rebellion, obtained the upper hand of the clergy of Hungary; as soon as the Pope declared against him, he prohibited the remission of any revenue to Rome; and even after the war with Ladislas was over, the King still retained in his own hand the promotion to all benefices. To counteract the overpowering influence of the barons, Sigismund gave increased importance to the cities and the lower nobility. He instituted Diets in which two classes were represented, the *Status*, consisting of the barons and prelates of the kingdom, and the *Ordines*, consisting of the lower nobility of the district and the royal free cities. The preamble of the enactments made at the Diet held on the 15th April 1405 sets forth that deputies had been called from all the administrative districts and from the free cities; and that after consideration of their representations, the King had with the counsel and advice of his prelates, barons, and magnates, made certain important regulations.

The legislation thus enacted affords the best evidence of the wise and provident intentions of the King. It is concerned with the administration of justice, with the rights of the cities, with the royal revenues, and with matters of business, coinage, and minting. Affairs of clerical jurisdiction were to go to the clerical courts, lay matters to the lay courts; in cases of disputed jurisdiction, the King, with the advice of his prelates and barons, was to decide as to the court having jurisdiction. Papal solicitors were not allowed to plead in disputes between laymen. The unsuccessful party to a suit was obliged to pay a ninth or a tenth part of the value to the judge. In the free cities suits were to be brought in the first place before the city judge, with an appeal to the royal treasurer (*Magister Tavernicorum*), and a second appeal to the King. The nobles and the free cities were confirmed in their power of punishing evildoers and lawbreakers. Those whom the arm of justice could not reach were to be outlawed, a notice of the crime and sentence being sent to all courts with a view to apprehension and punishment. The regulations for the cities enacted that every walled city had the right to send deputies to the Diet, that smaller market towns and villages in danger from the Turks might surround themselves with walls and thus acquire the dignity of royal free cities. Beside the customary revenue, each city was also to make, on New Year's Day, a donation in proportion to its taxes, and each head janitor was to pay six florins. In the case of a visit from the King the city had to provide only for his table, but each craft was called on to present a specimen of its handiwork. To affairs of trade and commerce Sigismund paid particular attention. Imports from foreign countries had to pay a thirtieth of their value, but the import of salt was forbidden, as also was the export of gold, silver, and copper; detailed regulations were published in these respects. Uniform weights and measures were established with exceptions in favour of tithes, mining rights, and ecclesiastical revenues. The staple-right of Buda was abolished for home merchandise. Foreign traders were not allowed to deal in retail, nor were native dealers allowed to trade with foreign wares as if they were home products. The regulations concerning the coinage enacted that the Hungarian gold florin was to pass as worth a hundred pfennigs, that coiners were punishable with death, that in every city there was to be a royal money-changer who alone could change gold for silver or *vice versa*; all gold and silver from the mines was to be sold to the royal overseer at a fixed price; no one was allowed to trade in the precious metals, which could only be given to smiths for making plate and jewellery; beside goldsmiths and others duly authorised, no one was allowed to possess touchstones, smelting-pots, or nitric acid, or to practise analytical chemistry. The rights of coinage and the monopoly of gold and silver were evidently very valuable. Sigismund also alleviated the lot of the peasants by abolishing the state of villenage and by allowing them, on payment of a quittance to their landlord, to migrate to a city or to another holding. He also recompensed his beloved Kumanians for their help in time of war by making them free of tolls, and responsible only to the courts of their own captains.[1] His legislation throughout was businesslike and straight-

[1] Aschbach, i. cap. xiii. for the foregoing details.

forward; much of it was intelligent and beneficial; in parts it was in advance of the general feeling and economy of his time.

The lighter side of Sigismund's character displays many agreeable and kingly traits. He was a man of unbounded activity, as ubiquitous in the saddle as that Paladin of romance, his grandfather, King John of Bohemia, who died at Crecy. He was very fond of fishing and of hunting, and after a night in the ballroom would rise early in the morning for his favourite sport. His activity kept his frame limber and supple, so that he was still spare and well-proportioned when he became King of the Romans. His long tawny beard would have done credit to Otto the Great or to Frederic Barbarossa. He was great at the tourney and the joust, accomplished in the tilting-yard; his prowess won all hearts at Cracow and, later on, at Constance. He delighted in magnificent apparel, and yet he was a ' student of books, and amidst the distractions of his broken life he always spared some leisure time for reading, finding, as he said, that the pressure of business needs the relish of knowledge. . . . He helped poor scholars where he could, as men whom nature meant to top the world, and he would sometimes say that though he could make a thousand knights in a single day, he could not make one scholar in a thousand years.'[1] He was fond of proverbs and apothegms; a man of quips and sentences. ' Kings would be blessed if they had no flatterers about them,' said he; ' the flatterer is worse than the crow, for the crow picks out the eyes of the dead, but the flatterer the eyes of the living.' ' I kill my enemy by sparing his life.' ' You cannot love a king unless you are afraid of him.' ' No prince deserves to reign who cannot shut his eyes and ears.' ' A donkey has a better time than a prince, for his master at least leaves him alone while he is eating.' Such are some of the sayings attributed to Sigismund. He could be all things to all men; stately and majestic as Solomon in his glory when occasion required, he could wheedle a merchant out of his money with friendly, unceremonious talk, or he would doff his bonnet to an oyster-wench and bandy a jest with her husband. When the envoys from Genoa refused to admit him into their town, he presented them with a copy of Justinian, and left them believing him to be

[1] Wylie (*C.*), 17.

86 POPE JOHN THE TWENTY-THIRD

a kindly, God-fearing man, strong in body, simple in diet, and hedged about with prudence.[1] His readiness of converse and of access extended to all ranks ; he surprised his guests in their bedrooms in the morning and won them to his wishes with graceful talk ; he told the peasants of Bohemia that his ancestor on the mother's side had held the plough, and that he was therefore the right king for the peasants ; when any one knelt to him with a petition, he held out his hand and begged him to rise ; he was polite to the lowly and had a good word for everybody.[2] Innocent plausibility, soft flattery, confidential converse, persuasive promises, and scathing scorn came with equal readiness from his lips ; pithy proverbs and biting wit alternated with poetic warmth and lofty sentiment.

Sigismund was, above all, a man who delighted to manage his own affairs ; he needed neither sponsor nor attorney. He made it his business to know all men's manners and to understand their natures. Though not so good a theologian as his half-brother, he was a good churchman, but he saw the need for reform. He made many a bitter jest at the avarice and licence of the clergy ; the difference between the married priest of the Greek Church and the celibate of the Latin, he used to say, was that the former had one wife while the latter had ten. He disliked the interference of the clergy in worldly affairs ; his friends and counsellors were mostly men of the world ; he was the first German king to appoint a layman as his chancellor. He was not bitten with the vulgar hatred of the Jews. He honoured relics as his father had done, but was on his guard against being deceived ; when purchasing the skeleton of Saint Elisabeth at Marburg he cautioned his agent to be present at the opening of the grave as he did not want to be put off with a ' bit of a dead cobbler.'[3] He was a good judge of men and of character ; and herein lay his salvation, for neither the towns nor the lower ranks of the nobles could have furnished him with adequate support had the higher nobility turned against him. In the pomp and pageantry which he loved, in the splendour of his apparel, in his gifts to fair ladies, Sigismund was guilty of the most reckless extravagance ; he had none of the wise

---

[1] Wylie (*C.*), 17, 19.   [2] Lindner, (*H. and L.*), ii. 288.
[3] *Ibid.* (*H. and L.*), ii. 289.

SIGISMUND

economy of his father Charles, none of the niggardly parsimony of his cousin Jost; he was ever on the verge of bankruptcy. His generosity and extravagance often brought him to comic straits; as a Frenchman said, the man who was ready to set the whole world in flames and to threaten the antipodes was constrained to behave like a beggar, to screw small sums from his nearest friends, to wear shoes patched by a cobbler and clothes so badly mended that you could see through the rents. He possessed not punctuality, the politeness of princes. He would drink with any one, but was not a drunkard, like Wenzel. He was an epicure, delighting in fish and fruit. He loved all pretty women, from the highest to the very lowest.

Although the new King of the Romans had spent so much time in warring, he had had a considerable amount of experience in peacemaking, both on his own account and as arbiter between other combatants. At the time of his election he was engaged in making peace between the Poles and the Teutonic Order after the desperate fight at Tannenberg. Sigismund had also a keen eye for political chances and his judgment might generally be trusted. His relations with the House of Habsburg prove this; he saw that Albert the Fourth was a better man and a better ruler than either Wilhelm or Leopold; and when Albert died, poisoned before Znaym, Sigismund stood by the widow and her young son Albert, the boy who was eventually to wed his own daughter Elisabeth. While in the countries immediately subordinate to him he had strengthened and consolidated his rule, in the neighbouring countries he had by treaties and alliances secured peace on his borders; the Venetians were the only people with whom he had not settled his differences at the time when he was elected King of the Romans.

Reference has already been made to Sigismund's alliance with Duke Albert of Austria, and also to the reforms by which he improved the condition of his people and increased the number and welfare of the towns in Hungary.[1] In addition to these principles of his policy there were also three other fixed ideas to which he was ever true both as King of Hungary and as King of the Romans. He believed firmly in the majesty and practical value, in the old and waning theory, of the Holy

[1] Droysen, 155-6.

Roman Empire. An attempt has been made elsewhere [1] to show the precise point of development which had been reached at this time in the relations between the Empire and the Papacy; the pretensions of the Empire had suffered through the humiliation of the Hohenstaufen, through the long quarrel of Louis of Bavaria with the Popes, through the concessions made by Charles the Fourth and by King Rupert. But Sigismund was minded to place those pretensions as high as had Frederic the Second; he still dreamed of universal suzerainty, and consequently suffered rebuffs at the hands of England, France, and Spain, reminding him that those countries were no longer in any sense vassals of the Empire. The Electors had no quarrel with Sigismund when he upheld the constitutional rules formulated by the Diets of Rhens and Frankfurt by neglecting to apply for any papal approbation and confirmation of his election; but he found the vassals of the Empire in opposition when he tried to assert strict imperial right against one of their number; they were ever ready to demand the performance of imperial duties, and Sigismund was generally ready to comply; while he, on the other hand, was ever ready to attempt the extension of imperial rights, which they were determined to resist. In this connection it must be remembered that the mediæval theory of the divinely ordained necessity of a one and only world-state still retained its vitality. The principle had been assailed, especially in France. John of Paris had held that although unity is required by divine law in the Church still the laity should live in different states; and Gerson inclined to the same opinion. But the general opinion still was that 'the Romano-German Kaiser, as immediate successor to the Cæsars, was by divine and human law possessed of the *Imperium Mundi*, by virtue whereof all peoples and kings of the earth were subject unto him.' [2] Lupold of Bebenburg held that even in lands which were not imperial the Emperor had 'immediate jurisdiction over the rulers and a mediate jurisdiction over the subjects in case of default of justice.' William of Ockham held that the Emperor could decide certain matters which kings could not decide, that he could perform certain reserved acts, and could make kings in lands that possessed

[1] *In the Days of the Councils*, chap. i.   [2] Gierke, 19.

none. Aeneas Sylvius at a later time asserted ' a true feudal lordship over all princes and peoples; they all have their temporalities from the Kaiser and owe him obedience; he has a right of correction, may issue commands *pro salute communi*, impose taxes, demand auxiliary troops, right of transit, provisions; he may decide disputes among sovereigns.'[1] Sigismund fully understood the theory of imperial right, although he was gifted with too much strong common-sense to allow him to push it to extremes.

In the second place the new King of the Romans believed, as did every one else, in the unity of the Papacy, but he believed also that it was the duty of the head of the Holy Roman Empire to restore the lost unity.[2] In the eleventh century Cardinal Petrus Crassus had held that it was the right of the Emperor to summon a general council; the Hohenstaufen had enunciated the same doctrine; and in the fourteenth century the same theory had been propounded by that doughty champion of papal rights, Augustinus Triumphus of Ancona.[3] For the last fifteen years Sigismund had evinced his anxiety to see the Great Schism ended, but he believed that this was the work of the Emperor of the Holy Roman Empire rather than of the King of France, whose intervention he dreaded and suspected; and now that he was elected King of the Romans, he was determined that the task should be undertaken under his own auspices, that it was he and no other sovereign who should convoke the council which was practically to put an end to the Schism which had rent Christendom for nearly forty years.

The third fixed idea of the King was the duty of beating back the unbeliever.[4] He had failed in this at Nicopolis; the defeat of Bajazet by the Tartars had averted immediate danger; but with the accession of Muhammad ten years later to sole sway over the Turks the peril to Christendom again became pressing; and it was to win allies for this end that Sigismund was to tarry so long away from Constance and to lose the commanding position and influence which he at first enjoyed in the Council. The King, as Droysen says, might be impulsive and easily accessible to new impressions, but the grandest ideas and the

---

[1] Gierke, 127.   [2] Sauerbrei, 11.   [3] Gierke, 124.
[4] Lindner (*H. and L.*), ii. 297; Sauerbrei, 13.

boldest plans caught firmest hold of him; he might not be persistent in action and determined in resolve, but he could be counted on to seize the happy moment and to dare the unexpected.[1] The tasks of Empire, its perils and its glory, seemed to captivate, to invigorate, to ennoble him. Nothing was more certain than that as King of the Romans he would be a complete contrast to the ineffective Rupert and to the sluggish Wenzel.

Such was the new King; masterful, arbitrary, and occasionally unscrupulous; of strong passions, but having learned the necessity to control them; politic, shrewd, bent on having his own way; essentially, a 'various' man. He was no hero; there were very few heroes in those days; he was of the earth, earthy; he was not cast in a heroic mould nor gifted with grandeur of soul; but he was a born ruler of men; he was neither noble nor magnanimous, but he was masterful and active. He was a man of varied experience, full of energy, determination, and power; a sworn foe to his enemies, a true friend to his friends. To bind the latter to him the more closely, in December 1408 Sigismund instituted the Order of the Dragon, designed especially for Hungary, though the lesser insignia were sometimes bestowed on foreigners. Its members were pledged to fight the infidels and the enemies of the kingdom, to uphold peace and unity, to observe obedience and fidelity to the King, to protect his throne, his Queen, and his children, to maintain the customs and constitution of the realm. The insignia of the new Order were a double chain of gold, bearing a golden cross and a golden dragon; the inscription was '*O quam clemens et misericors est Deus,*' and on the reverse, '*O quam pius et justus.*' The number of members was limited to four-and-twenty; they were entitled to unrestricted access to the King, to a share in the royal counsels, and to a special jurisdiction of five members of the Order for all disputes among themselves. Among the first members were the two Gara brothers, Count Hermann of Cilly, Pippo Span, Count Stibor, Johann of Maroth, and his brother Jacob, Peter von Pereny and others.[2]

In 1408 Sigismund married his second wife, Barbara of Cilly, a tall, handsome girl, sixteen years of age, rather freckled, but

[1] Droysen, 186.   [2] Aschbach, i. 263.

SIGISMUND 91

graceful and svelte, with long fair hair. Barbara was proud of her rank; but though her husband regarded her as a Penelope, she valued him at his right worth, and for all his amours she paid him back in his own coin. She believed in nothing beyond this world and this life, but she believed thoroughly in enjoyment; when she was a widow, she said, she would not mourn like a turtle-dove for her mate, but would live like a pigeon, frolicsome and free; in her more serious moments she declared that she would marry the King of Poland. Handsome Barbara scoffed at her handmaids when they prayed or fasted or did penance; she bade them enjoy themselves in this life, for it was the only one they had. She was all things to all men, if by any means she might win some, and she was quite ready to do the wooing when necessary.[1] She bore a daughter, Elisabeth, to her husband in 1409, but she never had a son.

On the burning question of the day, on the question of the Great Schism, every one knew that Sigismund would do his utmost to bring the unhappy disruption of the Church to a termination. He had taken a determined position since 1396,[2] when he was made Vicar of the Empire by his half-brother Wenzel. The King was invited by Pope Innocent the Seventh to the general council which he designed for ending the Schism; he had interfered energetically on behalf of Pope Gregory the Twelfth in the hope of bringing about a general council under his supervision and he had appealed to that Pope for help against the Turks and the heretics of Bosnia. It was certainly unfortunate that Gregory had sent Sigismund his letter, defending himself against the Council of Pisa just after the King of Hungary had approached Pope John; but, on the other hand, Sigismund had consistently opposed the Council of Pisa on the ground that it was being engineered by and on behalf of the French court; and he never applied for approbation and confirmation of his election to the Pope of the Council. There were indeed very strong reasons against his taking such a step. In the first place, there was the possibility, which was already contemplated by many, that the resignation or reduction of all three Popes might be necessary or advisable in the interest of Holy Church. In the next place Pope John the Twenty-third

[1] Æn. Sylv., 123, 130, 486.   [2] Goeller, 10.

was already sufficiently bound to him by their common enmity to King Ladislas of Naples; this would keep the Pope true to him and there was no need for him to bind himself further. In the third place, Pope John was bound hand and foot to the French alliance; he had been elected through the influence of the French Court, and he was at present engaged in furthering the schemes of Louis, Duke of Anjou; an alliance with France was scarcely a recommendation for an alliance with Germany. It was certain, when once Sigismund was elected King of the Romans, that the question of the termination of the Schism would not be allowed to lie dormant, though it was not certain what line he would take for its solution. It was also clear that he could not take up the question until he had settled his differences with Venice; a war with the Republic was immediately before him. But at any rate the Holy Roman Empire had found in him a master, and Christendom had once again a determined guide.

It was at this crisis that Pope John the Twenty-third made his second false move on the chess-board of European politics. His first mistake had been when his legates set the Gallican Church against him by claiming the papal dues as supported by the civil, by the canon, and by the natural law, thus ruthlessly upholding the claim to exactions against which the Church and the University were ready to fight, tooth and nail. His second mistake was even more serious. The Electors had defined at the Diet of Rhens on the 16th July 1338, the position of the man whom they chose to rule over the Empire; they had defined it still more clearly at the Diet of Frankfurt three weeks later (8th August 1338). 'As soon as any one is elected King by the Electors,' they had said, 'immediately by the election alone he is true King.' There was no need for papal confirmation nor approbation; the crowning at Aachen was a mere formality; the election alone raised the chosen prince to be King of the Romans. This was the constitutional law of the land. The King of the Romans did not become Emperor until he was crowned by the Pope, but he became King without any intervention of the Pope. Charles the Fourth indeed had sought and obtained the papal approbation before he styled himself King or used the royal seal; but in the Golden Bull he had ratified the constitutional law as settled at Rhens and Frankfurt, and the name of the Pope is not mentioned in that enactment. In 1376, when Wenzel was elected King of the Romans, the Pope was informed and his grace and favour solicited, but not his approbation; Wenzel was crowned, he used the royal title and seal without the Pope's approbation being sought for or obtained; the principle of the Golden Rule was scrupulously upheld. When Rupert was elected King of the Romans, he was anxious to obtain the Pope's help against his rival Wenzel; and he accordingly applied for the papal confirmation and approbation. Boniface the Ninth was quick to perceive the advantage which this gave him; for three years the case depended before the Curia; at last, when he thought it perfectly safe, on the 1st October 1403 Boniface confirmed the election; up to that time he had not recognised Rupert as King of the Romans, but only as elected to be King (*electus ad regem*). It would be an immense gain to the Papacy if the election were thus made dependent on the papal confirmation and approbation; and John determined to follow where his patron had led. But he was by no means in so strong a position as Boniface the Ninth, and Sigismund was by no means in so weak a position as Rupert. Boniface had been recognised by the greater part of Christendom as rightful Pope, whereas the greater part of Christendom now saw that the Council of Pisa had failed to establish unity in the Papacy, and John was therefore merely one of three Popes. Rupert again had only been recognised over the western half of Germany, whereas Sigismund was undisputed King of the Romans over the whole country. He took his stand on the constitutional law; he never applied for papal confirmation or approbation of his title as King of the Romans; and Pope John, on the other hand, never recognised him as anything more than elected to be King. Not until the Council of Constance was commencing, when Sigismund sent word of his coronation at Aachen, did John the Twenty-third acknowledge Sigismund to be King of the Romans. The slight was gross and impolitic; it did not tend to conciliate Sigismund, notwithstanding the efforts John had made to secure his election in the first place. Sigismund was firm in his seat; nothing that the Pope could do would displace him; so that the Pope's arrogance in upholding papal pretensions against the law of Germany resulted in evil to none but himself; it tended to alienate the very man whom it behoved him of all others to bind to him as his friend.

Having thus introduced and described the three chief characters in this history, the Pope, the Reformer, and the King, we can now proceed to the orderly sequence of events leading to that conciliar movement, whose volume and force probably no one of the three men at this time accurately gauged or even approximately imagined.

CHAPTER V

ROCCA SECCA

IN the spring of the year 1411 Baldassare Cossa, the strenuous cardinal who had successfully defended the Council of Pisa, whose fate was involved with the future defence of that Council, had been for a year Pope John the Twenty-third ; John Hus, the patriot and church reformer, was at that time the most popular and influential man in Bohemia ; and Sigismund, the stalwart monarch of Hungary, became undisputed King of the Romans. The lives and fortunes of these three men, during the next four years, are strangely and inextricably interwoven ; at the end of that time the first fell and was deposed, the second was burned at the stake, but accomplished more by his death than in his life, while the third lived on to be crowned Emperor and to rule the Holy Roman Empire for another quarter of a century.

The first year of his pontificate, which Pope John the Twenty-third spent in Bologna, was a presage of the trouble in store. There were deaths in his entourage ; the Cardinal of Ravenna died on the 8th October, and the Cardinal of Mileto on the 5th February.[1] A horrible pestilence desolated the city and drove the Pope to the Olivetan Monastery at San Michele in Bosco, on the beautifully wooded hill which lies a mile north of Bologna. Thence he returned on the 14th September to the Castle San Pietro, and on the 14th November he took up his residence in the Galliera Fortress. He moved from here to the Pubblico Palazzo and celebrated the Christmas festivities. Ambassadors meantime came from Rome to escort him to the Eternal City, and early in January Louis of Anjou and Paolo Orsini arrived for the same purpose. On the last day of February the Pope presented the Golden Rose to the Duke of Anjou. The spring

[1] Mur. xviii. 599.

was unpropitious. All through the province the rain poured incessantly; the prices of wheat, barley, and oats rose to famine rates. In Rome also the winter had been hard. A fox and five wolves had been killed in the Viridarium on the 23rd January and their bodies hung on the battlements of Saint Peter's; on the 29th of the same month there was such a storm that the Romans thought the end of the world was at hand.[1]

It was on the 1st April 1411 that Pope John, placing Uguccione de' Contrari in command of the troops, left Bologna. Except his boyhood and the few years which he had spent as private chamberlain to Pope Boniface the Ninth, nearly all his life had been passed in the pleasant city at the extreme edge of the Apennine Hills, but he was now to move south and, as became a Pope, to take up his residence in the foremost city of the antique world. The Marquess of Este accompanied him out of Bologna, the entire College of Cardinals and many chiefs of Italy and France were in his train, the Duke of Anjou and General Paolo Orsini were in command of the armed escort. They travelled through Tuscany without let or hindrance, halting a few days at Siena;[2] and on the 11th April at the hour of vespers they reached the Porta Sancti Pancratii on the Via Aurelia at the entrance to Rome. They remained there that night, heard Mass next morning at the Church of Saint Pancras, and at vespers on the 12th the Pope rode through the Transtiberis quarter, over the island-bridge where the Jews had their stalls, through the ' Field of Flowers ' with the Capitol on the right, across the Bridge of Saint Peter's leading directly to the Vatican. At the foot of the staircase the Pope alighted from his horse, mounted the steps, and made his obeisance to the chief of the Apostles; he entered the church with Duke Louis and the Cardinals, proceeded to the high altar, knelt there in lowly reverence, and then ordered that the sacred handkerchief of Saint Veronica be displayed to the Roman populace who had assembled in the Basilica. The bells were rung throughout the city for a whole week. On Sunday, the 13th April, Pope John celebrated Mass in Saint Peter's; and on the evening of the next day, Easter Monday, two hundred and forty-six of the Roman magistrates and nobles, bearing torches in their hands, visited

[1] Mur. xviii. 599; xxiv. 179, 1023.   [2] *Ibid.* xix. 424.

him to do him homage. Thus did the Pope again take possession of the city from which he had driven the troops of King Ladislas sixteen months previously.

The Pope's departure from Bologna was soon followed by trouble in that city. He had sent Oddo Colonna to be Legate in the Duchy of Spoleto, and had despatched Bishop Branda to conclude the peace between the Poles and the Teutonic Order.[1] In his own place as Papal Legate of Bologna with the rule over the province of Emilia he appointed his old friend and fellow-countryman, Conrad Caracciolo, the man whom he had tried to persuade the Cardinals to elect as Pope. He gave him Luigi da Prato as his counsellor. There was already trouble on the frontiers of the city. Carlo Malatesta had entered the service of the Pope's deadly enemy, King Ladislas of Naples, and on the 16th April he notified the Bolognese that he was about to begin hostilities which, however, would not be to their prejudice.[2] He advanced, ravaging the land as he came, to his castle of San Giovanni in Persiceto. Cardinal Caracciolo tried to persuade him to surrender the castle, but Malatesta had held it since the beginning of the Pope's lordship of Bologna and not unnaturally refused. The Cardinal then tried to take it by force, but the castle was strong, and the Bolognese horse and foot could make no impression on it, when the Papal Legate himself suddenly died.[3] Pope John subsequently appointed Henricus Minultulus, who was also a Neapolitan, to be Papal Legate, but for a time the city was without a ruler, and the force of soldiers in the place was small. There was much discontent and suffering at this time in Bologna; disease and scarcity oppressed the poor, and the influence of the nobles was hateful to many. The moment, which was opportune for a conspiracy, was seized; a revolution followed. The conspirators put Pietro Cassolini at their head. The rising occurred on the 11th May.[4] Seated on a bare-backed horse, with a pennon in his hand, Cassolini raised the cry ' Viva il Popolo e l'Arti '; the conspirators passed through the Piazza and took the Palace. The people followed. They turned out the magistrates and officials; eight Antients and a Gonfalonier of Justice were elected; and envoys were

---

[1] Raynaldus, viii. 330. [2] Finke (*Acta*), 6.
[3] Ghirar, ii. 586; Ciaconius, ii. 810. [4] Mur. xxii. 856; Ghirar, ii. 586.

sent to Venice for corn. Tribunes of the people were elected. The quarrel was with the nobility rather than with the Church; and the Captain of the Pope's troops, Uguccione, was allowed to remain in the city, the annual tribute to the Pope was also to be regularly paid.[1] The suddenness of their attack had rendered it successful, but the people did not feel safe as long as the Galliera Fortress was not in their hands. A deep ditch was run up to the walls within which Luigi da Prato and his soldiers had taken refuge. The garrison was small and insufficiently victualled; and they deemed discretion the better part of valour. They surrendered the fortress, and were allowed to march out with their belongings and a promise of the back pay due to them; while the Commune of Bologna on their side stipulated to render 'true and due obedience' to Pope John.[2] No sooner had the people got possession of the fort than they pulled down the walls and razed it to the ground. Luigi da Prato then went to Rome and reported the disaster to the Pope, who was excessively wroth. Carlo Malatesta again came to his castle of San Giovanni, and the people decided to attempt what the Papal Legate had failed to accomplish. The famine within their walls was so bad that they had only their lives to risk; and an army of fifteen thousand foot soldiers marched out, but they were useless against a strong fortress. The city was obliged to make peace with Carlo, and paid him thirty thousand liras.[3]

For a year Bologna was governed by the Antients and the Tribunes of the people under Pietro Cassolini. In the early months of 1412 the nobles took counsel together, but their conspiracy was discovered, and several of their number were cast into prison, tortured, and put to death. Finally deliverance was wrought through the Pope. He bethought him of one Giacomo Isolano, a doctor of great reputation and authority; and he promised him a cardinal's hat if he could overthrow the government of the Arti and re-introduce the former régime. Isolano knew that the nobility would be on his side; the government of the people was, moreover, rapidly degenerating into tyrannical extortion and injustice; the men in authority had grossly abused their power. Giacomo Isolano went to work

[1] Mur. xxiv. 180.   [2] Ghirar, ii. 587.   [3] Mur. xviii. 600; Ghirar, ii. 588.

secretly and prudently; he got together the nobility and their followers, armed them and hid them; and on the 14th August 1412, at two hours after midnight, he assembled them all in the Piazza, seized the Palace, and successfully effected a counter-revolution. The Antients and Tribunes were deprived of office; some were put to death; Pietro Cassolini and another, the chief offenders, were compelled to disgorge their ill-gotten gains, were imprisoned and then banished.[1] Giacomo Isolano was now in power, supported by the nobles and the Artificers. A third attempt was made to take the castle of San Giovanni in Persiceto, and a third time it was unsuccessful. The position was still precarious, and the Papal Legate, Henricus Minultulus, fearing a popular rising, hid himself in a private house with the intention of escaping to Ravenna. A pestilential fever seized the trembling Cardinal, and pale death carried him off on the 18th May. Shortly afterwards Giacomo Isolano felt that the time had come to make the final move; he sounded his followers and introduced the Bishop of Monte Fiascone into the city; he occupied the Piazza with troops; and on the 23rd September the banners of the Pope and of Holy Church were hung out, the cry of 'Viva la Chiesa' was raised, and the city returned to her old allegiance. At the same time the garrison of San Giovanni in Persiceto sent their keys also to the Bishop and submitted, turning out those soldiers who remained true to Carlo Malatesta. A stately embassy was sent to Pope John at Rome to assure him of the loyalty of the city. He appointed Cardinal Fieschi as Papal Legate, and the Genevese Cardinal made his solemn entry on the 30th October. Henceforward Bologna remained true to the Pope, though Forli was lost to him, having been persuaded by Carlo Malatesta to render obedience to Pope Gregory.

The primary object of Pope John the Twenty-third in coming to Rome was to push on vigorously the war with Naples. It was a critical time. For support outside Italy the Pope looked chiefly to the King of Hungary and to the Duke of Burgundy. Sigismund had already been once, and was soon to be the second time, elected King of the Romans; but he had his hands full at present; and until his pending war with Venice was over he would be unable to attend to the affairs of the Church. Jean

---

[1] Mur. xviii. 601; Ghirar. ii. 592.

100 POPE JOHN THE TWENTY-THIRD

sans Peur, Duke of Burgundy, also saw trouble ahead; for the young Duke of Orleans, nineteen years of age, had just married Anne, daughter of the powerful and warlike Count of Armagnac. On the other hand there was little to trouble the Pope personally in the affairs of Europe just then. The proceedings for the new election were satisfactory; Sigismund, the Pope's candidate, was sure to be elected. In France the trouble caused by his indiscreet envoys had been smoothed down; the Pope had granted the King the right to levy aids on the clergy for three years, and the collation to benefices was arranged to the liking of both King and Pope. The University of Paris was also in agreement with the Pope on this matter, for she needed benefices for her graduates, and found them more readily with the Pope than with the French bishops or with private patrons. There was peace between the Teutonic Order and the Poles. There was no danger at present from the Turks, for the sons of Bajazet were still fighting together. Martin the Humane, Pope Benedict's patron, was still reigning in Aragon; John the Second was King of Castile. The religious trouble in Bohemia did not appear important; a hint to Archbishop Zbynek would ensure compliance and peace. But in Italy itself there was need for immediate action.

The most determined enemy of Pope John the Twenty-third was King Ladislas of Naples. Louis, Duke of Anjou, in right of his father, the adopted son of Queen Joanna of Naples, claimed the kingdom. The Duke was now thirty-two years of age, three years younger than King Ladislas; and when in France last year (1410) he had married his little son, aged seven, to Katharine, daughter of the Duke of Burgundy. If the Pope could overthrow Ladislas and establish Louis in his place, he would feel secure in his temporal power. But for this he had to depend on himself alone. There was no power in Italy to help him. Venice would only be guided by her commercial advantage, and was occupied with the King of Hungary and on the side of King Ladislas. The Republic of Florence, disgusted with the manner in which the Duke of Anjou had mismanaged the war in 1410, fearing that they would have to pay all the troops, and being, moreover, by no means desirous of seeing a strong French rule established in Italy, had made a separate peace with the

King of Naples and had withdrawn from the alliance of the Pope and the Duke. They had already unsuccessfully attempted to induce the Pope and the Duke to make peace with the King; they now renewed that attempt, sending envoys to Ladislas, and at the same time sending them to Carlo Malatesta; but all their efforts for peace were unavailing.[1] War was inevitable.

Louis, Duke of Anjou, was brave with that impetuous French valour which had lost the Battle of Nicopolis. But he was no general; he despised the skilful and cautious tactics of the condottiere leaders; he had left his soldiers without pay in Rome. He was at the end of his resources, and the Pope would have to find funds. An expensive army had been maintained, and practically nothing had been done. This dilatory policy was costly and inexpedient; it by no means jumped with the Pope's humour. He had ordered the levy of a tenth on the revenues of the clergy in France, in Savoy, in Portugal, in parts of Greece and the Islands of the Aegean. He now proceeded to action. On the 23rd April, the Feast of Saint George, he blessed the standards for battle; he appointed the Duke of Anjou to be champion and protector of Holy Church; and on the 28th he delivered the consecrated banners to him and to Paolo Orsini and bade them go forth to war. On the 6th May he sent to their aid fresh troops under Berthold des Ursins and the Florentine general Sforza Attendolo, whom he had taken into his pay. Having thus made all his preparations for war, Pope John was at leisure to think of peace, and he issued his invitations for the coming œcumenical council to meet in April 1412. This was in accordance with the resolution of the Council of Pisa. Rome was named as the place of meeting; and if the war went well, there should be nothing to hinder a goodly assemblage of prelates. But the war was the first object.

Paolo Orsini had been known to the Pope ever since the time when he, as Papal Legate, took command of the troops in 1403, before Bologna, if not earlier. The Pope trusted the general beyond his merits. Paolo Orsini was a skilful soldier, but he had all the worst faults of a condottiere general; he was of the old school which took pride in fighting battles without losing a single soldier on either side or shedding a single drop of blood;[2]

[1] Raumer, 226.   [2] Gozzadini, 28.

he was moreover treacherous in so far that he was constantly ready to desert one employer for another who would pay him better; and he always considered his own interest as a condottiere general before that of the potentate in whose service he was fighting. On one occasion he stopped the French troops from following up an advantage, telling them that it was not the custom of the country to kill too many of the enemy.[1] Albeit he was, says the old French chronicler, a valiant man-at-arms, and powerful among the people and his friends, for he was of the greatest lineage there was, and he led the van with certain Frenchmen whom the King of Sicily, Louis of Anjou, brought with him.[2]

A man of quite a different kidney was Sforza Attendolo, a man for whom Baldassare Cossa had exhibited great friendship and familiarity when he was Legate of Bologna. Sforza Attendolo and Braccio da Montone were the leaders of the two new schools of condottiere soldiers, who had taken their rise from the Constable Alberico da Barbiano, the general who first taught the Italians to depend on themselves and to dispense with the aid of the accursed foreign mercenaries.[3] Sforza's parents were peasants; he was one of twenty-one sons; a native of Cotignola, which is near Barbiano. His name was Muzio Attendolo; his muscular strength brought him the name of Sforza. He was born on the 28th May 1369; so that he was about the same age as John Hus, and a year younger than Pope John and Sigismund. His youth had been spent with hoe and mattock; but the boy was dissatisfied; he dreamed of a life at arms. One day in the fields he threw his axe at a lofty oak-tree, resolving that, if it stuck, he would be a soldier, and that if it fell, he would remain a peasant. The axe stuck, and Sforza founded the ducal house of the Sforzas at Milan. He was tall, above the ordinary height, broad-chested, and slim-waisted, a man beautifully formed in all his members. His face was dark and swarthy, and his deep-set, gleaming eyes gave him a leonine appearance, very terrible to his enemies. To his friends he was kind and affable; to his soldiers he was ever thoughtful of their comfort; in adversity he was cheerful and confident.[4]

[1] Juvenal, 203.   [2] *Ibid*. 208.   [3] Gozzadini, 31.
[4] Mur. xix. 727.

ROCCA SECCA

Sforza was a born general, a leader much superior to Paolo Orsini.

The papal generals took their way toward Capua. King Ladislas, who was an able leader and beloved by his soldiers, knew of their coming and was prepared to meet them; he had thirteen thousand horsemen to their twelve thousand. In the hilly country which overlooks the Pontine Marshes towards Terracina, the hostile armies approached within five or six miles of each other; they were camped near the village of Ceprano; and the river Garigliano, joined by the little stream of the Liri, and swollen with the floods of spring, rushed between them. The river washes the base of the mountain on which is the citadel named after the village of Rocca Secca, the birthplace of Saint Thomas Aquinas. The army of King Ladislas was on the inner side, between the river and the hilly ground, while that of Louis was encamped on the opposite bank. So they remained for several days. The stammering, red-haired libertine, although he was a skilful general and beloved by his troops, was not a brave soldier; he was still as much a coward at heart as when craven fear of his father's fate had ruined his chance of the crown of Hungary; he was anxious to avoid a pitched battle and held back his soldiery. In the event of a hand-to-hand fight it was his custom to select a few cavaliers of known courage and fidelity, and to arm them at all points like himself; he hoped that the sight of these men in royal armour, these counterfeit presentments of himself, would rouse courage in different parts of his own force and would strike dismay into different parts of the enemy. There were those who attributed the artifice to a simpler motive.

The two armies were no sooner face to face than a quarrel broke out among the Duke's generals. Sforza wished to attack the enemy at once; Paolo Orsini thought that a fight should be avoided and that the war should be conducted in the usual dilatory method. Sforza, however, persuaded the Duke, and the necessary dispositions were made. King Ladislas watched his enemy in fancied security. On the 18th May, in chivalric fashion, he sent to the Duke a letter of defiance, inquiring when the battle would be joined. He felt sure that the rushing torrent of the Garigliano was a sufficient protection against his enemy.

The Duke rewarded the messenger and sent him back, but discovered a ford. Braccio da Montone, with fifteen hundred men, was despatched to make a reconnaissance; he met Tartaglia, the captain of the vanguard of Ladislas, who, with two thousand troops, was on a similar errand. There was a sharp encounter from which the French returned victorious. The Duke held it to be a favourable omen and determined to attack the unsuspecting enemy on the morrow.

The next afternoon, at the hour of vespers, when the Neapolitan army was taking its evening meal, Duke Louis led his soldiers across the river and fell upon the enemy unawares. Louis de Logny led the van; the Marquess of Controne, the Senechal of Eu, and other French nobles were with the troops.[1] It was a total surprise; the tents were pitched, the tables spread, the gold and silver plate laid out for a banquet for Ladislas, the soldiers were eating their food, when suddenly the French were on them. The King was panic-stricken; he hastily armed six cavaliers at all points like himself; he placed Count Sergian Caracciolo over them on account of his valour and fidelity; and he sent them forth to the fray.[2] The French soldiers came on with terrible shouts, which were answered by the enemy, and re-echoed by the hills around; a flight of arrows hurtled through the air, but there was little generalship on either side; the fight was immediately at close quarters, and the Neapolitans had been caught off their guard. Nevertheless it was a desperate struggle; for full three hours swords flashed, daggers gleamed, and battle-axes crashed on the heads of foes; it looked as if fire from heaven had fallen on the troops of Naples until, as the sun went down, they lost heart, gave way, turned and fled. The slaughter of horse and foot was great. The Legate of Pope Gregory was captured; so too were the Count of Carrara and his son, the Counts of Arpino, Celano, Loreto, and others; in all ten counts, many other Neapolitan nobles, and hundreds of men of lesser note were taken prisoners and held to ransom. King Ladislas fled for his life to the Castle of Rocca Secca, a few miles distant, situated on a height above the village which has given its name to the fight. Count Caracciolo met the King here. His royal coat, sky-blue

---

[1] *Religieux*, iv. 392.   [2] Mazella, 187; Mur. xxii. 23; Hardt, ii. 363.

and worked with golden lilies, had been torn off by the enemy; his breastplate, dinted with many a blow, had been abandoned at the tents; his golden helmet had been seized by the foe who thought they had captured the King; and he had himself finally escaped, his face bathed in blood.[1] Duke Louis of Anjou had won a great battle and King Ladislas was defeated. The conflict had been of the fiercest; it had been waged entirely by the troops under Sforza and the French contingent; Paolo Orsini had only appeared at the end of the day; as King Ladislas afterwards said to Sforza Attendolo, 'It was you with those horsemen of yours that routed me at Rocca Secca.'[2]

The conquering troops were allowed to rush, as mercenaries ever will, to glut themselves with booty. The tents of Ladislas were pillaged; the gold and silver plate was taken; the soldiers were rich from the loot and from the thirty thousand horses which they had captured.[3] The standards of King Ladislas and of Pope Gregory, which had fallen into the hands of the victors, were sent to Pope John at Rome. The Pope was overjoyed at the victory of Rocca Secca, fought on the Day of Saint Yves, the 19th May 1411; he thought that the object of the war was now accomplished, and that Louis instead of Ladislas was the future King of Naples; he hung the captured banners from the towers of Saint Peter's for all Rome to see; he ordered a solemn procession in which he himself, with the cardinals and prelates, took part; the Neapolitan banners were dragged along in the mud, and all the people shouted, 'Long live the Sovereign Pontiff and the victorious King Louis of Sicily.'[4] A rude awakening was soon to come. Hitherto Baldassare Cossa had been man and master of his fate; Rocca Secca was the tide in his affairs which, taken at the flood, had perchance led him on to fortune; omitted, all the after voyage of his life was bound in shallows and in miseries. Even while the rejoicings were in progress, there sounded a note of evil fortune; the news came that Carlo Malatesta had occupied nearly the whole of the Province Emilia,[5] and that the Papal Legate was a fugitive from Bologna. Worse news was soon to come.

[1] Mur. xxii. 23. [2] *Ibid.* xix. 650-2. [3] *Ibid.* xxiv. 180.
[4] Lenfant (*P.*), ii. 54; Hardt, ii. 364; *Religieux*, iv. 394. [5] Anton, iii. 477.

Had the ducal troops followed up their victory of Rocca Secca, they could have captured Ladislas, have overrun his kingdom, and the war would have been at an end. This, as was universally acknowledged, is what they should have done; and it was what Sforza would have done; it was what Louis, Duke of Anjou, who was in supreme command, should have insisted on. The traitor was again Paolo Orsini. He and Sforza had a great quarrel, but Orsini refused to recall the soldiery to follow the fugitives; he allowed them to go on with their pillaging. Paolo Orsini did not wish to see either Ladislas or the Duke so powerful that they could do without his help; once more he set his own interest as a condottiere general above his manifest duty to his employer.[1] After all, it was the business of the Duke of Anjou to decide the difference between the two generals and to see that the victory was properly utilised; he threw away the gift which the gods had cast into his lap, and he paid for his faults with the crown of Naples. He was, as Montaigne said later of the King of Spain after Saint Quentin, ' unworthy that ever fortune should cast so great a good into his lap: for what profit had he of it, if notwithstanding he give his enemie leasure and meanes to recover himself ? ' This was exactly what Louis did. He even allowed the prisoners to escape.[2] No one was more astonished at this utter want of strategy than was King Ladislas. He had expected to be pursued to Rocca Secca; he was allowed time to recover from his misfortune. ' On that day,' he said, ' I had lost my life and my kingdom; on the morrow I had saved my life but had still lost my kingdom; on the third day I had lost neither the one nor the other, but had regained them both.' [3]

Like our own King William the Third, Ladislas was a great man at making the best of a defeat. His troops began to rally at San Germano; the King occupied the passes; advance became impossible to the ducal troops; and Ladislas was soon in as strong a position as ever. The Duke had sent eight large ships and twenty galleys toward Naples in support of the expedition by land; but this fleet was beaten by the six ships and seven galleys of Ladislas. Nicolo Ruffo was warring in Calabria on behalf of the French Duke, but he also was defeated;

[1] Ammirato, v. 21.   [2] Blumenthal, 63.   [3] Mur. xix. 927; Anton, iii. 477.

Cortone and Catanzaro were taken from him, and he was
obliged to leave Italy and to make his way back to Provence.
At all points the Duke was worsted; in spite of his grand
victory he was defeated; his troops were short of provisions,
they could not live upon the country, and sickness broke out
among them; they had accumulated plenty of booty but
they demanded their back pay. When Pope John was expecting to hear of the capture of Naples, the news came that
Ladislas was in possession of all the passes, and that the Duke
in despair was leading back his army to Rome.[1] The disappointment was terrible, not only because it was so unexpected, but because it was so undeserved. On the 12th July
Louis of Anjou re-entered Rome.[2] His expedition was at an
end, and nothing remained for him but to return to France.
Once again he appealed to Pope John for money, but was told
that the Pope was as poor as he was. On the 3rd August he
was conducted by the cardinals to his galleys at Ripa Granda,
but not a single Roman baron was to be found in his escort;
he embarked for Ostia, and sailed thence back to Provence.
He reached Paris on the 11th January,[3] and died in France five
years later, without making any further attempt to recover the
crown of Naples.[4]

Now that King Ladislas's beard had been singed, it was
necessary to prepare for the revenge which that monarch would
not be slow to take. Pope John entrenched himself in the
Vatican, and ordered the magistrates to ensure the safety of the
Leonine City by constructing a walled-in passage from the
Palace to Sant Angelo.[5] His next thought was to raise money.
He enforced loans from the wealthy nobles and citizens; he
tried to raise the tax on wine from fifty to a hundred thousand
florins, though there had been great scarcity of wine during the
previous year; he levied a tax on all shoeing smiths, horse
marshals, and on potters and other artificers; he altered the
currency; he was at his wits' end to procure the necessary sinews
of war. All these measures naturally created considerable discontent; the merchants complained that they could not sell;
the shopkeepers closed their shops; the Romans were as

[1] Raynaldus, viii. 334.   [2] Mur. xxiv. 1026.   [3] Juvenal, 237.
[4] Sismondi, v. 298.   [5] Mur. xxiv. 1026.

delighted as ever at shows and processions, but as ready as ever to resist taxation.[1]

Pope John was at last convinced of the utter selfishness, if not treachery, of Paolo Orsini; he saw that the fruits of the victory had been lost through his criminal inaction, when a very different end to the campaign would have ensued had the advice of Sforza been followed. But he could not bring himself to dismiss from his service the old friend who had jousted with him at Bologna. At the same time he would not trust him at Rome or in the vicinity of King Ladislas. Carlo Malatesta was now a declared enemy, and it was necessary to send troops against him. Cardinal Giordano Orsini was sent as Papal Legate of the Ancona and Romagna borders, and Paolo Orsini with his army was sent with him. On the other hand the Pope recognised the ability of Sforza Attendolo and was anxious to bind that leader to himself. Fourteen thousand ducats were due to him for his military services, and the Pope devised a means of payment which was profitable to himself and pleasing to Sforza. He made the peasant's son Lord of Cotignola, and raised his native place to the dignity of a countship. Pope John doubtless thought that he had bound over Sforza by the tie of gratitude. But a disastrous fire broke out in Cotignola soon after it became a countship; and its Lord was acute enough to see that he could never have his own way so long as Paolo Orsini remained in the Pope's service. Had the Pope chosen between them and had he rejected the worse man, Sforza would have remained faithful; but now it was clear that he would be in a subordinate position, while if his services were transferred to King Ladislas, the military power of the King of Naples would be superior to that of the Pope of Rome. Sforza preferred to be first in Naples rather than second in Rome.[2] The Pope sent Cardinal Angelus de Anna to him with thirty-six thousand pieces of gold. Sforza inquired whether this was for past or for future service. The Cardinal answered that it was for the future, but that all arrears should be discharged as soon as God sent better times to the Pope. The general refused to take the money; he was indignant; he felt himself exposed to the outrage of Paolo Orsini, who had killed the general Mostarda with his own hand,

[1] Ciaconius, ii. 787.   [2] Mur. xxi. 104-5.

and who was unrestrained and all-powerful. He returned the gold and declined any longer to remain his debtor's general; his term was up and henceforth he owed no further allegiance to Pope John. 'I am leaving Rome,' he declared, 'because I do not trust Paolo Orsini.' He marched off with his horse and foot and joined the King of Naples. Thus Pope John lost and Ladislas gained the best general of the time.[1]

[1] Mur. xix. 654; xxi. 105-6.

CHAPTER VI

A CREATION OF CARDINALS

At the commencement of the month of June 1411, with King Ladislas triumphant in the south and Carlo Malatesta triumphant in the north, Pope John the Twenty-third must have felt that in Italy the toils were closing round him. Naples was absolutely lost; Bologna was in revolt; Venice and Florence were allied with Ladislas; Milan obeyed neither Pope nor Kaiser. Rome, for the present, was true to him; but in Rome the Pope did not feel secure. It was emphatically a time at which he had need of aid and counsel; and it was the function of the cardinals, in addition to assisting him at certain liturgical services, to counsel and aid him in the government of the Church.[1] But the number of the sacred college was small and was diminishing. There had been twenty-three cardinals alive, but only sixteen in Italy, when he was elected Pope. Four of these had died during the first year of his pontificate.[2] Among these was the aged Guy de Maillesec, Cardinal of Poitiers, the only member who had received his hat before the Great Schism had commenced. Another was Giovanni de' Megliorati, the nephew of Pope Innocent the Seventh. A third was his old friend Conrad Caracciolo, who had been with him in Bologna, and whom he had tried to get the cardinals to elect on the death of Alexander the Fifth. Five others were to die before the end of 1412; they were Antonius Calvus the Roman, popular in the city, who had stuck so long to Pope Gregory the Twelfth; Nicolaus Brancacius, who had been in like manner faithful to Benedict the Thirteenth; Antonio Caetani, Cardinal of Aquileia, who had been promoted at the same time as the Pope himself; Henricus Minultulus, the Papal Legate at Bologna; and Francesco Uguccione, the Archbishop of Bordeaux. Considering the four deaths, the failing health of others, the

[1] C.E., iii. 337.   [2] Ciaconius, ii. 810.

A CREATION OF CARDINALS

fact that two were absent on legatine duty, the number of cardinals who were in Rome and who were able to give the Pope aid and counsel had fallen very low. On the 6th June 1411, Pope John the Twenty-third made his first creation of cardinals. The list of new names is very noteworthy.

One of the besetting sins of the Popes of that time was nepotism. Urban the Sixth had protected and favoured his shameless nephew Butillo. Innocent the Seventh had made one of his nephews a cardinal; he had given the command of the Papal troops to another nephew, Ludovico, who had murdered eleven notable Romans in cold blood. Nepotism of the most open and unblushing character had ruined the finances and the good resolutions of Gregory the Twelfth. But against John the Twenty-third the charge of nepotism was never raised. Yet the Pope was one of a large family. One of his brothers was the Admiral Gaspar Cossa. Another brother was one of the three ' orators ' whom Alexander the Fifth had sent to Venice.[1] A third brother, as we know,[2] lived at Rome when Baldassare Cossa was appointed as Papal Legate to Bologna. Two of his sailor brothers had been captured by King Ladislas and condemned to death, and were only saved by the urgent intercession of Pope Boniface the Ninth. So recently as 1410 the same King had imprisoned the Pope's brothers at Naples.[3] The Pope also had sisters, and he promoted the son of one of them to be a cardinal. This was Thomas Brancacius, the only one of the new cardinals who had a bad record. It was said of him that he was fonder of arms and women than became a good churchman, and that he bore on his face a scar received in a brawl at night. But he belonged to the same family as Cardinal Nicolaus Brancacius;[4] and if, as seems probable, it was this nephew whom the Pope sent with Pippo Span to the King of Hungary, when endeavouring to effect a peace with Venice, then the new cardinal must have been a man of ability to be entrusted with so delicate a mission. Even his enemy, Dietrich von Niem, does not charge Pope John with nepotism, but admits that all the cardinals whom he raised to the purple were distinguished either for their birth or their learning.[5]

[1] Mur. xxii. 847.   [2] Hardt, ii. 346.   [3] Mur. (*A.*), ix. 58.
[4] Ciaconius, ii. 675, 803.   [5] Hardt, ii. 367.

Six only of the remaining cardinals were Italians. Francescus Landus was a Venetian patrician, a doctor of the civil and the canon law, who had taken part in the Council of Pisa and had been made Patriarch of Constantinople by Alexander the Fifth. Antonius Pancera de Portogruario had been made Patriarch of Aquileia at the time that his uncle, Antonio Caetani, had been made cardinal; he had been deprived of the dignity and reduced to poverty by Gregory the Twelfth, and was now created Cardinal of Saint Susanna by Pope John. Alaman Adimar, a noble Florentine, had been Bishop of Florence in 1400, and was made Archbishop of Pisa in the following year; he had taken a prominent part in the Council of Pisa; and had subsequently been sent as Papal Legate to France, where he was when the news of his promotion reached him. He was a man who loved the men of Pisa, and who was loved by them and looked upon as their father.[1] Branda de Castellio was a noble Milanese, a celebrated jurisconsult, who had been summoned to the University of Pavia by Gian Galeazzo Visconti, who had later been sent as Papal Legate to Germany by Boniface the Ninth, and had been rewarded for his services with the bishopric of Piacenza; he had lost the bishopric when he abandoned Gregory the Twelfth in 1408; he was now created Cardinal-Priest of Saint Clement. Lucio de Comitibus, the Protector of the Order of Saint John of Jerusalem, was the son of Hildebrand, a noble of Rome. Perhaps the most celebrated of the new Italian cardinals was Francesco Zabarella, a man with an European reputation, and certainly the most famous Italian prelate of his day. He was a native of Padua, and after the fall of the House of Carrara, he had been entrusted by his fellow-citizens to carry the keys of the city to the Signory of Venice. Especially eminent for his eloquence and his knowledge of the canon and the civil law, he was also well read in poetry and history; he won renown for his lectures in law, but he also taught the liberal arts, natural philosophy and oratory. He had been elected Bishop of Padua, but was promoted by Pope John to the more important diocese of Florence. On the burning question of the Schism, he held that it was the duty of the Emperor to convoke a general council, and in 1408 he wrote a

[1] Ciaconius, ii. 799.

A CREATION OF CARDINALS 113

treatise affirming that such a council had the right to depose the rival popes. There was no prelate whose promotion to the sacred college was more welcomed, or reflected greater honour on the Pope.[1] No sooner was he made cardinal than, as already mentioned, Zabarella was appointed to the commission of four cardinals to whom was intrusted the process of John Hus. Much was expected of this commission and, as Zabarella was a careful and painstaking man, it is a pity that he was not allowed to finish a work which was peculiarly perplexed and intricate and needed careful and delicate handling.[2]

Seven of the new cardinals were chosen from countries outside Italy. John, the Archbishop of Lisbon, was promoted at the request of the King of Portugal, whose counsellor he was. George of Lichtenstein was of a noble German family, and had been Bishop of Trent since 1391; he was a thorn in the side of Friedrich of the Tirol, but was a friend of Sigismund, and it was probably as a compliment to the King that he was offered the rank of cardinal; but he never came to Rome to receive his hat. Two of the new cardinals were Englishmen. Thomas Langley,[3] who was educated at Cambridge and in his youth attached to John of Gaunt, who made him his executor, was made Canon of York in 1400 and Dean next year. On the 14th March 1405, on the resignation of Bishop Beaufort, he became Chancellor of England. Later, in the same year, the chapter elected him to the Archbishopric of York, but Pope Innocent the Seventh, offended by the execution of the previous Archbishop Scrope, annulled the election, though he appointed him to be Bishop of Durham in the following year.[4] Langley was an ' able and prudent statesman, and is said to have been a good canonist, and otherwise well educated.' He built two hostels, and founded two grammar schools. He was employed on divers important missions of diplomacy. In 1409 he attended the Council of Pisa, ' accompanied by a splendid escort.' But he never appeared at Rome to take his cardinal's hat, as the King of England could not spare him.[5] The other English prelate was Robert Hallam or Hallum,[6] who became Archdeacon of

---

[1] Ciaconius, ii. 804-5; Valois, iv. 57, 229. [2] Berger, 74.
[3] *Circ.* 1370-1437. [4] May 17, 1406.
[5] *D.N.B.*, xxxii. 112-3; Wylie, ii.-iv. *passim.* [6] 1360 to 1370-1417.

H

Canterbury in 1400 and Chancellor of the University of Oxford in 1403. In 1405 the Pope had nominated him Archbishop of York, but King Henry the Fourth objected; and in the year following Hallam gave up all his preferments and went to Rome. On the 22nd June 1407 Gregory the Twelfth appointed him to be Bishop of Salisbury, and consecrated him at Siena. Of Hallam it was said that he loved not the death of a sinner, but rather that he should turn from his wickedness and live. He had rendered yeoman's service at the Council of Pisa, as has been already narrated.[1] The appointments of Langley and Hallam may have been only complimentary. King Henry wrote at once to the Pope asking that they might be allowed ' to decline the honour, on the ground of their great value to him as counsellors at home.' [2]

The remaining three cardinals were Frenchmen. It was the French government and the University of Paris which had hitherto been most prominent in their endeavours to end the Great Schism; and the appointment of these three French prelates shows that Pope John was fully sensible of the influence which France still possessed, and was anxious to enlist it on his side. It was at this moment that he granted to the French King the right to take aids from the clergy of his realm for three years in extension of the period expiring on the 1st October 1412. It was the French government which, beyond all others, had supported the Council of Pisa, and the Pope desired its aid still to uphold the authority of that Council. It would be an immense aid to him if he were able to get the support of the leading French theologians. He did not offer a hat to Jean Gerson, but the three whom he selected were men of mark and influence. They were Fillastre, Des Champs, and D'Ailly.

Guillaume Fillastre, the witty Dean of Reims, had been one of the brilliant escort selected to accompany the Duke of Orleans to Avignon in 1398; he had taken a prominent part in the fourth Council of Paris, where he had incurred the royal displeasure by his defence of Pope Benedict; he was at that time of the opinion, which he afterwards recanted, that all Christendom united had not the right to judge the sovereign pontiff;

---

[1] *In the Days of the Councils*, 354-5, 358-9.
[2] *D.N.B.*, xxiv. 99; Wylie, iii. 95.

A CREATION OF CARDINALS 115

he was a member of the imposing embassy sent by the King and the clergy of France to Pope Benedict the Thirteenth in 1407. He was now made a cardinal-deacon, but was soon raised to be Cardinal-priest of Saint Mark.[1]

Of greater note in France was Gilles des Champs, 'the sovereign Doctor of Theology.' He was a member of the Faculty of Theology in the University of Paris, and was Rector of the College of Navarre in succession to Pierre d'Ailly, whose pupil he had been. From the first he had been eager in all schemes for ending the Schism. In 1393, preaching for the University, he reminded the King that actions were worth more than prayers. After the ten thousand notes had been dropped in the coffer in the Cloister of the Mathurins, Des Champs was one of those who indited the famous letter to the King [2] on the three ways of ending the Schism. In the embassy of the royal dukes to Pope Benedict the Thirteenth, it was to Gilles des Champs that the opening discourse was entrusted, and he had expounded to the Pope the advantages of the 'way of cession.' That embassy had failed, as also next year failed the embassy of the Three Kings, in which Gilles des Champs again unfolded the same tale to the determined little Spaniard. In the third Council of Paris he had broken the wonderful unanimity of the French clergy by expressing a doubt whether it was lawful for them to subtract their obedience from a Pope who had not been condemned by an œcumenical council; he was a man who had the courage of his opinions even in face of overwhelming numbers. He was one of those who were sent to treat with Pope Benedict in 1399 at Avignon, and one of those who represented the King of France at the Diet of Frankfurt in 1400. He had been in Rome when Pope Innocent the Seventh died, and tried to procure the postponement of any fresh election. He was one of the members of the great embassy to Benedict the Thirteenth in 1407 to urge for the last time the 'way of cession' on that pontiff. In France he had filled the posts of Bishop of Coutance and of King's almoner. At the Council of Pisa he had given evidence against the French Pope. He was undoubtedly one of the ablest men in the Church in France; and the Pope now nominated him cardinal, but he never

[1] Valois, iii. 207, 460 *et seq.*   [2] *Religieux*, ii. 136-82.

received the title nor the scarlet hat as he never appeared at any public consistory at Rome.¹

In every way the foremost and most important of the new cardinals was Pierre d'Ailly, the Bishop of Cambrai. The details of his life, up to the Council of Pisa, have been sketched in the former work, *In the Days of the Councils*, and it is therefore unnecessary to recapitulate them here. Pierre d'Ailly, Jean Charlier de Gerson, and Nicolas de Clamanges were the three shining stars of the College of Navarre; and after his great pupil, the Chancellor of the University, D'Ailly was the foremost churchman of his time in Europe. Though a man of strenuous convictions, he had not the moral earnestness of the Chancellor, and Pierre d'Ailly would not have dared to preach the sermon with which, at the Feast of Epiphany in 1403, Gerson strove to awaken the conscience of Pope Benedict the Thirteenth. He had known the charm of the handsome little pontiff, and from the beginning the difficulties of the situation were more patent to his political and discriminating intellect than they were to Simon de Cramaud and the hot-headed members of the Norman nation in the University of Paris. Pierre d'Ailly was in earnest on the matter of reform, as is proved by his *Capita Agendorum*; for two hundred years after his death his proposals were quoted by the Protestants; but he was a practical reformer of an intelligent and rational kind. He disapproved of the multiplication of images and pictures in churches, of the solemnisation of new festivals, of the building of new sacred edifices when so many were in ruins, of the canonisation of new saints, of the prohibition of all work on feast days.² He was fully alive to the evils of simony, not only to the evils of the simony of the Roman Curia, which hit principally the bishops and abbots, but the simony of bishops and archdeacons, which hit the secular clergy, and the simony of parish priests which hit their poor parishioners. He knew that through the spread of this vice there were many under the ban of excommunication because they were unable to pay for justice, that there were hundreds of poor priests wandering about the country as beggars, that there were scores of corpses lying in the fields ' unhouseled, disappointed, unaneled, no reckoning

---

¹ Ciaconius, ii. 804; Valois, iii. *passim*.   ² Finke (*F.*), 103.

A CREATION OF CARDINALS 117

made,' because the relatives could not pay for Christian burial; and he longed to right these iniquities. But he was, above all, a conservative reformer; he desired a reform from within the bosom of the Church itself. The hierarchical building was to him as the ark of the covenant on which he would lay no impious hand; though he did not believe in the infallibility of the Pope, he believed in the infallibility of the Church, and would yield his own opinion to the finding of a general council. He was alien alike from the ultra-conservative party of the Curia, and from such radical reformers as Dietrich von Niem; but he was heart and soul in unison with such men as the Brethren of the Common Life and he protected the Monastery at Windesheim. Though he had been apprehensive from the beginning, still the failure of the Council of Pisa was a bitter disappointment to him; he determined, if the Church Universal lacked reform in its head and its members, to reform thoroughly his own diocese; though he was sixty years of age, he was still full of work and energy. From Pisa he returned to Cambrai, and plunged into the work there; he consecrated chapels; though the defender of the Immaculate Conception was not free from superstition, he tested thoroughly all signs and wonders, and harried mercilessly those sons of perdition, the Brethren of the Free Spirit. He was interested in the science of his time; he desired to reform the calendar; he wrote a tractate on physical geography, the *Imago Mundi*, which inspired Christopher Columbus, and another against the superstitions of astrology, the *Tractatus de legibus et sectis contra superstitiosos astronomos*. As a theologian, D'Ailly was not a deep or profound thinker, but of a nimble and ready wit, seizing an idea or following an argument to its furthest consequences, sometimes to an absurdity. He was an ardent student of divine philosophy, knowing the Vulgate from end to end, and interpreting it after the school of William of Ockham; he preached dogmatic theology rather than the gospel of morality; he had all a theologian's fine contempt for the civil and the canon law, emanations of human wit, rendering the children of this generation in their day wiser than the children of light; he preferred the Law of Nature and the Law of God.[1] He knew Latin like

[1] Tschackert, Appendix, 19.

his mother tongue, though he never wrote it with the Ciceronian diction of Nicolas de Clamanges. He was well read in all patristic lore ; he was acquainted with the Franciscan writers from John of Paris to Henry of Langenstein ; he knew the mystics from Dionysius the Areopagite to Bonaventura ; he had studied the classics, and the Greek and Arabian philosophers of the Middle Ages in Latin translations. With all this weight of learning he was eminently a practical man, not ashamed of occasional judicious flattery ; he could recognise an abuse, but he saw also its occasional utility ; he was unwilling to abolish first-fruits until an equivalent source of income for the Curia could be found. Throughout his life he was a loyal Frenchman, an upholder of authority, a stickler for the ancient paths. He devoted himself pre-eminently to questions of Church government and reform, and was conservative with a tendency to liberalism. John the Twenty-third had met Pierre d'Ailly at Pisa ; he knew and appreciated him. The Pope saw that a struggle was coming, and that in that struggle Pierre d'Ailly would be a great force on one side or the other. If John, like Benedict, could win the Bishop, could procure him for his friend and defender, then his extensive learning, his rich experience of the Church, the Court, and the University, his acquaintance with Church policy, and the elasticity of his character would render him an invaluable supporter.[1] The Pope therefore offered to raise him to the purple, but the Bishop deliberated for some time before accepting the dignity ; ' tam sublimem dignitatem diu acceptare distuli,' he says, ' meque indignum multis rationibus excusavi.'[2] Before he proceeded to Rome he addressed to the Pope a letter [3] in which he points out that it is the duty of the Church of Rome, the head of all, to reform itself first ' in justice and morals ' before proceeding to the reformation of its members. This certainly betokened that the new cardinal meant to keep a free hand. Pierre d'Ailly had been disappointed in Pope Benedict, and he did not mean to bind himself hand and foot to Pope John.[4]

Such were the fourteen prelates whom Pope John the Twenty-third desired to promote to the purple. His aim was

[1] Tschackert, 170.   [2] *Ibid.* Appendix, 36.
[3] Gerson, ii. 882-3.   [4] Tschackert, 336-47.

A CREATION OF CARDINALS 119

to surround himself with men of knowledge and power. Though he kept one eye on the coming struggle for supremacy, his candidates were by no means blind adherents; some, the English, the French, and more than one of the Italian prelates, were men of conspicuous brilliancy and known force of character; and it would be necessary to go back for a long series of years to find a selection more renowned for merit and ability. Certain of them were men who were determined to put an end to the accursed trinity of Popes. Fortunately for them there was now at the head of the Holy Roman Empire a monarch who, as soon as his hands were free, was equally ready to do his part, who was determined to effect what was universally regarded as an indispensable preliminary to the reform of the Church, to restore the long lost unity of the Papacy.

A consistory was held on the 9th August 1411. Four of the new nominees never became cardinals; and Pierre d'Ailly did not come to Rome until the following year. Exactly who were present at this senate of the cardinals is not known. The most pressing business before them was the war with Ladislas, and the expected siege of Rome. Help was needed, and there was no help to be expected at this juncture from the King of the Romans, nor from the Court of France, nor from the Republics of Florence and Venice. By the advice of the College Pope John took up the process against the King of Naples where Pope Alexander had left it; he cited him to appear on the 9th December, and pronounced sentence of excommunication against him in the event of his failure; he preached a crusade, calling on the faithful of all nations for aid against the usurper. At the same time he proclaimed a crusade against the Moors in Spain.[1] The call to arms fell, however, on idle ears. Very few red-cross knights from France answered the appeal;[2] no white-cross knights arrived from England, for the King sent his troops rather to aid the Burgundians in France; the crusade in Spain was regarded merely as a political move against Pope Benedict the Thirteenth; nothing came of an attempt to capture Avignon;[3] and in Bohemia the preaching of the crusade and the issue of indulgences had a most disastrous result.

[1] Raynaldus, viii. 323, 334.   [2] *Religieux*, iv. 608.   [3] Blumenthal,

120 POPE JOHN THE TWENTY-THIRD

The preaching of a crusade against a Christian prince was perhaps barely constitutional. A crusade was originally an expedition undertaken, in fulfilment of a solemn vow, to deliver the Holy Places from Mohammedan tyranny; though ' since the Middle Ages the meaning of the word had been extended to include all wars undertaken in pursuance of a vow, and directed against infidels, *i.e.* against Muhammadans, pagans, heretics, or those under the ban of excommunication.'[1] In this sense of the word, crusades had been preached against John Lackland and Frederic the Second, so that there were precedents for the present action of the Consistory. To all those who should assist in purse or person the usual plenary indulgence was offered. They were to receive ' pardon for all their sins, remission of pain and guilt, and a passage for their souls straight to heaven without the pain of purgatory.'[2] Two hundred years earlier, as Villehardouin tells us, because the indulgence was so great, the hearts of men were much moved, and many took the cross for the greatness of the pardon. It was hoped that the same result would follow now, but the times were altered. At the time of the fourth crusade no one doubted the efficacy of an indulgence. Even now, though knights might not serve in their persons, the simple might contribute of their means. In the doctrine of indulgences, as understood by the Catholic Church, there is nothing pernicious, but much that is beneficial. For an indulgence is of no effect unless the sin has already been forgiven through contrition and confession. An indulgence is simply the remission of the temporal punishment which remains due to sin, after its guilt and eternal punishment have been remitted in the sacrament of penance;[3] and plenary indulgences, which cancel all temporal punishment due to sin, could be granted by the Pope alone. The qualifications as to contritions and confession were attached to the present pardons; ' but there can be no doubt that in practice they bleared men's eyes, and were often regarded as selling them leave to sin.'[4] The indulgences were sent to every Christian country for sale, and among others to Bohemia, and it was here that a violent outburst of popular indignation was aroused, so that the old religious trouble broke forth afresh.

[1] *C.E.*, iv. 543. [2] Wylie, iii. 471. [3] Pastor, vii. 334. [4] Wylie, iii. 472.

A CREATION OF CARDINALS 121

The arbitration award formulated by King Wenzel on the 6th July 1411 [1] had brought peace between the two former friends, but recent enemies, Zbynek and John Hus. The Archbishop was defeated. Overruled by his temporal and abandoned by his spiritual lord, he was commanded to agree with his adversary quickly, and he agreed. He even promised to send to the Pope a letter stating that he knew of no heresy in Bohemia or Moravia, that he was reconciled with the reformer, and that there was no need for his appearance at Rome.[2] The excommunication and the interdict were to be removed. The letter was drafted, but was never sent. On the 1st September Hus had read before a congregation of the University in the Caroline College his own letter to the Pope, expressing his full submission, his declaration that he had never taught any heresy, and his readiness to withdraw any error that might be proved against him or to suffer the death of a heretic. He thanked his followers for their withdrawal from the obedience of Gregory the Twelfth, and entreated the cardinals to show mercy to him and to excuse his personal appearance.

The peace, however, was of short duration. The iron had entered into the Archbishop's soul. He became half-hearted and dilatory, the King became impatient and angry. The Archbishop complained that forged papal interdicts had been issued,[3] that the courtiers had interfered with his rights, and he demanded an audience. This Wenzel refused. Zbynek then left Prague, declaring that he was no longer safe, and went to Leitomysl, the residence of the 'iron bishop,' John, a bitter enemy of King Wenzel, and a strong opponent of church reform.[4] Thence he wrote to the King, stating that he was on his way to visit Sigismund. He started on his journey, but died at Presburg on the 28th September. Hus thought of their former friendship and expressed his great sorrow at the Archbishop's death. Shortly before this, on the 7th September, and shortly after this, on the 2nd December, the two Papal Bulls, proclaiming the crusade against King Ladislas, were published.

At this time there appeared at Prague, on their way to Hungary, two envoys from the King of England who, having sent troops to aid the Duke of Burgundy, wished to draw

[1] *Vid. sup.* p. 66.   [2] Berger, 74.   [3] Helfert, 277.   [4] Luetzow, 144.

122   POPE JOHN THE TWENTY-THIRD

Sigismund into his alliance. They were Sir Hartung van Clux, who had won his spurs in the campaign against Scotland in 1400 and who had subsequently served against Owen Glendower in Wales; and Master John Stokes of Cambridge, who was also a trusted diplomatist of King Henry the Fourth.[1] They were 'probably the bearers of an official intimation from Archbishop Arundel that Wyclif's books had been again condemned as heretical and publicly burnt at Oxford.'[2] They were asked the news as to Lollardy. Sir Hartung said nothing; but John Stokes declared that Wyclif was now held in England to be a heretic, and that any man who studied his books, even with the best intentions and the firmest faith, must eventually be led astray.[3] John Hus protested, called on him to make good his words, and fastened his challenge to the Cathedral door. Stokes declined the encounter at Prague, seeing that he was on diplomatic business, but he offered to accept the challenge later at Paris or at Rome. On the appointed day, Hus was at the disputation room. He declared that John Wyclif was no heretic, that the University of Oxford had given him a clean sheet, and that the King of England's father had backed him up. If Wyclif was a heretic, then all Oxford men, who had been reading his works for thirty years past, must be heretics. There was more truth in Hus's words than perhaps he knew, for the University of Oxford had been wonderfully staunch to the Master of Balliol, and as Archbishop Courtenay, himself once Chancellor of Oxford, declared, Oxford was indeed the University of heresies.[4] The reformer defeated his absent antagonist. 'In such a cloud of banter Hus rode off an easy winner, but his opponent did not forget his beating; and among the bitterest accusers of Hus at Constance we shall meet the name of Stokes the Englishman.'[5]

The new Archbishop of Prague was Albik (or Albert) of Unicov, 'an elderly, conciliatory, opulent, well-intentioned man, whose home life was irreproachable,'[6] who had formerly been court physician to King Wenzel, and who was probably now elected through his influence. Soon after he assumed office, the papal representative for the sale of indulgences for

[1] Lenz, 32-3.   [2] Wylie, iii. 470.   [3] Luetzow, 146; Wylie, iii. 470.
[4] Rashdall, ii. 429.   [5] Wylie, iii. 471.   [6] Luetzow, 148.

A CREATION OF CARDINALS 123

the war with Ladislas arrived at Prague. This was Wenzel Tiem, Dean of Passau, an unscrupulous man, utterly unfit for the task in such a country as Bohemia. The recollection of the sale of indulgences in 1393 still lingered, and the new Archbishop took the precaution to publish regulations to prevent the worse abuses and to prohibit the taxing of penitents in the confessional. Tiem took no heed of these restrictions. He farmed out archdeaconries, deaconries and single churches, reserving the three principal churches in Prague for himself. The priests who were his farmers are thus described by Tomek in his *History of the Town of Prague*. ' Naturally, worthy priests were not suitable for such an unholy trade, and the business thus fell into the hands of priests who were either misers or gamblers, lived in concubinage, or practised other vices of the period. These men bargained shamelessly with the faithful in the confessionals and committed infamous actions of every description.'[1] The abuse of indulgences had for some time been a subject on which church reformers in Bohemia had been zealous, and now the abuse was in their very midst.

Early in June John Hus invited all members of the University to attend a disputation to be held in the Caroline College on the 17th to consider whether it was in accordance with the law of Christ, and for the glory of God, the salvation of Christians, and for the good of the realm that the Pope's Bulls for raising the cross against Ladislas, King of Apulia, and his allies, should be commended to the faithful in Christ. Such a public controversy was bound to raise again the storm which had been stilled, and two Doctors of the Theological Faculty applied to the Archbishop to forbid it.[2] The meeting was held, and was attended by a crowd of doctors, masters, and students. Hus himself spoke with firmness but with moderation against the Bulls ; he relied on scriptural quotations, and maintained that God alone could forgive sins. His two old friends, Stanislas of Znaim and Stephen Palec separated themselves from him ; they would not oppose the papal decree ; they were in favour of submission on all points to the Pope. Hus had once before raised the standard of revolt. On the present occasion he was surpassed by Jerome of Prague, who spoke with fierceness and

[1] Luetzow, 150.   [2] Lechler, 57.

vehemence, obtaining thunders of applause from the students, who insisted on accompanying him home in triumph.

This had been an academic outburst; it was followed next day by a popular demonstration. King Wenzel was not in Prague. The leading spirit was a turbulent courtier, Wok of Waldstein, who was assisted by Jerome of Prague and other Masters. They took certain light wenches in procession through the town; round their necks were hung copies of the Papal Bulls. At the ditch of the New Town a pyre had been erected under a gallows, with an iron trough standing by to receive payments for indulgences. The Bulls were laid on the pyre and burned; into the trough instead of pence satires against the indulgences were thrown.[1] The King condoned his favourite's offence, but threatened with the death penalty all rioters. On Sunday, the 10th July, when the faithful were being admonished to purchase indulgences, three young men stood forth in three different churches of Prague and protested, saying that the indulgences were nothing but deceit and lies. It had evidently been pre-arranged. They were arrested and thrown into prison. John Hus and others went to the town hall to intercede for them, were told that nothing should be done, and on that assurance went home. As soon as the crowd had dispersed, the councillors ordered the three young men to execution, and they were straightway beheaded ' at the corner of the present Iron Street, at the northern extremity of the market-place.'[2] A woman threw cloths over the bodies, which were taken up and carried to the Bethlehem Chapel. A large crowd had by this time assembled; ' and the Master (John of Jicin) with a loud voice intoned the anthem, *Isti sunt Sancti*, which is sung of the holy martyrs, and all joining with loud voices in the singing they bravely and joyfully carried the bodies to Bethlehem, while all the mailed soldiers and councillors looked on. Many students also, common people, lords and ladies, followed the bodies with much crying and lament, but with great piety, and while accompanying them to their graves they heartily pitied the young men, saying they had not deserved to die.'[3]

---

[1] Helfert, 119. [2] Luetzow, 157.
[3] Ancient Bohemian Chronicler, quoted at Luetzow, 158.

John Hus had taken no part in the indecent procession of Wok of Waldstein, nor did he refer to the death of the three students in his sermon next Sunday at the Bethlehem Chapel. He maintained an attitude of moderation throughout, when a word of his from the pulpit would probably have produced a riot, if not a massacre of the Germans still in Prague. But his attitude on the question of the indulgences was one of open opposition to the Pope; Hus had set up his own individual opinion against that of properly constituted authority. On the matter of church reform, most of the men of light and leading in Europe were in accord with him; but they longed for a reform within the Church, not a revolt against it. They could not understand a man setting up his own opinion or belief against that of the Church. It was the part of a good churchman to accept the common belief, deviation from which would impair the solidarity of the Church. It was the duty of every individual clerk to obey the Pope. Seeing that Hus had now taken up a new standpoint, that entailing revolt from lawful authority, it is small wonder that certain of those who had hitherto been his closest friends were soon to become his bitterest enemies.

CHAPTER VII

THE COUNCIL AT ROME

As the year 1412 wore on the outlook in Rome for Pope John the Twenty-third became more and more gloomy. The heresy of Aegidius Cantor [1] probably did not trouble him; it was dealt with effectually by the Bishop of Cambrai. But his allies, the Duke of Anjou and the Republic of Florence, had fallen away; certain of the papal states were still in revolt, and Carlo Malatesta threatened to increase the obedience of Pope Gregory the Twelfth; the Pope's brother, Admiral Gaspar Cossa, died on the 23rd September 1411; the famine in Rome was causing a continuous rise in prices; the Pope's attempts to raise money had created widespread and serious discontent; his captains, Paolo Orsini and Sforza Attendolo, had quarrelled, and on the 19th May 1412,[2] the latter entered the service of King Ladislas of Naples. There was no help to be looked for from the King of the Romans, who was at war with Venice; there was no help to be expected from the Duke of Burgundy, who was at war with the Armagnacs. The Pope had preached a crusade against Ladislas of Naples and against the Moors of Spain,[3] but he had preached to deaf ears, and no help was forthcoming. Invasion and a siege of Rome were threatening. Nothing remained for him but to agree with his adversary quickly. Bitter indeed must have been the humiliation which drove the Pope to treat with his worst enemy, but there was no help for it.

Ladislas meantime had not been idle. He had captured one of the Pope's principal captains, and held him in prison; he had sent troops to occupy the Monastery of Saint Agnes outside the walls of Rome. An attack on the city had been repulsed by a petty German captain, who chased away the enemy and captured some of their horses. Paolo Orsini was still in Rome,

---

[1] Raynaldus, viii. 339. [2] Mur. xxiv. 1030; *vid. sup.* p. 109.
[3] Raynaldus, viii. 338.

THE COUNCIL AT ROME 127

but did nothing except follow the foe at a distance. The Pope did not trust him against the King of Naples and sent him to the March of Ancona against Carlo Malatesta.[1] John had no troops whom he could trust; he was obliged to enter into negotiations, and the Florentines were only too ready to help him. Florence and Ladislas hated and distrusted each other, but at present they were allies.

The King himself was not unwilling to treat. He had received a sharp lesson at Rocca Secca, and did not feel sure that he had seen the last of Louis of Anjou; he feared King Sigismund; and, moreover, the King of France had advised him to abandon Pope Gregory.[2] When the Pope therefore sent to Naples his fellow-countryman, Cardinal Raynaldus Brancacius, Ladislas received him gladly and professed his entire readiness to listen to terms. He assembled a council of prelates and notables, amenable to his wishes, and then he declared that by their advice he found that he had hitherto been mistaken in believing that Pope Gregory the Twelfth had been canonically elected; he was therefore ready to renounce Pope Gregory and to acknowledge Pope John the Twenty-third throughout his dominions; he agreed further to release all the relatives and all the captains of Pope John whom he had hitherto held in captivity. The Pope on his side renounced Louis of Anjou and recognised Ladislas as King of Naples; he appointed him to be Grand Gonfalonier of the Holy Roman Church; he agreed to pay him a hundred and twenty thousand florins and to give security until payment; and he promised to aid him in the conquest of Sicily.[3] It was arranged that all prelates of Gregory's promotion were to apply to Pope John within three months for confirmation; and the Pope looked to this to bring him in a goodly accession of revenue. On these terms was peace made between the two inveterate enemies; if the Pope thought he could trust King Ladislas, he was again mistaken in his estimate of humanity.

While these negotiations were pending, the aged Pope Gregory the Twelfth heard of them. The broken and weary old man was living under the protection of Ladislas. He rebuked

---

[1] Hardt, ii. 366; *vid. sup.* p. 108.   [2] Raynaldus, viii. 342; Hefele, vii. 16.
[3] Raynaldus, viii. 344; Hardt, ii. 367.

the King. ' Why,' he asked, ' do you agree with my adversary and keep me in ignorance ? ' The stammering King protested that no such agreement was in contemplation ; but next day, the 31st October, he sent word to the octogenarian pontiff to bid him and his depart if they would be in safety. Gregory was then at Gaeta, and the men of Gaeta loved the aged Pope and were enraged at the King's breach of faith. Two ships, one from the east and the other from the west, came to the harbour ; the citizens brought up the cargoes and offered the barks to their Pope ; and the old man, having declined the offered pension of fifty thousand gulden, set sail with his three nephews and his little court in the two ships. They were many weeks at sea in stormy weather, but on the 24th December they reached Ancona, where they were at last safe under the hospitable and honourable protection of Carlo Malatesta, Lord of Rimini.[1] Gregory issued an encyclical, and had already sent legates to Germany, in the hope of increasing the area of his obedience,[2] but all his efforts were in vain. The land of Carlo Malatesta was all that in Italy still acknowledged the obedience of Pope Gregory the Twelfth ; the rest of the peninsula was under the spiritual sway of Pope John the Twenty-third, who was proclaimed by King Ladislas through the whole of his dominions as Pope and sole spiritual Lord.

The peace between the King and the Pope was not signed and finally concluded until the 15th June 1412.[3] It was a sad, if not an absolutely disreputable, alliance. The Pope might indeed plead that ' bitter constraint and sad occasion dear ' had been his motives ; but Ladislas had been deceived in so far that he deemed the Pope's constraint to be far less bitter than it really was. When he discovered that he had been overreached, every one knew that the King would observe the peace only so long as it suited him ; and Pope John, as well as every one else, knew the utter perfidy and faithlessness of the man with whom he was dealing. The so-called peace was but a hollow truce. But for the present the advantage was on the side of the Pope. He had acquired a great increase in the territory acknowledging his obedience ; and the price of grain in Rome fell immediately

[1] Hardt, ii. 368 ; Brieger, x. 389.   [2] Blumenthal, 71.
[3] Raynaldus, viii. 344.

THE COUNCIL AT ROME 129

to one half its former rate.¹ But the Pope gained no increase of revenue. The clergy of southern Italy took as little heed of their change of spiritual master as did any of the Visconti or Ladislas himself of a sentence of excommunication. The chief advantage which the peace procured to the Pope was that it enabled him to hold his Council.

At the twenty-second session of the Council of Pisa ² it had been announced that the work of the reformation of the Church would be undertaken at a Council to be held in April 1412; and the place for the Council had subsequently been duly notified as Rome. The choice of the Eternal City as the place of meeting had caused some umbrage, for there were some who said that it was idle to try in Rome itself to correct the faults of the Church of Rome. The French clergy had wanted it to be held in Savoy or in France. Verona and Padua were proposed; even Germany was named.³ On the 29th April 1411 the Pope issued his Bull naming Rome as the place of meeting. Then arose the question of sending representatives from France.

Their mutual concessions had, under the influence of the Dauphin, brought about an understanding between the Pope and the French Court, but had not destroyed the Gallican spirit. The Parlement had taken up the cudgels; and the National Synod, held in January 1412, had complained of the pensions assigned to cardinals on French churches, of the abuse of the system of appeals to Rome, and of the promotion of foreigners to benefices in France.⁴ The French clergy at first thought of declining to send representatives to the Council of Rome, but eventually better counsels prevailed. It was decided that the energetic Pierre d'Ailly and Simon de Cramaud were to represent the University of Paris, and that the court interests should be entrusted to Chevenon, Bishop of Amiens, and Montreuil, one of the King's secretaries.⁵ The French Court, where the Burgundian influence was supreme, at this time supported the Gallican party among the clergy.

The Council had been convoked for the 1st April 1412, and benches had been arranged in Saint Peter's Church for its meeting. But, as peace with King Ladislas had not then been

¹ Mur. xxiv. 1031. ² *In the Days of the Councils*, 379. ³ Finke (*Acta*), 110.
⁴ *Religieux*, iv. 590. ⁵ Chastenet, 138; *Religieux*, iv. 730.

signed, the roads to Rome were not safe, and no prelates from foreign countries had come. On the appointed day the Pope, accompanied by the clergy of the city, left his palace and proceeded on foot to the Square of Saint Peter's, entered the church and made the circuit of it, followed by the cardinals, archbishops, bishops, and others, and at the foot of the great crucifix celebrated the Mass of the Holy Spirit; then he took counsel as to the date to which the opening should be adjourned. It was decided to hold the Council in December of that year. As soon, says the Monk of Saint Denys,[1] as they learned that the roads leading to Rome were safe, the bishops, archbishops, primates, and other members of the clergy of Italy, Hungary, Bohemia, England, Scotland, and the parts of Germany in the Pope's obedience, started to assist at the Council. Deputies, not less celebrated for their wisdom than for their persuasive eloquence, chosen from the four faculties of the venerable University of Paris, set out in the name of the King and of the Kingdom of France with a brilliant escort, as already arranged, furnished with instructions relating to the suppression or diminution of the heavy charges weighing on the Gallican Church. The worthy chronicler gives a rose-coloured account of the attendance, which was in reality disappointingly small. The two new French cardinals, Pierre d'Ailly and Guillaume Fillastre went to Rome on their own account; so too did Simon de Cramaud, who had recently been promoted to be Archbishop of Reims, who was soon to be made a cardinal; but they arrived tardily. From the University of Paris there were at least two doctors and two masters of theology; the Bishop of Amiens, the abbots of Clairvaux and Jumièges, together with a third abbot, and two masters appeared for the prelates of France, and two knights for the King.[2] The distance and the perils of the road kept prelates away. Ladislas of Naples looked with disfavour upon the assembly, because it was regarded as a continuation of the Council of Pisa; and his enmity was the chief cause of its failure. There is no reason to suspect the Pope himself in this matter, as some have done;[3] it was to the interest of John that the Council should be truly representative and œcumenical;

---

[1] *Religieux*, iv. 730.   [2] Finke (*Acta*), 162.   [3] Martene (*A. C.*), vii. 1406.

THE COUNCIL AT ROME 131

for, next to Bologna, there was no place in Italy where the Pope was so influential as at Rome, and there was no place therefore at which a Council could be held which should more faithfully promote his own views and interests. At Rome he held both swords. A successful Council at Rome, which should satisfy the anticipations of Christendom, would do much more than all else to strengthen and extend his obedience. It was a heavy blow to John the Twenty-third that the Council was from the beginning a failure in point of numbers and of authority.[1]

By the adjourned date the French representatives had arrived. Guillaume Fillastre reached Rome on the 16th June; Pierre d'Ailly, on the 1st December 1412. The regular embassy did not start until the autumn.[2] Ambassadors came from the King of the Romans, from the King of Cyprus, from Ladislas of Naples, and from the Republics of Florence and Siena. Very few of the clergy arrived from other countries.[3] Germany sent a representative, one Wilhelm Bloc.[4] An envoy from Pope Gregory the Twelfth was at this time in Rome.[5]

It was probably at one of the preliminary meetings that a ludicrous incident occurred. The Mass of the Holy Spirit had been said, the congregation were devoutly seated, and Pope John had taken his place on his throne, when a ghastly bird of the night, a screech owl, flew with horrid outcry from a dark corner of the church, and perched opposite the Pope, glaring at him fixedly with large threatening eyes. John reddened and perspired; finally he rose from his seat; and the congregation dispersed. But at the next assembly the bird again appeared, and again fixed its black eyes on the pontiff. Some of the cardinals laughed and said that the Holy Ghost had appeared in the bodily form of an owl. John ordered them to chase the bird of ill omen away. They rose in a body, waved their staves, shrieked at the owl, but it was some time before they made it budge. Finally they knocked it down and killed it.[6] But the memory of the evil omen remained.

Although some of the French envoys ventured to reproach the Pope with simony and evil conduct, still the general tone of

---

[1] Finke (*Acta*), 126.
[2] *Ibid.* (*Acta*), 116; Valois, iv. 205.
[3] *Religieux*, iv. 730.
[4] Reinke, 32, note.
[5] Finke (*Acta*), 126, note.
[6] Gratius, i. 402.

France had moderated and was now distinctly favourable to John the Twenty-third. This was due in part to the action of the civil power, and in part to the conciliatory attitude of the Pope. Though he had not scrupulously respected the rights of cathedral chapters and of monasteries in the election of their superiors, still court, clergy, and University had acquiesced in his measures. Several beneficiaries had even appealed to him, as to their natural protector, against the exactions of the civil power. The chief object of France now was to obtain a remission or a reduction of papal taxation. There was no grumbling at papal presentations to benefices, for the appointments made by the Pope were recognised as being generally better than those made by the ordinaries. Both systems had been tried, and both had their faults; but the undesirable foreigners for whom the Pope might occasionally provide were nothing like so numerous as the utterly unfit servitors and followers whom the ordinaries presented at their whim. The University and the Court could by presenting a list of their graduates and nominees get livings from the Pope for the majority. The Rector of the University, speaking before an assembly of the clergy, declared that although exactions and abuses were to be combated, still the Pope's right of collation to benefices, notwithstanding the provisions in the royal ordinances, which had never been carried into effect,[1] was sacred and inviolable.[2] The Pope, on his side, was ready to make concessions. There was not likely, therefore, to be much friction in the proceedings from the side of the representatives of France.

The majority of the work of the Council was transacted at those less formal congregations and conventions at which it was customary to prepare resolutions for the confirmation or vote of the general sessions of the whole body. Great freedom of speech was allowed. Pierre d'Ailly had, in 1411, sent to the Pope a proposal relating to a favourite scheme of his for the reform of the calendar, and this had been recommended for confirmation to the Council,[3] though nothing more was done. Jean de Montreuil, the head of the Court embassy, pronounced a discourse early in 1413, offering the King's salutation to the Pope, com-

[1] Finke (*Acta*), 116.   [2] Valois, iv. 195, 202, 208.   [3] Finke (*Acta*), 164-5.

plimenting him on his accession, and recommending to him
the officers of the King, the Queen, and the Dauphin; his real
mission was to obtain from His Holiness the right of nomina-
tion to certain benefices in France, and John acquiesced in the
demand;[1] the French ambassadors had travelled seven hundred
miles, and were not to return empty-handed. The Bishop of
Amiens obtained for himself the bishopric of Beauvais, and then
advised his colleagues to maintain silence on the different
requests which they were commissioned to make.[2]

The ambassadors from the University of Paris also laid
before the Pope their proposals for reform. The first four of
these related to the prorogation of the Council and the due
publication of the time and place for the adjourned meeting;
to which John answered that he would take the necessary action,
that he would publish the time at the first general session, and
would intimate the place three months later. The two most
important concessions made by the Pope to the University were
that he granted to their Chancellor the right of absolving
masters and scholars from papal censures, and that he allowed
that all their causes, which had hitherto gone to Rome, should
be in future adjudicated by the Bishop of Paris. On the
question of first fruits the University was moderate, and the
Pope, while reserving this 'laudable custom,' allowed that the
first half should be paid after six months, and the second at the
expiration of the first year after the promotion of the new bishop
or abbot. In reply to the request that he would reduce the
number of cardinals to twelve or to some other number not
burdensome to the Church, the Pope answered that he did not
intend to create any new cardinals, except in case of necessity.
He also returned a favourable answer to the request that
foreigners might not be appointed to benefices in France; and
he promised to await the result of elections and to confirm those
canonically elected, except when there was good cause to the
contrary. He further engaged scrupulously to observe the
constitution of the Council of Pisa that no prelate should be
transferred without his own consent. John also promised not
to join secular to regular churches, not to exempt any from the
spiritual control of their superiors, except on reasonable

[1] Finke (*Acta*), 149-51; Valois, iv. 214-5. [2] *Religieux*, v. 72.

grounds. He agreed to punish those who neglected duly to celebrate provincial Councils. With regard to the complaint against archdeacons and others of lightly issuing sentences of excommunication, he thought that the ordinary law sufficed or that the matter might be left to the disposition of the Council; and he made a similar answer to the allegation of oppressive visitations. The Pope promised to reduce the number of cases reserved to the Curia, to punish bishops who promoted clerks without resources or learning, and to see that ordinaries duly corrected their inferiors who were of vicious livelihood; he also engaged to restrict the number of reservations in accordance with a Bull of Benedict the Twelfth. Finally the Pope revoked the Bull of his predecessor in favour of the mendicant orders. The University had obtained from the Pope the promise that among clerks provided with benefices in France, the preference should be given to those who were Frenchmen, who had taken a degree in some French university or had served the King, the Queen, or one of the princes.[1] The French ambassadors had at any rate got something in the direction of reform from Pope John the Twenty-third.

The French Court was thoroughly satisfied with this modicum of success. When the Council was announced the Duke of Anjou, who had returned from his unsuccessful expedition, was hand-in-glove with the Duke of Burgundy; his son was betrothed to the Duke's daughter Katharine, who lived with Yolande, Duchess of Anjou. But while the Council was in progress, Louis of Anjou had deserted to the opposite camp of the Duke of Orleans, and had sent back Katharine in disgrace to her father, Jean sans Peur. There was now bitter enmity between the royal cousins; the Gallican party had lost the support of the Duke of Burgundy, who had espoused their cause as a goad to the Pope to back up the Duke of Anjou; and now the Dauphin himself was lukewarm. After the ambassadors returned, a royal proclamation was issued protesting against the drain of money from the kingdom, but subsequently nothing further was done. The ecclesiastical policy of France was as unstable as ever; it fluctuated as the influence of the Burgundian or the Armagnac party predominated; as a general

[1] Finke (*Acta*), 155-62; Valois, iv. 208-11.

THE COUNCIL AT ROME

rule the Duke of Burgundy favoured Pope John, because this Pope represented the Council of Pisa, and that Council had been held under the Duke's influence ; as a general rule, the Armagnacs favoured the opposite side ; but the support was not constant, nor was it consistent.[1]

All that had been done at Rome thus far had happened outside the Council proper. Apart from the ceremonial and the adjourned opening, there was only one, the first and last, regular general session, which was held on the 10th February 1413. This was concerned with the spread of heresy. The Pope recognised that the number of prelates present was so small that the Council of Rome was without authority, and that it must be prorogued. But at its single session it made an important pronouncement on the heresy which had originated in England and which had spread to Bohemia.

The most important proceeding of the Council of Rome was its condemnation of the works of John Wyclif. Wyclif was the last of the great schoolmen, and he was a Realist. At the time when he wrote the authority of William of Ockham was supreme and Ockham was a Nominalist. Ockham's philosophy was received by all the theological faculties at the different universities ; it was as unquestioned in the University of Paris as it had been by the German nations in the University of Prague. The difference between Realism and Nominalism was no small thing ; it was a difference far more bitter and deeper than that between rival political schools of to-day. To us it seems perhaps inconceivable that men should spend so much time and thought over these insoluble quibbles and quiddities, but to them divine philosophy was the theory of the universe, the groundwork of religion, the thing above all others worth living and fighting for ; to believe rightly was to be saved, to be heterodox was to be damned everlastingly. Students, armed with bows and arrows or with staves, would turn out in the streets and fight under the rival banners of Nominalism and Realism ; and the Nominalist University of Paris condemned Realism as heresy ;[2] men did not want to understand[3] or

---

[1] Bess, 99-101.   [2] Hauréau, II. ii. 458.
[3] 'The art of understanding adversaries is an innovation of the present century, characteristic of the historic age. Formerly, a man was exhausted by

convince their adversaries, they wanted to suppress them; they believed that those who propagated heretical opinions were causing the damnation of their fellows, and that they should therefore be put to death. Hence the consideration of Wyclif's doctrines was a matter of the most serious importance, and it is as well therefore to try to get a clear conception of the actual point in issue between the rival schools. For it will be shown later on that John Hus was burned, not only because he was a heretic, but also because John Wyclif was a Realist. In order to appreciate the point which the Council had to decide it is necessary to describe in outline the theories of the rival schools.

The Realist theory current at the time when William of Ockham wrote was to the following effect. Species are certain insensible qualities produced by sensible objects; they are extended and spherical; they dwell in intermediate space, where they in their turn produce still other species, connected with them, and forming a continuous series, reaching from the sensible object on the one hand to the sentient organ on the other. These species deposit on the sentient organ an individual impression, which causes it to form the primary sensation of the object. The primary sensation gives forth other species which proceed by the veins and the nerves to the inner sense, or intellect, on which they produce the psychological action of a sensation perceived. Thence a third kind of species are transmitted to the memory, where they become the representative idea or permanent image of the absent object. Inasmuch as the intellect differs entirely from the senses, it is necessary that in addition to the representative idea of the individual thing, there should also be its species which can act on the intellectual energy; relations can only exist between similar objects; hence these species which emanate from the individual ideas are no longer individual, but are in a sense universal. They are called the *species intelligibilis praevia*.

This was the theory which Ockham set himself to destroy. In the first place he would have none of the intermediate species.

the effort of making out his own meaning, with the help of his friends. The definition and comparison of systems which occupies so much of our recent literature was unknown, and everybody who was wrong was supposed to be very wrong indeed.'—Acton: *Lectures on Modern History*, 202.

THE COUNCIL AT ROME

There was nothing to prove their existence, and it was not right to multiply existences unnecessarily; *non est pluralitas ponenda sine necessitate*. It was not necessary for one object to act upon another that they should be in the same place; the sun proved that. All that was wanted for sensation was an exterior object and the mental sensibility to receive the impressions of that object. The object perceived and the subject perceiving it are the two causes of sensation; and sensations can be renewed by the imagination. Duns Scotus had taught that the exterior object was not the sole cause, but only the associate cause, the occasion, of the image which arises in the mind; that since the images remain in the mind after the act of appropriation, for the most part as phantasmata, but also in part as species which represent the intelligible, and since both can be called up by the memory, these intelligible species are themselves an actually producing power. William of Ockham, on the other hand, held that it is the *actus intelligendi* itself by which a thing is revealed to us, and that there existed no *species intelligibiles* to be inserted between the things and the activity of the spirit.[1] Sensible objects produce none of the insensible species affirmed by the realists; the quality of the external object produces on the sentient mind a quality of like nature, and this mental quality can itself become the object of further sensations. Nor again do the species predicated by the realists exist independently in the laboratory of our imagination, but the notions of things perceived remain after the first act of sensation, and can be evoked by the imagination for its own uses. Just as sensible species do not exist, no more do intellectual species. Even as sensation is the result of the relationship between the external object and the sentient subject, so is the intellectual act determined by the intelligence of the person and the matter perceived by him.[2]

On the vexed question of universals William of Ockham was precise. Universals are of three kinds, universals *ante rem*, universals *in re*, and universals *post rem*. Duns Scotus had taught ' that the general exists first as the original type, after which things are formed, that it exists secondly in them as the *quiditas* which gives the nature of the thing, and thirdly that

[1] Erdmann, i. 436, 504. [2] Hauréau, II. ii. 379 *et seq.*

it is discovered by our understanding, which abstracts it from the things, (hence *post res*) as that which is common to them.'[1] Universals *ante rem* were supposed to exist in the divine intelligence, subjectively they were the models which God used in creation. Now God, according to William of Ockham, was the most universal of universals; you can frame no precise image of God as you can of Socrates or of Bucephalus; the notion of God is a subjective idea, begotten of experience and framed by reason, representing the sum of diverse abstract qualities;[2] and universals *ante rem* in relation to Him must be either subjective or objective. They cannot exist in Him subjectively, forming part of His essence, because the essence of God is absolutely one, while these universals are manifold. They must therefore exist objectively; and the only difference between ideas human and divine is this, that with man the idea is born after an external object has been perceived, while in God the idea precedes the production of the object; and so far only can it be said that things exist in God. This stone is not in God because He knows it; the knowledge that He has of the stone is not the thing itself, but is a mental fact, the act of a thinking subject. To suppose that there are any subjectively representative images in the breast of the divine intelligence is to imagine pure chimeras.

The second class of universals are the universals *in re*. Certain philosophers before the time of Aristotle had invested universals with a separate subsistence; and this theory had been upheld by the school of Duns Scotus who styled such universals the common nature or substantial foundation of all

[1] Erdmann, i. 491.
[2] Hauréau, II. ii. 402. Ockham's idea of God is, as Hauréau points out, the same as that of John Locke. 'It is Infinity which, joined to our ideas of Existence, Power, Knowledge, etc., makes that complex Idea, whereby we represent to ourselves the best we can the supreme Being. For though in His own essence, which certainly we do not know (not knowing the real essence of a pebble or a fly, or our own selves), God be simple and uncompounded; yet I think I may say that we have no other idea of him but a complex one of Existence, Knowledge, Power, Happiness, etc. infinite and eternal: which are all distinct ideas, and some of them, being relative, are again composed of others; all which being, as has been shown, originally got from Sensation and Reflection, go to make up the Idea or Notion we have of God.'—Locke: *Essay Concerning Human Understanding* (ed. 1721), i. 268.

THE COUNCIL AT ROME 139

accidental differences. William of Ockham would not allow any subjective existence to such universals ; he would not allow that they had any real existence outside the mind distinct from the individual. Nor would he allow that universals exist united with individuals but formally distinct from them, as endowed with a separate existence, anterior to individual differences. Nor would he allow that each individual possesses two realities, one individual and the other common, the former dominating and individualising the latter. Universals, says he, do not exist outside the intellect ; individuals alone exist ; there is nothing intermediate.

As to the third class of universals, the universals *post rem*, he would not allow that these existed outside the intellect. An universal is an intellectual conception, *fictum quid*, existing objectively in the mind, a creation of the thought or intellect ; or it may be defined as a mental qualification signifying the manner of being which is common to external objects ; it represents the point of identity of individuals, but it has no separate subjective existence. An universal is an idea relating to several individuals and representing their natural similitude ;[1] it is found, *ante rem*, in the divine intelligence, and *post rem*, in the human mind ; universals are abstract notions, possessing merely a psychological existence.

Such was in outline the philosophy of William of Ockham, intelligible and trenchant. He was a metaphysician of the type of John Stuart Mill. In his own time his philosophy was called Nominalism in contradistinction to the Realism of Duns Scotus and his followers ; but inasmuch as it was confined to the region of logic it has been described in our day as Terminalism. His method ' may be said to have proceeded on the supposition that logic deals not with things nor with thoughts, but with terms arbitrarily imposed by ourselves. When we use certain terms in logic for the sake of convenience in drawing out a syllogism, we neither assert nor prove anything as to the relation of those terms to our thoughts or to existing realities. Argument is only true *ex supposito*. Duns Scotus, on the other hand, conceived the function of logic to deal with thoughts. As to the metaphysical basis, they were still more strongly opposed. Duns held

[1] Hauréau, II. ii. 404-20.

to the reality of universals in the more uncompromising form to which the mature mediæval realism ever attained : Ockham declined to go beyond the logical necessity ; he enforced the 'law of parsimony' and regarded them as terms in a syllogism.'[1]

The sphere of logic, however, was circumscribed to the domain of Reason ; Revelation and Faith were altogether beyond it. In the region of theology William of Ockham was strictly orthodox, except as regards the authority of the Papacy. The union of philosophic scepticism with orthodox theology was the result of his division of ' the human mind into watertight compartments, the total divorce of Faith from Reason—in other words, by a blind prostration of the intellect, in matters of Religion and Morality, before either external authority or subjective religious emotion or some combination of the two.'[2] According to Saint Thomas Aquinas certain truths of revelation were not to be proved by the reason ; and according to Duns Scotus theology was outside the pale of the sciences. Ockham carried this tendency still further ; he ' positively revelled in demonstrating the uncertainty or irrationality of dogmas which as a Theologian he was prepared to swallow with dutiful avidity.'[3] The earlier philosophy of the Middle Ages had tended to reconcile faith with reason ; and John Wyclif was not, like William of Ockham, prepared to divide the human mind into two ' watertight compartments.' He also differed from him on the question of the reality of universals. The situation cannot be better described than has been done by Dr. Rashdall. ' Medieval Realism dimly and blindly testified to the part which Mind plays in the constitution of the objects of our Knowledge—to the truth that in all our knowledge there is a rational element (if the term may be allowed) which comes not from any supposed external object but from the mind itself, and that these mental ideas, forms, relations—call them what you will—are not chimeras, illusions, imaginary entities, faint copies of unintelligible external things ; but, in the strictest sense of the word, Realities—not indeed in abstraction from that of which they are relations, but as real as any other element in things. In the dim witness which it bore to this metaphysical truth lay the strength of medieval Realism ; and

[1] *D.N.B.*, xli. 360-1.   [2] Rashdall, ii. 537.   [3] *Ibid.* ii. 538.

hence in part it was that medieval Realism was not stamped out by the Invincible Doctor.'[1]

John Wyclif was a realist, a Platonist who followed the method of Aristotle. His philosophy was grounded in part on the Bible, on the doctrine of the Logos. Like Saint Augustine and Saint Thomas of Aquino, he misread the third and fourth verses of the Gospel according to Saint John, or rather, he ran the concluding words of the third into the beginning of the fourth verse, reading, ' Quod factum est in ipso vita erat ' ; and he translated it to mean, ' Everything which was created was originally, and before its creation in time, an actual reality —actually pre-formed in the eternally existing Logos.' He believed in the independent existence of universals as grounded in God's thought and work ; he believed in the objective existence of ideas, as being God's thoughts. ' What God creates, He cannot possibly create by chance or unwisely ; He must therefore think it ; and His thought, or the archetype of the creature, is the idea ; and this same is eternal, for it is the same in time with the Divine knowledge.' God does not think arbitrarily, but according to the reason of things ; only realities can be thought. We do not, therefore, according to Wyclif, attain to true knowledge by looking at things as they are known to us merely by experience ; we must rather apprehend them as they pre-exist in the eternal reason. ' If we desire one day to see God in the heavenly home, we must here below consider His creatures in the light of those deep intellectual principles, in which they are known and ordered by Him, and we must turn our eyes towards that eternal horizon under which that light lies concealed.' True morality also depends on a well-ordered love for the universal ; sinful acts arise from a placing of that which is lower and individual above that which is higher and universal.[2] Such was the philosophy of John Wyclif ; it was contrary to that of William of Ockham.

In philosophy John Hus was a follower of Wyclif ; he was, like his master, a determined Realist, an enemy of Nominalism, which he regarded as the root of all philosophical error. ' With no very great dialectical faculty, there were motives enough for disinclining him to view the new Nominalism with any great

---

[1] Rashdall, ii. 536-7.   [2] Lechler (*Lorimer*), 225-32.

affection. And was not the other word a much better, healthier, more promising word ? Was it not better to feel always that we were dealing with realities ? Was not this needful, above all, in the highest region ? Was it safe to think of righteousness or justice or truth as if they were mere names ? Were not the ecclesiastics of the day doing this very thing ? No, Hus would teach the students of the University, just as he taught the King and the Court in the Bethlehem Chapel, to be Realists in their hearts and understandings, let Germans and Frenchmen talk about their Nominalism as they chose.'[1]

It was not to be expected that the Realist doctrines of John Wyclif would meet with any favour at the hands of the prelates in Rome. The majority of the cardinals and doctors were canon lawyers, who had no sympathy with the speculations of the schools, Realist or Nominalist, and who took no trouble to understand them. There was a deep gulf set between the canon lawyers and the theologians. Nor was Wyclif like to meet with better treatment at the hands of the latter party. William of Ockham had been a theologian, bitterly adverse to the canonists and the canon law; he had set up the Bible as an authority superior to the Decretals. In this he was followed by Cardinal Pierre d'Ailly and those who acted with him. But they were Nominalists, and the leading feature of Wyclif's theology was that in Nominalism was the seat of all theological error. The *Dialogus* and *Trialogus*, the only two books named in the decree of the Council, were written in the later years of his life when he was antagonistic to the whole mediæval system of Church government. In the *Dialogus* he defends his itinerant preachers, believing that the imposition of a bishop's hands is not necessary when the divine call and commission to the ministry are present, and maintaining ' that a single unlearned preacher effects more, by the grace of God, for the Church of Christ, than many who have graduated in schools and colleges.' The *Trialogus* treats, among other matters, of the doctrine of transubstantiation, but it is a work which requires very attentive reading. According to the received doctrine of transubstantiation, the visible elements were merely accidents existing without any underlying substance; but to Wyclif, as a Realist, the doctrine of the

[1] Maurice, ii. 35.

THE COUNCIL AT ROME 143

objective existence of the substance was dear; and as he said, 'the worst heresy that God suffered to come to kirk is to trowe that this sacrament is an accident without substance.' He denied that any material change in the bread and wine took place; he asserted that there was the real presence without any such change; he held that in the sacrament of the altar there is true bread, but at the same time the body and blood of Christ. In saying that after consecration there still remained true bread and true wine, Wyclif contradicted the orthodox doctrine; while his doctrine of consubstantiation, which ' misjoins the sacred body with the bread,' was as heterodox then as subsequently in the days of Martin Luther. At the same time he guarded himself against the error of Berenger, that the body and blood of Christ are only subjectively apprehended by the communicant; Christ had Himself said that His body and blood were really present, and Christ could not lie. But although he believed in a real presence, he did not believe in a corporeal and local presence. The presence in the consecrated host is an effectual, a spiritual, and a sacramental presence. Christ is present effectually as He is present everywhere in His Kingdom; He is present spiritually as He graciously indwells in the souls of the faithful; the sacramental presence is a miracle. 'By means of the sacramental words a supernatural change takes place, by means of which bread and wine remain indeed what they are in their own substance, but from that moment are in truth and reality Christ's body and blood. Not that the glorified body of Christ descends out of heaven to the host, wherever it may be consecrated in church; no! it remains above in heaven fixed and immovable, and only in a spiritual, invisible manner is it present in every morsel of the consecrated host, as the soul is present throughout the body. The host is not itself Christ's body, but undoubtedly the latter is in a sacramental manner concealed in it.'[1] Such is Wyclif's teaching on this most important matter; but there was no one present at the Council to represent the Realist view, so that the condemnation of his works was almost a foregone conclusion.

The decree which the Council of Rome passed against the errors of Wyclif and Hus is dated the fourth day of the Nones of

[1] Lechler (*Lorimer*), 196, 353-4; Figgis, 38.

February 1413, and is headed 'Joannis XXIII. Synodale decretum adversus Hussitas'; but it is a significant fact that the decree itself contains no mention of Hus or of the Hussites, but is concerned exclusively with John Wyclif and his works. It mentions the *Dialogus*, the *Trialogus*, and several other books, written and intituled by the name of the said John Wyclif, which certain persons in divers parts of the world have been curious to learn and to teach, not for the saving of souls and support of the faith, but rather for their own renown and the subversion of the catholic faith. The *Dialogus*, *Trialogus*, and the other unnamed works then with the Council were made over to a committee for examination and report. This committee consisted of certain cardinals and bishops, skilled in theology and in both laws. They found, by evidence of fact and by many 'definitive sentences,' that these works were full of false doctrine, which (according to Jerome) had been termed by our Saviour the abomination of desolation, like to corrupt all catholic learning as rabid poison. On this report, the Council in their zeal against such false, perverse, and pestiferous doctrine condemned the *Dialogus*, the *Trialogus*, and all other such books, written and intituled by the said John Wyclif, and ordered that they be publicly burned. No one was to read, teach or expound them; but the books were to be diligently sought out and publicly burned. If any one violated or contemned this decree, he was to be held suspect. Furthermore, all who desired to hold the said John Wyclif in remembrance were to appear within nine months and show cause why he should not be condemned as a heretic.[1]

The Pope then closed the abortive Council of Rome. He promised to send to France a legate to abolish abuses. He, on the 3rd March, issued a notice that the adjourned Council would meet on the 1st of December 1413, at a place which he would name within three months. He appears to have confided to Pierre d'Ailly his wish that this place should be Bologna, for the Cardinal informed the Republic of Venice accordingly;[2] but John himself said that he desired first of all to consult the King of the Romans.[3] He had not yet met Sigismund, who had been occupied with the war against Venice; but he knew that

---

[1] Mansi, xxvii. 506-7.   [2] Finke (*Acta*), 167.   [3] *Ibid.* (*Acta*), 238.

THE COUNCIL AT ROME 145

the King was eager to take up the entire question of church reform as soon as his hands should be free. Now that the Council of Rome had proved such a dismal failure, the eyes of all men waited more than ever on the King of the Romans. He was at this time in North Italy.

CHAPTER VIII

THE WAR WITH VENICE

SIGISMUND, King of the Romans, knew that before he could deal effectually with the Great Schism, he must be crowned with the silver crown at Aachen ; but before he could arrange for his coronation it was imperative to settle his differences with the Republic of Venice. In the matter of the Council of Pisa, Sigismund had throughout acted in concert with the Republic ; they had backed up the cause of the Venetian Pope Gregory the Twelfth ; the Venetians, moreover, had refused to acknowledge Antonius Pancera de Portogruario as Patriarch of Aquileia ; they had flouted the declaration of the Council in his favour and had acknowledged in his place Louis of Teck, the nominee of their fellow-countryman ; but since then, differences, many and serious, had arisen between the two hereditary enemies, Hungary and Venice. For the last thirty years the Republic had been embarked on a flood-tide of success. Their pride and pretensions had been aggravated thereby ; their animosity toward their old enemy had of late been more and more glaringly evinced ; until now it was becoming evident that the variance between the two States could only be adjusted by the stern arbitrament of war. Sigismund was not a man to commit the fault of the late King Rupert by taking in hand more matters than he could properly deal with at one time ; he therefore determined to postpone the questions of the Schism and the coronation until he was at peace with Venice.

The King was willing to avert war if possible, and to settle the differences by arbitration. It was no light matter to make war with Venice at this time, for the Republic was in an extremely flourishing condition. Three quarters of a century had passed since she had recognised that the passes through the Eastern Alps were essential for her commerce, and had occupied the Trevisan March ; with the exception of eight years she had

THE WAR WITH VENICE 147

held that territory ever since. It was more than thirty years since she had fought for dear life her 'most fatal war' of Chioggia (1379-80) and had settled her differences with that Republic and her allies by the Treaty of Turin (8th August 1381). Since that time she had pursued a selfish, trimming, and at times dishonourable, policy which had consistently proved to her own advantage. She had allied herself with Verona in 1385, and with Milan three years later against Padua, and she had then recovered Treviso (14th December 1388); she had lent her aid to young Francesco da Carrara against Milan in 1397; she had acquired Argos, Nauplia, Scutari, Durazzo, Alessio, and Corfu (1386-1402); she had defeated the French and Genoese fleets under Boucicaut at the naval battle of Zonchio on the 9th October 1403; after the death of Gian Galeazzo Visconti of Milan she had declared war on Francesco da Carrara of Padua, had occupied Vicenza and Verona, had taken Padua (22nd November 1405), and had committed 'her darkest crime' in the execution of Francesco and his two sons. Later still the Marquess of Mantua had left his son and state under the tutelage of the Republic; and the Marquess of Ferrara had ceded to them Guastalla, Brescello, and Casel-Maggiore on the Po. They had taken advantage of Pope Gregory's disagreement with the Patriarch of Aquileia to occupy certain of the chief towns and passes in Friuli, the north-eastern corner of Italy which lay between Treviso and the Julian Alps.

In their dealings, which more particularly affected the King of Hungary, they had evinced a spirit of uncompromising hostility. They had for many years neglected to pay him the seven thousand ducats which were due annually under the Treaty of Turin as compensation for the cessation of the Hungarian salt manufacture; they had helped the Dalmatian rebels; they had aided and abetted Ladislas of Naples in his attempt on the crown of Hungary; they had purchased from him the city of Zara and his rights in Dalmatia without inquiring whether he were rightful owner or not; they had bought up the Croatian lordship of Ostrovitza, they had occupied four islands, they had seized Sebenigo by main force.[1]

[1] Daru, ii. 252.

Moreover, since the death of Gian Galeazzo, Duke of Milan, they had been extending their sway in northern Italy without any regard to the rights of the Holy Roman Empire, of which Sigismund was now temporal lord ; through treaty with Milan they had acquired Verona, Bassano, Belluno, and Vicenza ; Feltre had opened its gates to them ; Padua had been conquered. Venice now held these cities and the Trevisan March ' together with the high tableland of the Seven Communes above Bassano. The boundaries of the Republic in Italy were now, roughly speaking, the sea from the mountains of the Tagliamento to those of the Adige—the Tagliamento to the east, the Alps to the north, and the Adige to the west and south.'[1]

On other sides than that of Venice the situation of Hungary, at the time Sigismund was elected King of the Romans, was precarious. After the victory of Ladislas, King of Poland, over the Teutonic Order at Tannenberg (1410), Sigismund had succeeded in negotiating a treaty of peace, which the Pope had ratified, between the Order and the King ; but Ladislas had, in April 1411, concluded an alliance with Venice against the King of Hungary ; and this was followed next month by an alliance between the same monarch and the Woivod of Wallachia, also directed against Sigismund ; and in October of that year Duke Ernest of Austria also joined the ranks of the King's enemies. Ernest was angry with Sigismund for taking his cousin Albert from his guardianship ; he had married Cimburga, the niece of the King of Poland, a princess very strong in the hands, and endowed by nature with that prominent jaw which became the distinguishing feature of all her descendants. On the 23rd February 1412, his younger brother Friedrich also entered into alliance with the King of Poland and with the King's brother, the Archduke of Lithuania. It was a most formidable coalition, but it was not in reality so formidable as it looked.

There was no chance really of renewed hostilities between Poland and the Teutonic Order ; neither the magnates nor the King of Hungary were anxious for such a risk ; and the aim of King Ladislas was simply to secure himself against King Sigismund ; he also did not wish for war. In November 1411,

[1] Brown, 248.

THE WAR WITH VENICE 149

accordingly, twelve of the Polish nobles met the same number of the Hungarian nobility and arranged a truce to last till the 15th August of the following year; and on the 15th March 1412, the Kings of Hungary and Poland met and made peace together. The terms were to the advantage of Poland; but it was agreed that, in the event of a war with the Turks or other unbelievers, the Woivod of Moldau was to help King Sigismund. The King of the Romans ever kept a watchful eye on that part of his imperial capitulation which pledged him to rid Europe of the enemies of Christianity. After the peace Sigismund entered into the most friendly relations with Ladislas, King of the Poles, who was his guest from Easter till the end of June 1412; the two kings hunted and feasted together, filling their days and nights with delight. On Corpus Christi of that year Sigismund held at Buda a magnificent court, at which guests and envoys from every land in Europe appeared to congratulate him on his new honour. The only drop of bitterness in the King's cup was the hostile attitude of the iron-handed Duke Ernest, who appeared at the festivities with ploughmen painted on his horses' clothing, and who tried to raise a conspiracy against the new King of the Romans. The King of Poland smoothed matters over, but Sigismund was not the man to forget a personal insult. Later on, in the spring of 1413, Duke Ernest also made his peace with the King.[1]

By his imperial capitulation the new King of the Romans had pledged himself to recover the lands which had been lost to the Empire,[2] and he knew very well that he could look for very little aid from the Estates of the Empire in effecting this recovery. Venice was not only the enemy of Hungary; she was the enemy of the Holy Roman Empire. It was in the latter capacity, as Lord of the Empire, that Sigismund made war on Venice to recover the territories belonging to the Patriarchate of Aquileia. He proclaimed this in his letter to Duke Leopold of Austria of the 11th November,[3] 1411; he set it forth at length in the circular letter which he sent to the States of the Empire on the 30th January 1412.[4] He recognised the importance and the difficulty of his undertaking.

[1] Huber, ii. 522-3.
[2] *Ibid.* ii. 523.
[3] Sauerbrei, 19.
[4] Aschbach, i. 430.

The prosperity of Venice at this time was unexampled. Her trade and commercial speculation had of late been advancing with a prodigious impulse. 'The argosies of the Morosini, the Cornari, and the Mocenigi traversed every arm of the ocean, and visited every port and inlet.'[1] Into the city itself there had been a great influx of new blood. Many German and other artificers who had sojourned there the requisite time were admitted as citizens, and privileges were granted to them. Natives from all parts of Italy, from the simplest trades to the most highly skilled, had taken up their residence; the citizenship had recently been thrown open to all who came to live in Venice with their families.[2] Gothic architecture was then in its glorious prime; Tuscan sculptors and Bolognese miniaturists worked in Venice; the Oriental feeling for colour was manifest in the early paintings. Morions and coats of mail for the common soldiers, crossbows of the finest workmanship, all the various pieces of armour worn by officers were manufactured in the city.[3] Every one, rich and poor alike, was trained to the use of the bow, and martial exercises were systematically encouraged. 'Venetian skill and courage in the use of arms were verily remarkable. Petrarch declares that this nation of sailors was so skilful in the handling of horses and of weapons, so spirited and so hardy, that it surpassed all other warlike nations whether by sea or by land.'[4] The people were rich; sumptuary laws had been enacted; the Doge appeared in public clad from head to foot in cloth of gold. The wealth of the Republic gave them the command of mercenaries. They could obtain the services of the best condottiere generals, and had no difficulty in filling one third of their ranks with foreign troops. Venice was therefore at this time exceptionally strong and prosperous; it was no light task to cope with such a foe; Sigismund was naturally willing to avert war and to resort to arbitration. Pope John the Twenty-third was ready to act as mediator; but there was little chance of his proving successful, for Venice was of all States the least amenable to papal influence; her policy was dictated by her commercial interest.

Both parties professed to be ready to refer their grievances

---

[1] Hazlitt, i. 741.   [2] Molmenti, i. 173.
[3] *Ibid*. ii. 88.   [4] *Ibid*. i. 206.

THE WAR WITH VENICE 151

to the Pope.[1] He was still at Bologna, and the King's representatives reached that city first. On the 10th February 1411, the Venetians issued their instructions to their envoys. They were anxious to impress on the Pope, as arbitrator, that Sigismund had no ground for quarrel with them; they had befriended him at his utmost need, and had heard of his recent election with joy; the purchase of Zara and the other territories had been perfectly regular, and their orderly government by the Venetians could not but be of advantage to the King; if they were reproached with failing to pay the seven thousand ducats due annually under the Treaty of Turin, the Pope must remember that Hungary also had neglected her obligations under that Treaty. What the Hungarians replied we do not know. The Pope, however, tried to persuade King Sigismund that Dalmatia was of little use to Hungary. As the royal representatives were not fully empowered, John sent his own nephew with Count Pippo of Ozora and one of the Hungarian envoys back for ampler powers. The envoys did not return to Italy; the Pope himself left Bologna on the 31st March; and when once in Rome, he was fully engrossed with the war against Ladislas of Naples and the consequent Bull. In September the Republic of Venice informed the Marquess of Montferrat that the Pope's nephew had not come back, but that they were still ready to send an embassy to Rome. They knew that the Pope by this time wanted Sigismund to come to Rome to defend him against the King of Naples, irrespective of whether peace had been made between the Republic and Hungary or not. It was clear that the attempted mediation of the Pope had come to nought, and that the only solution of the question between the two States was to be by war. Sigismund had chastised Bosnia and Dalmatia, and now set to work at his new task. On the 11th November 1411, he despatched an army of ten thousand men under his able and trusted general, the Florentine, Count Pippo of Ozora;[2] and he appointed Friedrich of Ortenburg to be Vicar of the Empire for the province of Friuli, in order that he might raise local troops.[3]

---

[1] Mur. xxii. 855.
[2] Aschbach, i. 337; according to Goeller, 94, Pippo's army reached Cividale on the 18th October.   [3] Sauerbrei, 22.

152   POPE JOHN THE TWENTY-THIRD

There was, about the time the war began, a rumour that Sigismund himself was coming to Italy with the intention of being crowned Emperor at Rome.[1] The Pope sent Berthold des Ursins to persuade the King to come and defend Rome; and the ambassador got as far as Venice, where he disclosed his mission to the Venetians. They reminded him that the Pope had promised not to crown the King until there was peace between Hungary and Venice; they were clear that the King's advent in Italy would be to their own disadvantage.[2] The Republic therefore said that they would do their best to prevent the King's journey to Rome. As Sigismund did not accompany his army, nothing more was heard of the project at this time; though when he did come to Udine later on, the rumour again revived. At the end of 1412 men said that he was going to Bologna to be crowned by Pope John there.[3] The Lords of Ferrara and Mantua were said to be adverse to the project, which was abandoned. What Sigismund really meant is shown in his letter to Kaiser Manuel.[4] He did not expect the Venetian war would hang on so long as it did; he thought it would be finished speedily; he then meant to go to Aachen to receive the silver crown, and in the following winter to go to Rome to be crowned by the Pope. This was the meaning of his embassies. But in endeavouring to humble the haughty Republic of Venice he had undertaken a heavier task than he imagined. He was quite ready to throw over his half-brother Wenzel; he never thought of taking the golden crown before the silver; but meantime he had the war with Venice on his hands, and this had to be decided before any coronation at all could take place.

Whether Louis of Teck sent on Maundy Thursday that year to Venice the bull and twelve pigs, representing the Patriarch and his twelve canons, which the Venetians received annually with derisive joy,[5] we do not know; but Pippo, crossing over from Istria speedily overran the Patriarchate and caused him to fly for refuge to Venice.[6] The Republic had an army in the field. Twelve thousand men had been sent under the command of Taddeo del Verme; but he had been superseded by Carlo

---

[1] Mur. xxii. 858.
[2] 'Ad damna et sinistra nostri dominii'; Finke (*Acta*), 98.
[3] Mur. xxii. 876.   [4] Finke (*Acta*), 396.   [5] Daru, i. 174.   [6] Mur. xxii. 857.

THE WAR WITH VENICE 153

Malatesta, Lord of Rimini, who had previously commanded Venetian troops against Gian Galeazzo and against Francesco da Carrara. A deep ditch was dug, twenty-two miles long.[1] The troops were raw; Malatesta was cautious and dilatory; the general 'with the leaden foot' excited much hostile criticism by the time he took to complete his dispositions. Count Pippo made good use of his time and of his adversary's inactivity. In December he crossed the Tagliamento and overran Friuli, famed for its swordsmen. There were dissensions between the landowners and the Patriarch of Aquileia; the agriculturists also disliked the commercial Republic which favoured the cities; the Hungarian general had consequently little trouble in crossing the Livenza and in making his way through the mountain gorges. He penetrated as far as the March of Treviso, and fought and won a battle of Conegliano, south of the hills below Belluno.[2] King Sigismund at Buda received nineteen conquered banners on the 5th January 1412. Pippo marched thence to Serravalle in the hill country, and took the place; his troops, who had previously threatened to cut off the hands of all who resisted them, behaved with such barbarity that ' the sad cries of boys and girls, the groans and wailing of wives, widows, and virgins went up to heaven.'[3] The right hands, the noses, and the ears of the prisoners were cut off.[4] On the 22nd April Pippo carried the Venetian lines, the troops scattering as he approached.[5] Feltre, Belluno, and seventy other places fell into the hands of the conquering general, whose own tenth share of the spoil amounted to sixty thousand ducats; the whole of the March seemed in his power; Treviso was summoned to capitulate. This, the chief city of the *Marca Amorosa*, had, except for eight years, been for the last three-quarters of a century Venetian; and she now proudly answered that she knew no lord save the Doge and Republic of Venice. Nevertheless the city would probably soon have fallen into Pippo's hands, had not his army dispersed to plunder, and had not he himself fallen so ill that he was obliged to retreat westward to Udine, and thence into Hungary.[6] He took the

[1] Mur. xxii. 856.   [2] *Ibid.* xix. 834.   [3] *Ibid.* xix. 835.
[4] *Ibid.* xxii. 860.   [5] Daru, ii. 259.
[6] Mur. xix. 835; xxii. 861; *A.S.I.*, iv. 137; Huber, ii. 524.

precaution to leave such strong garrisons in the conquered towns that the Venetians were unable to make much impression on them.

This retrograde movement of the Hungarian general was, however, so much to the advantage of the Venetians that Brunoro della Scala and Marsiglio of Padua, whom Sigismund had promised to reinstate in their lordships of Verona, Vicenza, and Padua, made no scruple of accusing the Florentine of having been bribed ; and the story got about that the Venetians had sent him two silver-gilt goblets, ostensibly filled with good wine, but really containing ducats.[1] There was not an iota of truth in the story, and Sigismund himself never doubted the good faith of Pippo.[2] The King sent Marsiglio and Brunoro into Italy with another army under the command of the Woivod of Transylvania, who won the first battle of Motta, where the Venetians lost nine thousand men.[3] The Hungarians, however, lost their general. So far the balance of success had on the whole been on the side of the Hungarians, but there was no preponderating advantage on either side ; the Republic took Serravalle and Udine ; Carlo Malatesta still held his own ; the province was divided between the combatants. Heavy expense had been incurred on both sides; and the Venetians had put on several extra taxes to meet the cost of operations. Both parties were glad of a breathing time, and agreed to a truce.

Pope John the Twenty-third, ever ready to ingratiate himself with Sigismund, re-assumed the office of mediator. The Republic hoped to get the Dukes Ernest and Friedrich of Austria, who had already given them some help, entirely on their side ; they also tried to win over the powerful King of Poland. But Sigismund was beforehand with them ; he had made peace with King Ladislas, and the Austrian brothers dared not enter the field alone against him. Negotiations for peace between Hungary and Venice were begun at Rome. The Republic held to their former terms, but demanded in addition the restitution of the places taken by Count Pippo. Sigismund agreed to the Pope's suggestion, he was ready to sell his claim to Zara, but he insisted on the rendition of Sebenigo.[4]

---

[1] *A.S.I.*, iv. 174.
[2] *Ibid.* 136 *et seq.*
[3] Aschbach, i. 340.
[4] Mur. xxii. 863.

THE WAR WITH VENICE 155

The Venetians offered him a hundred thousand ducats and the yearly tribute of a palfrey in acknowledgment of his suzerainty. The King's representative sent to Sigismund to know whether these terms were acceptable. Meanwhile the King of Poland intervened, and the Venetians told him that they were willing to raise their bid for Dalmatia. Count Pippo, who had alarmed the Republic by landing foragers on the Lido on the 10th June, regained Ostrovitza. The war in Italy recommenced. Carlo Malatesta captured several small places, but Udine held firm for the Hungarians; and Sigismund, elated at the success of Count Pippo, raised his demands and claimed the rendition of Zara. France and Burgundy intervened; the negotiations, which had failed at Rome, were recommenced at Buda. But all hopes of an understanding were vain; the renewal of the war, which had already occurred between the contending forces in the March, was inevitable; the Pope's attempt to befriend the King of the Romans and to procure peace had failed.

Hostilities began badly for Sigismund. On the 24th August at Motta,[1] Carlo Malatesta avenged the defeat of the Venetians earlier in the year by gaining a decisive victory over Count Pippo. The leaden-footed general had held to his camp by Motta on the Livenza River, and when taunted that the Hungarians were coming, he had always answered, 'Let them come.' They came and they took him by surprise. There were seven or eight thousand horsemen in all; three thousand of them were Hungarian lancers; one squadron was from Friuli; others were from Bohemia, well mounted and well armed. In their sudden onset, as they came on crying out *Carne, Carne,* they scattered the Venetian troops until Carlo Malatesta, donning his cuirass and mounting his horse, caused the trumpets to sound. Many of the Venetians, imagining in their terror that their general was already captured, took to flight, until one of their captains, Pietro Loredano, destroyed the bridge of boats over the river. The flying troops were rallied and led back by Ruggiero Cane of Perugia to where Malatesta and his men were bravely holding the enemy at bay; their timely arrival turned the fortune of the day. The fighting became fierce and general; the din and clamour were terrific; the battle was cruel and

[1] Mur. xxii. 869.

hard.¹ Taddeo del Verme was there and bore himself bravely ; he was wounded by a sword-cut in the face. Carlo Malatesta was wounded in three places, by a bolt from a cross-bow, by a lance, by a sword-cut in the thigh. But the Hungarians were repulsed ; five of their six banners were taken ; thirteen hundred of them were killed, four hundred were taken prisoners, twenty-five of these being rich warriors, girt with gold or silver belts and with their pockets full of money. The second battle of Motta was won for the Venetians.² But, as in the first battle of Motta, the victorious general was placed *hors de combat*. The wounds of Carlo Malatesta were so grievous that he could take no further part in active hostilities ; he retired to Venice for a cure, and thence to Rimini. The Venetians, although they celebrated the victory by a solemn procession round the Piazza of San Marco, were dispirited. More especially was this the case on the field. Men said that they saw a celestial horseman, the Spirit of Victory, fighting against them and for the men of Feltre and Belluno. The Republic despatched the loquacious chronicler of Treviso to engage the services of Pandulfo Malatesta, the Lord of Brescia, who had formerly commanded their troops against Padua, to replace his brother. Pandulfo was at Verona, but was in treaty with Duke Friedrich of Austria, and at first hesitated. One of the early fugitives from Motta came to him with the news that his brother had been captured by the Hungarians ; but the messenger from the Republic followed, bringing news of Carlo's victory and grievous wound, on which Pandulfo delayed no longer, but hastened to take command of the Venetian army.³

Marsiglio of Padua and Brunoro della Scala meantime persuaded King Sigismund, who was then in Istria, that the cities of the Trevisan March would submit if he promised to constitute them cities of the Empire ; and the King accordingly sent Count Pippo with sixteen thousand horse to obtain their surrender. The Florentine knew that he had little chance with the faithful city of Treviso itself, and accordingly marched off to Padua, where, however, Pandulfo Malatesta was before him. Pippo then turned north to Bassano, but here also he was

---

¹ 'Molto aspra e dura.'
² Mur. xix. 837 ; xxi. 957 ; xxii. 869 ; Aschbach, i. 344.   ³ Mur. xix. 839.

THE WAR WITH VENICE

repulsed; and at Vicenza the like fate befell him. Indignantly he called for Marsiglio and Brunoro and upbraided them; but they answered that it was no fault of theirs, the Venetians had been before them everywhere, and they had better march with all haste to Verona. Pippo marched accordingly, but at Verona also his overtures met with no favourable response, and the fighting which occurred was indecisive. He again tried Bassano unsuccessfully, and was drawn into an ambush at Asola. In disgust he placed his army in safety at Friuli, and went off to report the want of success to Sigismund.[1]

In addition to their success in Italy, the Venetians had met with somewhat of the like fortune in Dalmatia, where Sebenigo had surrendered to their general Mocenigo. It was clearly time for the King of the Romans to appear on the scene in person; and this he was now able to do, as he had given his award between the Poles and the Teutonic Order, he had made peace with Ladislas, the powerful King of Poland, and he had settled matters with the two Austrian Dukes. The war had already lasted much longer and had been much more costly than he had expected. Sigismund raised a loan from his new ally, Ladislas of Poland; he hired ships for the defence of Dalmatia from the Republic of Genoa; he got troops to help him from the Austrian Dukes Ernest and Friedrich, from Bavaria, and from his Vicar in Friuli.[2] With an army of forty thousand men he appeared before Udine on the 18th December, and took over the commandership in chief in the following February.[3] Hostilities were resumed in earnest; Udine, Cividale, and other places were more than once taken and lost; and the war assumed a particularly savage character; there was a third fight, which lasted for three days, before Motta;[4] the Venetians were repulsed, and Sigismund forced their commander himself to hew off the right hands of one hundred and eighty of the prisoners; the mutilated men were sent back to Venice for their countrymen to behold.[5] Count Pippo followed his master's example by cutting off the arms and gouging out the eyes of forty of his chief prisoners;[6] on which Pandulfo Malatesta threatened to kill all the Hungarians in his power

[1] Mur. xix. 840-3. [2] Sauerbrei, 25. [3] Goeller, 95; Sauerbrei, 25.
[4] Mur. xxii. 874; Aschbach, i. 345. [5] Altmann, 26. [6] Mur. xxiv. 182.

if such barbarities were permitted in the opposite camp. An attempt to renew negotiations, made at this time by Count Hermann of Cilly, King Sigismund's father-in-law, was fruitless. Pandulfo beat back the Hungarians, but was himself obliged to retreat. Count Pippo, on the other hand, had been everywhere unsuccessful; the Venetians had held their own, they had discovered and had punished conspiracies, they had kept the enemy at bay. Sigismund himself had met with some slight advantage, but Malatesta had burned Feltre and had been successful in many other places.

Sigismund now appealed to the Pope to stop the Venetians from warring in Dalmatia, on the ground that they had no right to carry the war into that country; but after his recent failure, John the Twenty-third was chary of interfering again, and did nothing. He hereby missed his chance, for the circumstances were now altered. The protracted and indecisive nature of the war, and his own want of any striking success, caused Sigismund to recognise that, in attempting to humble the haughty Republic as he had humbled Bosnia and Dalmatia, he had undertaken more than he could carry through, except at a ruinous cost of money and time; he was anxious to turn his attention to the pressing needs of the Empire and the Church; hence he was willing to listen to terms of accommodation. Venice also was weary of the war, which had cost her two millions of ducats and the devastation of her provinces. Count Hermann of Cilly again took up the role of mediator; and on the 17th April 1413 a truce for five years was concluded.

The Marquesses of Ferrara and Mantua, and Carlo Malatesta of Rimini, were included in the peace on the side of the Republic, and the Patriarch of Aquileia and the Castellani of Friuli on the side of the King.[1] Each party was to retain what it then possessed; the Venetians agreed to pay the King two hundred thousand ducats and to allow him free passage through their territory when he desired it. The old fear that Sigismund meant to get himself crowned Emperor had not yet subsided; a league for ten years was at this time formed against the King between Milan, Florence, Genoa, the Count of Montferrat and Pandulfo Malatesta, with the expressed object of preventing

[1] Mur. xxii. 880.

THE WAR WITH VENICE

Sigismund from being crowned in Lombardy by Pope John. The King and the Pope were to meet later in the year, but no attempt at a coronation was ever made; and the letter already quoted shows that no such design was ever entertained.

The King of the Romans now marched back to Friuli; he was received in the different cities of which he was in possession; and at the beginning of June 1413, he made his joyous entry into Belluno. Laymen and priests came forth to meet him with banners and crosses. The road was strewn with flowers and the King entered the city under a magnificent canopy borne aloft by four of the principal citizens, and took up his residence at the Bishop's palace. He confirmed the privileges of the city, and bestowed additional favours on the burghers. He remained in Belluno for a week, and during that time he was invited by the Ghibelines to a wedding. The King, ever ready for any scene of merriment, consented; and the bride, in her joy at his condescension, took off the wedding garland from her own head and placed it on his, vowing that thenceforward she would do nothing but enjoy herself.[1] From Belluno in the middle of June, Sigismund went to Feltre, where he concluded a truce between the Venetians and Duke Friedrich of Austria. While at Feltre the King of the Romans invested the Count of Goerz with jurisdiction over Feltre, Belluno, Serravalle, Cordignano, and Zumella, thus pursuing his policy of placing trustworthy men in command of the possessions of the Holy Roman Empire.

While at Feltre Sigismund received news of the utmost importance to him as Lord of the Empire. The fratricidal strife between the sons of Bajazet, his old enemy at Nicopolis, was at an end. In 1402 Bajazet the Turk had been conquered at Angora by Timur the Tartar, and he had died a year later in captivity. Rarely, says Finlay, 'has the world seen a more total defeat than that sustained by the Othoman army.'[2] Then began a war of succession between the three sons of Bajazet. Suleiman and Musa fought together; Suleiman was defeated and murdered. Musa then fought with his youngest brother, lost the battle and his life. Ten years had elapsed, says the same author, since Muhammad, ' then a mere youth, fled from

[1] Mur. xvii. 826.   [2] Finlay, iii. 482.

the field of Angora with only one faithful companion, until he reunited under his sway nearly all the extensive dominions which had been ruled by his father.'[1] He was now sole ruler of the Turks, and Sigismund, King of the Romans, was filled with the apprehension that the work which he had so signally failed to accomplish at Nicopolis would fall to be recommenced by him in the future. For it was part of the duty of the Lord of the Holy Roman Empire, as Sigismund had acknowledged in his imperial capitulation, to defend Christendom against the unbeliever. At Feltre also he learned of the treachery of the Duke of Spalatro, whom on the 1st August Sigismund deposed from the dukedom, declaring all his possessions forfeit.

That the truce with the Republic of Venice was not likely to ripen into a permanent peace seemed only too probable from the requests made by them at Feltre. Their envoy was Tomaso Mocenigo, who was accompanied by Francesco Foscari, the wisest Venetian, so the King declared, that he had ever seen or heard.[2] The future Doge begged Sigismund to allay the Schism in the Church, and to induce peace among the great nobles of Italy, demands with which the King was, to the extent of his ability, only too ready to comply; but he went on to request that the Republic might be invested with the lordship of Padua, Verona, and Vicenza, which Sigismund was determined to restore to his allies, Brunoro della Scala and Marsiglio of Padua. The promise of the Republic, moreover, to allow him free passage through Italy was not of any present value, inasmuch as he had made up his mind to receive the silver crown at Aachen before he thought of taking the golden crown of Rome. The great point, however, gained by the truce with Venice was that the King of the Romans was now free to deal with the Schism in the Holy Roman Church. Sigismund had always regarded with a jealous eye the efforts of the French court to restore unity to the Church; the work was pre-eminently a task for the temporal head of the Empire; and he was determined that he, and not the King of France, should heal the Great Schism which had now for thirty-five years distracted the Holy Roman Church.

[1] Finlay, iii. 484. [2] Mur. xix. 826.

CHAPTER IX

THE FLIGHT FROM ROME

WHILE King Sigismund was making his joyous entry into Belluno, Pope John the Twenty-third was in deadly peril of his life in Rome. There was still the old cloud between the spiritual and temporal heads of the Empire. Sigismund had never applied to the Pope for approbation and confirmation of his election; and John, on his part, never recognised Sigismund as King of the Romans, but simply as ' elected to be King.'[1] The King's attitude was still ambiguous; John knew that he might determine to terminate the Schism by deposing all three rival Popes.

Short and evil was the peace with Ladislas, King of Naples. It was made in June 1412; its immediate effect was to reduce the price of grain to one half its former rate;[2] and it enabled the Pope to hold the Council of Rome. Sforza Attendolo had left the Pope's service and taken the pay of Ladislas of Naples. John had obtained peace with the King, but had lost the services of the best general in Italy. The loss was his own fault, because he preferred Paolo Orsini to Sforza; but, nevertheless, it enraged him, and he professed to regard the action of Sforza as that of a traitor. He caused his effigy to be hung on all the gates and bridges of the city to a gallows by the right foot; in the right hand of the figure was a peasant's axe; in the left was a scroll, on which was written:

> ' I am the peasant Sforza of Cotignola, a traitor,
>   Who contrary to my honour have twelve times betrayed the Church;
>   My promises, my agreements, my contracts have I broken.'[3]

It was an absurd and petty outburst of spite against a valiant soldier, of which Baldassare Cossa in his earlier days would not

---

[1] 'Electres ad regem.' [2] Mur. xxiv. 1031. [3] *Ibid.*

have been guilty ; it is a significant mark of the failing strength of will and character.

The peace with Ladislas brought no increase of revenue to the Pope. The clergy of southern Italy took no heed of their change of spiritual master, and scarce any applied for confirmation of their position. The Pope was again confronted with the task of raising money. He ordered that a tax should be levied of two ducats on every barrel of wine brought to the city by water. The merchants retaliated by refusing to import, saying that they could sell the wine more profitably outside. The new tax was a blow to the King of Naples, for his merchants had reckoned on the peace to sell their wine and other merchandise to advantage in Rome ; and if their market was spoiled the King could not tax them so heavily as he wished. He tried to meet the difficulty by forbidding them to send wine to Rome, and by himself imposing a tax of two ducats per barrel on their sales elsewhere. The tension between the Pope and the King was becoming daily more strained ; and when, on the 3rd March 1413, John announced that the Council would re-assemble on the 1st December at some place other than Rome, Ladislas replied by an announcement that in that case he must occupy Rome to keep the peace there. In May he sent out his troops ; Sforza was sent north to besiege Paolo Orsini in Rocca Contrada, so as to prevent him from marching to the aid of the Pope ; the Neapolitan fleet sailed for the mouth of the Tiber ; and Ladislas himself set out for Rome. As his troops closed round the city, the price of grain rose again. Henceforth it was open war between the Pope and the King.

Pope John at this time determined still further to strengthen his College of Cardinals by including in it Simon de Cramaud, Archbishop of Reims, whom he raised to the purple on the 13th April 1413. The fighting Patriarch of Alexandria had been a prominent character all through the latter part of the Great Schism ; he had started as a Benedictine monk, winning renown for his theological and juristic knowledge, as well as for his acquaintance with men and affairs ; at the University of Paris he had been head of the stormy Norman nation ; he had presided at the Councils of Paris in 1398 and 1408, and had been at the head of the great embassy to Pope Benedict the Thirteenth

THE FLIGHT FROM ROME

in the latter year; he had been most active at the Council of Pisa. Altogether he was a man of such determination and activity that it was wiser to have him on one's side than in the opposition. In 1414, as soon as the Council of Constance had been decided on, he again took up the weapons of controversy, after the approved scholastic fashion, against Pope Gregory the Twelfth in defence of Pope John and of the Council of Pisa.[1]

Pope John the Twenty-third had been grossly deceived and betrayed by the King whom he ought never to have trusted; he had now to fight in defence of his favourite city and of his personal safety. He had made an alliance with the Count of Urbino; and he tried to win back his old friends, the Republic of Florence; but the wise Florentines were chary of entering on a quarrel with so powerful a King as Ladislas of Naples. They knew they could not trust him, but they feared to irritate him unnecessarily. The Pope, on his side, tried to pacify the Romans by removing the tax of one-third on wine, and by restoring to them their liberty. ' I place you on your own feet,' he said to them, ' and I ask you to act well and faithfully by your Holy Mother Church, and not to fear King Ladislas nor any man of this world, for I am ready to die with you for the sake of the Holy Church and the Roman people.' The Roman nobles answered, ' Holy Father, doubt not but that the whole of Rome is ready to die with you for the sake of Holy Church and for Your Holiness.' Two days later, on the 6th June, they held an assembly in the Capitol, and there resolved to die with their Lord the Pope rather than bow before the King of Naples; they were ready to suffer privation of bread and wine and every necessary; ' We Romans,' they said, ' are determined rather to eat our own children than be subject to that dragon.' In the evening of that day the whole of the Roman people came to the Pope and acquainted him with their resolve; he received them honourably and thanked them for their message. They were brave words, but empty of meaning.

On the night of the 7th of June the Pope with thirteen cardinals and the whole of the Curia removed from the Leonine City across the Tiber to show the people that he trusted them,

---

[1] Finke (*F.*), 15 *et seq.*

164 POPE JOHN THE TWENTY-THIRD

and he abode in the palace of Count Orsini of Manupello. The Neapolitan troops were outside the city before the gates. On the next night Rome was conquered by Ladislas. On the far side of the city, beyond the Esquiline, the wall by the Porta Capena near the Church of Santa Croce was broken down, the sleeping sentinels were overpowered, and Tartaglia, one of the King's generals, entered by the breach into the city with his troops crying, ' Long live King Ladislas and peace.' [1]

The Pope and the cardinals, roused from their sleep, took to their horses and left the city in flight to Sutri. Some of their followers were too old and feeble to ride, and made their escape on foot; others were overpowered by the heat next day and fell by the roadside dead. The enemy followed, but slew very few of them. All that they had been obliged to leave in the city was plundered. The main body of the fugitives reached Sutri, beyond the Lake of Bracciano, that night, the 8th June, but the Pope did not feel safe here, and before morning he set out again, with a considerable number of the Curia, for Viterbo, the walled city in the patrimony of Saint Peter, famed of old for its handsome fountains and its beautiful women. They reached the city next evening,[2] espied the enemy following them irresolutely at a distance, were received by the governor and the weeping matrons of Viterbo, and soon learned to their joy that the prefect of the pursuers had orders not to do them any injury.[3] For two years and two months only had Pope John held possession of Rome; he was never more to behold the Eternal City.

The Pope did not tarry at Viterbo, but pushed for Monte Fiascone, eight or nine miles on, where he remained until the 13th; thence he went to Aquapendente, and on the 14th to Radicofano, where he halted for two days. On the 17th he reached Siena,[4] with eleven cardinals in his train.[5] Here he stayed four days, feeling that he was for the time in comparative safety, and he cheered up the officers of the Curia by promising to recompense them for their losses.[6] But he was determined to make his way to his former friends and allies, the Florentines. Florence, as was so often the case, was divided into two factions;

[1] Mur. xxiv. 1035. [2] Finke (*Acta*), 171. [3] Hardt, ii. 381.
[4] Finke (*Acta*), 171. [5] Mur. xix. 424. [6] Hardt, ii. 382.

THE FLIGHT FROM ROME

one held for the Pope, and the other for Ladislas; the strife was bitter betwixt them; but both alike were taken aback at being asked to accommodate so important a guest. The King of Naples had, it was true, violated his word, for he had promised them to undertake nothing to the prejudice of the Pope, and not to assume possession of Rome; but there was a strong feeling that he was too powerful to be rashly offended. They solved the difficulty by not receiving His Holiness within the walls, but they offered him the Bishop's palace in the Faubourg Saint Antoine, and here, on the 21st June 1413, Pope John the Twenty-third took up his residence, and here he was visited next day by the signors, the Balia, and the principal citizens of Florence.[1]

The Faubourg Saint Antoine lay north of the city, outside the present Barriera del Ponte Rosso, and along the Via Vittorio Emanuele. The Bishop's palace was about two miles from the Duomo. It was destroyed in the siege of 1530; but on its site there now stands a *tabernocolo* or shrine, containing a bust of Saint Antoninus, Archbishop of Florence, who died in 1459. This is on the west side of the road; and on the other side of the way, a little further on, where the steep Via S. Marta runs up to the Capuchin Convent, there is a fresco of Saint Anthony, the patron saint of the suburb.[2]

On the day when the Pope fled, at the hour of tierce King Ladislas entered Rome, ' less as a conqueror than as a corsair.' Two thousand of the Romans had assembled, but finding that Pope John had fled and that they were without a leader, they deemed prudence the better part of valour, and welcomed the Neapolitans. For the first two days Ladislas remained at the palace of Saint John of the Lateran, but after that he went to the Vatican, where he found and imprisoned the Cardinal Louis de Bar, who had remained there at his post as guardian.[3] The King stayed at the papal palace for three weeks, appointed his own officers in the city, and soon let the Romans feel the change of masters. The Florentine merchants in Rome had hidden all

[1] Mur. xix. 955; xxi. 106.
[2] Guido Carocci: *I Dintorni di Firenze*, 211. My attention was first directed to this locality through the courtesy of Dr. Guido Biagi and of the Director of State Archives in Florence, to whom my thanks are due.
[3] Mur. xxiv. 1035

166 POPE JOHN THE TWENTY-THIRD

their wares and valuables; but when the King sent round criers to proclaim that all would be safe, they brought them out again; whereupon he seized them, ' not like a King, but like the worst of tyrants.'[1] The merchants were not alone in their suffering. Priests were plundered and massacred; the Pope's chapel was pillaged; jewels and relics were looted; horses were stabled in Saint Peter's; the churches of Rome were converted into inns and brothels. The Cardinal Chalant, when deputed to King Sigismund, drew a vivid picture of the miseries endured. ' Some of the cardinals were imprisoned,' he said, ' many priests and other ecclesiastics were massacred, and others were wounded. The officers of the Papal Court were robbed. The shrines of the apostles were profaned; horses were littered down in them as if they were in their own stables; the churches of the city were denuded of their crosses, their chalices, and their sacred ornaments; the insolent soldiery used the sacred vessels in the inns instead of glasses. Wives and holy virgins were violated; the most respectable citizens were banished and their goods confiscated. Never had impiety been carried to such horrible excess.'[2] Romans were tortured and sent to the galleys; merchants were swindled and plundered. A new coinage was struck.[3] The city suffered almost as if it had been sacked. The commandant of Sant Angelo was killed by a bomb. His successor was bribed by Ladislas to surrender the fortress; the traitor was rewarded, allowed to go to Naples, and there shortly afterwards he was assassinated and his property seized. On the 26th June news came of the surrender of Viterbo, Perugia, Cortona, and other cities. The King, who had turned out the Pope's officers and put his own in their places, remained in Rome until the 6th July, when he sailed to Naples, resolved now to take up in earnest his former project of gaining for himself the overlordship of Italy; he would capture Bologna and get possession of Pope John.

The Pope's general, Paolo Orsini, had been kept inactive all this time at Rocca Contrada. Braccio da Montone, who had been holding Bologna for the Pope, hastened from that city to help him, took Cesena, captured the concubine of Carlo Malatesta[4], arrived at Todi, and was obliged to retire on the citizens

---

[1] Anton, iii. 477-8. [2] Lenfant (*P.*), ii. 182.
[3] Hardt, ii. 382. [4] Mur. xix. 496.

THE FLIGHT FROM ROME

making terms with King Ladislas. The men of Todi, however, soon changed their minds; they recalled Braccio, and again raised the papal banners on their walls. The King tried to win over Braccio da Montone, but that general declined to break faith with the Pope. Then Ladislas played the same game with Paolo Orsini, who began to treat Braccio as he had formerly treated Sforza. Rocca Contrada was situate on a very steep hill, and for three months Sforza's troops besieged the place in vain. There was only a small garrison in the place, but as soon as their opponents approached, they rolled down huge stones on them and kept them at a distance. Eventually Paolo Orsini got out of the fortress and made his way to Urbino, Carlo Malatesta, who had come there ostensibly to aid Sforza, being suspected of abetting his escape.[1] No one felt safe very long in alliance with Ladislas, for no one trusted him. Before the winter commenced, however, all the southern and central parts of Italy, as far as the borders of Siena, were in his possession, and the Pope saw his victorious opponent approaching closer and closer.

In Rome itself Ladislas had left Julius Cæsar in charge at the Vatican and the Count of Troja in command of the city. The Pope's arms were everywhere pulled down and replaced by those of the King; there were executions and imprisonments, one Geronimo Cossa, among others, being sent to the galleys; the citizens gathered their vintage with fear and trembling. So the year wore sadly to its close amid tribulation and portents, a great fiery beam being seen at one time moving across the sky.

While Pope John was settled, a fugitive, at the Faubourg Saint Antoine outside Florence, King Sigismund was leaving northern Italy for the Tirol. He had not recovered Milan; the task which his predecessor had failed to accomplish was still unachieved. The King, however, made peace with the Austrian Dukes Ernest and Friedrich. There was little in common between the vain calculating monarch and these two imperious young sons of the Duke who had fallen at Sempach. But Sigismund had the art of making himself all things to all men, and he set himself to win the younger brother, Friedrich of the Tirol. The points of likeness and of contrast in their characters were, however, too marked for them to become real

[1] Mur. xix. 496-501; xxi. 106.

friends, apart from the fact that there was fourteeen years difference in their ages.[1] Both were masterful men, eager to rule and greedy of power; both were versed in all knightly exercises; both loved a jest and a practical joke ; both ardently admired female beauty. But Friedrich despised the pomp and pageantry which were dear to the heart of Sigismund ; he valued only the reality of power, regardless of its trappings ; he was firm and steadfast of purpose, whereas Sigismund was often fickle and an opportunist ; and the King of the Romans could, on occasions, be inconstant and false, while Friedrich was usually straightforward and true. Sigismund, however, became friendly with the young Duke, and entrusted to him the task of bringing about a reconciliation with his iron-handed brother Ernest, Duke of Styria. Friedrich succeeded, and a formal alliance for mutual defence was drawn up between the King and the two Dukes. Friedrich accompanied Sigismund to Feltre, and they lived together apparently in the most intimate brotherly love and confidence (May 1413). Even here, however, a little incident occurred sufficient to set the King against the Duke. They were walking together, arm in arm, Friedrich dressed as usual in a long flowing velvet robe. The King, who loved a practical joke at another's expense, saw some mud on ahead, and directed their steps toward it, whereby the Duke's trailing robe was befouled with black mud. Seeing himself the victim of the pleasantry, the Duke turned the laugh against the King by taking the end of his robe in his hand and flapping it round his companion's thighs, so that Sigismund was bespattered half way up with mire.[2] It was a little thing, but the King of the Romans, vain of his majesty, did not relish being made the laughing-stock of the camp ; he did not forget nor forgive.

On the 25th June the King and the Duke were at Trient. Thence they went to Salzburg, which they reached on the 1st July ; here they met Duke Ernest, and a truce for two years was concluded between him and the Archbishop of Salzburg.[3] The Bavarian Duke Stephen of Ingolstadt, who had lately made an unsuccessful attempt on the Tirol, was also at Salzburg ; and Sigismund was able to negotiate a truce for a year between the two Austrian brothers and the Dukes of Bavaria.[4] This was in

[1] *A.D.B.*, vii. 588
[2] Mur. xix. 826.
[3] Altmann, 27.
[4] Aschbach, i. 358.

THE FLIGHT FROM ROME 169

July 1413, and the King and Duke Friedrich went from Salzburg to Innsbruck. Here an event happened which has always had the credit of changing their apparent friendship into open and bitter enmity.

Duke Friedrich, who shortly before had married his second wife, Anna of Brunswick, a beautiful but pious dame, determined to do great and seemly honour to his suzerain lord, the King of the Romans, and prepared for him a noteworthy feast and a dance to which all the gentles and burghers of the city were bidden. Among the ladies present was the fair daughter of one of the citizens. Some one enticed the beauteous damsel aside into a secret place and dishonoured her. She was not consenting thereto, and as soon as she regained her liberty, there was an outcry. But she had not seen her ravisher's face, and knew only that he had a long beard. There were only two of the knights present who wore their beards long, and they were the King of the Romans, and Friedrich, the giver of the feast. Suspicion immediately fell upon the former. The Hungarian magnates were disgusted; Friedrich's wife was indignant at the dishonour done to the house; Sigismund was universally upbraided. But the King swore on his honour and by his kinglihood that he had not done this thing; he would he knew who had wrongly thrown the blame on him that he might be avenged; he should always think shame and dishonour on the man who had brought this undeserved reproach on him. Then the damsel was summoned, and she was asked to choose between the two, who alone had long beards. She answered that he had indeed a long beard, but that his speech was not the King's voice. The blame was thereupon thrown on Duke Friedrich, and King Sigismund gave the girl four hundred Hungarian gulden.[1] Such is the story as told by Eberhard Windecke, the King's faithful servant and secretary, told, probably, as far as possible, to his master's advantage. It would be interesting to know more precisely whether the King gave the four hundred gulden before or after the girl recollected that the voice was not the voice of Sigismund; it would be interesting also to know why the suspicion of every one fell upon him in the first place; and also why the King protested so much. Both he and the Duke were fond of a pretty face; but it is not

[1] Altmann, 49-50.

consistent with the character of Friedrich to act thus toward one of his own guests, in his own palace, in the proximity of the wife whom he had lately married. Whichever of the two was guilty, the effect was the same ; there was open and undisguised hatred between the Duke and the King.

But this was not the sole nor the chief cause of the animosity between the King of the Romans and the Duke of the Tirol. Friedrich, though romantic and chivalrous, was determined and energetic ; and in his government of the Tirol, he was at variance with nearly all the nobility of the land. His position was difficult ; he was set on being the real ruler, the nobility were equally set on his being merely *primus inter pares*. The Tirol was a land apart ; the nobles were numerous and powerful ; the tenantry were loyal and patriotic. Had the office of Count of the Tirol been abolished, and had the land become directly dependent on the Empire, it might have split up into a number of cantons, like Switzerland, but at the head of each canton there would have been the local nobility, and the disruption of the Tirol would have been certain to follow. Already the southern portion showed signs of slipping away from Germany to Italy ; Tirolese nobles were making alliances with Venice and with Milan. Only a strong and powerful ruler could maintain the unity of the country. The last popular ruler had been Margaret Maultasch, ' pock-mouthed Meg,' who, with the consent of the nobility, had made over the country to Rudolf of Austria on the 26th January 1363,[1] and who died at Vienna six years later. But the diminution of the power of the Count of the Tirol had begun in her father's time ; he was set on obtaining the crown of Bohemia, and recklessly mortgaged his possessions in Tirol to support his claims. His example was followed by his successors, the usufructuary mortgagees being the Tirolese nobility, who thus grew stronger as their ruler became weaker. Margaret's son, Meinhard the Third (1361-63), was entirely in their hands. In this condition the country passed to the House of Habsburg, who were strangers in the land, not bound to the old nobility by ties of love or hereditary attachment. After the death of Rudolf, his brothers Albert and Leopold became joint Counts of Tirol, but took very little part in the administration, so that a spirit of independence and

[1] Egger, i. 400.

THE FLIGHT FROM ROME 171

of opposition naturally arose in the Tirolese nobility. Tirol was a land intensely attached to its local institutions; it was governed by the tradition of its elders, and would brook no interference of the Roman or any other written law. A spirit of sturdy patriotism permeated not only the nobility but also the tenantry; so that when the victorious Appenzellers in 1406 came over the Arlberg to incite the Tirolese to strike for liberty, not a man moved to welcome or support them.[1] The Tirolese nobles assumed to be the foremost representatives and defenders of their natural customs and privileges, and they had hitherto generally rendered their Count dependent on their will. They were a conservative body, opposed to all change which was not to their own advantage; and hence there was bound to come a time when government of the land would become impossible in face of their opposition to any measure of reform, when there would be a set struggle between the old and the new ideas. This time came with the accession of Friedrich.[2] After the battle of Sempach and the fall of many of the old Tirolese nobles a new generation had sprung up who had no confidence in the government, who were more self-reliant and more self-confident in their landed possessions, and who were determined to hold their usufructuary mortgages as a special privilege of the land.

Not only had these mortgages increased so as to render the Count of the Tirol almost a beggar in his own country, but Friedrich's brother Leopold had made over the collection of revenue to Nicolas Wintler, the richest man in the Tirol, and he gathered in all the taxes and financed the country. Friedrich saw that the first step, if he was to be anything more than a nominal ruler, must be to get the finances into his own hands. From 1370 onward Wintler had been court-banker to the Austrian Counts, he had been their bailiff in the Inn Valley and on the Adige, and he had been their financial counsellor on all occasions. He was virtually ruler of the land. On more than one occasion he had redeemed Friedrich himself from the hands of innkeepers to whom the Duke could not pay his scot. Wintler was, in 1407, called upon by the Duke to account for all revenues which had passed through his hands; he refused on the ground that he had been appointed by Leopold, Friedrich's elder

[1] B. W., 99.   [2] B. W., 57-8.

brother, and was responsible to him alone. Friedrich then deprived Wintler of all his offices, and claimed to redeem the mortgages which he held. Heinrich von Rottenburg interfered on Wintler's behalf; but in 1409 a settlement was effected, whereby Wintler received five thousand ducats and the fortress Rungelstein, but was obliged to refund all the mortgaged property. His defeat and degradation ate into his soul and he died in 1413.[1]

Having got the finances into his own hands, Friedrich had now the sinews of war, and set to work to recover as much as possible of the property mortgaged. When he entered on the administration in 1406 he and his brother Leopold had issued a charter of liberties which set forth, among other matters, that all rights, customs, and privileges were to remain in force; but he speedily supplemented this by publishing a set of fundamental principles, the first of which was that it belonged to the ruler of the Tirol, and to no one else, to explain and interpret to the Estates what their privileges were, and the revision of all mortgage transactions was announced at the same time. The nobility held it to be a custom of the land that usufructuary mortgages were practically irredeemable and were without account. Friedrich was of the opposite opinion. He determined to fly for the highest game, knowing that if he hit his quarry there, he would have no difficulty elsewhere. Heinrich von Rottenburg, the sixth of that name, was the principal noble in the Tirol. He was intensely conservative and tenacious of what he conceived to be the good old customs; he was at the head of the Elephant League, which had been formed against Friedrich just as the League of Marbach was formed against his father-in-law, which Friedrich, like Rupert, had met by joining the League; he was vain and proud. Friedrich had often laughed at his pomp and circumstance; on one occasion seeing Heinrich strutting along, followed by his menials, he had followed in his train in mock humility, carrying his sword; Rottenburg turned round and said, 'Fritz, Fritz, when will you become serious?' to which Friedrich answered with an irony which escaped the other, 'When you become an utter fool.' The Duke now called upon Rottenburg to produce his mortgage deeds and to render account, and he, relying on the custom of

[1] *B. W.*, 199.

THE FLIGHT FROM ROME 173

the country, refused and shut himself up in his castle. There could be no suit before Tirolese elders for account and redemption, for Friedrich had expressly declared that he was not amenable to any such jurisdiction; he demanded a personal account. It was a case in which the strong arm must decide, and the Duke proved the stronger. He besieged Rottenburg, took him prisoner, and forced him to submit to his judgment, which was pronounced on the 19th November 1410. Heinrich von Rottenburg died next year.

Not satisfied with attacking the richest man in the Tirol, Wintler, and the most powerful noble, Rottenburg, Friedrich also proceeded against the highest ecclesiastic, Georg of Lichtenstein, who had been Bishop of Trient since 1391. He claimed to hold Trient, Bozen, and Vintschgau by donation from Kaiser Conrad the Second to Bishop Ulrich of Trient in 1027-28; but it was demonstrated that in 1363 an agreement had been made declaring that the Bishop of Trient was subject to the Count of the Tirol. Georg of Lichtenstein was intriguing with Italy and set Friedrich at defiance; but he was taken prisoner by the Duke and the nobility, and was compelled to resign his countship, the bishopric being secularised (1407). The University of Vienna, however, where Petrus de Pulka was at that time rector,[1] disallowed the secularisation; arbitrators were appointed, whose award afforded no solution; fresh trouble at once arose; Friedrich seized the countship and promised to pay the Bishop a thousand ducats yearly (19th December 1410). Georg of Lichtenstein, however, placed the Duke under the ban, and went off to his relations in Moravia, and then appealed to the Pope and the Kaiser to help him. There is no doubt that Friedrich's action had the effect of keeping the south Tirol true to Germany.

The policy which has been described had been initiated and so far carried out when Rupert was King of the Romans. Its aim was to preserve the unity of the Tirol; if a *Reichsunmittelbarkeit* had been adopted, if the Tirol had been made directly dependent on the Empire, the result under the weak and ineffective rule of Rupert would have been anarchy and con-

[1] Peter Zech (*c.* 1374-1430) was born at Pulka in southern Austria; he was several times Dean of the Philosophical and the Theological Faculties, and also Rector of the University of Vienna, which he represented at the Council of Constance (Pulka, 5).

fusion. Friedrich saw this, and tried to consolidate his powers into a *Landeshoheit*; 'something that was less than modern sovereignty, for it would still have the Empire above it, but more than feudal signory since classical thoughts about the State were coming to its aid.'[1] As King Rupert was his father-in-law he was in a fair way of effecting his purpose. But as soon as King Log was dead and King Stork reigned in his place, the aspect of affairs changed. The nobles found support with the new King of the Romans, and henceforth Sigismund became the centre of discontent, the moving force of all that was done in the Tirol, against Duke Friedrich.[2] The King received the Bishop of Trient in 1412 with open arms at Buda and took him under his protection, and Pope John the Twenty-third followed suit. Thus, in 1413, the Kaiser was the focus of revolt in the Tirol, and this is the chief cause of the deadly enmity between him and Duke Friedrich.

From Innsbruck King Sigismund marched south through the Brenner Pass to Brixen on the Eisak, with its cathedral and the Chapel of Saint John, in which the minnesinger Oswold von Wolkenstein was later to find burial. Here the King might have met his death. One morning his cook found a Bavarian in the kitchen, and asked him what he did there. He made some unsatisfactory reply, on which the cooks, being persuaded that he meant to poison the King, fell on him, beat him, and turned him out of the place. The noise attracted Sigismund, who scolded his men for treating the stranger so uncourteously. The Bavarian plucked up heart of grace, and departed. He went to the bridge and threw something into the water. A man of the city saw him, and pointed his action out to the King. The man was seized and on him were found an iron spoon and a gauntlet. He confessed that he had thrown poison into the river; he had intended to smear the stuff over the royal saddle, bridle, and stirrups; and his presence in the kitchen would show that he also meant to throw poison into the cooking-pots. He said that the Venetians had sent him to poison the King, that they had given him already three hundred ducats, and were to give him two hundred gulden more when he had done his work. Sigismund put him in prison, to hold as a witness against the Republic.[3]

[1] Gierke, 14. [2] *B. W.*, 150. [3] Altmann, 50.

THE FLIGHT FROM ROME 175

From Brixen the King turned west to Meran, where he met the Swiss envoys from Zurich, Bern, and Solothurn, who had come to obtain from the Head of the Holy Roman Empire a confirmation of their privileges. Sigismund had need of Swiss help if he was to fulfil the article of his imperial capitulation relating to Milan. Going for a few days to Bozen, where the sentence on the Duke of Spalatro was pronounced, he returned to Meran, where he arranged the truce between Duke Friedrich of the Tirol and the Republic of Venice and then confirmed the privileges of certain Swiss cities of the Empire. On the 5th August 1413 he was at Chur.[1]

The eleventh article of the capitulation or contract which, on the 22nd July 1411, Sigismund had made with the Electors of Mainz and Cologne runs thus :—' Item ist ez daz einche lande, ez si in Dutschen Ytalien oder Welschen landen, die dem heiligen riche zugehoren oder zugehoren solten, uber lang oder kurz deme selben riche verfallen und ledig worden weren, und darzu daz land von Meylan, daz wir die mit aller unser besten vermogde understen sollen zu unser gehorsam und widder zu deme riche zu brengen ane alle geverde.'[2] The King was now to make an effort to fulfil this promise and to bring the land of Milan into his obedience, and he knew that from the Electors themselves there was no help to be had. His own resources had been pretty well exhausted by the war with Venice, and he experienced the usual difficulty which beset the head of the Holy Roman Empire, of means to fulfil the duties which were attached to that high calling. His only hope was in the Swiss. There had, since the year 1402, been trouble between the cantons of Uri and Unterwalden on the one side and the Duchy of Milan on the other regarding the toll demanded for the cattle driven to the annual fair at Verese;[3] the Valle Leventina had transferred itself to the cantons from the Duchy; the peasants of the two cantons had taken Domodossola; and when the governor whom they appointed was arrested and their troops massacred, the Confederates again marched to the river which divided the two valleys of Ossola (1411), chased out the Milanese soldiers, and re-established their own dominion. Sigismund hoped that they might help him to undertake an expedition against the Duchy. The three original cantons, Uri, Unter-

[1] Aschbach, i. 360.   [2] *D. B.*, vii. 108.   [3] Mueller, iv. 46 *et seq.*

walden, and Schweiz, which had won their independence at the battle of Mortgarten, had been joined by five others, Lucerne, Zurich, Glarus, Zug, and Bern, so that the confederacy now consisted of eight cantons, distinguished for their bravery and valour. These cantons, with their allies of Solothurn and Appenzel, had, on the 28th May 1412, concluded a peace for fifty years with Duke Friedrich of the Tirol, guaranteeing them possession of their lands. They were anxious to remain on good terms with the head of the Empire, and for this reason the envoys of three cantons had visited Sigismund at Meran and had obtained from him a confirmation of all their freedom and privileges, for which, however, they had paid him four hundred gulden. The King now summoned the representatives of all eight cantons to Chur, where they met on Saint Bartholomew's Day (24th August) 1413.

Sigismund addressed them as follows :—' Good and faithful men, you know how the Lord of Milan, the Vicar of the Holy Roman Empire in Lombardy, had been disobedient to the Empire and has brought great loss upon it; he refuses to recognise our suzerainty and to receive his fief from us, as he is pledged to do. His disobedience grieves us sore, and we therefore have bethought ourselves of reducing him to subjection. Since you and your forefathers have always been true and have never deserted the Empire, we now beg and ask you as good and faithful men to grant us your help against the Lord of Milan in order to render him obedient.'[1] The envoys, not being empowered to pledge their cantons as desired, returned home, promising to send their reply. On the 8th September the King sent his messengers to Lucerne to hasten matters. The confederates could not agree. They answered that they must think over his proposal, and would send him their reply at Chur. Soon their determination was brought. It was a very weighty matter to undertake such a war far from their own land; there were difficult paths and passes to overcome; but they were willing that the King should take into his pay any who might volunteer for the adventure.

The reply was not all that Sigismund had hoped for, but he was fain to be content. He endeavoured to raise money; he assembled two thousand Swiss at Bellinzona; he expected

[1] Aschbach, i. 363.

other troops from Swabia, having written to Basel and Strassburg to send them to Feldkirch; he had the scanty force which he had brought with him. His numbers were absurdly inadequate, and his money was soon exhausted. North of the Lake of Lugano there was danger of a mutiny in the tiny army; 'No pay, no Swiss,' was the motto; the volunteers deserted; and the King was left with his Hungarian and German troops. He was joined by four hundred horse and three hundred foot from the Tirol, but he had to pay seven thousand ducats for this assistance, and was unable to keep them with him long.[1] He did not give up all hope of reducing the Duke of Milan to subjection, but he relied on negotiation rather than on force.

The task before Sigismund was nothing like so serious as that which had faced King Rupert. Gian Galeazzo had been a determined statesman in possession of all northern Italy as far as the confines of Venice and Florence. His sons had all his bad qualities and none of his good. Their dissensions had ruined them. Gian Maria, the eldest, had lost Como, Lodi, Cremona, Piacenza, Parma, Reggio, Bergamo, Bologna, Perugia, and other places; the second son, Filippo Maria, had lost Novara, Vercelli, Tortona, Alesandria, Verona, Vicenza, Belluno, Bassano, and all his small possessions in Piedmont; the illegitimate son, Gabriel, had lost all his possessions and had been executed at Genoa in 1408. Although Gian Maria was Lord of Milan, he was the mere tool alternately of the Guelfs under the Malatestas and the Ghibelines under Facino Cane. When the celebrated commander Facino Cane was sick unto death, his followers murdered the Duke Gian Maria on the 16th May 1412, intending to put two of the other Viscontis, Estorre and Gian Carlo, at the head of the government; but Filippo Maria, who married Facino Cane's widow, forestalled them, and on the 19th June was sole Duke of Milan. He determined to turn the other two Viscontis out of Monza, where they had fled for refuge, and they in their need appealed to King Sigismund, who was then in Friuli, warring with Venice. They promised to render him suit and obedience, which Filippo and his brother had refused since their father's death. Gian Carlo then betook himself to the King of the

[1] Kagelmacher, 7.

Romans, who sent ambassadors to Filippo Maria to induce him to suspend his hostilities against Monza. The Duke for the time consented, but as soon as Sigismund had made his peace with Venice, Filippo resumed the siege, in which Estorre Visconti lost his life, took Monza, made terms with the Genoese, with the Marquess of Montferrat, and with Pandolfo Malatesta of Brescia, and received comforting intelligence from King Wenzel of Bohemia, who was becoming very inimical toward his half-brother, the King of the Romans. Filippo Maria also tried, but without success, to make an alliance with the Venetians. He could, however, now await with composure the coming of King Sigismund.

The Duke was willing to negotiate rather than fight. He sent to Sigismund a proposal, offering to pay him twenty thousand ducats, if the King would invest him with the Duchy of Milan and would give into his hands his enemy Gian Carlo Visconti. The proposal reached Sigismund at Chur. The Duke expected that the King of the Romans would soon reappear in Italy at the head of a formidable army of Swiss. On the 23rd October he sent a brilliant embassy to the Papal Legate to swear fealty to the King, to promise him two thousand armed warriors, to make war as he wished, to keep the peace with his neighbours in Lombardy, to allow the King to march through or remain in any of his dominions, and to appear at his coronation.[1] All appeared now to have succeeded to the best of Sigismund's hopes; but for little more than a month was his good fortune to last. The Duke learned of the King's failure to get any aid from the Swiss, and his mood altered at once. He had now no reason to fear the King. Towards the end of November Sigismund moved on to Canturio, a small village near Como on the road to Milan, where he met the Duke.[2] The Milanese army was drawn up at a short distance, and Sigismund at first feared treachery. But Filippo Maria advanced to meet him with only three persons in his train, and the colloquy was held. The Duke desired to be formally invested with the dukedom, he wished the King of the Romans to be accompanied by a merely insignificant number of armed attendants into Milan, and he insisted on the surrender of Gian

[1] Kagelmacher, 9; Finke (*F.*), 10; Sauerbrei, 38. [2] Sauerbrei, 39-40.

THE FLIGHT FROM ROME

Carlo and his associates. Sigismund was not the man to put his head in the lion's den himself, nor to betray a friend and client to certain death; he deemed the terms unworthy of acceptance by the imperial majesty; and he refused to agree. So they parted, each having missed his aim. The King, however, conceived a high opinion of Filippo Maria. 'I was told,' he said, ' that he was a boy; if the Italian boys are like that, what very wise men their seniors must be.'[1] He had failed to recover to the Empire the territory of Milan; but he had put a garrison in Piacenza, and he had won over to his side Loterio Rusca of Como, Giovanni Vignate of Lodi, and Gabrino Fondulo of Cremona.[2] Moreover, he was about to accomplish a most important step toward securing the unity of the Church.

Pope John the Twenty-third was meantime at Florence, where he was obliged, imitating the evil example of his patron, Pope Boniface the Ninth, to raise money by the sale of expectancies and other graces.[3] Leonardo of Arezzo, the pupil of the celebrated Byzantine, Manuel Chrysoloras, who had been a boy when the Schism began,[4] was here his secretary, and of him the Pope made a confidant. Though his obedience extended to nearly the whole of Christendom, Pope John could not but feel that the toils were closing upon him. The ambition and the power of Ladislas of Naples, now as of yore his deadly enemy, had become overpowering. John knew that Ladislas was determined to win the overlordship of all Italy; he knew also that the King was determined to take him personally prisoner. The King of Naples had allied himself with Carlo Malatesta and with Filippo Maria in order to subdue Florence and Siena; he endeavoured also to win over Nicolas of Este, but was checked by King Sigismund. The situation was desperate.

The only hope for Pope John was in the King of the Romans One of his first acts therefore after his arrival at Florence was to despatch the Cardinal Chalant, the ambitious Savoyard, who, four years earlier, had dreamed of the tiara for himself, to Sigismund to implore his aid against Ladislas, whose troops were marching victoriously through Italy. The Cardinal made

---

[1] Mur. xix. 827.   [2] Sauerbrei, 40.
[3] Hardt, ii. 383.   [4] Mur. xix. 914.

an impassioned speech on the perfidy of the Neapolitan, and the King sent a messenger back to the Pope. John repeated his letters of entreaty, begging Sigismund to help the Church; the King replied that nothing but a general Council could bring unity and reform. The Pope knew that the King of the Romans was bent on holding an œcumenical council, one which should be of that universal weight and authority which had been so sadly lacking in the Council of Rome. He knew, too, that the project was in the air for the deposition of all three existing Popes, and that his own position was by no means sure. But with Ladislas on his traces, it was necessary to take immediate action, and Pope John the Twenty-third now made up his mind to make the first decisive move toward convoking an œcumenical Council. He had promised, when the Council of Rome broke up, that he would announce the time and place for its re-assembling, and the latter part of this promise was still unredeemed. He, like the King, was full well aware of the immense difference which territorial influence would exert on the assembled divines; he felt that if it were to be held at a place where he was powerless, he would be doomed; and he therefore desired that the Council should be convoked to meet in some city where he would hold ' both swords '; while Sigismund, on the other hand, was equally determined that it should meet where the Pope's influence would be at a minimum and his own power would be supreme. John unbosomed himself one day privately to his young secretary. "The chief consideration is the place at which the Council is held; and I do not want to go anywhere where the Emperor is more powerful than I am. I will therefore give my ambassadors the fullest powers and authority for them to display openly, but secretly I shall restrict their competence to the choice of certain fixed places.' He enumerated the places to his friend, and drew up a list which he proposed to give his envoys as their secret instruction.[1]

Such was his intention, but his own impetuous disposition got the better of him. He chose the two cardinals, Chalant and Zabarella, as his envoys, and with them was to go the eloquent Greek Chrysoloras. The two cardinals were much more devoted to securing the convocation of the Council than to

[1] Mur. xix. 928.

THE FLIGHT FROM ROME 181

providing for the safety of their chief. John called the two prelates to him, and Leonardo was the only other person present at the interview. The Pope spoke to his envoys at length; he urged them to use all diligence and impressed on them the weightiness of their mission; he explained to them the importance of the selection of a locality; he told them that he entrusted his own interests entirely to their prudence and fidelity; he waxed so eloquent that he tore to shreds the chart of his secret instructions, saying, ' I had intended to name certain localities for selection, excluding all others, but now I have changed my mind and trust entirely to your prudence and judgment.' And so he sent them on their way.

At the time Pope John sent his three ambassadors to King Sigismund, another embassy, purporting to have a like mission, was despatched. King Ladislas, having deserted Pope Gregory and betrayed Pope John, now turned his attention to the third member of the accursed trinity, Pope Benedict the Thirteenth. He had his spies everywhere, and knew of the correspondence between Pope John and Sigismund. He despatched an embassy to Pope Benedict and his protector, King Ferdinand of Aragon,[1] proposing a close league for the purpose of bringing about the unity of the Church. Ferdinand answered that he would send an embassy in return, and Pope Benedict appointed two envoys who were to accompany the royal ambassadors in order to hear the plan proposed by the King of Naples. Owing to the delay of the King of Aragon and the death of King Ladislas, the ambassadors were never sent. But when Ferdinand communicated with Benedict he mentioned a rumour, which was utterly without foundation, that France was about to return to her allegiance to the ' gallant spaniard,'[2] and such a rumour could only tend to confirm Benedict in his stiff-necked obstinacy.

On the 8th November Pope John the Twenty-third, with his Curia, left Florence, and on the 12th he again entered his beloved Bologna.

[1] Finke (*Acta*), 310-3.   [2] Burke, i. 322.

CHAPTER X

THE CONVOCATION OF THE GREAT COUNCIL

As soon as Pope John arrived in Florence, negotiations began between him and King Sigismund. The King heard of the adjournment of the Council of Rome until the 1st December, and sent messengers asking the Pope not to fix the place for the adjourned meeting until he heard from him. He had already made up his mind that a general Council, to be of any value, must be held outside Italy. In reply, on the 27th July 1413, John answered that he would send one or more cardinals to speak with the King and to arrange a meeting between them at which a fitting place for the Council might be settled; if, by God's grace, they thus met, the time and place could be arranged and published.[1] Sigismund thereupon sent back envoys to Pope John. Both the contracting parties were alive to the supreme importance of the place at which the Council should meet, and each was determined, if possible, to have his own way in the matter. The King would not entrust his envoys, in his own absence and in the presence of the persuasive Pope, with the power of fixing the venue; so that a further delay ensued; and it became evident that the Council would not meet on the 1st December 1413. That, however, was a matter of minor importance.

Meantime Sigismund in August wrote to King Henry the Fifth of England, telling him of his efforts with the Pope for a general Council to remedy the evils of the Church, and saying that he hoped to fix on a place convenient for all Christendom, easy of access, capable for accommodation, and abounding in all the necessaries of life.[2] He also wrote in the same sense to King Charles the Sixth of France, not forgetting to mention that this duty specially devolved on him as King of the Romans.[3] The Count Palatine and the Archbishop of Trier recommended Basel or Strassburg to the King as fitting places for the meeting

[1] Finke (*Acta*), 238.   [2] *Ibid.* (*Acta*), 239.   [3] *Ibid.* (*Acta*), 241.

CONVOCATION OF THE COUNCIL 183

of a Council. On the 30th August Pope John, being then 'apud Sanctum Anthonium extra muros Florentinos,' drew up a Bull, addressed to the Cardinal-Priest Antonio and the Cardinal-Deacon Francescus Cosma and Damianus and to the noble Byzantine knight Manuel Chrysoloras, empowering them to treat with his dearly beloved Sigismund, King of the Romans, respecting the convocation of a general Council, and suggesting Genoa or Nice as a place of meeting.[1] Five days later he entrusted to them the Bull giving them full discretion to determine the time and place for the Council;[2] and thus armed with full discretion they took their way.

The news of a suggested meeting between the Pope and the King of the Romans caused perturbation, more especially among the Venetians. The Marquess of Este and Uguccione de' Contrari informed them that the Duke of Milan was like to submit to the King, and that Sigismund was about to meet the Pope at Parma with a view to his imperial coronation. This bugbear still prevailed. The Republic answered that they could not prevent the meeting, but hoped that the King and the Duke might not come to terms; still less did they like the idea of Sigismund meeting the Pope at Parma or at Genoa, but would prefer that such a meeting, if it must take place, should be held at Friuli.[3] The Republic knew of the Pope's devotion to the King, and probably suspected that the feeling might be reciprocal, and hence they argued ill for the welfare of their ally, King Ladislas, if a meeting occurred in a place where John was all-powerful. They did not know the mind of King Sigismund.

The two cardinals, the Savoyard Chalant and the Florentine Zabarella, left Florence on the 6th September, and after a long and rough journey, found King Sigismund at Como.[4] On the 13th October they opened their case to him with long speeches full of flattery. Cardinal Chalant called the King the living corner stone of the Church; he reminded him that Pope John had held a Council at Rome in accordance with the resolution of the Council of Pisa, but that the evils of the time had prevented the attendance of all but a few, and that the Pope still deemed a general Council necessary for the common necessity of

[1] Finke (*F.*), 243.   [2] Palacky (*Doc.*), 513.
[3] Finke (*Acta*), 244.   [4] But see Kagalmacher, 8, note.

Christendom; and that he therefore entreated him, by the bowels of God's mercy, to concur with this project in order that there might be a notable congregation of the faithful for the reformation of the entire state of the Church militant. Cardinal Zabarella began by informing Sigismund that he was worthy of assuming divinity like one of the old Roman emperors; that Christ, before He ascended, had left His peace on earth in the keeping of the pontifical authority and the royal power; that the Pope had used his best endeavours to get a worthy head elected to the Empire, and that he regarded Sigismund as the only prince who could restore peace to the republic of Christendom, which by reason of various and inveterate afflictions seemed spiritually and temporally to be near its ruin.[1] The learned Zabarella, 'King of the Canon Law,' who thus reminded Sigismund of all that the Pope had done toward securing his election, made a favourable impression on the King of the Romans, who raised three of the suite to the dignity of Counts Palatine. The preliminary interviews were held at Saint Stephen's Church, in a little village called Vegni, near Como, and the fact that they lasted eighteen days suggests that the Pope's envoys did all in their power to carry out his wishes. At the end of that time, however, the King of the Romans had won his point, for Constance on the Boden See was agreed upon as the place for the meeting of the Council. Sigismund had already thought of Constance as in every way suitable; at this city of the Empire everything would be under the control of the head of the Holy Roman Empire, and the head of the Holy Roman Church would be comparatively powerless.

From his camp therefore at the Villa called Viglud, or in the vulgar tongue Vegni,[2] near Como, on the 30th October 1413,[3] Sigismund clinched matters by issuing a proclamation announcing that an œcumenical Council would be held at Constance, to open on All Saints' Day 1414, under the presidency of the Pope and the King of the Romans. He promised full security in

[1] Finke (*F.*), 243-8.

[2] I am unable to find any place of this name, but I would suggest that *Vig*lud or *Veg*ni may possibly represent the suburb of Como, which is now known as the Borgo *Vico*. This is covered with modern villas, built on a broad stretch of level ground lying between the foot of the hills and the lake, and very proper (formerly) for the encampment of a small force.

[3] Sauerbrei, 43.

CONVOCATION OF THE COUNCIL 185

coming, staying, and returning to all who had business thereat. He immediately wrote to the King of France inviting him to this sweet feast for the reformation of the Church and the reconciliation of East and West; he wrote also to Pope Gregory at Rimini, begging him to attend, offering him two thousand gulden a month while the Council lasted, and warning him that he could not afterwards plead ignorance of the summons.

When Pope John heard the news that Constance had been selected as the place for the meeting of the Council, he was overwhelmed with grief;[1] he was in despair, and he made no secret of his despondency; he felt that Fate was against him and that he was a doomed man. Before this, during his pontificate, there had been displays of emotion, outbursts of tears, of which the once masterful cardinal would have been ashamed; but from this time onward the old force and determination of the man who is master of his fate were more and more replaced by the shifty and indecisive steps characteristic of him who fears and tries to elude it. The Neapolitan fatalism settled heavily on his spirit. As he said later: ' I confess that it shows little prudence to place oneself in the power of persons unknown, and that the Council is not mine; but what can I do, when I have a fate that draws me on ? '[2] His only hope was that he might personally induce the King to change the venue, but Sigismund was not the man lightly to abandon the advantage which he had thus gained. The die was cast; the step was irrevocable.

Providence had been very kind to the King of the Romans; the Pope's extremity had been the King's opportunity. But for the embassy of Pope John, King Sigismund would have found it wellnigh impossible to summon an œcumenical Council; the ' Advocatus et Defensor Ecclesiae ' would have been as powerless as his predecessor.[3] France had no desire to move further; she stood by the Council of Pisa, which was her work; Spain and Provence were still true to Pope Benedict the Thirteenth; Italy was at the back of Pope John; there was no country which would effectively support Sigismund in convoking a general Council. But now the oppression of King Ladislas had thrown the Pope with the largest obedience into the King's arms, and the chief difficulty in the way of convoking a really œcumenical Council was overcome; and not only would such

[1] Mur. xix. 928.   [2] *A.S.I.*, iv. 262.   [3] Lenz, 49.

a Council be called together, but it would meet in a place where its power would not be overshadowed by that of the Pope who convoked it. The way was made easy for the King to show that he was really the temporal head of Christendom.

Pope John travelled from Bologna to Piacenza, and here, for the first time, the heads of the Holy Roman Church and Empire met. At Piacenza Sigismund met again his old friend, the Tirolean poet-knight, Oswald von Wolkenstein. The last of the minnesingers was a year older than the King of the Romans. Oswald was the second son of Friedrich, whose father Conrad, a scion of the ancient house of Villanders, had, in 1325, acquired Wolkenstein, had quartered the three blue peaks with the three clouds, and had assumed thenceforth the name of Count of Wolkenstein. Oswald had been a knight errant from his youth up. When a child his right eye had been shot out by an arrow. He had left his father's home at the age of ten, 'with threepence in his pouch and a little bit of bread,'[1] to fight the heathen under the auspices of the Teutonic Order. He had continued fighting for eight years, and had learned much in the meantime; he could groom a horse, could sing a song, could play on half a dozen different instruments, could speak the Slav language, knew something of the use of cannon, and could cook an excellent dinner. Then for a year he fought for Margaret of Denmark; and after that, he went to England to see the country of King Arthur and the Round Table. Being in England, he also visited Scotland and Ireland, and thence returned to Konigsberg on the Baltic. Here he took ship for the Black Sea, where he was wrecked and wellnigh drowned, 'pulling an oar in a Candian boat';[2] and thence he went by caravan to the Euphrates, and learned to love roses and rose gardens. He worked his way as ship's cook to Candia and Constantinople; and in 1391 he joined King Sigismund and served him under Hermann of Cilly, whom he had known in Prussia. With Sigismund he escaped after the battle of Nicopolis, accompanying the King back to Dalmatia, where he left him and returned to the Tirol. There he met the fair Sabina von Jaeger, a maiden of eighteen years, with whom he fell desperately in love; he sang to her, played to her, wrote poems

---

[1] Wolkenstein, 3.   [2] *Ibid.*

CONVOCATION OF THE COUNCIL 187

to her; but she perversely preferred a knight with two eyes, and to get rid of Oswald intimated to him that he ought to perform a pilgrimage to the Holy Land. This seemed to him quite natural, and he started, going by way of Alexandria and Cairo, visiting Bethlehem, Jerusalem, and other holy places, spending three years as a love-lorn pilgrim bent on devoting his sword to his lady and to our Lord. Naturally he fell into poetry ; the following is a specimen :—

> ' In the Syrian land 'neath a distant star
>   You may hear the angels sing ;
> Or you may perchance from the distance far
>   Yourself to the dark grave bring.
> Young was the Virgin when her son was born
>   Without pain to the holy maiden :
> The good news gladdened the world outworn,
>   But the Devil with grief was laden.
> In anger the wall of the stable he cleft,
>   Myself with mine eyes have seen the deep reft.
>
> ' Almighty God, the world is thine,
>   Thine are its greatest men,
> They may or dead or living be,
>   They may be born again.
> A child was born to the maiden fair
>   By God's own hand selected,
> How lowly, alas ! was the shelter there
>   Which the infant God protected.
>
> ' The ox and the ass did welcome the stranger,
>   Thy birthplace their stable, Thy cradle their manger ;
> The Virgin dwelt with Thee and Thou wert her son,
>   She saw Thee and knew Thee, the Omnipotent One,
> So He had decreed it whose will must be done.
>   O Holy Twain ! I Wolkenstein
>   With my whole heart give praise ;
>   O Son of God ! O Mother mine,
>   Help me in my last days.' [1]

Eventually, when Oswald got back to Sicily, the thought struck him that he had been some time absent from his love, and he hurried through Italy, reaching home on a bitter cold night in December 1400, to find his father on his deathbed and Sabina married to another. After his father's death Oswald obtained a

[1] Wolkenstein, 134-6.

share of the inheritance and remained some time in the Tirol. He accompanied King Rupert on his expedition into Italy, but learned to distrust that ineffective ruler, and fixed his hopes on the King of Hungary. He was well received by Gian Galeazzo of Milan, and returned once more to the Tirol. He was a thorough conservative, and was the originator of the Elephant League. In 1409 he met his future wife, Margareta of Schwangau, who was then a maiden of sixteen. In this year he bethought him of fighting the Moors ; he went by Heidelberg and Cologne, and then by ship with the Queen of Portugal to Spain ; he took part in the storming of Ceuta, visited Castile, and spent a year in Aragon, basking in the smiles of the Spanish ladies. Wherever he went his sword and his song made him welcome ; he was foremost in the lists and in the fêtes ; he was at home in the ladies' bowers ; and when he returned to Genoa in 1413, he had the scars of seven deadly wounds to prove his prowess in the field. From Genoa he went to Piacenza and joined King Sigismund, whose right-hand man he was to be in that monarch's contention with Duke Friedrich of the Tirol. Oswald von Wolkenstein thenceforth was the King's trusted intermediary in Tirolean affairs ; both poet and King alike wished evil to the Duke.

From Piacenza, about the 25th November 1413, King Sigismund and Pope John the Twenty-third made their way to Lodi. This place had been chosen for their conference rather than Genoa or Nice, as the King was in the midst of his negotiations with Milan. At Lodi they remained for nearly a month. An old Florentine merchant, who had ' seen many men's manners and knew many cities,' conversing with the King confided to him that he knew not which was the wiser man, he or Pope John. ' Which of us two, think you, is the sadder ? ' asked the merry monarch. ' The Pope, mayhap,' answered the merchant, ' for the hair is all gone from the top of his head.' Whatever his reason, the old Florentine was right, for the Pope felt that the pusillanimity of his envoys had betrayed him. At Lodi the conference between the two heads of Christendom was held.

The Pope represented to the King his sincere desire for a great Council, to be held anywhere the King wished so long as it

CONVOCATION OF THE COUNCIL

was in Italy, for it was impossible for His Holiness, so he asserted, to bring his cardinals and archbishops across the Alps. To this the King of the Romans replied that he also had three mighty archbishops, who were Electors of the Holy Roman Empire and great princes in Germany, whom he also could not bring across the Alps. Then followed a long consultation as to the place where the Council could be held. The King inquired whether there was no city near the Alps belonging to the Roman Empire. Count Ulrich of Teck recommended Kempten in southern Swabia. But Count Eberhard of Nellenberg answered that Kempten was indeed a city of the Empire, but that there was no sufficient accommodation there; whereas at a day's journey from Kempten lay the city of Constance on the Rhine and on the Boden See, a lake eight miles long and three miles broad, which was the seat of a bishopric and a place to which ships could come and go; not long before, said the Count, there had been war in Switzerland, and King Rupert and all the counts, lords, and knights had come there and had found shelter and food and drink; in fact, everything could be bought at Constance; meat, fish, hay, and fodder, everything that man or beast could want could be procured at Constance at a trifling cost. Then said Sigismund to Pope John, ' Seeing there is a bishopric in Constance, and that the city belongs to the Holy Roman Empire, is it not Your Holiness's will that the Council should be held there ? ' The Pope took counsel with his party, but it was a mere matter of form. His ambassadors had already agreed to the place, and it was manifestly useless to try further to persuade the King to change it; the Pope had perforce to concede, and it was agreed that the coming œcumenical Council should be held at Constance. Accordingly, on the 9th December 1413, Pope John the Twenty-third promulgated his Bull for the convocation of a general Council at Constance on All Saints' Day 1414, and promised that he personally would be there.[1] It is said that he also at Lodi advanced to the penurious King the sum of fifty thousand golden gulden, a story rather less improbable than the other that Sigismund took occasion to ask John to amend his evil livelihood.[2]

Ambassadors from Florence, Genoa, Venice, and other places

[1] Richental, 18.   [2] Finke (*Acta*), 177.

appeared at Lodi. The Florentines wished to secure themselves against King Ladislas, who was on the best terms with Venice and had entered into negotiations with the Marquess of Este. A league was made between the Pope, the Republic, and the Marquess, directed against the King of Naples, John securing the attachment of the Marquess by threatening to deprive him of the Vicariat of Ferrara. The Venetians refused to join any such league.[1]

At Lodi the King and the Pope had learned to know each other; they had also learned to distrust each other.[2] Sigismund was determined that all three Popes should abdicate or be deposed at the Council of Constance; and John knew that he had to fight for his own hand. Hitherto he had befriended the King in the matter of the Bishop of Trient against Duke Friedrich of the Tirol; now he turned round and began to make friends of the mammon of unrighteousness; while he was at Lodi, on the 23rd December 1413, in confirming a contract between the city of Rottweil and the Duke, he calls Friedrich his beloved son, and speaks of his devotion to the Church and to him.[3] The Duke himself, as soon as his envoys returned from Lodi, made a treaty for twelve years with the Pope's old friend and supporter, John of Nassau, Archbishop of Mainz, an enemy of Sigismund, and with Duke Charles of Lorraine and the Marquess Bernhard of Baden.[4] The Pope and the Duke were already casting in their lot together against the common enemy, but as yet there was no open breach; John had need of Sigismund against Ladislas of Naples, and did not despair of benefiting by his influence in the Council of Constance.

For three long years, in the bitterness of his heart, had Pope Gregory the Twelfth watched the progress of events without breaking silence; but now that he saw that a general Council was at hand, he resolved also to speak. He wrote to King Sigismund,[5] reminding him of his father's zeal for catholic truth and justice, approving his election as King of the Romans and future Emperor, and he called on all the faithful in Christ to acknowledge and obey Sigismund as their King who was to be

---

[1] Finke (*Acta*), 178.   [2] Schmid, 197.   [3] *Ibid.* 198.
[4] Lichnowsky, v. 154; Egger, i. 474.   [5] Hardt, ii. 462.

CONVOCATION OF THE COUNCIL 191

their Emperor. The affectionate tone of the letter formed a marked contrast to that which the aged pontiff sent about the same time to the Count Palatine; but for good or evil Pope Gregory was wellnigh powerless in the events which were preparing. He was duly invited to come to the Council of Constance, and was offered an allowance during his stay; but he, the one Pope whose title was undoubtedly just and canonical, had a smaller obedience than either of his rivals.

While he was still at Lodi, King Sigismund wrote to that stubborn little Spaniard, Pope Benedict the Thirteenth, inviting him also to the Council of Constance. He sent letters, moreover, to various kings and princes, enlisting their favour and assistance in the great work. The Pope and the King kept Christmas at Lodi, and travelled thence to Cremona, the town on the left bank of the Po, which had been faithful to Frederic Barbarossa in his wars with Milan. The Lord of this city was Gabrino Fondulo, and its recent history forms an instructive episode in Italian politics.

Cremona had been left by Gian Galeazzo Visconti, who, with all his faults, was a strong and able ruler who kept smaller tyrants in order, to his eldest legitimate son, Gian Maria; but soon after his death it was seized by Ugolino Cavalcabo and Gian Ponzono. Cavalcabo, being of opinion that the city was not large enough for two rulers, murdered Ponzono and became sole Lord of Cremona. He then tried to seize a suburb of Brescia, but was defeated and taken prisoner by the ducal troops, and would have been executed but for the intercession of one Andreas, a friend of Gian Maria. Andreas advised Cavalcabo to surrender all his claims and to become the liege man of the Duke of Milan. Gabrino Fondulo, who had been in the pay of Cavalcabo, heard of the plan and determined to prevent its execution. He persuaded Cavalcabo to entrust Cremona to a relative of his own; and he invited Ugolino, Andreas, and others of Cavalcabo's intimates to a supper to consider what was best to be done. The guests all came to the fortress which Gabrino held, and after the feast their host announced that to-morrow morning he would disclose to them somewhat to their advantage. They all retired to rest. While they slept Gabrino Fondulo, with a body of cut-throats, entered their chambers and killed them all as they slept. Thus he himself became Lord of Cremona.[1]

Gabrino Fondulo now welcomed Pope John and King Sigismund, and with them was the Venetian envoy, Tomaso Mocenigo, who had just heard that he had been elected Doge of Venice. Gabrino took his three illustrious guests up the Torrazzo, a tower four hundred feet high adjoining the cathedral in the Piazza del Comune. From this lofty height they could look out over the wide waveless plain of Lombardy, and as they gazed, Gabrino Fondulo and his men stood behind them. A thought, a temptation, entered his head, worthy of him who harboured it. As the Lord of the Holy Roman Church, the Lord of the Holy Roman Empire, and the Lord of the Adriatic stood on gaze, Gabrino was seized with the desire to precipitate them all three from the tower, breaking their necks, and thus introducing inextricable confusion into the spiritual, the temporal, and the commercial world. What a fishing there would be for fishermen like himself in the troubled waters! For some reason he did not give the word, and his project for the relief of Christendom remained unexecuted. But eleven years later, when he was executed at Milan by order of the Duke Filippo Maria, he confessed that there was nothing he regretted so much as having allowed that fateful moment to pass without carrying out his brilliant design. The Pope, the King, and the Doge were ignorant of the crisis they had passed through. After some further conferences the Pope betook himself to Bologna to brood over the state of Italy and his own precarious fortune, but King Sigismund remained until the middle of February at Cremona. He had interviews with the Venetian envoys; and seeing that he was not like to return to Hungary for some time, he appointed the Archbishop Kanysa and the Palatine Nicolaus Gara to be regents in his absence.

The Pope and the King had been in perpetual conference together for more than two months. The irony of fate seemed to have set these two men the task of reforming the Christian Church, a task for which they were singularly unfitted, because each of them lacked moral earnestness, neither of them, though possessed of intellectual ability above the average, possessed

[1] Mur. xix. 806.

CONVOCATION OF THE COUNCIL

any weight of moral conviction. Pope John was, like most of the Popes, a lawyer; he had no tincture of that theology which was so dear to the souls of two men so opposed as Jean Gerson and John Hus; and it was the theological spirit which was the soul of the reform movement. Nor was King Sigismund a theologian. His half-brother, King Wenzel, when not in his cups, delighted in a theological argument; he loved to hear a canon lawyer disputing with a theologian; he could appreciate John Hus. But Sigismund regarded such things with the straightforward common-sense of a man of the world. These were the two men set to preside over an assembly called to provide for the reform and unity of Christendom. The question of the place of meeting was soon settled. The Pope issued his encyclical on the 9th December. There remained, therefore, many weeks during which the two heads of Christian Europe were able to confer on other matters connected with the coming Council.

Of these conferences no record remains. One matter which in all probability was discussed by the Pope and the King was the religious trouble in Bohemia. This was a matter of peculiar interest to Sigismund. He was heir to the childless King Wenzel; he might conceivably be called on to take up the government before that King's death. Bohemia had an evil reputation as the home of Wyclifry. The Archbishop of Prague and the Chancellor of the University of Paris were in correspondence on the subject,[1] which was certain to be brought up at a Council, part of whose business it was to exterminate heresy. John Hus was the most influential ecclesiastic in Bohemia, and he was known to be in some points, though not in all, a follower and an admirer of the English reformer. Wyclif's works had been condemned by the Council of Rome, but no mention of Hus had been made in the condemnation. Hus had, it was true, been excommunicated, but merely for an error in conduct in not appearing personally at Rome, not for an error of doctrine. On the other hand, the late Archbishop Zbynek had expressly declared that Hus was not a heretic; and he had been ready to repeat this declaration shortly before his death. So far as orthodoxy went, Hus could point to a clean

[1] Palacky (*Doc.*), 523 *et seq.*

bill. Bohemia and Moravia were said to be full of heresy, but no one had been convicted of heresy. If Sigismund could clear the country of the foul imputation he would be doing a national service ; the clergy would welcome the return of peace and of security in their possessions ; and he would win the gratitude of Hus's party, which was strong not only among the populace but also among the nobles of the land. John of Chlum and other Bohemian nobles were in his train at the time he and the Pope were in conference, and kept him informed of the progress of events in Bohemia. What likelier expedient could there be than that John Hus should appear at the Council, should clear himself and his country before the assembled fathers of the imputation of heresy, and should restore the fair fame of Bohemia. In order that John Hus might attend the Council of Constance, it would be necessary that the King should grant him a safe conduct, and it was desirable that the Pope should relieve him from the ban of excommunication. That both steps were subsequently taken renders it probable that both matters were at this time previously arranged.[1]

John Hus had, in 1412, preached, but with much moderation, against the crusade proclaimed against ' Ladislas, King of Apulia, and Angelus Correr, who, with sacrilegious daring, calls himself Gregory the Twelfth ' ; but for this the Pope could not bear him any logical grudge, seeing that he himself had subsequently made peace with King Ladislas. The adversaries of Hus had secured as their agent at the papal court a German, Michael of Deutschbrod, a wily and utterly unscrupulous man, who had swindled the King by embezzling the money from certain royal mines, who had formerly been a priest in Prague, and who was afterwards appointed by the Pope to be advocate in matters of faith,[2] whence he is generally known as Michael *de Causis*. Through his agency a fresh papal Bull, proclaiming an aggravation of the sentence of excommunication against Hus, was sent to Prague in August 1412, and the city was again placed under an interdict. The King submitted to the indignity. None of the newly born were admitted to the Christian faith by baptism ; none of the dying received extreme unction ; none of the living were allowed to confess or receive

[1] Berger, 88 *et seq.*   [2] ' Procurator de causis fidei ' ; Luetzow, 152.

CONVOCATION OF THE COUNCIL 195

communion. Two attempts were made to wreck the Bethlehem Chapel, but both were defeated by the vigilance of the worshippers. Hus was deeply grieved at the trouble he had brought on the land. On the ground that all the faithful, and especially the princes, barons, knights, and others of Bohemia compassionated him for the excommunication which had so grievously been procured against him through the instigation of his adversary Michael *de Causis*, John Hus appealed, following the example of Chrysostom, of Bishops Andrew of Prague and ' Saint Robert ' of Lincoln, from the Pope to his Lord Jesus Christ. It is difficult to see the difference between such an appeal and the repudiation of all ecclesiastical authority. At the suggestion of King Wenzel he resolved to quit Prague for a time.

With the exception of a few secret journeys to the city during which he preserved his incognito, Hus remained absent from Prague, chiefly at the castle of Kozi Hradek, the property of the Lord of Usti, nearly all the time until he started for the Council of Constance. In the hope to bring peace and to calm the religious differences King Wenzel called a Synod which met at the Archbishop's palace in Prague on the 6th February 1413. The orthodox clergy, led by Stephen Palec and Stanislas of Znaim, were too bitterly rigid, and Hus's partisans, from the court downwards, were too numerous, for success ; the exacerbation and difference were as marked as ever ; the Synod of Prague was a failure. The King, however, did not give up hope ; he appointed a commission of four to hear both sides and to effect a settlement. But this also failed. The orthodox party insisted on defining the Holy Roman Church as that of which the head was Pope John, and the Cardinals its members ; to which the opposite section would only agree on the understanding that they were bound to accept the findings of this Church only so far as all good and true Christians could. Palec reproached the commission with weakness and partiality ; and it broke up. King Wenzel was extremely wroth ; he banished Palec, Stanislas, and two other University professors from the kingdom ; and Stanislas of Znaim died soon after.[1] This brought peace for the time, and the King followed up this

[1] Palacky, iii. 289-96,

measure by another equally drastic. He altered the composition of the Council of Prague, which had hitherto been mainly composed of Germans, the adversaries of Hus and his followers. The King ordered that henceforth twenty-five Germans and the same number of Bohemians should be nominated, of whom he would select nine of each nation; and on the 2nd November 1413, he executed two of the old counsellors ' pour encourager les autres.'

The time of his exile from Prague was that of Hus's greatest literary activity. It was then that he wrote his treatise ' On Simony,' in which he complains that the Pope's cooks, porters, equerries, and footmen ' have first claim on the most important benefices even in lands of which they do not know the language,' in which he suggests that bishops and parish priests should be elected according to God's will by the drawing of lots, and should be guided in the paths of truth and justice by the King; ' and he would not guide them in the path of truth and justice did he allow them, like negligent servants, to incur the wrath of the Highest of Kings; he would not thus fulfil the duties of his royal office.'[1] John Hus only knew King Wenzel whom he trusted, more than most men did, to fulfil the behests of the King of kings. Another work composed by Hus at this time in the Bohemian language was the 'Postilla,' in which he endeavoured ' briefly to expound with God's help the Gospel for all the Sundays in the year.' In his sermon on the Gospel for Palm Sunday he draws a contrast between the Pope, seated on his white war horse and smiling that he has so much praise, and ' our dear, tranquil, meek Redeemer riding into Jerusalem on his mule and weeping bitterly.' Of his Latin writings at this time the most important is the treatise ' De Ecclesia,' an abridgment of Wyclif's work, and founded on Saint Augustine's doctrine of predestination. All mankind is divided into two classes, those predestined to eternal bliss, and those foreknown (*presciti*) to eternal damnation. The former constitute the true Holy Catholic Church, and Christ is their only head; but the *presciti* also are members of the Church as at present constituted and since the Donation of Constantine the Pope has considered himself as Head of the Church and as Christ's Vicar on earth.

[1] Luetzow, 195.

CONVOCATION OF THE COUNCIL

To this period also belongs Hus's 'Answer to the Writings of Stanislas,' who had formerly been his friend, but who separated from him and became one of his bitterest enemies from the time that Hus ceased to acknowledge the supreme authority of the Pope.

The storm over the sale of indulgences had disgusted Albert with the archiepiscopal office ; he found it difficult to serve two masters, the Pope and the King ; he accordingly effected an exchange with Conrad, Bishop of Olmuetz, and became the titular Archbishop of Caesarea, and Provost of the Vysehrad, the previous Provost taking the bishopric vacated by Conrad. This chaffering of high ecclesiastical dignities naturally excited great scandal and indignation in Bohemia. The new Archbishop is described by Tomek as being neither better nor worse than the great majority ; ' like the others he only wished to acquire large worldly possessions as rapidly as possible.'[1] He was a weak and elderly man. But he had no sympathy with the advanced members of the Hussite party, who desired to regulate the organisation of the Church by the simple rule of the Bible, and to reject all later expansion and development of its institutions as unnecessary.

It was about the time that Pope John issued his encyclical that King Sigismund opened negotiations with John Hus. John of Chlum and Wenzel of Duba, both of them admirers and friends of the reformer, were in the King's train, and they undertook to transmit the royal proposals to Hus. The King promised him a safe conduct in going and coming, and a public hearing at the Council, in order that he might purge himself and Bohemia from all suspicion of heresy. Hus was at the time when he received the news at the castle of Heinrich Lefl of Lazan, who gave him the invitation, which he resolved to accept. There were those who warned him ; one of Sigismund's own envoys said to him, ' Master, be sure that thou wilt be condemned.' Hus went to Prague to consult his friends, and some of them tried to dissuade him, but his resolution was taken. He had no doubt in the integrity of his cause ; he thought he was going to hold an academical discussion, such as he had often held successfully in Prague ; to John Hus the invitation of King

[1] Luetzow, 169.

Sigismund was a call to the end of strife. His disputations in the University of Prague had been marred by the race-animosity of Czech and Teuton ; his condemnations before the papal court had been procured through the interested malice of personal enemies ; he had been belittled and vilipended all his life by the parish priests whose evil courses he had desired to reform ; but now, in the clear scholastic air of the Council, far from the smoke and stir of these local dissensions, he would reasonably and temperately plead his cause, citing passages from the Fathers and from Holy Writ, he would persuade the assembled fathers of his orthodoxy, he would justify the faith that was in him ; he was ready to recant any error that might be proved against him on authority that he acknowledged ; but eventually he would triumphantly purge himself and his beloved country of the monstrous scandal of heresy. Hus was determined to go to Constance.

From Cremona King Sigismund went to Piacenza to meet Carlo Malatesta, the Lord of Rimini. The letter and offer to Pope Gregory had been fruitless ; the aged pontiff said that he could not go to Constance. Malatesta, however, was of one mind with the King as to the necessity for a Council, and promised to use his influence to induce the old Pope either to undertake the journey in person or to send fully empowered representatives. Later on Gregory wrote to the King expressing his acquiescence, provided the Council was called and the time and place of meeting fixed by Sigismund himself ; provided also that the same number of each obedience attended, for Gregory apparently took it for granted that Pope Benedict the Thirteenth would neither attend nor be represented ; and provided finally that all points in dispute between the two parties were referred to the King of the Romans for decision.[1] His opposition to the Council was clearly weakening under the influence of his protector. On the 6th June Sigismund entrusted the negotiations with Pope Gregory to Count Amadeus of Savoy, but the Count took no steps in the matter, being engaged with the King of the Romans in his own dominions.[2] In July Sigismund gave full powers in this respect to Archbishop Andreas of Calocza, who was also entrusted by Pope John to

---

[1] Finke (*Acta*), 275.   [2] *Ibid.* (*Acta*), 196, 290.

CONVOCATION OF THE COUNCIL 199

publish the meeting of the Council in Romagna. The Archbishop in the first place approached the Republic of Venice, but they declined to interfere, on the ground that they did not acknowledge the Pope. The ambassador appeared at Rimini on the 30th July, delivered his credentials and the invitation to the Council, which was dated as far back as the 13th December 1413. He promised a safe conduct, both on the part of the King and of Pope John, a secure residence in Constance, and safe return, no matter what happened there. The Pope remarked on the delay in sending him an invitation by a fully empowered hand, while one had long since been sent to his old rival Benedict the Thirteenth; he stated that he was ready to work for the union of the Church and had already sent to the King his proposals. Later on the Archbishop referred to two articles in his instructions which contemplated the possibility of a condemnation of Pope Gregory. Naturally the pontiff asked who would preside over the Council, what would be the paramount authority, who would judge the Popes. The Archbishop could only point to the impartiality and high character of King Sigismund. Finally, however, the aged Pope gave way. He bitterly regretted that Sigismund had disregarded the dying advice of his father and had forsaken the successor of Pope Urban the Sixth, but he was willing to send his representatives to Constance on receiving safe conducts from Sigismund and from Duke Friedrich of the Tirol, and a monthly subsistence allowance of two thousand golden gulden.[1]

While at Cremona Sigismund again renewed negotiations with Milan, but again unsuccessfully. Having appointed Giovanni Vignate as his regent in Lodi, the King left Cremona and proceeded to Genoa. He was anxious to get the suzerainty of the Empire acknowledged in Piedmont and Savoy.

The Genoese had reserved the rights of the Holy Roman Empire even when they passed under the sway of France. In 1409 they had, as already narrated,[2] revolted against France, and had made Theodor, Marquess of Montferrat, their Doge for five years; but in February 1413 the Guelfs banished him from the city and elected a Doge of their own. As Sigismund

---

[1] Finke (*F.*), 22-5; (*Acta*), 196-203, 290-307.
[2] *In the Days of the Councils*, 389-90.

approached Genoa, marching in through one gate of their little town Gavi, north of the city, and marching out through the other, there was a heated discussion as to whether the King of the Romans should be admitted. They feared that he came with the intention of reinstating Marquess Theodor, to whom they had paid twenty-four thousand gulden for peace, and whom they feared as the mightiest lord in Piedmont. They sent an embassy to explain that they were compelled to keep their gates shut against him; Sigismund received the ambassadors graciously, made one of them a knight and appointed him Palatine, ' presented them with a copy of Justinian and left them with the impression that he was a kindly, God-fearing man, strong in body, simple in diet, and hedged about all round with prudence.'[1] From Genoa Sigismund marched on to Alessandria and thence to Asti.

In Asti, where he remained for some weeks, the King met the Marquess of Montferrat, whom he appointed Vicar of the Empire for the whole of Lombardy, and for whom he arranged an alliance with Milan against Genoa. Here Sigismund had another narrow escape for life. The governor secretly introduced eight thousand armed men, brought them into the city by night, and fell upon the King with intent to murder him. Sigismund sprang up, seized a banner in his left hand and a sword in his right, laid about him valiantly, crying out, ' Smite the varlets, God is with us.' So stoutly did his two thousand withstand their enemies, that the citizens rushed to their timely aid, and the treachery was foiled.[2] After leaving Asti the King used his influence to bring about a peace between the Marquesses of Montferrat and Saluzzo on the one side and the Counts Ludovico and Amadeus of Savoy on the other. He then went on toward Pavia.

One of the lords of Pavia, Castellino Beccaria, and his nephew had been seized and imprisoned by the Duke of Milan in October 1413; Lancellotto Beccaria had fled to his fortresses, defied Filippo Maria, and now implored the aid of Sigismund to obtain the release of his brother and nephew; the Duke frustrated his hopes by executing them both; and the King of the Romans was powerless to avenge his vassals, and was

[1] Aschbach, i. 380-2; Wylie (C.), 17.   [2] Altmann, 51; Aschbach, i. 383.

CONVOCATION OF THE COUNCIL 201

obliged to content himself with promising Lancellotto an annual pension of five thousand ducats.

Thus far the efforts of King Sigismund in northern Italy had been crowned with success; he had practically re-established the suzerainty of the Empire everywhere except at Milan. The government of France, whatever the attitude of the Duke of Burgundy might be, had renounced all their pretensions to Genoa, and regarded with a favourable eye the restoration of the imperial authority in Italy.[1] The Duke of Milan alone remained recalcitrant; with him the King had still to deal.

On the 17th June Sigismund was received with much honour and festivity in Turin, the capital of Savoy. A University had been founded in 1405 by Louis of Savoy with a Bull from Pope Benedict the Thirteenth; the King of the Romans had granted a charter in 1412, and Pope John, who was then acknowledged in Piedmont, had followed it up by another charter in the following year.[2] Sigismund now recognised that he could do nothing further against Milan at present. From Cremona he had written for troops to eight large towns in Germany, and they had not refused, but had procrastinated,[3] when a speedy compliance was essential; for there was trouble also north of the Alps to be accommodated, and Sigismund had convened a Diet at Speier for the 8th July. The King therefore remained but a short time at Turin, and then, accompanied by the two Counts of Savoy, whose dominion stretched to the Lake of Geneva, and by Theodor of Montferrat, he went by the Saint Bernard Pass down the Rhone valley into Switzerland. His intention was to go to Aachen to be crowned with the silver crown, and thence to make his way to the Council of Constance. In spite of all that he had accomplished with so much toil, his old enemy, John of Nassau, Elector of Mainz, was able to twit him with having failed hitherto to recover the Duchy of Milan.

On the 17th January 1414, Pope John came from Cremona to Mantua, where he remained with his friend Francesco of Gonzaga until the 7th February if not later; on the 22nd he was in Ferrara; and he returned to Bologna on the 26th February. On the 19th March he began the restoration of his fortress at the Galliera Gate, which had been destroyed when

[1] Valois, iv. 236.   [2] Rashdall, ii. 57.   [3] Sauerbrei, 50, 56.

the people revolted three years earlier. This castle had originally been built by Cardinal Du Pouget in 1330, and was known as one of the most beautiful fortresses in Italy; it was pulled down four years later; was rebuilt by Baldassare Cossa in 1404, and destroyed again in 1411. The Pope now employed an engineer, Giovanni of Siena, to reconstruct it for the third time, but it was destroyed again two years later.[1] In Bologna Pope John awaited the approach of his deadly enemy, Ladislas of Naples, who was bent on taking the city and on making the Pope his prisoner.

On the 14th March 1414, the King of Naples rode into Rome. Seated on his horse, surrounded with Roman and Neapolitan barons, he entered the Lateran Church, and had the heads of the holy apostles, Peter and Paul, the most sacred relic in Rome, displayed before him. Three days later he appointed new conservators for the city; and on the day following the Romans were terrified by a fearful storm and the fall of two thunderbolts. Ladislas remained in Rome until the 25th April, when he moved out with his army and marched to Isola.[2] Paolo Orsini, after his escape from Rocca Contrada, bethought him of retrieving his shattered fortunes from the purse of the King of Naples, and accordingly deserted to Ladislas, who received him graciously.[3] The King of Naples, in 1413, hoped that he had won over to his cause the Pope's ally, Nicolas, Marquess of Este. Sforza's son was with the Marquess for education in the art of war, and the general had persuaded the King to send the Marquess the royal sceptre and standard, appointing him captain of his troops, and giving three thousand gold florins for their pay. Sforza himself stood security for the money; and great was his chagrin and disappointment when, early in 1414, Nicolas returned the banner and sceptre and renounced the captaincy. The King was no less disappointed than his general, though he thoroughly trusted Sforza's good faith. Without the aid of the Marquess it was in vain to attempt to gain Bologna; Ladislas was obliged to give up the desire of his heart; he advanced into Umbria and attempted to take Foligno, which was faithful to the Pope. Florentine troops came to the aid of the town, and the King fell back on

---

[1] Gozzadini, 12.   [2] Mur. xxiv. 1042.   [3] *Ibid.* xix. 42, 657.

CONVOCATION OF THE COUNCIL 203

Todi, which he besieged. The town is on a steep hill, and was defended by Braccio da Montone. Here, as the siege dragged on, the leaders of the Neapolitan troops tried the plan of appearing one by one before the walls, to tempt the papal troops to try conclusions with them. When the turn of the arch traitor, Paolo Orsini, came he was vigorously attacked by his former comrade, Braccio, and had been like to have the worst of it, but that Sforza, seeing his danger and magnanimously sinking his private difference for the common weal, rescued him and brought him back safe to camp. The resistance at Todi was too stubborn to be overcome, and Ladislas returned to Perugia, which had submitted in the previous year. He opened negotiations with Florence; and the Republic, trembling at his success, was ready to desert Pope John; for a moment the King thought he might even win over Sigismund to his side. The anxiety in Bologna was so great that the officers of the Curia sent their valuables to Ferrara and Venice for safe custody, and the Pope himself made ready to flee to the former place. But the unexpected was to happen. Paolo Orsini at this time began to attempt, or was thought by the King to be trying, some new treachery. Ladislas was not so long-suffering as Pope John had been, and straightway clapped him in chains.[1] The King of Naples had hitherto been successful beyond his deserts, but the fateful hour of the red-haired libertine was now come.

King Ladislas was deeply enamoured of the fair daughter of a physician of Perugia; the Florentines heard of his lechery, and found means to bribe the girl's father. The doctor took the bribe, sent for his daughter, talked to her of the King's love till the girl was overjoyed, and then began to hint doubts of his constancy until she fell into despair. He could give her, he said, a drug which, poured into the King's wine, would act as a love philtre and ensure his constant affection. The damsel took the drug. Ladislas visited her, troubled and in pain; she poured the drug into his golden goblet, drank thereof herself in her innocency, and the King drank after her. The deadly poison took immediate effect on her weak frame; and the King's robuster constitution was also unable to withstand its effects.[2] Rome was still under the King's sway; and the bells in all the

[1] Mur. xix. 659; Finke (*Acta*), 182.   [2] Crivelli, 117.

churches had been duly rung on the 5th July when the news came of the imprisonment of Paolo Orsini. At the end of the month the tidings arrived that the King was returning, sick unto death. A hammock (*vara*) and then a chair were prepared for him; and on the night of the 30th July, King Ladislas of Naples was carried from Passerano to the Church of Saint Paul outside the city walls, was taken thence to the river hard by, and was placed with his prisoner, Paolo Orsini, on a galley destined for Naples. He had entered the Church of Saint John on horseback; he left the Church of Saint Paul a dying man, in a chair. This was the last the Romans saw of him.[1] The galley reached Naples. The King, in his agony, thirsted for the blood of the traitor Paolo Orsini, and cried out to have him killed in his presence. His sister Joanna, to appease him, said falsely that Paolo had already been executed. King Ladislas died on the 6th August 1414; and Pope John the Twenty-third was thus freed from his direst enemy.

The temptation to return to Rome to secure possession of the capital of his temporal dominions was great, and the Pope at first thought of taking the journey and of postponing the great Council. The rumour ran, alike in Portugal and in France, that it was put off for five months. John also contemplated going to Avignon to meet the French princes; galleys were freighted to convey him from Pisa, and ambassadors came to him from 'the sinful city.' But the cardinals represented to him that the occupation of Rome would only be for the temporal welfare of the Church, whereas the Council of Constance was for its spiritual benefit; that he might depute his vicars or legates for the lesser, but that it devolved on him alone to discharge the higher duty. Better thoughts prevailed; the Pope gave up the idea of going either to Rome or to Avignon; he determined to keep his word; he sent Cardinal Hannibaldus to Rome and himself prepared to set out for Constance.[2]

[1] Mur. xxiv. 1045.   [2] *Ibid.* xix. 929.

CHAPTER XI

PRELIMINARY NEGOTIATIONS

THE Council of Constance had been convoked, but it remained to ensure that it should be really œcumenical, really representative of Christendom. Pope John the Twenty-third might be trusted, for his own protection, to bring with him a goodly number of the Italian clergy ; and King Sigismund could ensure the attendance of other prelates of the Empire, as well as those of Hungary and Bohemia. But the King was specially anxious that England and France should be fully represented at the Council.[1] If the prelates of the Empire, of France, and of England attended in goodly array, it would not matter much whether the three rivals Pope were present or not. There were also Spain and other countries to be considered. A year was certainly not too long for the preliminary negotiations if the Council was to be really œcumenical.

The great difficulty naturally was with France. That nation had hitherto been foremost in attempting to heal the Great Schism, and the King of the Romans had taken their work out of their hands. The Council of Pisa had been held under French, mainly under Burgundian, protection ; and France was inclined to regard its work as final, and to consider Pope John as undoubtedly the only lawful Pope. The Duke of Orleans coincided in that view, although his father-in-law, the Count of Armagnac, was still an ardent supporter of Pope Benedict the Thirteenth. Sigismund not only pointed out that the Council of Pisa was a failure, as its failure to effect any reform proved, but he also insisted that he could not be crowned Emperor save by a Pope acknowledged by all Christendom. He described the aim of the Council as being to decide which of the three pretenders was the legitimate Pope, entitled to crown him Emperor,

[1] Finke (*Acta*), 376.

a view which would commend itself to the Armagnac party, less inclined to Pope John than were the Burgundians; while in his invitation of the same date (9th November 1413) to the King of France he was careful to intimate that the Council was convoked by Pope John the Twenty-third.[1] Charles the Sixth, in his answer, referred to his own labour in the cause of the Church, which he hoped had attained its end; he said that he himself regarded Pope John as the legitimate possessor of the apostolic seat, and intended to obey him until he renounced his right, but that at the same time he would not detain any one who wished to go to the Council of Constance.[2] The reply was dictated while the Duke of Burgundy was in power; but Providence had meantime again worked for the King of the Romans by banishing the Duke and restoring the Armagnacs. The King had no intention of resting content with this answer, but his difficulty in treating with the French Court was complicated, not only by the civil war between the Armagnacs and Burgundians, but also by the diverging interests and influence of the various royal princes who made up the former party.

As to the main division Sigismund soon made up his mind. He had, in the spring of 1412, been on friendly terms with John of Burgundy, and tried to persuade Pope John to join him in reconciling Burgundians and Armagnacs;[3] but in the course of that year affairs in the Duchy of Luxemburg caused a change in his feeling. Antoine de Brabant, the Duke of Burgundy's brother, had, in 1409, married Sigismund's fair niece, the heiress of Goerlitz, and now began to prosecute her claims in the Duchy on the strength of her marriage-contract made with King Wenzel. This roused the nobility of the Duchy against the Duke; they appealed to the King of the Romans, and Sigismund forbad them to pay any homage to the usurper of Brabant or his wife. He himself had been no party to the relinquishment of rights nor to the mortgage made by his half-brother; and Luxemburg still formed part of the Holy Roman Empire. He therefore abandoned the party of Burgundy, whom he suspected of siding with his brother of Brabant, and attached himself to that of the Armagnacs. The Duke of Anjou, he

---

[1] Mansi, xxviii. 5; *Religieux*, v. 206; Finke (*Acta*), 220.
[2] *Religieux*, v. 208.   [3] Finke (*Acta*), 217.

PRELIMINARY NEGOTIATIONS 207

thought, might be trusted to welcome a Council convoked by the Pope who had backed him in Italy, and by the King who openly supported him.[1]

The civil war between the Burgundians and Armagnacs was raging in France. On Monday, the 22nd August 1412, the Duke of Orleans and his friends met the Duke of Burgundy and his near a nunnery on the open plain outside Auxerre, and there they made peace; the common people rejoiced greatly and cried out, *Gloria in excelsis Deo*.[2] But the peace was nothing better than an armed neutrality. On the one side stood the Orleanists and Armagnacs; on the other was Jean sans Peur, and his army, supported by the University and the people, and more especially the butchers, of Paris.[3] Reform was demanded; the Estates were summoned; the University was consulted; but Paris was in a ferment. On the 28th April 1413, the butchers, under Caboche, the friend and ally of the Duke of Burgundy, rose, marched on the Bastille, and took prisoner the governor, Pierre des Essarts, while another party penetrated to the Dauphin's hotel. The Cabochiens ruled Paris. On the 9th May one of their orators denounced the evil courses of the Dauphin; on the 22nd a deputation appeared at the royal palace; on the 26th a Cabochien ordonnance of reform was published and was approved by the King. This measure, however, was not sufficiently democratic to satisfy the butchers; there were executions and murders; until the Parisians and the University grew sick of their tyranny. Then came the peace of Pontoise (28th July); the Dauphin secretly recalled the heads of the Armagnac party to deliver the King; the Cabochiens were put to flight; the Duke of Burgundy escaped to Lille (29th August), and Paris became Armagnac; the green bonnets with Saint Andrew's cross were replaced once more by the large white crosses with the device, 'The right road.' Civil war recommenced.[4] The little children in Paris had sung:

> Duc de Bourgogne,
> Dieu te ramaint à joye:

but now the cry was, 'Faulx traistre, chien bourgoignon, je regny Deu, ce vous ne serez pilliez.'[5] But the Duke reappeared

[1] Valois, iv. 254. [2] Monstrelet, 248. [3] Coville, 148.
[4] Lavisse, IV. i. 351. [5] Tuetey, 46.

before Paris on the 7th February 1414, with his troops and encamped at Saint Denis, which was abandoned to him; while the gates of the city were straightly shut for a fortnight. His friends said that he was angry only with the Duke of Anjou for sending back his daughter 'like a poor or simple dame to her father';[1] but Jean sans Peur was compelled to depart, being declared a rebel, banished as a traitor without pity or mercy, the ban and the arrière-ban being called out to combat him.[2] This change in the position of parties in France helped King Sigismund in his negotiations.

For the success of the Council it was necessary that there should, as far as possible, be peace in Europe; and Sigismund's great aim was to avert the war which threatened between England and France. He was in constant diplomatic relations with both countries, kept them both aware of this fact, and hoped to make peace by bringing about a marriage between King Henry of England and Princess Katharine of France. He desired universal peace, from which 'that parricide,' the Duke of Burgundy, was alone to be excluded. With France, England, and the Empire against him, Jean sans Peur might be treated as a negligible quantity. Pope John, on the 27th April 1414, charged Cardinal Adimar to address special letters of convocation to the Council, to France and the neighbouring countries; and Sigismund was also active in the same direction. In the beginning of March he wrote to Charles the Sixth, to the Dauphin, and to the Dukes of Orleans, Anjou, and Berri, telling them that he had intended to visit Avignon and to come thence to Paris, but that he had refrained on hearing that the Duke of Burgundy was encamped before its gates with an armed multitude; he begs therefore that one of the royal dukes, with some doctors of the University, will meet him in Provence or at Asti. At the same time he wrote to the University of Paris asking them to send some masters of theology and other doctors with the royal princes, so that he might disclose to them the secrets of his heart.[3] Not until May did he receive an answer. The civil war prevented any of the royal princes accepting his proposal, and it was suggested that he should come to them. Affairs in Italy, however, detained Sigismund;

[1] Tuetey, 48.   [2] Monstrelet, 320.   [3] Finke (*Acta*), 358-67.

he promised to despatch these as soon as the French ambassadors reached him, and again he asked that doctors and theologians from the University might be sent to him that he might take counsel with them concerning the inner things of his heart, which were so weighty and important that he could not trust them to writing.[1]

On the 25th June 1414, King Sigismund, being then at Trino in the land of the Marquess of Montferrat, signed a solemn treaty with the King of France. The Houses of Valois and Luxemburg had been close friends for a hundred years, and the King desired to renew the old treaties. He promised to be faithful in word and deed and to assist the French King against all his enemies, especially against John, who called himself the Duke of Burgundy.[2] War was at this time brewing between England and France, and Sigismund, in writing to Charles the Sixth, shortly after signing the treaty, made no secret that he was in diplomatic relations with King Henry the Fifth;[3] on that side he clearly desired to keep his hands free, but on the side of the Duke of Burgundy he was most anxious for the French alliance, dreading lest the two brothers of Burgundy and Brabant might interfere with him as he went to Aachen to be crowned. Universal peace, and the crushing of Jean sans Peur, were his objects. He heard that Pope John, who was a consistent ally of Burgundy, had endeavoured to reconcile the Duke with France; and he wrote to the King and to the Duke of Orleans, entreating them to make no one-sided treaty which should leave him out in the cold. On the 25th July he again sent two messengers to King Charles. In reply the King asked him to come to Verdun; and then, when the rumour came of Pope John's projected visit to Avignon, Sigismund was asked to come to Lyons; but to both invitations he answered that it was impossible, that in order to appear at the coming Council as *advocatus ecclesiæ* he must first comply with the wishes of the Electors and get himself crowned. He sent Duke Louis of Bavaria to explain the pure intent of his mind more fully, and begged the King to send some of the royal princes together with doctors of the University to the Council of Constance.[4]

[1] Finke (*Acta*), 367-70.
[2] Lenz, 44.
[3] Finke (*Acta*), 371.
[4] *Ibid.* 380.

The kaleidoscope of French politics now took another turn, much to the chagrin and dismay of the King of the Romans. The King of France, leaving Peronne and taking Bapaume, went to Arras to besiege the Duke of Burgundy; and there, with his son, the Duke of Aquitaine, and the Dukes of Orleans, Bourbon, and others, he laid siege to the place and many feats of arms were done.[1] On the 25th July there came to the King's camp the Duke of Brabant and his sister, the Countess of Mainault, and took counsel with the Duke of Aquitaine, who was married to the daughter of the Duke of Burgundy, and a peace was concluded.[2] The treaty was signed on the 4th September; the civil war was at an end. The Cabochiens were sacrificed to the fury of the Armagnacs,[3] but Jean sans Peur was reconciled to the brother of the man whom he had so foully murdered, and the troops escaped from the bloody flux which was decimating their numbers; never were peals of bells more joyous than those which sounded at Paris on the 13th September when the news was known.[4] King Sigismund was more disgusted than surprised; from Heilbronn on the 14th October he wrote a letter full of reproach; he complained that it was at the King's instance that he had proceeded aggressively against the Duke for whom he was now betrayed, and that it was common rumour that the latter meant to attack Aachen; and after mentioning that he was in all points in accord with his half-brother the King of Bohemia, he again asked that the royal princes, the prelates and doctors and other worthy men of France should attend the Council of Constance.[5]

King Sigismund had, after all, secured his chief point. A preparatory assembly of the clergy was convoked at Paris on the 1st October; and it was arranged that each ecclesiastical province should depute its archbishop, together with bishops, abbots, masters, and notable clerks to the Council; each archbishop was to receive ten francs a day, each bishop eight, the abbots five, and the others two or three. France was to be fully represented at the Council, although the French representatives were not to arrive in time for the opening. But then, neither would the King of the Romans.

[1] Juvenal, 280-1.   [2] Monstrelet, 343.   [3] Juvenal, 288.
[4] Tuetey, 56.   [5] Finke (*Acta*), 383-6.

PRELIMINARY NEGOTIATIONS 211

The Duke of Burgundy was also to be represented, and indeed his murder of the Duke of Orleans was to furnish the assembled fathers with abundant food for discussion and deliberation. The assassination had occurred on the 23rd November 1407; the doctrine of political assassination had been elaborately upheld by Jean Petit on the 8th March 1408;[1] the contrary thesis had been maintained on the 11th September by the Abbé Serisy;[2] as soon as the Armagnacs came back to Paris in 1413, Jean Gerson took up the question, and the King ordered the Bishop of Paris to investigate the justification of the Norman doctor. On the 13th February 1414, the Bishop, without mentioning the Duke nor Jean Petit by name, formally condemned the principle as contrary to good faith and morality, and recommended that the justification be burned.[3] Jean sans Peur, against whom the people now sang songs in the streets of Paris, protested against this sentence; and the matter was referred to the Council of Constance. The University of Paris was also to be represented, and well she deserved to be; for in great measure the assembling of the Council was due to her diplomacy and still more to the 'ideas which had gradually shaped themselves into something like a new theory of ecclesiastical polity in the minds and writings of the Parisian theologians.'[4]

Diplomatic relations between the King of the Romans and the English Court were facilitated by the residence, as English agent with Sigismund, through the entire reign of Henry the Fifth, of the knight Hartung van Clux. Although his name was Flemish, Hartung was an English subject, and in 1411 he had been sent,[5] together with John Stokes, by his King to Sigismund, by whom he was thereafter consistently trusted and occasionally employed. The aim of Henry the Fifth was to obtain the aid of Sigismund against Charles the Sixth; the aim of Sigismund was to bring about peace between England and France in the interest of the Council and of Europe. There had been confidential relations between Henry the Fourth and Rupert, the two Kings whose positions in their kingdoms were

---

[1] Barante, iii. 107-43.
[2] *Ibid.* 160-83.
[3] *Ibid.* iv. 150.
[4] Rashdall, i. 546.
[5] *Vid. sup.*, 122.

so similar; Rupert's son Louis had married Henry's daughter Blanca, 'more an angel than an Angle in her looks.'[1] Now Louis had transferred all his interest in the Empire to Sigismund; he believed himself to have been the chief instrument in his election; he was his enthusiastic supporter; he had worked with Pope Gregory the Twelfth to induce that pontiff to acknowledge the Council of Constance: so that the diplomatic relations between the King of the Romans and the King of England were almost a logical continuation of those between their predecessors.

The first letter from King Sigismund to King Henry the Fifth was despatched in August 1413, and at the same time he sent a letter of the same tenor to the King of France, and probably to other monarchs also.[2] The threefold aim of King Sigismund's life was to restore the shattered suzerainty of the Holy Roman Empire, to bring about a General Council, and then to lead a crusade against the Turks. He was at this time engaged in the first project, these letters concerned the second, the time for broaching the third had not yet arrived. These letters were written while he was in diplomatic relations with Pope John, but before anything definite had been arranged as to the time or place of the great Council. He complains of the delay and of the increasing necessity for Church reform. Inasmuch as the matter concerns all Christendom he asks the King of England also to take anxious thought and to favour him with his opinion whether the most fitting place for a Council would be in Italy or in Germany; it must be a place easy of access, capable of holding a large number of visitors and of providing them with the necessary supplies. He also wrote to the Count Palatine and to the Archbishop of Trier to inquire as to the suitability of Basel or Strassburg. He was clear that the place selected should not be in Italy.

In 1414 Sigismund told the knight Hartung van Clux that he desired with his whole heart to make a treaty of friendship with Henry the Fifth; and accordingly on the 23rd July 1414, the King of England commissioned two knights, Walter Hungerford and John Waterton, and a Doctor Simon Sydenham to conclude a treaty with the King of the Romans and of Hungary. About

[1] Lenz, 57.   [2] Blumenthal, 106; Finke (*Acta*), 239 *et seq.*

PRELIMINARY NEGOTIATIONS   213

the same time[1] Sigismund sent to Henry by Clux a long letter full of his plans for the Council; he wanted peace between England, France, and the Empire, for they could do all things if they stood together; ' si enim Deus pro nobis, quis contra nos '? he hoped to visit the King of France and to forward the project of Henry's marriage with the French princess Katharine; he trusted that all three Popes would be at the Council of Constance, but even if they were not there, the reformation of the Church could be effected under such august patronage without their presence; and he asked that certain of the excellent English theologians, doctors, and others might come on ahead to confer with him before the Council opened. What deep-laid scheme Sigismund cherished for which these preliminary conferences were requisite does not appear; at any rate, none of them ever came off, unless perchance he took counsel with the English bishops at Aachen. The English ambassadors met the King of the Romans at Coblenz about the middle of August;[2] and at the end of that month Sigismund again wrote to Henry the Fifth, ' Lord of England and France,' pressing for an alliance of the three powers against John of Burgundy, and offering to give the Duke's possessions in Flanders to the King of England.[3] Sigismund was quite ready to dispose of vacant realms, even before they were vacant, as Lord of the Holy Roman Empire. No treaty was at this time concluded between the two Kings,[4] but Henry's help for the Council of Constance was secured. He had, like other sovereigns, received his formal invitation, together with the *Edictum Universale*, long before; and on the 20th October the envoys were appointed. At their head was the Earl of Warwick, Governor of Calais, and with him were Lord Fitzhugh and Walter Hungerford; the clerical members were Robert Hallam, Bishop of Salisbury, who had taken part in the Council of Pisa, and whom Pope John had desired to make cardinal; John Catterick, Bishop of Saint David's and later of Lichfield; and Nicholas Bubwith, Bishop of Bath.[5] They were authorised to conclude a treaty of alliance with Sigismund; and with an escort of eight hundred horses they made their way through

---

[1] Finke (*Acta*), 373.   [2] Lenz, 60.   [3] Finke (*Acta*), 377.
[4] *Ibid.* 387.   [5] Ramsay, i. 191.

Flanders and Brabant to Aachen, where their King intended them to add additional splendour to the coronation of the King of the Romans.

The negotiations with the kingdoms of Spain, the stronghold of Pope Benedict the Thirteenth, met with two preliminary obstacles. In the first place there were the communications with King Ladislas of Naples, which were brought to an end by the death of the monarch. In the second place King Ferdinand of Aragon objected to the opening sentence of Sigismund's letter of invitation; the King of the Romans exhorted his illustrious serenity of Aragon in virtue of his imperial office as defender and advocate of the Catholic Church; and the King remonstrated that they of Spain had never recognised the Emperor as their superior. It was explained that the expression was a mistake of the office sending out the letters, although the same expression had been used in the letter to the King of France. This preliminary difficulty was smoothed over. In his letters to parts which acknowledged the obedience of Benedict, King Sigismund was careful to notify that the Council of Constance was convoked by him, and no mention was made of the intruder Baldassare Cossa. In May 1414 three embassies reached Spain; Ottobonus of Bologna, a doctor of the civil and canon law, much employed in embassies by Sigismund, came on behalf of the King of the Romans; four ambassadors came on behalf of the King of France; and the Patriarch, John of Constantinople, represented Pope John the Twenty-third. The first ambassador proposed to the King of Aragon, and subsequently to Pope Benedict, a meeting with Sigismund at Marseilles, Nice, or Savona; and was himself present when the King of Aragon and the Pope met subsequently at Morella. As to the Patriarch of Constantinople the King was at first inclined to refuse to see him, but he subsequently issued a safe conduct; his commission was merely to the King and not to the Pope. The French ambassadors met Ferdinand at Saragossa on the 30th May, and two of them went in June to Castile, while the other two returned home in August.[1] In these negotiations the difficulty was with the aged Pope Benedict the Thirteenth. He was unassailable by argument, refused to look facts in the face,

[1] Finke (*Acta*), 205-9.

and would see things only in the light of his own particular theory. Originally the last of the cardinals to forsake Pope Urban the Sixth, when the Great Schism began, he never afterwards appeared to have any doubt of the righteousness of the step he so tardily took. Before he himself became Pope, he was the most persuasive and successful defender of the right of Clement the Seventh. Benedict was a pious, just, and strong man, of clean livelihood and averse from simony, who, in happier times, would have made an exemplary Pope. But Fate was against him; he found nothing but trouble and hardship in his pontificate; he suffered siege, persecution, and the subtraction of obedience at the hands of the nation which had been most obsequiously subservient to his predecessor. The effect of his long trial was that his character hardened, and his very virtues suffered atrophy; his firmness degenerated into obstinacy, and his strength into perversity. He had become incapable of considering fairly any point of view but his own; he could not judge fairly any man who did not agree with him and believe in him. In these negotiations he calls the Council of Pisa a conciliabulum or a congregation, and gives the same name to the coming Council of Constance; he always dubs his rivals as intruders; he descends to call Gregory by the vulgar nickname of Errorius. He acknowledges that under subsisting difficulties of law and fact it is almost impossible to convoke what shall really be a General Council;[1] he suggests separate Councils of each obedience, and the selection by each of certain arbitrators to meet,[2] a recourse to the discarded 'way of compromise';[3] he gravely argues the question whether the one-third elected by the rightful obedience could confer with the other two-thirds elected by the schismatics; he scouts the idea of going to Constance for which, moreover, there was not time before All Saints' Day, but he is willing to meet Sigismund at Nice between April and July next year, he desires him meantime to procure a condemnation of the Council of Pisa,[4] and he himself postpones the re-opening of the Council lately held at Perpignan until Easter 1415.[5]

[1] Finke (*Acta*), 323. [2] *Ibid.* 320.
[3] Cf. *In the Days of the Councils*, 178.
[4] Finke (*Acta*), 332. [5] *Ibid.* 338.

Luckily, King Ferdinand saw things with different eyes from Pope Benedict; he was not the whole-hearted supporter his predecessor, King Martin, had been; he desired rather the unity of the Church; he knew that he had not long to live, and his words, therefore, carried the more weight; ' the tongues of dying men enforce attention like deep harmony.' He was almost as bitter against that 'most dread lord Baldassare Cossa' as was Benedict himself, and was persuaded that Benedict was the one undoubted true Pope and highest pontiff of the Universal Church,[1] but he was determined that something should be done. After the arrival of the ambassadors he repeatedly sent to the Pope to arrange a meeting; he himself went to Morella on the 1st July, and Pope Benedict the Thirteenth appeared there on the 18th of that month. Morella is a little place in the hills, north-west of Peniscola, near the Catalonian border of Valencia. Here was held the meeting which ultimately determined the attitude of the Spanish kingdoms to the Council. It was a splendid assembly; not only were the Curia of Benedict and the family of Ferdinand present, but also a large number of bishops and theologians, including the celebrated Vincenzo Ferrier, and the ambassadors of France, Castile, and the Empire. There were ecclesiastical pomps and processions, in which the Pope appeared in all his diminished glory, with his Curia and his Cardinals;[2] and there were lengthy consultations which lasted up to the middle of September. Sigismund had told Ferdinand that the two other Popes would abdicate; the point was whether Benedict would do the like; in that case a new Pope could be chosen at Constance. This corresponded with the advice given at the Council of Perpignan.[3] Benedict professed to be ready thus to give peace to the Church, but made conditions and reservations.[4] He wanted the proceedings of the Council of Pisa, in the first place, to be set aside. There was a debate as to whether a General Council was the proper mode of securing the abdication of the Popes; it was suggested that each Pope should appoint a commission from among the members of his obedience, the three commissions to meet and form a general commission; and it was decided that

---

[1] Finke (*Acta*), 332.   [2] *Ibid.* 328.
[3] *In the Days of the Councils*, 314.   [4] Finke (*Acta*), 334 *et seq.*

the decision of such a general commission would be valid, notwithstanding that two-thirds of them were schismatics.[1] The project for a meeting of all three Popes at some handy place on the nearer side of the Alps was also broached; but more to the point was it that a meeting of Ferdinand and Benedict with Sigismund, such as eventually occurred, was debated, although the aged Pope, who knew the localities well, proposed that in this case his fleet and that of the King of Spain should rest in the comfortable little harbour of Villa Franca, while Sigismund's galleys were to ride in the tiny Port de Limpia at Nice, exposed to the sudden gusts of the Mediterranean.[2]

The upshot of the conference, as Benedict left for San Mateo while Ferdinand stayed on until the end of September at Morella, was that two different embassies with different instructions were sent to the King of the Romans. Pope Benedict spoke of his meeting with Sigismund; his envoys had nothing to do with the Council, which he only mentioned in connection with his request that the proceedings at Pisa might be quashed. Ferdinand expressed his desire to meet Sigismund with Benedict; he wanted the Council to be postponed for two months at least; in case of refusal his ambassadors were not to insist, but were to join with any others of their way of thinking to delay the proceedings; he also suggested that representatives of the three obediences should meet, and proposed that Benedict should stay at Perpignan while King Sigismund could come to Arles.[3]

Not much actual headway had been made in the present; but the ground had been cleared for the future. Ferdinand had himself despatched ambassadors and had so recognised the Council of Constance; moreover he had instilled into the minds of the clergy of Castile and Aragon, into the greater part of the obedience of Benedict, that the one great aim to pursue was the unity of the Church; and in the future they would be ready to follow his lead rather than that of the obstinate octogenarian whose scruples and reservations no man could foresee or compass. Benedict himself knew that he was losing ground, for he wrote to the Count of Armagnac,[4] explaining that, although he

---

[1] Finke (*Acta*), 324.   [2] *Ibid.* 331.
[3] *Ibid.* 334 *et seq.*   [4] *Ibid.* 354-8.

utterly refused to acknowledge the Council of Constance, yet he was willing to assent to arrangements for the meeting of the three Popes, but that the abdication of one Pope would be of no avail. He was, in fact, willing to agree to what he knew was impossible, but he would not do what the Council of Perpignan had urged. He knew that he was the Catholic and true Vicar of Christ, and he meant to live and die in that opinion.

One of the dreams that passed through the ivory gate and floated before the Council of Constance was the reconciliation of the Greek and Latin churches. The pilgrimage of the Kaiser Manuel to the European Courts and the elevation of the Candian Filargi to the papal throne seemed to bring it near fufilment. The Emperor of the Grecian part of the Empire sent to Alexander the Fifth John Chrysoloras, a nephew of Manuel Chrysoloras who was already in Italy, and both uncle and nephew appeared at the papal court. Pope John expressed his desire to procure peace and union between the Greeks and the Latins, and Jean Gerson in France had indicated this as one of the tasks of the new Pope. Before, during, and after his war with Venice, King Sigismund wrote to Kaiser Manuel, setting forth his eagerness for the union of the two churches, for such an union would be an invaluable prelude to a crusade against the blaspheming Turks; if the Greek Church acknowledged Rome as her Mother, he was confident that everything else could be amicably arranged; he himself would continue to be Emperor of the Romans and Manuel of the Greeks. Nothing was done in the way of actual help to Constantinople at this time, but thus it came about that an embassy from Rome on the Bosphorus was present at the Council of Constance.

During these negotiations the King of the Romans was making his way to the place of his crowning. At Romont he met the deputies of Bern, who invited him to their city. The march lay through Freiburg. Three miles from Bern a grand procession met the King. He was escorted by eight hundred horsemen; and with him were Amadeus of Savoy, and Theodor of Montferrat, with six hundred cavaliers. It was the day of Saint Ulrich, the 3rd July 1414. Five hundred beautiful boys, none of them over sixteen years of age, the comeliest bearing the banner of the Empire, and all crowned with garlands and wearing scutcheons of the imperial eagles in their hair, came to greet him. 'A new world has risen before us,' said the King. Then came the clergy, regular and secular, with crucifix and pyx, singing hymns. At the gate of the city appeared the mayor and council with the foremost citizens in two lines to present the keys of Bern. 'Take them back,' said Sigismund to Petermann von Krauchthal, the mayor, 'and guard the city well.' Four bannerets held a costly baldachino above his head, and the senate and the council of two hundred lined the streets, as the King rode into Bern. He was conducted to the celebrated Clocktower, where the cock crows and the bears march round every hour, and thence to his lodgings at the Dominican convent. Here all was made ready for a splendid reception; his bed was covered with silken sheets, embroidered with gold; the walls of the room were hung with costly tapestry. In the refectory of the convent, and indeed all through Bern, there was feasting and merriment. The good Swiss wine ran freely for all strangers; the frail beauties of Bern could be visited without payment. On the morrow the King received a grand deputation from all the Swiss towns and cantons. For three days did the Lord of the Holy Roman Empire tarry at Bern, and Sigismund declared that although he had been received with honour in many places, nowhere had he been so well treated as at Bern. He confirmed all the old and granted new privileges to the city; he received the homage of Amadeus of Savoy; he confirmed the privileges of the Canton of Uri.[1] It was his policy to keep on good terms with the Swiss, who had, only two years before, made a peace for fifty years with his enemy, Friedrich of the Tirol. He was accompanied by their envoys as far as Basel.

Now, four years after his election, Sigismund entered the German Empire, which sadly needed a strong ruler. The Archbishop of Mainz was in high dudgeon; King Wenzel was grumbling and discontented, and the Elector of Saxony, Duke Ernest of Austria, the Duke of Brabant, and the Dukes Ernest and Stephen of Bavaria were on his side; there was open strife between Prince Louis, brother of the Queen of France, and the other members of the House of Wittelsbach; the

---

[1] Mueller, iv. 184; Aschbach, i. 387-9.

Meissen inheritance was in dispute; the roads were unsafe throughout the Empire; a spirit of revolt against the magistracy had in many places declared itself; the old leagues for mutual defence had been renewed; and there was a disputed election to the Archbishopric of Cologne. The Count Palatine and the Burggraf Friedrich of Nuernberg were the most faithful and consistent supporters of the new King of the Romans. At Cologne the Archbishop Friedrich had died on the 9th April 1414, and part of the chapter elected Bishop Wilhelm of Paderborn, a brother of Duke Adolf of Bergen, to succeed him, while the majority chose Friedrich of Mors, a nephew of the previous Archbishop, who received the support of John of Nassau and of King Sigismund,[1] and was confirmed by Pope John the Twenty-third. Wilhelm was confirmed by Pope Gregory the Twelfth, and the Duke of Bergen entered the archbishopric with an army. Such was the unsettled state of the land when Sigismund, on the 11th July, came to Strassburg.

The Count Palatine, the Archbishop of Trier, the Duke of Lorraine, and the Markgraf of Baden greeted the King as he entered the city amid the joyous shouts of the inhabitants. Sigismund remained for a week at Strassburg, dancing and delighting the ladies with his wit and good humour, and sending them gold rings at his departure in memory of their pleasant intercourse. On the 19th he went to Speier, entering the city under a costly canopy, the top bearing the black eagles and the sides embroidered with the arms of the Empire, the Electors and of Hungary. The King had summoned a Diet of the South German magnates to meet here; but with the exception of Friedrich of Nuernberg and those who came in his train no one appeared. Sigismund was angry and disgusted, but had no other alternative than to fix another day in the middle of August for Coblenz. He halted for a fortnight at Speier, confirming the privileges of many cities, for which, however, they had to pay his chancery dearly. At the beginning of August the King moved on to Mainz, where the Archbishop, John of Nassau, avoided him; and on the 8th he proceeded by ship to Bingen, and thence, on the 12th, reached Coblenz.

Here, again, the King was made to feel the bitterness of the

[1] Coeln, i. 51.

PRELIMINARY NEGOTIATIONS 221

dignity without power which was the lot of the Lord of the Holy Roman Empire; for except those who were already with him, not a magnate from Bohemia, from Saxony, from Bavaria, not even the Archbishop of Mainz had appeared in answer to his invitation. Eberhard Windecke, who was not with the King but was in Berlin at this time, says that Sigismund was so wroth that he was minded to return to Hungary without being crowned.[1] This was probably untrue;[2] but the King left Coblenz on the 9th or 10th September, and went with the Count Palatine, carefully avoiding Mainz and its Archbishop, by Alzei and Worms to Heidelberg. Here he stayed for a week and sent out invitations to Frankfurt and three other cities for a Diet to be held at Heilbronn on the 3rd October. On the 25th September the King came to Nuernberg, and here the tide began to turn in his favour; probably the nobles began to realise what a state of anarchy would ensue if he threw up the government and returned uncrowned to his own kingdom of Hungary. At Nuernberg Sigismund was welcomed by the clergy and laity of the city, by the Burggrafs Friedrich and Johann, by the Elector Rudolf of Saxony, by Duke Johann, brother of the Count Palatine, by the Bishops of Wuerzburg, Bamberg, and Eichstedt, and by many lords and envoys of Franconia. On the 30th he arranged for the peace of Franconia for three years.

From Nuernberg the King went to Heilbronn, receiving the homage and confirming the privileges of different towns on the way; and here he arranged for the peace of Swabia, Alsace, and the Rhine lands; here also [3] he was joined by Queen Barbara, who had come from Hungary to be crowned with him at Aachen. A dispute with Frankfurt concerning the tax on the Jews caused the King to avoid that city on his way from Heilbronn to Speier, where he, on the 18th, signed the safe-conduct for John Hus. From Speier Sigismund went down the Rhine to Coblenz, where, on the 29th October, for the first time, he met John of Nassau, the warlike Archbishop of Mainz. The King tried to win the favour of the mighty Elector; he made him bailiff and preserver of the peace for the Wetterau, and gave him the revenues of its four chief cities; but the Archbishop would not

[1] Altmann, 52.   [2] Lenz, 61-2.   [3] *Ibid.* 63.

be appeased. The reason is conjectured to have been that Sigismund had not kept his promises to his half-brother, to whom John of Nassau had become security;[1] and Wenzel was known now to be in league with the Duke of Brabant to intercept Sigismund on his way to Aachen; but whatever the reason, the irate Archbishop refused to take any part in the coming coronation and returned to his own place.

The troops which Antoine de Brabant was able to collect were not strong enough to oppose the forces sent to the assistance of the King by the Count Palatine, the Count of Guelders, the Archbishops of Trier and Cologne, and the citizens of Aachen. Sigismund and Barbara, with her escort of eight hundred Hungarian prelates, barons, and knights, rode safely into the old capital of Karl der Grosse. On the 8th November 1414, Theodoric of Mors, who had not as yet been consecrated, performed the ceremony of consecration, gave the King and Queen the Holy Communion, and crowned them both.[2] It was a magnificent assemblage; of the magnates of the Empire the Archbishop of Mainz, the King of Bohemia, and the Wittelsbachs of Bavaria were alone absent; a hundred counts, six hundred knights, and the ambassadors from many foreign powers graced the ceremony. The Count Palatine received a golden Bull confirming his electoral right, restricting the succession in his house to the eldest heir male, and appointing him Steward of the Empire; Rudolf of Saxony and his brother Albert were also confirmed in their rights as Elector and as Marshal of the Empire; other privileges also were granted. Having thus been crowned King of the Romans, Sigismund wrote to Pope John the Twenty-third to acquaint him with the fact and to announce his approaching arrival at Constance.

[1] Aschbach, i. 409. [2] Coeln, 52.

CHAPTER XII

THE JOURNEY TO CONSTANCE

'You may go to Constance as Pope, but you will return as a private man,' said the friends of Pope John to him; and, although he appreciated their warning, he was determined to go. His intention was that the Council of Constance should be formally recognised as a continuation of that of Pisa; but his expectation of this cannot have been sanguine, for he knew that both his rivals who had been declared heretic and schismatic, and who had been deposed at Pisa, had been invited to appear at Constance. He distrusted Sigismund, but had not abandoned all hope of keeping him on his side; if the King had never applied to him for approbation and confirmation of his election, neither had he on his side ever acknowledged Sigismund as King of the Romans; although, as soon as he was informed of his coronation at Aachen, he gave him that title. At his back Pope John had the Italian clergy; he trusted also in the Duke of Burgundy, in the Archbishop of Mainz, in the Markgraf of Baden, and in Duke Friedrich of the Tirol; he trusted most of all in himself, his wealth, and his eloquence. He made up his mind, therefore, to go to Constance; he could not in honour do otherwise.

King Sigismund had written to the magistrates there, and they had made a treaty for the Pope's benefit, in which they contracted that he should be received in their city with all due honour and ceremony, that he should be recognised as the true and only Pope, that he should enjoy full liberty to remain and to depart without let or hindrance, that he should exercise spiritual and temporal jurisdiction, and that they would proceed promptly against any of their citizens who should undertake aught against any member of his court or against any one who had come to the Council, the Pope observing a reciprocal obligation towards them, that the Pope's safe conducts should be respected, and that they on their side would see that all the roads were free and practicable in order that no one might suffer hurt in coming or going.

In order that all things might be ready for his coming, Pope John sent on ahead the three cardinals, Zabarella, Antoine de Chalant, and Jean de Brogni, commonly known as the Cardinal de Viviers. He was now the oldest cardinal in the College, but Jean de Brogni had begun life as a swineherd, had got a gratuitous education at Rome, had become a Carthusian monk, had won the favour of Philip of Burgundy, had been made cardinal-priest in 1383 by Clement the Seventh, and cardinal-bishop in 1398 by Benedict the Thirteenth. He arrived at Constance on the 12th August with a couple of carriages and eighty-three horses, and alighted at the house of Albert von Buettelspach, the Cathedral Dean. The Dean, who was lame, was carried down in a chair to meet the Cardinal, who greeted him and asked his hospitality, saying that he trusted to remain under his roof until Christendom was again united under one sole chief. They talked in Latin, and the Dean answered, ' This day is salvation come to this house.'[1] The cardinals made everything ready for the arrival of the Pope.

In this they were assisted by one who had been especially appointed by the city in this behalf. This was the worthy chronicler Ulrich von Richental, a burgher of the middle class, who lived in a house known by the sign of the Golden Hound, ' den guldinen Bracken,' opposite the church of Saint Stephen.[2] As soon as the Council was decided on Count Eberhart of Nellenburg had written to Richental, bidding him arrange for fodder, hay, straw, and beds. Early in June came the Count with the Bishop of Augsburg and Herr Frischans, and they arranged the right quarters for each guest, and placarded the inns and houses where each was to lie.[3] Very busy all through the Council was Richental in providing accommodation for man and beast; not for some years did he find time to record his lively recollections of what had occurred.

On the first day of October 1414, Pope John the Twenty-third with a suite of six hundred men, left the city which he loved so

[1] Richental, 24.   [2] Marmor, 8.   [3] Richental, 24.

THE JOURNEY TO CONSTANCE 225

well, travelling by water, probably going down the river Reno until it joins the Po, and then up the great river to Ferrara, the residence of Nicolas of Este, whom Ladislas of Naples had vainly tried to seduce from his allegiance. From Ferrara they went up the river to Verona, and from here their way lay up the Valley of the Adige, through which the Kings of the Romans with their hated German troops were wont to march to be crowned with the golden crown of Empire at Rome. They came to Trient. Trient, says Heine, lies old and broken amid a circle of fresh green hills that look down like young gods on man's decaying handiwork. Broken and decaying now is the lofty castle hard by, which dominated the city, a romantic building of a romantic age, with its pinnacles, projections, and battlements and its large round tower. The town also is built in the spirit of romance, and wonderful at the first sight are the old-time houses with their bleached frescoes, their crumbling images of the saints, their turrets, oriels, and lattice windows, their gables which stand out resting on old grey columns, themselves in need of support. So spake the poet who, when he entered the cool cathedral, discovered how very good the Catholic religion was in the summer time. In 1414 Trient was the seat of Bishop Georg of Lichtenstein; Duke Friedrich had seized the castle to ensure the South Tirol against Milan and Venice; he held that the rights, fiefs and mortgages belonged not to the Bishop but to the Count; Georg had appealed to Sigismund who had taken his county under the imperial protection.[1] The quarrel was a very pretty quarrel when Pope John passed through on his way to Constance. A jester in his train warned him that if he went beyond Trient he was lost.

Ten miles further on they halted at the little village of Saint Michael on the Adige, where there was a monastery, which had formerly been well endowed and flourishing. The frequent wars, and the heavy duty of hospitality to nobles and others on their way to Italy, to say nothing of frequent floods, had crippled the monks and reduced their monastery to a state of ruin. The Pope, therefore, while granting to the prior the right to use episcopal vestments and ornaments, appropriated to the abbey the living of Mezzotedesco on the Adige in order to in-

[1] *B. W.*, 236-7.

crease his revenue. War, hospitality, and tempest were the ruin of many a monastery. Still wending their way up the Etschland the next halt was at the village of Tramin, about ten miles from Saint Michael. The Pope had in the year previous sanctioned the building of a new church at Tramin, and was now met with the request that the parish might be independent of the mother church at Kaltern, about seven miles off. Though the distance is not great, there were difficulties in bringing water for baptism and the holy oil for chrisms, and for this reason Pope John granted the request and ordered that in future Tramin should be independent of Kaltern.[1]

On the 15th October, a fortnight after leaving Bologna, Pope John and his retinue reached Meran, the ancient capital of the Tirol, on the right bank of the Passer. Here he was welcomed by Duke Friedrich, with whom, since the days at Lodi, he had been in friendly communication. Friedrich was at this time thirty-two years of age, proud, ambitious, determined, and active; he was smarting under the affront which King Sigismund had put upon him and at his intrigue with his vassals. He had strong castles and possessions near Constance, and his alliance would be invaluable to the Pope. He was already in league with the Archbishop of Mainz, the Pope's devoted friend, and with the Marquess of Baden, with whom, three months later, the Pope made a treaty and to whom he presented sixteen thousand florins of gold.[2] John now appointed Friedrich to be captain general of the papal troops on an annual salary of six thousand ducats, and the Duke in his turn promised the Pope safe conduct against every man.[3] The Pope and the Duke were concerting against the common enemy, and at that time neither of them could foresee the consequences, disastrous to both, which were so soon to result from their treaty of alliance.

From Meran the papal party retraced their steps to Bozen. As, on their way to Meran, they had passed by the busy little town, nestling amid the dolomite peaks, the Pope had caught sight of the new Benedictine monastery, which was nearing completion in the neighbouring village of Gries, at the base of

[1] Schmid, 202-3.   [2] Lenfant (C.), i. 18.
[3] Lichnowsky, v. 164 ; Egger, i. 476.

THE JOURNEY TO CONSTANCE 227

the Guntschna Berg. The position and the magnificence of the convent pleased him. To the prior, who had been there since 1408, he gave the right to consecrate the chalices and church ornaments and to wear episcopal vestments except when a bishop or papal legate was present, and he exempted the monastery entirely from episcopal control.

From Bozen the way lay by the bridle path up the valley of the Eisak past Klausen to Brixen, the seat of Bishop Ulrich, a little town noted for the mural paintings in its cathedral cloisters and for the frescoes in the Chapel of Saint John. The Bishop made a petition to the Pope on behalf of his friend and counsellor Canon Hilprand; and John granted to the said Canon the right to hold in plurality his canonries in Trient, which he was afraid of losing, and Brixen together with the rich living of Fliess in the Oberinnthal. Another canon of Brixen, Johann Vogelin, a secretary to Duke Friedrich, obtained canonries in Brixen and Trient together with the living of Tysens. A third canon, Vockenlander, complained to the Pope of a priest, Michael Perger, that he had wounded and taken captive another priest, had practised usury, and committed other unseemly acts. Perger was degraded and the living was given to the canon. A few miles from Brixen is the Augustine monastery of Neustift, in which also the Pope granted the use of episcopal vestments; and from here he went up the Brenner to Innsbruck.

Innsbruck was at that time a handsome city, whose inhabitants were noted for their piety. The Brethren of the Blessed Virgin Mary had built a new church in honour of Saint Dorothea and had endowed two benefices for its priests. The Pope confirmed the endowments and granted certain rich indulgences to the new and popular church, and also to the monastery in the neighbouring suburb of Wilten.

After Innsbruck the road led west. About twenty-two miles distant is the small village of Stams, with a large Cistercian monastery, whose prior the Pope empowered to consecrate the church ornaments and to initiate novices into the minor orders. The cavalcade now climbed the steep valley of the Inn, the Innthal; there were nine cardinals, many bishops, the whole Curia, in all six hundred persons in the Pope's train. After

Landeck the valley, which passes the old castle of Wiesberg, contracts, and the brawling Rosanna forms waterfalls by its side, until at last, to the left of the precipitous glacier of the Riffler, Saint Anton is reached. Then begins the climb up to the Arlberg Pass, nearly six thousand feet above sea-level, the road winding through a wild and sequestered valley. The wind bites shrewdly as it whistles over the newly fallen snow on the Arlberg toward the end of October; and the way is beset with danger. Pope John was in a carriage, and in the Pass, somewhere near the little hospice of Saint Christopher, the vehicle overturned and rolled into the snow. There was general consternation, and inquiries as to whether the Holy Father was hurt. But the humour of the situation seemed to tickle the Pope's fancy, for he began to drolly intone his own epitaph: ' Hic jaceo in nomine Diaboli,' adding, ' and I should have done much better to stop at Bologna.' And all the villagers who assisted to set up the carriage were horrified, as well they might be, seeing that they understood not a word of what he said. After this mishap they proceeded to Klosterle, and looking down over the Klosterthal, saw the Lake of Constance gleaming in the distance. A touch of his old sardonic humour came over Pope John as he gazed; he remarked, ' Foxes trapped here.' (Hic capiuntur vulpes.) The quiet city on the southern bank, where the Rhine flows out of the lake, was the battle-ground for the coming struggle.[1] No further occurrence marked the journey; they came by Feldkirch to Kreuzlingen, outside Constance, and descended at the Monastery of Saint Ulrich. It was between noon and one o'clock on Saturday the 27th October when Pope John arrived; he remained there that night, and conferred on the Abbot, Erhard Linden, the pontifical mitre.

Sunday, the 28th, was the Day of the Saints Simon and Judas. At eleven in the forenoon after the morning refection the procession was formed. The Pope, clad all in white like a priest at the altar, and with a simple white mitre on his head, was accompanied by his cardinals, archbishops, bishops, and prelates, and by the Curia; he was met at the door of the monastery by the clergy of Constance bearing the

[1] Richental, 25; Schmid, 204-5; Lenfant (C.), i. 19.

THE JOURNEY TO CONSTANCE

holy relics; among them were the Abbots of Reichenau, of Kreuzlingen, and of Petershausen, and the canons of the cathedral and of the churches in the town. Four of the chief magistrates conducted the Pope to his white horse, richly caparisoned in scarlet, which stood under a canopy of cloth of gold, while the Counts Rudolf of Montfort and Berthold des Ursins held the bridle. Eight white horses in red trappings led the way; then came a priest bearing the staff and the cross; then followed a white hackney carrying a silver-gilt chest with a monstrance in which was the Holy Sacrament. Then followed His Holiness surrounded by the burning tapers of the guild and of the canons; and near him was a priest who scattered small coin to relieve the press. Behind the Pope's canopy rode the cardinals, two and two, with their servants and pages, holding up their red mantles; and on their heads were broad red hats with long silken bands. So they came to the lower court where they dismounted and went into the cathedral. There the Te Deum was sung, and the bells pealed through the city until vespers. Then the Pope walked on foot through the Chapel of Saint Margaret to the bishop's palace, and the cardinals departed to their own places. There was a quarrel over the horse which the Pope had ridden; it was taken by the Burgomaster, who alleged ancient custom.[1] Thus did Pope John the Twenty-third establish himself in the city of Constance three days before the day fixed for the opening of the Council. He at any rate was in time and had kept his word.

John Hus had also to make the journey to Constance, but he started under a double misapprehension. Hus was a Bohemian of the Bohemians; he had never been out of the country, and personally knew nothing of any other land. He was in a sense the spoiled child of Bohemia, for Fortune had been very kind to him. For several years the confidant of his archbishop, he had enjoyed the constant favour of the Court; he was the Queen's confessor, the King liked him, there were many nobles who would have protected him against Pope or Emperor, he was the idol of the Bohemian population and worshipped by all the pious ladies of Prague. He had suffered excommunication, but was not cast down, for he had been excommunicated for re-

[1] Richental, 25-7.

cusancy and not for heresy; and it had done him no harm. He was a patriot and wanted Bohemia for the Bohemians; his foes were the Teutons, who in church and state wrought only for their own hands and took no thought for the sons of the soil; they were rich and malicious; they had withstood him in the University and had maligned him to the Pope. He had fought with them and had overcome them; there was now one fight more; if he could reach Constance, he would emerge victorious, clearing himself and his country of the foul stain of heresy which the Teutons had falsely cast upon them. But to reach Constance he had to travel through a land teeming with his enemies, and he doubted not that they would be ready, were he not sufficiently guarded, to waylay and to murder him. This was his first misconception; the Teutons out of Bohemia bore him no animosity, but he thought otherwise. He had often thought of the crown of martyrdom, and he now had a presentiment that he should never return to Prague. Before he started on the journey he wrote a letter to his disciple Martin, which was not to be opened by him unless and until he heard that Hus was dead; he also wrote a farewell address to his faithful brothers and sisters in Christ Jesus, assuring them that if he were condemned at Constance it would not be for any heresy, that he was starting on his journey without any safe conduct into the midst of his worst enemies, and that they might never see him in Prague again.[1] The second misconception of John Hus was that, if once he reached Constance, he would there hold an academic disputation with adversaries who, like himself, would be more open to sweet reasonableness, who would be less prejudiced and intolerant, than had been the Teuton professors whom he had met and vanquished in the University of Prague. That his adversaries would be many and learned he knew; all that he desired was a calm and temperate discussion;[2] he was ready to recant any opinion which could be proved from the Bible to be erroneous. But he knew not the temper of the times. In truth it was often nigh as dangerous for a realist to appear among a congregation of nominalists as

[1] Palacky (*Doc.*), 73-5.
[2] Hus, if a sincere Catholic, should have remembered that the Catholic Church teaches but does not discuss.

THE JOURNEY TO CONSTANCE 231

for a Christian boy to walk through a Jewry singing *Alma redemptoris* night and morning.

Hus was anxious that his appearance at Constance should be with the proper credentials of orthodoxy. He had called upon any one who had aught against him to appear at the next provincial synod at Prague. This was held on the 27th August, but Hus and his advocate, John of Jesenice, who had already appeared for him on more than one occasion, could not obtain entrance. Hus then posted a notice on the castle gate calling on the King and his counsellors to bear witness to his orthodoxy, and in continuation of this notice his advocate, with a large number of the Bohemian nobility, appeared on the 30th August before the papal inquisitor, Nicolas, titular Bishop of Nazareth. Jesenice asked the inquisitor whether he knew of any error or heresy in Master John Hus, or if any one had thus incriminated Hus before him. The inquisitor replied in the negative, saying that he had many times conversed with John Hus, that he had ate and drunk with him, and had listened to many of his discourses and had never found in him any error or heresy, but in all his words and works had found him to be a true and faithful Catholic, neither had he discovered anything in him that smacked of heresy or error. A notarial instrument was drawn up to this effect and was duly signed by the inquisitor, and sent to King Sigismund.[1] After this three barons, in an assembly of the notables, held at Saint Jacob's Cloister in Prague, asked the Archbishop whether he could accuse Master John Hus of any error or heresy, and he too answered that he knew of no heresy and made no accusation; on which the three barons went off to King Sigismund and acquainted him with what had happened. Sigismund had determined to take the Master under his protection; he intended that he should enter Constance in his train, and commissioned John of Chlum and Wenzel of Duba to accompany John Hus to his camp.[2]

All preparations were made for the journey. Money and necessaries were forthcoming from friends. Two lords provided a good horse apiece. The University also provided financial aid. A comfortable carriage was forthcoming. Ten days later than the day on which Pope John left Bologna John Hus and his

[1] Palacky (*Doc.*), 239 *et seq.*; Berger, 100.   [2] Berger, 101.

party left Prague. They were joined at Pilsen by Henry of Chlum, surnamed Lacembok, and by John of Reinstein, surnamed Kardinal, the latter and John of Chlum being sent as representatives of the University of Prague.

As soon as Hus set foot in Germany, he found how groundless his fears had been; he was received everywhere with open arms as the champion of church reform. Bernau was the first town beyond the border; the priest and the people received Hus, took him to the inn, and drank with him a mighty can of wine, the vicar declaring that he would always be his friend. At Neustadt and at Weiden great crowds welcomed him. At Sulzbach the travellers alighted at an inn, where a local court was being held. Hus presented himself before the seniors and consuls there assembled, saying, ' Here am I, Master John Hus, of whom I doubt not you have heard much evil; therefore ask of me what you will.' And they treated him with the greatest kindness. Thence the road lay through Herspruck to Lauf, where Hus stayed the night with the vicar, conversing with him and with a jurist and others.

On the 19th October they reached Nuernberg in the valley of the Pegnitz, that ' quaint old town of art and song,' whose

> ' burghers boasted, in their uncouth rhyme
> That their great imperial city stretched its hand through every clime.'

Some business men who had gone on before had heralded their coming, so that the squares were full of spectators eager to catch a glimpse of the Bohemian reformer. Before Hus had dined a note was brought to him from a parish priest who was anxious to talk with him; and then came Wenzel of Duba to tell him that the magistrates and citizens wished to confer with him. After dining, Hus betook himself to them, and the magistrates proposed that they should speak in private, but Hus answered that he was wont to preach in public and preferred that every one who wished should hear what he had to say. Then they talked until the going down of the sun; and at the end they said to him : ' Certainly, master, that which we have heard is Catholic doctrine, such as we have taught and held and do still teach and hold; and if there is naught else against thee, thou

THE JOURNEY TO CONSTANCE

wilt return with honour from the Council.' A Carthusian monk was the only one who dissented; all the rest wished Hus good cheer. Here as in other towns through which they passed a public notice was posted on the gates of the city saying that Hus was ready to meet all his critics and opponents at Constance.[1] Up to that time, Hus said that he had not met a single enemy.[2]

When the master was at Nuernberg, the King of the Romans was at Speier, and Hus ought to have gone to Sigismund and to have placed himself under his protection. He was told that the letter of safe conduct was ready and waiting for him. But the man who knew nothing of the outside world refused to follow the directions of the man who knew something of it, and the consequence was sad. Instead of entering Constance in the train of the King of the Romans as the champion of the orthodoxy of Bohemia, John Hus heard the sounds of the joyous entry far away from an underground cell in the Dominican monastery. If he had not trusted to his own judgment, resolving to press on to Constance, if he had complied with the desire of Sigismund, one cannot say what the ultimate consequence would have been; but assuredly, as the King said, things would have gone differently, and John Hus would have been treated with more respect and have received a more patient hearing than was actually the case. The change of plan was his own work,[3] and it brought retribution. Wenzel of Duba went to the King to tell him that John Hus was going straight to Constance.[4]

From Nuernberg Hus's party went on through Ansbach and Ulm to the imperial city of Biberach, where again they had a long theological discussion. In this, however, Hus took little part; but John of Chlum spoke so learnedly that the citizens took him for a doctor of theology and his companions thereafter humorously called him the Doctor of Biberach.[5] A day's march ahead was the Bishop of Lubeck, who warned the folk of the coming of the heretic; but the warning merely increased the general curiosity, and brought greater crowds than ever on the route. Going by Ravensburg the party, under John of Chlum, reached Buchhorn, now called Friedrichshafen, on the Boden

[1] Palacky (*Doc.*), 76, 245. [2] Lechler, 75. [3] Palacky (*Doc.*), 76.
[4] Berger, 104. [5] Palacky (*Doc.*), 93-4.

234 POPE JOHN THE TWENTY-THIRD

See.[1] Here they took boat and came across the lake to Constance, reaching the city on the 3rd November.

Hus lodged with a widow called Fida, whose house is still to be seen, in the street which was then called Saint Paul's but is now named after the reformer, near the Snezthor. The next day Hus's enemies began their work; Michael *de Causis* posted on the door of the cathedral an information of accusation against John Hus as being a man excommunicated, pertinacious, and suspected of heresy. On the same day John of Chlum and his uncle Lacembok went to the Pope to report the arrival of Hus. The town had presented the Pope with sixteen casks of wine, forty sacks of oats and with a silver-gilt goblet; moreover His Holiness knew the mind of King Sigismund in the matter of John Hus; so he answered the knights cheerfully, saying, ' He may remain safe in Constance. I will not let any one interfere with him, even though he had killed my own brother.' Hus was now firmly convinced that his worst enemies were his own countrymen. A day or two later the Lord Wenzel of Duba returned with King Sigismund's safe-conduct [2] for Hus.

The reformer had come from Prague to Constance without having, and without needing, any safe conduct. That which he now received has been the subject of violent controversy. Safe conducts in those days were political and judicial. The latter are for appearance before a tribunal; they provide for safety in coming, remaining, and returning; they are issued only by the supreme judge of the court; they are for a certain specified

---

[1] Luetzow, 210.

[2] The following is the text of the safe conduct :—

'Sigismundus dei gratia Romanorum rex semper Augustus et Hungariæ, Dalmatiæ, Croatiæ, etc. rex

'Universis et singulis principibus, ecclesiasticis et secularibus, ducibus, marchionibus, comitibus, nobilibus, proceribus, ministerialibus, militibus, clientibus, capitaneis, potestatibus, gubernatoribus, præsidibus, teleonariis, tributariis et officialibus quibuscumque, civitatum, oppidorum, villarum et locorum communitatibus ac rectoribus eorundem ceterisque nostris et imperii sacri subditis ac fidelibus, ad quos præsentes pervenerint, gratiam regiam et omne bonum. Venerabiles, illustres et fideles dilecti!

'Honorabilem magistrum Joannem Hus, sacræ theologiæ baccalaureum formatum et artium magistrum, præsentium ostensorem,

'De regno Bohemiæ ad concilium generale in civitate Constantiensi in proximo transeuntem,

'Quem etiam in nostram et sacri imperii protectionem recepimus et tutelam,

THE JOURNEY TO CONSTANCE

time; and they express that their object is to enable appearance to be made and innocence to be proved. The safe conduct to Hus was not of this kind; it was of the ordinary political kind. Hus had not been cited before any tribunal; he himself insisted on this;[1] nor could Sigismund have given him a judicial safe conduct, had he been so cited. The King rated his prerogative very high; but he, and every one else, knew that he had no jurisdiction in a spiritual court. His safe conduct was intended to ensure safety for Hus and his belongings during his journey to Constance, his residence there, and his return; but it was intended to give this assurance only against the exercise of unlawful power, not against the exercise of lawful authority. The words concerning the going, abiding, and returning are the usual words found in all political safe conducts. If Hus were called upon by a competent court to account for any fault committed before his arrival at Constance, or during his stay there, then the King's safe conduct afforded him no protection.[2]

King Sigismund had convoked the Council of Constance for All Saints' Day 1414, but not until a week later was he crowned at Aachen. He did not tarry, but left the city two days later, and arrived at Cologne on the 11th November. Here he confirmed the city's privileges, subsequently, however, revoking any privileges which were to the disadvantage of the Archbishop. The Pope wrote to the King to hasten his coming; but it was not until the end of the month that Sigismund left Coblenz, and even then he went up the Lahn as far as Wetzlar to receive the homage of the towns of the Wetterau. On the 12th December

vobis omnibus et vestrum cuilibet pleno recommendamus affectu, desiderantes, quatenus ipsum, dum ad vos pervenerit, grate suscipere, favorabiliter tractare, ac in his, quæ celeritatem ac securitatem ipsius concernunt itineris, tam per terram quam per aquam, promotivam sibi velitis et debeatis ostendere voluntatem, nec non ipsum cum famulis, equis, valisiis, et aliis rebus suis singulis per quoscumque passus, portus, pontes, terras, dominia, districtus, jurisdictiones, civitates, oppida, castra, villas et quælibet loca alia vestra sine aliquali solutione datii, tributi et alio quovis solutionis onere omnique prorsus impedimento remoto transire, stare, morari et redire libere permittatis, sibique et suis, dum opus fuerit, de securo et salvo velitis et debeatis providere conductu ad honorem et reverentiam nostræ regiæ majestatis.

'Datum Spiræ anno domini MCCCCXIIII., XVIII. die Octobris regnorum nostrorum anno Hungariæ, etc., XXXIII. Romanorum vero quinto.

'Ad mandatum Domini regis: Michael de Prziest canonicus Vratislaviensis.'
[1] Palacky (*Doc.*), 88.   [2] Berger, 105-11.

Sigismund and Barbara made their joyous entry into Frankfurt, where the King was welcomed with the customary honours and received the customary gifts. Old privileges were confirmed, and promises for the future given. The King meant that the troubled state of the land should be quieted and that the peace should everywhere be preserved. John of Nassau, the proud Elector of Mainz, met Sigismund at Frankfurt, and they travelled together to the electoral city. Sigismund received its homage, and confirmed its privileges and those of the Archbishop and the clergy. On the 16th he left Mainz and travelled by the Rhine as far as Speier; thence he went by land through the territories of the Counts of Wuertemberg and Swabia straight for the Boden See, reaching Ueberlingen on Christmas Eve. This old town, whose mediæval walls and towers are still in perfect order, was visited by Frederic Barbarossa in 1135, and in 1397 it became a free city of the Empire.[1]

[1] Capper, 122-3.

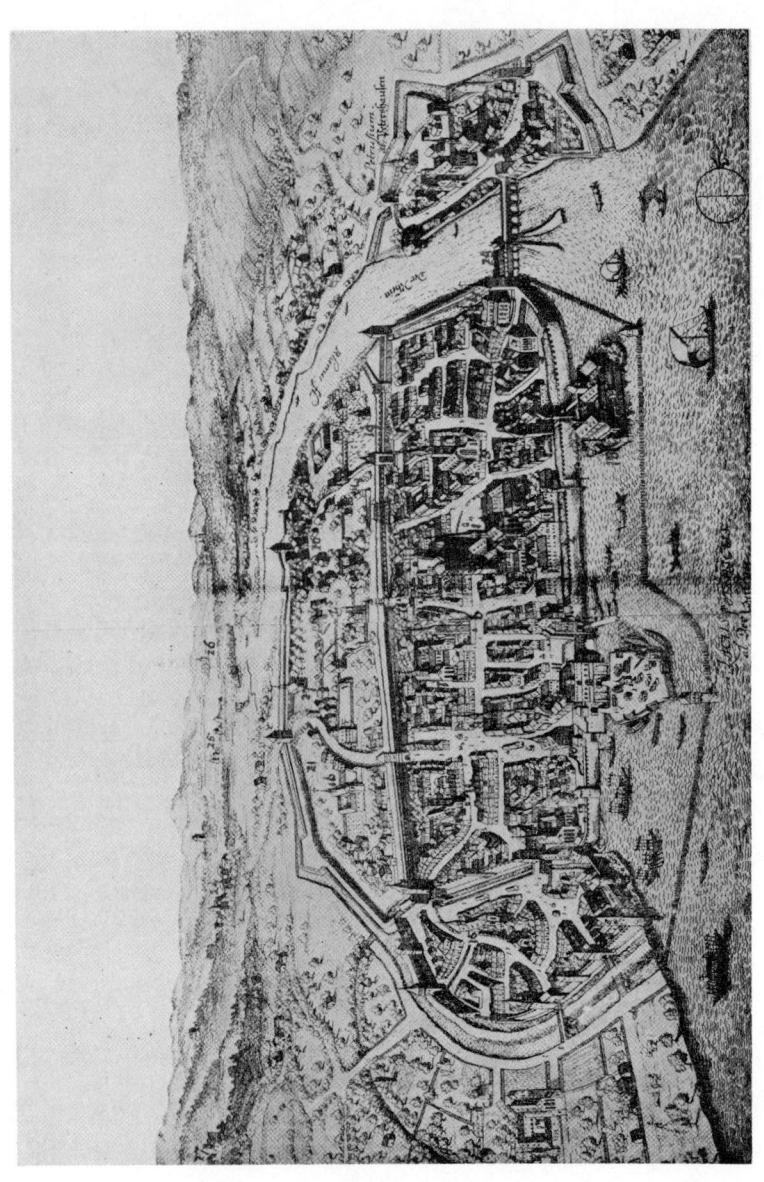

Bird's-eye View of Constance and its Environs at the time of the Council. Reduced from the map published by Von der Hardt in his *Rerum Concilii Oecumenici Constantiensis*, 1697.

CHAPTER XIII

CONSTANCE

CONSTANCE, said Eiselein writing in 1850, is the same now as it was in the days of the Great Council; and of the city itself this is still substantially true. It is still a mediæval city; many of its streets are paved with cobblestones, and any one, with a copy of Von der Hardt's map in his hand, can easily find his way about the town. But there have necessarily been changes in the past five hundred years. The old wooden bridge over the Rhine was some yards further down the river than the present bridge of stone; and the suburb of Petershausen, which lies beyond the river, where at that time stood the Benedictine Abbey in which King Sigismund was lodged in order that his unruly troops might be well out of the way, is now covered with villa residences. On the further side of the town, in the suburb of Kreuzlingen, the old Augustinian Abbey still stands but is now used as a normal school. The third suburb, Paradise, to the south-west of the city, which was then an open space available for tournaments or any outdoor pastimes, still boasts a few apple-trees and some open ground, but much of it is taken up with small houses and with intersecting roads.

The old walls of the city have disappeared and have been replaced by a broad boulevard with an avenue of trees; and the drain which separated Constance from Kreuzlingen has been filled in and a street built over it. Of the thirty towers and gateways which existed at the time of the Council only seven remain; the one which guarded the old wooden bridge, and the Pulverturm a little further down the river, the Snezthorturm, built in the fourteenth century, and the Schlachtthorturm, built about the same time, the tower near Saint Paul's Church in which Jerome of Prague was imprisoned, and also the tower which served as the last place for the incarceration of John Hus. There are two others of more recent date.

Within the circuit of the old city walls there have also been changes. The nave of the Cathedral with its columns still stands as in the days of John Hus, but nearly every other part is more recent. The nave was fitted up with three rows of benches, one raised above the other, for the accommodation of the prelates; and about ten or twelve yards from the western door there is a flag stone, the only one still remaining from those days, on which the Reformer stood to hear his sentence, and from that day onward, says tradition, that stone has never been dry. The two nunneries, near the bridge, are now utilised as a normal school for women. The Church of Saint John is no more; and the old Church of Saint Stephan, in which the auditors sat during the Council, has given place to one built later in the fifteenth century. A Stadthaus, or town hall, now stands on the site of the Franciscan Monastery in which John Hus and Jerome of Prague were tried, and in which Duke Friedrich of the Tirol swore to be true to his liege lord, King Sigismund. The churches of Saint Laurence, Saint Paul, and Saint Judas have disappeared; so too has the old Schoten Church, once a Benedictine monastery, dating from the beginning of the eighth century. The railway station occupies the sites of the old town granary and of the monastery of the Austin Friars, though a Church of Saint Augustine hard by still preserves the memory of the ancient cloister. The Dominican monastery on the lake has been transformed into the Insel Hotel, a most worthy institution, where one may still wander through the old convent gardens and eat one's food in the stately refectory.

Hard by is the Kaufhaus, just as it stood when used for the Conclave of the Council; the old fish and fruit markets can still be traced; the Rosgarten Museum is the old guildhouse of the butchers; the houses occupied by King Sigismund and Queen Barbara when they arrived from Ueberlingen, the house in which Zabarella died, the house assigned to John of Nassau, and numerous others still exist as they were in the days of the Council. The streets are everywhere the same, although the names of some have been changed. Constance to-day has hardly stepped out of the Middle Age; it is a thoroughly picturesque and lovable city of the quaint mediæval world.[1]

[1] *A. F.*, 19 *et seq.*

CONSTANCE

'The first building of the city of Constance,' says Gabriel Buceli, 'was the work of the grandchildren of Noah, no long time after the deluge.' If the worthy Benedictine Father had said that Constance was founded about the time of the flood or earlier, he would have received corroboration from the fact that remains of a large settlement of lake-dwellers were found when the new harbour was excavated.[1] Both tradition and history however, assign the foundation of the city to the fourth century; it is supposed to be named after the Emperor Constantius Chlorus; enormous blocks of masonry and some very broad piers were laid bare by some excavations in the year 1552. The undoubted site of a Roman settlement, the part which was earliest provided with buildings and bastions, is the so-called Island, always known as the Niederburg. This included the part of the town to the west between the river, the southern walls and the city walls by the Schreibergasse and Langgasse as far as the house which goes by the name of 'Zum Spiegel.' Here stood the old Benedictine monastery which was, in 701, replaced by the cathedral, the monks moving to the Rubbish Heaps (Schoten) outside the town to the west. Within the same limits stood the somewhat later church of Saint John. The bishopric was transferred from Windisch to Constance in 560, and to keep alive the memory of the transfer the newly elected bishop always rides into the town from Gottlieben by the Hochstrasse.

Toward the end of the seventh century the town was extended on one side to the Schotenthor, and on the other the old palace, near the ecclesiastical court-house, the residence of the Bishops of Constance for two hundred years, was brought into the town by a new wall. The small Church of Saint Nicolas, afterwards called Saint Stephan's, was still without the walls. Salomo the Third subsequently built the present episcopal palace south of the church in the cathedral-yard.

It was to this Bishop, at the commencement of the tenth century that the third enlargement of the town was due. The new lines ran from the upper cathedral-yard to the site of the Kaufhaus, and thence to the square where the subsequent Hagelisthor stood, and thence to the north, taking in the church of Saint

[1] Capper, 149.

Stephan. The Kreuzlinger Monastery and the Conrad Hospital adjoining were founded in 938 by Conrad the First, Bishop of Constance and Count of Altdorf; and in 1110-20 the monastery was restored and enlarged by Bishop Ulrich. The Church of Saint John was built in 930; that of Saint Paul in 938; Petershausen fifty or sixty years later; the Cathedral, which had fallen down in 1052, was rebuilt four years later by Bishop Rumoald.

In the twelfth century several Reichstags were held in Constance, and it was here that, in 1125, the fierce feud between the Guelfs and Ghibelines took its rise. Frederic Barbarossa, the greatest of all the Emperors since Karl der Grosse, held a Reichstag here in March 1153, when he was in the prime of early manhood ; he held others in 1155 and 1162 ; he held his last court on the banks of the Boden See when he was sixty-two years of age, in 1183, when the celebrated Peace of Constance was signed. His grandson Frederic marched on Constance, and baffled his rival Otto thirty years later. Before this time, in 1202, the nunnery ' at the Ferry ' was founded ; but fifty years after, the nuns bought the knightly castle of Veltpach near Stekboren, and some other nuns from Pulenbrunnen took the abandoned convent and dedicated it to Saint Peter. In 1240 the little Church of Saint Mary under the lime-trees was made over to the Franciscans, but shortly after this they obtained ground to build a monastery, and then they gave their old home to some pious ladies. Though buildings were springing up, Constance was unlucky at this time ; twice within seven years a terrible fire laid the city in ashes. Three years after the second conflagration, the Dominican convent in the Niederburg was founded, in 1253 ; and fifteen years later the building of the Augustinian monastery, for which the town gave the site, was commenced. The Snezthor and the Schlachtthor, with the town wall between them, were built in 1286 ; and the Plantengasse about the same time. By the edge of the lake (*in foro litoris*) there were several houses at the beginning of the thirteenth century ; and in 1225 the Hospital of the Holy Ghost was founded by the citizens Heinrich von Bizenhofen and Ulrich Blarer. In 1276 the Church of Saint Laurence was built, the southern side, where the women sat, being over the foundation of the old city wall.

The fourth enlargement of the town occupied from 1286 to

CONSTANCE 241

1324. It began at the south-west end, stretched up to Paradise to the place where the Snezthor stands, proceeded thence downwards round the Platz where later the Augustinian Monastery was built, and joined the old town at the Merkstade, or *in foro litoris* or *in foro mercatus* as it was also called. The fourteenth century was an era of prosperity. The linen industry (*Tela di Constanza*) increased and became famous through Europe; leagues for mutual protection were formed with the Swabian cities; the guilds disputed the government of the town with the noble families who had hitherto monopolised it; and the Jews were occasionally persecuted in good mediæval fashion. But at the end of the century there were three disastrous fires in eleven years.

In 1405, after the Neugasse had been burned down, the town was again enlarged by a new enclosing wall erected from the Snezthor as far as the Paradisegasse, and thence to the river. Five years later a sixth enlargement was effected, an enclosing wall being carried as far as Kreuzlingen. Petershausen and Paradise were from time immemorial part of Constance, forming suburbs to the north and west.[1] Such was the gradual growth of the city of Constance, similar to that of many another mediæval town, up to the time of the Great Council.

At this time the Bishop was Otto the Third, son of Markgraf Rudolf of Hochberg, who had been chosen on the 2nd February 1411, and was a mighty and a learned prelate; under him were twenty-four canons and his chaplains, beside the canons prebendary and chaplains of Saint Stephan and Saint John. There was a monastery of Benedictine monks at Petershausen, one of the Augustines at Kreuzlingen, beside the houses of the Dominican and the Franciscan Friars in the town, and two convents of nuns.

The total population of Constance at the time of the Council was between five and six thousand; the citizens being divided into eighteen guilds, the fishermen, shipmen, shoemakers, tailors, and others, and each guild being ruled by two masters. The town was governed by a council, elected annually from the guilds, the highest office being the Burgomaster, the second the Imperial Bailiff, and the third the city Amman. Linen

[1] Eiselein, 1-9; *A. F.*, 1-10.'

was the chief product of the place, but in the market of Constance were to be found goods from the furthest ends of the earth.[1]

The town council, or local senate, had to take thought for the expected inrush of visitors, and it was known that the number would be very large. The actual number present during the Council is not accurately known; Mueller conjectured that it was more than a hundred thousand, Richental estimated it at eighty thousand, Dacher and Urstitius put it at sixty thousand each.[2] There were thirty thousand horses in the city, and thirty-six thousand beds were provided for strangers. Buildings for the accommodation of visitors were erected round Saint Stephan's Church and round the Augustinian monastery; in fact every available bit of vacant space was utilised.[3] During the four long years through which the Council lasted there was a continual stream of visitors coming and going, for it was the sight of Europe; many came to see the learned men; others came to get married; numbers flocked into the city to see the tournaments and other shows; students came in hundreds to look for livings.[4] The local senate had to care for the board and lodging of all these.

It was decided, in the first place, that every citizen was to provide lodging for a certain number of strangers, according to the size of his house; but this arrangement failed utterly to supply the necessary accommodation, and misery often acquainted a man with strange bedfellows. The quarters for the more important guests were assigned beforehand; placards were posted, and were removed when the occupant came and affixed his own coat of arms outside his lodging. Disputes with regard to letting were sure to occur; and for the settlement of these a Board was appointed consisting of six persons, three being auditors from the Curia, and the other three being city counsellors; the number was afterwards increased to eight, one being appointed from each nation of the Council, and four from the Senate of the city. At the same time the College of Auditors, twelve in number, sat three times a week at the church of Saint Stephan to settle disputes as to possession.[5]

[1] Eiselein, 32-4.   [2] Rossmann, 28.   [3] Ibid. 47.
[4] Ibid. 30.   [5] Ibid. 52.

CONSTANCE 243

Cases of theft and other offences came before the auditors, who were lenient as the times went. They transported scores of offenders beyond the boundaries, thanking God they were rid of knaves; a juvenile offender brought them by King Sigismund was thus allowed to get off; and of the fifteen men whom they condemned to death several thus cheated the gallows.

The ordinary police arrangements were undertaken by the city and were admirably performed, the city police not fearing to defend even Jews against papal officials.[1] The gates of the city were shut every evening at sundown, and if any traveller arrived after they were closed, he was conducted to his lodging without payment. If, however, as was often the case, he was a foreigner whose speech was unintelligible, he was provided with board and lodging free of charge for the night, and next morning was taken to the cathedral, that being the place where men of all nationalities most did congregate.[2] The charge for a furnished room with a clean bed was a gulden and a half the month (about fifteen marks), and the linen was changed once a fortnight.[3] Stabling for a horse was to be had at two pfennigs the night.

A tariff of prices was also arranged to prevent disputes and to avoid the higgling of the market in divers tongues. At first the prices were set too high. A bushel of wheat was to be sold for eighteen schillings, about ten marks, but the price soon fell to thirteen schillings; the bushel contained about one hundred and fifty litres of modern measure. Similarly the bushel of oats was originally fixed at thirty schillings but soon fell to fifteen;[4] and in this case the bushel contained about two hundred and forty litres. Of meat there was good store; in two of Richental's illustrations we see the butchers cutting up the joints, while the dogs under the benches are eating the offal. Beef was sold at three pfennigs the pound; lamb and pork at four; but lean pork was dearer.[5] Of the larger game there was not much variety; the flesh of the wild boar was sold at seven pfennigs a pound, that of the red deer was cheaper. Hares were also in the market. A loaf of white rye bread was to be had for a pfennig, or fourteen for a schilling; bread was brought in from the country and by river; and in Constance the bakers

[1] Rossmann, 56.   [2] *Ibid.* 57.   [3] Richental, 38.
[4] Eiselein, 35-6; Rossmann, 37-8.   [5] Richental, 40.

244 POPE JOHN THE TWENTY-THIRD

trundled their little round ovens in wheelbarrows through the streets, selling cakes, ringpuffs, and pasties, made of meat, fish, or chicken, well spiced and seasoned.[1] Partridges and pigeons were five or six hallers apiece; thrushes, as popular a dish as they were with the Romans in the time of Antony, were four or five hallers; fieldfares and blackbirds were more expensive; an ordinary fowl cost three pfennigs. Eggs were at first bought up by the wealthy, but it was ordered that they should all be sold in the open market, that rich and poor alike might purchase at a haller (about a penny) apiece. Salmon, otter, and beaver were sold at eight pfennigs the pound. Fish generally was dearer than it would otherwise have been because of the three fasts a week, when no one ate the flesh of any warm-blooded animal. There was a trade in dried fish with Bern and also with Lombardy, and a pound of dried cod was sold for twenty pfennigs or a little more; the familiar felchen of the Swiss lakes cost a schilling; pike, carps, and eels were eighteen pfennigs the pound; a measure of common loach was thirty pfennigs; miller's thumbs were two-thirds the price; herrings were one or two pfennigs. A very good criterion of the value of money is found in the fact that an ordinary workman got ten pfennigs a day and his food, or eighteen pfennigs a day if he found himself; so that a labourer's food must have cost about eight pfennigs a day.[2] A pound of butter cost about a shilling, a pound of tallow about ninepence. A quarter of onions sold for half a crown; carrots for one-third of the price. A large head of cabbage was two pfennigs, a small cabbage one. Saffron was two florins the pound, cinnamon one-half and pepper one-third this price. Hay was brought in by boats, and as many as thirty large ships might be seen unloading at Saint Conrad's Bridge at one time;[3] as both oats and hay were dear, horses must have been expensive to keep. Hus complained of the scarcity of fruit and of hay, and said that horses were being sold very cheap,[4] the reason being that very few could afford to keep them. Such was the scarcity of wood that some of the neighbouring forests were cut down.[5] Wine varied much in price. A measure, three pints, of the common stuff given only to

---

[1] Richental, 39.   [2] Rossmann, 38.   [3] *Ibid.* 41.
[4] *Ibid.* 42.   [5] *Ibid.* 41.

servants cost two pfennigs; the ordinary wine of the country cost three or four times as much; Rhine wine was twenty pfennigs the measure, and Malvoisy was twice that price.[1] Do what they might, however, the local senate could not prevent grumbling. Oswald von Wolkenstein complained that all the best victuals were bespoken for clerical stomachs, to the great discomfort of the hungry layfolk; mushrooms, said he, cost a schilling a piece, and an egg sixteen hallers; meat was scarce and cabbage might be howled for. You have to eat with a small spoon and remain hungry, remarked the poet; you may have slops, but there is a short allowance of roast meat, and wild fowl and fish are under ban; the wine is as sour as sloes.[2] Poets are ever a querulous race, but the deputies from the University of Vienna also complained of the high prices.[3]

When the King and the Pope, the envoys from European nations, and the crowd of Teuton and other nobles and princes were all assembled, Constance was thickly thronged. There were twenty-nine cardinals, more than three hundred bishops and lofty prelates, hundreds of doctors from the universities, besides Greeks and Muhammadans, Armenians and Russians, Africans and Ethiopians. The worthy chronicler Richental set draughtsmen to work; they depicted the priests of the Orthodox Church with their long black beards, their swarthy countenance, and their foreign garb; Hungarians with mighty moustaches and slit eyes; comfortable prelates and stern warriors; no less than the sturdy butchers with turned-up noses and the raw butcher-boys.

Not only were large crowds expected of those who had work or pleasure at the Council, but also there were many of those who came to minister to their necessities. Artisans and craftsmen came in from the country round. In order to prevent disputes between these and the men of Constance, the outsiders appointed delegates to confer with the senate and to report measures for the exercise of their trades. Workshops had to be erected and dwelling-places provided. The squares, walls, neighbourhood of churches were all utilised; many dwelt in the cellars, and others on the roofs of houses.[4] A record of

[1] Eiselein, 35-6.   [2] Wolkenstein, 37.
[3] Pulka, 9.   [4] Rossmann, 47.

these outsiders was made, and there were more than two thousand six hundred of them; goldsmiths, merchants, pickpockets, shoemakers, cobblers, furriers, druggists, ironsmiths, bakers, cooks, barbers, tailors, and others. There were also those who came to provide amusement; musicians, actors, merry-andrews, strolling players, and the like, came in their hundreds. There was abundance of public amusement all through the Council; dancing, singing, and music went on all through the day and far into the night in the squares. There were peasants' plays from the Tirol and miracle plays; coursing, tournaments, visiting, and excursions were the order of the day. But the dancing was perhaps the most popular amusement. Many of the knights and of the clergy also soon had enough of the dissertations and disquisitions, and those who did not repair home to tell of the wonders they had seen remained to enjoy themselves. The daughters of the castle came to the dance; many a cavalier had his beard plucked out when he wooed too fiercely, or lost his costly agate to some cutpurse as he rolled home drunk.[1] Queen Barbara, ever ready for frolic and flirtation, gave dances at which the burghers' wives were resplendent in their beauty and their finery. There being so many ghostly fathers assembled, troops of naughty damsels, light o' love, flocked in from all sides to minister to their carnal pleasures; one report says that there were fifteen hundred of them; Dacher counted seven hundred and then discreetly stopped;[2] they lived thirty in a room; they put up in bathrooms or sheds; and those who could find no better lodging were content with the empty wine-butts which lay about in the streets.[3] No wonder that it took Constance many years after the Council was gone to recover her wonted morality!

Many of the rich ecclesiastics did their share to aid or amuse the multitude. Some, like Archbishop Eberhard of Salzburg, fed crowds of paupers every day at noon; and the city at one time had to start building new walls as a relief work, paying eighteen pfennigs a day as wage; Bishop Hallam of Salisbury exhibited plays, showing the Birth of Our Lord, the Coming of the Three Kings, and the Slaughter of the Innocents. The number of horses encouraged tournaments and other equine

[1] *B. W.*, 259.   [2] Hardt, vi. 45.   [3] Richental, 183.

displays; bolsters and sacks of sand were sometimes placed on the horses by way of variety.¹ There were processions, in which the Florentines carried off the prize for splendour, while the English won applause for the novelty and sweetness of their singing.² Women who could sing were special objects of wonder and curiosity.³ Each of the great lords brought his own minstrelsy. When Sigismund, the ' beadle of the Empire,' was away from Constance in Spain, France, and England, business slackened and pleasures became more rife. The prelates took to making picnics in the neighbouring forests; their cooks prepared them food and drink at some shady place in the glades, *neque deerant meretrices.* Every man, even the most severe, could amuse himself at Constance.

During the Council there were representatives of every country of Europe in the city; there were Arabs, Ethiopians, Armenians, and white Russians. Thirty different languages were talked in the streets. The Pope's penitencers, twelve in number, sat in the cathedral to hear confessions, four in the apse, four by the baptistery, and four at Saint Peter's altar; and over each of their shriving boxes was a notice, stating the languages in which the ghostly father was ready to hear confession. The town was a veritable babel of tongues.

It was a gay, a motley scene. There were cardinals in scarlet hat and mantle, with pages bearing their long trains; dukes or counts entering the city with their full complement of attendant cavaliers and squires; the ambassadors of Prester John speaking a language which no man could understand; youthful bishops in parti-coloured jackets with winged sleeves making a leg and flirting with a lady; sleek Florentine bankers and merchants, at the head of them Cosimo de' Medici, the Pope's treasurer;⁴ scores of hungry friars with platters, looking for a pittance at the house of some rich lord or prelate; little boys in brown and blue blouses, women with their heads wrapped up, men in brown hats gathered round the fish stalls; mountebanks and fiddlers, students and beggars; all were there. There also were on view natural curiosities such as are seen at this day at an Indian fair; among others was the

---

¹ Rossmann, 64.   ² *Ibid.* 59-62.
³ *B. W.*, 260.   ⁴ Wessenberg, ii. 85.

strange beast which the King of Poland had sent from Lithuania to King Sigismund, an animal bigger than a war horse, like a black ox, but with larger head and short thick neck and with more beautiful horns. At the tables outside the inns sat scholars from Prague or Heidelberg, singing songs of the fatherland, while stern English or Scotch knights looked stolidly on; Grecian spice merchants vended aromatic drugs and perfumery; Grecian maidens with dark hair and darker eyes offered finery for sale; musicians with the lilies of France on their back sang to the lute or the viol. All this and much else might have been seen every day of the week at Constance. Yet, notwithstanding this mighty assemblage of all sorts and conditions of men, the peace within the city itself was well kept, though there was murder and robbery outside the walls; several men were expelled from Constance during the four years, but only two were killed in street brawls. It was, on the whole, a merry and good-natured throng; viewed in its social aspect, and taken apart from its religious and business side, the Council of Constance was the Vanity Fair of the fifteenth century.

The literary activity during the time was very great, for there were in the city a greater crowd of prominent and talented men, from the three literary cardinals, Fillastre, d'Ailly, and Zabarella downward, than had ever met in one place before. The ranks of the Curia contained noted humanists, such as Leonardo Bruni of Arezzo, the private secretary of Pope John, who remained for a few months only, and Poggio[1] of Florence, who stayed in Constance nearly the whole time of the Council. The humanists ransacked the neighbouring libraries of Reichenau and Saint Gall; they were disgusted at the want of care with which the manuscripts were treated, and were delighted with rich finds, such as Quintilian's *Institutes*, the works of Valerius Flaccus, the Commentaries on Cicero, and the *History* of Ammianus Marcellinus. Copies of the classics and of theological and canonical works were made in Constance by copyists working for their daily bread. The sermons of d'Ailly and Gerson, official protocols, circular letters of the Council, religious and political tracts were copied and disseminated by the hundred. The delegates

[1] Poggio, 1381-1459; Wessenberg, ii. 112.

from Poland utilised their stay in Constance to collect abstracts of learned works for their own libraries. Dietrich Vrie wrote a history of the Council in execrable hexameters. The preaching was nearly all in Latin, but occasionally in the vulgar, as when Andreas Lascari preached in German, with a Teuton priest by him to prompt him when he was at a loss for a word. Bartolommeo da Monte Pulciano, a booklover and collector, wrote verses slightly better than those of the dramatist, Antonio Loschi ; he and Agapito Cenci, author, translator, and commentator, were the pupils of Manuel Chrysoloras ; Jean de Montreuil represented the French humanists ; Giovanni de Serravalle commenced his translation of Dante's *Divine Comedy* ; there were scores of lesser lights.[1]

Poets also there were, though German poetry was then at its lowest ebb. Thomas Prischuch of Augsburg sang the praises of King Sigismund, the faults of Pope John, and the stainless beauty and virtue of Queen Barbara ; Arnald of Villanova told of geomancers, hydromancers, cheiromancers, pyromancers, necromancers and of those who sought the philosopher's stone at Constance ; Johann Englemar expressed his hope that the Kaiserdom would flourish which had long hung on a barren tree; Fichard was hot and eager against that fool King Wenzel who had sent heretics in his embassy, against the impecunious Markgraf of Baden, and against John of Nassau, who limped like a dog when he would, who was a poisonous snake, and had already lived too long for his bishopric :

> 'Johannes ist din name ;
> Jehenna is der flamme,
> den dir der Teufel hat bereit.'

Eberhard Windecke, the King's banker and travelling companion, mingled with the poets and occasionally borrowed from them for his history ; he looked with no favourable eye on the minever mantles of the papal scribes :

> 'Sint wilkomen, here kortesan !'

was his greeting. But there was one true poet at the Council of Constance, he who was known by some as the Tirolean Ulysses, by others as the Tirolean Skald.

[1] Finke (*B.*), 60-74.

One of the earliest arrivals was the minnesinger, Oswald von Wolkenstein. He had been to Schwangau and betrothed himself to the beauteous Margareta, and had stayed several weeks in her castle, ' the world forgetting, by the world forgot '; but he tore himself away to come to the Council. He had the affairs of the League to look after, and was hand-in-glove with King Sigismund's chief supporters, with Friedrich of Nuernberg, with Louis of Brieg and Louis of Oettingen, with Louis the Bearded, the French Queen's brother, and with the Count Palatine, and Bishop Eberhard of Salzburg; all of them staunch adherents of the King and opposed to Duke Friedrich of the Tirol. Oswald wrote two humorous short poems on the money-getting ways of the men of the Boden See, one of which has already been quoted, while in the other he narrates how they emptied his pockets and drained him as dry as an empty bottle. He affected to despise the empty glitter of the balls and the venality of the ladies; but in another sweet little poem he confesses that he has found perfect Paradise amid the notes of the cathedral music, and that all the sorrows of his heart are healed :—

> ' Women here, like angels wooing,
> Beautiful, in splendour bright,
> They have been my heart's undoing,
> They possess my dreams at night.
> One there is of beauty rarest,
> Never shall I her forget,
> Of delights and joys the fairest,
> She within my heart is set.
> The fairest fair
> In their dainty dresses,
> With jewels rare
> In their auburn tresses;
> The rose-red lips
> And their blushing faces,
> Whence sorrow trips
> And leaves no traces.' [1]

Oswald von Wolkenstein was not the only poet who was overpowered by the beauty of the ladies of Constance. ' So great is the host of most dainty dames and damsels who surpass

[1] Wolkenstein 33.

the snow in the delicacy of their colouring,' wrote Benedict de Pileo, ' that you may rightly say of Constance as Ovid declared of Rome, that Venus herself reigns in this city.'[1] There was something to suit every taste in Constance on the Boden See. ' A mad world, my masters.'

[1] Finke (*B.*), 69.

CHAPTER XIV

THE COUNCIL BEFORE CHRISTMAS, 1414

THE Council of Constance was by universal consent the largest, the most influential, and the most splendid gathering that had ever been held in the Middle Ages. Not only was it an œcumenical church conference called for the extinction of the Great Schism which had vexed Christendom for wellnigh forty years, for the reformation of the Church in its head and its members from those abuses which are so vividly set forth by that ardent reformer, Nicolas de Clamanges, and for the extirpation of the new heresy which threatened the very foundations of the Catholic Church, but it was also, in a certain measure, a political congress dealing with matters of European interest, with which was combined a Diet of the Empire. The King of the Romans was the backbone of the Council. The Council of Pisa had failed because neither Pope nor Emperor had any part therein, and because the cardinals who convoked and conducted it had no power of enforcing its conclusions. The head of the Holy Roman Empire was recognised as the advocate and defender of the Church; and it was admitted even by so determined a papalist as Augustinus Triumphus that it was his right and duty to convoke a General Council;[1] King Sigismund had undertaken the great task, and he was backed up not only by the Pope with the largest obedience, but by the most influential of the Christian nations of Europe; so that he might reasonably look for success in his undertaking. The work of the Council, however, does not fall within the scope of the present sketch, further than as it concerns the fortunes of Pope John the Twenty-third and the patriot reformer John Hus.

The Council was convoked for the first day of November 1414, and on that day Pope John the Twenty-third celebrated the

[1] Gierke, 124.

Mass in the Cathedral of Constance. But the assemblage of prelates was small in contrast with the stately gathering at Pisa on Lady Day 1409. The old Cardinal of Poitiers, nephew of the Pope who had promoted him to the purple before the outbreak of the Great Schism, the cardinal who then presided at the opening ceremony, had died in 1412, and there were now with John simply the nine cardinals who had accompanied him from Italy. As soon as the Mass was finished Cardinal Zabarella, the junior in the Sacred College, rose and announced that Pope John the Twenty-third had resolved at Lodi to celebrate at Constance a General Council in continuation of that at Pisa, and that it would be opened on the 3rd of November. The opening was subsequently postponed until the 5th. The terms of Zabarella's announcement showed how earnest the Pope was that the Council should be considered as a mere continuation of that in which his two rivals had been declared heretic and schismatic and had been formally deposed; if he could only succeed in getting the assembly to adopt this view, it followed that he was to be recognised as the canonical Pope. On the 2nd November six more cardinals rode into Constance.[1]

On the 5th November the Council was opened. Neither the King of the Romans nor any of the Electors, nor any ambassadors from any of the courts of Europe, nor the representatives of Popes Benedict or Gregory, had as yet arrived; but there were present fifteen cardinals, two patriarchs, twenty-three archbishops, and a large number of other prelates, about three hundred in all,[2] who passed in solemn procession into the cathedral. Pope John celebrated the Mass of the Holy Ghost, and a Cluniac monk preached a sermon. Cardinal Zabarella then mounted the pulpit and announced that, by order of the Pope and with the approbation of the Council, the first session would be held on Friday the 16th. The Council now being formally open, the congregation dispersed.[3]

The date fixed for the opening of the Council was so far favourable in that it was the peaceful season of the year, when the roads were generally free from troops and the traffic was thereby unimpeded. But in other ways it was unfavourable. Constance in the spring or early summer, when the apple and

[1] Richental, 28.   [2] Hardt, iv. 13.   [3] Mansi, xxvii. 532; Hardt, iv. 13.

pear blossoms sparkle, like a carcanet of pearls, along the borders of the lake, or Constance in the early autumn, backed by its wondrous semicircle of snowy mountains, from Hohe Sentis round to the Jungfrau, clear cut against the blue sky, is a place of beauty and a joy to the beholder; but it is otherwise in the winter, when the cold mist hangs heavy and grey over city and lake, and germs of disease infest the air; and it is little wonder that the Pope, accustomed to the dry heat and dry cold of Bologna, soon fell a victim to the chilly mists; this was the reason why the first session was so unduly postponed.[1] Later on there was a general epidemic of the *Noli me tangere*,[2] which laid so many of the prelates low that it was impossible to hold the second session until after a still longer interval.[3]

On the 10th November there arrived five more cardinals, with a large number of archbishops and prelates, and also the Patriarch of Constantinople and the Grand Master of the Knights of Rhodes. But more cheering to the sick Pope than anything else was the news from Rome. After the death of King Ladislas, his sister Joanna the Second had seized the city and her generals were in possession when the Pope's Legate arrived. The Romans, however, were tired of the Neapolitan tyranny, and Cardinal Hannibaldus soon chased out the hostile troops and brought back the Eternal City once more to the papal obedience. Pope John ordered a solemn procession of thanksgiving, and took occasion in the same congregation to forbid any member leaving the Council without his permission.[4]

John Hus, meantime, was abiding quietly at the house of the widow Fida, ' the second widow of Sarepta.' He was awaiting in confidence, and was busily preparing his case for the public disputation which he was to hold in the presence of King Sigismund, before whom he expected, after a great fight, to obtain a great victory; his enemies, he knew, dreaded his public speech, and for the time he was content to sit behind his little window, watching the giddy crowds which now began to throng the streets.[5] His old enemy John, the iron Bishop of Leitomysl, was in Constance, and his spies kept watch on Hus.

---

[1] Martene (*A. C.*), vii. 1408.
[2] An ulceration of the face, more especially of the nose.
[3] Finke (*F.*), 164. [4] Hardt, iv. 14. [5] Luetzow, 214.

Pope John sent two bishops and a doctor to the reformer to propose that his matter should be quietly arranged; but Hus was bent on a public triumph and declined.[1] The cardinals, however, were shocked that he daily read Mass regardless of the fact that he was still excommunicated. They represented the matter to the Pope and a sharp discussion ensued. John settled the matter by suspending of his own authority the interdict and the sentence of excommunication which had been passed against Hus three years before; but the Master was requested, in the interest of the public peace, to avoid the more important processions and ceremonies, though he was free to roam about Constance and to go into any church he pleased. Pope John was evidently doing his best to anticipate the wishes of King Sigismund in the matter of John Hus, although the reformer's voluntary appearance in Constance might be taken in some measure to palliate his former recusancy. But Hus took no advantage of the permission granted; he continued to read Mass in his own room; he welcomed the crowd of neighbours who flocked thither; he expounded his doctrine to them, and laboured to clear himself of any suspicion of heresy; his winning personality charmed his hearers and dismayed his adversaries. They went to the Bishop of Constance, who sent two officials to forbid Hus to read the Mass; and when the Master protested and pointed out that the sentence of excommunication had been suspended by the Pope, his protest was accepted, but the people were forbidden to frequent his dwelling.

By reason of the prevalent sickness and of the paucity of numbers it was impossible to make any headway with the business of the Council, but at a congregation of doctors in theology, held on the 12th November, it was proposed that the members of the Council should be divided into nations, and that all matters should be debated in the nations in the first place, and that then representatives from each nation should meet for general discussion, what was proposed at one session not being concluded until the next.[2] These doctors in theology were probably, for the most part, early arrivals from Paris; at any rate, their proposal of the division of the Council into nations

[1] Palacky (*Doc.*), 79; Berger, 115.   [2] Hardt, ii. 189-90.

was an innovation which had far-reaching consequences, disastrous to Pope John. It was further proposed that the first matter was to secure the unity of the Papacy as a necessary preliminary to the reform of the Church in its head and its members, and it was hoped that this might be effected in the person of that most constant Pope who had convoked the Council, and who had, at so much trouble, toil, and expense, crossed the mountains and come to Constance. This was laid before Pope John at a general congregation on the 15th November; there were other proposals also, concerning the abdication of all three Popes, which the doctors thought it wiser to keep for the present in the background.[1]

The first general session of the Council of Constance was held on Friday, the 16th November 1414. The Mass of the Holy Ghost was celebrated by Cardinal Giordano Orsini, the other prelates sitting in their copes. The Mass over, they put on their pontifical robes and their white mitres, and then sang an anthem. Then followed prayers, silent and audible, another anthem and the litany. The benediction and the gospel came next. The Pope then preached a sermon on the words, 'Speak ye every man the truth with his neighbour; execute the judgment of truth and peace in your gates,' and at its close he intoned the *Veni Creator Spiritus*. Cardinal Zabarella then left his place and, standing by the Pope, read the preamble to a Bull announcing that the Pope had convoked this Council to carry on the work begun at Pisa. The Bull of convocation was then read by a secretary; it set forth that the work of reform of the Church had been postponed at Pisa for three years, after which it had again been taken up at Rome and had again been postponed because of the paucity of numbers, and then it described briefly the negotiations with King Sigismund and the convocation of the present Council. Cardinal Zabarella then, on behalf of the Pope, ordered a solemn Mass to be celebrated every Thursday in all the churches of the city, enjoined on all the duty of prayer, fasting, and meditation, more especially in connection with the duty of suppressing the heresies of John Wyclif. The officers of the Council were then nominated. Count Berthold des Ursins, who had held the Pope's bridle at his entry into

[1] Lenfant (*C.*), i. 46.

COUNCIL BEFORE CHRISTMAS, 1414 257

Constance, was made guardian of the Council. Arragon of Malaspina, Paul de Juvenac, Pierre Donat, Hermann Dowerch, Thomas Polton, and Jean de Tremblay were appointed notaries, with four other sub-notaries or scribes under them. Jean Basir, Jaques de Tamplo, Angelo de Ballionibus, and Pierre Paul de Justinopoli were charged with the collection of votes. As advocates there were nominated four doctors of law, Pierre de Anchorano, the celebrated jurist of Bologna, Simon of Perugia, Raphael de Fulgose, and Ardessin de Novarre. Jean de Scribani and Henricus de Piro were named proctors; and the duty of assigning to members their proper places was laid upon Baronius de Pistorio, Jean Ponset, Barthélemy de Pando and Michel de Blosonis. These appointments were then put to the assembly, and the prelates with one accord answered *Placet*.[1] The business being concluded, the second session was fixed for the 17th December.

Three days later there occurred a little excitement to ruffle the hitherto undisturbed serenity of the Council. Pope Gregory the Twelfth, in answer to the brusque invitation conveyed by Archbishop Andreas of Calocza, had determined to send his representatives to the Council, and had for this purpose selected the recreant Dominican Giovanni, Cardinal of Ragusa, the man who originally had so strenuously supported the double cession, and who had then turned round and become its most vehement opponent, who had backed up the Pope in his alliance with King Ladislas of Naples and in his refusal to meet Pope Benedict. He was certainly an unpromising envoy to send to a Council bent on the abdication of the Popes. When the Cardinal was three or four miles from Constance, he sent messengers to the representatives of King Sigismund and to the senate and magistrates of the city asking for accommodation, and was told that the convent of the Austin friars had been assigned to Pope Gregory. Hereupon Cardinal Giovanni sent and affixed outside the convent the arms of Gregory together with the keys and triple crown. This public display of the papal insignia by his rival was more than Pope John could bear; he sent during the night and had them torn down. A general congregation was held in the papal palace next day, the

[1] *Religieux*, v. 466.

20th November, and a heated discussion ensued. There were many who contended that the Cardinal had a right to affix the insignia outside the convent; but the majority were of opinion that this was wrong, as Constance was in the obedience of Pope John, and, moreover, Pope Gregory himself had not appeared.[1] It was felt that there had been hasty action on both sides. No definite conclusion was reached; and although Pope John had his way, he must have felt that he was not undisputed master in the Council of Constance.[2]

The early days in the Council must have been very depressing. Every one knew that there were great schemes in the air, but no one dared put his hand to them until the more important and responsible actors arrived on the scene. Crowds of tradesmen and artisans were pouring in from the countryside, but numbers of ecclesiastics were confined to their lodgings through illness. On the 17th all the cardinals went in procession to meet Pierre d'Ailly, Cardinal of Cambrai, just returned from his German mission, who now entered Constance with more than two score followers.[3] Rumour falsely said that he was the son of a butcher; but he and his pupil, Jean Gerson, were to prove themselves the most powerful men in the Council of Constance, the backbone of the conciliar movement. A few days later there arrived Count Hermann of Cilly, the father-in-law of King Sigismund, and the ambassadors of Albert of Austria, who was betrothed to the King's daughter Elisabeth, but who was too young himself to come to the Council.

On the 28th November, eleven days after the arrival of Pierre d'Ailly, a step was taken which led to consequences of European importance. This had reference to John Hus. A cart of hay had been seen outside the house of the widow Fida, and the spies who watched Hus immediately reported that he was trying to escape. The story was believed by many, and among others by the chronicler Richental; but it has been conclusively proved to be absolutely false. Hus never made the slightest attempt to leave Constance; he had, indeed, never set foot outside the widow's house.[4] He was only anxious for the King's arrival that he might meet his opponents in fair academi-

[1] Schwab, 495.
[2] Hardt, iv. 20-1.
[3] Tschackert, 184.
[4] Helfert, 179 *et seq.*

cal disputation; and his two most determined adversaries, as he knew, were Stephen Palec and Michael *de Causis*. The former was a Bohemian, a conscientious man, who had been a close friend of the reformer, but who had separated from him when Hus showed signs of revolting from papal authority, when he appealed from the Pope to Jesus Christ and his own conscience; Palec was himself an earnest reformer and was simply fighting for the orthodox faith. Michael *de Causis*, on the other hand, was a Teuton, a convicted swindler, a very clever advocate in the spiritual courts, a man who would do anything for money. These two and the spies went to the cardinals. Whether Hus had actually tried to escape or not, it was clear that he might be persuaded to make the attempt and to evade the jurisdiction of the Council; and this danger had to be reckoned with.

As Hus was sitting at dinner, there appeared at his house the Bishops of Augsburg and Trient, together with the Burgomaster of the city and a soldier, and addressed John of Chlum. They said they had come from the cardinals at the Pope's order to inform Hus that, inasmuch as he had previously desired to speak with them, they were now ready to hear him. The worthy knight rose in anger, saying, 'Do you not know, most reverend fathers, why and how Master John Hus came here? if you are ignorant, I will tell you. When Wenzel of Lestna and I were in Friuli with our Lord the King, and were about to return to our own country, he told us to act as guardians to Master John for his safe conduct to this Council. Know, therefore, that you must do nothing contrary to the honour of our Lord the King.' Then John of Chlum turned to the Burgomaster and to him in German he said, 'You know very well that if the devil himself came here to have his case tried, he ought to have a fair hearing.' He then addressed himself again to the bishops, informing them that Sigismund had especially enjoined that John Hus was to say nothing in his matter except in the King's presence. To which the Bishop of Trient answered that they had only come in the interest of peace and did not wish for any uproar. What effect the episcopal admonition of the warlike Georg of Lichtenstein produced upon the equally pugnacious John of Chlum we do not know. The two bishops, the burgomaster, the knight, and the soldier must have nearly filled the small upper chamber in the widow's house; but there was sitting at the table, unnoticed by them, John Hus himself, and he now spoke to the right reverend fathers. 'I did not come here to see the cardinals, nor did I ever desire to speak with them,' said Master Hus, 'but I came to the General Council, and there will I speak as God shall direct me, concerning whatever I may be asked; yet at the request of my lords the cardinals, I am ready at once to come to them, and if I am asked concerning any matter, I trust that I shall rather choose death than deny any truth known to me from the Scripture or otherwise.' Thus, of his own accord, and in defiance of the better judgment of his valiant protector, John Hus decided to go with the bishops. They and the burgomaster had surrounded the house with armed men. As Hus descended the staircase the widow Fida met him, and he invoked God's blessing on her, to which she replied with tears. The bishops could not conceal their joy at having so peaceably captured the heretic. 'You will no longer officiate or say Mass now,' remarked they tauntingly. Hus mounted a sorry nag and, accompanied by his jailors and by John of Chlum, rode to the bishop's palace, hard by the Cathedral. The first false step that John Hus made was when he declined to join King Sigismund at Speier, preferring to come straight to Constance; the second was when he neglected the King's injunction that he was to say nothing except in his royal presence. He was a man of simple trusting mind, who did not appreciate the antagonism which the suspicion of heresy had raised against him.

Having arrived, Hus saluted the cardinals, who said to him: 'Master John, many and wonderful things are said of you, that you believe and teach many errors in the kingdom of Bohemia, and now we have called for you to ask if it is so.' He answered: 'Most reverend fathers, be it known to Your Holiness that I would rather die than hold a single article in error. And, look you, I have freely come to this sacred Council and am ready humbly to be corrected and to amend anything in which I have erred.' The cardinals answered: 'These are certainly good words'; and having so said they went away, leaving Hus in charge of the guard and John of Chlum with him.

While the cardinals were away there came to John Hus a

Franciscan friar Didacus, an expounder of Holy Writ, tempting him and saying : ' Reverend master, I am an unlearned monk, and have heard many strange doctrines ascribed to you, which I would gladly know whether you hold or not; and firstly they say that you believe that after consecration there remains in the sacrament of the altar merely material bread.' Hus denied this. Three times the friar repeated this question, and thrice it was denied. Then John of Chlum waxed angry and asked who he was, and what he meant by not taking a straightforward answer. To which the friar answered that he was an unlearned man seeking instruction, and forthwith began to question Hus as to the union of the divine and human nature in Christ. The Reformer now himself began to suspect his questioner, and remarked to John of Chlum in Bohemian that the man was not as simple as he made out, for he was asking questions on the most profound subjects; and turning to the friar he rebuked him for his duplicity. Didacus then thanked Hus for what he had said and hinted that Hus would have said more, but was afraid that John of Chlum would not understand. As soon as he had gone the Pope's guards asked Hus if he knew who the friar was, and told him that he was Master Didacus, well known to be the subtlest theologian in all Lombardy. Hus remarked : ' If I had known that, I would have peppered him differently with the Scriptures ; if they are all like him, with the aid of God and of Holy Writ I shall fear none of them.'

At four o'clock in the afternoon the cardinals returned and began to deliberate what was to be done with John Hus. Stephen Palec and Michael *de Causis* urged them by no means to let him go; they danced round the room, exclaiming, ' Ha ! ha ! we have him now, and he shall not escape till he has paid the last farthing.' There was a scene of confusion. John of Reinstein had come to fulfil his duty as one of the King's guardians of the safety of Hus, and Palec attacked him. Then Mladonowicz and a monk began to quarrel ; Palec joined in ; but having rather the worst of the argument he and the monk left the palace. The cardinals then sent to John of Chlum to say that he might go away if he liked, but that Hus would remain in the palace. The Bohemian knight, being very wroth at the artifice by which the reformer had been captured, went at once to the Pope; 'Holy Father,' he said, 'this is not what your paternity promised me and my uncle of Lacembok.' He repeated to him word for word what had passed at the interview on the 4th November, and concluded by saying that he was not going to be silent, but warned everybody who had violated the safe-conduct of his Lord the King. Pope John stretched out his hand toward the cardinals and answered: 'My brethren will bear me witness that I have never ordered him to be taken prisoner'; and afterwards, speaking privately to John of Chlum, he said: 'You see very well how matters stand between me and the cardinals; they have forced him upon me and I must keep him in captivity.' Pierre d'Ailly may have used his influence with the Pope.[1] This was all the satisfaction which the knight got from the Pope; he was obliged to leave John Hus in custody. On the days following, John of Chlum went about the city, publicly accusing the Pope and the cardinals of breach of faith, showing the King's safe-conduct to all who could read, and finally affixing a manifesto in Latin and German on the door of the cathedral, charging the Pope with contemning and vilifying the King's safe-conduct and the security and protection granted by the royal and imperial majesty.[2] Then he left Constance and went off to find the King of the Romans. He reported to him all that had happened. Sigismund was very wroth; he swore that he would have John Hus out of captivity again, if he had to break down the prison doors.

Pope John the Twenty-third was no longer, mentally or physically, the strong man he had been at the Council of Pisa; he was becoming heavy and gouty in body, vacillating and fatalistic in mind. Pisa had been his Council; the Council of Constance, as he told Valori, was not his, but what could he do when Fate dragged him on. Ever since Rocca Secca, the tide had flowed against him. King Ladislas had chased him out of Rome; the Florentines had relegated him to a suburb of their city; the two cardinals and Chrysoloras whom he trusted had failed him; Sigismund had refused to give way on any point, and had driven him with an iron hand; and now he knew that he was on the eve of a bitter fight to retain that papacy which had been the goal of his ambition. He realised already,

[1] Tschackert, 184.   [2] Palacky (*Doc.*), 247-54.

COUNCIL BEFORE CHRISTMAS, 1414   263

as the King of the Romans was later to realise, that the Council was stronger that either Pope or King. He could not depend on the College of Cardinals; some were neutral, others were adverse, his own friends were often weak; while the new French prelates whom he had promoted, Fillastre and d'Ailly, were strong men who knew their own mind, and were not to be won by blandishment. Pope John the Twenty-third had to fight for his own hand; he knew that King Sigismund would be angry at the incarceration of John Hus; but the Council had the undoubted right to detain him pending inquiry; and as they insisted on the detention, the Pope in self-defence gave way. Whatever he may have said later, it was the truth he told, as already narrated, to John of Chlum; he did not dare offend the Council.

Hus remained in custody at the palace. To the Bohemian patriot, who knew practically nothing of the world outside Bohemia, it must have seemed, despite the taunts of his enemies, that some temporary mistake had been made, which would soon be set right. Neither he nor the King had ever dreamed of a trial. Sigismund had promised to see his matter safely through the Council and naturally thought, after the assurance of the Archbishop and the papal inquisitor, that Hus would have no difficulty in clearing himself and Bohemia of the aspersion of heresy. Hus thought so too.[1] The posting of the accusation on the door of the cathedral he had regarded as the ordinary preliminary which he had often himself adopted before a public discussion. But here there had been no attempt at any disputation. The cardinals had asked him a single question to which he had replied in meekness and humility, and they had expressed themselves satisfied with his answer. Although stupefied by what had happened, he knew he could trust the good knight, John of Chlum, to do his best to rectify the error and to get his liberty restored. His friend Mladonowicz brought him his fur coat, which was very necessary at the end of November, and a supply of money. At eleven o'clock at night he was taken to the house of a precentor where a cardinal was living, and there Hus remained under guard.

A week passed away, and at the end of that week Hus was

[1] Berger, 128.

taken, not to the house of the widow Fida, but to the Dominican Cloister at the edge of the lake, and was confined in a tiny cell, eight feet square by nine feet high, in close proximity to one of the city drains. Here he soon fell ill from fever and constipation. And as he lay, sick and weary, men came to him with extracts from his treatise *De Ecclesia*, asking if they were his. Then, if not before, John Hus must have realised that his enemies had stolen a march upon him, that there was to be no academical discussion, but that there was to be a trial, though he knew not on what charge, for no information had as yet been filed. But he was a man with many friends. Not only were there the multitudes in Prague, to whom he had preached in their own tongue, who loved and revered him as a prophet sent from God, but there were also the Bohemian nobility, to whom he was the apostle in the crusade against the Teutons, the foremost champion in the work of winning back Bohemia for the Bohemians; there were the trusty knights who were with him on his journey; there was, above all, the King of the Romans who had granted him a safe-conduct: he would certainly be liberated when once Sigismund reached Constance, if not sooner. Meanwhile, the Pope sent his own physicians to attend him, and under this kindly treatment the patriot reformer was speedily restored to health. But he remained in the underground cell of the Dominican monastery from the 6th December until the 3rd March, the day after the second general session of the Great Council.

To conduct the preliminary inquiry against John Hus the Pope appointed three judges, John, Patriarch of Constantinople, a Frenchman who was later a cardinal, the Italian Bishop Bernhard of the Citta di Castello near Perugia, and the German Bishop Johann of Lubeck. As soon as Hus realised that he was to be tried, he applied for the aid of a lawyer. This request was refused, as under the canon law no aid could be given to a heretic; had any advocate appeared on behalf of Hus, he would himself have been deemed a fautor of heresy. Professional advice was, however, just as necessary in those days as in the present in a cause involving nice legal distinction and argument, and Jean Gerson afterwards declared that had it been allowed to John Hus, the Reformer would never have been

COUNCIL BEFORE CHRISTMAS, 1414 265

convicted of heresy.[1] The witnesses examined were Muensterberg, doctor in theology, and Master Storch from Leipzig, both of whom had been with Hus in Prague, Stephen Palec, Zeifelmeister from the Prague diocese, a monk, Petrus of Saint Clements, a fierce enemy of Hus, the Abbot Peter of Saint Ambros in Prague, and others.[2] Now that Hus was safely in custody there was no need for haste in the conduct of his case. Michael *de Causis*, however, was indefatigable; thinking to support his charge concerning communion in both kinds he had intercepted and procured a copy of a letter from Hus to Jacobel, and of the latter's reply; these were shown to Hus and were admitted by him.

In the intervals between the hearings Hus busied himself in writing treatises for his friends in Prague; those on Marriage, on the Ten Commandments, on the Knowledge and Love of God, on Penitence, on Man's Three Enemies, and on the Lord's Supper were composed in the underground cell of the monastery. Hus's kindliness and gentle nature won him the love and sympathy even of his prison guards; he had no trouble in getting his treatises sent on their way nor in communicating with his friends.

Meanwhile, on the 1st December, the Council appointed a further and very strong commission to deal with the charge of heresy, probably to examine the evidence which the three judges collected; on this body were four cardinals, D'Ailly, Calvus, Brancacius, and Zabarella, who were assisted by a Dominican and Franciscan friar and by six other learned men.[3]

Prelates of high degree were now pouring into Constance from all sides. The Archbishops of Riga, Vienna, and Genoa arrived on the 1st December; the Bishops of Salisbury, Bath, and Hereford, the Abbot of Westminster, the Prior of Worcester and the Earl of Warwick on the 7th. On this latter date there was a congregation of cardinals and prelates at the palace, though the Pope himself was not present. A few of the Italian cardinals, forming the party of John the Twenty-third, proposed a resolution recognising the present Council as a continuation of that of Pisa and confirming all that was done at the former Council. Cardinal d'Ailly opposed this on the ground that the

[1] Luetzow, 223.   [2] Hefele, vii. 71.   [3] Hardt, iv. 23.

two Councils were quite independent. A third proposition was made by the Cardinals Castellio, Chalant, Brancacius, and Zabarella; it referred to certain points in which they thought the Pope was wanting in correctness and decorum; he cut the Masses short, did not give proper audiences, and was sometimes even jocose. Zabarella, from the days at Como onward, was more devoted to King Sigismund than to Pope John.[1] A week later another congregation was assembled, in which the initiative was again taken by the Pope's party who proposed to proceed by 'way of fact' against the two Popes who had been deposed at the Council of Pisa. This was again opposed by the Cardinal of Cambrai, who urged that, although that Council might have been legitimate, it was not infallible, and that therefore it was better neither to confirm nor to contradict what had been done there, but to listen courteously to the legates of the two Popes and to the ambassadors of the princes in their obedience, and not to proceed to the 'way of fact' until the method of gentleness had first been tried and had been proved ineffectual.[2] Pierre d'Ailly was rapidly assuming a commanding position in the conduct of the Council, and Pope John realised what a mistake he had made in promoting him to the sacred college.[3] He had already in the heat of argument uttered his famous contention that the Council was above the Pope and could depose him; and it was difficult for the party of Pope John, who took their stand on the Council which deposed two Popes, to gainsay this; when the Pope takes the lead in the Council, he is still, contended the cardinal, only a part of the Council, and the part has a smaller authority than the whole. Pierre d'Ailly was the most formidable opponent of the Pope who had yet appeared on the scene.

The second session of the Council had been fixed for the 16th December, but it was not held on that date, nor until long afterwards, and the reason is not far to seek. The resolutions passed at the congregations were not binding on the Council, but those passed at the general sessions were authoritative and final. Now the Council of Constance was thus far in marked contrast with the Council of Pisa. That Council was conducted by the cardinals, who were of one mind as to all that was to be

[1] Hardt, iv. 24-5. [2] *Ibid.* ii. 196-7. [3] Tschackert, 193.

done, and its unanimity was therefore wonderful; the envoys of King Rupert and the representatives of Pope Benedict, when they appeared, were few and uninfluential, and were readily flouted. But in the Council of Constance there was dissension from the commencement. It was an open secret that many of the prelates desired the abdication or deposition of Pope John the Twenty-third, and here was he at the head of the Council, and with a strong following behind him. Pierre d'Ailly had taken a line of his own, and there were other cardinals also in opposition, but parties were still in a fluid state and had not yet settled down under their leaders. Moreover, the King of the Romans had not yet arrived, and it was uncertain what line he would take on certain important points. He had written to Pope John announcing his speedy arrival, and it was known that he was extremely wroth at the action taken in the matter of John Hus. Every one felt that nothing definite could be done until he came, and the day of his coming was at hand. On the 21st December the French prelates and ambassadors, a mighty crowd, arrived; and on Christmas Eve King Sigismund reached Ueberlingen, and immediately sent off an express to the Pope asking him to delay the Mass next morning, as he himself would be present in the Cathedral.

We may be certain that the whole of Constance was awake that night to watch the fleet, the boats lighted up with innumerable torches, as it swept over the dark waters of the lake under the star-lit sky past the Island of Mainau, and rounded the corner of the bridge within hail of the Dominican monastery. It was two o'clock in the morning, and the young moon had set when the disembarkation commenced. The King of the Romans, every inch a monarch of men, tall and majestic, handsome and manly, with long, flowing beard and hair turning grey, more grave and thoughtful than he had been when first King of Hungary, but still full of activity and good humour, was accompanied by his wife, that fascinating pagan Queen Barbara, twenty-two years of age,[1] svelte and winsome,

'that fairer was to sene
Than is the lilie upon his stalke grene,
And fressher than the May with floures newe.'

---

[1] Aschbach, i. 132.

With her were her father and her brother; also the King's sister Elisabeth, Queen of Bosnia; and his niece Anna, Countess of Wuertemberg; and others, including a couple of Turks and a thousand horsemen. It was a cold night, and the King was to lodge at the House with the Steps (which is still standing);[1] but the royal party were taken straight from Saint Conrad's Bridge to the Stadthaus, where, before a blazing fire, they drank warm Malmsey wine. Shouts of joy greeted the King and Queen as they moved along the street; and John Hus, who should have ridden in Sigismund's train, could hear faint sounds of the merry din from his underground cell in the Dominican cloister.

[1] *A. F.*, 31.

CHAPTER XV

REX SUPER GRAMMATICAM

HAVING refreshed himself and rested at the Stadthaus, King Sigismund was escorted under a lofty canopy to the Cathedral, Queen Barbara and Elisabeth of Bosnia following under another canopy, also held aloft by four stalwart citizens. At the Cathedral they were welcomed by Pope John, resplendent in his pontifical attire and in a mitre which glittered with gold and precious stones. Inside the sacred edifice, on the right of the papal throne, there had been prepared a throne for the King, on whose right sat the fair Queen Barbara, and between them her father, the Count of Cilly, holding the golden apple in his hand. Friedrich of Nuernberg, Elector-designate of Brandenburg, bore the imperial sceptre; and Rudolf, the Elector of Saxony, as Marshal of the Empire, carried the drawn sword. While Scribani and his fellow ushers were placing the members of the Council in their seats, the King assumed the stole and dalmatic of a deacon to enable him to take part in the holy office. The Mass on that Christmas Day was celebrated by Pope John the Twenty-third, but the Gospel for the day was read by King Sigismund; and it must have been with a spirit of proud complacency that he pronounced the words, ' There went forth a decree from Cæsar Augustus,' for he was the modern representative of the old Roman Emperor, and it was by his decree that there was now here assembled the greatest peaceful gathering that the world had ever seen. He was fulfilling the traditional office of the head of the Empire in bringing peace to the Church; and he had done more than any other sovereign since the days of Frederic the Second to restore that Empire to the proud position which it occupied in the days of the first three Othos. The full tale of pomp and magnificence, so dear to the heart of King Sigismund, so trivial in the mind of Pope

John, was told out; three full Masses were celebrated; at the conclusion the Pope presented the King with a sword; and it was not until past high noon that the congregation dispersed. In thus timing his first public appearance at the Council of Constance for the High Mass on Christmas Day 1414, King Sigismund had concentrated on himself the full splendour of spiritual and secular significance.

Three days later, on the 28th December, Pierre d'Ailly preached one of those political sermons for which he was so celebrated. He took as his text half a verse from Saint Luke: 'There shall be signs in the sun and in the moon and in the stars'; and the words were significant. The sun and the moon as symbolising the Pope and the Emperor were an emblem of which Innocent the Third had been particularly fond, and with which all d'Ailly's hearers were well acquainted; but the Cardinal added a third member to the emblem as being foreshadowed in the Scripture, a member which was in the Council of Constance eventually to become stronger and more important than the other two. Who were these like stars appearing? These, said the Cardinal of Cambrai, are this sacred General Council in which the Church Universal is represented; the stars are the multitudinous variety of the ecclesiastical estates; they are placed in the firmament not only to assist by their additional light the sun and the moon, but also to influence them by their own manifold virtue.[1] The sermon, although it was not finished,[2] was a manifesto of the conciliar party, the chiefs of which were Gerson, D'Ailly, and Zabarella, thrown down before the Pope and the King of the Romans. That party held that a General Council represented the Church Universal, and was therefore entitled to exercise papal power and also the power of cardinals, bishops, and priests; the Pope was merely a member of the body of the Church, and was no more above the Church than the part can be above the whole; the General Council, on the other hand, could direct and moderate, could repress abuses of power, could depose the Pope, imprison him, and even put him to death.[3] Such were the views of the conciliar party, who now in the sermon of Pierre d'Ailly claimed scriptural authority to shine forth as the stars in heaven. It

---

[1] Hardt, i. 436-50.　　[2] Tschackert, Appendix, 47.　　[3] Gierke, 156-9.

REX SUPER GRAMMATICAM

was the conciliar party which became dominant in the Council, and which guided its destinies. For the present, however, it had not got the upper hand ; but it had already made trial of its strength with the Pope in the matter of John Hus, and it was now to make trial of its strength in the same matter with the King of the Romans.

The matter of the imprisonment of John Hus had to be settled between the King and the Council. Sigismund had threatened to break down the walls of the prison. The nobles of Bohemia wrote to him to complain that, whereas Hus had gone to Constance to clear himself and his country from the suspicion of heresy, he had been thrown into prison, before his case was heard or specified (*causa indicta et incognita*), in defiance of the safe-conduct granted him by the King. There were angry discussions on New Year's Day between the prelates and Sigismund. John the Twenty-third disclaimed all responsibility, and the King soon found that the Pope was powerless against the cardinals and the Council. Sigismund threatened to leave Constance and to abandon the Council to its own devices if his royal majesty was thus openly contemned ; but the prelates replied by pointing out that John Hus was strongly suspected of heresy, that heresy was a damnable crime against God and man, that a heretic who disseminated heresy was the worst of all heretics, and that the canon law forbad any faith to be kept with a heretic. Heresy in those days was regarded, it must be remembered, as a more hateful and dangerous crime than is anarchism in the present century. The King's safe conduct, it was pointed out, was *ultra vires* ; he had no jurisdiction in a spiritual case, and he could not shelter a heretic. Sigismund was obliged reluctantly to acknowledge the force of this reasoning ; but still there was the ugly fact that he had given Hus a safe-conduct, that he believed and that nearly every other layman believed, and that the nobles of Bohemia and Moravia to a man believed, that this was sufficient for the protection of John Hus, and that Sigismund would have to bear the odium of its breach. Finally the worshipful prelates used their last argument ; it was the same argument as the King's, the abandonment of the Council. If the Council, one of whose professed objects was the suppression of heresy was, not competent to deal with such cases, then they would abandon it altogether rather than be made a laughing-stock before all men; the King must choose between the Council and John Hus; if he insisted on the release of their prisoner, then the Council was at an end; if he wished the Council to proceed, then the prosecution of Hus must also proceed according to the spiritual law thereto applicable. Sigismund had no choice but to submit; if the Great Council fell through because he refused to give way on a point in which he was in the wrong, then not only would he become the jest of Europe, but he would have allowed one of the three great objects of his life to miscarry; he had got into a false position, and to get out of it he must abandon John Hus. He did so; but at the same time, he secured for the reformer the privilege of an open trial.

It is interesting to consider dispassionately the problem of John Hus, because it touches certain points of more modern thought. John Hus left Prague, as he boasted, without any safe-conduct, but there is no doubt that he depended on the royal promise to furnish one. He thought he was going to Constance for an academical disputation; he expected that the Council would engage in a theological debate, and that the learned fathers would calmly discuss his views as to the Church and church government. Hus set the Book above the Church, the written Word above Tradition, as the supreme authority; and he imagined that his position was defensible. He thought that the Council would debate the question on its merits, and would then impose their decision on the faithful as a law of belief; and he declared himself willing to accept their decision. But such was not the method of the old orthodoxy. 'To know what was of faith was not a question of speculation and argument, but of observation.' The Council could witness to the constant and universal belief of the Church, but it refused to go further and to add logical conclusions to the existing body of settled belief.[1] Hus utterly misunderstood the function of the Council.

Then again no man knew better than he did the temper of his adversaries, of Stephen Palec burning with zeal for the orthodox faith and Michael *de Causis* unscrupulous and

---

[1] Tyrrell, *Christianity as the Cross-Roads*, 23-47.

ready to take any unfair advantage; he knew that they regarded him as an heretic, and he must have known that it was most probable that they would accuse him of heresy. Had he complied with the wish of King Sigismund and entered Constance in his train, had he regarded his injunction and refused to say a word except in the royal presence, then, as the King said, perchance his affair would have taken another turn. But on both points Hus, of his own accord, disregarded the royal injunctions; he came to Constance and then, contrary to the wish of John of Chlum, he went to speak with the cardinals. He thus placed himself in their power, and they had to decide as to his liberation or detention.

It is at this point that the apparent hardship of Hus's case strikes us. We in England are wont to pride ourselves on the fact that a man is presumed to be innocent until he is proved to be guilty; and it appears to us as if Hus was at once presumed to be guilty and was imprisoned and denied the privilege of an advocate on the ground that he was a heretic. But in England a man is not treated as innocent, whatever the presumption may be, when once a *prima facie* case has been made out against him; he is then either detained or is required to give security for his appearance as an ' under trial ' prisoner. Now, as soon as Hus was before the cardinals, the wily Michael *de Causis* had certain allegations ready. The first charge was that John Hus had sanctioned communion in two kinds, which was actually practised in Prague. This, however, was an innovation since Hus's departure, for which he was in no way responsible. It was also alleged that Hus had taught that the material bread remained after consecration. This was false; but there was something in the charge. Hus had coquetted with Wyclif's doctrine, as had Stephen Palec and Stanislas von Znaim,[1] in his early days, and had thus given a handle to his adversaries, though he had speedily renounced this heresy and had become a staunch defender of the orthodox doctrine. But there was against him the fact that he was an open admirer of Wyclif, who had denied transubstantiation; and there was the further fact that he was a realist and that the denial of transubstantiation was, so it seemed to the nominalists,

[1] Hefele, vii. 34.

the logical consequence of Realism. Hus might reply that he was content with the doctrine which had satisfied Saint Anselm, or that he was ready to believe that a miracle was worked whenever the elements were consecrated; his judges had not heard him on this point, and to them it seemed that a convinced realist must believe as Wyclif believed. The opinion was, in fact, universal, as the writings of Dietrich von Niem show,[1] that the Wyclifites in Prague were heretical on the doctrine of transubstantiation; and it was only natural that this heresy should be attributed to the influence of the leading Wyclifite, John Hus.

Furthermore, Michael *de Causis* had made certain extracts from Hus's treatise on the Church, and the reformer had admitted that these extracts were from his book. They might be garbled, and some might be susceptible of explanation; but taken as they stood, with the meaning which Michael assigned to them, they required explanation, and appeared to back up the charge of heresy. It was alleged that no priest in sin could validly administer the sacrament—a point which Hus denied—and also that laymen could administer. Then, again, Michael said that Hus taught that the Church did not simply mean the Pope, cardinals, archbishops, bishops, and clergy; whereas on this matter there were pillars of orthodoxy, such as Gerson and D'Ailly, who held the same view; and that the Church ought not to hold any property, the Donation of Constantine having been the source of much evil. This was a point open to much argument. The proposition that the Church would have no power if the Pope and all the clergy were in a state of deadly sin, was certainly of merely academical importance.

It was more to the point when Hus was accused of contemning the sentence of excommunication and of holding that the barons in Bohemia could institute priests. He was further charged with defending the articles of Wyclif, which had been condemned in the Earthquake Council; but his accusers showed the cloven hoof when they alleged that Hus was the cause of the Teutons being driven from Bohemia and of the attacks on the local clergy.[2] Hus's judges, being strangers to Bohemia, were

[1] Erler, 200.   [2] Hefele, vii. 71.

REX SUPER GRAMMATICAM 275

naturally unable to see that it was as patriot, no less than as Reformer, that Hus had offended. Thus, setting aside those points which Hus might reasonably hope to maintain, still until the other charges were met and explained, there was certainly a strong *prima facie* case against John Hus, sufficient to justify his detention in custody. There was, therefore, nothing unusual or unjust in his imprisonment; on the other hand, the unusual features in his trial for heresy were that he was allowed to see the witnesses against him and that he was allowed to speak publicly in his own defence. He was answerable for his own misfortunes, and he found more favour than was customarily granted in those days to men accused of the fearful crime of heresy.

Jean Gerson, the Chancellor of the University of Paris, had also entered the lists against Hus; he had drawn up a catalogue of twenty heterodoxies which he had discovered in Hus's treatise *De Ecclesia*; this was sent to Constance and shown to Hus. ' O that God would give me time to defeat the falsehoods of the Parisian Chancellor,' wrote the Reformer,[1] who complained that he had much ado in his prison to answer all the charges made against him. From Bohemia itself came bitter enemies and indiscreet friends. A Bohemian bishop, who gave himself out to be King Wenzel's confessor, appeared and announced that the King had never encouraged either Hus or the Wyclifites, but that he had sent Hus to the Council in order that his doctrines might be examined and an authoritative pronouncement made. About the same time came Cristanus Brachadicz, who said that he was King Wenzel's astronomer; he was a pronounced utraquist, taking his stand on the text, ' Except ye eat the flesh of the Son of Man and drink His blood, ye have not life in yourselves.' He was promptly clapped in prison.[2]

Prelates and envoys with their followers were rapidly filling the free city on the Boden See. The English contingent numbered eight hundred; that from France must have been at least a thousand. There was, however, much to be settled before a second session could be held, and this was done at the congregations. On the 29th December King Sigismund held a general congregation, at which the Pope and all the cardinals and prelates appeared; he told them of his negotiations with

[1] Palacky (*Doc.*), 97.   [2] Pulka, 15.

Popes Benedict and Gregory and that he had promised to meet the former at Nice in June, to confer with him and the King of Aragon ; he expected the Legates of both Popes at the Council, and he asked that some cardinals should be appointed to confer with him on the business to be done. This was a sufficient indication that he did not mean necessarily to work hand-in-glove with Pope John ; and the cardinals were appointed accordingly. A week later, on the 4th January, as the Legates of Pope Gregory were daily expected, another congregation was held to decide on the manner of their reception. There was a stormy discussion. Pope John and his partisans were indignant at the thought of receiving Cardinal Giovanni in his red hat ; they demanded that an audience be refused to his colleague, the Patriarch of Constantinople ; they protested against the grant of safe conducts to the Legates of Benedict the Thirteenth ; they appealed to the authority of the Council of Pisa which had declared both Gregory and Benedict to be heretic and schismatic. But King Sigismund and Cardinal d'Ailly were full well aware that the essence of politics is compromise, and they proposed that the Legates of both Popes should be received with the honours which they demanded, and their opinion was adopted. Pope John was again defeated and felt the ground crumbling beneath his feet.

At this time, and for some weeks later the members hoped and believed that the Council would have finished its work by Easter. Suspicion was rife that the impecunious King was being bribed to uphold the Council of Pisa and Pope John the Twenty-third ;[1] but Sigismund was more honest than men thought. On the 8th January arrived the legates of Pope Benedict, and they were at first scornfully entreated by the King, because they were not armed with full powers for all purposes. They were received in full congregation on the 12th, and announced that their master was agreeable to the proposed meeting at Nice. But not on that day, nor until long afterward, did they receive a definite answer from King or Council. On the 17th January came the ambassadors from Pope Gregory. At their head was the bearded Prince Louis, Count Palatine ; Giovanni Domenici, Cardinal of Ragusa, wore his red hat, and

[1] Pulka, 15.

the Patriarch of Constantinople a black hat ; they were followed by the Bishops of Speier, Worms, and Verden. The ambassadors presented a Bull, granted by Pope Gregory, empowering them to treat ; and the Elector declared that although Gregory would in no way acknowledge the authority of Pope John, he would adopt any ' way ' approved by the Council to procure the union of the Church ; and the Elector added that in any case he and the prelates would hold Gregory to the judgment of the Council. They were ordered to present their proposals in writing, and the hearing was adjourned until next day, when the Elector gave in a memorial signifying their acquiescence in the ' way of cession,' and their readiness to submit to the decision of the Council. Pope John approved this memorial if it referred only to the abdication of Popes Gregory and Benedict, but if they meant anything further by it, then they ought to explain themselves better. The Pope was absent from several of the congregations and assemblies held under the seal of secrecy ; but he was perfectly acquainted with all that passed, for every night prelates came to see him, and he had very little difficulty in inducing them, if necessary under an absolution, to disclose all that had happened. He saw perfectly well that the King of the Romans and the most influential of the cardinals were hostile to him, and he could only await events.[1]

Although he was out of favour, Pope John the Twenty-third was nevertheless acknowledged by the Council as the only legitimate Pope ; on the 6th January 1415 he had solemnly blessed the people from his palace, and on the 1st February he celebrated a still more important function, the Canonisation of Saint Brigitta, the Swedish saint who was a contemporary of Catharine of Siena and who died in 1373. She had instituted an Order, that of the Holy Saviour, of monks and nuns, and had foretold the death of Pope Urban the Fifth ; her revelations were in high repute, and her life in Rome was pious and charitable ; she had been on pilgrimage to Jerusalem ;[2] she was the mother of Saint Catharine of Sweden.[3] She had already been canonised on the 7th October 1391 by Pope Boniface the Ninth during the Schism, and the Swedes now desired a renewal,

[1] Hardt, ii. 389 ; iv. 36-41.   [2] Hefele, vii. 80.   [3] *C. E.*, ii. 782.

278 POPE JOHN THE TWENTY-THIRD

under the authority of the œcumenical Council, of the universal precept. Ambassadors from Sweden, Denmark, and Norway appeared and pressed their demand on the grounds of her piety, her pilgrimage, her revelations and the abundant miracles wrought during her life and after her death; they produced a numerous troop of doctors and licentiates who swore on the great altar to the reality of the miracles. A Danish archbishop after celebrating Mass, elevated a silver statue of the Saint, who was canonised by the Council; the *Te Deum* was sung, the bells rang out, and the prelates enjoyed a splendid feast. Subsequently Brigitta was canonised a third time by Pope Martin the Fifth in Florence four years later.[1] On the same day, it being Candlemas, Pope John in the presence of the cardinals, the King of the Romans, and the Grand Master of Rhodes, sprinkled the tapers with holy water, read five collects over them, and blessed them; his chaplain threw the tapers down to the crowd, who were overjoyed to get sixty pounds of wax, and fell over one another with great laughter in their haste to secure the booty. After refection the Pope blessed other tapers and sent them to the houses of the lords spiritual and temporal, so that a hundred pounds weight of wax was distributed that day.[2]

Sigismund had fully decided to throw over the Pope. At first they had been friendly and there was some talk of the Pope lending the King money, but John, already fearful for his dignity, did not wish to lose his treasure also, and declined.[3] Sigismund felt that he was master of the situation. Occasionally he went too far and had to draw back. On one occasion, for example, he espied a certain Martin, who said that he came from the Duke of Milan. Sigismund disbelieved him, threatened to hang him, and cast the man into prison. At this high-handed action there was a general outcry, and the King was obliged to release his prisoner.[4] Sigismund soon learned to respect the opinion of the Council.

Matters were drawing to a crisis. Every one felt that the only way of healing the Great Schism was that all three Popes should either abdicate or be deposed, but no one ventured publicly to bring forward this proposition. The two cardinals,

[1] Richental, 53; Hardt, iv. 707. [2] Richental, 54.
[3] Mueller, iv. 193. [4] Martene (*A. C.*), vii. 1410.

REX SUPER GRAMMATICAM 279

Fillastre and D'Ailly, were working together, as they had worked in 1406 when they defended Pope Benedict the Thirteenth, and as they had worked quite recently when they crossed swords with the Italian party in December. Guillaume Fillastre now mounted the breach and openly declared that it was the duty of Pope John to resign ; he urged that the more firmly John was persuaded that he was the true Pope, the more incumbent was it on him as a good shepherd to make this sacrifice for his flock. A copy of the speech was sent to Sigismund, who sent abstracts to the nations. The Pope heard and was furious.[1] But the die was now cast. The Cardinal of Cambrai now advocated the same course ; although the Council of Pisa, he argued, had been legitimately convoked, and although to the election of Pope John no exception could be taken, yet they had to face the fact that neither of the other two Popes had resigned, and that each had a considerable obedience, and that action in case of all three was therefore advisable ; in counselling Pope John to abdicate they did not wish to derogate from the authority of the Council of Pisa, nor to put him on a level with heretics and schismatics, but to confer on him the high distinction of doing honour to Christendom and of showing his own humility by exposing the obstinacy of his rivals. At the same time both cardinals expressed the opinion that the Council, as representing the Church universal, had the power to depose even a legitimate Pope if peace could not otherwise be restored to the Church. The partisans of Pope John might vigorously protest, but the reasoning of the cardinals found favour with the influential. The two French cardinals and the Florentine Zabarella, all of whom Pope John had promoted, and the Bishop of Salisbury, whom he had desired to raise to the purple, were four of the Pope's most vigorous ecclesiastical opponents, and the latter two were high in favour with King Sigismund. Opinions on the proposal of cession were so divided that it seemed as if it would be necessary to settle it by vote ; and then the questions arose as to who were entitled to vote, and as to how the votes were to be reckoned. This matter soon came up for determination.

Prelates of every degree, dukes, counts, and ambassadors,

[1] Tschackert, 199.

each with his retinue of knights and squires, came thronging into Constance so that by the middle of February the little city was full to overflowing. If King Sigismund was elated by the arrival of a magnificent Milanese embassy from Filippo Maria, the heart of Pope John was no less gladdened by the coming of Friedrich of Austria and John of Nassau. The Archbishop of Mainz, first Elector of the Empire, had ridden into Constance, clad in mail under his scarlet tunic,[1] at the head of eight counts and six hundred horsemen; a faithful friend of the Pope, he was like him at heart rather a soldier than a churchman. Very martial in his tastes was John of Nassau; he had not been long in Constance before men were whispering the large sum he had paid one of the burghers for the favour of his wife; he lodged at the Sign of the Sun, near the church of Saint Paul.[2] Duke Friedrich rode in, on the Friday after Candlemas, on the same day as the Dukes of Bavaria and Lorraine, the Burggraf of Nuernberg and others, at the head of twelve counts, Oswald von Wolkenstein among the number, and six hundred horsemen;[3] he abode at the Kreuzlingen Abbey, and had delayed his coming as long as possible, because of the affairs of Trient, and of the enmity of King Sigismund, who had summoned him, contrary to the custom of the Tirol, to do homage at Constance. The King was obliged to acknowledge that Friedrich was entitled to receive investiture within his own duchy, but he remained displeased at his wishes being thwarted. Oswald von Wolkenstein was the agent of the League of the Adige, and was in close attendance on Sigismund; the vanguard of the nobles had arrived, and tried to persuade the King to summon the Duke before the Council.[4] Trouble was brewing; Friedrich expected a stormy time at Constance, but he little knew all the woe that was in store for him. The Pope meantime felt himself safer when once his sworn protector was within hail. He had also a powerful ally in Bernhard, Markgraf of Baden, to whom he had, out of pure generosity, as he phrased it, *de nostra mera liberalitate*, given the sum of sixteen thousand florins.[5]

Early in February the question of voting came up for discussion. The Councils of Pisa and of Rome had allowed

---

[1] Martene (*A. C.*), vii. 1410.   [2] Richental, 43; *A. F.*, 34.
[3] Richental, 49.   [4] *B. W.*, 260.   [5] Hardt, ii. 148-9.

professors and doctors in theology to vote ;[1] but Pope John, relying on the large number of his Italian prelates, was anxious to revert to the earlier practice and to restrict the privilege to bishops and abbots and their superiors in rank ; he desired especially to exclude all secular votes. But here again he was opposed by the French cardinals. Pierre d'Ailly pointed out that the composition of councils had varied at different times, and that on some occasions all Christians had been allowed to vote ; he pleaded more especially for the doctors in theology as being more than others competent to form a right opinion ; he also thought that all doctors of the civil and of the canon law should vote; and finally he proposed to include all rulers or their proctors or ambassadors as being interested in the extinction of the Schism in their respective realms. Fillastre, Cardinal of Saint Mark, followed in the same strain ; he would allow even priests and deacons, who came in contact with the people and knew the actual needs of Christendom, for an ignorant king or bishop, said he, is no better than a crowned ass. This was felt to be too republican, but the opinion of the Cardinal of Cambrai carried the day. It was agreed that all doctors should be admitted to the Council, as well as all the secular representatives of kings, princes, republics, towns, and academies, but the secular voters were not to intervene in matters of the faith.[2] Pope John felt that it was wellnigh impossible for him to have any influence over such a motley crew. Worse, however, lay behind.

For the last fortnight there had been heated argument and discussion as to whether voting in the Council was to be by heads or by nations ;[3] and on the 6th and 7th February the all-important question of how the votes were to be reckoned came before the congregation. The Pope desired that the ancient custom of voting by heads should be retained. The Italian clergy were far more numerous than the others and were, for the most part, devoted to him ; he had, moreover, created fifty chamberlains, or house-chaplains, each of whom was entitled to vote. If the votes were counted by heads he had a reasonable hope of securing a majority. But from the first the clergy at the Council had divided themselves into nations and

[1] Hefele, vii. 83.   [2] Hardt, ii. 224-5.   [3] Pulka, 14.

the different nations deliberated apart. The Italian nation sat in the refectory of the Dominican Monastery. Besides Italians, all the east of Europe, Turks, Bosnians, and Tartars, were included in this nation. The French nation sat in another hall of the same convent. The Germans, including Bohemians, Hungarians, the Scandinavian nations, Poles, Russians, and Flemish, sat in the Franciscan convent. So, too, did the English nation, which included not only Scots and Irishmen, but also any stray Arabs, Persians, Medes, Egyptians, Ninevites, Ethiopians, and men from the kingdom of Prester John, but which, after all, was the smallest nation of the four. Later on, when the Spaniards arrived, they formed a fifth nation and sat in the convent of the Austin friars. The division into nations had therefore been in full swing for upwards of three months.[1] The system of voting by nations found favour with the French cardinals for it was the system adopted in their own University of Paris. The English and the Germans meeting in the same building were able to confer together, and Hallam, Bishop of Salisbury, proposed to the Germans that the Council should adopt the system of voting which prevailed in the universities. In the congregation on the 6th February members of these two nations rose and protested against individual voting; they proposed that a certain number of deputies should be appointed by each nation and that the ultimate decision should rest with them. The French next day gave in their adhesion to this plan. The nations were to deliberate apart, and in his own nation every member had the right to speak, and the greater part of the discussion would take place there, and would result in resolutions of the nations. Each nation was to be under its own president, who was to be changed once a month. When the nations had decided on their resolutions, their deputies were to meet in a general congregation, and were to discuss and settle matters. In this way difficulties would be smoothed away, and the Council in its general session would merely add the weight of its authority to what had been already decided between the deputies of the nations.[2] There was no definite decree, but the

[1] Richental, 50-2.
[2] Hardt, i. 157-60; ii. 230-1; iv. 40; v. 67; Finke (F.), 256-7; Creighton, i. 319.

REX SUPER GRAMMATICAM

constitution of the Council was thus settled by the three nations, and the Italians were powerless to resist. The great defect of this arrangement was that it ignored the Cardinals; in the all-important preliminary deliberations they were, as a body, left out of account altogether. The English and Teuton nations were eager for reform; the French nation would follow the lead of its two cardinals; on any important question, therefore, there would be three votes to one against Pope John. The Pope understood this and recognised that his doom in the Council was sealed. The constitution by nations was settled, and each nation assumed a character of its own. The Teutons were known for their straightforwardness and firm constancy; the French for their distinction, their erudition and their gift of exposition; the English, for their candour and sagacity; while the Italian nation was distinguished for their subtlety, their craftiness, and their persistency. Such, at least, is the judgment of a German professor.[1]

About this time a covert attack was made on the character of Pope John by some anonymous Italian who published a memoir containing a variety of disgraceful charges. The Pope was alarmed, and consulted some of his most trusted cardinals. 'It would never have happened,' said he, 'if I had only remained in Italy.'[2] He protested his innocence of the graver charges but acknowledged that his private life had not been blameless; he had, however, never been guilty of heresy, the one sin for which a Pope could be deposed; and he thought it might be advisable to make a clean breast of his other offences before the Council. But the English and German nations resolved that it was better to avoid the scandal which a public inquiry would entail; they thought that the anonymous memoir should be dismissed with silent contempt; and this course was adopted by a congregation of the nations.[3] The serpent was thereby scotched, not killed.

Thus far everything had gone most propitiously for King Sigismund and most unfavourably for Pope John. They distrusted each other; they were on the brink of open enmity. The Pope felt that he was the abler and more intellectual man; he looked with contempt upon Sigismund's pretensions; he

[1] Wessenberg, ii. 117-8.   [2] Mueller, iv. 192.   [3] Hardt, ii. 391-2; iv. 41.

regarded his adversary as an illiterate Teuton. A ludicrous incident is related which strengthened the Pope's belief and which made the King for the time being a laughing-stock. None of the Electors knew Latin, and the King of the Romans, though voluble, was shaky. Sigismund had been indefatigable in his attendance at the congregations, and at one of them he exhorted those present to work with their will for the extinction of the accursed Schism. 'Date operam,' said he, 'ut illa nefanda schisma eradicetur.' Then was heard the piping voice of a querulous cardinal. ' Domine, schisma est neutri generis.' Great was the wrath of King Sigismund. ' I am the King of the Romans,' he exclaimed, ' and superior to grammar.' ' Ego sum Rex Romanorum et super grammaticam.' It was not a joke ; it was meant in earnest. It was the Cardinal of Piacenza who had presumed to correct the Lord of the Holy Roman Empire, and he backed up what he had said by quoting Priscian and others. Sigismund inquired who these authorities were, and was told that they were learned grammarians. ' And am I not Emperor and above them ? cannot I make a new grammar ? ' said the monarch, and turning to the cardinal with his ready wit, he added, ' Placentia, Placentia, you may please others, but you do not please me, for you make me of less account than Priscian,' and everybody laughed at the unlucky cardinal. The story may be a fable, but *se non e vero e ben trovato*; it shows the popular estimate of Sigismund's learning. Mr. Wylie [1] says that the earliest form in which he has been able to trace the story dates from about eighty years after the King's death ; but there are many who, with Carlyle, always remember Sigismund as the *Rex super Grammaticam*.[2]

[1] Wylie (C.), 18.   [2] Menzel, ii. 157.

CHAPTER XVI

THE QUESTION OF RESIGNATION

THE universal desire of the Council now was that all three Popes should voluntarily resign their dignities, and there seemed a reasonable prospect that this might be accomplished. Pope Gregory was ready to abdicate provided his rivals did the like and were not allowed to preside at the Council. Pope Benedict had said that he was willing to meet the King of the Romans at Nice, and this meeting was recognised as having the same end in view. Cardinal Fillastre proposed that the Council, or at any rate its commission, should adjourn to Avignon, and that a place should be arranged for the meeting of the two Popes, John and Benedict, and the two kings, Sigismund and Ferdinand. The Italian nation had stood out as long as possible on the authority of the Council of Pisa, but had now become convinced that the pressure of general opinion was too great, and that the inevitable must be faced. Pope John saw that he must give way, and resolved to do so with the best grace possible. The deputies of the nations visited him and in vague and general terms hinted at his resignation. To their delight he received their proposal most cheerfully and immediately convened a general congregation to carry it into effect. It was the 16th February. The King of the Romans was present, and all the prelates, princes, and deputies of the nations. The Pope called on Cardinal Zabarella to read the form of resignation which His Holiness himself had prepared. The Florentine, who was honest as well as eloquent, and who was himself strongly in favour of the resignation, was a favourite with the Pope as well as with the King. Zabarella read forth the following ' formula of cession.'

' Our most holy Lord the Pope here present, although in no way obliged thereto by vow, oath, or promise, yet for the repose of the Christian people, has proposed and resolved of his own free will and accord to give peace to the Church even by resignation, provided that Peter de Luna and Angelo Corario, who were condemned and deposed at the Council of Pisa as heretics and schismatics, also legally and sufficiently resign their pretended popedoms, and that in manner, circumstance and time to be forthwith declared and concluded by a treaty forthwith to be made to this effect by our Lord the Pope, or his proctors, and the deputies of the nations.'[1] This formula was considered next day by the deputies, who found it to be vague and needlessly offensive. The Pope thereon prepared another, which was declared to be even less acceptable. Not wishing to offend him by repeated criticism, the deputies themselves prepared a 'formula of cession,' which the King presented to the Pope. But John disliked this as being couched in almost the same expressions as Pope Gregory had used; he rejected it, and also a second which was proposed to him. In these negotiations the remainder of the month wore away.

Arrivals still continued. Louis of Bavaria Ingolstadt, brother of the beautiful Isabella of France, came at the head of an embassy from Charles the Sixth, and his arrival cheered the Pope. With him, on the 5th March, the Archbishop of Reims and the Bishops of Evreux and Carcasonne, accompanied by two hundred and fifty horsemen, appeared at the gates of Constance. They requested audience in a general session; it was granted them in a general congregation on the 11th March. The Bishop of Carcasonne commenced with a few pleasing generalities, but he proceeded to uphold the action of the Council of Pisa, to demand that the intrigues of those who had there been justly condemned should be baffled, and to suggest that the present Council should be adjourned to some more fitting place. This, of course, meant that the Council was to be moved from Teuton soil to France, and King Sigismund would not hear of any such suggestion; the embassy had to submit, but they had poured balm into the heart of Pope John and were manifestly adverse to the King of the Romans.

The King of Poland also sent two ambassadors who brought two harangues, for the Pope and the King, exhorting them to

[1] Hardt, ii. 232-3.

THE QUESTION OF RESIGNATION 287

restore peace to Christendom and to Poland, and reminding them that it was at the persuasion of the Pope that the King of Poland and the Grand Duke of Lithuania had laid down their arms when they might have conquered the Teutonic Order, in the hope that the Council would make a just settlement between them and their adversaries. But the most important embassy which arrived at this time was that from the University of Paris, with the Chancellor, Jean Charlier de Gerson, who was empowered both by the King and by the province of Sens, at its head. This celebrated man soon became, and was known as, the 'soul of the Council.' He represented the King of France and also the University of Paris ; but he fought for his own convictions. The convictions of Pierre d'Ailly were nearly the same as those of his celebrated pupil ; but throughout the Council the Cardinal of Cambrai stood by the sacred college ; hence there was occasionally a divergence in the line of action taken by the two theologians. The French embassy included Dachery, Jean de Spars, Gentian, better known to posterity as the Religieux de Saint-Denys, and Jean de Templis. They were welcomed with great effusion by Pope John, who, however, soon found that he could not count on their unconditional assistance. King Sigismund, on the other hand, was delighted at their accession to his forces. He introduced them to the German nation,[1] explained what had already been done, and hoped that they would work with the English and the Teutons to push through the ' way of cession ' in the face of the Italians. The ambassadors answered that they were perfectly ready to join in any just and reasonable measures, and that they thoroughly approved the ' way of cession ' ; they complimented the King on his energy and diligence, and trusted that he would continue the same, seeing that without his presence and protection all their toil would be in vain.

A new ' formula of cession ' was now prepared for presentation to the Pope, and it was rather more rigorous in its terms than those which he had already rejected. But patience was becoming exhausted. The German nation insisted that the Council was the sovereign judge, that the ' way of cession ' was the most efficacious, and that Pope John might be ordered

[1] Hefele, vii. 85.

or threatened or even compelled by the secular arm to adopt this means of ending the Great Schism. On the advice of the ambassadors of the University of Paris, the Pope was to be required not merely to promise, but to vow and swear that he would resign.[1]

Next day, the 1st of March, a general congregation was held at the palace occupied by the Pope. The King of the Romans, the Patriarch of Antioch, who was president of the French nation, and the deputies of the four nations, were present. The Patriarch presented the formula to the Pope, and asked him to read it. John did so, accepted it with every appearance of cheerfulness, and then read it aloud. It ran thus :—

' I, Pope John the Twenty-third, in order to secure the repose of Christendom, declare and promise, vow and swear to God, to the Church, and to this holy Council, freely and spontaneously to give peace to the Church by means of my own resignation, and to do and carry this into effect in accordance with the determination of the present Council, if and when Peter de Luna and Angelo Corario, called Benedict the Thirteenth and Gregory the Twelfth in their respective obediences, shall similarly either in person or by their legal proctors resign their pretended popedoms : and even in any case of resignation or death or otherwise, if my resignation may give peace to the Church and extinguish the Schism.'[2] The concluding words of the formula are not free from ambiguity. The Pope, to the joy of all, read it through. He was immediately thanked by King Sigismund, by the cardinals, by the deputies and by the members of the University ; a *Te Deum* was sung ; and the second general session of the Council was announced for the next day.

On the 2nd March 1415 was held the second general session of the Council. Pope John celebrated the Mass, and at its conclusion seated himself in front of the great altar, facing the congregation. The Patriarch of Antioch handed him the formula of cession which had been accepted the day before. The Pope read it in a loud voice. When he came to the words ' I vow and swear,' he rose from his seat, knelt before the altar, placed his hand on his breast, and added, ' I promise to fulfil

---

[1] Hardt, ii. 236-7 ; Lenfant (*C.*), i. 112-3.   [2] Hardt, ii. 240.

THE QUESTION OF RESIGNATION

this.' Then he resumed his seat and concluded the formula. Sigismund, ever impulsive and theatrical, took off his crown and threw himself at the pontiff's feet, kissed them, and thanked him most humbly for his action. The Patriarch of Antioch, in the name of the Council, did the like. A *Te Deum* was sung, and all the church bells in the town broke out into a peal of joyous music. The congregation was in tears, for every one believed that now at last the Great Schism was to be ended.

But Fate had been dragging the Pope on, and he now began to reflect and to repent. Two days later, in a general congregation held in the Dominican monastery, from which John Hus had just been transferred, the King of the Romans promised the ambassadors of Benedict the Thirteenth and of the King of Aragon to come to Nice as they desired in the month of June; and in order to treat with the King and the rival Pope it was deemed necessary that the conditional promise of Pope John should be ratified beyond recall. He was asked by the prelates in a general congregation to promulgate a Bull notifying his resignation to Christendom; but the Pope flared up at the suggestion and abused those who had made it. Sigismund then approached Pope John, who proved more tractable and promulgated the desired Bull [1] on the 7th March. But even this did not satisfy the King, who wanted to make sure that the Pope should not change his mind when he himself was no longer there to control him. On the 9th March accordingly, in a general congregation, John was urged to appoint Sigismund and certain prelates as his proctors to carry through the abdication; but the Pope, who was backed up by the Italian nation, angrily refused to place himself thus unconditionally in the hands of his adversaries. This refusal aroused the King's suspicions, and he ordered that the lake and the city gates should be watched night and day to prevent any one leaving Constance.[2]

Next day Pope John tried to reconcile the King by presenting him with the Golden Rose.[3] This was the greatest compliment which the Pope could pay to a Christian monarch, and Sigismund received the trophy with expressions of thankful respect; he carried the Rose in procession through the town, and

---

[1] Hardt, iv. 53-4.   [2] *Ibid.* 54.   [3] Cf. *In the Days of the Councils*, 402.

deposited it in the Cathedral as an offering to Our Lady. The Pope entertained the King and the princes, ecclesiastical and secular, at a grand banquet. But Sigismund's suspicions, once aroused, were not thus to be allayed. The next day (11th March) he called a congregation and broached the subject of a new Pope for the Church, thus signifying in the most pointed way that he no longer considered John as pontiff. John of Nassau, Archbishop of Mainz, arose in wrath and declared that unless Pope John the Twenty-third were re-elected, he would recognise no Pope. Unhappily the worldly character of this prelate lent no weight to his protest, and the only result of his interference was that the members of the assembly began discussing together the disgraceful charges which had been previously made against the Pope, which John hoped were now buried in oblivion. Pope John and King Sigismund were now at open and undisguised enmity.

King Sigismund with Pope John the Twenty-third made precisely the same mistake as the French prelates had made eight years earlier with Pope Benedict the Thirteenth.[1] More tact and less brusqueness might possibly on each occasion have led to a different result, but unfeeling and inconsiderate haste was fatal to the smooth conduct of negotiation. The absurdly premature proposal of the 11th March was a wanton insult, intended and received as such. The King and the Pope continued to meet, but all decorum of intercourse was at an end between them. John made no effort to conceal his real opinion of his adversary, but called him a barbarian, a fool, and a drunkard. He twitted the King with his attempt to borrow money of him, and Sigismund indignantly denied the accusation. 'You Italians,' he said, ' seem to think you are beyond everybody in knowledge and power, but I consider you the dregs of the earth.' ' And do you suppose,' the Pope retorted, ' that you are now sitting alongside me because you are a Luxemburger ? I tell you that if you were not the King of the Romans you would be sitting at my feet ; it is to the King of the Romans that I grant this honour, not to the mere barbarian.' All hope of a peaceful settlement had disappeared ; there was open strife between the two heads of Christendom ;

[1] Cf. *In the Days of the Councils*, 257.

THE QUESTION OF RESIGNATION 291

each was ready to get the better of the other by force or by guile. At times, however, they managed to treat each other with outward respect.

It was a critical situation, and it is important to comprehend exactly how matters stood at this time. Pope John had promised to resign; King Sigismund had promised to go to Nice with a view to the resignation of Pope Benedict. The Pope proposed that he also should go to Nice, either with the entire Council or with its representatives, in order that he might resign there. Cardinals d'Ailly and Fillastre supported this suggestion; they were anxious that the Pope should resign, but at the same time they were dignitaries of the Church and careful of the dignity of its head; they were the moderate party, half-way between the English nation, who wanted to imprison the Pope, and the Italians, who desired that John alone should be recognised as universal Pontiff. But Sigismund would not trust the Pope off German soil. The King was backed up by the Archbishops of Milan and Riga, by Jean Mauroux, the Patriarch of Antioch, and, above all, by Robert Hallam, Bishop of Salisbury. The Bishop was credited with the desire to burn Pope John, and with having said that he himself was his superior; what he actually did say was that the Council was superior to the Pope. Pope John, beside his prelates from central and southern Italy, who dwelt in 'the Valley of Jehoshaphat,' was supported by the warlike Archbishop of Mainz, the man who had made and had unmade King Rupert, by the Markgraf of Baden, and above all by Friedrich of the Tirol. The Duke, however, knew that he was an object of suspicion to King Sigismund, and he kept ostensibly away from the papal palace, alleging that he had nothing to do with Baldassare Cossa or his money. But his devotion to Pope John was well known.

Under these circumstances the Pope saw no help for himself in Constance; beside which, he was constantly ill. The weather during the whole winter had been atrocious; winds had been blowing from opposite quarters; there had been only three fine days from the autumn to the spring.[1] The rain had been so abundant and continuous that the rivers had overflowed their banks and the fields were under water. Constance itself

[1] *Religieux*, v. 478.

was enveloped in a thick mist; and Pope John, accustomed to the dry cold of Bologna, was continually indisposed; he was attacked by gout induced by five years of comparative inactivity following on a strenuous life, and was unable to get about as usual. He contemplated flight; and he hoped that the Council, being thus deprived of its head, would break up, and that he would be a free man once more. He had a guarantee that he was free to leave the city when he pleased, although this merely contemplated his quitting Constance when his work and that of the Council was finished. He knew that the King had set guards on the lake-front, on the walls, and on the gates. He determined to try if it were possible to leave Constance. The man whom he chose to make the attempt was one of his oldest and most trusted friends. Cardinal Petrus Stefanescus Hannibaldus, sprung from an old Roman family, had been protonotary in the court of Pope Boniface the Ninth when Baldassare Cossa was private chamberlain there; he had lately returned from Rome which he had won back to Pope John from Queen Joanna the Second of Naples.[1] The Cardinal tried to leave Constance, and was stopped at one of the city gates. It was as the Pope had thought; open flight was impossible; a disguise was necessary. John called a congregation in his palace, and bitterly reproached the magistrates of Constance with their faithlessness; but they threw the blame for the breach of their guarantee entirely on the King.

Next day, the 15th March, Sigismund prepared his counterblast. He assembled a congregation of the French, English, and German nations and explained that he had posted the guards on the advice of certain cardinals. John of Nassau had left the Council, and there had been several cases of prelates secretly following his example. It was represented that some of these had left because they were too poor to afford the cost of living, and it was agreed that such cases should be helped from a common fund.[2] The deputies present then resolved that the Pope should be requested to appoint proctors, the King of the Romans and certain prelates, to carry out his resignation; he was but a man, they said, and might alter his mind at the

---

[1] Ciaconius, ii. 723; *vid. sup.* p. 254.   [2] Martene (*A. C.*), vii. 1411.

THE QUESTION OF RESIGNATION 293

instigation of the devil;[1] they were further of opinion that he should promise himself not to leave, nor to permit any one else to leave, the Council until the union of the Church under one head had been accomplished.[2] Jean Mauroux, Patriarch of Antioch, conveyed the resolution to the Pope. This prelate was now leader of the French nation and high in favour with King Sigismund. Pierre d'Ailly, on the other hand, had taken no part in a general session for a month past, in protest against the manner in which the influence of the college of cardinals was being effaced by that of the nations.[3] The mysterious silence observed by him and by Guillaume Fillastre was held to be suspicious, and they were distrusted by the English and German nations. Pope John assembled a congregation at his palace on the 16th March, and in reply to the resolution of the nations, he promised not to dissolve the Council until the Schism was extinct, but he refused to appoint proctors on the ground that he was quite ready to effect his resignation in person and would prefer to do so in presence of his rival, Pope Benedict the Thirteenth, at Nice. In this resolve he was supported by the Cardinals d'Ailly and Zabarella, who had reasons for believing that Benedict would not resign otherwise than in person.[4] But the English and the Teutons expressed their discontent;[5] they did not trust the Pope.

The difference of opinion between the nations was accentuated in an assembly held at the Franciscan cloister next day, the 17th March. The English and German nations again insisted on the absolute necessity for the appointment of proctors; but the French, who appeared to think that these two nations were taking the conduct of the Council entirely into their own hands, stood out and demanded time for reflection. The Italians tried to profit by the dissension by sending five cardinals to draw the French to their own way of thinking; and Pope John complained openly that he and his friends were no longer safe in Constance.[6]

Tuesday, the 19th March, was a day long remembered for its manifold disputes and discussions. The English nation began by demanding in the presence of the King of the Romans that

[1] Schwab, 505. [2] Hardt, iv. 55-6. [3] *Vid. sup.* p. 282.
[4] Valois, iv. 281. [5] Hardt, iv. 56. [6] *Ibid.* 57.

the Pope be forthwith taken into custody; and John was persuaded that, but for the opposition of the French, this course would actually have been adopted. Sigismund had heard how the Italians had been tampering with the French; taking the English and German deputies and his own council with him, he marched off to the French nation at the Dominican monastery and presented to them the resolution taken by the English and Germans demanding that the Pope should forthwith appoint proctors to perform his resignation. The French nation represented to the King that they had the privilege of consulting separately; whereupon the English and German deputies withdrew. Sigismund and his counsellors remained. The Frenchmen again demurred; the King might remain, but his council ought to depart. Sigismund became enraged, and left the chamber, exclaiming, ' Now we shall see who is for the union and faithful to the Empire; I shall find out the men who mean to dishonour me.'[1] Indignant at this intimidation, Pierre d'Ailly left the assembly. Four other cardinals, who were present, found the King still in the monastery and asked him if they were free to deliberate. Sigismund had cooled down considerably and apologised for his outburst, telling them that the French were free to deliberate, but that no one else must be present. Luckily at this moment the French ambassadors appeared and joined their countrymen. They saw the folly of standing out against the King and the other two nations. A resolution was on their advice passed that the Council should not be dissolved nor transferred, and that the Pope should not leave it, but should appoint such proctors as the Council might nominate.[2] Thus the three nations were once more reunited against Pope John the Twenty-third.

That afternoon, shortly after vespers, the King went to visit the Pope, whom he found lying down. ' How are you, Holy Father?' inquired Sigismund. ' I am out of sorts,' answered Pope John, ' for the climate of this place does not suit me, and I cannot stand it.' The King assured him that there were many safe and pleasant spots close to Constance to which the Pope could retire to recruit; he had only to choose one, and Sigismund would arrange everything; the only thing on which the

[1] Hardt, ii. 258; iv. 58.   [2] *Ibid.* iv. 58.

THE QUESTION OF RESIGNATION 295

King insisted was that the Pope must not leave Constance in any secret or unseemly guise before the Council broke up ; provided he promised this, the King would be responsible for his safety. To which the Pope answered that he had no intention of leaving Constance before the Council was dissolved ; but he naturally did not explain whether his leaving the city would, in his opinion, itself dissolve the Council.[1] To an Italian, accustomed to the dry air of Bologna, the dampness of Constance must have been depressing and unsalutary ; but a Teuton could not understand why the Pope complained of the climate. How could Baldassare Cossa with any reason complain that the climate did not suit him ? asked his secretary, Dietrich von Niem. Although Constance may be a small town compared with other German cities, continues Dietrich, still it is beautiful and delightfully situated, with a climate that suits any stranger and any age. There are boats on the lake and in the rivers. There is an excellent government of the town. All round are vineyards, fields, meadows, and groves, so that it is like the land which the Lord hath blessed. It would be difficult to find any place like it where everything necessary and healthful for the life of man would be similarly forthcoming.[2] Such was the opinion of Dietrich von Niem ; such was not the opinion of Pope John the Twenty-third.

King Sigismund was perfectly well aware that the Pope meditated flight, and he had spies everywhere, even in the papal palace, to watch his movements. Pippo Span of Ozora visited the Pope two or three times a day ; he even penetrated into the Pope's bedchamber ; though, when the time came, a servant in the bed deceived the King's spy.[3] John of Nassau and Friedrich of the Tirol were the two men whom Sigismund suspected of being the Pope's aiders and abettors. Since Friedrich had come to Constance on the 4th February, he had become on still worse terms with the King. Irritated at the Duke's refusal to do homage at Constance, Sigismund turned to the Swiss and asked them for a promise of assistance against Friedrich, but they, mindful of the fifty years' peace, hesitated. The Duke, being alarmed, promised to satisfy the King. Each party now intrigued against the other to gain the Swiss. Friedrich made

[1] Hardt, ii. 395-6. [2] *Ibid.* 397-8. [3] *A.S.I.*, iv. 182.

Sigismund great offers if he would help him against the stiff-necked mountaineers. If the King accepted, the Duke meant to betray him to the confederates; but Sigismund was too wily to be thus caught. He sent for the Swiss deputies, and in Friedrich's presence unfolded to them the Duke's offer. They were naturally astonished. The Duke was disgusted, could not explain, but asked for some delay in order to collect the reports of his officers in Switzerland. Sigismund expressed his astonishment at Friedrich's having complained of the Swiss on imperfect information. The deputies saw that they were being used as tools in a personal quarrel and refused to alter the *status quo*; they adhered to the fifty years' peace. This passage-at-arms increased Sigismund's suspicion of Duke Friedrich. He charged him with being privy to the plot of Pope John; and when Friedrich denied, he warned him to have nothing to do with the Pope's attempt to escape.[1]

Despite all the King's precautions, the Pope and Duke Friedrich were in communication. The Duke did not mean to lose the advantage which the Pope's aid would give him in his quarrel with the Bishop of Trient and others. He did not despair of John's cause. When he could not see the Pope himself, he used Ulrich von Silvenhorn as his intermediary and messenger; he was a Swabian, for the Duke would not take any of the Tirolese into his confidence.[2] The present situation between the King and the Pope was intolerable; it could not last. For the 20th March Friedrich had arranged a grand tournament to be held in the open ground at Paradise, just outside the city; he was to lead the knights on one side, and Friedrich of Cilly, son of the King's father-in-law, was to lead their opponents. All the secular and many of the spiritual nobles would be present; the townsfolk would all be at the show; the streets of the city would be deserted; this was the opportunity.[3]

In those days of stress and strife, no one except his closest friends and his bitterest enemies had time to think of the Bohemian patriot reformer lying in custody. At first, when, through the kindly care of the Pope's physicians, he had re-

---

[1] Mueller, iv. 191.   [2] *B. W.*, 265.
[3] For another view see Valois, iv. 285 note.

THE QUESTION OF RESIGNATION 297

covered from his illness, he was tolerably cheerful and looked forward to his release by the King; but his hope gradually died away. His patience and benignity won upon his custodians, and the clerks from the papal camera and his warders were alike kind to him.¹ The Bishop's chamberlain allowed him visitors, and Hus burst into tears when he saw his old friend Christian, the Rector of Prague. He sent and received letters; he communicated freely with John of Chlum who still resided with the widow Fida. He was allowed lights, so that he could write all night long if he pleased. Though discomfited, he was not cast down, for he suffered in good hope. What most troubled him was the enmity of his old friend Palec, and the trickery of Michael *de Causis*, who had waylaid some of his letters and had taken copies. It was at this time that the question of communion in both kinds first arose in Bohemia; Master Jacobel had written to Hus for a decided opinion, but Hus was not very friendly toward the innovation, although he admitted to his friends in Constance that communion in both kinds was in accordance with the custom of the early Church.² The correspondence between him and Master Jacobel was therefore not amicable; but Michael Deutschbrod, eager to get additional evidence against the reformer, had managed to seize and copy it.³

When the judges came to see Hus early in January, he was taken to the refectory. They showed him articles of accusation drawn from passages in his writings. 'These had,' says Mladonowicz, 'been falsely and unfairly extracted from the *De Ecclesia* by Palec, who had mutilated some sentences at the beginning, others in the middle, others at the end, and who had invented things that were not contained in the book at all.' Hus pointed this out to his judges, but they answered that the articles had been drawn up by the Bohemians. The Archbishop (or probably the Patriarch John) taunted Hus with possessing seventy thousand florins. 'What had become of that cloth full of money,' asked Michael, 'and how much have the barons in Bohemia got of yours?' One of the bishops accused him of inventing a new law, and the other with preaching all that was contained in the articles of accusation. Hus

---

[1] Palacky (*Doc.*), 87.   [2] *Ibid.* 91.   [3] *Vid. sup.* p. 265.

could only protest.¹ When they had left, he set to work writing explanations of the extracts, and he also wrote comments on the forty-five articles for which Wyclif had been condemned for heresy in England ; but in all he professed to write under correction ; he was willing to submit to the verdict of the Council and to retract any expression which was proved to him to be erroneous. Even yet he did not realise that he was to be tried for heresy. He wrote a petition before notaries, and sent to the Council a supplication through the Patriarch, praying that he might be allowed to answer academically (*more scholastico*) or might be permitted to pronounce a discourse.² The only offences with which he could, he thought, be charged were his opposition to the crusade against Ladislas, his officiating while excommunicated, his appeal from the Pope, and his coming to Constance without a safe-conduct.³ When the allegation that he had appealed from the Pope was read to him, Hus laughed, and he might have laughed still more heartily had he known how matters were likely to go with Pope John. But yesterday ' he might have stood against the world ; now . . . none so poor to do him reverence.'

But while the Council was agitated with the question of the Pope's resignation, Hus was left alone ; eight weeks went by since his last audience with the commissioners.⁴ Meanwhile, he had fallen ill again and was horribly troubled with gravel, from which he had never previously suffered, and with grievous vomiting and fever ; he seemed likely to die ; he was taken out of his prison. Then he was transferred to the Franciscan cloister.⁵ He was still imprisoned there on the 20th March 1415.

[1] Palacky (*Doc.*), 92. [2] *Ibid.* 91. [3] *Ibid.* 89.
[4] *Ibid.* 99. [5] *Ibid.* 98.

CHAPTER XVII

THE FLIGHT

THE tournament held in the lists at Paradise on the 20th March 1415 was a gorgeous function. All the houses in the town were closed, though the shops and booths displayed their wares and finery. The Jews' quarter near the Judenthurm in the Ziegelgraben had its houses barricaded, and the premises occupied by the fifty-eight money-changers were also strictly guarded. All the inhabitants of the city streamed out through the gateway past the Capuchin monastery to the open ground known as Paradise. The lists themselves were usually sixty paces long by forty in breadth, and at the two ends were the lodges of the combatants, whereon were displayed their arms, banners, and helmets, those of Friedrich, Duke of the Tirol, and of those who fought on his side, being in the station at one end, and those of Friedrich, Count of Cilly, and his associates, at the other. On one side of the lists was the royal stand, provided with semi-circles of benches, rising in tiers one above the other, where sat, resplendent in the majesty of the Holy Roman Empire, King Sigismund, a perfect chevalier, who once in the lists at Constance played the same part as Le Noir Faineant in the tournament at Ashby de la Zouch. Unhappily a chivalrous knight of those days could, to his private enemies, be fully as mean and treacherous as any man of honour of the modern times. Below the King, on the lowest tier, with the prize of the tourney on a cushion before her, was the Queen of the Tournament, the fair and fickle Barbara, casting loving glances ever and anon at the young Tirolese knight, Tegen von Villanders;[1] whose relative the minnesinger, Oswald von Wolkenstein, with the peacock's plume in his hat

[1] Cf. Herman Schmid, *Friedel und Oswald*; a romance full of historical inaccuracies, but giving a vivid picture of the social life at this time.

and the Queen of Aragon's ring in his beard, pointed out the celebrities to the youthful Margareta and her father, Berthold von Schwangau, who had recently, to Oswald's surprise and delight, arrived in Constance. The slight, dark-eyed Swabian girl, whose blond hair waved in curls over her little ears and fell to her shoulders, with her dainty nose and chin and perfect throat, as the laughter broke from her rosy lips and showed her white teeth, was the cynosure of neighbouring eyes. Gathered round King Sigismund were the princes, dukes, and dignitaries of the Empire, with the ambassadors and strangers of rank from every country of Europe and beyond, all glittering in costly apparel; while facing him, on the further side of the lists, was the pavilion for the citizens of Constance. Here sat the burghers in holiday attire, with their fair wives and daughters, who danced at Queen Barbara's balls, whose beauty captivated the heart of many a gallant knight whose speech they could scarce understand. Between lay the sanded battle-ground, with the long barrier to separate the combatants as they tilted at one another.[1] The tournament began early in the afternoon, as soon as the bell rang for vespers, and it was the general rule to continue the combats until the stars came out in the sky. But on this occasion, before that time, there came into the lists a messenger, one Ulrich Saldenhorn, who rode up to Duke Friedrich and whispered in his ear. The Duke, apparently unmanned, rode his last bout with his antagonist, was defeated[2] and unhorsed, dragged off the ground by his squires, and released from his armour. He left the lists without attracting attention. The young Count of Cilly was the victor of the tourney; but Duke Friedrich had received the fateful news for which he was anxiously waiting. The Pope had fled from Constance.

[1] The modern sport which most resembles the mediæval tournament is pig-sticking with the long spear against a good old fighting boar. Both are sports for the steed no less than for the rider. The horse must gallop his hardest and straightest; a shy at the critical moment is fatal. The spear was held steadily and firmly; there was no thrusting or jobbing; the impact carried the full weight of both horse and rider. Finally the aim was to strike the opponent full on the breast, so that the stroke did not glint or glance off. Pluck and momentum were the secret of success.

[2] Richental, 62.

THE FLIGHT

While all the world of Constance was at the tournament, Pope John, attended only by a youth and a priest, issued from the palace near the Cathedral. No one would have recognised the Pope; he walked heavily from the gout in his feet; he was dressed in grey like a groom, and had a grey shawl thrown over his head to conceal his features; he carried a crossbow after the manner of stable-boys. His companions were also disguised. Pope John mounted a sorry nag, and made his way along the Inselgasse. He dared not try the Bridge, knowing that there would be a watch on the gate. The three fugitives made their way through the Eserthurm and, leaving the old Benedictine cloister at the Rubbish Heaps on their right, they went along the road by the river past the Castle of Gottlieben to the little village of Ermatingen on the Rhine, five miles from Constance. Here they halted at the house of the village priest, who gave them to drink. They waited here for Duke Friedrich of the Tirol.[1]

When Friedrich first heard of the Pope's flight, he was astonied. He expected it, but John had carefully concealed all the details from him and from every one. The crisis, now that it had arrived, had come at a most awkward time for him, when King Sigismund had just succeeded in undermining the confidence of the Duke's Swiss allies. He knew not what to do; he had pledged his word to the Pope; he had no objection to seeing the Council dissolved; but his action would place him in irreconcilable enmity both with the King and the Council; he could hope for no quarter from either. From the lists he hurried to the house of a friendly Jew, known by the sign of the Winnowing-fan, and sent for his bailiff. 'You have begun this without me, and you must finish it without me,' answered Hans von Lupfen. Then entered his trusty steward, Hans von Diessenhofen, who encouraged the Duke. 'What has been begun must be loyally carried through: here am I, my lord, Hans the steward will never abandon you.' The worthy Hans then got three horses saddled; and taking a single page with them, they set out for Ermatingen. Here they found the Pope. The flight and the meeting were long

[1] For an examination of the different accounts of the flight see Finke (*B.*), 23 *et seq.*

remembered in the little village, where the Vigil of the Miller's Thumbs commemorated the Pope's disguise and his simple refreshment.[1] From Ermatingen the party rode on to Steckborn, five miles further down the river, where they found a boat, which carried them, passing under the old wooden bridge at Stein, down the Rhine to Schaffhausen. It was long past midnight when they arrived.

Schaffhausen, so called from the boat-sheds, or skiffhouses, built in the eighth century as rude depots for the cargoes of vessels coming from the Boden See, is situated just above the beautiful Falls of the Rhine, and was held by the Dukes of Austria on mortgage from the Empire. Even to-day the town is distinguished above every city in Switzerland by the mediæval character of its houses, its gates, and its citadel. Behind the town was the castle, standing on a small hill, with a 'thick ring of walls set with tall bastion towers, and its covered viaduct-like way sloping down the hill-side.'[2] Here the Duke and the Pope took shelter, and in the morning John wrote to King Sigismund. 'Thanks be to the all-powerful God, my dearest son, we are now here at Schaffhausen, in a free and good climate; and we came here without the knowledge of our son, the Duke of Austria, and with no intention of receding from our intention of resigning, but in order that we may do so in freedom and in good health as we undoubtedly intend doing.'[3] Pope John appreciated the danger of having too many confidants, and probably the only person who knew for certain that he meant to escape at that particular time was the chief of the Burgundian embassy;[4] so that what he said of the Duke was in so far true that Friedrich knew that the Pope intended to fly, but had not been told that he meant to make the attempt at that particular time; although his subsequent conduct shows that he knew that this was probable. To certain of the cardinals the Pope wrote complaining bitterly of the King's oppression,[5] he also sent letters to the King of France and the Duke of Berri stating that a party had arisen in the Council engrossing all power, threatening his freedom and that of the Council, and through its violence hindering the work of

[1] Finke (*B.*), 27.   [2] Mayhew, 303.   [3] Mansi, xxvii. 577.
[4] Valois, iv. 302.   [5] Aschbach, ii. 65.

THE FLIGHT

restoring peace to the Church.[1] His great hope was in the Duke of Burgundy, Jean sans Peur, to whom he wrote begging him to await his ambassadors and not to dismiss the troops with which he might come to the aid of the sovereign pontiff.[2]

Now, at last, at Schaffhausen the two arch-conspirators, the Pope and the Duke, were face to face, and were able to discuss each other's plans. They had scarcely met, had only seen each other by stealth, since the day, more than five months ago, when the Pope passed through Meran. Friedrich had only been in Constance six weeks; he had communicated with Pope John occasionally by messenger. The reason he had accepted the Pope's offer on the journey to Constance was that, being an enemy of King Sigismund, he wanted the Pope's aid in dealing with his refractory bishops of Brixen, Chur, and Trient. He had promised John his protection, but apparently he thought that moral support would alone suffice, for he made no further preparation. He was not devoted to the Pope, who had been opposed to him before the meeting at Meran, but he was ready to redeem his word as became a scion of the House of Austria. But he was not ready to do more. Pope John's desire, in escaping from Constance, was to get to France, to Burgundian soil. On the 23rd March he wrote to his Curia to follow him at once to Schaffhausen, thinking thus to break up the Council. King Sigismund guessed his design, and sent out messengers accordingly to intercept his flight over the border. The Pope relied on Duke Friedrich to help him, because Friedrich's brother Leopold had been married to Katharine of Burgundy, who had dealt favourably with her youngest brother-in-law in the arrangements made on her husband's death.[3] But Friedrich was by no means inclined to favour the Pope so far. A Pope on the soil of France might or might not be grateful to the Duke of the Tirol, but other motives would necessarily produce a prior influence on his mind. If Pope John was to be of any service to Duke Friedrich, now that he had kept his word with him, he must remain in the Duke's power so that he might use him either for his own ends in Tirol or in treating with his enemies. If the Pope were once on Burgundian soil,

[1] Mansi, xxvii. 577. [2] *Ibid.* xxviii. 13. [3] Lichnowsky, v. 140.

Friedrich would have no asset in dealing with Sigismund; he would be utterly helpless.

In escaping from Constance, Pope John had made a great, and irreparable mistake. Had he remained, he would certainly have had to resign the papacy; but the French cardinals and the moderate party in the Council, who held the balance between the fanatic English and Germans on the one side and the Italians on the other, would have ensured that his resignation was made with all due grace, and that his future was richly endowed. Instead of this, he had risked all on a gambler's throw, and, as he must have realised very soon after leaving Constance, he had lost everything. A bold stroke, such as he had made, might have had a different result had Pope John had to do merely with Pope Gregory or Pope Benedict, men of vacillating or protracting disposition, but he had to do with the foremost man of action of the time, and King Sigismund rose to the occasion magnificently. As soon as Pope John heard of the King's action in Constance, he must have realised that his own cause was irretrievably lost. From this time forth his fatalistic disposition produced a marked change in his character. He had hitherto kept his word, as for example in opening the Councils of Rome and Constance, even to his own hurt; but he became not ashamed now to descend to an occasional falsehood. In the long letter which he addressed to the University of Paris he claimed for himself the praise of instituting the prosecution of John Hus for heresy.[1] This was false; and as the large-browed Verulam saith, ' There is no vice that doth so cover a man with shame as to be found false and perfidious'; and in another place he says, ' The virtue of adversity is fortitude'; but Pope John was a fatalist, he had not fortitude.

It was about the time of vespers, three o'clock in the afternoon, when Pope John left Constance. That same evening the news of his flight leaked out and became generally known. The city was in the direst confusion. The universal opinion was that the Council was now perforce at an end. The Bishop's palace which the Pope had occupied was immediately sacked. The shops were all closed in terror. The burgomaster called

[1] Hardt, ii. 253.

the citizens to arms. The King's guards occupied every square and street. Hundreds of Austrians and Italians left the town during the night on foot, on horseback, or in boats. Those who remained feared lest the Pope might march at the head of an army on the city. The lords and dignitaries, spiritual and temporal, knew not what to expect. The town was in an uproar. Every one awaited the worst. At break of day King Sigismund and the Count Palatine Louis, preceded by trumpeters, paraded the town; the trumpeters and the King himself with a loud voice proclaimed that all was well, that no man was to think of leaving Constance, that the persons and possessions of all were safe and were guaranteed by the royal protection; Pope John had fled stealthily, but let no man be afraid.[1] Influential members of the Council, like the Chancellor Gerson, supported Sigismund.[2] Having thus calmed the public distress, the King then assembled all the prelates and secular dignitaries and assured them that he would, at the peril of his life, maintain the Council. The King's resolution and courage appeased the tumult in all minds. The lords, spiritual and temporal, knew that the Council was safe and would continue; the shopkeepers re-opened their shops; the Florentine bankers and money-changers were reassured; the town was quieted and the ordinary life of the place resumed its wonted aspect.

King Sigismund held a congregation of the four nations on the 21st or 22nd March at the Franciscan Monastery to consider the situation and to read to them the short letter received from the Pope. The cardinals having assembled at the palace hard by, it was resolved to ask their advice. Sigismund went with the deputation. The cardinals announced that they were ready to go on with their work in conjunction with the four nations, even in the Pope's absence, and that if they found that this hindered the reformation or the unity of the Church, then they would utterly abandon Pope John, but that in the first place they thought a deputation should be sent to him, and that nothing should be undertaken to his detriment meanwhile. On the 23rd March, before the embassy was despatched, Jean Gerson preached a sermon upholding the authority of the

[1] Richental, 63.   [2] Tschackert, 211.

Council, but the cardinals refused to attend and listen to his discourse.[1]

Three cardinals accordingly, Giordano Orsini, Amadeus de Saluzzo, and Guillaume Fillastre, were deputed, and accompanied by Regnault de Chartres, Archbishop of Reims, proceeded to Schaffhausen to have an interview with the Pope.

The King of the Romans meantime turned to the business of the Empire. An attempt was made to dissuade him from vengeance on the Duke of Austria, on the grounds that it might dissolve the Council, raise the price of provisions, and drive the Pope further away from Constance.[2] Sigismund was not to be moved. As soon as the congregation of the nations was dismissed, the princes of the Empire assembled at the monastery, and before them the King impeached Friedrich, Duke of Austria, of treachery to the Empire and the Church by the abduction of the Pope; he asked their aid in righting the wrong done to the Empire, and they all with one accord consented. It was resolved that the Duke be summoned to appear and answer before the King of the Romans and the Council of Constance.[3]

The patriot reformer, John Hus, felt the evil effects of the Pope's flight; hitherto he had been the Pope's prisoner, and his captivity had been tolerable. He heard of the flight and wrote to his friends of the universal perturbation. On the 24th March all his guards fled and he had nothing to eat; he asked his friends, if they loved the poor Goose, to see that the King sent him guards or let him out of prison that evening.[4] He took a childish delight in thus playing upon his name (Hus =Hans=Goose). That same evening an armed force of a hundred and seventy men, sent by the Bishop of Constance, conveyed Hus to the Castle of Gottlieben, about three miles from the city, on the banks of the Rhine. Here he was watched by German guards, who were not kind to him as the Italians had been; he was chained by the hands by day to a post, and at night his feet were similarly secured. He could write no more letters and could see no more friends; he now endured the horrors of a mediæval prison.

---

[1] Schwab, 507.
[2] Finke (*F.*), 170.
[3] Hardt, iv. 64; Hefele, vii. 93.
[4] Palacky (*Doc.*), 99-100.

The Castle on the Rhine at Gottlieben, still standing, used by the Bishop of Constance for his prisoners. In this castle both Pope John the Twenty-third and John Hus were incarcerated.

THE FLIGHT

From Thursday the 21st March until Good Friday the 29th, Pope John remained in Schaffhausen, and probably officiated in the church there occasionally during Passion Week.[1] During this time he had not given up the hope of retaining some influence over the Council. He had ordered the Curia and the cardinals to join him, under pain of excommunication, within six days. Some of the Curia came; on Palm Sunday four of the cardinals, those commonly known as the 'Italianissimi,' from their hostility to Sigismund not only in his church but also in his Italian policy, fled from Constance. They were the Cardinal of Pisa, Alaman Adimar, the Pope's nephew Brancacius, the Savoyard Antoine de Chalant, and Branda de Castellio, Cardinal of Piacenza. Next day three more arrived, and among them was Oddo Colonna, the future Pope Martin the Fifth. The Pope wrote long letters to the Kings of France and Poland, the Duke of Orleans and the University of Paris, detailing all that had been done from the commencement of the Council, and dilating upon the delay, the hostility, and the suspicious conduct of Sigismund, King of the Romans. Much happened also in Constance during this week. As soon as ever the Pope had fled a manifesto against him and the cardinals was posted on the door of his palace, in which John was charged with tyranny, homicide, simony, and jobbery; and when the Duke of Austria was publicly accused, several lords and towns of his obedience at once renounced their fealty. Perhaps the most important event of all was the sermon delivered on Saturday the 23rd March by Jean Gerson, who now came forward and became the leading spirit of the Council.[2]

Jean Gerson came to Constance as one of the representatives of the King of France, but he was as bitterly opposed to the policy of the Armagnac party in upholding Pope John as he was to the damnable doctrine of tyrannicide preached by Jean Petit for the benefit of the Duke of Burgundy. With regard to Jean sans Peur, Gerson had upheld in the cathedral of Notre Dame in Paris that the Duke ought to be humiliated, and to make proper satisfaction for his sin, in order to ensure the salvation of his soul.[3] With regard to the Pope, Gerson held him to be inferior to the Council, and he now openly stated his views.

[1] Finke (*B.*), 34.   [2] Hardt, ii. 265-74.   [3] Monstrelet, 353.

As this sermon was approved by the Council and constituted its plan of action, it will be as well to give the mere outlines. The Chancellor took for his text the words of the fourth Evangelist, 'Walk while ye have the light, lest darkness come upon you.' It was entirely a political sermon, intended to explain the position of the Council with regard to the Pope; and the preacher began by informing his audience that it was delivered by the order of the ambassadors of the King of France and the University of Paris. It set forth that the head of the Church is Jesus Christ, under whom, as vicar and secondary chief, is the Pope, apart from whom, however, through the assistance of the Holy Spirit, the Church possesses the faculty and power of life. The Church has in Jesus Christ a spouse from whom she can never be divorced, but she is not allied in the same fashion to the vicar of her spouse; she, or a general council representing her, is a model (*regula*) drawn up by the Holy Spirit and given by Christ in order that every one, even the Pope, should listen to her and obey her, on pain of being accounted a heathen man and a publican.[1] The orator then proceeded to define and describe a general council. It is an assembly of the whole hierarchy of the Catholic Church, bound to listen to every Christian who desires to be heard, convoked by legitimate authority in a certain place to deal with and regulate the good government of the Church in faith and morality; although it cannot deprive the Pope of his *plenitudo potestatis*, it can place limits on its use. A general council, continued Gerson, referring to Pisa and to the present state of affairs at Constance, may be called and may continue in existence without the express consent or mandate of the Pope. His next proposition had special reference to the Schism, and ran thus:—When the Church or a general council has prescribed to the Pope a certain way of ending the Schism, he is bound to accept it, and to resign the papacy if that method has been proposed to him, though he is doubly praiseworthy when he himself of his own free will offers so to do. A general council, he continued, is called upon to extirpate errors and to correct the erring, without distinction of persons; and in saying this, he alluded not only to the Wyclifite heresy but also to the

[1] Hardt, ii. 272.

THE FLIGHT

defence of political assassination by Jean Petit. Jean Gerson wound up his discourse by recommending the continuance of general and provincial councils as the most efficacious means to church reform. This discourse was received with the greatest enthusiasm by the King and the nations.[1]

The cardinals meantime sat apart and formed a separate chamber from the congregation of the nations; they had refused to attend to hear the sermon of Jean Gerson, knowing that it would meet with their disapproval; they were naturally prejudiced in favour of the Pope, though they felt that his flight had placed them and the French ambassadors at a disadvantage beside the more determined party of Jean Mauroux, Patriarch of Antioch, and the members of the University of Paris. The deputation of the three cardinals, followed by the royal embassy, consisting of Louis of Bavaria, Colard de Calleville, and the Archbishop of Reims,[2] reached Schaffhausen on Saturday evening, and remained with the Pope all Palm Sunday and Monday.[3] The cardinals besought Pope John to adhere to his intention of resigning and to give way on the matter of the proctors; the royal ambassadors entreated him not to go further away; they offered to procure him guarantees for his safety and to prevent war breaking out between King Sigismund and the Duke of Austria.

Regnault de Chartres, Archbishop of Reims, returned to Constance in advance of the other ambassadors. He brought a letter from the Pope to the cardinals. John appointed each and all of the sacred college as his proctors to effect his resignation in case both his rivals died or abdicated, and he proposed also to name four prelates, one from each nation, from a list prepared by the Council, to act with the cardinals.[4] Apparently he was ready to deliver himself, bound hand and foot, into the power of the Council. After reading this letter in a congregation on the 25th March, the Archbishop named the prelates from the English, French, and German nations, leaving the Italians to name their own; and he proceeded to explain that the Pope had left Constance simply for change of air and not because of any ill usage, that indeed his great desire

[1] Schwab, 507.
[2] Bess, 171; Valois, iv. 288.
[3] Finke (*F.*), 170.
[4] Hardt, iv. 69.

was to make the journey to Nice in company with King Sigismund in order that the contemporaneous resignations might be effected there. Nothing in fact would have suited the design of Pope John better than such a journey, for he knew the temper of Pope Benedict. In some of his other letters to Constance, however, the Pope stated that he was in fear of violence on the part of the King and his courtiers.[1] As a matter of fact the motives which had induced the Pope to fly from Constance were three; it was partly anxiety for his health because of the damp climate, and partly anxiety for his personal safety because of the King's enmity,[2] but it was mainly in the hope that he would thereby checkmate his opponents by provoking the dissolution of the Council; and compared with the cogency of this third motive, the other two were merely pretexts. John was mistaken in his calculation, for his flight simply accelerated his own destruction.

The cardinals continued in opposition. They were discontented with their position. They saw that they were gradually losing influence in the Council and were of less account than the nations. They had claimed to be treated as a nation, and to be specially mentioned in all letters emanating from the Council; but both requests had been refused.[3] Nine of them had joined the Pope at Schaffhausen.[4] The third general session of the Council was now convened for the 26th March; there was no Pope to preside; and if a cardinal did not preside, the college was like to lose its influence completely. At the same time they were unwilling, under the circumstances and until they knew something more of the Pope's mind, to acknowledge the authority of the Council in his absence. To save the situation, D'Ailly and Zabarella attended; the other cardinals refused, some alleging illness, the others saying that they ought to await the return of the deputation from Schaffhausen.[5] The Cardinal of Cambrai presided; and a resolution was passed, in the spirit of our own Long Parliament more than two hundred years later, that the Council should continue in session until its work was completed. But at the conclusion the two cardinals entered a protest that they adhered to their obedience so long

---

[1] Lenfant (*C.*), i. 139. [2] Mur. iii. 855. [3] Martene (*A. C.*), vii. 1412.
[4] Finke (*F.*), 170. [5] Tschackert, 214.

THE FLIGHT

as the Pope persisted in his desire to resign. The cardinals would not desert the Pope unless and until he failed to fulfil his formal promise to resign the papacy.

Later in that same day the three cardinals and two others returned from Schaffhausen. They were privately of opinion that the Council was virtually dissolved through the absence of the Pope, who possessed and retained the right to dismiss it when he chose. Their report was made before a congregation held on the 28th. It differed in some slight degree from that of the Archbishop of Reims. Any three of the college were empowered to effect the 'act of cession,' but they were to act in concert with eight prelates whom the Pope would select from a list of thirty-two to be nominated by the nations; the Pope promised not to dissolve nor transfer the Council, and he would himself remain in the neighbourhood of Constance. But he wanted the cardinals and the functionaries of the Curia to come to him; a sufficient number of the cardinals might remain at Constance, but the officials were commanded to repair to Schaffhausen within six days, under pain of excommunication. Moreover, all these concessions, such as they were, were made conditional on freedom and protection being granted to him and to Friedrich, Duke of Austria.

King Sigismund, however, now that he had got his enemy in his power, did not mean to release him until he had thoroughly humiliated the proud Duke. The Pope's proposal was scornfully rejected. A fourth session of the Council was to be held on Saturday the 30th March, and on the day preceding Sigismund called a congregation of the English, French, and German nations to decide on what should be brought forward. Four resolutions were adopted and were submitted to the cardinals, who would not agree to them as they stood. They communicated to the King a proposal of the Pope that Sigismund and two cardinals should be empowered to effect the Pope's resignation, that the Pope would undertake not to remove the Curia without the consent of the synod, and would cancel his former orders. The nations distrusted the Pope and could not agree; Sigismund was anxious not to alienate the cardinals, as their departure would effectually have broken up the Council; it was agreed that they should appear at the Council to-morrow,

312 POPE JOHN THE TWENTY-THIRD

and that the propositions should be passed in the form to which the cardinals had agreed. These propositions superceded to all effect those which had been passed in the second session.

At the fourth general session of the Council of Constance, held on Saturday the 30th March 1415, the following three resolutions were passed :—(1) The Synod of Constance, legitimately assembled in the Holy Spirit, constituting an œcumenical Council and representing the Church militant, derives its power direct from Christ, to which Council every one, of whatever state or dignity, even the Pope, is bound to render obedience in all that relates to the faith or to the extirpation of the Schism ; (2) The Pope shall not summon from Constance, without the consent of the synod, the Curia or its officers whose absence would entail the dissolution of the Council ; (3) All penalties pronounced by the Pope since leaving Constance against any dependants or members of the Council are invalid.[1]

Unlike the cardinals Sigismund utterly declined to believe in the good faith of John the Twenty-third. He was convinced that the Pope's design was to protract negotiations, to vacillate and procrastinate, in order to break up the Council ; and in this design his propinquity to Constance assisted him. Guards were stationed on the city walls ; armed men were posted along the roads ; but it was impossible to prevent desertions ; and every day's delay was in the Pope's favour. Schaffhausen was only thirty miles from Constance, and as soon as the deserters arrived there they were under the protection of the Duke of Austria. It was necessary to deal with the Duke, and that speedily. Friedrich of the Tirol had friends in Constance ; but his treachery to the Empire and the Council was so glaring that not a voice had been raised in his defence at the assembly of the Teuton notables. He had been summoned to appear and answer ; the three days' grace had expired ; the ambassadors had returned, and the Duke had made no sign. The King resolved to proceed to sterner measures. The ambassadors from the University of Paris, who had entreated their King not to remove his countenance from the Council because of the Pope's flight, took alarm, and now begged Charles to interfere

[1] Hardt, iv. 86 *et seq.* ; Hefele, vii. 101.

THE FLIGHT

lest the King's measures against Friedrich should themselves cause the dissolution of the Council. But Sigismund was wiser than the ambassadors.

On the 25th March he called another assembly of the princes of the Empire, who found Friedrich guilty. The King pronounced the ban. All the Duke's lands and subjects were released from their obedience to him and reverted to the Empire; it was forbidden to give him lodging or shelter, to provide him with food, forage, help, or counsel, to keep the peace or to abide with him. The fathers of the Council approved of the secular ban, although they declined to add at that time a sentence of excommunication. The whole of the Empire, lords and cities, clergy and laymen, were informed of the ban, and were told that all leagues, contracts, and alliances with the Duke were null and invalid. The Swiss confederates, with the exception of the men of Bern, who desired further time for consideration, declined at that time to break their fifty years' peace; but the nobles of the Tirol seized their opportunity. The Patriarch of Aquileia, the Bishops of Trient and Freisingen, the widow and the daughter of Heinrich of Rottenburg, the Counts of Jungingen, Bodmann, Waldburg, and Sulz all produced their claims against Friedrich. Within a few days four hundred lords and cities sent in their cartels of defiance; even Hans von Lupfen was among the number. Military operations began on the 28th; Conrad of Weinsberg bore the banner of the Empire, and Friedrich of Nuernberg commanded the troops. Stein on the Rhine was captured that night; Diessenhofen opened its gates.[1] On Black Thursday, as Pope John with seven cardinals was on his way to the church at Schaffhausen, a messenger brought him the news. He turned back at once, told the cardinals what had happened, and advised them to shift, each man for himself. At the same time he asked them to accompany him in the further flight which he intended to make next day, but they all, even his own nephew, declined. They were afraid, says Cardinal Fillastre, they should, like the Pope, become the prisoners of Friedrich of the Tirol, for the Duke had sworn to make the Pope and the cardinals pay for the war which they had forced upon him.[2]

[1] Brandis, 87-9.   [2] Finke (F.), 170.

314 POPE JOHN THE TWENTY-THIRD

The Spanish ambassadors, who had at last received their marching orders, made their way through the roads crowded with soldiers, to Schaffhausen that Thursday; they were admitted into the town, and witnessed the universal confusion and uproar. Prelates and cardinals were darting hither and thither in disguise, hoping to make their way back to Constance. The envoys saw some one in a country cart, muffled up, and mistook him for the Pope. It was on Good Friday, and clothed in his pontifical robes, that Pope John, in the midst of torrential rain, quitted Schaffhausen, accompanied by Duke Friedrich.[1] They rode twenty-four miles that day as far as Waldshut, a little village that lies high above the Rhine. Ten miles next morning took them on to the Castle of Laufenburg, where the Rhine separates the Swiss Jura from the Swabian range. The green waters of the stream glide between pink rocks over the Lesser Falls, which give their name to the 'City of the Current.'[2] The Pope and the Duke came to angry strife; John wanted to continue his flight in order to escape from the imperial troops; Friedrich insisted on a halt and promised the Pope every security; the dispute waxed so hot that the Cardinal Hannibaldus and the Bishop of Gap, who had accompanied the Pope, disguised themselves and fled, but fell into the hands of the enemy. John had to recognise that he was not his own master and to remain at Laufenburg. He stayed at the hostelry known by the sign of the Peacock.[3]

The space of eight days during which Pope John the Twenty-third tarried at Schaffhausen, forms a period apart in his career, distinct from the time before and after. Although he had left Constance, he had not formally broken with the Council and was by many still regarded as its head. In fact, at the third session the Council was described as a *reputed* general council because the Pope did not preside. John had a body of cardinals with him at Schaffhausen, and retained all the dignity of his high office. But the days there were a transition state which could not last, and their duration did not depend on the will of the Pope. He was between King Sigismund and Duke Friedrich; he was no longer master of his fate, but was between the upper and the nether millstones. On Good

[1] Finke (*B.*), 34-5.   [2] Mayhew, 265.   [3] Finke (*B.*), 36.

Friday he was compelled to quit Schaffhausen ; had he returned to Constance he became the King's puppet ; continuing his flight he remained the Duke's prisoner. He chose the latter course ; he became a fugitive from the Council, desiring to escape to France, but remaining a prisoner in the hands of his jailor.

CHAPTER XVIII

THROUGH THE BLACK FOREST

THE second flight of the Pope cleared the air to a great extent. He could no longer allege the climate as the reason for leaving Constance; in the Bull which he issued from Laufenburg he gave as his reason the fear for his personal safety and the apprehension of the effect which the news of the violence to him might have on his rivals to the prejudice of all hope of extinguishing the Schism.[1] But the King was ready to meet this plea. He called a congregation at which the Archbishop of Reims and Cardinal Chalant again announced to the audience that John had assured them that he had no reason whatever to complain of the King's conduct toward him. Desertions, however, continued. Safe-conducts had been offered to the cardinals found at Schaffhausen, but the majority answered that they wished to return, not to Constance, but to Rome. John of Nassau had deserted immediately after the Pope left Constance. Others followed his example daily. Five cardinals fled, besides archbishops and bishops and officers of the Curia.[2] The congregation nominated three commissioners from each nation to receive and examine the applications of those who wished to quit the city and to punish those who left without permission. The fifth general session of the Council was called for Saturday, the 6th April.

This was the most important session yet held. The King of the Romans was present, and Cardinal Giordano Orsini presided. Only seven other cardinals were present; they were Antonius Pancera, Guillaume Fillastre, Antoine de Chalant, Amadeus de Saluzzo, Francesco Zabarella, Alaman Adimar, and Angelus de Anna. The cardinals Jean de Brogni, Pierre d'Ailly, Louis Fieschi, and Francescus Landus, although they were in

[1] Hardt, iv. 102.   [2] Richental, 65.

Constance, did not attend, alleging as an excuse that they wished to avoid giving offence. Although the Cardinal of Cambrai had taught that a Council derives its authority from Christ, and not from Peter or Paul, as the head of the Church,[1] still a Council without a Pope was repugnant to him ; he doubted whether a resolution of the four nations without the participation of the college of cardinals could be held valid as a decree of the Council ; his preference for a Council with a Pope at its head indeed explains his insistence later on the election of a new Pope before the question of church reform was considered. The division between the college and the nations was becoming every day more marked.[2]

It was deemed advisable at this session to confirm the first resolution passed at the fourth session ; and this was done with the addition of words importing that every one was bound to render obedience to the Council not only in the matter of the extirpation of the Schism but also in reform of the Church in its head and its members. No respect for the feelings of Pope John was any longer evinced. Then followed an article which had been proposed at the preliminary congregation but had not been brought before the fourth session ; it ran thus :—Whoever, of whatever condition or dignity he be, even of the papal, shall obstinately refuse to obey the decrees of this Council, or of any other general Council legitimately assembled, shall be liable to penitence and to punishment, even though secular aid have to be invoked (*etiam ad alia juris subsidia, si opus fuerit, recurrendo*). The prohibitions to the Pope to remove any of his officers from Constance were renewed ; and the last resolution asserted that Pope John and all members of the Council had enjoyed, and did enjoy, full liberty.[3] The Monk of Saint-Denys and other authorities say that further resolutions were passed at this fifth session regarding the duty of the Pope to resign, threatening him with deposition, blaming his flight, and assuring him full security for his person and his possessions if he returned to Constance.[4] It was agreed to write to all countries in Christendom to notify the flight of the Pope and the continuance of the Council. The punishment of all leaving

[1] Huebler, 376. [2] Tschackert, 216.
[3] Hardt, iv. 98. [4] *Religieux*, v. 600 *et seq*.

Constance without permission was made over to the King of the Romans and the President of the Council, Cardinal Jean de Brogni being appointed three days later to take the place of the absent Pope in all matters save holding consistories. Sigismund was also requested to write to Pope John and to offer him a safe-conduct for his return to Constance. Zabarella still professed to believe in the Pope, who had not, he contended, written or said anything showing that he was not ready to fulfil his engagements. The King promised to write and to send the safe-conduct, but remarked that he very much doubted whether the Pope would be willing to return, or whether the Duke of Austria would permit him to do so if he wished.

This session of the Council also concerned itself with the question of heresy. It was reported that according to the opinion of the doctors of theology and canon law the condemnation of Wyclif's works by the Council of Rome in 1412 ought to be confirmed and the books to be burned. Inasmuch as the commission appointed by Pope John on the 1st December to inquire into the case of John Hus had done little or nothing, and might be held to have expired with the flight of the Pope, a new ' commission of belief ' was appointed and was directed to take over the register of the process from the former commissioners.[1] Pierre d'Ailly, who was recognised as the foremost theologian in the sacred college, was made president, and with him were associated Cardinal Fillastre, the Bishop of Dole, and the Abbé of Citeaux; they were to deal with the matter of John Hus, with the doctrine of Jean Petit on political assassinations, and also with the condemnation of the forty-five articles of Wyclif, considering the censures of the Universities of Paris and Prague on the tenets of the English reformer, and also the question whether his bones ought to be exhumed from the hallowed soil in which he had been buried.

The importance of this fifth session of the Council of Constance lay in its claim to superiority over the Pope. The nations and the University of Paris had won a victory over the cardinals and the French embassy; the latter might enter a secret protest, but they dared not openly dissent.[2] The Council of Pisa had assumed superiority; the Council of Constance

---

[1] Tschackert, 222. [2] Valois, iv. 298.

affirmed it in full session. It was a tenet which was to be hotly discussed in the future, and it was not finally decided until the nineteenth century. The Council of Constance declared itself to be an œcumenical Council, but its pretension was at a later time ratified only as regarded its last four sessions, those held under the presidency of Pope Martin the Fifth.[1] Its earlier resolutions have no authoritative character. But although its infallibility and superiority were later discredited, they formed at the time the only theory adequate to deal with the Great Schism and to effect the deposition of Pope Benedict the Thirteenth. The Council forms in every respect a marked contrast to that of Pisa, which was wholly uncanonical; the cardinals governed the Council of Pisa, they were governed by the Council of Constance.

The war, for it was nothing less, against Duke Friedrich was prosecuted vigorously. The men of Schaffhausen were ready to open their gates as soon as the Pope and the Duke had left, and they took the opportunity to get rid of the Austrian dominion by paying off the amount due on the mortgage, so that Schaffhausen became once again a free city of the Empire. The Swiss, threatened with being placed under the ban of the Empire, agreed to take arms against the Duke on the conditions that they might retain every place they conquered, and that the King of the Romans would not make peace with the Duke without including them in it. Frauenfeld and Winterthur in the Thurgau Canton were taken; Feldkirch was besieged. The Count Palatine, as a precautionary measure, occupied certain places in Alsace belonging to the Duke, who was reduced to despair by the revolt of his Swiss allies.

It was at this juncture in France that the Dauphin seized the reins of power, summoned the provosts, the University, the merchants and the burgesses to the Louvre, and announced that he intended to govern the country.[2] He forbad his cousins and his uncles to follow him. As if by presentiment Pope John, while at Laufenburg, began to shower ecclesiastical benefactions on the Duke of Guienne, and he accompanied these with spiritual favours which the young prince, who had exiled his wife to Saint-Germain-en-Laye in order to prosecute

[1] *C. E.*, iv. 425.   [2] Monstrelet, 361-2.

his amour with 'la belle Casinelle,' certainly did not merit. But while the Pope thus had his eyes turned toward France, it had become dangerous to remain any longer in Laufenburg.

In the early morning of Tuesday, the 9th April,[1] Pope John left the little town by the Rhine Falls. He was again disguised, and carried a bow and a quiver. Six men accompanied him; none of them belonged to the Curia; the Abbot of Podiobonizo was the only Italian among them. The seven fugitives struck across the Black Forest; on the first night they reached Todtnau in the Wiesental. The next day they passed Muggenbrunn, Halde, Giessheubel, Horben, and the monastery in the picturesque valley of the Guenterstal, two miles from Freiburg. Here in Freiburg im Breisgau at the Dominican Cloister Pope John was to remain, with the exception of a week's wandering, for more than a month. As he wrote from Freiburg on the 11th April, it is probable that he reached the cloister on the 10th. At about the same time five or six cardinals, an archbishop, a bishop, several other prelates and officers of the Curia, returned to Constance.

Freiburg found special favour in the eyes of Dietrich von Niem;[2] its broad streets and squares, its fountains and runlets pleased him. But its chief glory, which the stolid Teuton never mentioned, is its cathedral. Its finest parts are the work of an unknown architect of the eleventh century, so that the cathedral is the earliest masterpiece of mediæval architecture. The steeple springs out of an octagonal turret which itself rises naturally from a square tower; and it is more slender and graceful than that of Vienna, Strasburg, or Antwerp; it is perfect in its clean wonderful proportion. The hollow perforated octagonal turret is the earliest and boldest example of its kind; as the moonlight streams in broad luminous beams through the red-stone interstices, 'the finely varied devices of the lattice-work shine out in all the deep contrast of light and shade, the pierced embroidery of the steeple is picked out in silver—here revealing some handsome trefoil design, there displaying the petal-shaped tracery of a Gothic window, and anon the web-like mullions of a rosace.' The ribs of the deep

---

[1] The exact date is uncertain; it was either the 8th, 9th, or 10th: Finke (*B.*), 37.   [2] Hardt, ii. 399-400.

THROUGH THE BLACK FOREST   321

arch in the porch are embossed with statuettes; the ' stained windows of the interior are even more handsome and gorgeous perhaps than those of the Alsatian Munster, while the old carved screens and pulpits, and early German altar-pieces are rich bits of mediæval beauty.'[1] Freiburg had been held by the Austrian dukes since the summer of 1368.[2] There is little wonder that the Pope and those of the Curia who followed him, when they entered the city, were struck with its beauty and elegance.[3] No cardinals came after John; but there were bishops, chamberlains, and other officers of his court still in his train. They remained with him until the 3rd May, when they returned to Constance. ' When the honey failed, the flies no longer swarmed around.'[4]

Pope John was now in Freiburg, no longer in imminent fear of the troops of the Empire, but hoping for a speedy and happy issue out of his trouble. He was in correspondence with Jean sans Peur, who had sent a bodyguard to the Rhine in Alsace to meet him; the Duke had been profuse with his gifts of wine in Constance during the winter; his ambassadors were at the Council, and in the Pope's confidence. They wanted him to fly to Avignon and to settle there under the Duke's protection. Moreover, John expected an armed force to arrive from John of Nassau, the Archbishop of Mainz, his old friend and King Sigismund's enemy. The Pope knew that he had nothing further to hope from the Council; trusting in the armed assistance which he expected, he wrote as one combatant would write to another. He still professed to be willing to resign, but the war against the Duke of Austria must cease, and he must be made Cardinal Legate in perpetuity for the whole of Italy, with Bologna and Avignon ceded to him, with a pension of thirty thousand florins secured on the cities of Venice, Florence, and Genoa, and with perfect freedom from account for any of his actions in the past or the future.[5] However, he could not help seeing that the days of his power might be limited, and he resolved, like the unrighteous steward, to make the most of the time left to him. He bestowed on the new Archbishop of Cologne the administration of the diocese of

---

[1] Bader, 160 *et seq.*; Mayhew, 186 *et seq.*   [2] Bader, 343.
[3] Hardt, ii. 402.   [4] Finke (*B.*), 38-9.   [5] Hardt, ii. 403-4.

Paderborn; he appointed a number of Italian archbishops and bishops; he granted rewards to all who had served him faithfully.[1]

An assembly of the nations at the Franciscan monastery read the Pope's letter on Saturday, the 13th April. They naturally regarded the offer to resign as a dishonest subterfuge intended merely to gain time for the flight to Burgundy; and they prepared a long letter to all secular powers describing what had happened. In this the Pope's conduct was consistently manifested in the most unfavourable light, as dictated entirely by his own self-interest; every one knew, they said, that he intended to flee from Constance, and that King Sigismund had declared that he had rather the Pope did this than give any handle for reproach against himself for breach of his word or for interference with the Pope's liberty of action.[2] At the same time they passed a decree against the mendicant Friars, who were known to be working in the Pope's interest, prohibiting them from leaving the city and from holding any chapters during that entire year. Sigismund also revoked the safe-conducts which had been granted at Schaffhausen, as he found they were being used not merely for returning to, but also for leaving, Constance. Cardinal Hannibaldus had turned his steps toward Italy, and was accompanied by Benedict de Pileo, who was caught and taken to Neuchâtel, having a most gruesome experience before he regained his liberty. The security and good regulations for police which obtained at Constance were not observed outside the city, as many of those who left the Council discovered to their cost.[3] The Pope and the Council were thus now at hopeless variance.

In these troublous days the bad climate of Constance claimed its first noted victim. Manuel Chrysoloras, the celebrated Grecian, died on the 15th April, and was buried in the church of the Dominican Friars. A touching epitaph in Latin was afterwards composed by Aeneas Sylvius, which set forth how the learned ambassador rested there in foreign soil, a matter of little import, since heaven was always at the same distance from this house of his bondage.[4]

[1] Finke (*B.*), 39. [2] Hardt, iv. 107-11.
[3] Finke (*B.*), 68. [4] Lenfant (*C.*), i. 176.

The members of the University of Paris continued to be very wroth with the lukewarmness of the cardinals and the villainy of Pope John. They announced that he had written to the King of France, and to the Dukes of Berri and Orleans, traducing those three pillars of the Council, King Sigismund, the Patriarch of Antioch, and the Bishop of Salisbury; and they stated their own fixed determination to proceed with the good work.[1] On the 11th April, at Pierre d'Ailly's lodging, Jean Gerson took advantage of the suspicion resting on the Duke of Burgundy of abetting the Pope's flight to stir up the question of Jean Petit's doctrine, proposing that any one who opposed its condemnation should be considered as a fautor of heresy.[2] If he did not desire the death of the Duke, the Chancellor at least desired his public humiliation. The gauntlet, thus thrown down, was taken up in the name of Jean sans Peur on the 15th May.

The sixth general session of the Council was held in the cathedral on the 17th April in the presence of the King of the Romans, clad in cope and dalmatic, with the royal crown on his head, and the imperial sceptre, the golden apple, and the sword borne before him. Jean de Brogni, Cardinal de Viviers, the oldest member of the sacred college, now seventy-two years of age, presided on this occasion as on all others until a new Pope was elected. All the cardinals then in Constance, save Pierre d'Ailly, were present. Mass having been celebrated by a Polish archbishop, an 'act of cession' was read and approved, which was to be sent to the fugitive Pope. By this act he was required to select proctors from the list submitted to him, any two of whom were empowered, in the face of the opposition of the others or even of the Pope himself, to effect his resignation. The Council then nominated four proctors from each nation from whom the Pope was to select two from each nation to act with any others whom he might appoint. The Cardinals Fillastre and Zabarella and certain other members of the Council were deputed to carry the document to Pope John, to procure his choice of proctors, and his decision of the place at which the resignation was to be effected; if he declined to return to Constance he was to fix on Ulm, Ravensberg, or Basel; two

[1] Pulka, 17.   [2] Valois, iv. 318.

days' grace were to be allowed for this purpose and ten days for the subsequent journey; or the Pope might promulgate a Bull declaring himself to be no longer Pope; if he refused all these methods, then the Council would proceed against him as a notorious schismatic and heretic. Meantime, until his answer was received, all proceedings against him were to be in abeyance.[1]

It was also necessary at this session to take cognisance of the matter of heresy, the attention of the Council being called thereto by the proceedings of that firebrand among reformers, Jerome of Prague. He and a disciple had come to Constance secretly on the 4th April and had gone to a hostelry in Saint Paul's Street. He, however, beat a hasty retreat, leaving his sword behind him, and went with his disciple to Ueberlingen. Here the valiant knight plucked up courage and wrote to King Sigismund and to the Council asking for a safe-conduct. The King refused; the Council offered Jerome a safe-conduct for coming to Constance, but not for leaving it. Jerome then wrote a manifesto in the Latin, German, and Czech languages, which he procured to be affixed to the doors of all the churches and monasteries in Constance, saying that he had come there to defend himself and his country from the charge of heresy, and that he required a safe-conduct to ensure that he should not be clapped in prison before being heard; having so done, he departed to Bohemia.[2]

The Council in its sixth session also took up again the question of the 'commission of belief.' The president, Pierre d'Ailly, was not present and it was felt that he required some supervision; four deputies from the four nations were therefore appointed as a controlling body to receive the report of the commission concerning Wyclif's heresies and to proceed against John Hus's '*usque ad definitivam sententiam inclusive*.'[3] The Council further resolved, being actuated by a desire to clear foxes out of the Lord's vineyard, to summon Jerome of Prague to appear before them within fifteen days, and they declared expressly that their safe-conduct would only avail until he

---

[1] Hardt, iv. 113 *et seq*.   [2] Richental, 78.
[3] Mansi, xxvii. 610; Tschackert, 223; for another view as to the new appointments see Huebler, 5.

appeared and would not shield him against the arm of justice.[1]

Party feeling was now running very high. The nations and the cardinals were at variance; and the former sent their resolutions to the latter so shortly before the time appointed for a general session that the cardinals had not time to deliberate thereon, and resented the slight. A proposal was indeed made, though it was not pushed,[2] at this session to exclude the Pope and all the cardinals from the consultations on the ground that they were interested parties in the question of Church reform. The cardinals manifested their displeasure in a congregation held the next day and upheld the rights of the Roman Church against a general Council; but the congregation would not agree that the Church was the head of the Council where the matter in dispute was the removal of a schism which had been caused by the cardinals. A similar dispute arose over the question whether the condemnation of the Wyclifite heresy was to issue in the name of the Pope or of the Council or of both. Pierre d'Ailly desired the condemnation to issue from the Council without any mention of the Pope; he declared that the Council was superior to the Pope and could depose him. But the Cardinal was opposed; even the Patriarch of Antioch, who had so bitterly withstood Pope John, now declared that the Pope was not subject to the Council and that the condemnation must issue in the name of the pontiff. The worthy Patriarch clearly thought that if John succeeded in escaping to Burgundy it would be wise not to have exasperated him too far. As he was then preparing their instructions for the ambassadors to Pope John he took the opportunity to ask the Pope's advice on the question, and he was thereafter bitterly upbraided for this unseemly complaisance and flattery. None but the most determined or honourable men dared steer a perfectly straight course at this time.

The stately embassy, led by the two cardinals, journeyed by Basel up the Rhine valley to Freiburg, arriving there on the 21st April. But the Pope was no longer there. Duke Friedrich had followed him to Freiburg, and had received news of one disaster after another. The men of Bern had overrun the

[1] Mansi, xxvii. 611. [2] Tschackert, 217.

Aargau Canton and had taken even the castle at Habsburg, the cradle of his race. The men of Zürich took Mellingen; those of Lucerne took Sursee; the combined forces captured two other towns. Baden in the Aargau was besieged. Although Breisgau, the Black Forest, and the Tirol were still true to him, the Duke began to lose heart. Ruin was staring him in the face. Help might come from Burgundy and Styria, condottiere troops might be hired by the Pope from Milan and Venice; but this would take time, and meantime King Sigismund had an army of forty thousand men in the field against him. The Duke felt powerless.[1]

Pope John's hopes were set on the Duke of Burgundy, to whom he was ready, men said, to advance large sums of money. But here also he was deceived. At the time when the Pope's messenger reached Jean sans Peur, there arrived also a messenger from the Council, giving the King's version of the story. The Duke who had assassinated his cousin was not a man to have any sentimental attraction toward the Pope. He was a long-headed, self-seeking politician; he saw that John had made a fatally false move, that he had lost his place and influence, that he was no longer able to induce the Council to reverse the decree of the Bishop of Paris and to uphold the doctrine of Jean Petit. The Pope was therefore useless to John of Burgundy. The Duke repulsed his messenger with great indignation, and refused to believe what he said in opposition to the messenger of the Council.[2] He despatched ambassadors to Constance to exculpate himself from all complicity with the Pope. Meanwhile, King Sigismund cut off all further communications across the border.

But the Pope had not given up all hope. In order to be as near the promised land as possible, John went on the 20th April to Breisach, the picturesque old town on the Rhine, at the foot of a lofty crag on a spur of the Kaiserstuhl. The ambassadors from Constance sent a messenger to him on the 22nd, and themselves followed next day. At first they could find no trace of His Holiness; even his servants and his intimates did not know where he was. At length, at seven o'clock in the evening, Bindachius de Ricasoli, a friend of the Pope

[1] Aschbach, ii. 76-7.   [2] Pulka, 20.

who had followed him from Florence, appeared and told them that John had been very ill for a day and a night and was lying at that moment at the hostelry, but would like to see them. It was arranged that the embassy should wait on him next day.

Of the two cardinals who introduced the ambassadors, Zabarella was eminent in learning and in popularity ; every one expected that he would be the next Pope ; it was hopeless for the Pope to try to seduce him from his allegiance to the Council. But John tried to win over Cardinal Fillastre ; he allowed him the privilege of making transfers of benefices, bringing in valuable first fruits, and the cardinal, notwithstanding his zeal for reform, was quite ready to reap this benefit from the mammon of unrighteousness. The cardinals introduced the embassy. The ambassadors, after saluting the Pope with all reverence, acquainted him with the instructions of the Council, and begged him to betake himself to one of the cities they named. Pope John's answer was sufficiently clear and explicit. He still meant to resign ; unfortunately he had been obliged, from fear for his safety, to leave Constance and to wander from place to place, followed by his enemies ; but he had never intended to return to Italy, his plan being far otherwise. He meant to betake himself to France, for the French Kings had ever been protectors of the popes and opponents of the Schism. He had therefore sent messages to the French nobles ; the Duke of Burgundy was waiting for him with two thousand men ; and when once he got to France he would resign and do all that was desired. He would consider the proposals of the embassy and would give them his answer ; but meantime he wished the two cardinals to speak alone with him. The ambassadors took their departure and Fillastre and Zabarella remained. They urged him to comply and then all would be well ; they spoke long and earnestly with him, but failed to persuade him. Fillastre himself gives the account of the interview.[1]

Pope John had determined to make one more dash for liberty. Next morning—it was the Day of Saint Mark, the 25th April— he disguised himself in a short jacket and long black mantle and went, with a single attendant, from the hostelry toward the bridge over the river. The gatekeeper refused to let him pass.

[1] Finke (*F.*), 172-3.

A wayfarer turned up who conducted the Pope to a second gate, but the gatekeeper here also refused him egress. A third gate, the Spekthor, was tried; the Pope waited in a barn; but all these customs-gates were in the hands of the men of the town and they were on the side of the Council. Meantime, a troop of the Duke's cavalry took the old road up the Rhine toward Basel; they were going to the little village of Neuenburg; and Pope John, seeing the Austrian cavalry, went with them, hoping to escape across the river in a boat. But he reckoned without his captor; Friedrich had no intention of allowing his valuable bird to escape from the cage so easily. It was a long march; but they arrived about midday, and there were Burgundian troops on the other side of the Rhine. Never had liberty looked so near. But no sooner had the troopers reached Neuenburg than a fearful tumult broke out in the town. A cry was raised that the men of Basel and Strassburg were about to besiege the place in the interest of the Council. The townsfolk were in an uproar. They ran to arms. One party dashed off to seize the water supply. There was universal confusion. The Pope remained in Neuenburg until eight o'clock in the evening, and then gave up hope; he little suspected that the whole tumult had been got up by Duke Friedrich to prevent his escape.[1] John had not slept the night before; he had now to mount a sorry little black nag and to take his way through the dark night to Breisach. They reached there in the early morning, but had to wait an hour and a half, and then to go round to another gate. The Pope was utterly broken down by anxiety and fatigue. He burst into a fit of convulsive sobbing; he wailed and moaned; he knew not where he was; he only knew that he was betrayed.

Friedrich of the Tirol had resolved to abandon the cause of Pope John. The Swiss were continuing their victorious career; they had taken Reichensee, Merenberg, and Vilmeringen; they were besieging Baden. Basel, Strassburg, Colmar, and other towns were in arms against him. The Duke was being crushed. His cousin, Louis of Bavaria Ingolstadt, wrote to him, and advised him to submit. Friedrich believed in Louis, and resolved to follow his advice. This meant that he was to

[1] Finke (*F.*), 175-6.

THROUGH THE BLACK FOREST 329

betray Pope John. The Pope had fallen into the trap; he had been caught in this, his third endeavour to escape, and was now to be delivered as a peace offering by Duke Friedrich to King Sigismund. The King had played his cards well, and had captured both his enemies.

When the ambassadors heard of the Pope's new flight, they were thunderstruck; they took their way back to Freiburg in despair; their embassy had failed; they intended to return at once to Constance. At the entreaty of the burgomaster and the Council of Freiburg they consented to await for a few hours the arrival of Louis of Bavaria. At eleven in the forenoon the brother of the French Queen rode into Freiburg, had a short interview with the cardinals, and then hurried on to Breisach to meet Friedrich of the Tirol. He was just in time. Four hours later, and the Pope would probably have slipped out of the Duke's hands.[1]

A fortnight earlier the Markgraf Rudolf of Hachberg and the envoys of Basel and Strassburg had met the Duke and the Pope at Freiburg and had endeavoured to make peace between them and the Council; but Friedrich had scornfully told them that as long as the Council lasted, so long should the Pope remain with him. The last fortnight had broken the Duke's spirit. Louis of Bavaria spared him not, but upbraided him with his foolhardiness and stupidity; Friedrich was meek as a lamb. The Count informed him that the King and the nobles were resolved on his destruction; there was no remedy save in absolute submission. Friedrich agreed; the Pope was to be sacrificed.

On Saturday, the 27th April, the Duke and the Count escorted the unwilling Pope from Breisach, leaving his valuables behind; and at Umkirch they met the cardinals. Fillastre and Zabarella set before the pontiff the alternatives of honourable resignation or disgraceful deposition; and in the evening the Bishop of Carcasonne spoke to him earnestly in the same strain. The Pope took the night for reflection, but failed to realise his position. In the morning he announced that he was willing to resign, but not at Constance nor at any of the places proposed; he would resign in Burgundy, Savoy, Italy, or Venice, always

[1] Pulka, 21.

providing that fitting provision were made for his future, and that his two rivals took the same step ; he asked for three new proctors, Regnault de Chartres, Géraud du Puy, and Jean Dachery, to be appointed, and promised to hand over his declaration of resignation to Berthold des Ursins ; finally, he would only resign if peace was made with the Duke of Austria.[1] Clearly did he not know that Friedrich had already betrayed him ; but so it was.

As Pope John was brought back to Freiburg, the women of the town tore their hair and wailed, and the men rushed together to arms, fearing that the city would be besieged. But Louis of Bavaria calmed their fears by telling them that the Pope was brought back in order to pacify the King and the Council.[2]

From the end of April Pope John was a prisoner in the charge of the burgomaster and council of Freiburg ; twelve guards watched him by day, and twenty-four by night. The town was occupied by the imperial troops, and the Pope was the prisoner of the King of the Romans.[3] Escape was impossible. Some absurd and disgraceful rumours were indeed circulated at Constance,[4] but they were started ' more out of malice than integrity ' by that hatred, envy, and all uncharitableness which was then so rife against the fallen pontiff.

[1] Hefele, vii. 114. [2] Pulka, 22.
[3] Finke (*B.*), 47. [4] Pulka, 22.

CHAPTER XIX

THE DEPOSITION OF POPE JOHN

UPON the college of cardinals, upon the Italian nation at the Council, and upon every friend of Pope John the Twenty-third the news of his last desperate attempt to escape fell with a weight of deadening despair; while the Pope's enemies were exultant and began to bruit abroad the most gross and outrageous scandals.[1] When the ambassadors returned, no one took any interest in their story, for the news of the Duke's submission was known, and it was felt that the time of grace for the Pope was past. His enemies gloried in his flight; there were processions and prayers for the peace of the Church. The two Dukes of Austria and Bavaria had ridden on Saturday, the 27th April, to Schaffhausen; Louis had left Friedrich here, and galloped on through the night to Constance, bringing the news to the King on Sunday morning after Mass. On the 30th April Friedrich came back to Kreuzlingen and met Sigismund that same evening. ' Your transgression will not be forgiven until you have brought back your prisoner,' were the King's first words. Next day, Wednesday, the 1st May, the Duke went to the hostel near the Bishop's palace and remained there in custody, awaiting his appearance before Sigismund and his court.[2]

The seventh general session of the Council was held on the 2nd May. It was a stormy meeting; certain of the bishops lost their temper; other members broke forth into abuse; the entire assembly was on tenterhooks. Pope John's proposals were read and rejected, and he was summoned to appear before the Council within nine days; he was cited as a heretic, a schismatic, a simoniac, as immoral and incorrigible; he was

[1] Cf. Hardt, ii. 402; Pulka, 22; Hefele, vii. 113 note.
[2] Finke (*B.*), 47.

threatened with suspension and deposition; the safe-conduct despatched to him expressly reserved the right of punishment. The Council was in no humour for further trifling. At the same session permission was granted for institution of process against Jerome of Prague, who was at that time lying in prison at Hirschau in Bavaria; Duke Johann of Bavaria had, on the 23rd April, sent word to King Sigismund of his capture of the heretic; and he had also despatched to the same address the letters found on Jerome, wherein certain of the Bohemian nobles complained that he had been granted neither a hearing nor a safe-conduct. The Council took no heed of the imprisonment, but merely directed Master Heinricus de Piro of Cologne to proceed further against Jerome at the next session. Next day, the 3rd May, Pope John's old friend, John of Nassau, Archbishop of Mainz, sent his envoys to the Council; they were simply heard and dismissed.

Notwithstanding the Pope's captivity, the mind of the Council at this time was as unsettled and various as the face of the earth on an April day.[1] Nothing yet was finally settled, and all kinds of rumours prevailed. Men said that an Italian money-changer had offered the King three hundred thousand florins '*pro domino papa*,' but that Sigismund had refused the bribe.[2] Meanwhile, the eighth general session of the Council was held on Saturday, the 4th May, to deal with the question of the Wyclifian heresies. Cardinal Viviers as usual presided; eight other members of the college were present, and the King in all his regalia. The Patriarch of Antioch celebrated Mass; and the Bishop of Toulon preached from the text, 'The Holy Spirit shall guide you into all truth.' Piro and Scribani then rose and demanded that the followers of John Wyclif, inasmuch as they had not appeared, be declared contumacious; he represented that Wyclif was a notorious heretic who had died impenitent; and he asked that his bones be exhumed and that the forty-five articles extracted from his works and already condemned by the Universities of Oxford and Prague be condemned by this general Council. The Archbishop of Genoa then read the confession of faith framed by the Twelfth General Council to which all present expressed their adherence. The

[1] Pulka, 21.   [2] *Ibid.* 23.

THE DEPOSITION OF POPE JOHN

Archbishop then read the forty-five articles.[1] 'These and many other errors has Wyclif set forth,' said he, ' in his *Dialogus*, *Trialogus*, and other works, and had wrought much sorrow and

[1] The following is the text of these celebrated articles :—

ARTICULI XLV., WICLEFI
PUBLICA SENTENTIA NUNC CONDEMNATI, PER PILEUM ARCHI-
EPISCOPUM GENUENSEM PRÆLECTI

I. Substantia panis materialis, que similiter substantia vini materialis, manent in sacramento altaris.

II. Accidentia panis non manent sine subjecto in eodem sacramento.

III. Christus non est in eodem sacramento identice que realiter in propria persona (in Vind. Lips. que Goth. præsentia) corporali.

IV. Si Episcopus vel sacerdos est in peccato mortali, non ordinat, non conficit, non consecrat, nec baptizat.

V. Non est fundatum in Evangelio, quod Christus missam ordinarit.

VI. Deus debet obedire diabolo.

VII. Si homo debite fuerit contritus, omnis confessio exterior est sibi superflua que inutilis.

VIII. Si Papa sit præscitus que malus, que per consequens membrum diaboli, non habet potestatem super fideles ab aliquo sibi datam, nisi forte a Cæsare.

IX. Post Urbanum sextum non est aliquis recipiendus in Papam, sed vivendum est more Græcorum sub legibus propriis.

X. Contra Scripturam sacram est, quod viri Eccle. habeant possessiones.

XI. Nullus prælatus debet aliquem excommunicare, nisi prius sciat, eum excommunicatum a Deo, que qui sic excommunicat, fit hæreticus ex hoc vel excommunicatus.

XII. Prælatus excommunicans Clericum, qui appellavit ad Regem que ad concilium regni, eo ipso traditor est Regis que regni.

XIII. Illi qui dimittunt prædicare, sive verbum Dei audire, propter excommunicationem hominum, sunt excommunicati, que in die judicii traditores Christi habebuntur.

XIV. Licet alicui diacono vel presbytero prædicare verbum Dei absque autoritate sedis Apostolicæ vel Episcopi Catholici.

XV. Nullus est Dominus civilis, nullus est prælatus, nullus est Episcopus, dum est in peccato mortali.

XVI. Domini temporales possunt ad arbitrium suum au,erre bona temporalia ab Ecclesia possessionatis habitualiter delinquentibus, id est, ex habitu, non solo actu delinquentibus.

XVII. Populares possunt ad suum arbitrium dominos delinquentes corrigere.

XVIII. Decimæ sunt puræ eleemosynæ, que parochiani possunt propter peccata suorum Prælatorum ad libitum suum eas auferre.

XIX. Speciales orationes applicatæ uni personæ per prælatos vel religiosos, non plus prosunt eidem, quam generales, cæteris paribus.

XX. Conferens eleemosynam fratribus, est excommunicatus eo facto.

XXI. Si quis ingreditur religionem privatam qualemcunque, tam possessionatorum, quam mendicantium, redditur ineptior que inhabilior ad observantiam mandatorum Dei.

vexation of souls, especially in England and Bohemia; they have been rejected by the Universities of Oxford and Prague, been condemned by the Archbishops of Canterbury, York, and Prague, and the last named has ordered Wyclif's books to be burned; lately, also, the Council of Rome condemned the same writings. This present Council has had these articles examined by cardinals, bishops, abbots, masters of theology, and doctors of the civil and canon law, and they have found that many of them are heretical, others are erroneous, others blasphemous and offensive to pious ears. It has also been found that Wyclif's books contain many other like doctrines.' Taking the extracts as they stand, no one can doubt that, to an orthodox churchman of that day, the Archbishop's description of them was perfectly fair. John Hus and his followers did not defend all the articles; they urged that some were capable of explanation in an orthodox sense, and that others suffered through being torn from their context; certain of them were, of course, mere copies of the tenets of the Fraticelli and Spiritual Franciscans, and had already been condemned by the Church. The Council of Constance now decreed that it confirmed the sentences of the

XXII. Sancti instituentes religiones privatas, sic instituendo peccaverunt.
XXIII. Religiosi viventes in religionibus privatis, non sunt de religione Christiana.
XXIV. Fratres tenentur per labores manuum victum acquirere, que non per mendicitatem. Prima pars est scandalosa que præsumtuose asserta, pro quanto sic generaliter que indistincte loquitur. Et secunda erronea, pro quanto asserit, mendicitatem fratribus non licere.
XXV. Omnes sunt Simoniaci, qui se obligant orare pro aliis, eis in temporalibus subvenientibus.
XXVI. Oratio præsciti nulli valet.
XXVII. Omnia de necessitate absoluta eveniunt.
XXVIII. Confirmatio juvenum, clericorum ordinatio, locorum consecratio, reservantur Papæ que Episcopis propter cupiditatem lucri temporalis que honoris.
XXIX. Universitates, studia, collegia, graduationes que magisteria in eisdem, sunt vana gentilitate introducta, que tantum prosunt Ecclesiæ sicut diabolus.
XXX. Excommunicatio Papæ vel cujuscunque prælati non est timenda, quis est censura Anti-Christi.
XXXI. Peccant fundantes claustra, que ingredientes sunt viri diabolici.
XXXII. Ditare clerum est contra Christi mandatum.
XXXIII. Sylvester Papa que Constantinus Imperator erraverunt Ecclesiam dotando.
XXXIV. Omnes de ordine mendicantium sunt hæretici, que dantes eis eleemosynam sunt excommunicati.
XXXV. Ingredientes religionem aut aliquem ordinem, eo ipso inhabiles sunt ad

THE DEPOSITION OF POPE JOHN 335

three Archbishops and the decree of the Council of Rome; that it condemned the forty-five articles together with the *Dialogus, Trialogus,* and all other writings of Wyclif; that it was forbidden to expound or read them except for purposes of confutation; and that the writings and treatises should be publicly burned.[1] It was also ordered that the body of John Wyclif be exhumed from the consecrated ground in which he had been buried. The Archbishop was then about to read two hundred and sixty further extracts, but this was postponed. After the session the citation to Pope John to appear was posted on the Snezthor; and three cardinals and many connected with the Curia returned on this day from Schaffhausen to Constance.

To the friends of John Hus the condemnation of the forty-five articles must have been a severe blow of evil omen, for it committed the Council on many points which Hus regarded as open to argument. Wyclif, like many other philosophers, occasionally clinched his reasoning with a paradox which could only be rightly understood in the light of the preceding argument. He held that all dominion was founded upon grace.

observandum divina præcepta, que per consequens perveniendi ad regna cœlorum, nisi apostataverint ab eisdem.

XXXVI. Papa cum omnibus clericis suis possessionem habentibus sunt hæretici, eo, quod possessionem habent, que omnes consentientes eis, omnes scilicet Domini seculares, que laici cæteri.

XXXVII. Ecclesia Romana est Synagoga Satanæ, nec Papa est immediatus que proximus Vicarius Christi que Apostolorum.

XXXVIII. Decretales Epistolæ sunt apocryphæ, que seducunt a fide Christi, que clerici sunt stulti, que student eas.

XXXIX. Imperator que Domini seculares seducti sunt a diabolo, ut Ecclesiam dotarent de bonis temporalibus.

XL. Electio Papæ a Cardinalibus per diabolum est introducta.

XLI. Non est de necessitate salutis, credere, Romanam Ecclesiam esse supremam inter alias Ecclesias. Error est, si per Romanam Ecclesiam intelligatur universalis Ecclesia, aut Concilium generale, aut pro quanto negaret primatum summi Pontificis super alias Ecclesias peculiares.

XLII. Fatuum est, credere indulgentiis Papæ que Episcoporum.

XLIII. Juramenta illicita sunt, quæ fiunt ad roborandum humanos contractus que commercia civilia.

XLIV. Augustinus, Benedictus que Bernhardus damnati sunt, nisi pœnituerint de hoc, quod habuerunt possessiones, que instituerunt, que intraverunt religiones. Et sic a Papa usque ad infimum religiosum omnes sunt hæretici.

XLV. Omnes religiones indifferenter introductæ sunt a diabolo. Hardt, iv. 153-5.
[1] Hardt, iv. 150 *et seq.*

To him ' it was the personal relation, the immediate dependence of the individual upon God, that made him worthy or unworthy ; it was his own character and not his office, however exalted in the eyes of man, that constituted him what he really was. The Pope himself, if personally a bad man, lost *ipso facto* his entire right to lordship.' This is the thought underlying articles 4, 8, 15, and 26. Here, however, as so often in his writings, ' an important distinction has to be settled. Every good man,' though lord of all things, ' is not on that account at liberty to assert his possession of them in contravention of civil right : so also he cannot claim to disobey the civil ruler because that ruler is personally unworthy of his post ; his rule is at least permitted by God. Thus Wyclif expressly repudiates the inference which might naturally and logically be drawn from his premises. God, ran his favourite paradox, ought to obey the devil ; that is, no one can escape from the duty of obedience to existing powers, be those powers never so depraved.'[1] This explanation of the sixth article ought to have satisfied even the fathers of the Council. We do not know what number of copies of the reformer's works were then in Constance ; nor do we know the names of the cardinals, bishops, abbots, doctors, and masters to whom they were submitted for examination ; although we may be sure that men like Pierre d'Ailly and Jean Gerson would be well acquainted with, and have studiously and carefully examined, the works of the Master of Balliol. But the value of the vote of the general session of the Council must necessarily depend on such preliminary examination and discussion ; and if this was entirely one-sided and inadequate then the friends of John Hus had every reason to fear for the fate of him who had publicly defended certain of the condemned articles. If John Hus himself, as he lay fettered in the Castle of Gottlieben, heard of the condemnation, he must have felt that, although he had expressly declined to defend the forty-five articles,[2] he too had been condemned unheard as a fautor of heresy. He knew now that he was fighting for his life ; his only hope lay in the defence which he would make at his public examination. The new commissioners visited him occasionally for the purpose of their

[1] Poole, 301.   [2] Palacky (*Doc.*), 92.

THE DEPOSITION OF POPE JOHN

investigation; they found him weak and weary through hunger and suffering; he was meek and patient; his spirit was broken.

The next day, the 5th May, was still more notable in the history of the Council. It was Sunday, and there was a great gathering of the chief prelates of the four nations and of the secular princes and nobles in the Franciscan cloister. King Sigismund sat on a throne at the far end of the long room. He had at first declined ever to make peace with Friedrich of Austria again; and now, although he had been brought to a more conciliatory frame of mind, he was still determined to humble his adversary to the dust. Duke Louis of Bavaria, Burggraf Friedrich of Nuernberg, and Count Nicolas Gara appeared at the door, leading the unhappy Duke Friedrich, who kneeled three times at the entrance. In answer to the King's question what they wanted, Duke Louis spoke :—' At the request of my cousin Friedrich, Duke of Austria, I ask the King to pardon him in that he hath contemned your royal majesty and the Council; he hereby makes over to the King's grace and power his body, his land and his people, all that he has; he promises, moreover, to bring back Pope John provided, for his honour's sake, that no injury befall the Pope's body or his goods.' The petitioner and those who accompanied him then approached the royal throne. ' Is that what you request ? ' said the King; and the Duke answered in so broken a voice and pleaded for grace so humbly that Sigismund's anger began to lighten. Sigismund held out his hand to the Duke, saying, ' Sorry indeed are we that you have committed this fault.'[1] Then Duke Friedrich swore and subscribed a deed, whereby he made over all his lands, from Alsace to the Tirol, to the King to hold until it should please him to return them; and he further contracted to bring Pope John back to Constance and to remain himself as hostage until all his promises were fulfilled. When this deed had been read before the assembly, King Sigismund, swelling with pride, turned to the envoys from Venice, Genoa, Milan, and Florence, and said :—' You know how mighty and honoured are the Dukes of Austria; but now you see what a King of the Teutons can do; I am the mightiest prince over all other

[1] Richental, 68.

princes and states.'[1] This was the most triumphant moment of Sigismund's life at Constance. His troubles were to begin.

The King immediately sent his delegates in all directions to take possession of the Duke's lands and to receive homage from the occupants. Tirol and the cities Waldshut and Villingen objected. The Tirolese nobility might be dissatisfied with their Duke, but they had no mind to be handed over like cattle to a changeable and penurious King of the Romans, who might mortgage Tirol as if it were an imperial city; they would only recognise as Count of the Tirol one who was in possession with their will and assent. Sigismund had not the money to raise an army and march to the Adige; he remained sulkily discontent with the failure of his plan for the ' Land in the Mountains.'[2] With his allies, the Swiss, he also disagreed. He sent orders to stop the sieges of Baden and Wildeck. The cantons of Bern and Zurich sent back an answer in the name of the confederates that they could not withdraw their troops from Baden because the city was to be delivered to them after eight days. 'You will not only have the Duke for your enemy, but me also, if you disobey my orders,' said the King in his wrath. But having cooled a little he sent the messengers back to Baden to persuade their fellow-countrymen to comply; and with them went the Counts Conrad of Freiburg and Friedrich of Toggenburg to take possession of the fortress in the King's name. But, before they came, the city had been already stormed, and all the Habsburg archives and deeds had been burned. The confederates excused themselves on the grounds that they had been unable to restrain their troops and that it was only a fair revenge for the breach of the peace at Winterthur.[3] The King professed to be satisfied with this excuse, but asked that the places taken should be surrendered to him. The Swiss again demurred; they had taken the places at their own cost, and had been promised beforehand that they should retain what they captured. Sigismund reminded them that they were at peace with Duke Friedrich, and had only acted on behalf of the Empire, and that their action was unjustifiable on any other ground; he wanted the suzerainty of the captures, which they might occupy; only he must have the revenues and

[1] Richental, 70. [2] *B.W.*, 269. [3] Aschbach, ii. 80-1.

THE DEPOSITION OF POPE JOHN

the control of the management. Zurich, the richest canton, now took up the negotiation and advanced the money which the penurious King needed.

The days of Pope John's captivity at Freiburg were spent in doing good to them who had done good to him. He had already rewarded the city of Freiburg; he now bestowed a dispensation on the trustees of the cathedral of Saint Stephan at Breisach, which stood in need of new bells and much repair, and he released the burgomaster and the council from an interdict placed on them by the Bishop of Constance. He gave three thousand gulden to his faithful equerry, Bindachius de Ricasoli, who had served him long and faithfully; and he also nominated several bishops.[1] On Ascension Day, Thursday the 9th May, the envoys from Constance appeared to take their prisoner to the Council. They were Friedrich, the Burggraf of Nuernberg, and the Archbishops of Besançon and Riga, with a troop of several hundred horsemen. Most of the Pope's officials had left on the 3rd May; there were still with him the two trusted Archbishops of Reims and Acerenza, whom he had recently promoted, the Bishops of Arezzo and Oleron, and a few of his servants—a sorry train for the spiritual lord of the Holy Roman Empire. The Pope received the envoys and promised to accompany them to Constance; he complained of the evil counsels adopted toward him; and he wrote secretly to the Cardinals Zabarella, d'Ailly, and Fillastre, asking them to act as his proctors in the process instituted against him. It was an extraordinary request, considering the activity of these three cardinals in the Council, an attempt to draw to his own side the three members of the college who had been most conspicuous in promoting the work which the Pope was endeavouring to overthrow. The nine days allowed for his appearance elapsed, and still Pope John delayed his departure. The Burggraf refused to lay his hand on the Lord's Anointed; he would only protect the escort. At length they got off, and on the 19th May they reached the ancient town of Radolfzell, at the end of the Zeller See, where the Pope had to put up at an inn.

The ninth general session of the Council was held on the

[1] Finke (*B.*), 47.

13th May. As the Pope had not appeared within the time allowed, Henricus de Piro, as promoter of the persecution, applied that he be suspended, that evidence be taken, and that the process for his deposition proceed. Cardinal Zabarella then rose and informed the Council of the Pope's letter and request with which the three cardinals were utterly unwilling to comply; and Piro also insisted on the necessity for the Pope's personal appearance. Five prelates then proceeded to the church door and called on Pope John to appear; naturally they received no reply. Another day's grace was allowed by the Council, but they appointed a body of thirteen commissioners to take evidence. The two hundred and sixty extracts from the works of John Wyclif were also condemned at this session. On the same day the Teutons held a congregation in furtherance of the prosecution of the Pope and proceeded to take evidence. King Sigismund laid before the same congregation a letter from Carlo Malatesta and a copy of a Bull from Pope Gregory the Twelfth authorising the Lord of Rimini and all others of his obedience to recognise the Council of Constance.[1]

Next day the tenth general session was held. Pope John was again solemnly summoned, and as he did not appear, he and his adherents were declared to be contumacious. Cardinal Fillastre then reported that ten witnesses had already been examined, and that from their depositions it was sufficiently proved that the Pope had dissipated the Church goods, had practised all manner of simony, and had caused scandal and confusion to Christendom, so that he deserved to be deposed from the spiritual and secular control of the Church; he admitted that there was no evidence of heresy. The other members of the commission making the preliminary investigation corroborated the Cardinal. Pierre d'Ailly had given evidence against the Pope on many points. On the motion of Henricus de Piro, the presiding cardinal and the four presidents representing the nations then assented to a decree of suspension, which was read out by the Patriarch of Antioch. The decree runs thus :—' In the name of the holy and undivided Trinity, the Father, Son, and Holy Ghost; Amen. Since we have surely

[1] Mansi, xxvii. 647.

THE DEPOSITION OF POPE JOHN 341

known that Pope John the Twenty-third, from the time of his accession till now, has scandalously misgoverned the Church, has through his damnable life and infamous conduct given an evil example to the people, has notoriously by simony distributed bishoprics, monasteries, priories, and other church benefices, has wasted the property of the church at Rome and other churches, has neglected all admonition and still continues to oppress the Church, we therefore declare the aforesaid Pope John to be suspended from all spiritual and secular control and hereby prohibit him from exercising the same ; and we direct that a process for his deposition be introduced : at the same time any further obedience to him on the part of the faithful is hereby forbidden.' The Monk of Saint-Denys wanted to make provision for the collation to benefices, but this was postponed until the issue of the final sentence against the Pope.[1] At this session Pierre d'Ailly and three other cardinals did not appear.

The fate of John Hus had been cruelly aggravated by the Pope's flight, and although his sad lot might escape the notice of the fathers at Constance, it raised universal commiseration among the nobles of Bohemia. On the 8th May the Barons of Moravia had sent to King Sigismund a letter of indignant protest, complaining that the patriot had not only not been freed from captivity, but had been kept in still viler duress. This was followed on the 12th May by another letter of similar tenor from two hundred and fifty barons of Moravia and Bohemia to the King and by a third to the courtiers, praying that they would use their endeavours also to set Hus at liberty. The matter was brought before a congregation of the four nations by Peter Mladonowicz on the 14th May. He read a letter from the nobles of Bohemia and Poland then in Constance complaining that John Hus was held in the straitest bondage notwithstanding the royal safe-conduct and the fact that no sentence had been passed against him, while heretics who had been condemned at Pisa walked about free at Constance ; they had endeavoured to obtain respect for the safe-conduct and a public hearing for Hus, but hitherto without result, and Hus was now in viler durance to the dishonour of Bohemia, a country which

[1] Mansi, xxvii. 654.

had ever been obedient to the Roman Church. The petitioners requested that, out of respect to the royal safe-conduct and to the fair fame of Bohemia, the Council would now make a speedy end of the matter. In conclusion the Bohemian nobles begged that no credence might be given to the lies that Christ's blood in Bohemia was taken about in flasks, and that cobblers were allowed to hear confession and to administer the sacrament. On hearing these last words, the iron Bishop of Leitomysl ejaculated, ' This is meant for me and my friends,' and he asked for time to answer these accusations. The Bohemian nobles were promised an answer next day.[1]

Next day, Wednesday the 15th May, a Bull of Pope Gregory the Twelfth was read in a congregation of the four nations presided over by the King. The Pope, who expressed his willingness to recognise the Council so far as it was convoked by King Sigismund and not by Pope John, and provided that Baldassare Cossa was taking no part therein, declared that he was ready to resign his high office. An answer to this Bull was returned later. It was on this date, as already mentioned, although his letters to the French nation were received eleven days later, that the Duke of Burgundy demanded that the Council should do justice between him and his enemy, Jean Gerson. Unfortunately for the Duke, Friedrich of the Tirol at this time disclosed to Louis of Bavaria the details of a plot which he said had been formed by the deposed Pope with the Republics of Florence and Venice, and in which the Duke of Burgundy and the Count of Savoy were implicated. Its object was to entrap or to kill King Sigismund as he passed through the lands of Burgundy or Savoy on his way to meet Pope Benedict and Ferdinand of Aragon. Gerson, speaking simply for himself and not on behalf of the French King or the University of Paris, took advantage of the excitement caused by Friedrich's revelation, to demand from the Council justice against the Duke of Burgundy for himself. Jean sans Peur wrote to exculpate himself from all complicity in any plot against Sigismund; he threw all the odium of the rumour on his enemy, Louis of Bavaria; who in his turn shifted the entire blame to the shoulders of the imprisoned Duke of Austria.

[1] Palacky (*Doc.*), 258, 547 *et seq.*

THE DEPOSITION OF POPE JOHN 343

King Sigismund thought it prudent to conceal his route;[1] and he determined that, if possible, the Duke of Burgundy should be condemned before he started on his journey south.

It was on the 16th May that the 'iron' Bishop John of Leitomysl appeared again before the Council. He reiterated the allegation that communion in both kinds was administered to men and women in Bohemia, and that the sacramental wine was taken in bottles to the sick. He denied having said that a cobbler had given the sacrament, though he feared it might come to that; he had heard that a woman had snatched the host from a priest and had communicated, saying that a holy layman was better than a sinful priest, for the latter could neither consecrate nor absolve. The Council on this day gave its promised answer to the Bohemian nobles, setting forth that Hus had only obtained his safe-conduct a fortnight after he was imprisoned, an allegation which the nobles had no difficulty in refuting two days later. They further pointed out that Hus had been summoned to Rome, had only sent a proctor, and had then been excommunicated; notwithstanding which they alleged that he had preached in Constance; to which the nobles retorted that he had never left his lodging. They promised, however, to take up the process against him as speedily as possible. The Bohemian nobles begged the Council not to place any credence in the charges of the Bishop of Leitomysl, which were founded on mere hearsay; it was well known to the whole world, they said, that they were good Catholics who had never protected heresy nor heretics. As a matter of fact, it was for John Hus the patriot rather than John Hus the theologian that the nobles were anxious to secure fair play.[2]

A few days later, on the 23rd May, Jerome of Prague was brought in chains to Constance, haled before a congregation, and questioned as to his flight; he excused himself on the ground that he had no safe-conduct. Jean Gerson thereupon charged him with disseminating many erroneous conclusions in the schools at Paris concerning ideas, universals, and other scandalous matters. It was the old strife of realist and nominalist. Jerome began to reply. A Master from Cologne accused him with teaching errors there also, but could not recollect an

[1] Finke (*F.*), 178.   [2] Palacky (*Doc.*), 259-65.

example at the time. A third opponent then alleged that at Heidelberg Jerome had likened the Holy Trinity to water, snow, and ice. Jerome offered to retract anything that was erroneous; but a tremendous hubbub arose, and shouts of ' Let him be burned ! ' to which he meekly answered, ' Let me die in God's name if it so please you.' Hallam of Salisbury then interposed: ' Not so, Jerome, for it is written, I have no pleasure in the death of the wicked.' The prisoner was then delivered into the custody of the Archbishop of Riga, and was imprisoned in the tower of Saint Paul's Church until he could be tried.

It was, in truth, impossible for the Council to proceed with the process either of John Hus or of Jerome of Prague while the more important matter of Pope John was still undecided. Many bishops, priests, and curials were examined by the commission, and on the 16th May an indictment containing seventy-two articles was published. The articles ranged from the time when Baldassare Cossa was a bad boy, disobedient to his parents, up to his recent flight to Nuernberg. Eleven articles concerned his misconduct in Constance. The indictment was very badly drawn; several charges run over two or three articles ; and others are repeated. The most serious charge, that of simony, of which John was notoriously guilty, occupies twenty-five articles ; and he is thrice charged with the death of his predecessor. Adultery with his brother's wife, and unchastity with nuns and virgins, oppression of the poor, tyranny extending to sentences of death and banishment, neglect of the admonitions of the cardinals, of the French ambassadors, of the King of the Romans, the whole story of his life was painted in the blackest colours. It was not so black a catalogue of crime as had been charged against Pope Boniface the Eighth, but if his accusers believed it, they must have felt that it was an indictment of the whole papal system quite as much as of the individual Pope ; unfortunately it is impossible, as the historian remarks,[1] to discriminate exactly how much is due to sheer malice and how much to vague, unfounded hearsay. The only charge of heresy was that the Pope did not believe in the immortality of the soul or the resurrection of the dead.

On the 18th May the Archbishop of Riga appeared at Con-

[1] Hefele, vii. 131 note.

THE DEPOSITION OF POPE JOHN 345

stance and informed the deputies of the nations that Pope John was at an inn at Radolfzell, that he had wept bitterly, had bemoaned his faults, and had entreated the Council to take pity on him; the Archbishop asked that proper provision be made for his custody. Of two officers of the signet who had been with the Pope at Freiburg, one had left and the other wished to follow the Pope with the signet, but John had disallowed this; the man, through spite, had gone to the Burgomaster of Radolfzell and had reported that the Pope meant to make another attempt to escape. The headman of the town on hearing this had made his way to the inn, had entered the Pope's bedroom, and had found Pope John in bed, and the faithful Bindachius de Ricasoli sleeping in the same room. Four guards, one from each nation, the Bishops of Asti, Augsburg, and Toulon, and Dr. Fyton of England, were sent to Radolfzell to watch the Pope. The Bishop of Toulon was a declared enemy of Pope John, whom he had described as Judas, and immediately began to upbraid him; he told him he had been suspended for making away with the Seal and Fisherman's Ring, with the registers of petitions and bulls; that the Council had sent them over because they had heard of his last attempt to escape; that they meant to dismiss all his servants and were come to guard him and bear him good company. The Pope made a civil answer to words which he was unaccustomed to hear from a bishop. He pleaded that of his intimates, two Olivetans, his chaplain, a squire, a caterer, a cook, and a physician might remain with him; and when his guards hesitated, he burst into tears, saying, 'I had them even when I was a scholar at Bologna, but I bow to the Council's order; do with me as you will.' The guards took pity and left him his servants. The Pope made over all the registers and the seal that he had with him, and he was removed to a strong tower.

King Sigismund, who had been in Radolfzell when the Pope arrived, and who had spoken with the Burggraf of Nuernberg but had refused to see Pope John, took charge of his custody and placed three hundred Hungarian troops on guard. On that same day, the 24th May, the Bishop of Toulon went back to Constance, carrying the Pope's written defence. On that day also there came to Radolfzell five cardinals, Orsini, d'Ailly,

Chalant, Saluzzo, and Zabarella, all of them men who wished the Pope well, but who came to communicate to him the decree for his suspension. They could not now give him the customary salutation; they could only kiss his hands and mouth. He told them that he had sent in his defence by the Bishops of Toulon and Augsburg and that he was perfectly ready to resign and would give security for so doing. They had to tell him that nothing short of the most ready and ample submission on his part would be of any avail; hesitation or obstinacy would be fatal; the allegations against him were so black that lifelong imprisonment or other punishment was most probable; if he would at once abdicate, then there was a hope that only those transgressions would be noted against him which were notorious and which he certainly dared not deny, his wasting church property, his simony, his evil rule, his encouragement of the Schism, and his flight. They impressed on him that he must perform the act of resignation in the most public manner possible, and that he must then remain in honourable custody until a new Pope was elected. The Pope was hopeless and broken-hearted; he declared that he was ready either to resign or be deposed, as it pleased the Council; he asked only that his honour, his person, and his position might be respected. He made a last appeal to the King for whom he had done so much, and he signed himself simply ' Baldassare.'

On Saturday, the 25th May, the eleventh general session of the Council was held. The mandatories of the commission then read out fifty-four [1] of the seventy-two articles of indict-

[1] The following is the text of the fifty-four articles:—

ARTICULI LIV

PUBLICE HODIE OBLATI CONTRA PAPAM JOHANNEM 23. PER ANDREAM LASCHARIS EPISCOPUM POSMANIENSEM PRÆLECTI

ART. I. Imprimis denunciant, dicunt, afferunt, ponunt, que si necesse fuerit probare intendunt, quod dudum tempore Bonifacii Papæ IX. sic in sua obedientia nominati, præfatus Dominus Johannes, tunc Balthasar De Cossa appellatus, per illicita media se procuravit Familiarem que Cubicularium præfati Domini Bonifacii. Et deinde inter dictum Dominum Bonifacium que quoscunque alios, pecunias habentes, que dare volentes pro beneficiis que aliis spiritualibus, se mediatorem, proxenetam que tractatorem fecit, palam, publice que notorie.

ART. 2. Item, quod dictus Dominus Johannes, tunc Balthasar appellatus, per hujusmodi illicitum quæstum, que Simoniacam pravitatem, ac procurationem que meditationem Simoniarum, que alia media illicita, in paucis temporibus acquisivit

ment which were held to be proved against Pope John ; and

que congregavit multam iniquitatis mammonam copiosumque pecuniæ thesaurum. Propter quod ex tunc divitis nomen que statum assumsit, ac ædificia sibi comparavit. Et sic fuit que est verum, publicum que notorium. Sicque, ut prædictur, dictum, tentum, creditum que reputatum communiter ab omnibus ipsius notitiam habentibus. Et adhuc dicitur, tenetur que reputatur, ac fuit que est de præmissis diffamatus manifeste, palam, publice que notorie.

ART. 3. Item, quod deinde præfatus Dominus Johannes, tunc Balthasar nuncupatus, mediante hujusmodi Simoniaca que damnata pecunia promotus fuit ad Cardinalatum, pro quo solvit magnam summam pecuniarum, que appellatus fuit Dominus Balthasar Cardinalis sancti Eustachii. Et sic fuit, que est verum, publicum que notorium. Ac de ipsis omnibus idem Dominus Johannes fuit que est publice diffamatus, palam que manifeste.

ART. 4. Item, quod postquam dictus Dominus Balthasar, tunc Cardinalis sancti Eustachii appellatus, civitatem Bononiensem ut legatus fuisset ingressus, viis tyrannicis pecunias quærens terras Ecclesiæ ac cives, habitatores earum, modo inhumano, impie, inique que crudeliter rexit que gubernavit, ac à Christiana pietate que à justitia divina humanaque totaliter alienus, diversas datias, gabellas, exactiones, extorsiones que onera insupportabilia eis imposuit. Talliarum que exactionum que onerum alias inauditorum fuit inventor. Et tam per illos modos quam alios consimiles, exactivos que nimium onerosos, per tyrannidem que de facto totaliter subditos oppressit. Quo dictam civitatem, comitatum (communitatem) que terras Ecclesiæ que cives depauperavit, devastavit, que depopulavit, ita, quod tempore sui regiminis, mala, tyrannica que violenta sua gubernatione causante, multi fuerunt mortui, multique profugi, multi exules, banniti, exhæredati, depauperati que deperditi. Et ita, ut prædicitur, fuit dictum, tentum, creditum que reputatum, que communiter ab omnibus divulgatum. Et adhuc dicitur, creditur que reputatur, ac fuit que est verum. Ipseque Dominus Johannes de omnibus præmissis fuit que est graviter diffamatus, palam, publice que notorie.

ART. 5. Item, quod Dominus Johannes tunc Balthasar appellatus, tantum practicare scivit post mortem bonæ memoriæ Domini Alexandri Papæ Quinti, quod in Romanum Pontificem electus extitit, que se Johannem Papam XXIII. appellavit, que ab aliis se nominari que appellari fecit. Et dum crederetur mutatione nominis que honoris de vitiis in virtutes mutatus, fallax fuit opinio. Quinimo contra sanctorum Patrum decreta, que contra laudabiles Romanæ Ecclesiæ consuetudines veniendo, velut paganus divina officia contemsit, officium pastorale non debite in divinorum administratione exercuit, missis que vesperis papalibus interesse non curavit, horas canonicas dicere, jejunia, abstinentias, ceremonias, que alia canonica instituta, ad quæ omnes Christiani que præsertim clerici que Ecclesiastici adstringuntur, juxta formam Ecclesiæ servare sprevit, que si aliquoties celebravit, hoc fuit currenter, more venatorum, que armigerorum, que plus, ne culparetur totaliter de hæresi, que ne expelleretur à papatu, quam devotionis vel charitatis causa. Sicque, ut prædicitur fuit dictum, creditum, tentum que reputatum ; diciturque, tenetur que reputatur, atque de iis fuit, que est publica vox que fama.

ART. 6. Item, quod dictus Dominus Johannes fuit que est pauperum oppressor, justitiæ persecutor, iniquorum columna, Simoniacorum statua, carnis cultor, vitiorum fex que à virtutibus peregrinus Consistoria publica fugiens, ac totus

as each article was read, the number and quality of the witnesses

somno que aliis carnalibus desideriis deditus, vitæ que moribus Christi totus contrarius, infamiæ speculum, que omnium malitiarum profundus ad-inventor, adeo que in tantum Ecclesiam Christi, scandalizans, quod inter Christi fideles, vitam que mores suos cognoscentes, vulgariter dicitur diabolus incarnatus.

ART. 7. Item, quod dictus Dominus Johannes Papa vas omnium peccatorum, pro pecuniis, repulsa dignos (in Lips. ac Goth. repulsis dignis), indignos ad officia que beneficia promovit, gratias non gratis, beneficia, vacantes prælaturas que dignitates Ecclesiasticas non magis meritis, sed plus offerentib' post venditionem expositam contulit, que conferri mandavit, literasque bullatas per mercatorum que nummulariorum manus, ut de mercibus mercari solitum est, vendidit atque jussit, que mandavit. Sicque ut prædicitur, fuit dictum, tentum, habitum que reputatum, atque vendi jussit, que mandavit. Sicque ut praedicitur, fuit dictum, tentum, habitum que reputatum, atque fuit que est verum publicum et notorium.

ART. 8. Item, quod propter præmissa, in clero ac in populo, totaque universali Ecclesia grave scandalum, graviusque Domino Johanni Papæ que curiæ Romanæ infamia, exortum fuit que suscitatum, atque orta que suscitata.

ART. 9. Item, quod propter hæc que alia Reverendissimi Patres que Domini sanctæ Romanæ Ecclesiæ Cardinales dictum Dominum Johannem Papam XXIII. anno primo pontificatus sui, inter se que ipsum solum fraternaliter diversis vicibus corripuerint, ipsumque precibus humilibus, que devotis atque salutaribus monitis cum instantia requisiverint, ne Romanam que universalem Ecclesiam per hujusmodi spiritualium merces que venditiones scandalizaret. Et sic fuit que est verum publicum que notorium.

ART. 10. Item, quod Dominus Johannes Papa ob præmissam fraternam monitionem animum in aliquo non immutans, avaritiæ coercitate infectus, ex post continue pristina Simoniarum mercimonia continuans, pejora prioribus perpetravit, que ubi prius sub typo justitiæ non nisi suis familiaribus, commensalibus, datam coronationis suæ in expectativis gratiis confinxit, postea post fugam ab urbe Romana, cuilibet indifferenter, pro certa florenorum summa videlicet pro XXV. florenis auri de camera, dicta data coronationis publicæ venditioni exponebatur, ad scandalum sedis Apostolicæ, que totius fidei Christianæ. Et sic fuit que est verum, publicum que notorium.

ART. 11. Item, quod dictus Dominus Johannes Papa in vitiis invalescens fortius, que non se corrigens, certos referendarios ac cubicularios ac secretarios creavit, fecit que ordinavit mediatores, proxenetas ac procuratores groslarum que pingvium Simoniarum, Ecclesiarum cathedralium, abbatiarum, monasteriorum, prioratuum que beneficiorum vacantium reservatorum, quodque sub nube mediorum fructuum nondum nactorum (in Lips. natorum) vel perceptorum, ante supplicationem vel saltem recuperationem literarum Apostolicarum impetrantem solvere opportuit certam summam ex pacto, que nisi impenetrans mox solvisset, rediit vacuus absque cujusvis onere provisionis. Et sic fuit que est verum, publicum que notorium.

ART. 12. Item, quod idem Dominus Johannes registratoribus literarum apostolicarum per expressum inhibuit, ne cuiquam sumtum ex registro literarum apostolicarum traderent, nisi prius que ante omnia pecuniam promissam solutam fore probaretur. Propter quod multos litigantes, qui tantam summam solvere non potuerunt, in clara sua justitia ob probationis defectum succumbere oportuit.

deposing thereto was stated. A single example will suffice :

Sicque avaritia que malitia dicti Domini Johannis Papæ causantibus, iniquitas æquitati prævaluit. Et beneficia possessa fuerunt absque canonico titulo contra canonicas sanctiones palam que publice.

ART. 13. Item, quod dictus Dominus Johannes Papa ultra in supra proxime articulis nominatos, certos in Romana curia mercatores deputavit, qui beneficia vacantia curiæ tribus vel pluribus diebus ad libram ponderarent, que plus offerentis supplicationem reciperent, que signari facerent, in dedecus sedis Apostolicæ, que perditionem animarum multarum. Et sic fuit que est verum, publicum que notorium.

ART. 14. Item, quod supra dictus Dominus Johannes Papa, ne aliqua supplicatio absque Simonia que solutione signaretur, omnibus que singulis Referendariis injunxit, ut nullus sibi supplicationem signandam aliquam præsentaret, nisi nomine Referendarii eam præsentantis signata esset : Quodque nullus, quancunque supplicationem de vacantiis signari obtineret nisi valorem totius vel mediae summæ in supplicatione expressæ prius realiter recepisset, que ipsi Papæ responderet, que traderet. Alioquin talis Referendarius haberet tantundem solvere de suo proprio, in pœnam transgressionis hujusmodi prætensi mandati apostolici. Et sic fuit, que est verum, publicum que notorium.

ART. 15. Item, quod dictus Dominus Johannes Papa, ultra præmissa sæpe que sæpius contra Deum, que propriam suam conscientiam, ementibus plerisque bullas vendidit. In quibus scripsit, beneficia obtinentes que officia ea in suis manibus resignasse. Et tunc, per hujusmodi confictam que mendosam resignationem, quæ nunquam accidit, contulit] vel conferri mandavit pro pecuniarum certa concordata quantitate, multos sic funditus, usque ad mendicitatem depauperando palam que publice.

ART. 16. Item, quod per hoc dabatur occasio multis beneficia emendi, conscientiam laxandi, que temeritas timorem Dei postponendi. Devenitque res ad tantum, quod qui majorem summam in supplicatione expressit que exsolvit, signaturam absque difficultate obtinuit.

Idem de Sacramentis, indulgentiis, dispensationibus, que aliis Ecclesiasticis que spiritualibus donis. Sicque, ut prædicitur, fuit dictum, tentum, creditum que reputatum, diciturque, tenetur, que reputatur palam que publice.

ART. 17. Item, quod Dominus Johannes Papa unum que idem beneficium sæpius pluribus que diversis personis, vel etiam uni que eidem repetitis vicibus vendidit, que plerumque uni venditum per anticipationem ante Datam alteri ementi conferebat : Et sic similiter de gratiis expectativis, declarationibus, que surrogationibus, que per impositionem silentiorum jus jam quæsitum absorbuit. Per quæ quasi tota Ecclesia est labe Simoniaca deturpata, indignis repleta, tam in superioribus, quam in inferioribus prælatis, omnique gradu Ecclesiastico lacessita, que per consequens quasi irreparabiliter scandalizata.

ART. 18. Item, quod Dominus Johannes Papa canonice electos, idoneos, usque ad saturitatem appetitus sui solvere non valentes, confirmare recusavit, quodq : indignos que minus idoneos, ad summas desideratas ascendentes, scandalose duxit promovendos que promovit. Plerosque etiam invitos de suis Ecclesiis transtulit, ut viduatas carius vendere posset, in scandalum que dedecus Christi fidelium plurimorum, palam que publice.

ART. 19. Item, quod deinde dictus Papa Johannes Concilio Pisano astrictus pro reformatione Ecclesiæ in capite que in membris in urbe Romana concilium

'Item, quod propter præmissa in clero et populo, totaque univer-generale convocavit. Et ibidem in pluribus sermonibus etiam ante que post que publice correptus que monitus minime se emendavit, quinimo temporis successu continue diabolico instinctu incorrigibilis pejora prioribus perpetravit. Et sic fuit que est verum publicum que notorium.

ART. 20. Item, quod dictus Johannes indulgentias in mortis articulo, prædicationem crucis, item a pœna que culpa absolutionem, Ecclesiarum que altarium portatilium concessiones, ac Episcoporum consecrationes, que Abbatum benedictiones, reliquias sanctorum, ordines sacros, potestatem in confessionibus absolvendi a peccatis, actusque, qui per solas Spiritus Sancti operationes ad gratiam ministrari debebant, pro pecunia vendidit numerata. Per quæ de novo Ecclesia sancta Dei in persona dicti Domini Johannis graviter dissamata fuit, que notorie scandalizata.

ART. 21. Item, quod anno Domini Millesimo quadringentesimo duodecimo, que de mense Augusti ejusdem anni, quidam Nicolaus De Pistorio, mercator Florentinus, que dicti Domini Johannis Papæ assertus Secretarius, laicus conjugatus, nuncius que legatus Apostolicus per dictum Dominum Johannem tunc deputatus, venit ad partes Brabantiæ, habens ab eodem Domino Johanne Papa potestatem exigendi que percipiendi quoddam subsidium, quod fuit decima pars fructuum omnium beneficiorum in cameracensi, Tornacensi, Leodiensi que Trajectensi civitatibus que diœcesibus, quodque non solventes excommunicare posset per certum ad hoc deputandum subdelegatum, ac suspensionis in collegia, conventus que capitula, interdictique sententias in eorum Ecclesia, quæ sibi hujusmodi fructuum pecunias non traderent. Per quod Ecclesiastica censura ad ludibrium que derisum que tota septentrionalis Ecclesia graviter fuit que enormiter scandalizata.

ART. 22. Item, quod dictus Dominus Johannes Papa supradicto Nicolao mercatori, ut præfertur, in legatione existenti, concessit, indulsit que commisit, ut idem Nicolaus quibuscunque hominibus utriusque sexus ad suæ libitum voluntatis deputare posset confessores, ut quod hujusmodi deputati confitentes absolvere possent à pœna que a culpa, certis tamen pecuniarum taxis mediantibus. Quas quidem prætensas indulgentias idem mercator publicavit que publicari fecit in certis locis, civitatibus que villis, videlicet Trajecti, Mechlinæ, Antwerpiæ, que alibi, de quibus maximas pecuniarum summas exhausit que extorsit, Christi fideles seducendo, que statum que ritum totius Ecclesiæ catholicæ enormiter scandalizando.

ART. 23. Item, quod præmissa omnia que singula fuerint que sint vera, publica que notoria, atque pro veris publicis que notoriis apud clerum que populum civitatum que diœcesium prædictarum, per cunctosque Christi fideles ibidem asserta, credita, visa, audita, palpata, que ut talia habita que reputata, atque de ipsis que eorum quolibet fuit que est publica vox que fama, fuitque que est de præmissis omnibus que singulis dictus Dominus Johannes Papa publice diffamatus.

ART. 24. Item, quod de anno Domini millesimo, quadringentesimo XIImo., Pontificatus dicti Domini Johannis anno tertio, nonnulli Ambassiatores tam ex parte Illustris Regis Francorum que Prælatorum regni Franciæ, quam ex parte almæ universitatis Studii Parisiensis, Romæ apud sanctum Petrum in Palatio Apostolico que in camera magna paramentorum, multitudine Cleri que nobilium ibidem in publica audientia congregata, dicto Domino Johanni Papæ XXIII.

sali ecclesia, grave scandalum, gravisque Domino Joanni papæ diffamiam, Simoniacam que malam vitam, malamque famam, per totum que universum mundum divulgatas, exposuerunt, asserentes, Ecclesiam Dei mirabiliter ob id scandalizatam, monentes sæpe que sæpius caritative, que requirentes eundem Papam Johannem, quatenus a Simoniæ mercibus cessaret, atque fructus ante fiendas gratias que signaturas, que antequam beneficiandus percepisset eosdem, Cameræ apostolicæ solvendos que dandos, tolleret que resecaret, seque in vita que moribus emendaret, cum frequenti instantia fuerunt exhortati. Sicque fuit que est verum, publicum que notorium.

ART. 25. Item, quod dictus Dominus Johannes XXIII. Papa à supradictis que nonnullis aliis Prælatis que Ambassiatoribus tam Ecclesiasticis, quam secularibus, quin etiam Doctoribus que Magistris universitatum, humili que devota monitione correptus, a criminibus prædictis, que a scandalis supradictis non cessavit, imo continuavit, mala pejoribus accumulando. Et sic fuit que est verum, publicum que notorium.

ART. 26. Item, quod dictus Dominus Johannes Papa fuit que est de præmissis omnibus que singulis, publice que notorie per totum mundum, que cuncta Christianitatum regna totaliter divulgatus, que diffamatus, atque pro tali que ut talis, in Romana curia que extra, ubicunque ipsius notitia habetur, habitus, tentus, nominatus que reputatus, atque tenetur, habetur que reputatur pro tali que talis, palam que publice.

ART. 27. Item, denunciant, ponunt que probare intendunt, quod supradictus Dominus Papa bona temporalia Ecclesiæ Romanæ, urbem videlicet Romam que patrimonium Ecclesiæ in Italia, Pessime que scandalose rexit, oppressiones, angarias que gabellas, ut thesaurizaret, adauxit, que aliquas de novo adinvenit, totamque subditorum substantiam, quantum in eo fuit, exhausit, que sibi imbursavit, ipsoque Ecclesiæ subditos depauperavit, turpiaque lucra undique scandalose recolligens, pluresque terras Romanæ Ecclesiæ sine evidenti necessitate vel utilitate hypothecavit que impignoravit, aliquas vero perpetuo alienationis titulo distraxit, que cum Communi Florentino de alienando Bononiam tractavit, urbemque Romanam que terras patrimonii Ecclesiæ proditorie capi, invadi, que occupari permisit, que tacite consensit. Et dum nuper de mense Junii Anno Domini Millesimo, quadringentesimo decimo tertio, scil. in crastino, Romano populo missam in Ecclesia sancti Laurentii in Damaso pro consolatione pacis que victoria belli, contra quendam Ladislaum Apuliæ Regem per ipsum Papam Johannem confici spopondisset, Romanum populum deserens, curialesque suos que oves in manibus luporum que inimicorum suorum tradens, ex culpa sua recessit scandalose. Propter quod multi Cortesani interenti, trucidati, capti que spoliati, etc. aliqui violenter per marinarios ad galeas capti, que in perpetuam servitutem redacti fuerunt. Itaque fuit que est verum, que est publica vox que fama.

ART. 28. Item, quod propter præmissa que ipso culpante que causam dante, multa crimina, videlicet sacrilegia, adulteria, homicidia, spoliationes, rapinæ, furta, in urbe Romana fuerunt commissa. Et ita fuit que est verum, publicum que notorium.

ART. 29. Item, quod communis que vulgata omnium hominum opinio, assertio, credulitas ac fama manifesta fuit que est, quod dictus Dominus Johannes Papa tam in præmissis quam aliis innumerabilibus casibus que universaliter in omnibus male que pessime administravit, tam in spiritualibus quam in temporalibus, que quod fuit que est bonorum Romanæ Ecclesiæ que cæterarum Ecclesiarum, que

ex tunc Romæ infamia, exortum fuit et suscitatum, atque exorta
rerum Ecclesiasticarum ac etiam temporalium ad Ecclesias pertinentium,
maximus, que plus quam de aliquo alio fuit lectum vel auditum, delapidator,
devastator, ac dissipator, que pessimus que inutilis ac damnosus administrator,
atque universali Ecclesiæ que toti populo Christiano scandalosus, veneficus,
homicida, fratrum interemtor, carnis vitia per omnia colens, incontinens, que
infinitis criminibus irretitus, malæ famæ, que pessimæ conditionis : Adeo, quod
in Italia que quasi tota, capto vocabulo que similitudine a quodam inhumanissimo
gentium armorum Capitaneo, Boldrinus appellato, etiam Papa Boldrinus
vocitatur. Et sic fuit que est verum, publicum que notorium.

ART. 30. Item, quod de præmissis omnibus idem Johannes Papa fuit que est
publice que notorie diffamatus, que per totum mundum divulgatus que infamatus,
que quod de ipsis que eorum singulis fuit que est publica vox que fama, que ut
talis que pro tali fuit que est ubique, ubi de ipso notitia habetur, dictus, tentus,
creditus que reputatus, dicitur, tenetur que reputator palam, publice, communiter
que notorie pro tali que ut talis.

ART. 31. Item, quod præfatus Dominus Johannes Papa nonnulla diversa bona,
mobilia que immobilia diversarum Ecclesiarum, que monasteriorum titulorumque
Dominorum Cardinalium, tam Episcopatuum quam aliorum presbyteralium que
diaconalium, Collegiorumque que prioratuum, Ecclesiarum parochialium, que
capellarum, altarium, hospitalium, cæterorumque locorum Ecclesiasticorum dictæ
urbis Romanæ, que præsertim Ecclesiarum Principis Apostolorum de urbe, sancti
Johannis Lateranensis, que alia ad Canonicos que personas Ecclesiasticas dictæ
urbis spectantia, nec non de bonis monasteriorum sancti Petri que Pauli, sancti
Alexii, sancti Fabiani (in Lips. S. Gabbæ, in Goth. S. Salæ) que aliorum
monasteriorum, tam virorum quam mulierum, sola avaritiæ cæcitate seductus
vendidit, alienavit, dilapidavit que dissipavit, que aliqua eorum ad nihilum
redegit, adeo, quod in plerisque cessat servitium divinum. Et ubi erant x., xx.
vel xxx. religiosi, hodie non sunt nisi unus, duo vel tres, quasi fame morientes.
Et sic fuit que est verum, publicum que notorium.

ART. 32. Item, quod idem Dominus Johannes Papa etiam jura mobilia
que immobilia Ecclesiarum cathedralium que collegiatarum, monasteriorum,
prioraturum, studiorum, collegiorum, hospitalium, Ecclesiarum parochialium,
Capellarum que cæterorum beneficiorum que officiorum Ecclesiasticorum extra
dictam urbem, tam in civitate que districtu Bononiensi, quam in aliis civitatibus,
villis, que locis dicti patrimonii Ecclesiæ Romanæ, quam extra ubicunque
existentia, etiam vendidit, alienavit que dissipavit. Et præsertim plura bona
Episcopatus Bononiensis, que Ecclesiæ sancti Petronii Bononiensis, que præsertim lapides, ligna que totam materiam, de quibus debebat compleri, que
ædificari que fabricari dicta Ecclesia, que pecunias annuas ad dictam fabricam
ab antiquo ordinatas recepit, que opus omnino cessare fecit. Similiter curias,
possessiones prædia, que bona mobilia que immobilia ad dotationem totalem
Collegii Gregoriani in dicta civitate Bononiensi per sanctissimum Dominum
Gregorium Papam XI. fundati, pro sustentatione quinquaginta scholarium
pauperum, etc. etiam vendidit que alienavit : Ita quod de mobilibus ibi nihil
remansit, que de immobilibus vix posset sustentari congrue unus scholaris solus,
que domum tradidit satardis (Sacardis) habitandam, qui totaliter eam destruxe-
runt, que eam vendidisset, si reperisset emtorem. Et sic que est verum publicum
que notorium.

et suscitata. Iste articulus probatur per unum cardinalem de

ART. 33. Item, quod dictus Johannes Papa præmissis non contentus, sed etiam literarum studia per Salarii distractionem que subtractionem subtiliter extinguere conatus, doctoribus studii Bononiensis per plures annos, que maxime a promotione sua ad Papatum stipendia eorum ab antiquo tempore dicti Studii eis debita, que unde vivere que provide studere que legere debebant, fundata, abstulit que removit, que taliter fecit, quod tam mobile que solenne studium quasi ad nihilum respective devenit. Et sic est verum.

ART. 34. Item, quod non solum dilapidavit bona que jura prædicta, mobilia que immobilia Ecclesiarum, sed etiam super personas Ecclesiasticas urbis Romanæ que civitatis Bononiensis ac in toto patrimonio Ecclesiæ gravissima onera, tallias que exactiones insupportabilia imposuit, facultatesque Ecclesiarum, unde personæ Ecclesiasticæ vivere que Deo servire debebant, ex eis extorsit, que sibi applicavit. Imo etiam super alios prælatos Ecclesiasticos aliarum terrarum, que dominiorum secularium diversa onera, tallias que exactiones solvendas dominis temporalibus que comitatibus secularibus, que præsertim regni Franciæ, comitatus Sabaudiæ, Provinciæ etiam, nec non communitatibus Florentiæ, Venetorum, Senarum, que pluribus aliis, cum quibus in pretio participavit, imposuit, adeo que in tantum, quod dicti Ecclesiastici fuerunt que sunt tanta paupertatis angustia afflicti, ut post propriorum patrimonialium bonorum consumtionem, necessitate famis libros, calices que ornamenta Ecclesiarum vendere sunt coacti. Sicque ut prædicitur, fuit dictum, tentum, creditum que reputatum, diciturque, tenetur, creditur, que reputatur, palam que publice que notorie.

ART. 35. Item quod propter præmissa tota Ecclesia Dei notorie fuit scandalizata. Et ita fuit que est verum, palam, publicum que notorium.

ART. 36. Item, quod horrida, que detestandorum criminum Domini Johannis Papæ antedicti fama, imo infamia, crebris que in consummationem multiplicatis vicibus, non solum semel, sed pluries que sæpe Christianorum Principum totiusque populi Christiani, proh dolor, aures penetravit, que in tantum, quod Serenissimus que invictissimus Princeps Dominus Sigismundus, Romanorum que Hungariæ, etc. Rex semper Augustus, in Lombardia existens, ad civitatem Laudensem applicuit, dictumque Dominum Johannem Papam ibidem advenientem humili que devota prece rogavit, quatenus, attento, quod quasi totus mundus in ejus persona scandalizatus est, suaq: crimina mundus dissimulare non posset, mores que vitam emendaret in melius, que ut ad unionem sanctæ matris Ecclesiæ, tunc que nunc tripartitæ, summis vigiliis que cura intendere dignaretur, ut astrictus per Pisanum Concilium tenebatur : Et concilium generale in aliquo loco, securo cuncto Christiano populo que commodoso indicere suasit, que ut Ecclesia in capite que in membris reformaretur, etiam devote supplicavit.

ART. 37. Item, quod dictus Dominus Johannes Papa XXIII. precibus dicti Serenissimi Principis, Romanorum que Hungariæ, etc. Regis, in parte condescendens, amplius a vitiis hujusmodi scandalosis que præsertim Simoniaca hæresi abstinere spopondit, que hanc civitatem Constantiensem, pro loco multitudinis capace, que alias habili que idoneo, pro concilio generali celebrando, elegit, quod anno Domini millesimo quadringentesimo decimo quarto de mense Novembris inchoandum indixit, que per mundum publicavit. Et sic fuit que est verum publicum que notorium.

ART. 38. Item, quod deinde dictus Papa Johannes Bononiam rediens in pristinam que pejorem Simoniam recidivavit, falsas Datarum anticipationes

veritate et notorietate, et per unum magnum magistrum, et vendidit, jus quæsitum pro numerata pecunia litigantibus abstulit, que ad solventium instantias eorum adversariis perpetuum plerisque vicibus silentium imposuit, de facto, turpiter que scandalose. Et sic fuit que est verum publicum que notorium.

ART. 39. Item, que ne per viam justitiæ oppressi relevarentur, idem Papa Johannes nuper anno Domini Millesimo, quadringentesimo decimo quarto, plerisque vicibus Dominis auditoribus per suos referendarios, que præsertim per Dominum Jacobum de Camplo, nunc Electum Pennensem, dici fecit que mandavit, ne materias anticipationum datarum admitterent in judicio, que ne datarum registratores aut alios officiales quovismodo compellerent in his materiis, privationem juris alterius concernentibus, veritati testimonium perhibere, justitiam notorie opprimendo. Et sic fuit que est verum publicum que notorium.

ART. 40. Item, quod propter præmissa que plura alia reverendus Pater Episcopus Sarisburiensis, que alii Christianissimi Principis Regis Angliæ illustres Ambassiatores, dictum Dominum Johannem Papam XXIII. monuerunt que corripuerunt caritative, supplicantes eidem, quod Simoniam que beneficiorum venditionem desereret, que se in vita que moribus emendaret, alioquin dubitaret, propter scandalum, subtractionem obedientiæ, que alia inconvenientia secutura. Quod que ipse Dominus Johannes incorrigibilis factus hujusmodi monita salutaria sprevit, ipsumque que alios Prælatos duris que asperis verbis minatus est que injuriatus palam que publice. Et sic fuit que est verum publicum que notorium.

ART. 41. Item, quod deinde præfatus Dominus Papa ad Constantiam veniens, post diversas persuasiones, exhortationes que rogamina, per hoc sacrum generale Concilium Constantiense devote factas que facta, ut pacem Ecclesiæ daret, que papatui cederet, cum alia tutior, promptior que securior, quam via cessionis, non esset, ad unionem perfectam in Ecclesia Dei consequendam, attentis scandalis, ex persona sua jam exortis, propter quæ existentes in aliis obedientiis retrahebantur ab Ecclesiæ unitate, hoc anno Domini millesimo, quadringentesimo decimo quinto, die Sabbati, secunda Mensis Martii, in Sessione generali Constantiensi que in pleno concilio generali Constantiensi universam Ecclesiam repræsentante, Ecclesiæ Dei, sponsæ suæ, promisit, vovit que juravit cedere papatui sponte que libere, dare pacem Ecclesiæ per viam suæ simplicis cessionis papatus, juxta deliberationem ejusdem Concilii, prout in quadam schedula conscripta, quam suamet voce intelligibili, viva que alta legit que dixit, juravit, vovit, promisit, que alia fecit, prout in eadem schedula, ad quam se referunt promotores que procuratores antedicti, continetur, cujus tenor sequitur que est talis. Ego Johannes Papa XXIII. propter quietem populi Christiani profiteor, spondeo, voveo, juro que promitto Deo que Ecclesiæ, que huic sacro concilio sponte que libere dare pacem ipsi Ecclesiæ per viam meæ simplicis cessionis papatus, que etiam eam facere que adimplere cum affectu juxta deliberationem præsentis Concilii, si que quando Petrus De Luna, Benedictus XIII. que Angelus Corrario, Gregorius XII. in suis obedientiis nuncupati, papatui, quem prætendunt, per se vel procuratores suos legitimos similiter cedant, que etiam in quocunq : casu cessionis vel decessus, aut alio, in quo per meam cessionem poterit dari unio Ecclesiæ Dei ad extirpationem præsentis schismatis.

ART. 42. Item, quod Dominus Johannes Papa se huic sacro Concilio submisit, que ejus sententiae que judicio stare promisit in omnibus que singulis, quæ

etiam unum magnum priorem.' Among the charges dropped

pertinent ad reformationem Ecclesiæ tam in capite quam in membris. Et hoc est verum, publicum, notorium, que ita ab omnibus tenetur que reputatur.

ART. 43. Item, quod dictus Dominus Johannes, postquam fuit in hac civitate Constantiensi, que post concilium jam inceptum, sæpe que sæpius, que maxime in publica Sessione omnibus audientibus cunctos (monuit) avisaverit, quatenus contra ipsum dicerent, que objicerent, quicquid vellent, cum ipse vellet (intenderet) stare determinationi hujus sacri Concilii de his, quæ tempore sui papatus gesserat, que administraverat. Et hæc sunt publica, notoria que manifesta, que ita ab omnibus tanquam notoria habentur, tenentur, que reputantur.

ART. 44. Item, quod deinde, ut hujusmodi professio, votum, juramentum que promissio juxta deliberationem Concilii ad practicam cessionis papatus que per consequens perfectæ unionis in Ecclesia Dei consequendæ ponerentur, dictus Dominus Johannes Papa requisitus, quatenus procuratores aliquos ad præmissa adimplendum constitueret, ut dictus Serenissimus Princeps que alii, per hoc sacrosanctum generale Concilium deputandi que eligendi, in civitate Niciensi Petro de Luna, Benedicto XIII. in sua obedientia nuncupato, bonam Domini Johannis voluntatem ostenderent, que ut similiter cederet, prout cum Ambassiatoribus Petri de Luna que illustris Principis Domini Regis Arragonum tractatum que conclusum extitit, fuit pro parte nationum que hujus sacri Concili humiliter que devote rogatus que requisitus.

ART. 45. Item, quod post hujusmodi requisitionem dictus Dominus Johannes Papa dolose cogitavit se absentare que clam recedere velle. Et super hoc fuit publica vox que fama.

ART. 46. Item, quod fama hujusmodi recessus Papæ Johannis tunc instantis ad aures Serenissimi Principis, Domini Sigismundi Dei gratia Romanorum que Hungariæ, etc. Regis deducta, idem Dominus Rex in præsentia Reverendissimorum in Christo Patrum que Dominorum Cardinalium, Patriarchæ Antiocheni, Episcoporum multorum, Ducum que Comitum atque Prælatorum multitudine copiosa, hortatus est que rogavit dictum Dominum Johannem, ne a civitate Constantiensi recederet, neve ante perfectam unionem hujusmodi sacrosanctum generale Concilium dissolveret, persuadens, quantum, meritum apud Deum, quantamque laudem humanam habiturus esset, si per ipsum perfecta unio fieri posset, dans que offerens (concedens) uberiorem salvum conductum atque salvam guardiam, que plenissimam securitatem personæ, que bonorum, omniumque familiarium que cortesanorum, etc. Quodque dictus Dominus Johannes recedere nunquam cogitasset, respondit, sed utique remanere ac perficere, que adimplere cum effectu velle ea, quæ vovit que juravit. Et sic fuit que est verum publicum que notorium.

ART. 47. Item, quod ex tunc dictus Dominus Johannes Papa videns, Concilium hujusmodi, que totum mundum, ad sanctæ Ecclesiæ Dei, jam XXXVIII. vel circa annis scissæ que divisæ unionem que reintegrationem, nec non extirpationem hæreseos que vitiorum, ac ipsius Ecclesiæ in capite que in membris reformationem anhelare, diabolico spiritu instigatus hoc sacrosanctum concilium dissolvere quærens, ut reformationem Ecclesiæ, hæresium atque schismatum extirpationem prædictam, evadere que impedire posset, que suam malam vitam continuare, ad præterita vitia que ambitiones reincidens, contra vota, professa, promissa, ac Deo que Ecclesiæ jurata id facere facto renuit. Et nuper, hoc anno

probably from want of evidence [1] were those relating to the death of Alexander the Fifth, to several alleged instances of simony and maladministration, and also the charge of heresy. The remaining fifty-four constituted a sufficiently black record, if they were proved. But, as we know, ' a scientific law of evidence comes very late in legal history,' and cross-examination, that surest provocative of bare, crude fact, was in those days unknown.[2] Men were satisfied with very little corroboration of that which they already regarded as probable or plausible, and Rumour painted full of tongues was accepted for confirmation strong as Holy Writ. Pope John knew this, and determined not to contest any of the findings ; it would have

millesimo, quadringentesimo decimo quinto, die Mercurii XXI. (in Lips. que Goth. XX.) mensis Martii, in noctis tenebris habitu indecenti que dissimulato, laicali more, non ut Romanum decuit Pontificem, gregem sibi commissum ut mercenarius deserens, ab hoc sacro generali Constantiensi concilio contumaciter se absentando aufugit que recessit, in scandalum generalis Concilii que totius populi Christiani. Ita fuit que est verum publicum, notorium que manifestum.

ART. 48. Item, quod de post dictus Dominus Johannes ad oppidum Schaffhusen se retraxit, que nonnullos Cardinales, Episcopos que Prælatos, ac etiam Cortesanos que Principum Ambassiatores à præsenti civitate Constantiensi ad se venire jussit, que mandavit ac practicavit. Et nihilominus sub certis prætensis pœnis que censuris ipsos ad se vocavit, que venire jussit, que eum sequi volentibus aut non volentibus mandavit, ut de hoc sacro loco recederent. Et sic per suam fugam oves spargere, concilium sacrum dissolvere, schisma nutrire, que perpetuo Dei Ecclesiam tenere monstrosam hæresibus que divisam, vitiis deformatam, proposuit, que quantum in eo fuit, voluit, deliberavit que fecit. Et sic fuit que est verum publicum notorium que manifestum.

ART. 49. Item, quod ex post de dicto oppido Schaffhusen, ipsa die Veneris sancta, tempore divini officii, hora tertiarum, iter arripuit versus oppidum Lauffenberg, que deinde ab oppido Laufenberg iterum transformato habitu turpiter ulterius versus oppidum Brisacum gressus suos direxit, scandalose à dicto Concilio que civitate Constantiensi plus que plus contumaciter se elongando, totisque conatibus, practica que opera datis, ire visus est in Burgundiam. Et sic fuit que est verum publicum que notorium.

ART. 50. Item, quod nuper hoc anno Domini millesimo quadringentesimo decimo quinto, que de mense Aprili ejusdem anni, dictus Johannes Papa per Reverendissimos Ambassiatores, Oratores, nuncios que epistolas, pro parte hujus sacri concilii generalis ad ipsum, tunc in præfato oppido Brisaco residentem, destinatos que destinatas, quatenus more pii pastoris, qui animam suam posuit pro ovibus suis, cujus actionis, ut autoritatis præsidentia, ita vitæ exemplo que doctrina, insecutor esse dignaretur, ad gregem suum desertum rederit, Constantiam, vel saltem ad unam de tribus civitatibus, seu oppidis, locis utique insignibus, videlicet civitatem Basiliensem, Ulmam, seu Ravensburg, civitati

---

[1] Valois, iv. 309.
[2] Jenks, *Law and Politics in the Middle Ages*, 276, 280.

THE DEPOSITION OF POPE JOHN 357

been useless. The Council sanctioned the process on these fifty-four points and summoned Pope John to appear and answer in person and to receive sentence on the 27th. When the Bishops of Posen and Lavaur appeared on the 26th at Radolfzell, with two abbots and certain notaries, and brought him the indictment, inquiring whether he meant to enter any defence, the Pope answered that he had done much, even before he was elevated to the papacy, toward regaining the unity of the Church, and had also in Constance promised to abdicate; that he most sincerely regretted ever leaving the city, for death would have been more profitable to him than flight; he did not propose to offer any defence, but he submitted to the orders of the Council, as he had already declared.

Constantiensi que loco Concilii vicinam, de unione Ecclesiæ, gratia Dei perficienda in brevi, secum cum omni benignitate que charitate tractare possent, charitative cum debita reverentia rogatus fuit, monitus que requisitus : Promittentes eidem que offerentes ex parte dicti sacri Concilii salvum conductum plenissimum, tunc jam paratum, que sigillo magno Regio seu imperiali sigillatum, que eidem Domino Johanni lectum, donatum que ostensum, securitatem vitæ que status que provisionem honestissimam condecentem statui suo, si reverteretur, atque vota, jurata que promissa adimpleret, prout iidem legati que Ambassiatores id à prædicto Concilio habuerunt in mandatis, obtulerunt, quemadmodum in instrumentis publicis desuper confectis, ad quæ se referunt promotores que procuratores prædicti, latius continetur.

ART. 51. Item, quod dictus Dominus Johannes Papa, in reprobum sensum datus, monita hujusmodi more aspidis, aures obturantis, ne audiat, obaudiens, se in crastinum responsum dictis Ambassiatoribus que legatis velle dare asserens, ipsos ex tunc redire jussit. Nec crastino expectato, post mediam noctem ante diluculum, non dato responso, ad oppidum Nuenburg auffugiens se transtulit habitu transformato, que sic sacrum Concilium dissolvere, unionem que reformationem Ecclesiæ, extirpationem hæresium que vitiorum impedire, que suam vitam detestandam continuare posset, quæsivit, prout que continuavit imo in profundum malorum deditus pejora prioribus committere non expavit, supra dictis monitis, precibus que requisitionibus minime condescendens. Et sic fuit que est verum publicum que notorium.

ART. 52. Item, quod supra dictus Dominus Johannes Papa fuit que est homo duræ cervicis, pertinax, peccator induratus, incorrigibilis, Ecclesiam Dei notorie scandalizans, fautor schismatis, aliasque talis, quod papatu que ejus administratione se reddidit indignum. Et pro tali habetur, tenetur, nominatur que reputatur.

ART. 53. Item, quod dictus Johannes Papa fuit que est de præmissis omnibus que singulis publice que notorie talis divulgatus que diffamatus, atque pro tali que ut talis in Romana curia que extra, que ubicunque ipsius notitia habetur, habitus, tentus, nominatus que reputatus pro tali que ut talis, palam que publice.

ART. 54. Item, quod de præmissis omnibus que singulis fuit que est publica vox que fama. Hardt, iv. 237-48.

The Council of Constance, he continued, was holy and infallible, and he would never oppose it. He would make no comment on the evidence, but would leave his defence to the Council which could not err, and to them he commended himself. He promised the Bishop of Lavaur to appear in person at the session next day, and again assured him of his submission.[1]

The bishops returned from Radolfzell on the 27th and reported the result of their mission to the four nations. The next session was postponed until the 29th May, and deputies were sent to the Pope, who received them courteously and promised to do whatever was required of him. He was no longer the proud and haughty fighting cardinal who had engineered the Council of Pisa; he was a humble and broken man seeking forgiveness for his faults. He did not appear at the twelfth session of the Council, held on Wednesday, the eve of Corpus Christi Day. Sigismund was present, surrounded by the princes of the Empire; fifteen cardinals and a numerous array of prelates and doctors appeared at this important assembly. The Bishop of Lavaur narrated the details of the mission to the Pope, and Henricus de Piro then moved for the decree of deposition. The Council passed in the first place a precautionary decree, providing that in the event of the apostolic see becoming vacant no step for refilling it should be taken except with the assent of the Council. The decree of deposition was then read by the Bishop of Arras, assisted by the deputies of the four nations, the Patriarch of Antioch for France, Bishop Nicolas of Merseburg for Germany, Antonio of Concordia for Italy, and Patricius Cortagensis for England. It ran as follows:—The Holy General Council of Constance, legitimately assembled under the Holy Spirit, having invoked the name of Christ and having God alone before its eyes, having maturely regarded and considered the articles made in this case against Pope John the Twenty-third and the proofs thereof, together with his spontaneous submission, hereby pronounces and declares (1) that his withdrawal from the city and Council secretly by night in disgraceful disguise was illegal and scandalous to the Church and the Council, disastrous to the peace and union of the Church, helpful to the Schism and contrary to his

[1] Mansi, xxvii. 701.

THE DEPOSITION OF POPE JOHN 359

own promise; (2) that Lord John is a notorious simoniac, a squanderer of church goods and privileges, an evil manager of the Church both in spirituals and temporals; (3) that by his detestable and unseemly life and conversation he has brought scandal on the Church and Christendom both before and after his elevation to the papacy, that all admonition has been fruitless and he is therefore worthy to be deposed; (4) that this Holy Council hereby releases all believers from fidelity and obedience to him and forbids them to call him Pope or to obey him; (5) that she at the same time declares that he shall live for the future in some sure and fitting place under the inspection of Sigismund, King of the Romans and of Hungary, and that she reserves to herself the right to impose on him such further penalties as he may have deserved; and (6) finally, that she decrees that neither Baldassare Cossa nor Angelo Corrario nor Peter de Luna shall in the future be chosen to be Pope.[1]

To the question whether this decree is approved, the President of the College of Cardinals in the first place answered *Placet*; the four representatives of the nations made the same answer; and they were followed similarly by all others present. Cardinal Zabarella wished to make some explanation, but was obliged to remain silent. The Archbishop of Riga then produced the Pope's seal, which was solemnly broken up by a goldsmith, who also destroyed the papal arms. The Archbishop was then discharged from his duty as guardian of the Pope; and a deputation was appointed to wait upon the Pope with the sentence of his deposition. They came to Radolfzell on the 31st May and were well received by Pope John, who requested two hours for reflection. At the end of this time he met them again and told them that he accepted the sentence, confirmed it, and would never do aught to invalidate it, swearing solemnly to this effect. He removed the papal cross from his room. He protested that he was sorry that he had ever been Pope, expressed a desire to plead in his defence before the Council in case any further accusations or punishments were contemplated, and recommended himself to their mercy. A protocol to this effect was taken down and laid before the representatives of the four nations on the 1st June.

[1] Mansi, xxvii. 715.

360 POPE JOHN THE TWENTY-THIRD

This was the end, after a reign of five years and fifteen days, of the pontificate of Pope John the Twenty-third ; his cardinalate had been brilliantly successful; his pontificate was eminently disastrous. As a condottiere general he had captured Bologna, had kept it, and had extended its sway ; as ruler, he had governed firmly and well, bringing peace and prosperity to the city ; he had arranged the Council of Pisa, had defended it against King Ladislas of Naples, and had made the triumphal march to Rome ; at the death of Pope Alexander the Fifth, when war was imminent, he had been summoned by the war party to the papacy ; and at the battle of Rocca Secca it looked as if the choice had been justified. But from that point the tide of Fortune changed, disaster followed disaster, until now Pope John had sunk to the lowest depth of public degradation. Apart from his moral and spiritual failings, he had not the statesmanlike gifts nor the statuesque qualities which go to the making of a successful Pope ; yet of him, might it not be said that he was ' *capax imperii, nisi imperasset* ? '

Thus was the first step taken toward the extirpation of the Great Schism.

CHAPTER XX

THE TRIAL OF JOHN HUS

THE ambassadors sent by King Sigismund and the Council to announce to the King of France the deposition of Pope John the Twenty-third were attacked on the 8th June by a band of Lorrainers and Burgundians under the Marshal of Lorraine and Henri de la Tour, a devoted servant of the House of Burgundy. Three of the suite were killed, the rest were dragged off to the castle of Saulcy. The embassy was promptly delivered by the Dukes of Bar and Lorraine, and the castle was rased to the ground. The King of France thanked the Duc de Bar, but the Duke of Burgundy was very wroth at the destruction of his castle. The news of the deposition was not well received. The court party, the Armagnacs, who stood by the Council of Pisa, were naturally displeased at the disgrace of the Pope who represented that Council. Equally displeased was the Duke, a declared enemy of King Sigismund; for Jean sans Peur had now lost the Pope who was to shelter him from being placed under the ban of Christendom. The Dauphin went so far as to clap the spokesman of the University into prison for a few days.[1] Meanwhile, the Duke of Burgundy's enemy, Louis of Bavaria, was in high favour with Queen Barbara; and the deposed Pope and his protector were in the clutch of her husband, King Sigismund.

Duke Friedrich of the Tirol, despoiled of all his property, and henceforth to be known as 'Friedrich with the empty pockets,' was, like Baldassare Cossa, the prisoner of the King of the Romans. His submission has been described by one historian as the most foolish,[2] by another as the wisest,[3] step of his life. It was understood that, after performing what he had contracted, Friedrich was to be reinstated in full possession as

[1] Valois, iv. 314, 326 *et seq.*   [2] Mueller, iv. 230.   [3] *B.W.*, 211.

an act of grace, but not of right.[1] He had prevented the Pope from escaping to France and had brought him back to safe custody in Freiburg; more than this he could not do, as he was in custody himself; he had, moreover, paid a heavy fine.[2] On the pretext, however, that the Tirol had not submitted, King Sigismund persisted in keeping the Duke captive. His wife, that fair saint, Anna of Brunswick, interceded for him unavailingly. The King would not give way; Friedrich remained a prisoner.

Baldassare Cossa, the King's other prisoner, now no longer Pope John, was by Sigismund made over to the Count Palatine for watch and ward; and Louis, the foremost adherent of the rival Pope Gregory, was only too glad to accept the charge, and lost no time in confining the ex-Pope in the castle of Gottlieben, which the Bishop of Constance used as his stronghold. All his old servants were taken from Baldassare Cossa and all his correspondence was cut off. There were many in Constance who pitied the unfortunate prisoner and who interceded for him with the Council, but the Bearded Prince was obdurate. Baldassare Cossa's confinement in Gottlieben began on the 3rd June; that of John Hus, who had been confined in the same castle since the 20th March, ended at the beginning of that month. It is just possible that the two prisoners, the Pope and the patriot, may have seen each other at Gottlieben. The trial of Pope John had concluded; that of John Hus was about to commence.

The reformer meantime was weak and ill. He suffered from headache and toothache; he was troubled with spitting of blood and with pains in the bladder; at night he was perplexed with evil dreams; snakes tried to bite him, but could not; men tried to efface the picture of Christ in his Bethlehem Chapel, but it shone out more beautiful than before. His sensitive nature yearned for sympathy; he wrote to the Bohemian nobles in Constance telling them that they were angels of God sent to him in his great temptation. He still hoped that God might deliver him from death and imprisonment, but he was bitter against the King, who had allied himself with the Council to the detriment of divine truth.

[1] *B.W.*, 268.   [2] Aschbach, ii. 83.

THE TRIAL OF JOHN HUS

'The Council,' he said, 'calls itself holy and infallible, but I have heard Teutons say that it will take Constance thirty years to clear itself of the sins which the members have committed within its walls.' He had clearly small hope left in man; he was ready to fall into the hands of the living God.[1]

While John Hus had lain chained in the castle of Gottlieben he had not been able to communicate with his friends, and the visits of the commissioners had impressed him with a sense of his danger. Very early in the month of June he was removed to the Stadtthurm adjoining the Franciscan cloister at Constance,[2] and was again able to write. His letters, couched in a spirit of pious resignation, show that the thought of death by fire was imminent in his mind, that he was resolved to fight the good fight of faith, and that his chief desire was publicly to express the belief that was in him, so that all Christendom might know his final opinion.[3] He had realised that not only his old enemies the Teuton nominalists of Prague, but the French also, were an *irritabile genus* who would not suffer a heretic to live. There was no such thing as toleration of opinion in those days; and the most religious followers of William of Ockham, the most ardent advocates of church reform, were persuaded that the logical outcome of realism was pantheism, that the realist doctrine was anti-catholic and had always been condemned by the Church, and that it was the duty of the Council, as the supreme court of Christendom in matters of faith, to stamp it out mercilessly.[4] John Hus fully realised their feeling now; he felt that he and his master John Wyclif, whose works in his possession he affectionately left to his friend Mladonowicz, were right in many points; and although he still expressed his openness to conviction, he was determined to die rather than retract a syllable of divine truth. His friends had again petitioned the Council on the 31st May, asking for his release; they had drawn attention to his declaration that he sought only the glory of God and the good of His Church, that he had never taught anything that he believed to be contrary to the true faith, and was ready to retract anything

[1] Schwab, 590-2.   [2] Marmor, 93.
[3] Palacky (*Doc.*), 101 *et seq.*   [4] Erdmann, i. 523-5.

that was unorthodox. The Bohemian nobles objected to the unfair and misleading manner in which extracts had been made from Hus's writings, and asked that he might be allowed to argue calmly and precisely with Masters of Holy Writ, seeing that he was ready in all points to submit himself to the findings of the Council. They sent a copy of their petition to King Sigismund, begging him for the honour of his own safe-conduct to use his influence on behalf of the patriot reformer.[1] The answer they received from the nations was that Hus could not be delivered from custody, but that the first hearing of his case was fixed for Wednesday, the 5th June. The day which Hus had so anxiously expected during the past seven months had come at last.

The refectory of the Franciscan monastery was crowded on the morning of Wednesday, the 5th June; nearly all the clergy in Constance, even those of the lowest degree were present, anxious to get a glimpse of the man whose teaching had spread through Bohemia, Poland, and Moravia. At first, however, John Hus was not present. The proceedings began ominously enough by reading the words of the Psalm, ' Unto the wicked God saith, What hast thou to do to declare my statutes, And that thou hast taken my covenant in thy mouth ? ' and the following verses. Then the garbled extracts and a false copy of a letter from Hus were read. His friends took fright; Mladonowicz ran to Wenzel of Duba and John of Chlum, and the two knights went off to King Sigismund to protest against the procedure. The King at once sent the Count Palatine and the Burggraf of Nuernberg to the congregation with an order that they were not to arrive at any determination in that matter, that the work of John Hus on the Church and his tractates to Stanislas and Palec were themselves to be placed before the congregation, and that they were to hear Hus patiently in person, and that they were to submit their conclusions to him in order that he might lay the matter before certain doctors for consideration.[2] Sigismund hereby arrogated a jurisdiction which did not belong to him, but later he made no attempt to exercise the final right of judgment. John Hus was accordingly brought before the congregation. He acknowledged the three

[1] Palacky (*Doc.*), 266 *et seq.*   [2] *Ibid.* 274-5.

works to be his and professed his readiness to correct any errors which they might contain. By a mistake another tractate had been handed in together with the *De Ecclesia*, but to his relief this was returned, although Michael *de Causis* called out for it to be burned.[1] Hus saw the iron Bishop of Leitomysl and congratulated him on his promotion; but received only the surly answer, ' What have I done to you ? ' The first article of the indictment was then read together with the relevant depositions, and Hus then began to explain that his meaning had been misunderstood. But he was interrupted by a furious uproar and cries of ' Stop your sophistries and answer " Yes " or " No." ' Others began to jeer at him. Seeing no chance of explaining his meaning, Hus remained silent. Then he was assailed with shouts, ' Ah! you are silent; that shows you admit your errors.' Finally two articles of the indictment were struck out, but there was no hope of continuing the hearing in the excited state of the assembly. The further hearing was therefore adjourned until Friday, the 7th. This tumultuous and disorderly audience was far from being the academic discussion which the reformer had expected and his friends had desired. As he left the refectory in the custody of the Archbishop of Riga, he held out his hand to his friends and bade them not be afraid for him; and as he passed down the steps he blessed the people and laughed, going away cheerfully amid the shouts of their derisive laughter.[2]

The first day of the trial was over, and John Hus was still of the same determination not to retract anything which was not proved to him to be erroneous. A certain doctor advised him to submit absolutely to the Council. ' If the Council says you have one eye, when you have two, you ought to agree that it is so.' But Hus was not of that mind; he would not retract anything he had written for fear of condemning Saint Augustine or the Holy Fathers; on the other hand, he would not admit the false testimony of those who said he had preached what he had never taught, nor would he abjure any such alleged doctrine for fear of being perjured. On the 6th June he wrote to John of Chlum, hoping that King Sigismund would be present at his trial on the morrow; he asked that his friends would pray for

[1] Palacky (*Doc.*), 105. [2] *Ibid*. 276.

him and for Jerome of Prague that they might be constant until death.[1]

The proceedings on the second day of the trial, the 7th June, were conducted with more attention to decorum and order. The King was present; a large guard of armed men was in attendance; and it was announced that any person infringing the harmony of the assembly would be at once ejected. An hour before the audience opened there was a total eclipse of the sun. The first charge read against John Hus was that he had maintained that after consecration of the elements material bread remained, or in other words, that he did not believe in the Catholic doctrine of transubstantiation. Hus denied that he had ever believed or taught any such doctrine, he had never taught that material bread remained after consecration. Then Pierre d'Ailly rose. The cardinal was incensed against John Hus, for he regarded his realism as inimical to his own schemes of church reform.[2] 'Do you believe in the existence of universals?' he asked. 'I do, even as Saint Anselm and others have maintained,' was the answer. 'Then it follows,' argued the cardinal, ' that after consecration the material bread must remain ; for after consecration, if the bread is changed into the body of Christ, there either remains the ordinary substance of material bread or there does not ; if it remains, then the proposition is proved ; if it does not remain, then the universal must disappear with the singular.' Hus answered that there ceased to be any material bread in that particular Host, seeing that it had been changed or transubstantiated into the body of Christ, but that the other accidents of bread remained. What Hus meant was that although the accidents or properties of bread remained, the substance was changed and was something very different, namely, the body of Our Lord. The cardinal's argument was that it was absurd to say that the accidents remained and not the substance, that the universal name *bread* merely described the particular properties or accidents which, according to Hus, remained after consecration. Whether Hus was logical or not, at any rate he was thoroughly orthodox on the subject of transubstantiation. It might require a miracle to transform the substance of bread into the body of Christ,

[1] Palacky (*Doc.*), 103-6.   [2] *Ibid.* iii. 349.

and Wyclif had doubted whether God would be at the trouble of constantly working unnecessary miracles, but Hus had no such difficulty; he was prepared to believe in constant miraculous intervention. Indeed, it is hard to see how any one who believes in the Incarnation and the Resurrection can find any difficulty in accepting the doctrine of transubstantiation, especially when he considers that a miracle constantly and consistently repeated becomes equivalent to a mere law of nature. The nominalists of the school of Gerson and d'Ailly separated philosophy from Christian doctrine, and unfolded the ideal content of belief without any regard to science;[1] where the two clashed, they held that faith was superior to reason, divine knowledge to human understanding. With regard to the sacrament they took Christ's words, *This is my body*, literally as expressing a fact superior to human reason and removed from its sphere. The nominalists were mystics, and they made no attempt to reconcile human and divine philosophy, as did realists like Wyclif; and Gerson and d'Ailly failed to see that in not attempting the reconciliation they were just as illogical as was John Hus when he refused to follow Wyclif to the logical conclusion in the theory of transubstantiation.

Hus thought that he had vanquished the Cardinal in the argument;[2] but d'Ailly simply refused to believe Hus because he saw that he was illogical. The Cardinal of Cambrai was nearly twenty years the senior of Hus; in his own diocese he had as bishop dealt summarily and severely with heretics, and he had no fancy now for disputing in public with one.[3] He was a convinced nominalist, and was certain that a realist must be in the wrong;[4] and, as Renan says, 'on n'est jamais bien tolérant quand on croit qu'on a tout à fait raison et que les autres ont tout à fait tort.' The result of this philosophical prejudice was that the nominalist doctors refused to believe John Hus, and preferred rather to trust the evidence of the false witnesses against him. For, notwithstanding his asseveration, there was a certain amount of evidence that Hus had taught the Wyclifian doctrine; there were witnesses from Prague, one of whom added that the Master had jeered at Saint Gregory,

---

[1] Erdmann, i. 517.   [2] Palacky (*Doc.*), 106.
[3] Tschackert, 226.   [4] Schwab, 586.

calling him a jester and a rhymster ; there was Hus's old enemy, Stokes the Englishman, who deposed that he had seen in Prague a tractate ascribed to Hus containing the objectionable doctrine ; there were two other Englishmen who attacked him at the trial and charged him with captious answering after the manner of Wyclif ; as Zabarella pointed out, there were at least twenty witnesses to the fact. The Cardinal animadverted on the reformer's distrust of such men as Palec and Gerson ; he might have added his own name. Hus could only answer that God and his conscience were his witnesses that he had never taught nor believed this Wyclifian heresy. The evidence against Hus might be untrustworthy, and probably much of it would have broken down on cross-examination ; but that art was unknown in those days, and there was only the bare word of John Hus to contradict the evidence against him.

The next allegation against Hus was that he had taught the Wyclifian heresies. Hus was a great admirer of the English reformer, and in his treatise *De Ecclesia* and in other works he had copied his master *verbatim et litteratim*.[1] But he had thought for himself, and there were many of the condemned forty-five articles with which he disagreed. He had, he said, no particular ground for following Wyclif, who was not his father nor a Bohemian, and for whose errors the English must concern themselves. He admitted that he had not concurred in the unqualified censure of the University of Prague. Wyclif was alleged, but possibly erroneously,[2] to have maintained that a bishop or priest, being guilty of mortal sin, has no power to ordain, or consecrate, or baptize. Hus explained that he held that he might do these acts, though he did not do them worthily. There was a dispute as to whether he had made this limitation in his works, but his tractate against Palec was produced in his defence. On the question of tithes, Hus held to Wyclif's doctrine that they were freewill offerings, maintaining in opposition to the Cardinal of Cambrai that they were as free as were the works of mercy ordained in the twenty-fifth chapter of the gospel of Saint Matthew (v. 33, *et seq.*). On Hallam of Salisbury objecting that the poor were unable to exercise works of mercy, Hus admitted that the command was to those who

[1] Loserth, 182 *et seq.*   [2] Lechler (*Lorimer*), 237.

THE TRIAL OF JOHN HUS

had and were able to give ; and as regarded tithes, he explained that although they had originally been free, they had now, through long submission to them, become obligatory. This was an admission which certainly should have conciliated all holders of benefices. Hus stated that although he had not agreed with the condemnation of the forty-five articles, yet he did not desire obstinately to maintain any of them ; in other words, he dissociated himself from Wyclif and wished to be judged on his own merits.

The third charge against the Bohemian reformer was that he had regarded the earthquake which happened during the Council at London as a sign of the divine displeasure, and had expressed the wish that his soul might be with that of John Wyclif ; to which he answered that he had liked Wyclif's philosophical works before his theological writings were known in Bohemia, and had expressed the wish because he had never heard aught but good of him. He denied that he and his friends had defended Wyclif's heresies, adding that so far as he knew there never had been, nor was there at that present, a heretic in all Bohemia. In burning the books which had been delivered to him with a request that the errors might be indicated, the Archbishop of Prague had gone beyond the orders of the Pope, and therefore Hus had appealed against him to Alexander the Fifth and then to John the Twenty-third, and after waiting two years in vain for an answer, he had appealed to Christ. At this there was a general laugh, but Hus continued that he knew no juster or mightier judge than Christ, who deceiveth none, nor is deceived of any. Palec objected that audience in the Roman Curia had not been denied to Hus, but that his personal attendance had been deemed necessary because he was suspected of heresy. Hus also denied that he had urged his followers to attack his adversaries with the sword ; he had not referred to the material sword but to the Word of God.

These first five articles of the indictment had regarded Hus as a theologian, but the sixth touched him as a patriot, for it charged him with stirring up strife and causing the ruin of the University. He defended the action of King Wenzel in giving three votes to the Bohemian nation, and he pointed with his finger toward Albert Barentrall, who had been at that time

2 A

Dean of the Faculty of Arts and who was then present in the refectory, as being one of the Teutons who had sworn not to obey the royal decree but rather to emigrate. The Dean himself was not allowed to answer, but Doctor Johannes Nas took up the parable and reminded Hus of the anger of the King, who had threatened him and Jerome of Prague with death. Palec also added that not only foreign but Bohemian doctors also had been driven into exile through the machinations of John Hus. The reformer, however, answered that this was not true, for he was not in Prague when they left the city. He remarked that he should have expected more order and decorum in a council. Pierre d'Ailly then reprimanded Hus. 'Master John, you spoke more quietly of late when you were in the tower at Gottlieben than you are now doing; this is not right.' To him Hus replied, 'Reverend Father, that is because you then spoke gently with me, whereas here all cry out upon me, so that I know that they are my enemies.' 'Who cries out?' asked the cardinal. 'When you speak, they listen in silence.' But Hus persisted and referred to the King's orders that any one who interrupted should be expelled, adding that they ought to be silent or he could not hear the questions. The next charge also had reference to the disturbances in Prague, which Hus attributed to the disobedience to the King's order of neutrality between the rival Popes; Archbishop Zbynek had placed the city under an interdict, had robbed the sepulchre of Saint Wenzel, and had fled to Roudnice, followed by the prelates and clergy. Both Johannes Nas and Pierre d'Ailly objected to this version of what had occurred, the latter saying that as he came back from Rome he had met certain prelates who complained that all the clergy had been robbed of their livings and evil entreated. 'Master John,' continued the cardinal, 'when you were brought to the papal palace we asked you why you had come, and you told us that it was of your own free will, and that if you had not wanted to come, neither the King of Bohemia nor the King of the Romans could have compelled you.' To which Hus answered proudly, 'I said that I came of my own free will, and if I had not wished to come, there are so many and so great lords in Bohemia in whose castles I could have hidden, so that neither this King nor

THE TRIAL OF JOHN HUS

that could have made me come.' Thus spake John Hus the patriot, but the cardinal shook his head and murmured at his boldness. But his stalwart friend, the baron John of Chlum, came to the rescue. 'He speaks the truth, and true it is: I am but a poor knight in our country, but I could hold him safe for a year, gainsay me who will. And there are many and mighty lords who love John Hus, who have very strong castles and could protect him as long as they please against both Kings.' This stormy scene closed the hearing for the day.

As Hus was about to be led back in custody, Pierre d'Ailly turned to him and said, 'Master John, you assured us when you were in the castle that you would submit humbly to the Council: I advise you so to do, and not to persist in your error but to accept instruction, and the Council will be gracious to you.' King Sigismund also addressed him:—' Listen, John Hus! Some have said that it was only fifteen days after your imprisonment that I gave you a safe-conduct. That is not true. I promised it you before you left Prague, and ordered Wenzel of Duba and John of Chlum to accompany and protect you, so that you might come without let or hindrance to Constance, and might have a public hearing and defend your faith. This has come to pass; you have had a public, peaceful, and proper hearing. I thank the Council for what they have done, although certain have maintained that I could not grant a safe-conduct to one suspected of heresy. And therefore I give you the same advice as the cardinal, not to be obstinate, but to submit yourself unreservedly to the mercy of the Council in all that has been proved against you or admitted by you; then, out of consideration for me and my brother and the kingdom of Bohemia, will they deal graciously with you and only inflict some slight penance. But if you obstinately hold fast to your own contentions, woe be to you; they know well what they must do, and I declare to you that I will never take the part of a heretic, but would rather myself burn any one who persists in his heresy. Therefore I counsel you to submit entirely, and the sooner the better, to the mercy of the Council, and not to run into still worse error.' Hus thanked the King for his kindness in granting the safe-conduct, and added that he had come there not desiring to obstinately defend anything, but humbly to improve himself when he should be instructed as to his errors. The third hearing was fixed for the next day.[1]

The advice which the King and the cardinal gave John Hus was meant in good part. Sigismund had been for nearly six months in daily communication with the fathers of the Council, and had learned the futility of his notion that Hus could clear himself and his country of the suspicion of heresy. D'Ailly was naturally imbued with the prejudices of his University; and the University of Paris treated realism as heresy pure and simple.[2] To be a heretic in those days was worse than being an anarchist in our own. Heresy not only destroyed the souls of the faithful; it brought plague, pestilence, and famine in its train; it had brought, it might again bring, battle, murder, and sudden death. It was the leprosy of the soul, foul and contagious; in those days, when all the world was one religion, a heretic was accursed, alike of God and of man, fit only to be destroyed with fire, so long as he continued in his heresy. Seeing, therefore, that Hus had dissociated himself from the arch-heretic Wyclif on many points, but that he still remained obdurate on others, what kinder advice could the King and the Cardinal give him than to submit himself to the highest ecclesiastical authority in Christendom, and to submit to the slight penance it would impose? Hus, however, was a man of 'too much thinking to have common thought'; he believed that he had in no wise deviated from the Catholic teaching; he felt that to give way would be to suffer an impeachment of his own integrity. He had ever striven to be the good and faithful pastor of his flock, to lead them in the way of truth, and for their sake he would not, without manifest proof, admit that he had erred. His integrity was to him 'dearer than life, stronger than death, higher than purest love'; he felt that he had rather die than falsely own himself a heretic.

The next day, the 8th June 1415, the third and last day of the trial of John Hus, was occupied with the discussion of his views on the Church and on Church government. Thirty-nine extracts had been made from his works, twenty-six being from the *De Ecclesia*, seven from his tractate against Palec, and six

---

[1] Palacky (*Doc.*), 273-85; Hefele, vii. 149-57.   [2] Hauréau, iii. 458.

from that against Stanislas of Znaim.[1] Special stress was laid on the nineteen extracts from the *De Ecclesia* which had been made by Jean Gerson ; these the Chancellor had designated as

[1] The following is the text of these articles charged :—

'ARTICULI EXTRACTI DE TRACTATU M. J. HUS DE ECCLESIA'

1. Tantum una est sancta universalis ecclesia, quæ est prædestinatorum universitas. Error, pro quanto asserit, sicut et asserit, solam universitatem prædestinatorum esse sanctam universalem ecclesiam.

2. Sicut Paulus numquam fuit membrum diaboli, licet fecerit quosdam actus actibus ecclesiæ malignantium consimiles, similiter Petrus, qui in grave incidit perjurium ex permissione domini, ut fortius resurgeret.

3. Nulla pars ecclesiæ ab ea finaliter excidet, eo quod prædistinationis caritas, quæ ipsum ligat, non excidit.

4. Prædestinatus, non existens in gratia secundum præsentem justitiam, semper est membrum sanctæ universalis ecclesiæ. Error, intelligendo de omni prædestinato.

5. Nullus locus dignitatis vel humana electio vel aliquod signum sensibile facit membrum sanctæ ecclesiæ catholicæ.

6. Numquam præscitus est membrum sanctæ matris ecclesiæ.

7. Judas numquam fuit verus discipulus Christi.

8. Convocatio prædestinatorum, sive sint in gratia sive non secundum præsentem justitiam, est ecclesia sancta universalis, et illo modo ecclesia est articulus fidei.

9. Petrus non fuit, nec est caput sanctæ ecclesiæ catholicæ principale.

10. Si vocatus Christi vicarius Christum sequitur in vita, tunc est ejus vicarius; si vero vadit viis contrariis, tunc est Anti-Christi nuntius, contrarius Petro et domino Jesu Christo et vicarius Judæ Schariothis.

11. 'Omnes simoniaci et sacerdotes criminose viventes, ut filii infideles infideliter sentiunt de septem sacramentis ecclesiæ, de clavibus, officiis, censuris, moribus, ceremoniis et sacris rebus ecclesiæ, veneratione reliquiarum, indulgentiis et ordinibus in ecclesia.'

12. 'Dignitas papalis a Cæsaribus inolevit. Papæ præfectio et institutio a Cæsaris potestate emanavit.'

13. 'Nullus sine revelatione assereret rationabiliter de se vel de alio, quod esset caput ecclesiæ particularis sanctæ.'

14. 'Non oportet credere, quod iste quicumque Romanus pontifex sit caput cujuscumque particularis ecclesiæ, nisi deus eum prædestinaverit.'

15. 'Potestas papæ vicaria frustratur, nisi ipse papa conformetur Christo vel Petro in moribus et in vita, nec aliter a deo recipit procuratorium potestatem, quia nulla alia sequela est pertinentior.'

16. 'Non quia papa vices tenet Petri, sed quia magnum habet dotationem, ex eo est sanctissimus.'

17. 'Cardinales non sunt manifesti et veri successores collegii aliorum apostolorum Christi, nisi vixerint more apostolorum servantes mandata et consilia domini Jesu Christi.'

18. 'Nullus hæreticus ultra censuram ecclesiasticam est relinquendus judicio seculari morte corporis puniendus.'

notoriously heretical. Gerson agreed with Hus in regretting the breaches of church discipline; but he held that the reformer's zeal was not according to knowledge, that errors were

19. Mundi nobiles debent compellere sacerdotes ad observantiam legis Christi.

20. Obedientia ecclesiastica est obedientia secundum adinventionem sacerdotum ecclesiæ, præter expressam auctoritatem scripturarum.

21. 'Quod excommunicatus a papa, omisso judicio papæ et concilii generalis, si appellet ad Christum, præservatur, ut excommunicatio hujusmodi non afficiat eum.'

22. 'Si homo est vitiosus et agit quidquam, agit vitiose; et si est virtuosus et agit quidquam, tunc agit virtuose.'

23. 'Sacerdos Christi, vivens secundum legem ejus, habens scripturæ notitiam et affectum ad edificandum populum, debet prædicare, non obstante prætensa excommunicatione; et infra: quod si papa vel alius præpositus mandat sacerdoti sic disposito non prædicare, non debet obedire.'

24. 'Quilibet prædecantis officium accepit, qui ad sacerdotium accessit, et ejus mandatum debet exequi, excommunicatione prætensa non obstante.'

25. 'Censuræ ecclesiasticæ sunt Anti-Christianæ, quas clerus excogitavit ad sui exaltationem et populi subpeditationem, si ipsis clericis laici ad eorum non obedierint voluntatem.'

26. 'Non debet poni interdictum in populo, quia Christus, summus pontifex, nec propter Joannem baptistam, nec propter suas injurias posuit interdictum.'

ARTICULI EXTRACTI EX TRACTATU FACTO CONTRA M. STEPHANUM PALECZ

1. 'Si papa, episcopus vel prælatus est in peccato mortali, quod tunc non est papa, episcopus vel prælatus.'

2. Gratia prædestinationis est vinculum, quo corpus ecclesiæ et quodlibet ejus membrum jungitur ipsi capiti insolubiliter.

3. 'Si papa est malus et præsertim præscitus, tunc ut Judas apostolus est diabolus, fur et filius perditionis, et non caput sanctæ ecclesiæ militantis, cum nec sit membrum ecclesiæ militantis.'

4. 'Papa vel prælatus malus vel præscitus non est vere pastor, sed æquivoce, sed vere fur et latro.'

5. 'Papa non est, nec debet dici sanctissimus, etiam secundum officium, alias rex etiam deberet dici sanctissimus secundum officium et tortores, præcones, diaboli deberent dici sancti.

6. 'Si papa vivit Christo contrarie, etiam rite, legitime et canonice electus secundum humanam electionem ascendit aliunde in papatum, quam per Christum.'

7. 'Condemnatio XLV. articulorum Wiclef per doctores facta est irrationabilis et iniqua, et causa per eos allegata est ficta, videlicet quod nullus ex eis est catholicus, sed quilibet eorum aut est hæreticus, aut erroneus aut scandalosus.'

ARTICULI EXTRACTI DE TRACTATU FACTO CONTRA M. STANISLAUM DE ZNOYMA

1. 'Non eo ipso, quo electores vel major pars eorum assenserint una voce secundum ritus hominum in personam aliquam, eo ipso persona illa est legitime

THE TRIAL OF JOHN HUS

not to be reformed by other errors, that demons were not to be driven from the Church by Beelzebub, but by the finger of God ; he regarded Hus's own ideas on the Church and on Church government as utterly erroneous and heretical.[1] The extracts were read out, and some of them were admitted by Hus to be correct. The others were carefully compared with the original works, and this comparison showed that in some instances modifications and distinctions had been drawn which altered the sense ; and on other extracts also Hus's oral explanations put a less offensive signification. In other instances the Cardinal of Cambrai pointed out to King Sigismund that the extracts had been actually toned down ! But the main stumbling-block, his argument as to the constitution of the Church, his allegation that the Church could be governed as well by priests scattered throughout the world without a head as by the Pope, remained.

Hus's treatise on the Church was indeed a masterly work, which, because of its immense citation of authorities, was declared by the Cardinal to combat the authority and plenary power of the Pope no less than the Kuran combated the Catholic faith.[2] It was based on the work of John Wyclif, some parts of it being copied verbally ; but it did not follow Wyclif into his more violent heresies in which he declared the Roman Church to be the synagogue of Satan, and the election by the cardinals to be the work of the devil. But both reformers built their constitution of the Church on a totally different basis from that adopted by the Catholic Church. They held that the Church is the whole body of the predestinate ; that no man

electa, vel quod eo ipso est manifestus et verus successor Christi, vel vicarius Petri apostoli in officio ecclesiastico sed eo ipso, quo quis copiosius operatur meritorie ad profectum ecclesiæ, habet a deo ad hoc copiosius potestatem.'

2. 'Papa præscitus non est caput ecclesiæ sanctæ dei.'

3. 'Non est scintilla apparentiæ, quod oporteat esse unum caput in spiritualibus regens ecclesiam, quod semper cum ipsa militante ecclesia conversetur.'

4. 'Christus sine talibus monstruosis capitibus per suos veraces discipulos sparsos per orbem terrarum melius suam ecclesiam regularet.'

5. 'Petrus non fuit universalis pastor ovium Christi, nec Romanus pontifex.'

6. 'Apostoli et fideles sacerdotes domini strenue in necessariis ad salutem regularent ecclesiam, antequam papæ officium fuerat introductum : sic facerent, deficientes per summe possibile papa, usque diem judicii.'—Palacky, *Doc.*, 286-307.

---

[1] Schwab, 587.   [2] Gerson, ii. 901.

who is 'foreknown' by God to damnation is a member of the Church, and that all the predestinate, though they be in sin, are members, since they will ultimately be saved by divine grace. The Church is thus a mystic and indeterminate body, since not only does no man know of another whether he is elect or not, but no Christian can be absolutely sure of his own standing in grace.[1] Hus held that the temporal power of the Pope was derived from the Donation of Constantine, and he rejected the Cardinal's suggestion that it could be based on the simultaneous decree of the œcumenical Council; he agreed with many others that the Donation had been the beginning of evil. He contended that unless the Vicar of Christ followed the paths of virtue, he was not the true Vicar and pontiff of the Church; if he followed the contrary paths he was the messenger of Antichrist. When this article was read [2] the presidents looked at each other, smiled, and shook their heads. They believed that the powers that be are ordained of God; the Catholic doctrine is that the Church is 'a body of men united together by the profession of the same Christian faith, and by participation in the same sacraments, under the governance of lawful pastors, more especially of the Roman pontiff, the sole Vicar of Christ on earth'; and the conditions of membership are that a man profess the true faith and have received the sacrament of baptism, that he acknowledge the authority of the Church and her appointed rulers, and that he enjoy the canonical right to communion with her.[3] Hus's teaching loosened the bonds of authority. He believed that those who are simoniac and who live in sin, pollute their priestly power and have only a dead faith; he did not scruple to apply the same doctrine to the cardinals, alleging that they were no true successors of the apostles unless they lived like them, following the precepts and counsels of their Lord Christ. This particularly touched the Cardinal of Cambrai, who, for all his piety and reforming zeal, was believed to have a keen eye to the loaves and fishes, and to be fully persuaded that the workman was worthy of his hire. He reproached John Hus with having preached such a doctrine to the laity to the scandal

[1] Lechler (*Lorimer*), 295.   [2] Palacky (*Doc.*), 289.
[3] *C.E.*, iii. 745, 755.

of the Church. The Master excused himself on the ground that there were priests and learned men among his audience, but Pierre d'Ailly persisted that he had done wrong. Jean Gerson also not only altogether dissented from Hus's theory as to the constitution of the Church, but he condemned his strictures of the clergy as rash.[1] It was clear that they were subversive of discipline. Hus trusted that God would one day judge between him and the Parisian chancellor.[2]

The question of ecclesiastical censures then came up. John Hus thought that the Pope should not impose interdicts, because Christ had never done so; he contended that a heretic should be gently and piously reasoned with, that the scripture should be explained to him, and that such instruction ought always to precede any punishment. He relied on the words of Our Lord, who said that one who would not hear the scripture was to be to them as a heathen man and a publican; but Christ had not gone further than that. There was great murmuring at this explanation. A passage from his work was then read in which he compared those who inflicted such censures to the scribes and Pharisees who had delivered Christ to Pilate. The tumult increased, and they turned angrily to Hus demanding whether he likened those who delivered a heretic to the secular arm to those who had betrayed Christ. He answered that those who gave an innocent man to death were like the chief priests, the scribes, and the Pharisees. He could not appease the uproar, and the Cardinal of Cambrai again remarked that the expressions in his book were worse than those given in the extract, and he reiterated this opinion in reference to a later article on the same subject. Hus, who drew a distinction between venial sins and others, contended that obedience was not due to an unjust excommunication, which in his eyes was equivalent to a benediction. He admitted that he himself had appealed from the Pope to Christ, because he had received no answer to his appeal to Rome for two years. The Cardinal of Cambrai asked whether he exalted himself above Saint Paul who had appealed to Cæsar; and Hus answered that Paul was acting under the command of his Master, but that the ultimate appeal lay to Christ. Those in the assembly laughed at him

[1] Schwab, 587. [2] Palacky (*Doc.*), 97.

and asked whether he had not celebrated Mass while he was still under sentence; he admitted this, but explained that he had appealed, though he had not received absolution from the Pope.

As regards the articles charged against Hus in the indictment, it will be noted that the extracts were not in all cases true copies of his words, but were often in the nature of an abstract or epitome of the text; and this gave rise to frequent discussions as to the fairness of the same. The Master was allowed to explain his real meaning, and in some cases it was found that the article charged was less objectionable than the doctrine expressed in the work. Having finished the articles taken from the *De Ecclesia*, those taken from the two tractates were then considered; and these, with one exception, concerned the power and office of the Pope. In regard to his dissent from the judgment of his University on the forty-five articles of Wyclif, Hus explained that he did not wish to defend the errors of John Wyclif or of any other person, and that his simple reason for not joining in the condemnation was because no scriptural proofs had been adduced to justify the condemnation.

With reference to the Church of Rome, Hus believed that the grace of predestination was the chain which bound the Church and its members to its head, and that that head was Christ, neither Peter nor the Roman pontiff having ever been the universal pastor of Christ's flock; that there was no reason why there should be one sole head on earth ruling the Church in matters spiritual, and that Christ through his own true disciples could govern the Church better than it had been governed of late by its 'monstrous heads.' Hus here referred to the deposition of John the Twenty-third and the approaching resignation of Gregory the Twelfth. 'I maintain,' he said, ' that in the time of the apostles the Church was infinitely better governed than it is at present. And at present we have no head, and yet Christ does not cease to rule the Church.' At this all laughed at him. The apostles and the faithful priests of the Lord, he contended, had governed the Church wisely before ever the office of Pope was introduced, and they could do so until the Day of Judgment. There was a chorus of 'Lo, he prophesies!' But Hus persisted in the truth of his contention, and remarked that they had no Pope at present and might not have for the next two years. But the angrier part of the discussion raged round the question of the worthiness of the Pope. Hus contended that it was not through the mere fact of a canonical election, but from his works, that a true pope was known, and that if a pope, bishop, or priest was in mortal sin, he was not then pope, bishop, or priest. When the article was read John Hus added, 'Truly he who is in mortal sin is not worthily a king before God,' and he quoted the instance of Saul who had neglected to execute the fierce wrath of the Lord against Amalek.

King Sigismund was at this moment standing in the refectory window talking with the Count Palatine and Friedrich of Nuernberg. He had lost all sympathy with John Hus now, and pointed him out to his two companions as the greatest heretic in Christendom. He was not listening to the discussion, but the presidents of the assembly called on Hus to repeat what he had said as it touched the royal office. The prisoner did so, when Sigismund, with bluff common-sense, answered him: 'John Hus, no one of us lives without sin.' Pierre d'Ailly then angrily intervened: 'It is not enough for you to libel the spiritual office in your writings and dogmas, but you must also seek to cast down the royal office and kings from their estate.' Palec also rose and pointed out that Saul was still king, and that David would not allow him to be touched because of his royal unction. 'A man may be a true pope, king, or bishop,' said he, 'though he be not a true Christian.' John Hus then inquired why Baldassare Cossa had been deposed if he was the true Pope. King Sigismund answered: 'The fathers of the Council have indeed found that Baldassare Cossa was the true Pope; but on account of notorious misdeeds, by which he scandalised the Church of God and despoiled her goods, he has been deposed from the papacy.' John Hus in other articles had maintained that if the Pope were a bad man and foreknown by God to damnation, then he was not the head of the Church militant, but was a thief and a robber; and he explained that he limited this to the assertion that he was not really and truly such before God, though he still was as regards his office and reputation before men; Hus again referred to the case of the

Pope lately deposed. A spirited argument between Palec and Hus followed on the question of those who entered the fold through the canonical election, but not 'through the door.' Hus concluded by stating that any one who entered on a benefice by means of simony, not with the intention of working in God's Church, but rather with that of living delicately, voluptuously, and luxuriously, had got in by some other way, and had not entered by the lowly gate of our Lord Jesus Christ, and according to the gospel he was a thief and a robber. John Stokes, the Englishman, could not resist the temptation of a final fling at his old adversary. ' Why do you boast of these writings and doctrines and arrogate to yourself the title of them ? ' he asked. ' These doctrines and opinions are not yours, but Wyclif's, whose path you are following.' It was quite true ; the doctrines of John Hus on the Church and on Church government were derived from the works of John Wyclif. The hearing proper on the articles charged in the indictment was now over.[1]

[1] Palacky (*Doc.*), 285-308. It is hardly necessary to point out that the Catholic doctrine on Church government is 'that the Pope or Bishop of Rome, as the successor of Saint Peter, possesses authority and jurisdiction, in things spiritual, over the entire Church, so as to constitute its visible head and the viceregent of Christ upon earth,' the Holy See being the centre of unity and the fountain of authority; that the high dignity of supreme pontiff may be awarded without reference to the exemption of its holder from sin and crime ; and that the rock, designated by Christ, upon which He promised to build His Church was not Himself but Peter, the first Bishop of Rome. See Wiseman's *Doctrines and Practices of the Catholic Church*, Lecture VIII.

CHAPTER XXI

THE CONCLUSION OF THE TRIAL

As soon as the hearing was terminated, Pierre d'Ailly, Cardinal of Cambrai, turned and addressed the accused. 'Master John ! there are two ways open to you to choose from ; you can either surrender yourself absolutely to the mercy of the Council, content to do as it shall dictate, and then the Council will, out of reverence to the King of the Romans and his brother of Bohemia, and for your own welfare, deal with you in a spirit of piety and humanity ; or, if you still wish to defend any of the former articles and desire a further audience, this shall be granted to you ; but take notice that there are here great and learned men, doctors and masters, who entertain such strong opinions adverse to your articles that it is to be feared lest you fall into still more grievous error by further defending them. I am now giving you counsel and not speaking judicially.' Others also counselled him to the like effect. ' Certainly, Master John, it were better for you to surrender yourself completely to the mercy of the Council, and not pertinaciously to continue in error.' John Hus bowed his head humbly and made reply : ' Most reverend fathers, I came here of my own free will, not to defend any point pertinaciously, but humbly to submit myself to the instruction of the Council wherever I had laid down aught wrongly or defectively ; I ask, therefore, that an audience be granted me in order that I may set forth my meaning in the articles charged against me and may adduce the writings of the Fathers ; and if my reasoning and proofs be insufficient, I will submit myself humbly to instruction by the Council.' On this many in wrath cried out that Hus was speaking captiously and perversely, that he sought instruction instead of leading and correction from the Council. Hus answered : ' God is my witness that I speak sincerely and not captiously ; I desire to submit myself humbly to the Council for instruction, for authoritative decision, and for correction.' Then the Cardinal of Cambrai, accepting this as submission on the part of the Master, said to him : ' Master John, since you are willing to bow to the mercy of the Council, and submit to its decision, know that sixty doctors, on its behalf, have unanimously resolved that you must humbly acknowledge your error in the articles you have held, that you must abjure them and swear never more to hold nor preach nor teach them, that you publicly renounce and retract them, and hold, write, and preach the contrary.'

On hearing this sentence Hus burst forth and conjured the right reverend father not to expose him to the risk of damnation by requiring him to abjure the doctrine that material bread remained in the elements after consecration, a tenet which had falsely been alleged against him, which had never entered into his heart ; many things had been alleged against him which he had never believed, so that it would be contrary to his conscience to abjure such articles. Some tried to reason with him and to persuade him that such a course was not abjuration ; but he objected that he could not conscientiously take such an oath. ' Does not your conscience testify that you may have erred and still be erring ? ' they asked. Then the King intervened. ' Listen, Hus ! why should you not abjure all those articles which you say are false and have been falsely alleged against you ? I, for my part, would willingly abjure every error, no matter whether I had held it or not.' ' My Lord the King,' said Hus, ' that is not the correct meaning of the expression.' Cardinal Zabarella then informed Hus that a certain limited (*satis limitata*) form of abjuration would be prepared and submitted to him for consideration and decision. Sigismund then told Hus that he might abjure and renounce his errors and throw himself on the mercy of the Council, but that if he persisted in upholding them, then the fathers of the Council had their laws and would give judgment accordingly. This of course meant that Hus was to abjure or to be burned. He answered, ' Most serene prince, I desire not to hold any error, but rather to submit myself humbly to the determination of the Council ; only, in order that I offend not before God and my

THE CONCLUSION OF THE TRIAL 383

own conscience, let me not be said to have held errors which I never believed, which never entered my mind. I only asked that an audience be granted me that I may set forth my belief in certain points which have been alleged against me, more especially in regard to the Pope, the heads and members of the Church, in which my meaning has been mistaken; for I admit that, although the Pope or bishops or prelates may be foreknown by God to damnation and are in mortal sin, so that they are not really such meritoriously nor worthily before God, still they are such so far as their offices are concerned, even though they be unworthy ministers of the sacraments.' Much more he said to the same effect on the distinction between those who were officially but not worthily officers of the Church. King Sigismund answered him. 'Listen, John Hus! what I said to you yesterday, I say again to-day, and I will not repeat it, for you are old enough to understand. You have heard that the lords of the Council have offered you the choice of two alternatives, either that you submit in everything to the grace of the Council, and the sooner the better, and abjure and renounce every error, those written in your books, those admitted by you, and those proved against you by the witnesses, and that for these errors you perform the penance assigned with a contrite heart, and swear never to hold them more but to believe and teach the opposite; or else, if you still hold to them, the Council will of a surety proceed according to law.' A certain aged priest from Poland remarked that the law on the point was quite clear. Hus again repeated that he was open to instruction. Again did many members of the assembly cry out on the Master that he was obstinate, confirmed in his errors, unwilling to submit to the decision and correction of the Council. A certain plump priest, dressed in a gorgeous raiment, who was sitting in the window, objected to Hus being allowed to abjure, because he had already sent a letter to his followers telling them that if he were compelled to recant it would be with his mouth only and not with his heart, so that his word could not be trusted. Hus protested against the unworthy suspicion. 'I have made public protestation,' he said, 'in my tractate against Stanislas, that I am ready faithfully to submit to the decision of our Holy Mother Church as every faithful Christian ought to do.' Stephen Palec then rose and remarked very pertinently : ' What would be the good of my saying that I did not want to box Master Albert's ears, if I did box them ; that is what you are doing ; you say you do not want to defend any errors, and especially Wyclif's errors, and still you do defend them.' He read to the Council five articles of Wyclif's errors, which they had condemned, against which he and Stanislas had preached at Prague when Duke Ernest of Austria was there ; these same five errors Hus and his allies had defended in the schools and publicly. ' I have with me here your writings in their defence,' he continued, ' and if you will not produce them, I will.' Hus asked him to produce them ; but the King said, ' If you have them, it were well that you produced them for the Council to examine ; if you do not, then others will.' And again Hus asked that they might be produced.

Procedure in those days was very lax, and it seemed as if the trial were to be reopened, for at this stage a certain comment on some opinion of the Pope's was produced and was alleged to have been made by Hus. He, however, denied that he had ever seen the comment, and stated that he disapproved of it. The long hearing and agitation was telling upon the weary man ; he had not slept the night before for toothache and headache, and now he began to shake with fever. But the audience continued nevertheless.

The next point brought up against him concerned the three students executed at Prague for uproarious conduct.[1] He was charged with bringing back their bodies in triumph to the Bethlehem Chapel, with having the Mass for Martyrs chanted over them, and with doing all he could to canonise them. To this he answered that it was true that they had been beheaded, but all else was false, for he was not in Prague at the time. Dr. Johannes Nas then gave the whole history of the tumult, tracing its origin to Hus's preaching against the indulgences ; and he was corroborated by Palec.

The next offence charged was that Hus had read a copy of a letter purporting to come from the University of Oxford in support of John Wyclif. This he admitted, stating that the letter bore the seal of the University and was brought to Prague

[1] *Vid. sup.* p. 124.

THE CONCLUSION OF THE TRIAL 385

by two of its students; one of them was Nicolas Faulfisch of good memory, now dead, and he knew not who was the other. Palec explained that Faulfisch was not an Englishman, but a Bohemian, who had brought with him a stone from Wyclif's grave, which was worshipped by many at Prague. Other Englishmen then produced a letter which purported to come from the Chancellor of the University of Oxford, containing two hundred and sixty extracts from Wyclif's writings to be submitted to the Council for condemnation. Stephen Palec then rose and explained that in all he had done he had been actuated solely by zeal for the true faith and not by any personal animosity against John Hus; to which Michael *de Causis* added, 'So have I.' Hus answered, 'I stand before God's judgment seat, and He will judge us both according to our merits.' The Cardinal of Cambrai concluded the proceedings by congratulating Palec on the fairness and leniency with which he had made the extracts charged against the accused.

As the Archbishop of Riga was about to take Hus back into custody, John of Chlum held out his hand to the prisoner and consoled him; and Hus was very grateful for this mark of sympathy toward one who was rejected of all and despised as a heretic. The cardinals and prelates rose to depart, and the guards left the hall. John of Chlum, Wenzel of Duba, and Mladonowicz drew near the window, and the King thought they were going to follow the prisoner. Sigismund then spake to the prelates who remained: 'Reverend Fathers! you have heard that what he has confessed and what has been proved against him is sufficient for his condemnation; therefore if he will not renounce and abjure his errors and preach against them, let him be burned or do with him according to your law. And be you well assured that though he should promise to recant and should recant, you cannot trust him, nor would I trust him, for he would go back and sow other worse errors, and the last heresy would be worse than the first. Therefore forbid him all preaching. And send those condemned articles to my brother in Bohemia, to Poland also, and to every land where he has secret disciples and adherents, and let the bishops and prelates punish such people and tear them up, root and branch; and let this Council write to all kings and princes to favour especially such of their prelates as have worked in this Council for the extirpation of these heresies. You know how it is written that in the mouth of two or three witnesses shall every word be established ; while the hundredth part of the evidence here given would suffice for his condemnation. And you must make an end of his other secret disciples and adherents, as I am shortly going to leave you, and especially with the man who is now in custody.' They asked him, ' Do you mean Jerome ? ' and he answered, ' Yes, Jerome ' ; to which they said that they would soon arrange that matter, which was much simpler, seeing that Jerome was but the disciple of Hus. And Sigismund added, ' I was but a young man when this sect first took its rise in Bohemia, and now see how it has increased and multiplied.' His audience, very glad at heart, then took their leave of the King.[1]

Thus was John Hus tried and condemned for heresy, and there can be no doubt that the condemnation was in accordance with law. Heresy is error pertinaciously held and manifestly repugnant to the faith ; and Hus's doctrine of church government was contrary to the teaching and tradition of the Catholic Church. Pierre d'Ailly and Jean Gerson agreed with him in regarding Christ and not the Pope as the head of the Church ; others had advocated a plurality of Popes ; but the doctrines of Wyclif and Hus, in distinguishing between the worthy and the unworthy priest, brought the officers of the Church before the tribunal of the individual conscience. Not that it was ever alleged against John Hus that he exalted the individual conscience to the post of supreme authority, and no one would repudiate the suggestion more heartily than he. But as a matter of fact this is the tendency of his teaching. What else was the meaning of his appeal from the Pope to Christ ? it was simply an appeal to his own sense of what was right and just.

This arose from his love for Holy Writ. Like all the Bohemian reformers he was devoted to the Bible. He regarded Christ's law, as set forth in the New Testament, as a sufficient guide for the life of Christians, for the governance of the Church, and for the attainment of salvation.[2] In this he was only following John Wyclif, one of the distinctive features of whose

[1] Palacky (*Doc.*), 308-15.   [2] Lechler, 111.

THE CONCLUSION OF THE TRIAL

teaching was that he insisted on the supreme authority of Holy Scripture. It contains, he contended, that which is necessary and indispensable for salvation, and all that is necessary can either be found in it or be deduced from it. Man's reason is a lesser and imperfect guide; the Fathers and Tradition are admissible only in so far as they are consistent with the Scripture. In this Wyclif and Hus were at variance with the teaching of their time. William of Ockham and Jean Gerson,[1] for instance, claimed authority for the Scripture and for church teaching in combination; they thought of the two as being always in harmony, the latter supplementing the former and not needing to be tested by it; whereas Wyclif and Hus distinguished clearly between the two, and regarded the Scripture as the authority by which the doctrines of the Church and the Fathers were to be tried.

The difficulty lies, of course, in the question of interpretation; for the Scripture is occasionally hard to understand, and it must have been still harder when every text was susceptible of four different meanings. There was not only the literal sense of the words, which Wyclif always took as his starting point, insisting upon this as the indispensable basis of all thorough and deep understanding of the Scriptures; there were also the symbolical, the moral, and the mystical interpretations. Both reformers had done much to render the Scriptures accessible to the mass of the people of their country in the vulgar tongue; and this increased the importance of the question of interpretation; for although learned men like Wyclif and Hus, in the interpretation of a difficult text, might and did study with attention and reverence the opinions of the Fathers, these aids to correct interpretation were not within the means of the vulgar to whom they had rendered the sacred word accessible. For the right interpretation of Scripture both Wyclif and Hus relied upon the Holy Ghost; God Himself would enlighten the inquirer to a right understanding of His word. This right of private interpretation was precisely the point which the council of doctors of the theological faculty at Prague had brought against the followers of Hus; they interpret the Scriptures out of their own heads, they said, and take no thought for the

[1] Hauréau, iii. 465.

interpretation given by the community of the wise men of the Church.[1]

The appeal to the Holy Ghost in the interpretation of Scripture, like the appeal to Christ against the Pope's decision, was in reality an exaltation of the individual conscience against church Tradition; and in this respect John Hus was a precursor of the Reformation. But it is necessary clearly to understand the doctrine of the Catholic Church in dealing with the Protestant opinion thus advanced by Hus. The Holy Roman Church has always evinced the deepest reverence for the Scriptures, she has embodied them in the Breviary, the Missal, and the Psalter for daily use by the clergy, on whom she has enjoined the study of Holy Writ, bidding them to meditate and ponder thereon. Nor did she at any time during the Middle Ages issue any general prohibition of the translation or the reading of the Bible in the vulgar tongue. But, on the other hand, she did not regard all portions of the Scripture as easy to understand or as being of universal application. It must be remembered that Christ delivered His teaching orally, that Tradition thus preceded the written word; it does not follow therefore that the Word contains the whole of His teaching and never requires to be supplemented by Tradition. Even when instruction was subsequently imparted by letter, it was at times of local and not of universal application. Saint Paul, writing to the Gentiles who were full of good works, preached faith; whereas Saint James, writing to the Jews who were strong in the faith, inculcated good works.[2] But the Holy Roman Church has always held that the interpretation of the Bible was a matter of which the Church alone, and not the laity, could judge. The office of teacher, as Pope Innocent the Third laid down, belongs not to the whole body of the faithful but to a special class, and he who does not belong to this class must prove his special calling. It is against the fallibility of human judgment and its liability to error that the Church has guarded; and the verdict of history shows that precaution has not been unnecessary. Heretics at all times have appealed to the Bible, not only to refute the true faith, but also to refute

[1] Palacky (*Doc.*), 476; Lechler (*Lorimer*), 238-49; Lechler, 111-12.
[2] St. Evremond; cf. Hauréau, i. 177.

one another. As the milk-white Hind, in Dryden's poem, puts it :—

> 'Did not Arius first, Socinus now,
> The Son's eternal Godhead disavow?
> And did not these by gospel texts alone
> Condemn our doctrine and maintain their own?
> Have not all heretics the same pretence
> To plead the Scriptures in their own defence?'

And in another place :—

> 'Mark how sandy is your own pretence
> Who, setting Councils, Popes, and Church aside,
> Are every man his own presuming guide.
> The sacred books, you say, are full and plain,
> And every needful point of truth contain;
> All who can read interpreters may be.
> Thus, though your several churches disagree,
> Yet every saint has to himself alone
> The secret of this philosophic stone.'

If the truth is one and not multiform, then there is sound sense in the contention that blind guides should be prohibited, and that expert teachers should alone be trusted for its discovery; and, moreover, in an age of little education and of faulty translation, it is readily conceivable that reading the Scripture in the vulgar tongue might, with good reason, be discouraged.[1] The consistent teaching of the Catholic Church from the beginning has been that which was formulated by Pope Pius the Fourth :—' I admit the Holy Scriptures according to the sense which our Holy Mother the Church has held, and does hold, to which it belongs to judge of the true sense and interpretation of the Scriptures.'

John Hus was therefore rightly condemned as guilty of heresy, but it did not necessarily follow that he was to be burned. The lowest classes were always most violent in their pursuit of the crime. The mob, says M. Luchaire,[2] living in perpetual terror of the scourges which decimated it, and convinced that plague, famine, and war were marks of the divine anger, thought they might disarm God's wrath by exterminating His enemies. In the upper classes there was less fanaticism,

---

[1] Michael, iii. 231-5.   [2] *Innocent III. : La Croisade des Albigeois*, 36.

and it was not rare that the priest was more tolerant than the layman because he was more enlightened. As one mounted in the Church hierarchy, religious passion decreased. King Sigismund spoke with the voice of the crowd when he demanded the burning of Hus; the more influential fathers of the Council desired not his death, but his recantation; and they did what in them lay to make the recantation as feasible and easy as possible. They did not sympathise with the lower orders of the clergy who had caused such a disgraceful scene on the first day of the trial.

Hus was expecting a final audience; he thought that the King and Cardinal d'Ailly had promised it him; and he besought his friends to secure it. He did not trust Sigismund, who had condemned him before his enemies had done so, and had deceived him about the safe-conduct.[1] The King's change of attitude toward John Hus, though he knew it not, had set the entire Bohemian nation against him; the patriot was to be avenged by long and fierce wars in the near future. After the third day of the trial Hus was troubled with evil dreams; he felt that neither he nor Jerome of Prague would leave Constance alive; and for himself, if he was not to have a final audience, he desired nothing further than instant sentence of death. He wrote on the 10th June to his friends in Bohemia bidding them stand fast in the faith, asking their gratitude to the lords of Bohemia, Moravia, and Poland who had been steadfast to him, and telling them to pray for the King of the Romans and for King Wenzel and Queen Sophia.[2] Two other letters, of the 13th and 16th June, bear a similar testamentary character.

Hus's expectation of a speedy sentence was not fulfilled, for time was given for repentance and recantation. The Council held a general session on the 15th June to deal with the question of communion in both kinds which had been referred to them by the iron Bishop of Leitomysl. A commission of theologians had considered the matter and had reported unfavourably to the Bohemian innovation. The Council decreed that although Christ had instituted the sacrament after supper and had ministered to His apostles in both kinds, nevertheless the authority of the canons and the custom of the Church had

[1] Palacky (*Doc.*), 114.   [2] *Ibid.* (*Doc.*), 117.

THE CONCLUSION OF THE TRIAL 391

held that, save in cases of sickness or necessity, the sacrament shall only be received fasting, by the priest in both kinds, but by the laity, for the avoidance of scandal, under the form of the bread only, in which form both the body and blood of Christ is communicated. They decreed that this custom of the Church was to be observed as a law, and that offenders were to be punished. The only effect of this decree on John Hus was to cause him to declare himself definitely in favour of communion in both kinds, and he laughed at the Council for condemning as an error the sacrament as instituted by Christ Himself.[1] Jean Petit's doctrine of political assassination also came up for consideration at the thirteenth session, and a commission was appointed.

During these final weeks of Hus's imprisonment, many attempts were made to induce him to recant. Some one, possibly an abbot, sent him a form of abjuration, but Hus felt that he could not accept it, and when his friend tried to reason with him and to persuade him that any guilt in recanting what he did not believe would recoil on those who forced him so to do rather than on himself, he declined to be persuaded. He could not recant what was true, nor would he pretend to recant what he had never believed; he had his faithful flock to think of as well as himself. An Englishman told him that all the magistrates in England had recanted the errors of Wyclif at the King's order, although they had never held them. Stephen Palec, who had called Hus the worst of all heretics barring John Wyclif, tried to persuade him that there was no ignominy in recantation. 'What would you do?' asked Hus, 'if you knew that you had never believed the errors charged against you? Would you recant them?' His old friend burst into tears and confessed that it was a hard situation.

Hus's tractates were publicly burned on the 24th June, but neither did this discourage him; he rejoiced rather that his enemies had read certain of his works more attentively than they read their Bibles. But he was now full of scorn for the Council; they pretended to have read his works, whereas they were men of all nations, very few of whom understood Bohemian; they had gone on their bended knees and kissed

[1] Palacky (*Doc.*), 128.

the feet of John the Twenty-third, whom they knew to be a man full of sin; he likened them to the scarlet whore of the Revelation. He wrote to his friends in Constance and in Prague, exhorting them to preserve his letters and to stand fast in the faith; he congratulated Wenzel of Duba on his approaching marriage; he sent several letters to John of Chlum, thanking him for his firm friendship and speaking kindly of his wife and family; he advised the University of Prague to avoid dissension and to consider only God's honour, telling them that he had declined to withdraw any article which was not proved by the Bible to be false. He remembered King Wenzel, and sent a message of kindly encouragement to Queen Sophia. He bribed the guards to take out and bring in his letters. His inveterate enemy, Michael *de Causis*, tried to stop this, and told the guards that, with God's help, he hoped soon to burn this heretic, over whom he had expended so much money.

On the 27th June Hus was not without hope. Efforts to procure his recantation were redoubled. Many tried to persuade him that he might lawfully abjure what he had never taught; but Hus insisted that in that case he must be allowed first to swear that he had never held these errors. This could not be allowed, since the errors to be forsworn were in his works. Hus maintained that the opinions, as he understood them, were not heretical. On the 1st July he wrote as follows :—' I, John Hus, fearing to offend God and to swear falsely, cannot abjure all the articles which false witnesses have testified against me, for before God I have never preached, held, nor defended that which they ascribe to me. As for the articles correctly extracted from my works, I say that, if any of them contains anything false, then I utterly abhor it; but fearing to offend against the truth and the opinion of the Fathers I cannot abjure them. And if it were possible that my voice could reach the whole world, as every falsehood and sin of mine will be manifest at the Day of Judgment, so would I right willingly recant every falsehood or error that I have ever thought or spoken.'

On the 5th July Cardinals d'Ailly and Zabarella made a last effort. They had a proposition which they thought he could accept. He was to declare that he abjured and recanted all the articles written with his own hand and so extracted from his

THE CONCLUSION OF THE TRIAL

works, and that he had not taught the articles alleged against him by the witnesses; or if he had taught them, he had done wrong, for they were erroneous, and he would never hold them in future. King Sigismund approved the formula and sent Louis of Bavaria, John of Chlum, Wenzel of Duba, and certain prelates to fetch the prisoner. They came to the Franciscan Cloister. Hus was brought in; he had already seen the formula. John of Chlum, his stalwart friend, spoke to him feelingly and in straightforward fashion. 'See now, Master John, I am a layman and know not how to counsel you; but if you feel that there is anything obnoxious in any of the matters laid against you, do not fear instruction and recantation; but if you conscientiously feel that you are not guilty in any matter, then by no means go against your conscience and lie in the sight of God, but rather stand fast until death in the truth you have known.' A finer exhortation was never uttered, and it coincided exactly with the sentiment of John Hus. He was in tears as he replied, 'Lord John, rest assured, and may God be my witness that I would with right good will humbly recant anything erroneous or contrary to the law of God or Holy Church that I may have written or preached; but I wish them to show me better and more reasonable writings than those which I have written and taught, and then will I right readily recant.' One of the bishops asked Hus if he pretended to be wiser than the whole Council. Hus answered that he made no such pretension, and that if the very least of the Council would instruct him with stronger proofs from Holy Writ he would at once recant what he had written. The bishops as they departed remarked, 'How obstinate he is in his heresy.' Hus was taken back into custody once more; the last attempt at procuring a recantation had failed; sentence was to be passed next day.[1]

The end was now close at hand. Hus's line of argument from first to last was clear and logical. He stood for Christ's law, for God's Word. If you could prove to him that anything he had said was contrary to Holy Writ, he was ready to recant it; but if not, then he claimed to judge every church tradition or doctrine by his own interpretation of the Scripture. He was

[1] Palacky (*Doc.*), 126-48, 316, 559-61.

not ready to accept a formal pronouncement of the Council without proof that it was in accordance with Holy Writ; but if there were such proof he was ready to submit, and there was no charge which he repudiated with such consistency as that he was obstinate in error. The head and forefront of his preaching and of his life's work, he said, had been to lead men back from their sins; to this end he had preached the gospel truth to them, and for this he was ready to die. He was, above all else, a reformer; but he was a reformer who held heretical views on the constitution of the Church and on church government. This was his offence. He had come to Constance expecting an academic discussion; he had met not argument but decision. He was told that his views were heretical and that he must abjure them; but he refused to acquiesce in a verdict the justice of which he disputed. 'Herein,' said Dr. Lechler, ' lies the greatness of Hus, that in spite of his humility and childlike character, in spite of his great self-distrust, he did not allow himself to be intimidated by the unanimous opinion of a great Council representing so large a part of the learning, intellectual power, and ecclesiastical authority of the time, that he preferred to bear the shame of being considered an obstinate heretic, and even to suffer the pangs of death at the stake, rather than consent to a recantation which he knew to be a falsehood.'

CHAPTER XXII

MARTYRDOM

THE date for the degradation and cremation of John Hus arrived. On this same day, the 6th July, the Council pronounced its first decree in the matter of the doctrine of Jean Petit. King Sigismund had announced that he would not start on his journey south until decision in this case had been given; the ambassadors of Jean sans Peur were at deadly enmity with Jean Gerson and his adherents; the Fathers of the Council were reluctant to place so powerful a prince as the Duke of Burgundy outside the pale of Christendom; and the result was a compromise. The question whether the thesis of Jean Petit did as a matter of fact purport to justify tyrannicide was left undecided; but the doctrine of political assassination was condemned in general terms without any names being mentioned. The scruples which the Fathers felt in condemning the man who had confessed that he planned the murder of his cousin, the Duke of Orleans, did not exist in the case of the patriot reformer of Bohemia.

Hus was condemned by the Council of Constance because he was what was afterwards known as a Protestant. He might venerate the Virgin Mary and believe the orthodox doctrine of transubstantiation, but he did not believe in the infallibility of the Church. He held the Protestant dogma that the written Word of God alone is the true standard and rule of faith; he rejected the Catholic dogma that there also exists a living authority, established by Christ in His Church, with His security against error, which can in cases of necessity issue decrees declaring what is true and what is false; he did not believe in Tradition, the unwritten Word of God, delivered by Christ to His apostles and by them to their successors. Therefore he was judged a heretic.

On Saturday, the 6th July 1415, the cathedral square at Constance was thronged with spectators, and the sacred edifice itself was crowded. King Sigismund sat there in royal state, surrounded by the chief officers of the Empire; and facing him was a crowd of magnates and nobles, spiritual and temporal, then attending the Council. The aged Cardinal of Viviers presided. When the High Mass, the litanies, and prayers were finished, the prisoner, John Hus, was introduced and was stationed in the middle of the nave near a table on which were placed the full vestures of a priest. The Bishop of Lodi preached a sermon from the text, 'That the body of sin might be destroyed.' Silence was strictly enjoined on all, and the proceedings of the day began.

Henricus de Piro first demanded, as proctor of the Council, that Hus's writings and books be burned. Then fifty-eight out of the two hundred and sixty condemned articles of Wyclif were read, the rest being taken as read, and condemned. The case against John Hus himself was opened by a description of his strife with the Archbishop of Prague, after which the articles for which he was condemned were read. What these were is not quite clear. They included those which had been charged against him on the 8th June,[1] with the exception of numbers 5, 16, 19, 21, and 26, from the *De Ecclesia*, and numbers 2 and 5 from his tractate against Stanislas of Znaim. But those charges also which were held to have been proved by the oral testimony of witnesses were also read, and after each charge, as in the case of Pope John, the number and civil condition of the witnesses, but not their names, were given. One of these was to the effect that Hus had associated himself with the three persons of the Trinity. This was supposed to be a logical conclusion from the pantheistic tendency of his realism. Hus was an ardent realist, but as a philosopher he was often not consistent in his reasoning; and his opponents, who were men of great logical ability, failed to make due allowance for this fact. To them every realist was a monster of impiety, who desired to explain by the reason that which could only be apprehended by faith. When a conclusion seemed to them logically to follow from realistic premises, they were satisfied with very little oral

---

[1] *Vid. sup.*, p. 372 *et seq.*

MARTYRDOM

evidence that it had actually been maintained. A solitary doctor had given evidence against Hus on this point. Hus asked for his name, but it was not given. As the several articles held to be proved were read, the prisoner attempted to reply, but was told by Cardinal d'Ailly to wait until the end. He objected that a reply then would be impossible, but Cardinal Zabarella ordered the beadles to impose silence on Hus. He folded his hands, saying, ' I beg you, for God's sake, to hear me, that those present may not think I have believed heresies; afterward you can do with me as you will.' He knelt down and cried aloud that he entrusted his cause to the righteous judgment of God. When the article condemning his appeal to Christ was read, he broke silence, exclaiming, ' Good Jesus, the Council condemns Thy procedure and commandment, which Thou gavest when Thou wast compassed by Thy enemies and committedst Thy cause to Thy heavenly Father, and gavest us an example.' He repeated his former explanation as to the reason why he had felt justified in celebrating Mass while under a sentence of excommunication; and he declared that although he had come to Constance willingly, yet he had been provided by King Sigismund with a safe-conduct. Hus is said to have looked at the King, who is said to have blushed at the remembrance of his perfidy, a blush which Charles the Fifth did not wish to repeat in the case of Luther at Worms. Hus's friend Mladonowicz, however, knows nothing of this incident. With the exception of these slight interruptions, the prisoner remained silent while the charges alleged to be proved against him were being read.

Then followed the sentence. It had been hoped that Hus might at the last moment submit and recant; and in this case he would have been sentenced to imprisonment for life. But there was no recantation. The more drastic sentence was therefore pronounced. It began by setting forth succinctly the reasons for his condemnation. At the part which mentioned that he had for many years been confirmed in his errors, Hus interrupted with the protestation, ' Never have I been obstinate, nor am I so now; but I have always desired to be instructed from the Bible.' When his books were condemned to be burned, he asked, ' How can you judge my books when you have adduced no stronger proofs from the Scripture than are therein contained, and how can you condemn my Bohemian works which you have never seen ? ' The sentence continued : ' Inasmuch as this Holy Council has satisfied itself that John Hus is stubborn and incorrigible and declines to return to the bosom of Holy Church and abjure his heresies, therefore the Holy Council of Constance decrees his deposition and degradation, and commissions the Archbishop of Milan and the Bishops of Feltre, Asti, and five others to carry out the degradation in presence of the Council, and since the Church has no further part in Hus, it delivers him to the secular arm and the secular judgment.'

John Hus knelt while the sentence was pronounced ; at its conclusion he prayed in a loud voice, ' Lord Jesus Christ, by Thy infinite mercy I pray Thee forgive all my enemies : Thou knowest that they have falsely complained against me, have brought false witnesses against me, and have fabricated false charges against me ; pardon them in Thy eternal mercy.' There were some who laughed at this prayer. The seven bishops then clothed him with the priestly garments as if he were to read Mass. When they endued him with the alb, he remarked that the Jews had put a white cloth on Christ and mocked Him when they led Him before Pilate. When he was fully clothed he was called upon for the last time to recant ; he rose, turned to the crowd and spake through his tears : ' See how these bishops call on me to recant, but I fear to do so, for I should lie in God's sight and before my own conscience, and should violate the truth, for never have I maintained these articles which have been falsely alleged against me, but have written, taught, and preached to the contrary. Therefore can I not recant, for I should grieve the many to whom I have preached, and all who publish the Word of God in truth.' The bishops, remarking on his obstinacy, then began the work of degradation. They took from him the chalice, calling him Judas, and declaring that they took from him the cup of salvation. Hus answered, ' I trust in the Lord, the Almighty God, in whose Name I suffer this blasphemy ; He will not withhold from me the cup of salvation, which I trust to drink with Him this day in His kingdom.' So the fearful ceremony proceeded. When they came to the tonsure, a dispute arose as to whether the entire head should be shaved clean or merely the existing tonsure disfigured. Sigismund laughed at the bishops for not knowing their work better. The tonsure was defaced at the four sides. The prisoner was now ready to be made over to the secular arm. A paper cap was placed on his head with the remark that his soul was committed to the devil. Hus answered, 'I commit you to my most merciful Lord Jesus Christ; as without complaining He bore for me a sharper crown of thorns, so will I humbly wear in His name and for the truth's sake this lighter but shameful crown.' The cap was two feet high; three ghastly devils, tormenting a soul, were painted on it; and it was inscribed, 'This is an arch-heretic.' As Hus was made over to King Sigismund, the usual hypocritical prayer was tendered that he might not be put to death.[1]

The last scene of the religious tragedy now commenced. King Sigismund turned to the Count Palatine: 'Sweet cousin Duke Louis, Elector of the Holy Roman Empire and our High Steward, since I am he who bears the temporal sword, take thou this man in my stead and treat him as a heretic.' The Count then called the Warden of Constance to him and said: 'Warden, take this man, because of the judgment against him, and burn him as a heretic.' The warden made him over to the town police and the executioner with strict orders that Hus was to be burned with all that was on him; not a girdle nor a penknife nor a shoe was to be removed.[2] His books were burned in the cathedral square as he left the church, whereat he smiled. He was not bound or fettered, but one of the Count's men marched on either side, two of the town police walked before and behind him, and a force of a thousand armed men marched on guard. As they marched, he prayed, 'Jesus Christ, Son of the living God, have mercy on me.' They went behind the Cathedral down the Plattenstrasse, past the church of Saint Laurence, and then turning to the right, they made their way out of the city through the gate that led to Paradise. Turning round by the Capuchin Cloister they reached a vacant piece of ground near the drain which ran down to Kreuzlingen. A cardinal's mule had been buried here a few days previously.

[1] Palacky (*Doc.*), 317-21; Hefele, vii. 193-211.   [2] Richental, 80.

Here the pyre was prepared.¹ Hus, seeing the wood and straw, cried out, ' Jesus Christ, Son of the living God, who didst suffer for us, have mercy on me.' Many who heard him were touched. As he prayed his paper cap fell off, and he smiled as the assistants replaced it, saying he must be burned with the demons he had served. He was asked if he would like to confess, and a wide space was cleared. Richental then brought a priest, Ulrich Schorand, a chaplain of Saint Stephan's Church, who had ridden to the place. Ulrich said to Hus : ' Dear Master, if you will repent of the heresy for which you are to suffer, then will I willingly shrive you ; but you, being a priest, know that one cannot shrive nor grant absolution to a heretic.' Hus had already confessed that morning before leaving his prison ; he now answered, ' It matters not, I am not in mortal sin.' He assured the bystanders that he was innocent of the sins laid to his charge, and tried to preach to them, but this Count Louis would not permit.²

The executioner then led Hus to the stake. Two faggots of wood were placed beneath his feet. He was standing facing east, and some of the spectators objected that a heretic should not face the rising sun ; so he was made to stand facing west. A chain was placed round his neck, and he was bound to the stake ; wood and straw were then piled round him until they reached his chin. Count Louis and Marshal Pappenheim then advanced and asked him if he would recant and save his life. Hus lifted his eyes to heaven and said, ' God is my witness that I have never taught or preached all the false things sworn against me, but have ever in all my words and acts and writings endeavoured to save men from their sins. I die joyfully to-day in the truth of that gospel which I have written and taught and preached.' Hearing him say this, Pappenheim and Louis left him to his fate. The fire was lighted. Hus sang in a loud voice, ' Christ, Son of the living God, have mercy on us ; Christ, Son of the living God, have mercy on me.' A third time he uplifted his voice, ' Thou who art born of the Virgin Mary,' but the wind blew the flames in his face ; his lips and his head were seen to move ; a great cry of bitter anguish burst from

---

[1] Eiselein : *Begruendeter Aufweis des Plazes bei der Stadt Constanz*, 1847, 10 *et seq.*   [2] Palacky (*Doc.*), 322 ; Richental, 81.

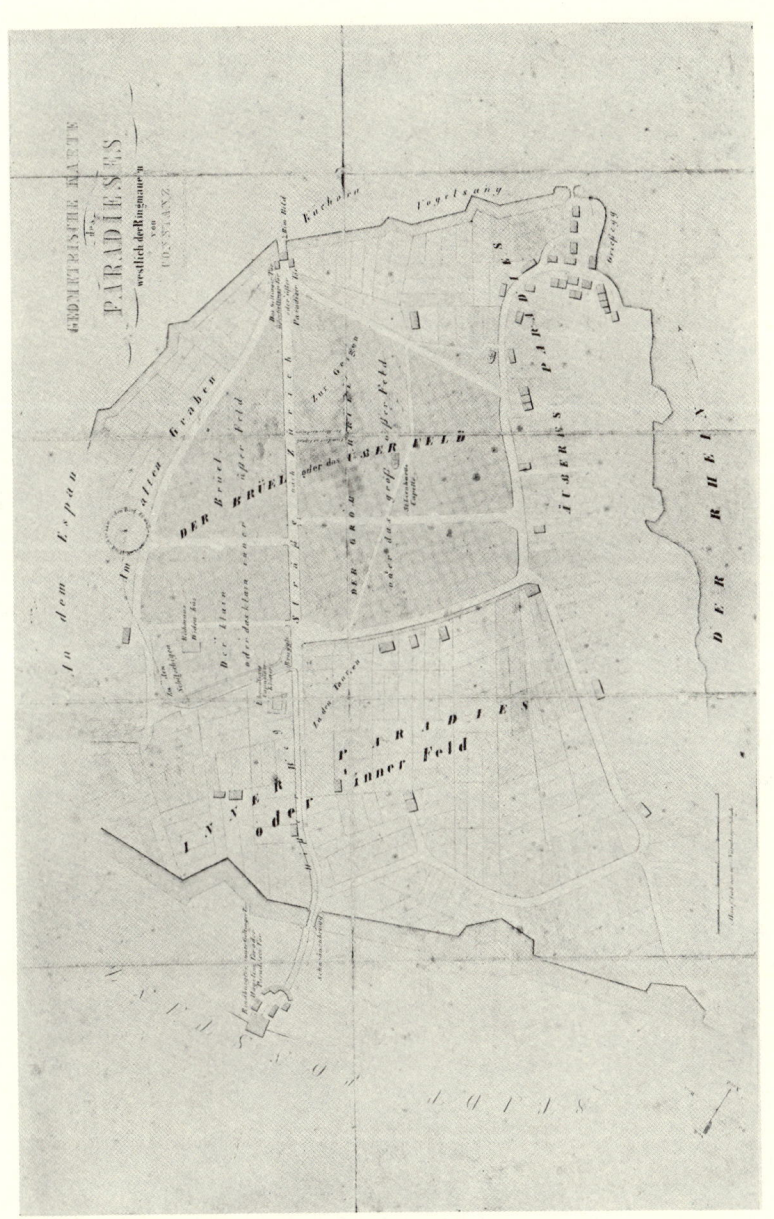

Geometrical Plan showing the exact spot, now marked by a monument, where John Hus and Jerome of Prague were burned. Reduced from the plan published by Eiselein in his *Begruendeter Aufweis des Plazes bei der Stadt Constanz*, 1847.

MARTYRDOM

him; and then all was still.[1] His spirit passed away; he died a death of fearful agony, a martyr for the faith that was in him. As Æneas Sylvius, at that time a boy of ten years, afterwards said, 'No one of the ancient Stoics ever met his death more bravely.'[2]

'As the flames flickered down, the beadles knocked over the stake with the charred body still dangling by the neck, heaped on more wood, poked up the bones with sticks, broke in the skull, ran a sharp stake through the heart, and set the whole ablaze again amidst a sickening smell from the carcase of the buried mule, as the ground cracked and lifted under the scorching heat. Duke Louis then told them to throw in the shoes and jacket which would otherwise have been the executioner's perquisite, lest the Bohemians should get possession of them and keep them as relics; and when the second fire had died out, the jumbled embers were thrown into a barrow together with some shovelfuls of earth and tipped into the Rhine.'[3] In later years men said that Hus blessed an old woman who had helped to pile the faggots, saying, 'O sancta simplicitas'; and others alleged that he prophesied, 'To-day you are burning the Goose,[4] but from my ashes will rise a white swan whom you will not burn.' But none of his contemporaries know of this reference to Martin Luther. John Hus was dead, burned as a heretic, but his work lived after him. His life was consistent, but his death was greater and more powerful than his life; he died because he would not utter what to him was a lie; his gospel, although he never thus expressly formulated it, was the proclamation to after ages of the liberty and the responsibility of the individual conscience:

> 'to thine own self be true,
> And it must follow, as the night the day,
> Thou canst not then be false to any man.'

---

[1] Palacky (*Doc.*), 323; Richental, 81.
[2] Æn. Sylv., 105.
[3] Wylie (*C.*), 170-1.
[4] *Vid. sup.*, p. 306.

CHAPTER XXIII

THE BEADLE OF THE EMPIRE

KING SIGISMUND had delivered John Hus to the Count Palatine to be treated as a heretic, and the patriot reformer had been done to death accordingly; he had also delivered to him his other prisoner, the ex-Pope Baldassare Cossa, who was imprisoned in the castle of Gottlieben on the 3rd June, all his old servants being taken from him two days later. The Count took his prisoner to Mannheim, halting for a short time at Heidelberg on the way, and confined him in the Eichelsheim Castle.[1] The old Pope remained here a year; and then an unsuccessful attempt to enable him to escape was made. It was frustrated, and the Count promptly drowned the governor of the castle in the Rhine. It was suspected that that strenuous churchman, John of Nassau, Archbishop of Mainz, was at the bottom of the scheme, and Louis thought it safer to remove his prisoner from his propinquity. He accordingly took Baldassare Cossa to the castle at Heidelberg, where he dragged out two more weary years. During all this time Cossa had only his cook and two chaplains—perhaps the Olivetan monks—with him; his guards and attendants were all Germans; he could not understand them, nor they him; their sole intercourse was by nods and signs.[2] Dietrich von Niem says that his prison was pleasant and spacious, but Cossa himself told a different tale. 'He gave me gall to eat, and in my thirst he gave me vinegar,' said the ex-Pope, 'no room had I for movement, but I lay in a narrow bed with cramped limbs; I wore soiled clothes; no good have I received from the Palatine, but I was a scorn and a mockery to men.' The Count himself considered that, although he had not treated Cossa as a cardinal, he had treated him very well as a mere prisoner. Cossa is said to have solaced

[1] Finke (*B.*), 52. [2] Mur. iii. 855.

his confinement by composing Latin verses on the vanity of all earthly things. More than three years thus passed in captivity, and during this time much happened, which we will only glance at briefly.

On the 15th June,[1] Carlo Malatesta, that noblest and most honourable of all the princes of the time, rode into Constance, furnished with full proctor's powers by Pope Gregory the Twelfth. This Pope had, on the 13th March, promulgated a Bull purporting to convoke the Council, and on the 4th July his Legate, the Cardinal of Ragusa, called a general session, the fourteenth, over which, at the Pope's special request, King Sigismund presided. At this session Carlo Malatesta, as the proctor of Gregory, resigned the papacy, the resignation being subsequently confirmed by his principal. Angelo Corrario was made Cardinal Bishop of Porto and Legate of Ancona, with first rank in the college after the future Pope, and with a full indemnity for everything he had done as Pope. Thus did he, the canonical pontiff, atone for the years of vacillation and duplicity which had brought the Council of Pisa and the subsequent misery and distraction to himself and the Church. He died in 1417, just before a new Pope was elected.[2]

Out of the three Popes, one having resigned and another having been deposed, there remained only the third to deal with. This was the Spaniard Benedict the Thirteenth, a pontiff who, in happier times, would have been a worthy successor to Innocent the Third, whom he resembled in character. In his moral life Benedict was chaste and pure, thereby being far superior to John the Twenty-third; he was also an enemy of simony and nepotism, and enjoyed an ascendency thereby over Gregory the Twelfth. But he was as firmly convinced that he was the Lord's anointed as could have been the most strait and particular saint among Scottish covenanters; he was fully persuaded that those of his own obedience constituted the Church universal to the exclusion of all others. It had been arranged that he was to meet the King of the Romans at Perpignan in June, and thither he repaired punctually, even as Pope John had appeared punctually at Constance; and on the night of the last day of June he summoned King Sigismund by

[1] Aschbach, ii. 425.   [2] Ciaconius, ii. 752.

public outcry, condemned him as contumacious for not appearing, and left the city.

At the sixteenth general session of the Council of Constance, held three days after the burning of John Hus, the fifteen deputies were chosen who were to accompany the King. The cardinals had desired that four of their number might be named, but it was felt that they would not be acceptable to Benedict, so that only bishops and doctors were chosen. The Count Palatine, to whose allegiance to the Council no objection could be taken now that Pope Gregory had resigned, was appointed its protector during Sigismund's absence. The seventeenth general session, held on the 15th July, blessed the King and placed him under the special protection of the Church during his mission. It was feared that his enemies might attempt to intercept him, and penalties, spiritual and secular, were fulminated accordingly; but no such attempt was made.

On the 18th July,[1] King Sigismund, having given his royal seal to the municipal council of Constance, having listened to a sermon by Jean Gerson, and having been duly blessed by the cardinals and the fathers of the Council, left the city. He was accompanied by all his Hungarian prelates and nobles and by an escort of four thousand horsemen; Queen Barbara quitted her dances in the city and went with her lord as far as Basel, returning home thence. The King continued down the Rhone valley, and entered Narbonne on the 15th August. Here he was detained for a month by negotiations with Benedict the Thirteenth, who at first refused to leave Valencia unless he were provided with a safe-conduct and were recognised as Pope by the King of the Romans. Sigismund could not give a safe-conduct in foreign territory, and refused to recognise Benedict except as cardinal; the obstinate octogenarian was obliged to give way, but he appeared at Perpignan accompanied by such a crowd of knights and horsemen that it seemed as though they had come for a fight rather than for a peaceful conference. Sigismund entered the city on the 18th September, and was received with all pomp and solemnity as King of the Romans.

After the Council of Pisa Pope Benedict the Thirteenth had

[1] Huebler, 5, note; Lenz, 71, note.

THE BEADLE OF THE EMPIRE 405

been hoping against hope. At times a ray of success seemed to brighten his prospect. Scotland and Aragon had remained faithful; Navarre had returned to his obedience; the greater part of Sicily had declared for him. For a long time, before and after the death of King Ladislas, he had hoped to secure the Kingdom of Naples, until this dream was finally dissipated by the marriage of Queen Joanna to the Count de la Marche, and her adhesion to the Council of Constance. The aged pontiff cherished illusory hopes of winning back the Kingdom of France. He was determined in no way to acknowledge the Council of Pisa nor to send any ambassadors to Constance. He maintained that, being the only cardinal promoted before the Great Schism, he was the only one whose title was clear, the only man who, even if he himself resigned, had a right to elect the new Pope.[1] It was manifest that negotiations with a Pope who made such pretensions would be difficult; but nothing daunted the King of the Romans.

While on his march southward Sigismund had despatched two envoys, Hartung van Clux and another, to endeavour to bring about a truce between England and France; but the English army was in such a desperately bad state from sickness and privation that the French deemed themselves certain of victory and refused to let the envoys proceed. They learned their mistake at the battle of Agincourt which followed soon after.

Sigismund reached Perpignan[2] where there was a goodly assembly. Regnault de Chartres, Archbishop of Reims, represented the King of France; Jacques Gelu, Archbishop of Tours, and other French delegates were present; the French contingent numbered seventy-five persons in all. There were numerous conferences, secret for the most part, on the expediency of transferring the Council; but the King of the Romans put his foot down on this proposition as soon as he heard of it, and it was abandoned. Sigismund and Ferdinand, backed by the Kings of Castile and Navarre, did their best, but were unable to persuade Pope Benedict to resign. He argued that, now that one of his rivals was deposed and the other had resigned, he was the only Pope, and that the right way to end

[1] Martene (*T.*), ii. 1648-50.   [2] Altmann, 63, note.

the Schism was to recognise him as such. The King of the Romans was disgusted at the failure of his efforts.

Moreover, he was in danger of his life, though this was a circumstance which would not weigh heavily on the mind of so brave a warrior as Sigismund. A fire mysteriously broke out close to his dwelling. Then there was a sharp fight between the Catalans and the Hungarians. The young Prince of Aragon galloped to Sigismund's aid; the King thanked him and assured him that he knew how to show himself in the hour of danger as a King and not as a dastard knave. Mysterious desertions also occurred. The young Count of Wurtemberg disappeared with his three hundred horsemen without taking leave. Some suspicious characters, designated from Constance as poisoners, were discovered with two counsellors of Duke Friedrich of Austria who had come to interview the King. At the beginning of November Sigismund left Perpignan in despair for Narbonne, intending to return to Constance. Envoys from Spain and Scotland determined him to halt while an ultimatum was presented to Pope Benedict.

Negotiations were accordingly recommenced with the octogenarian, but he proved intractable, deaf alike to reason and to threats. On the 13th November he departed secretly to Colliore, a small fort on the seacoast near Perpignan, intending to sail away to Sardinia, but his galleys were seized. A deputation waited on him here, but three days later the Pope fled to the rock-bound fortress of Peniscola,[1] a family possession, in which he, with his tiny court of cardinals, rested secure. Even the Pope's confessor, the celebrated Dominican Vincenzo Ferrier, deserted his cause for that of the Council. Finally the Kings of Aragon, Castile, and Navarre renounced their obedi-

---

[1] Upon the retirement of Pope Benedict to his rocky fortress, Oswald von Wolkenstein, who was with King Sigismund, burst into something that was intended for satirical poetry:—

> 'O Peterkin, you naughty cat,
> You wicked-tempered little brat,
> Your stubborn old bald head, I vow,
> Has got the better of you now.
> Kings, lords, and lands once held you true,
> But hear what now they think of you!
> They whistle to you with a whiff
> To dance upon the edge of a cliff.'—*B. W.*, 280.

ence; the Kings of Portugal and Scotland followed suit; and Pope Benedict was left, abandoned by all Christendom except Peniscola. To a Pope who loved holiness and hated simony, the prospect, though extremely limited, was not utterly dreary; here, on this miniature Gibraltar, a fortress inaccessible by water, but rising more than two hundred feet out of the sea, connected with the mainland by a narrow strip of sand, Pope Benedict the Thirteenth remained until his death on the 29th November 1422.[1] The Capitulation of Narbonne was drawn up on the 13th December 1415, and next day the Archbishop of Tours wrote to the Fathers of Narbonne that the union was now at last an accomplished fact.[2] The obedience of Aragon was withdrawn on the 6th January 1416, that of Castile on the 15th of the same month, that of Navarre six months later, and finally Pope Benedict was deserted by the Count of Foix. The spirit of the octogenarian was unbroken, and when the ambassadors from the Council called on him to resign, he reminded them how the remnant of the world had once been saved from the overwhelming flood, and pointing to his rocky crag of Peniscola, he exclaimed, 'Here is the Ark of Noah and the true Church.'[3] From the month of January 1416 the Council of Constance was acknowledged by all the Christian countries of Europe and the Great Schism was terminated.

The glad news was received with the greatest delight in Constance, where the assembled fathers were anxiously awaiting the King's return. The expenses of their long absence from home were weighing on those who had delegated them, and they were anxious to bring the Council to a conclusion by next Easter if possible. But King Sigismund had been invited by the Dauphin to visit Paris. Already, in December, the fathers at Constance had written to the King urging him to return speedily for the work of Church reform and the election of a new Pope. The Dauphin died, but Sigismund still held to his visit to the French capital, though John of Burgundy was said to be approaching it with forty thousand troops. Sigismund was to be received with all ceremony, and to have all his expenses paid; the prospect was too alluring; he wrote to the Council at Constance pointing out how peace between France and England

[1] Valois, iv. 452.   [2] Martene (*T.*), ii. 1655.   [3] *Ibid.* (*T.*), ii. 1672.

would tend to the unity and reformation of the Church; he promised to be back in Constance as soon as the embassies and envoys arrived there from the courts and churches of Spain.

King Sigismund spent a merry Christmas at Avignon. He made the grim walls of the papal fortress re-echo to the joyous sounds of balls and tourneys; all the expenses of his court were defrayed by the Avignonese, who made the King a present into the bargain of three thousand golden florins. The impecunious monarch sent his secretary to borrow more money from the Count of Savoy, and he himself reached Lyons on the 22nd January. Sigismund was revolving a new project. He had practically restored the suzerainty of the Empire in northern Italy; he had put an end to the Great Schism; and now he thought of his third darling project, a crusade against the Turks. It was true that there was still much to be done in the Council; there was a new Pope to be elected; and there was the reformation of the Church to be effected in its head and its members, a reformation which the King and many others thought would be more feasible while the Church itself was without a head. But, on the other hand, the battle of Agincourt had been fought on the 28th October; and Sigismund was fired with the idea of making peace between England and France, and leading the troops of both countries against the misbelievers to avenge the defeat of Nicopolis. ' If the French had only allowed our envoys to go to the King of England,' he said, ' this misfortune would never have happened to them; but now will we ourselves go, and with God's help see what can be done.'

From Lyons King Sigismund went to Chambery to invest Count Amadeus of Savoy; the ceremony was performed with great pomp in a wooden building which, being rickety, gave way and provided an unexpected dénouement to the scene. Sigismund reached Paris on the 1st March; the chief nobility, with Prince Louis, the Queen Isabella's brother, came out to meet him, and he rode into the city in full armour, but with his helm at his saddle-bow, decked with the insignia of the Dragon, and took up his quarters at the Louvre. But he had overestimated the authority in France of the Lord of the Holy Roman Empire; he might persuade the weak-minded King that the deposition of Pope John the Twenty-third had been necessary in the interest of the Church, but Bernard of Armagnac, who was still in deadly strife with Jean sans Peur, was hostile to King Sigismund and to his project of peace with England. The King himself unhappily accentuated the bad feeling. He visited the Parliament one day to see a case decided; took the royal seat, as a matter of course; and when one of the parties to the suit was like to have been prejudiced by his want of knightly rank, the impetuous King sprang up, drew his sword, and dubbed the litigant a knight on the spot. The party of Orleans at once resented this exercise of imperial rights. When he had been in Paris ten days, Sigismund gave a grand supper to one hundred and twenty ladies of Paris in the Bourbon Hotel,[1] but he served them with spiced dishes and abundance of wine in the German fashion, which was deemed a want of good breeding. His impecuniosity also made him the laughing stock of the wealthy court. He presented his guests with a little knife and a ring apiece, not worth more than a silver coin; he gave nothing to the offertory when he went to the Mass at Notre Dame, he gave nothing to the cathedral, he bestowed a crown on the choir children. His mission to Paris was a failure; at the end of six weeks he left for England and a French embassy accompanied him.[2]

Sigismund now knew that his hope of leading French and English troops in a crusade against the Turks was futile. Although the Armagnacs had sent the Archbishop of Reims and an embassy with him, there was but little hope of peace. The English had captured Harfleur, which was a solid advantage; they had won the battle of Agincourt, which both gave them moral ascendency by making the French reluctant to meet them in pitched fight, and also secured a large amount of ransom money; but Henry the Fifth insisted on the terms of the Treaty of Bretigny, and the French, who 'were not yet brought low enough to accept such spoliation,' insisted on the rendition of Harfleur. Bernard of Armagnac, 'a ruthless, unscrupulous border baron, with more of the buccaneer than the statesman in his character,' was now Constable of France, and took the earliest opportunity of leaving Paris. Jean sans Peur remained

[1] Tuetey, 69.   [2] Lavisse, IV. i. 372.

an enemy and a rebel to his country, and on the 24th June 1416 negotiated a private peace with the King of England. Count William of Holland, the father-in-law of the new Dauphin, joined King Sigismund in his efforts to secure peace, but the Armagnacs patriotically defended France; they blockaded Harfleur, and prepared to cut off its communication by sea with England.[1]

Sigismund left Paris on the 8th April, narrowly escaped a popular rising at Abbeville, and reached Calais on the 27th, where he was royally entertained by the Earl of Warwick, the 'Father of Courtesy.' He left on the last day of the month, and after a favourable passage of five hours reached Dover. As soon as his ship had cast anchor, the Duke of Gloucester, with drawn sword, rode into the water to inquire whether the royal guest intended to exercise any act of suzerainty or jurisdiction within the realm of England; and on receiving a reply in the negative the King of the Romans was allowed to land. He was received with every honour, for the greatest expectations had been aroused by this unprecedented visit. The Earl of Oxford met him at Rochester, the Duke of Clarence at Dartford. On the 7th May he entered London, the King meeting him between Deptford and Southwark. The royal apartments at Westminster were assigned for his use, and he was created a Knight of the Garter on Rogation Sunday, the 24th May. Henry the Fifth completely won the heart of Sigismund by his courtesy and liberality. Sigismund sent over a private embassy to Paris, and prayers were offered in London and elsewhere for the success of his efforts. He went down into Kent in the latter half of June; he and King Henry still hoped to effect some arrangement. Though Bernard of Armagnac was still opposed to any terms being made, the French Council arranged a meeting of envoys at Beauvais, at which a protocol was signed for a meeting on the 16th August between Boulogne and Calais to arrange for a truce.[2]

Meantime, however, the Genoese, the allies of the Armagnacs, had made an attempt to destroy the English fleet which was to relieve Harfleur. They failed, but they ravaged the Isle of Wight. Sigismund, disgusted with the French treachery after

[1] Omna, 258-61: Ramsay, i. 234. [2] Lenz, 104 *et seq*.

THE BEADLE OF THE EMPIRE 411

all he had done on their behalf and at their request,[1] definitely threw in his lot with the English. He made a league with Henry the Fifth at Canterbury on the 15th August, recognising him as King of France; and each King agreed to support the other in all claims against that country. The war between England and France was renewed; Harfleur was relieved; and the French fleet, with the Genoese carracks and the Spanish galleys, were defeated in the Seine on the 14th August.[2] Ten days later Sigismund crossed over to Calais for the conference, and a truce for four months was signed on the 3rd October. The King of the Romans had failed to bring about peace, and had now to make his way back to Constance.

This was somewhat difficult, for the King had quarrelled with Count William of Holland, and could not get from the Duke of Burgundy the safe-conduct which he desired. He sailed on some little English coasting vessels to Dordrecht and so to Nimwegen, and thence through the friendly territory of Juliers to Aachen,[3] where he remained for some weeks, leaving it on the 24th December. He spent Christmas at Liège, and on the first day of the new year (1417) he was at Luxembourg. He reached Constance again on the 27th January 1417, after an absence of a year and a half, and was there received with the utmost pomp and rejoicing. Much had happened during his absence, and the position of parties was now seriously changed.

The activity and usefulness of the Council of Constance were somewhat circumscribed during the absence of King Sigismund by his express orders that nothing was to be done in the matters of church reform and of the election of a new Pope until his return. He was in constant correspondence with the Council, and exercised a continual supervision over its action, although during his absence the person of most commanding influence was Jean Gerson, Chancellor of the University of Paris and delegate of the King of France. The Cardinals d'Ailly, Fillastre, and Zabarella had fallen comparatively into the background. The French nation proposed to abolish annates (first-fruits) and other papal exactions, but were not able to propose an equivalent for the revenue which would thus be lost; Jean Gerson

[1] Lenz, 109.   [2] Ramsay, i. 238.   [3] Aschbach, ii. 172.

discoursed eloquently against simony, and the Council suspended an abbreviator for that sin and for forgery ; the reform of the Benedictine Order was mooted, but nothing was done pending the King's return.

One matter of the highest importance with which the Council did concern itself, though without coming to any definite decision, during the King's absence was the doctrine of political assassination set forth by the Cordelier Jean Petit in his long justification of the Duke of Burgundy on the 8th March 1408. The assassination itself, as Jean Gerson said, was a *causa sanguinis*, but its justification, the doctrine of the legality of political assassination, was a matter for the spiritual court.[1] But the proceedings of the Council of Constance in this matter show how much less satisfactory than a Pope, in all matters not touching the temporal power of the papacy, is an œcumenical council as the supreme court of spiritual appeal, for the matter was one in which political interests were concerned, and in which members of the Council itself were parties in the political strife. Jean Petit had postulated eight truths, and had deduced therefrom nine conclusions.[2] After the death of the Duchess of Orleans the affair had slumbered until 1413, and meanwhile, in 1411, Jean Petit had died. Jean Gerson, who had once been a protégé of the Duke of Burgundy, fiercely condemned the doctrine of Jean Petit, and he appeared at the head of a deputation of the University of Paris, with which the young Dukes of Orleans were associated, which persuaded the King to allow the question to be re-opened. The case was heard before the Bishop of Paris, assisted by the Inquisitor of Heresy and the most prominent masters of the theological faculty, and they condemned the propositions of Jean Petit. The King published their sentence on the 16th March 1414. The Duke thereupon appealed to Pope John the Twenty-third, who appointed a commission of three cardinals, Orsini, Zabarella, and Pancera, who began their inquiry at Rome and concluded it at Constance, where, on the 15th January 1416, they upset the finding of the Bishop of Paris on the grounds of irregularity of procedure and want of jurisdiction. Meanwhile, the Council had met and the political difficulties had increased. As soon as

[1] Hefele, vii. 269.   [2] Barante, iii. 107-43.

Pope John the Twenty-third fled from Constance, the Duke of Burgundy, who had hitherto relied on his assistance, altered his tactics ; he assured the Council that he had not known of the Pope's design and was ready to arrest him if he appeared in Burgundy, that he had assisted Jean Petit with the facts of the case, but did not pretend, as a mere layman, to deal with the theory, that he was ready in all matters of belief to submit to the decision of the Council. The Duke of Burgundy was at this time suspected of a design to prosecute still further the doctrine of political assassination by entrapping Sigismund on his journey to the south of France, but this was discovered to be a fabrication of the King's prisoner, Friedrich, Duke of Austria. All this served, however, to embitter the party feeling with which the case was conducted. As the thirteenth general session of the Council had appointed a commission to deal with this and other cases,[1] Cardinal d'Ailly was, notwithstanding the protest of the Bishop of Arras, who represented the Duke, added to the other three cardinals, together with a certain number of doctors and prelates of each of the four nations. Jean Gerson would not rest content with the vague decree passed by the Council on the 6th July 1415, and determined to bring the matter again before the Council.

The contest between the Gallican and Burgundian factions of the French nation waxed hot, and the other nations were gradually drawn into the fray. The Chancellor of the University fought rather for his own hand than for the King of France, who, before the battle of Agincourt, was reconciled for a time to the Duke of Burgundy ; nor did Gerson at this time represent the University of Paris, which explained that the nine propositions condemned did not coincide with those set forth by the Norman doctor. Gerson was backed up by Pierre d'Ailly, who was, however, more inclined to compromise ; he would have condemned the obnoxious doctrine without mentioning the Duke. An anonymous pamphlet was issued stigmatising him and Gerson as firebrands and calumniators, and denouncing King Sigismund as a mere puppet in the hands of Prince Louis of Bavaria. Both the Chancellor and the Cardinal were formally accused by the Bishop of Arras of heresy ; and when

[1] Hardt, iv. 335.

Gerson cleared himself, he was again attacked by the Franciscan Giovanni de Rocha; he defended his orthodoxy, but lost his temper; he declared that John Hus would never have been sentenced had he enjoyed professional advice, and that he himself would rather plead before a jury of Jews and infidels than before the commission. The Franciscan friars worked hard for the Duke; and the Burgundians left no stone unturned, but were profuse with presents of wine and money, until they won the majority of the commission; on the 15th January 1416, more than sixty out of the eighty members found that the sentence of the Bishop of Paris was irregular and that the propositions of Jean Petit were not objectionable. The King of France was very angry at this decision, and declared that he had the assent of the King of the Romans in condemning the perilous doctrine; and Jean Gerson at once appealed against the ' hole-and-corner ' finding. The strife between the Gallicans and the Burgundians then broke out afresh before the Council; there were heated meetings, some of which broke up in tumult; Gerson pronounced an eloquent discourse on the 5th May, finishing with a passionate personal appeal to his two former friends, the Bishop of Arras and Pierre of Reims; the Bishop tried to reply on the 9th and 11th, but could not make himself heard for the noise. Eventually the Council agreed to postpone decision until after the King's return.

After the peace of Canterbury King Sigismund became reconciled with John of Burgundy and was an open enemy of the King of France; and this change of attitude was speedily reflected in the Council. Jean Gerson and Pierre d'Ailly took up arms against the English nation. It was absurd, said the Cardinal of Cambrai, that England, which only constituted the thirty-sixth part of Christendom, should count as a quarter or a fifth in the Council. The Spaniards, when they arrived, demanded precedence; and this dispute was only settled by the Germans ceding to them the third place among the nations. The dispute waxed hot and wearisome. The Patriarch of Antioch, Jean Mauroux, abandoned his countrymen and stood by the King of the Romans. It was said that Mars governed the Council; and Mars meant Sigismund's four most intimate counsellors, the Archbishop of *M*ilan, the Patriarch of *A*ntioch,

THE BEADLE OF THE EMPIRE 415

the Archbishop of *R*iga, and the Bishop of *S*alisbury.¹ So violent and intemperate became the discussions that at one time a cardinal assaulted an archbishop, a patriarch hit a protonotary, a Spanish prelate hurled an Englishman into the mud, and the English were caught in arms meditating a coup on the Cardinal of Cambrai. *Tantæne animis celestibus iræ!* The story of these debates is long and dreary, but the outcome of the whole was that the English nation maintained its right to separate existence, and with the Teuton and the Burgundian faction of the French nation backed up King Sigismund on his return to Constance.

Although the fathers at Constance had experienced some difficulty in deciding as to the guilt of John Duke of Burgundy, they found none in dealing with the heresy of Jerome of Prague. Jerome was a scholar of parts, educated and brilliant, a veritable knight-errant, but bitten with a taste for the realist philosophy, a man of wit and eloquence, as ready to maintain a thesis in any university as to break a lance in any court of Europe. He had travelled widely, had experienced many adventures, lacked not discretion, but had a gift of opportune disappearance. Four months of the horrors of a mediæval prison, the want of the customary necessities of life, illness, the advice of his judges and of well-meaning and pious friends, broke his spirit for the time; and when Jerome appeared at the nineteenth general session of the Council, on the 23rd September, he made a full recantation of his heresy. 'The Lord hath no pleasure in the death of the wicked,' said Bishop Hallam, ' but that he turn from his way and live'; and the Cardinals Orsini, Pancera, d'Ailly, and Zabarella were likewise of opinion that Jerome's recantation should be accepted, and that he should be released; but sterner counsels prevailed, and Jerome was haled back to prison again, though he was treated with more consideration than before. Michael *de Causis* and Stephen Palec then began to find fault with the terms of the recantation; they and Jean Gerson and the Patriarch of Antioch procured fresh judges to be appointed, and the process was re-opened. When a new indictment of forty-five, backed by another of a hundred and two, articles was prepared against him, and Jerome was

¹ Finke (*F.*), 204.

again produced before the Council, he had been in a damp, dark dungeon for three hundred and forty days ;[1] recantation had availed him nothing ; he saw that justice was to be meted out to him by a different measure than had been used for Hus, that he was an inferior and necessary victim, that the Council had determined on his death. He resolved to meet it like a man; and it required a truly noble and heroic soul to face that fearful agony. He was produced again before the Council on the 23rd May, when he had been exactly one year in prison, and the session continued until the 30th. Jerome retracted his recantation as being the greatest sin of his life. He was required to answer the charges against him, and demanded to state his own case in the first place ; when this was refused, he entered on his defence and proclaimed to the Council and the world his opinion of the judgment with which they judged him. He was sentenced and burned on the 30th May 1416. The Florentine papal secretary, Poggio Bracciolini, who was an eye-witness of the trial and the execution, has left in a letter to his friend Leonardo of Arezzo, an account which may be roughly thus summarised :—

'A few days after I returned to Constance,' says Poggio, ' the case of Jerome, said to be a heretic, was publicly tried, and I mention it to you both because of its importance and because of the man's extraordinary eloquence and learning. I confess that I have never seen any one who, especially in a capital case, more nearly approached the eloquence of those ancients whom we so much admire. The language, the eloquence, the arguments, the expression, the tone, the readiness with which he answered his opponents and set forth his own case were wonderful ; it is sorrowful that such noble and excellent talent should have been applied to the study of heresy. I do not pretend to judge in the matter ; I merely acquiesce in the opinions of those who are wiser than I am. I will not describe the case in detail, but will merely refer to the more striking episodes, so that you may judge of the man's learning. Much was alleged against him and was confirmed by witnesses to prove that he was a heretic, and he was required to answer the charges in detail. He objected that he ought first to state his own

[1] Helfert, 211.

case, and afterwards to enter on his defence ; but when this was not allowed, he stood in the midst of the assembly and spake thus :—What an injustice is this, he said, that after being kept in the strictest confinement for three hundred and forty days, in dirt, squalor, and filth, in fetters, with the lack of everything, while you were listening to my calumniators, you will not hear me for a single hour ; they after so long a time have persuaded you that I am a heretic, an enemy of the faith, a persecutor of churchmen, and I have no chance of defending myself ; you have made up your minds to sentence me before you have any chance of knowing aught about me. Remember that you are men and not gods, that you are mortals and will not live for ever, that you are liable to mistake and error, to be deceived and led astray. The lights of the world, the most learned men of the earth, are said to be here; but it is, above all, fitting that you take care to do nothing rashly, carelessly, or unjustly. I am the poor creature whose life is at stake, and it were indeed unworthy and of evil example that the wisdom of so many should decree aught unjustly against me. This and much else he said amid the dissent and murmurs of many who interrupted his discourse. It was ordered that he should first make answer to the charges brought against him and should be allowed to speak afterward. The different heads of the indictment were then read out, and he was required to answer ; and it is incredible how cleverly he replied and with what arguments he defended himself, and yet he said nothing that was unworthy of a good man. If he believed all that he said, then there could no cause of death or of offence be found in him ; for he alleged that it was all false, and that the crime laid to his charge had been invented by his enemies. When he was charged with being a calumniator of the Apostolic See, an opponent of the Roman pontiff, an enemy of the cardinals, a persecutor of prelates and of the clergy, and hostile to the Christian religion, then with a piteous voice, and spreading out his hands, he rose and exclaimed, Where shall I turn me now, conscript Fathers ? whose help shall I implore ? how shall I offer prayer or entreaty ? How can I turn to you when my persecutors have alienated your minds from me by representing me as the enemy of all those who sit in judgment on me. If you believe them, then indeed there is no hope for me. He used reproof, censure, and even jest. Being asked what he held as to the Sacrament, he answered that before consecration there was bread, but at and after consecration there remained only the true body of Christ, and no one but a baker would think there was bread. The proceedings had to be carried on to the third day. Jerome, amid much confusion and opposition, got the liberty of speaking.'

Poggio narrates how Jerome instanced from sacred and profane literature the cases of righteous men who had been unjustly condemned, even by councils of priests, because of the false testimony against them. He explained the reasons of the enmity against him so eloquently that he moved the minds of all toward pity. He told them how he had come willingly to exculpate himself; he set forth his life and his course of learning, his zeal and earnestness for truth; in matters of faith, he said, the ancient and most learned have not hesitated to explain their differences of opinion, not in order to prejudice the faith but to ascertain the truth. Saint Augustine and Saint Jerome had differed thus without any suspicion of heresy. Every one now thought that Jerome was about to recant his errors or to ask pardon for them. But he did nothing of the kind; he began to praise John Hus, who had lately been burned, calling him good, just, and holy, and unworthy of such a death; he said that he himself was ready to suffer and to yield himself to his enemies who had so impudently lied against him, who would have to render an account of their words to God whom they could not deceive. Great was the sorrow of those who stood round, who had hoped that so excellent a man might repent and be saved. But Jerome appeared to welcome death, and continued in his praise of John Hus. There were frequent interruptions during his speech, but he turned on his adversaries, causing them to blush and be silent. At times, when the murmuring increased, he would be silent, or he would reprove the audience; again and again he begged them to listen, but his face never grew pale; he remained firm and intrepid. Very eloquent was he when he reminded them how he had lain three hundred and forty days in a dark and fœtid dungeon, at which, as a brave man should, he did not complain,

THE BEADLE OF THE EMPIRE 419

but wondered at the inhumanity of others toward him. ' Yet, notwithstanding all these disadvantages,' continues Poggio, ' Jerome adduced as many of the wisest and most learned men as witnesses to his opinions, he brought forward as many divines to back him up, as if he had spent all that time in study in the greatest ease and quietude. His voice was soft, clear, and resonant; he had the dignity of an orator in expressing indignation or in moving pity; he stood fearless and intrepid, not afraid of death, but even welcoming it like another Cato; a man worthy of being for ever remembered. I do not praise him if he held anything contrary to the Church; but I admire his learning and his knowledge, his eloquence and his skill in argument; though I fear that all was given him to his own hurt. Finally he was allowed two days for repentance; and many of the wisest men went to see him to try to move him from his fixed intent. Among them was the Cardinal of Florence, who essayed to turn him to the right path. But since he persisted in his errors, he was condemned by the Council for his heresy, and was burned. With a smiling, joyous, and cheerful countenance he went to his fate; he feared not the fire nor the torment nor death. No one of the Stoics ever suffered death with so steadfast and brave a resolution as he exhibited. When he came to the place he himself took off his coat, and knelt down before the stake to which he was bound. Large logs, and straw, were piled round him breast-high; and when they were lighted he began to sing hymns, until the fire and smoke stopped him. This showed his bravery that when the lictor wanted to throw on wood from behind so that he might not see it, he called to him, Come here and light the fire in front; if I had been afraid of this, I should never have come to this place when I might have run away. So was this marvellous man burned; I saw his end and witnessed his actions.'

The foregoing is an abstract of the account written by a cultured Florentine on the day of the execution of the second martyr at Constance; the crowd laughed and cheered; the lower orders of the clergy applauded; but the higher ranks of the prelates, the cultured men of the Council, shuddered and were grieved. Of the effect which these two executions exercised on the kingdom of Bohemia there is no need to speak here.

Of the many other events which happened at Constance during the absence of the ' Beadle of the Empire,' as Sigismund was wittily named by Baldassare Cossa, the only one which need be mentioned here concerns the King's unfortunate prisoner, Friedrich of the Tirol. In the day of his humiliation he had undertaken to do more than he could effect without leaving Constance. His brother Ernest had taken possession and had won over the nobility, whose apathy toward Friedrich had aroused popular discontent. Georg Lichtenstein, Bishop of Trient, applied to the Council for reinstatement, and that body, on the 21st November 1415, decreed that Friedrich was to reinstate and to recompense the Bishop within thirty days. According to the constitution of the Tirol the Council was incompetent to interfere in its affairs ;[1] and in any case Friedrich, so long as he was a prisoner in Constance, was unable to execute their decree. Moreover, he suspected that the iron hand of his brother would be readier to grasp than to unloose his possessions. Friedrich felt himself powerless, bankrupt in pocket and in repute ; he determined to break parole and to escape. He fled from Constance on the 6th March 1416 ; he found that he had lost none of his old popularity with the peasants and the town-folk ; and on the 6th May he appeared at Brixen with an army. He secured the neutrality of the nobility in the contest between him and his brother by confirming their ancient privileges. Ernest had to retire to Styria, but Friedrich was placed under the great ban by the Council on the 28th February 1417.

[1] *B.W.*, 287-8.

CHAPTER XXIV

THE LAST DAYS OF BALDASSARE COSSA

BALDASSARE COSSA was under watch and ward of German gaolers in Heidelberg Castle when King Sigismund returned to Constance. Up to the time when the King left the Council, on the 21st July 1415, he had been the guiding spirit, and all had gone according to his wishes; but when he returned on the 27th January 1417 he found the situation sadly changed. King Ferdinand of Aragon had died on the 2nd April 1416 soon after his and Sigismund's envoys had brought to the Council the news of the Articles of Narbonne. Ferdinand's son Alfonso the Fifth followed in his father's footsteps, and his embassy was formally received by the Council at its twenty-second general session on the 15th October 1416; the ambassadors from the Kings of Navarre and Portugal had already arrived. Trouble then began. The Portuguese did not want to be incorporated in a Spanish nation; the English disputed priority of rank with the Aragonese and with the French; the Count of Palatine and the Burggraf Friedrich had much trouble in preventing bloodshed. An attempt was made to amalgamate the small English nation with that of the Teutons; but their right to form a separate nation was acknowledged by the Council in its thirty-first session, held on the 31st March. This was of great moment to the King, as his alliance with England had alienated the French nation, and he had now only the Teutons and the English, and to some extent the Burgundian faction of the French nation on whom he could rely. His influence as leader of the Council had vanished owing to his long absence. The Castilian embassy appeared on the 29th March 1417, and at once raised pretensions as to the coming election of a Pope and as to the constitution of the College of Cardinals which suggested that they were still at heart in favour of the Spanish Pope

Benedict; not until the thirty-fifth session on the 18th June were they formally united with the other members of the Spanish nation, and even after that date their pride troubled the harmony of the Council.

The process against Pope Benedict was commenced in the twenty-third general session on the 5th November, and on the 28th of that month he was publicly summoned to appear and answer within two months and ten days. Two Benedictine monks waited on the Pope at Peniscola; he received them, supported by his three cardinals and his clergy, justified himself, and once again excommunicated the Council of Constance; it was clear that he would neither appear nor send representatives. At the twenty-ninth session on the 8th March he was declared contumacious. A commission was appointed to hear evidence; its report was duly made, and Benedict was again cited to appear. As soon as the Castilians had given in their tardy adherence, the Council proceeded in its thirty-seventh general session, on the 28th July 1417, to pronounce the decree of deposition. This was announced in Constance the same day, and information was immediately sent throughout the Empire and the Kingdom of Hungary. The Great Schism was now ended; it had endured for thirty-nine years. Its termination was the great achievement of Sigismund, King of the Romans.

The Council of Constance had now put an end to the Great Schism and had burned two heretics; it might therefore be held to have accomplished two of the three great objects for which it had been convoked; but the third, the reformation of the Church in its head and its members, was as yet untouched. Every one was agreed that the reformation was necessary, and that the Council ought to undertake it; the only question was whether it should be undertaken before or after a new Pope had been elected. The King and the German nation were of opinion that its reformation could only be properly carried out while the Church was still without a head; Hallam of Salisbury was of the same opinion, and he carried the English nation with him; but the other nations were unanimous that the reformation could only be rightly effected under the auspices of a supreme pontiff. They feared the arrogance of King Sigismund, who had told the Bishop of Cuença that, the Church being

LAST DAYS OF BALDASSARE COSSA 423

without a head, there were no longer any cardinals, and that therefore he alone had the right to elect a Pope. He was said to be determined that the new Pontiff should be either a Teuton or an Englishman. Others were afraid lest the monarchical regime of the Church should be transformed by the Council into a democracy, the Pope being subordinate and the sacred college a mere nullity. Out of the twenty-four cardinals only two, backed by a few solitary ecclesiastics in the French, Italian, and Spanish nations were on the side of Sigismund; the great majority of the Council, headed by Pierre d'Ailly, were against him.

The year 1417 was spent in angry discussions and recriminations. The King, and the English and German nations, because of their anxiety to do without a Pope while carrying the good work through, were dubbed Wyclifites and Hussites; and on one occasion, when Sigismund and his party left a session in anger, the cry arose, ' Let the heretics go.' Jean Gerson and Cardinal d'Ailly were strenuous in their exertions to get a Pope elected before the work of reformation was touched. Cardinal Zabarella, formerly a warm partisan of the King, headed the cardinals in their opposition, and so excited himself in the strife that he fell ill and died on the 26th September; men said that he would have been the next Pope. A still more grievous loss was Robert Hallam of Salisbury, who died on the 4th September; his death was followed by the defection of the English nation. The Castilian embassy left the city and had to be brought back by force. The King threatened to imprison the cardinals, and they applied for their safe-conduct in order to leave Constance and to elect a Pope in peace. Sigismund had lost all control of the Council. His two faithful cardinals proved faithless; the Archbishop of Riga and the Bishop of Chur, whom he had hitherto fully trusted, were won over by the cardinals. Still the King of the Romans would not give way.

At this crisis, Henry Beaufort, Bishop of Winchester who had been on a pilgrimage to the Holy Land, came to Ulm; and it was resolved to refer the matter to him for decision. His probity and wisdom were trusted by both sides. He accepted the commission, and entered Constance in the garb of a pilgrim carrying his cross. Sigismund had already reluctantly agreed to the precedence of the papal election ; the points still in dispute referred to the particular articles of reformation which were to be undertaken, and the guarantee to be given by the cardinals that the work should be taken up before the Council was dismissed. The Bishop negotiated a compromise ' A guarantee of reform was to be embodied in a decree of the Council; those points in the report of the commission of reform on which all the nations were agreed were to be laid formally before the Council for its collective approval ; and commissioners were to be appointed to determine the method of election.'[1] The compromise was adopted by the Council on the 30th October 1417.

A list of eighteen articles was accordingly drawn up, which included most, though by no means all, the points urgently demanding reform. It was decreed that on this occasion the election should be made by the cardinals, now twenty-three in number, assisted by thirty prelates, six being appointed by each of the five nations. This plan was the outcome of endless deliberation and compromise. Bishops Richard of London, John of Norwich, Nicholas of Bath, and John of Lichfield, the Abbot of Bury, and the Dean of York were the English electors ; Jean Gerson was not included among the French.[2] The new Kaufhaus was fitted up for the Conclave, and the electors entered it on the 8th November.

The 9th was spent in arranging the method of voting. It was expected that the election would be long and hotly contested, as each nation was determined that, if possible, the new Pope should be chosen from its midst. National animosities ran so high that practically there was no chance of an English, French, or German being selected. The first scrutiny of votes, taken on the 10th November, showed that four cardinals were well ahead of the other candidates. The Bishop of Geneva, the Archbishop of Tours, and the Polish Archbishop of Gnesen were also among the favourites ; indeed at one time it looked as if Jean de Bertrands, the Bishop of Geneva, would be elected —he had seventeen or eighteen votes—but the cardinals insisted that the new Pope should be chosen from their body.

[1] Radford, 76-7. [2] Hardt, iv. 1473.

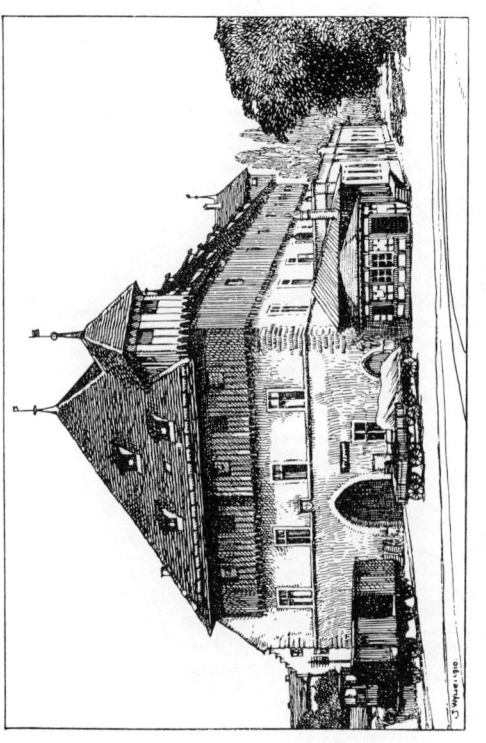

The Kaufhaus, or Merchants' Hall, of Constance, still standing, built in 1388 by Master Arnold, and used on the eighth to the eleventh November 1417 for the election of Pope Martin the Fifth toward the conclusion of the Council.

Beaufort, whom the French cardinals regarded with suspicion,[1] worked hard and successfully to spoil the chance of Pierre d'Ailly,[2] whom the English generally denounced as 'the father of all evils.' There being no chance of an Englishman being elected, the English electors gave their votes for Oddo Colonna, and the Archbishop of Gnesen resigned his pretensions in favour of the same cardinal. The German electors then abandoned their opposition and made common cause with the English and Italians. The French and Spanish electors still stood out, until they realised that it was hopeless to expect the necessary majority of two-thirds in favour of either a Frenchman or a Spaniard. Thus it happened that on the forenoon of the 11th November, as the King of the Romans was in procession with the nobles and prelates before the Kaufhaus, praying to the Holy Ghost to speed a fortunate election, the announcement was made that the choice of the electors had fallen on the Cardinal Deacon Oddo Colonna. The roof of the Kaufhaus was usually covered with ravens, rooks, crows, and the like birds of sombre hue, but when the electors entered all these black-plumaged visitants flew away; and when they came out, announcing the new Pope, there came a flight of fully two thousand little birds, not a black one among them, and covered the roof of the Kaufhaus in happy omen to Oddo Colonna.[3]

The newly elected Pope was the son of Agapito Colonna, who had himself been a cardinal of Pope Urban the Sixth. Oddo Colonna was promoted to the College by Innocent the Seventh; he had abandoned Gregory the Twelfth in 1408; and had taken part in the elections of Alexander the Fifth and Pope John. He was fifty or sixty years of age, a good, simple man, moderately well read, an enemy to intrigue, and loyal to his friends; he had been among the first to follow Pope John in his flight to Schaff-hausen and was the last cardinal to return to Constance. Notwithstanding this, he had uniformly been on good terms with King Sigismund, with his fellows in the college of cardinals, and with the Council. In pocket he was as poor as Alexander the Fifth;

'Papa Martino
Non vale un quattrino,'

---

[1] Finke (*F.*), 227, 231.   [2] Gascoigne, 155.   [3] Richental, 123.

sang the street urchins of Florence. But he was not a particular friend to reform, and he began by introducing for his chancery the very same regulations as his predecessor had adopted. He was crowned on the tenth day after his election.

On the day after the new Pope was crowned, 22nd November, the five nations approached him on the question of Church reform, and he appointed six cardinals to discuss the matter with their representatives. The subject was thorny; opinions as to the malignancy of the evils and as to the nature of the remedies differed in the different nations; the discussions were stormy and without result; two months passed away without anything definite being done. Indignation became universal; two of Pope Benedict's cardinals threatened to rejoin their old master unless something was done to stop simony; the German nation appealed to the Pope; the French complained to King Sigismund. The King of the Romans washed his hands of the whole affair. 'When we insisted on taking the reform of the Church before the election of a Pope,' he answered, ' you were of a different opinion and would have a Pope first. Now you have got him, go to him and ask for reform. We can now no longer act as we could when the papal see was vacant.' The Pope told the German nation that he was willing to fix the number of cardinals at twenty-four, but in other matters they received no satisfactory reply. The opinion of Pope Martin the Fifth was that the Council had lasted too long already, and that the work of reform should be deferred, because of the time and deliberation necessary, until some more seasonable opportunity; because, as Jerome says, ' every country has its peculiar manners and customs, which cannot be easily removed without great disturbance.'[1] There was much virtue in the remark of the Saint and in the action of Pope Martin. On the 21st March 1418 he published concordats with the four nations —none was made for Italy—granting a certain measure of reform to each; but no general scheme, applicable to the Church Universal, was formulated. This modicum was the whole measure of reform obtained by the Council of Constance. For its failure in this respect, as for its success in others, King Sigismund is in the main responsible. Had he returned to

[1] Platina, 349.

LAST DAYS OF BALDASSARE COSSA 427

Constance from Chambery, he would have retained his hold and guidance of the Council; the French nation would not have been alienated from him; he would have had the majority at his back and would have approached the subject of reform with more hope of success. As it was, the Council had defeated Pope John the Twenty-third, but Pope Martin the Fifth defeated the Council.[1] The reform of the Church in its head and its members, which Christendom had so anxiously expected from the Council, as a whole had failed.[2]

The Council of Constance was now near its end, but there was still a matter of importance to be determined before it was dissolved; this was the reconciliation between Sigismund and Friedrich of the Tirol. If the King could have worked his own will, he would have prosecuted his claims against the Duke to the uttermost; he desired to sell or mortgage his lands as escheats to the Empire and to run him out of his duchy. Friedrich had now recovered possession of the Tirol; the great landowners preferred to be under a duke of their own to being immediately dependent on the impecunious King of the Romans. Moreover, Friedrich wanted to recover the Aargau canton, and had borrowed money from the Venetians to repay the mortgage-debt. The Council, when it placed the Duke under the ban, had commissioned Sigismund to carry out the order; but the King found opposition among the magnates of the Empire. They did not desire to see imperial claims too inconsiderately pressed against one of their own number; and neither they nor the Swiss were ready to aid the King in a war against the Tirol. Count Louis of the Palatine, not so friendly as formerly with Sigismund, did not forget that Duke Friedrich was his brother-in-law; he and Louis of Bavaria and the Archbishop of Salzburg had effected a reconciliation between Friedrich and his brother of Styria, and Ernest had appeared near Constance with an army and had complained to the King of the manner in which the house of Habsburg was humiliated. Sigismund feared that the ducal brothers might ally themselves against him with Venice and Milan; he saw that he must give way; and he entered into negotiations. Basel was willing to give up its claim to the country between it and Schaffhausen, but the Swiss con-

[1] Radford, 64. [2] Aschbach, ii. 339.

federates held the King to his word and refused to give up the Aargau. On these terms the parties were reconciled. The King and the Duke met in the garden of the Augustinian cloister at Constance, and on the 8th May Pope Martin, who had throughout befriended the Duke, removed the sentence of excommunication.

The forty-fifth and last general session of the Council of Constance was held on the 22nd April 1418; the Cardinal Antoine de Chalant read a Bull wherein the Pope dismissed the assembled Fathers with full absolution for their sins. Pope Martin left Constance in great pomp on Whit Monday, the 16th May; and King Sigismund, after arranging for the payment of his own and his followers' debts, left without state or circumstance on the 21st May 1418. 'So,' says Aschbach, ' did the Council of Constance, the greatest and most splendid assembly which Western Christendom had ever seen, after lasting three years and six months, come to an end without any tumult, although there were men of different nations there who were for part of the time at war with each other, without any rise in the prices of provisions, and without any extraordinary sickness. Friend and foe alike agreed that this was the work of the King of the Romans, who spared no endeavour, no danger and no cost to attain this end.' For good or for evil the Council had met and departed; it had done its best to terminate the Great Schism and to suppress heresy; it had secured a modicum of reform from the Pope. It was then as it was in the days of the French Revolution. Men thought that the spiritual world could be reformed by framing a new constitution. Something may be done in that way, but not enough. The Fathers at Constance deemed that Christendom could be reformed by decrees correcting abuses and thus making a new constitution for the Church, ' a Gospel of Brotherhood, not according to any of the Four old Evangelists, and calling on men to repent and amend each his own wicked existence that they might be saved; but a Gospel rather... calling on men to amend each the whole world's wicked existence, and be saved by making the Constitution. A thing different and distant *toto cœlo*, as they say: the breadth of the sky, and farther if possible.'

Pope Martin the Fifth had been elected on the 11th November

LAST DAYS OF BALDASSARE COSSA 429

1417, and King Sigismund lost no time in asking him to take charge from him and from the Count Palatine of his predecessor, Baldassare Cossa. On the 7th January 1418 the King ordered the Count to make over his prisoner. Two days later the Pope sent word to his acquaintance, Conrad of Soest, the Heidelberg professor who had appeared as an envoy of King Rupert at the Council of Pisa, and to Paolo Capranica, one of the papal secretaries, to take charge of Baldassare Cossa, and to consign him afresh to the Count Palatine as a prisoner of the Church and of the Pope. Martin the Fifth was determined to be safely back in Italy before he released his predecessor from confinement.

Efforts for the release of Baldassare Cossa were, however, not wanting. In October 1418 a Florentine appeared before the Council at Venice with a letter from Bartolommeo de Montegontio, a trusted secretary of the former Pope, stating that the liberation of Baldassare Cossa had been projected between the Count Palatine and the Count of Savoy, but that in the first place a sum of two hundred thousand ducats was wanted. Count Louis was willing to release his prisoner if he could get his price. Baldassare Cossa himself was ready to pay fifty thousand; the Duke of Genoa and others hoped to raise further sums; it was hoped that the Republic of Venice would send a goodly sum to the Count of Savoy. The Council, however, declined on the ground that they knew not whether the former Pope was alive or dead.

At the same time, while Pope Martin was tarrying in Mantua, Cosimo de' Medici took the matter up, and sent an embassy to Milan. This was more successful. By an arrangement with Baldassare Cossa and Pope Martin, Galeotto Ricasoli, a member of the same family as that Bindachius to whom Pope John the Twenty-third had been so generous at Freiburg, approached the Count Palatine and arranged with him the release of his prisoner for the sum of thirty-five thousand golden guldens. Baldassare Cossa was ready to pay the amount to the Bardi bankers, and this was done at the Castello Adelberghe. But the Count was not going to release his prisoner until he had the money in his own hands, and this took time. The exchange was at length effected through a Venetian house which had dealings with Germany. The money was at length ready for receipt by the firm of Wilhelm Rummel of Nuernberg; and on the 16th April 1419 Wilhelm junior, the head of the firm, appeared at Heidelberg with the representatives of the Bardi house, and the money was paid over there. The ex-Pope was then made over at Basel to the care of the Bishop of Lebus, Conrad of Soest, and a member of the papal Curia. He was no longer a prisoner in the Castle of Heidelberg, but he knew not what his fate would be.

Baldassare Cossa was warned by the Medici and others to escape from his papal guards, and, above all, not to go to Mantua, if he wished to avoid further imprisonment. He provided a plentiful supper for his guards, plied them well with the rich wine of Tuscany, and while they slept the sleep of the drunken, he rode off to the castle of Sarzana, which belonged to the Medici. Thence he sent a messenger to the Republic of Venice, who advised him to submit unconditionally to Pope Martin. Cossa was ready to comply, and had already got a safe-conduct. The papal guards had by this time rejoined him, and accompanied him toward Florence. When they were near the city, he begged them to allow him to ride on, or themselves to ride on, as he wished to enter Florence like a free man.[1]

One day, shortly after the middle of June 1419, as Pope Martin was officiating in the cathedral at Florence, there appeared before him Baldassare Cossa, an aged man before his time, broken down by nearly four years' captivity. He threw himself at Martin's feet, and acknowledged him as the true and only, the canonically elected Pope. All present were affected at the sight and wept for joy, more especially the former cardinals of the deposed Pope. Although Martin was not altogether unprepared, no one was more rejoiced than he; he took pity on his former friend; on the 23rd June he bestowed on him the bishopric of Frascati, and on the following Tuesday raised him once more to the sacred college as Cardinal Tusculanus. The Pope gave Baldassare Cossa a ring; the cardinals greeted him with the kiss of peace. He preached a sermon in his own defence, setting forth what he had done for the Church,

[1] Finke (*B.*), 52-8.

for which he was ready to die. He paid a formal visit to the four Spanish cardinals who had joined the obedience since his time, and left the impression that, after all, he was a good man.[1]

In August, his confessor, Matteo of Viterbo, who had been with him at Mannheim, visited Venice. Baldassare Cossa thought of visiting Genoa, Milan, and Venice, partly on pilgrimage, partly to bring about a Lombard league against his enemy, King Sigismund. The Doge of Genoa was his friend, but the Republic of Venice, although they were ready to receive him with honour, did not look favourably on his plan. Cossa himself was too broken and ill to attempt the journey. He wrote to Benedict the Thirteenth in his lonely retreat on the rocks of Peniscola advising him to prefer the unity of the Church to his own advantage; and in his letter he complained of his own indisposition. His working days were over; he was living with his faithful adherent and banker, Cosimo de' Medici, and in his house in the Via dei Buoni,[2] he died on the 22nd December 1419.[3]

Baldassare Cossa, Pope John the Twenty-third, was in no sense a hero; he was simply a strong man, placed in a position for which he was eminently unfit, struggling with adversity. He had been trained in a bad school; he was one of the Popes who thought only of increasing the temporal importance, wealth and power of the Church, neglectful of her spiritual needs and interest. As a fighting cardinal he had been uniformly successful after the fashion of Gil Albornoz, and his memory was never stained with any ' massacre of Cesena ' as was that of Robert of Geneva, Pope Clement the Seventh. At Bologna he had been honourable and even generous in his dealings with his rivals, the Gozzadini, before their rebellion;[4] and his rule had brought peace and prosperity to the city he loved so well. For his services in connection with the Council of Pisa, the Cardinals, at the instigation of the French, had rewarded him with the papacy, for which he was eminently unfit.[5] As a

[1] Platina, 352; Finke (B.), 58.
[2] It was later the Palazzo Orlandini, and is now occupied by an insurance office. The Riccardo Palazzo, the home of the Medici, where Lorenzo and others first saw the light of day, was not built until eleven years later.
[3] Ciaconius, ii. 794; Finke (B.), 59.   [4] Gozzadini, 217, 310.   [5] Erler, 228.

man he was not worse than his time, he was not more worldly minded, he possessed not less religious feeling, than the generality of prelates; but being Pope, he was accounted the embodiment of all the ills from which the Church was suffering.[1] He contributed in a great degree to the election of Sigismund as King of the Romans. His troops won the battle of Rocca Secca. Up to this time all had gone well with him. But now the wheel of Fortune turned and he became the victim of untoward circumstances. What could he do, as he said, when Fate was against him? He was driven out of Rome and forced to implore aid from King Sigismund. He was compelled to convoke the Council of Constance. He had hitherto lived a life of military adventure; he was ignorant of the religious feeling of Europe. He possessed neither 'the learning nor the moral character to enable him to hold his own in the face of the Council.'[2] Had he held to his resolution to resign the papacy, he might have been treated as honourably as was Gregory the Twelfth. But he lost nerve, and 'then blundered more and more lamentably.' He was betrayed by King Sigismund, and then by Duke Friedrich; the Council had no pity on him; he was deposed and imprisoned. He sinned much, and was bitterly punished. As Reumont sums up, he 'was the incarnation of the spirit of worldliness which long before his time had led the Papacy terribly astray, and it is like the sign of an overruling Providence that the Master of anti-ecclesiastical tendencies and of purely political ends should attain the summit of power at the moment when the conscience of Christendom rose against the lowering of the highest office and the degradation of the most exalted institution on earth.'[3]

Over against the mighty Duomo of Florence, on the right-hand side of the high altar in the Baptistery, in that octagonal building, the most ancient church in the city, which replaced the old Temple of Mars, there rises high above the heads of the worshippers the tomb of Pope John the Twenty-third. It was raised by the bounty and gratitude of Cosimo de' Medici, the father of his country, to the papal patron whose wealth is said to have laid the foundation of the fortunes of that famous house. The tomb is one of the earliest works in

[1] Erler, 229.   [2] Creighton, i. 345.   [3] Pastor, i. note.

LAST DAYS OF BALDASSARE COSSA

the Renaissance style, and was fashioned by Michelozzo and Donatello in the years 1424 to 1427. The bronze figure of the storm-tost pontiff, recumbent on one side, looks out over the Florentine children who are brought there to be baptized; it is the work, often imitated, of Donatello, who sculptured also the guardian Madonna and Child. The story goes that Pope Martin objected to his predecessor being described in the inscription as 'formerly Pope'; and that the artist replied in the words of Pilate, 'What I have written, I have written.' It is an unlikely tale, for Oddo Colonna was one of the cardinals who elected Baldassare Cossa. Be that as it may, there the fallen pontiff

> 'is in his grave;
> After life's fitful fever he sleeps well: . . .
> Nothing can touch him further.'

INDEX

ABRAHAM (or Nicolas of Welenowic), 37-8.
ADALBERT, Ranco, 29.
ADIMAR, Aliman, Archbishop of Pisa, afterwards Cardinal Priest of S. Eusebeo, 20, 112, 208, 307, 316.
AGINCOURT, battle of, 405, 409, 413.
AILLY, Pierre d', Bishop of Cambrai, afterwards Cardinal Priest of S. Crisogono, known as the Cardinal of Cambrai, 6; his character and attainments, 116-8; created Cardinal, 118; 119, 126; at the Council at Rome, 129-32, 142, 144; 248; arrives at Constance, 258; present at the first hearing of Hus, 262; appointed a member of the commission on heresy, 265; opposes the party of Pope John, 265-7; his political sermon, 270; 274; opposes Pope John as to the reception of Pope Gregory's legates, 276; advocates the resignation of Pope John, 279; opposes Pope John in the question of voting, 281; his action compared with that of Gerson, 287; supports the proposal of Pope John to go to Nice, 291; absents himself from the congregations of the Council, 293; protests against the intimidation of King Sigismund, 294; presides over the third general session, 310; is absent from the fifth general session, 316; made president of the commission of belief, 318; absent from the sixth general session, 323-4; declares the Council superior to the Pope, 325; 336; is asked by Pope John to be his proctor, 339; refuses and gives evidence against the Pope, 340; visits the Pope at Radolfzell, 345; takes part in the trial of Hus, 366-7, 370-2, 376-7, 379, 381-2; 386, 390, 392, 397; falls comparatively into the background, 411; appointed to the commission to deal with the doctrine of Jean Petit, 413; backs up Gerson and is accused of heresy, 413; an enemy of the English nation, 414; is in favour of accepting Jerome's recantation, 415; Beaufort works against him at the papal election, 425.
ALBERT of Austria, 76, 78-9, 87, 148, 258.
ALBERT (or Albik), Archbishop of Prague, 122-3, 197.
ALEXANDER the Fifth, 1, 3, 12, 17, 20, 43-4, 46-8, 54, 112, 119, 134, 356, 360, 369, 425.
ALFONSO the Fifth of Aragon, 421.
AMADEUS de Saluzzo, Cardinal Deacon of S. Maria Nova, 306, 311, 316, 345.
AMADEUS of Savoy, 198, 200-1, 218-9, 342, 408, 429.
ANDREAS, Archbishop of Calocza, 198-9, 257.
ANDREW of Brod, 35.
ANEZKA, daughter of Thomas of Stitny, 33.
ANJOU. *See* Louis, Duke of.
ANNA, Angelus de, Cardinal Priest of S. Pudenziana, 108, 316.
ANNA of Brunswick, second wife of Friedrich of the Tirol, 169, 362.
ANNE of Bohemia, first wife of Richard the Second, 33.
ANTIOCH, Patriarch of. *See* Mauroux.
ANTONY of (or Antoine de) Brabant, 77, 206, 209-10, 219, 222.
ARMAGNAC, Count Bernard of, 205, 217, 409-10.
Armagnacs and Burgundians, 1, 134-5, 205-7, 307, 361, 409-10.
ARRAS, Bishop of (Martin Porée), 358, 413-4.
ARUNDEL, Archbishop of Canterbury, 21-2, 122, 334.

BAR, Cardinal Louis de, 165.

436 POPE JOHN THE TWENTY-THIRD

BARBARA von Cilly, second wife of King Sigismund, 82, 90-1, 222, 236, 238, 246, 249, 267, 269, 299-300, 361, 404.
BARBIANO, Alberigo da, 15, 102.
BEAUFORT, Henry, Bishop of Winchester, 113, 423-5.
BELLUNO, 148, 153, 156, 159, 177.
BENEDICT the Thirteenth, 13-14, 17-18, 110, 114-6, 119, 162, 181, 191, 198-9, 201, 205, 214-5; at Morella with King Ferdinand, 216-7; 224, 253, 257, 267, 276-7, 285-6, 288-91, 293, 304, 310, 319, 342, 359; appears at Perpignan to meet King Sigismund, 403-4; his hopes after the Council of Pisa, 404-5; refuses to resign, 405; retires to Peniscola, 406-7; process against him in the Council, 422; 426, 431.
BERNHARD, Markgraf of Baden, 190, 220, 223, 226, 291.
BERRI, Jean, Duc de, 20, 208, 323.
BERTRANDS, Jean de, Bishop of Geneva, 424.
Bethlehem Chapel in Prague, 33, 38, 43, 46-7, 49, 124-5, 384.
BINDACHIUS de Ricasoli, 326, 339, 345, 429.
BOLOGNA, 3, 6, 10, 13-15, 41, 47-9, 97-9, 144, 151-2, 177, 181, 192, 201-2, 321, 360, 431.
BONIFACE the Ninth, 5, 21, 30, 79, 111-2, 277.
BORDEAUX, Archbishop of. See Uguccione.
BRACCIO da Montone, 15, 102, 104, 166-7, 203.
BRANCACIUS, Nicolas, Cardinal Bishop of Albano, 110.
BRANCACIUS, Raynaldus, Cardinal Deacon of SS. Vito e Modesto, 9, 127.
BRANCACIUS, Thomas, nephew of Pope John, Cardinal Priest of SS. Giovanni e Paolo, 111, 151, 307.
BRANDA de Castellio, Bishop of Piacenza, afterwards Cardinal Priest of S. Clemente, 13, 23, 68-9, 97, 112, 266, 284, 307.
BREISACH, 326-9, 339.
BROGNI, Jean de, Cardinal Bishop of Ostia, also called the Cardinal of Viviers, 9, 224, 316, 318, 323, 332, 396.
BRUNORO della Scala, 154, 156-7, 160.
BUBWITH, Nicholas, Bishop of Bath, 213, 265, 424.
Burgundians and Armagnacs, 1, 134, 205-7.

BURGUNDY, Duke of. See Jans sans Peur.
BURGUNDY, Katharine of, 134, 303.
CAETANI, Antonio, Cardinal of Aquileia, 110.
CALLEVILLE, Colard de, 309.
CALVUS, Antonius, Cardinal of Mileto, 110.
CAPRA, Barthelemi della, Archbishop of Milan, 291, 398, 414.
CARACCIOLO, Conrad, Cardinal Priest of S. Crisogono, known as the Cardinal of Malta, 8, 22, 97, 110.
CARACCIOLO, Count Sergian, 104-5.
CARCASONNE, Bishop of. See Puy.
CASSOLINI, Pietro, 97-9.
CATTERICK, John, Bishop of Lichfield, 213, 424.
CHALANT, Antoine de, Cardinal Deacon of S. Maria in Via Lata, 9, 166, 179-80, 224, 265, 307, 316, 345, 428.
CHAMPS, Gilles des, 115-6.
CHARLES the Fourth, Emperor, 25-8, 53, 68, 70-1, 87-8, 92.
CHARLES the Sixth, King of France, 20, 76, 206, 208-11, 307-8, 312, 323, 408, 413-4.
CHARTRES, Regnault de, Archbishop of Reims, 286, 309, 311, 316, 330, 405, 409.
CHEVENON, Bishop of Amiens, 129-30, 133.
CHLUM. See John, and Henry.
CHOWKA, the boy, 81.
CHRYSOLORAS, Manuel, 180, 183, 249, 262, 322.
CILLY (or Cilli), Hermann von, 82, 90, 158, 186, 258, 269.
CILLY, Friedrich von, son of Hermann, 296, 299-300.
CLAMANGES, Nicolas de, 6, 116, 118, 252.
CLUX, Sir Hartung van, 122, 211-3, 405.
COLONNA, Giovanni, 10.
COLONNA, Nicolo, 10.
COLONNA, Oddo, Cardinal Deacon of S. Giorgio in Velabro (see also Martin the Fifth), 48-50, 65, 97, 307; elected Pope, 425; 433.
CONEGLIANO, battle of, 153.
CONRAD, Archbishop of Prague, 197.
CONRAD of Soest, 429-30.
CONRAD WALDHAUSER, 29.
CONSTANCE, city of, selected for the Council, 184-5; the selection confirmed, 189; Pope John reaches the city, 228; description and history of

INDEX 437

the city, 236-41; 253-4, 275-6; bad weather during the winter, 291-2; Niem's opinion of the city, 295; Sigismund leaves the city, 404; returns to it, 411; 423.

CONSTANCE, Council of, 184-5, 189-91, 194, 197-9, 201, 204-18, 223-4, 235; number present at, 242; lodging and police arrangements, 242-3; prices current, 243-5; nature of the crowds, 245-8; amusements, 246-7; literary activity, 248-51; its importance, 252; the Council opened, 253; arrivals, 254; sickness, 254-5; the division into nations, 255-6; the first general session on the 16th November 1414 and the appointment of officers, 256-7; discussion as to Pope Gregory's arms, 257-8; the early days, 258; postponement of the second session, 266-7; the question of Hus's imprisonment, 271-2; the question of voting decided, 280-3; adjournment to Avignon proposed, 285; congregation at which Pope John reads a formula of resignation, 288; second general session on the 2nd March 1415, 288-9; the Pope asked to notify his resignation and to appoint proctors to effect it, 289; the Pope again asked to appoint proctors, 292-3; dissensions in the Council, 293-4; congregation held after the Pope's flight and three cardinals deputed to him, 305-6; Gerson's sermon approved, 308; proctors named, 309; the cardinals lose their influence in the Council, 310; third general session on the 26th March 1415, 310; congregation preliminary to the fourth session held, 311; fourth general session on the 30th March 1415, 312; congregation held to exculpate King Sigismund, 316; fifth general session held on the 6th April 1415, at which the superiority of the Council to the Pope is proclaimed, 316-9; sixth general session held on the 17th April 1415, 323-4; seventh general session held on the 2nd May 1415, 331-2; eighth general session held on the 4th May 1415 to deal with the Wyclifian heresies, 332-6; ninth general session held on the 13th May 1415; tenth general session held on the 14th May 1415 and Pope John suspended, 340-1; Bull of Pope Gregory read in congregation, 342; Bishop of Leitomsyl heard and the Bohemian nobles answered, 343; Jerome of Prague brought up, 343-4; indictment framed against Pope John, 344; eleventh general session held on the 25th May 1415 and fifty-four articles held to be proved against the Pope, 346-57; twelfth general session, which deposes Pope John, held on the 29th May 1415, 358-9; the trial of John Hus on the 5th, 7th, and 8th June, 364-86; the sentence and execution, 395-401; the thirteenth general session, 413; the fourteenth general session, at which the resignation of Pope Gregory was accepted, held on the 4th July 1415, 403; sixteenth general session held on the 9th July 1415, 404; seventeenth general session, to speed Sigismund on his way, held on the 15th July 1415, 404; news of the Capitulation of Narbonne received, 407; the Council during the King's absence, 411-2; the doctrine of Jean Petit on political assassination before the Council, 412-4; the change in parties on the King's return, 414-5; the trial and execution of Jerome of Prague, 415-9; Friedrich of Austria put under the ban, 420; the Spanish nation in the Council, 421-2; the process against Pope Benedict, 422; the questions of church reform and of election of a new Pope, 422-3; the election of Oddo Colonna, 424-5; the question of church reform shelved, 426-7; the Council dissolved, 428.

CONSTANTINOPLE, Patriarch of. *See* John.

CORTONA, 16, 107, 166.

COSIMO de' Medici, 247, 429, 432.

COSSA, Baldassare (*see also* John the Twenty-third), at the death-bed of Pope Alexander the Fifth, 1; his qualifications and disqualifications for the papacy, 3-7; elected Pope, 7; 17, 41, 52, 55, 161, 292, 342, 344, 359; made over after his deposition to the Count Palatine, 361-2; 379; confined at Mannheim, 402; and at Heidelberg, 402-3; 420, 427; made over to the custody of Martin the Fifth, 429; efforts for his release, 429; his release effected, 430; appears at Florence and is reconciled to Pope Martin, and re-appointed Cardinal, 430; projects a visit to Venice, 431; dies, 431; his character, 431-2; his tomb, 432-3.

COSSA, Admiral Gaspar, 16, 111, 126.

438 POPE JOHN THE TWENTY-THIRD

Cossa, Geronimo, 167.
Cramaud, Simon de, 116, 129-30, 162-3.
Crusade preached against King Ladislas of Naples, 119-20; its effect in Bohemia, 123-5.

Didacus, the Franciscan Friar, 261.
Diessenhofen, Hans von, 301.
Dragon, Order of the, 11, 90.

Earthquake Council, the, 36, 274, 369.
Eberhard, Bishop of Salzburg, 246, 250, 427.
Elisabeth, widow of Louis the Great of Hungary, 70-4.
Elisabeth, daughter of King Sigismund, 87, 91, 258.
English Nation in the Council of Constance, 282-3, 287, 291-4, 309, 311, 414, 421-3.
Ernest of Austria, Duke of Styria, 69, 148-9, 154, 157, 167-8, 219, 384, 420, 427.
Ernst of Pardubitz, Archbishop of Prague, 27.
Este, Nicolas d', Marquess of Ferrara, 9, 96, 147, 152, 158, 179, 183, 190, 202, 225.

Facino Cane, 177.
Faulfisch, Nicolas, 38, 385.
Feltre, 148, 153, 156, 159-60.
Ferdinand, King of Aragon, 181, 214-7, 289, 405-6, 421.
Ferrara, Marquess of. *See* Este.
Ferrier, Vincenzo, 216, 406.
Fida, the widow, 234, 258, 260, 264, 297.
Fieschi, Louis, of Geneva, Cardinal Deacon of S. Adriano in Foro Romano, 99, 316.
Filippo, Maria, Duke of Milan, 177-9, 183, 192, 200, 280.
Fillastre, Guillaume, Dean of Reims, made Cardinal Priest of Saint Mark, 114-5; at the Council of Rome, 130-1; 248, 263; declares it the duty of Pope John to resign, 279; opposes him in the question of voting, 281; supports the suggestion that he should go to Nice, 291; awakens the distrust of the English and German nations, 293; deputed to Schaffhausen, 306; returns, 311; 313; present at the fifth general session, 316; member of the commission of belief, 318; on deputation to Pope John, 323, 325-7; at Freiburg, 329; asked by Pope John to be his proctor, 339; 411.
Florence, 10, 12-13, 100, 119, 127, 131, 158, 163-5, 177, 179, 182-3, 189, 321, 342, 426.
Forgacz, Balsius, 73-4.
Frankfurt, 13, 55-6, 61-6, 88, 92, 115, 221, 236.
Freiburg im Breisgau, 218, 320-1, 325, 329-30, 339, 345, 363, 429.
French Nation in the Council of Constance, 282-3, 293-4, 309, 311, 411, 421, 423, 426-7.
Friedrich, Burggraf of Nuernberg, 58-64, 220-1, 269, 313, 337, 339, 345, 364, 379, 421.
Friedrich of Austria, Duke of the Tirol, 69, 113, 148, 154, 157, 159, 167; his character, 168; the affair at Feltre, 168; accompanies King Sigismund to Innsbruck, 168-9; the affair of the burgher's daughter, 169-70; his rule in the Tirol, 170-4; 176, 188, 190, 199, 219, 223, 225; his alliance with Pope John at Meran, 226; 238; arrives at Constance, 280; suspected by King Sigismund, 291, 295-6; in communication with Pope John, 296; holds a tournament at Paradise, 299-300; hears of the Pope's flight, 300-1; goes with him to Schaffhausen, 302-4; is summoned to appear at Constance, 306; is undefended at Constance, and is placed under the ban of the Empire, 312-3; military operations against the Duke, 313; accompanies the Pope, who is his prisoner, to Laufenburg, 314-5; the war against the Duke, 319; Pope John's efforts on behalf of the Duke, 311, 321, 330; the Duke overwhelmed with disaster, 325-6; betrays the Pope, 328-30; comes back to Constance and meets King Sigismund, 331; his submission in the Franciscan cloister, 337; possession taken of his lands, 338; discloses a plot, 342; Friedrich 'with the empty pockets,' 361; the King's prisoner, 362; 406, 413; escapes from Constance, 420; is reconciled with King Sigismund, 427-8; 432.
Friedrich of Ortenburg, 151, 157.
Friuli, 147, 151, 153, 155, 157-9.

Gabrino, Fondulo, of Cremona, 179, 191-2.
Gara, Nicolas von, 73-4, 81-2, 192.
Gelu, Jaques, Archbishop of Tours, 405, 407, 424.

INDEX

GENOA and the Genoese, 2, 14, 157-8, 183, 188-9, 199-200, 321, 410-1, 431.
GENOA, Archbishop of. *See* Marini.
GEORG of Lichtenstein, Bishop of Trient, 113, 173-4, 225, 256, 296, 313, 420.
GEORGE of Knyehnicz, 38.
German Nation in the Council of Constance, 282-3, 287, 292-4, 309, 311, 340, 421-3, 426.
GERSON, Jean Charlier de, Chancellor of the University of Paris, 6, 21, 116, 193, 211, 248, 264, 270, 274-5; arrives at Constance, 287; helps King Sigismund to quiet Constance, 305; his attitude toward Jean sans Peur, 307; his sermon on the Council, 305-9; raises the question of Jean Petit's doctrine, 323; 336; charges Jerome of Prague with heresy, 343; 367-8, 373-4, 377, 386-7, 395, 404; contends against the doctrine of Jean Petit, 412-4; appears against Jerome of Prague, 415; 424.
GIAN CARLO VISCONTI, 177-9.
GIAN MARIA of Milan, 177.
GIOVANNI, the Dominican Cardinal, called the Cardinal of Ragusa, 257, 276, 403.
GNESEN, the Polish Archbishop of, 424-5.
Golden Rose, the, 95, 289-90.
GONZAGA, Francesco da, Marquess of Mantua, 147, 152, 158, 201.
GOTTLIEBEN, 306, 336, 362-3, 370, 422.
GOZZADINI, the, 17, 431.
GREGORY the Twelfth, 3, 10, 13, 17-19, 36-7, 41-2, 52, 55, 58-9, 66, 91, 111-2, 114, 121, 126-8, 131, 146, 163, 181, 190-1, 194, 198-9, 212, 215, 220, 253, 257-8, 276-7, 285-6, 288, 304, 340, 359, 363, 378; resigns the papacy, 403; 404, 425, 432.

HALLAM (or Hallum), Robert, Bishop of Salisbury, 113-4, 213, 246; arrives at Constance, 265; 279; proposes the system of voting by nations, 282; a strong supporter of King Sigismund, 281, 323, 344, 368, 415, 422; his death, 423.
HANNIBALDUS, Petrus Stefanescus, Cardinal Deacon of S. Angelo in Pescheria, 204, 254, 292, 314, 322.
HEDWIG, daughter of Louis of Hungary, 72-3.
HEIDELBERG, 402, 421, 429-30.
HENRICUS de Piro, proctor of the Council, 257, 332, 340, 358, 396.

HENRY of Chlum, surnamed Lacembok, 232, 234, 262.
HENRY the Fourth of England, 113-4, 211-2.
HENRY the Fifth of England, 182, 208-9, 211-3, 409-11.
Holy Ghost in the form of an owl, 131.
HORWATHI faction in Hungary, 72-5, 80, 82.
HUGO of Hervost, 13.
HUNGERFORD, Walter, 212-3.
HUS, John, 6, 22-3, 25; his early career, 31-2; at the Bethlehem Chapel, 33; in favour with the Archbishop of Prague, 34-7; defends the works of Wyclif, 36; breaks with the Archbishop, 38; receives the forged letter from the University of Oxford, 38-9; his doctrine as to transubstantiation, 39-40; his patriotic work, 40-1; his efforts for neutrality and for the alteration of the constitution of the University of Prague, 41-3; summoned by the Archbishop to answer certain charges, 43-4; appeals to Pope John against the Archbishop's order, 45; excommunicated by the Archbishop, 46; preaches in the Bethlehem Chapel, 46; cited to appear at the papal court, 48; receives a letter from Richard Wiche, 48; summoned to Bologna but does not go, 49-51; excommunicated for contumacy, 50, 64; his process entrusted to a commission, 65, 113; reconciled with the Archbishop and writes to Pope John, 66, 121; the peace with the Archbishop broken, 121; the encounter with Stokes at Prague, 122; holds a disputation on the Papal Bulls at the Caroline College, 123; intercedes for the three students, 124; his changed attitude toward the Pope, 125; his philosophy, 141-2; not mentioned in the decree of the Council at Rome, 143-4; his position in Bohemia, 193-4; is excommunicated and appeals to the Lord Jesus Christ, 194-5; his exile from Prague and literary activity, 195-7; resolves to go to the Council of Constance, 197-8; 221; his journey to Constance made under a double misapprehension, 229-30; starts with credentials of orthodoxy, 231; leaves Bohemia, 231-2; at Nuernberg, 232-3; determines to go on alone, 233; from Nuernberg to Constance, 233-4; arrival reported to the Pope, 234; his safe conduct,

234-5; 237-8; at the house of the widow Fida, 254-5; his alleged attempt to escape, 258-9; appears before the Cardinals and is imprisoned, 259-64; the preliminary inquiry, 264-5; writes treatises, 265; 267; King Sigismund acquiesces in his imprisonment, 271-2; the question of John Hus, 272-5; in custody, 289, 296; visited by the judges, 297-8; 304; removed to Gottlieben, 306; 318; his attitude toward the forty-five articles, 334-5; how affected by their condemnation, 335-6; the petition of the nobles on his behalf, 341-2; the Bishop of Leitomsyl before the Council, 343; Hus imprisoned at Gottlieben, 362-4; the first day of his trial, 364-5; asks King Sigismund to be present, 365; the second day of his trial, 366-371; advice of King Sigismund and of Pierre d'Ailly, 371-2; the third day of his trial, 372-80; his dispute with the King, 379-80; the address of Pierre d'Ailly and the supposed submission of Hus, 381-2; dispute with the King and others, 382-4; further points brought up against Hus, 384-5; Sigismund's address to the fathers as Hus is led back in custody, 385-6; his condemnation for heresy, 386-90; efforts to make him recant, 390-3; his position, 393-5; sentence and degradation, 396-9; the burning of John Hus, 399-401; 402, 414, 416, 418.

INNOCENT the Seventh, 37, 91, 111, 113, 115, 425.
INNSBRUCK, 169, 227.
ISOLANO, Giacomo, Cardinal Deacon of S. Eustachio, 98-9.
Italian Nation in the Council of Constance, 282-3, 285, 289, 291, 309, 331, 423, 426.

JACOBEL (or Jacob) of Stribo, the Utraquist, 32, 265, 297.
JAGELLO of Lithuania. *See* Ladislas of Poland.
JEAN PETIT and the doctrine of political assassination, 211, 307, 309, 318, 323, 326, 391, 395, 412-4.
JEAN SANS PEUR, Duke of Burgundy, 20, 76, 78, 99, 126, 134-5, 201, 206-11, 213, 223, 321, 323, 326-8, 342-3, 361, 395, 407, 409, 411-5.
JEROME of Prague, 31-2, 41, 123-4, 237-8; comes to Constance secretly, 324; is summoned to appear before the Council, 324-5; process instituted against him, 332; 370, 386, 390; his trial and execution, 415-9.
JOANNA of Naples, 72, 79, 254, 292, 405.
JOHANN of Goerlitz, 63, 76.
JOHANN von Pomuk, 43.
JOHN, Archbishop of Lisbon, made Cardinal, 113.
JOHN, Baron of Chlum, 194, 197, 231-4, 259-63, 273, 297, 364-5, 371, 385, 391-3.
JOHN, Duke of Burgundy. *See* Jean sans Peur.
JOHN of Reinstein, surnamed Kardinal, 232, 261.
JOHN, Patriarch of Constantinople, 214, 254, 264, 276-7, 297-8, 323, 325.
JOHN, the 'iron' Bishop of Leitomsyl, 121, 254, 342-3, 365, 390.
JOHN the Second, King of Castile, 100, 406.
JOHN the Twenty-third (*see also* Baldassare Cossa), his accession, 7-10; receives an embassy from Hungary, 10-13; remains at Bologna, 14, 22; prohibits use of the Bull in favour of the mendicant orders, 16; his correspondence with Carlo Malatesta, 17-19: his dealings with France and the University of Paris, his first false move, 20-1; his dealings with England, 21-2; limited sympathy with religious movements, 24; informs the University of Prague of his accession, 44; receives appeal against the Archbishop, 45; entrusts the process against Hus to Cardinal Colonna, 48; lays the question of burning Wyclif's books before the University of Bologna, 49; importance to him of the new election of the King of the Romans, 52-3; works for Sigismund, 55, 58, 64; is backed up by the Archbishop of Mainz, 57, 59, 61; interferes in the process of Hus, 65-6; the extent of his acknowledgment by Sigismund, King of the Romans, 66, 68-9; his attitude toward Sigismund, 91-2; his second false move, 92-4; the first year of his pontificate, 95; leaves Bologna and goes to Rome, 96-7; appoints Caracciolo and afterwards Minultulus to be Papal Legate of Bologna, 97; prompts Giacomo Isolano to put down the revolt there, 98-9; takes up the war with Naples, 99-101; his two generals, 101-3; receives news of the victory of Rocca Secca, 105;

INDEX 441

receives news of the discomfiture of the Duke of Anjou, 107; takes measures of defence at Rome, 107; his dealings with Sforza, who leaves his service, 108-9; his precarious condition in 1411, 110; makes a creation of cardinals, 111-9; his outlook in 1412, 126; makes peace with Ladislas of Naples, 127-9; holds the Council at Rome, 130-45; attempts to mediate between the King of the Romans and the Republic of Venice, 150-2, 154-5; refuses to mediate, 158; his attitude toward King Sigismund and toward Sforza Attendolo, 161; disappointed by the peace with King Ladislas, 162; makes Cramaud a Cardinal, 162-3; tries to animate the Romans against King Ladislas, 163; flies from Rome before Ladislas and reaches Florence, 164-5; raises money at Florence, 179; sends the Cardinals to King Sigismund to arrange for the convocation of a Council, 179-83; hears that Constance has been selected, 185; meets King Sigismund at Placenza, 186; travels with him to Lodi, 188; the conference at Lodi, 188-9; begins to take measures against the King, 190; with King Sigismund at Cremona, 192; a lawyer but not a theologian, 192-3; his conferences with King Sigismund, 193-4; returns to Bologna, 201-2; his indecision about Constance on hearing of the death of King Ladislas, but decides to go, 204; the Council to decide between him and his two rivals, 205-6; his projected visit to Avignon, 209; his ambassador in Spain, 214; his desire for union between the Greek and Latin churches, 218; his preliminary arrangements at Constance, 223-4; leaves Bologna, and goes by Verona to Trient, 224-5; at St. Michael on the Adige, 225-6; at Meran, 226; at Bozen, 226-7; at Brixen and Innsbruck, 227; the accident in the Arlberg Pass, 227-8; the arrival at Constance, 228-9; celebrates Mass and opens the Council, 252-3; receives news of the submission of Rome, 254; suspends the sentence of excommunication against Hus, 255; attends the first general session, 256-7; has the arms of Pope Gregory torn down, 257-8; allows the imprisonment of Hus, 262; learns the strength of the Council, 262-3; appoints three judges for the preliminary inquiry of Hus, 264-5; his party defeated in congregation, 265-6; receives the news of King Sigismund's arrival, 267; overruled as to the reception of his rival's legates, 275-6; absents himself from the congregations, 277; canonises Saint Brigitta, 277-8; is urged to resign, 279; is defeated on the question of voting, 280-3; is anonymously attacked, 283; his attitude toward King Sigismund, 283-4; resolves to resign, 285; his formula rejected, 286; accepts another formula of resignation, 287-8; celebrates Mass and reads his formula of resignation at the second general session of the Council, 288-9; refuses to make his promise unconditional, 289; presents King Sigismund with the Golden Rose, 289-90; at hopeless variance with the King, 290-1; finds it impossible to leave Constance openly, 291-2; promises not to dissolve the Council, 293; the King's visit, 294-5; in communication with Duke Friedrich, 296; leaves Constance in disguise, 300-1; goes to Schaffhausen, 301-2; writes to King Sigismund and others, 302; at Schaffhausen with Duke Friedrich, 303; his mistake, 304; deputation sent to him, 305-6; at Schaffhausen during Passion Week, 307; the embassies reach him, 309; his letter to the Cardinals, 309; the motives for his flight, 310; return of the Cardinals with John's reply, 311; the resolution of the Council at its fourth session, 312; Pope John flies from Schaffhausen to Laufenburg, 314-5; his Bull issued from Laufenburg, 316; proceedings of the Council against him in the fifth session, 317-8; the Council claims superiority over the Pope, 318-9; John's measures in favour of the Dauphin, 319-20; he flies from Laufenburg to Freiburg, 320; in Freiburg, 321, 330; goes to Breisach, 326-7; his last effort at Neuenberg, 327; brought back a captive, 328-30; the effect upon his followers of his attempt to escape, 331; cited to appear before the Council, 331-2; the Duke promises to bring him back, 337; John promises to accompany the envoys to Constance, 339; does not appear, is declared contumacious and suspended, 340-1; indictment framed against him, 344; is brought to Radolfzell, 345; visited by certain cardinals and appeals to King Sigismund, 345-6; the fifty-four articles held to be proved against Pope John, 346-57; he submits to the Council, 357-8; is deposed, 358-9; the end of his reign, 360; the news sent to France, 361; 369, 378.

JOST, Markgraf of Moravia, cousin of King Sigismund, 45; his candidature, 54, 56-9, 61; elected King of the Romans, 62; his death, 63; his character, 76-7; 78-9, 82, 87.

JUVENAL des Ursins, 20.

KARLSTEIN, Castle of, 26, 65.
KATHARINE of Burgundy, 100, 303.
KATHARINE of France, 208, 213.
KONTH, Stephen, 80-1.
KRIZ the Shopkeeper, 33.
Kumanians, the, 80, 84.

LACEK, Baron of Krawar, 48, 66.
LACEMBOK. *See* Henry of Chlum.
LADISLAS, King of Naples, 2-3, 10-11, 13-14, 16-18, 30, 55, 69, 74-5, 82-3, 79, 92, 97; his war with the Pope and the battle of Rocca Secca, 99-101, 103-9; 119, 123; makes peace with the Pope, 126-9; 130-1, 147-8, 151, 161; breaks the peace and drives the Pope from Rome, 162-5; in Rome, 165-6; gains all Italy as far as Siena, 166-7; 179-81, 183, 185, 190-1, 194; enters Rome, advances into Umbria, and returns to Perugia, 202-3; his death, 203-4; 214, 225, 254, 257, 262, 298, 360, 405.
LADISLAS, King of Poland, 43, 72-3, 77, 82, 148-9, 155, 157, 248, 286-7, 307.
LANDUS, Francescus, made Cardinal, 112; 316.
LANGLEY, Thomas, 113.
LAUFENBURG, 314, 316, 320.
LAVAUR, Bishop of, 357-8.
LEITOMSYL, Bishop of. *See* John.
LEONARDO BRUNI of Arezzo, 179-81, 248, 416.
LEOPOLD of Austria, 149, 171-2, 303.
LODI, 177, 188-91, 253.
LOUIS, Duke of Anjou, 2, 8, 10, 14-16, 75, 92, 95-6, 100-7, 126-7, 134, 206-8.
LOUIS the Bearded, Count Palatine, son of King Rupert, 52, 56-62, 191, 212, 220-2, 276, 305, 319, 362, 364, 379, 399-402, 421, 427, 429.

LOUIS of Bavaria, brother of the Queen of France, 219, 286, 309, 328-31, 337, 342, 361, 393, 408, 413, 427.
LUCIO de Comitibus, made Cardinal, 112.
LUIGI da Prato, 97-8.
LUPFEN, Hans von, 301, 313.

MAILLESEC, Guy de, Cardinal of Poitiers, 110, 253.
MALATESTA, Carlo, Lord of Rimini, 3, 9, 13, 17-19, 22, 53, 69, 97-9, 101, 105, 110, 126-8, 153-6, 166-7, 179, 198, 340, 403.
MALATESTA de' Malatesti, Lord of Pesaro, 8.
MALATESTA, Pandulfo, Lord of Brescia, 156-8, 178.
MANFREDI, Gian Galeazzo, 22.
MANNHEIM, 402, 431.
MANTUA, Marquess of. *See* Gonzaga.
MANUEL, Kaiser, 152, 218.
MARAMAUR, Pandulfus, Cardinal Deacon of S. Nicola in Carcere Tulliano, 14.
MARGARET MAULTASCH, 54, 170.
MARGARETA of Schwangau, wife of Oswald von Wolkenstein, 188, 300.
MARIA, first wife of King Sigismund, 71-5.
MARINI, Pileo de', Archbishop of Genoa, 332-5.
MARSIGLIO of Padua, 154, 156-7, 160.
MARTIN the Fifth (*see also* Oddo Colonna), 319; his election and character, 425-6; shelves the question of church reform, 426-7; dissolves the Council and leaves Constance, 428; takes charge of Baldassare Cossa, 429; arranges his liberation, 429-30; makes him Cardinal, 430; his criticism on the inscription on Cossa's tomb, 433.
MARTIN the Humane, King of Aragon, 100, 216.
MATTHIAS of Janow, 29.
MAUROUX, Jean, Patriarch of Antioch, 288-9, 291, 293, 309, 332, 358, 414-5.
MEGLIORATI, Giovanni de', Cardinal of Ravenna, 110.
MELORIA, fight off, 14-16.
Mendicant Orders, 16, 134, 322, 414.
MERAN, 175-6, 226, 303.
MICHAEL *de Causis* of Deutschbrod, 194-5, 234, 259, 261, 265, 272-4, 297, 364, 385, 392, 415.
MILAN, 112, 147-8, 158, 167, 175-6, 188, 200-1, 326, 427, 431.
MILAN, Archbishop of. *See* Capra.

INDEX 443

MILHEIM, Hans, 32.
MILIC of Kremsier, 29.
MINULTULUS, Henricus, Cardinal Bishop of Sabina, 97, 99, 110.
MLADONOWICZ, Peter, 261, 263, 297, 341, 363, 385.
MOCENIGO, Tomaso, Doge of Venice, 160, 192.
MONTFERRAT, Theodor, Marquess of, 151, 158, 178, 199-200, 209, 218.
MONTREUIL, Jean de, 129, 132.
MORS, Friedrich of, Archbishop of Cologne, Elector of the Empire, 55-9, 61-4, 175, 220.
MORS, Theodoric of, Archbishop of Cologne, 222, 235, 321.
MOTTA, the three battles of, 154-7.
MUHAMMAD, son of Sultan Bajazet, 89.

NARBONNE, 404, 406; the Capitulation of, 407, 421.
NAS, Johannes, 49, 370, 384.
NASSAU, John of, Archbishop of Mainz, Elector of the Empire: his efforts during the election of the King of the Romans, 54-64; consents to the election of Sigismund, 66-8; 175, 190-1, 201, 219-23, 226, 236, 238; arrives at Constance, 280; supports Pope John, 290-1, 295; leaves Constance, 292, 316; 321, 332, 402.
Nations in the Council of Constance, 255-6, 281-3, 293, 305, 309-11, 322, 325, 337, 342, 345, 358-9.
NAVARRE, King Charles of, 405-7, 421.
NELLENBERG, Count Eberhard of, 189, 224.
NEUENBERG, 328.
NICOLAS of Altronandis, 13.
NICOPOLIS, battle of, 29, 89, 186, 408.
NIEM, Dietrich von, 7, 117, 274, 295, 402.
Nominalism and Realism, 135-43.

OCKHAM, William of, 35, 117, 135-40, 363, 387.
Olivetan Monks, 44, 95, 345, 402.
ORDELASSI, Giorgio, 22.
ORLEANS, Duke of, 100, 205, 208-11, 307, 323, 409.
ORSINI, Giordano, Cardinal Priest of S. Lorenzo in Damaso, 108, 256, 306, 316, 345, 412.
ORSINI of Manupello, Count, 164.
ORSINI, Paolo, 10, 16, 95-6, 101-3, 105-6, 108-9, 126-7, 161-2, 166-7, 202-4.
OTTO the Third, Bishop of Constance, 241, 255, 304, 306, 362.

OXFORD, University of, 21-2, 24, 35, 38-9, 49-50, 332, 334, 384-5.

PADUA, 112, 129, 147-8, 156, 160.
PALEC, Stephen, 32, 36, 41, 123, 195, 259, 261, 265, 272-3, 297, 364, 368-9, 372, 384-5, 391, 415.
PANCERA, Antonius de Portogruario, Patriarch of Aquileia, nephew of Cardinal Caetani, made Cardinal, 112; 146, 316, 412, 415.
PARIS, Bishop of, 21, 211, 326, 412, 414.
PARIS, University of, 2, 16, 20-1, 24, 100, 114, 129-30, 132-3, 198, 207-9, 211, 287-8, 304, 307-8, 312, 318, 323, 361, 372, 393.
PAYNE (or Clerk), Peter, 38.
PERPIGNAN, 404-6.
PERUGIA, 166, 177, 203-4.
PIPPO SPAN, Count of Ozora, 10-13, 23, 55, 81-2, 90, 111, 151, 153-8, 295.
PISA, Archbishop of. *See* Adimar.
PISA, Council of, 2-3, 6, 12-14, 17-19, 41, 53-4, 57, 91, 93, 101, 112, 114-7, 129-33, 146, 163, 183, 205, 215-6, 223, 252, 256, 262, 265-6, 276, 279-80, 285-6, 308, 318-9, 340, 358, 360-1, 403-5, 431.
PLATINA, 5, 53.
POGGIO, Bracciolini, 248, 416-20.
POSEN, Bishop of, 357.
PRAGUE, city of, 26-7, 33, 38, 47-8, 50, 65, 121-5, 229-31, 273, 370-1, 384.
PRAGUE, University of, 24, 27, 35-6, 38, 42, 45, 50, 66, 123, 230, 318, 332, 334, 368-9, 378, 413.
PROKOP, cousin of King Sigismund, 29, 63, 77, 79, 82.
PUY, Géraud du, Bishop of Carcasonne, 286, 329-30.

RADOLFZELL, 339, 345, 357-9.
Realism and Nominalism, 135-43, 366, 396.
REIMS, Archbishop of. *See* Chartres.
Religieux de Saint-Denys (Gentian), 287, 317, 340.
RHENS, 88, 92-3.
RICHENTAL, Ulrich von, 224, 242-3, 245, 258, 400.
RIGA, Archbishop of, 265, 339, 344, 359, 365, 415, 423.
ROBERTI, Nicolo, 8.
ROCCA CONTRADA, 162, 166-7, 202.
ROCCA SECCA, battle of, 103-6, 127, 262, 360, 432.
ROME, 10, 96-7, 105, 107, 119; Council at, 128-45; 161-7, 203-4.

ROTTENBURG, Heinrich von, 172-3, 313.
RUDOLF of Saxony, Elector of the Empire, 54, 56-9, 62, 66-7, 219, 221-2, 269.
RUPERT, King of the Romans, 2, 12-13, 29-30, 34, 36, 52, 55, 57-8, 60, 78-9, 88, 90, 93, 146, 172-4, 188-9, 211, 267, 291.

Safe Conduct given by King Sigismund to John Hus, 194, 197, 234-5.
SCHAFFHAUSEN, 302-3, 306-7, 309-16, 322, 335, 425, 427.
SCOLARI, Filippo. *See* Pippo Span.
SEBENIGO, 147, 154, 157.
SFORZA ATTENDOLO (or d'Attendolo), 15, 101-6, 108-9, 126, 161, 167, 202-3.
SIENA, 15-16, 96, 131, 164.
SIGISMUND, King of Hungary and afterwards King of the Romans, 10-13, 17, 19, 22-3; his attitude toward Bohemia, 28-9; his candidature, 53-64; his influence on the process of Hus, 65-6; his imperial capitulations, 66-7; his election as King of the Romans, 62, 67; his attitude toward Pope John, 68-9; his former life and character, 70-94; the turning point in his career, 82; his three 'fixed ideas,' 88-90; 99-100, 131, 144-5; his grievances against Venice, 146-9; attempts arbitration, 150-1, 154-5; his war with Venice, 151-8; makes a five years' truce, 158; goes to Friuli, Belluno, and Feltre, 159; receives news of the accession of Muhammad, 159-60; nature of the truce with Venice, 160; his attitude toward Pope John, 161; leaves North Italy, 167; with Duke Friedrich at Feltre, 168; goes with him to Trient, to Salzburg, and to Innsbruck, 168-9; the affair of the burgher's daughter, 169; the chief cause of the deadly enmity between him and the Duke, 170-4; escapes poisoning at Brixen, 174; goes to Meran, Bozen, and Chur, 175; appeals to the Swiss for assistance, 176-7; his negotiations with Filippo Maria, 177-8; with Pope John concerning the convocation of a Council, 179-81; sends envoys to the Pope, 182; writes to King Henry the Fifth, 182; his conference with the Cardinals at Como, 183-4; issues proclamation for the Council, 184-5; Providence works for the King, 185-6; meets Pope John at Piacenza, 186; travels with him to Lodi, 188; the conference at Lodi, 188-9; writes to Popes Gregory and Benedict, 190-1; with the Pope and Gabrino Fondulo at Cremona, 191-2; the King no theologian, 192-3; his conferences with the Pope concerning Bohemia, 193-4; opens negotiations with Hus, 197-8; his negotiations with Pope Gregory, 198-9; and with Milan, 199; at Genoa, 199-200; at Asti, 200; at Pavia, 200-1; at Turin, 201; preliminary negotiations with France, 205-9; makes a treaty with France at Trino, 209; is invited but unable to come to France, 209; is disgusted at the treaty between the Burgundians and the Armagnacs, 210; secures the representation of France and Burgundy at the Council, 210-1; his negotiations with England, 211-3; and with Spain, 214-7; and with Kaiser Manuel, 218; his progress through Switzerland, 218-9; enters Germany, 219-20; at Strassburg, Speier, and Mainz, 220; his disappointment at Coblenz, 220-1; goes to Nuernberg and Heilbronn, and meets John of Nassau at Coblenz, 221; is crowned at Aachen, 222; writes to the magistrates of Constance, 223; his journey from Aachen to Ueberlingen, 235-6; 249-50, 252, 255-8; is wroth at the imprisonment of Hus, 262-4; arrives at Constance, 267-8; reads the Gospel in the Cathedral, 269-70; acquiesces in the imprisonment of Hus, 271-2; holds a congregation, 275-6; receives the ambassadors of Pope Gregory, 276-7; throws over Pope John, 278-9; receives embassy from Milan, 280; *Rex super grammaticam*, 284; hears the Pope's formula of resignation read, 285; withstands the French embassy, 286; welcomes the embassy from the University of Paris, 287; hears the Pope read an acceptable formula of resignation, 288; his delight, 289; receives the Golden Rose, 289-90; at open enmity with Pope John, 290; will not trust Pope John off German soil, 291; stops the flight of Cardinal Hannibaldus, 292; explains his action, 292-3; stormy interview with the French Nation, 294; visits Pope John, 294-5; his negotiations with the Swiss and Duke Friedrich, 295-6; present at the tournament, 299-

300; receives the Pope's letter and takes measures to prevent his further flight, 302-3; quiets the confusion in Constance, 305; reads the Pope's letter in congregation, 305; summons Duke Friedrich to appear, 306; calls a congregation, 311; takes measures against the Duke, who is placed under the ban, 312-3; calls another congregation, 316; promises to write to Pope John, 318; his war against Duke Friedrich, 319; revokes safe conducts granted at Schaffhausen, 322; present at the sixth general session, 324; captures the Pope and the Duke, 329-30; meets Duke Friedrich, 331; rumours of bribery, 332; receives the formal submission of Duke Friedrich, 337; takes possession of his lands, 338; lays before the Council the Bull of Pope Gregory, 340; receives a letter on behalf of Hus, 341; the plot to waylay the King, 342; takes Pope John into his custody, 345-6; present at the twelfth session of the Council, 358; sends ambassadors to France to announce the deposition of Pope John, 361; resists the entreaty of Anna of Brunswick, 361-2; makes over Baldassare Cossa to the Count Palatine, 362; corrects the proceeding in the trial of Hus, 364; is present on the second day, 365-6; his advice to Hus, 371-2; his dispute with Hus on the third day of the trial, 379-80; addresses Hus again, 382-3; his advice to the Council, 385-6; the effect of his change of attitude toward Hus, 390; sends prelates to Hus, 393; his attitude toward Jean sans Peur, 395; present at the condemnation of Hus, 396; his blush, 397; delivers Hus to execution, 399; is blessed by the Council, leaves Constance, and reaches Narbonne, 404; despatches envoys to France, 405; is unsuccessful at Perpignan with Benedict the Thirteenth, 405-6; the Capitulation of Narbonne concluded, 407; the King at Avignon and at Chambery, 408; at Paris, 408-9; in England, 410-1; returns to Constance, 411; reconciled with the Burgundians, Mars in the Council, 414-5; the 'Beadle of the Empire,' 420; change in the King's position in the Council, 421; the majority against him, 422-3; the question of reform and of the election of a new Pope, 423; gives way and a new Pope is chosen, 424-5; consequent failure of the project for reform of the Church, 426-7; reconciliation with Duke Friedrich, 427-8; leaves Constance at the close of the Council, 428; orders Baldassare Cossa to be made over to the new Pope, 429; 432.

SOPHIA, second wife of King Wenzel, 33, 42, 47-9, 390, 392.
Spanish Nation in the Council of Constance, 282, 414, 423.
SPEIER, 13, 220-1, 233, 236, 260.
STANISLAS of Znaim, and the Tractate against him, 32, 34, 36, 41, 123, 195, 197, 273, 364, 373, 383-4, 396.
STEPHEN, Duke of Bavaria, 59, 219.
STEPHEN PALEC. See Palec.
STIBOR, Count of Transylvania, 64, 66, 81-2, 93.
STOKES, Master John, 122, 211, 368, 380.
Swiss, the, 175-8, 295-6, 313, 325-6, 328, 338-9, 427.

TAGLIACOZZO, Count of, 16.
TANNENBERG, fight at, 43, 61, 87, 148.
TECK, Louis of, 146, 152.
THOMAS of Stitny, 29.
TIEM, Wenzel, Dean of Passau, 123.
TODI, 166-7.
TOULON, Bishop of. See Valentin.
TOURS, Archbishop of. See Gelu.
TREVISO, 146-8, 153, 156.
TROJA, Count of, 167.
TURIN, Treaty of, 147, 151.
TWARKO SCHURA, King of Bosnia, 80.

UDINE, 154-5, 157.
UGUCCIONE de' Contrari, 96, 98, 183.
UGUCCIONE, Francesco, Archbishop of Bordeaux, Cardinal Priest of SS. Quattro Coronati, 4, 110.
URSINS, Berthold des, 101, 152, 229, 256, 330.

VALENTIN, Vital, Bishop of Toulon, 332, 345-6.
VENICE and the Venetians, 12, 18, 22, 57, 69, 73-4, 87, 101, 119, 126; their policy and prosperity, 146-50; war with King Sigismund, 151-8; peace made, 158; 160, 174, 177, 183, 189-90, 199, 203, 321, 326, 342, 427, 429, 431.
VERME, Taddeo del, 152, 156.
VERONA, 129, 147-8, 156-7, 160, 177.
VIGNATE, Giovanni, 179, 199.
VITERBO, 164, 166.
VIVIERS, Cardinal of. See Brogni.

WARWICK, Earl of, 213, 265, 410.
WENZEL of Duba, 197, 231-4, 259, 364, 371, 385, 392-3.
WENZEL, King of Bohemia, 27-30, 36-7, 41-3, 47-50, 52-9, 62-7, 77-9, 82, 87, 89, 93, 121-4, 152, 178, 193-6, 206, 210, 219, 222, 249, 275, 369-70, 381, 390, 392.
WERNER, Archbishop of Trier, Elector of the Empire, 56-62, 66-8, 212, 222.
WICHE, Richard, 48.
WILHELM of Austria, 72, 79-80, 87.
WILLIAM of Holland, 410-1.
WILSNACK, the bleeding wafer at, 34.
WINTLER, Nicolas, 171-3.
WOK of Waldstein, 124-5.
WOLKENSTEIN, Oswald von, 174; his early life and adventures, 186-8; at Constance, 245, 250, 280, 299-300; 406.

WYCLIF and Wyclifism, 6, 24, 29-31, 33, 35-41, 66, 122, 135-6, 140-4, 193, 196, 256, 273-4, 298, 308, 324-5; condemnation of the forty-five articles, 332-6; 363, 367, 369, 372, 375, 378, 380, 384-7, 391, 396.

ZABARELLA, Francesco, Cardinal Deacon of SS. Cosma e Damiano, known as the Cardinal of Florence, 65, 112-3, 180, 183-4, 224; at Constance, 248, 253, 256, 265, 270, 279, 285, 293, 316, 318, 323, 327, 340; takes part in the trial of John Hus, 368, 382, 392, 397; 411-2, 419; his death, 423.
ZARA, 147, 151, 154-5.
ZBYNEK, Zajic of Hasenburg, Archbishop of Prague, 34, 36-50, 54, 65-6, 100, 121, 193, 334, 369-70, 396.